2002
The Supreme Court Review

2002
The

"Judges as persons, or courts as institutions, are entitled to
no greater immunity from criticism than other persons
or institutions . . . [J]udges must be kept mindful of their limitations and
of their ultimate public responsibility by a vigorous
stream of criticism expressed with candor however blunt."
—*Felix Frankfurter*

". . . while it is proper that people should find fault when
their judges fail, it is only reasonable that they should recognize the
difficulties. . . . Let them be severely brought to book,
when they go wrong, but by those who will take the trouble
to understand them."
—*Learned Hand*

THE LAW SCHOOL

THE UNIVERSITY OF CHICAGO

Supreme Court Review

EDITED BY

DENNIS J. HUTCHINSON

DAVID A. STRAUSS

AND **GEOFFREY R. STONE**

THE UNIVERSITY OF CHICAGO PRESS

CHICAGO AND LONDON

INTERNATIONAL STANDARD BOOK NUMBER: 0-226-36319-8

LIBRARY OF CONGRESS CATALOG CARD NUMBER: 60-14353

THE UNIVERSITY OF CHICAGO PRESS, CHICAGO 60637

THE UNIVERSITY OF CHICAGO PRESS, LTD., LONDON

The paper used in this publication meets the minimum requirements of American National Standard for Information Sciences–Permanence of Paper for Printed Library Materials, ANSI Z39.48-1984. ∞

FOR MADELINE

"Like the gentle night that holds us. . . ."
The Masses (August 1917)

CONTENTS

MARK TUSHNET

VOUCHERS AFTER ZELMAN

Celebrating their victory in *Zelman v Simmons-Harris*,[1] supporters
of school vouchers declared the case to be today's equivalent of
Brown v Board of Education.[2] *Zelman* upheld the constitutionality of
Ohio's program providing vouchers that Cleveland parents could
use to supplement their own payments of tuition in private schools,
including religiously affiliated schools, against a challenge that the
program violated the Constitution's prohibition on laws "respecting an establishment of religion."[3]

The invocation of *Brown* resonated deeply. Just as *Brown* was
the capstone of an extended process of litigation organized by an
ideological interest group (the National Association for the Ad-
vancement of Colored People) in the course of which the Supreme
Court whittled away at the constitutional defenses of segregation,
so *Zelman* resulted from a similarly extended process of litigation,
in which ideological interest groups played a similar role.[4] The
supporters of vouchers were concerned with a different dimension
of the analogy, though. For them, *Zelman* promised quality educa-

Mark Tushnet is Carmack Waterhouse Professor of Constitutional Law, Georgetown
University Law Center.

Author's note: I have benefited from comments by Marty Lederman, Ira Lupu, and
James Ryan, and from reading a draft of Ira C. Lupu and Robert W. Tuttle, *Zelman's
Future: Vouchers, Sectarian Providers, and the Next Round of Constitutional Battles*, forthcoming
in 78 Notre Dame L Rev (April 2003).

[1] 122 S Ct 2460 (2002).

[2] Clint Bolick, Vice President of the Institute of Justice, quoted in *Tax-Funded School
Vouchers Upheld*, Bloomberg News (June 27, 2002), available in LEXIS/NEXIS, News
Group File.

[3] US Const, Amend I (held applicable to the states through the Fourteenth Amendment
in *Everson v Board of Education*, 330 US 1 (1947)).

[4] For a discussion of the ways in which the litigation processes differed, see Section III.

tion to African American children in our nation's distressed inner-city schools, just as *Brown* had promised African American children in the segregated South education of a quality equal to that provided white children there. The irony of the analogy is that just as *Brown*'s promise went undelivered, so too might *Zelman*'s.

I begin this essay by examining *Zelman* itself and, in particular, the doctrinal background against which it was decided, showing that, like *Brown*, while *Zelman* might not have been strictly dictated by the precedents, it certainly was compatible with them, and perhaps more compatible with them than any alternative outcome. After exploring *Zelman*'s precise holding, I turn in the second section to the decision's doctrinal implications, with particular attention to three questions: whether voucher programs can exclude religiously affiliated schools; whether voucher programs can insist that recipient schools comply with various state regulatory requirements, including curricular requirements and nondiscrimination rules; and, finally, whether a credible argument now can be made that states *must* offer voucher programs to ensure that parents who have religious commitments to nonpublic education are treated equally with parents who are willing to send their children to public schools.

The third part of this article steps back from doctrine to locate *Zelman* in the political economy of religion and public education. Drawing heavily on the work of Dean John Jeffries and Professor James Ryan, I argue that *Zelman* fits well into a political world in which so-called movement conservatives have taken an increasingly large role, and that *Zelman*'s promise, as described by its supporters, may well be defeated by the unwillingness of taxpayers to invest substantial resources in the improvement of education in the nation's inner cities.

I. ZELMAN'S DOCTRINE

Zelman dealt with one of the nation's few school voucher programs, the adoption of which has been inhibited by a combination of constitutional and political obstacles that have proven difficult to overcome.[5] Originally put forward by proponents of wide-

---

[5] I discuss the political process—the obstacles and the way in which some have been partially surmounted—in Section II.

spread competition in education,[6] voucher programs have become
an important component of some proposals to improve the educational opportunities available to children attending what are sometimes called failing schools. The Ohio program at issue in *Zelman*
was typical of such programs. It was adopted by the Ohio state
legislature in response to widespread agreement that Cleveland's
public schools were failing to provide basic educational services to
large numbers of the students attending them.[7]

The program had two components. First, children whose parents decided to keep them in Cleveland's public schools could receive payments for tutorial assistance.[8] More than 1,400 students
received these tutorial assistance payments. Second, children
whose parents enrolled them in private schools, or in public
schools that charged tuition, could receive tuition assistance. Of
course, public schools generally do not charge tuition to students
whose families reside in the school district, but some school districts allow nonresidents to enroll their children in the district's
schools, usually only when space is available in the schools, and
charge these nonresident students tuition. Ohio's program authorized payment of $2,250 to public schools in districts adjacent to
Cleveland that accepted Cleveland's students. No adjacent districts
did so, however.

The more important component of the Ohio legislation involved private schools. The statute made private schools eligible
for tuition payments if the schools did not discriminate on the
basis of race, religion, or ethnic background, satisfied statewide
educational standards, and did not "advocate or foster unlawful
behavior or teach hatred of any person or group on the basis of
race, ethnicity, national origin, or religion."[9] Families whose in-
comes were less than twice the poverty line could receive 90 percent of private school tuition, up to a limit of $2,250, and private

---

[6] See, for example, Milton and Rose Friedman, *Free to Choose: A Personal Statement* 158–
71 (Harcourt Brace Jovanovich, 1980) (proposing a general voucher system, although giving
examples, most of which involve inner-city schools).

[7] Presumably to avoid state law strictures on special legislation, the statute actually made
the program available in all systems under federal court orders directing that the state
superintendent of schools take over the systems, but Cleveland was the only system that
satisfied this requirement.

[8] Children from low-income families could receive 90 percent of the cost of tutorial assistance, up to a limit of $360. Other children could receive 75 percent of the cost.

[9] 122 S Ct at 2463.

schools accepting children from such families could not require their parents to pay more than $250. For other families, the payments were 75 percent of tuition costs, up to a limit of $1,875. The state issued checks in the appropriate amounts to the parents, who then endorsed the checks to the private schools. A total of 3,765 students used the vouchers at private schools in the year the Court focused on. Notably, these vouchers are insufficient to cover the full cost of private school education; in the case of the low-income families, private schools that accept vouchers necessarily subsidize the students (because of the $250 limit on direct payments from the parents), and in many other instances private schools choose to subsidize students who pay with vouchers, refraining from raising their tuitions to a level that covers the entire cost of educating those students.

A final element of Cleveland's education system played an important part in the Court's constitutional analysis. Cleveland operates classic public schools, neighborhood based and subject to management by the city itself. But, like many urban school systems today, Cleveland also operates charter or community schools, and magnet schools. Cleveland's community schools have their own school boards, hire their own teachers, and design their own curricula, subject to general oversight (but not detailed management) of city officials. Nearly 2,000 students attended community schools. The city operates 23 specialized magnet schools, which emphasize particular subjects like the arts, foreign language, or science, and are attended by more than 13,000 students. The Court pointed out that the state provides over $4,000 for each student enrolled in classic public schools and magnet schools, and $4,500 for each student enrolled in a community school—in both cases, substantially more than the voucher program provided to parents who enrolled their children in private schools.[10]

Zelman resolved an Establishment Clause challenge to the Ohio statute. The challenge was driven by two facts. A substantial majority of the private schools receiving vouchers—46 of the 56 private schools in the program—were affiliated with religious institu-

---

[10] See, for example, 122 S Ct at 2468 n 3 ("Program students who receive tutoring aid and remain enrolled in traditional public schools . . . direct almost twice as much state funding to their chosen school as do program students who receive a scholarship and attend a private school.").

tions.[11] And, nearly all of the students who received vouchers—96 percent—used them at religiously affiliated schools.

Zelman was perfectly suited to Chief Justice Rehnquist's characteristically brisk opinion-writing style: setting out the facts, listing the relevant cases, describing each in a paragraph, asserting that the precedents' holdings clearly dictate the outcome, and distinguishing, in a paragraph or two, the strongest precedent offered against the holding, usually by quoting language from that precedent showing that the precedent does not preclude the Court's present holding. The only departure in *Zelman* from the Chief Justice's model opinion was a short section, seemingly inserted as a response to Justice Souter's dissent, in which the Chief Justice elaborated some important components of the Court's holding that might have gone underdeveloped in the absence of a provocative dissent.

The Chief Justice's opinion began by distinguishing between government programs "that provide aid directly to private schools" and those "of true private choice, in which government aid reaches religious schools only as a result of the genuine and independent choices of private individuals."[12] He noted that the Court's "direct aid" doctrine might be thought to be in flux, but he described the Court's cases dealing with programs of true choice as "consistent and unbroken" in their holdings that such programs do not violate the Constitution. The three cases he described in detail began with *Mueller v Allen*,[13] where then-Justice Rehnquist wrote for the Court to uphold a state program authorizing parents to take tax deductions for educational expenses, including tuition costs. The tax deductions were available to all parents, even those with children in public schools. Ninety-six percent of the benefits were claimed by parents with children in private schools, most of which were religiously affiliated, but the Court found that insufficient to establish the program's unconstitutionality. In *Zelman*, Chief Justice Rehnquist described *Mueller* as demonstrating that it was "sufficient" that the program there was "one of true private

---

[11] The Court uses the term, also prevalent in public discourse, *religious schools*, but I prefer the more accurate *religiously affiliated schools* (or variants of that term) to avoid the implication that every dimension of education at a religiously affiliated school is distinctively religious.

[12] 122 S Ct at 2465.

[13] 463 US 388 (1983).

choice, with no evidence that the State deliberately skewed incentives toward religious schools."[14]

Witters v Washington Department of Services for the Blind[15] upheld a state program giving vocational scholarships to persons with disabilities, as applied in the case of a student who used the scholarship money to study at a religiously affiliated institution preparing to become a pastor. Justice Marshall, who wrote the Court's opinion, anticipated the implications of the case for general voucher programs and included language suggesting some Establishment Clause limits on such scholarship programs. But, as Chief Justice Rehnquist pointed out in *Zelman*, a majority of the Justices, in separate opinions, emphasized that none of them shared Justice Marshall's misgivings.

Zobrest v Catalina Foothills School District,[16] the Chief Justice's third case, upheld a federal program allowing recipients of grants for education for persons with disabilities to use the money to pay for a sign-language interpreter helping the recipients in their religious education classes. According to the Chief Justice, *Zobrest* showed that "the circuit between government and religion was broken" when parents chose religious instruction as the best education for their children.[17]

Finally, the Chief Justice distinguished the major precedent pointing against vouchers. In 1973 the Court struck down a New York program that gave tax credits to low-income parents who sent their children to private schools and tax deductions to higher-income parents who did so.[18] *Mueller* had already distinguished that case on the ground that "public assistance amounting to tuition grants was provided only to parents of children in *nonpublic* schools,"[19] a distinction available in *Zelman* as well. In addition, the Court in *Zelman* emphasized that the program as a whole, which included grants for repairing old private schools as well as the tax credits and deductions, was designed to bail out financially

---

[14] 122 S Ct at 2466.

[15] 474 US 481 (1986).

[16] 509 US 1 (1993).

[17] 122 S Ct at 2467.

[18] *Committee for Public Education & Religious Liberty v Nyquist*, 413 US 756 (1973). Then-Justice Rehnquist dissented in *Nyquist*.

[19] 463 US at 398 (emphasis in original).

troubled private religious schools and "thus provided direct money grants to religious schools."[20] The distinction *Mueller* drew between the tax deduction program it upheld and the one the Court earlier invalidated was thin; invoking it in *Zelman* was no innovation, though.

The Chief Justice's argument from precedent was for all practical purposes unassailable.[21] *Mueller* left open the possibility that the Court might distinguish between choice-based programs involving tax deductions and those involving government grants, perhaps on the ground that a reasonable observer might interpret a flow of money from the government to a religiously affiliated recipient—albeit through an intervening recipient—as government endorsement of either the religion or the recipient's choice of a religious institution as the ultimate recipient, whereas that observer might not interpret in the same way a person's choice to spend money on religious education knowing that the cost will be reduced by a tax deduction taken later. Whether that distinction is at all plausible—I do not find it to be—it was eliminated by *Witters*, which involved a flow of money from the government to the religiously affiliated institution. Perhaps after *Witters* one might have distinguished between flows of money to institutions of higher education, and flows to elementary and secondary schools, but *Zobrest* eliminated that possibility.

Why then was there any question about the outcome in *Zelman*? Perhaps only because of the Court's—or, better, Justice Thomas's—unsuccessful effort just two years earlier in *Mitchell v Helms*[22] to make the constitutionality of government programs turn entirely on whether they were neutral between religious and nonreligious institutions. *Mitchell* involved a Louisiana program in which the state lent equipment to private schools. Justice Thomas, writing for only four justices, proposed a rule that would uphold

---

[20] 122 S Ct at 2472. For the "direct grant" characterization, the Chief Justice cited the pages of *Nyquist* in which the Court described one aspect of the program at issue there, which did indeed provide direct grants for maintenance and repair of private schools' physical facilities. It is at least misleading to transfer that accurate description of one aspect of the program to the tax credit and deduction aspect, which was the one relevant to the issue in *Zelman*.

[21] The precedential difficulty was created by *Nyquist*, which one might fairly regard as repudiated by *Mueller* and the cases that followed *Mueller*.

[22] 530 US 793 (2000).

any statute that provided aid to private institutions as long as the criterion for distributing the aid was neutral as between religion and nonreligion. Justice O'Connor concurred only in the judgment, arguing that "in terms of public perception, a government program of direct aid to religious schools . . . differs meaningfully from the government distributing aid directly to individual students who, in turn, decide to use the aid at the same religious schools."[23] But the failure of a majority to agree on a test that made neutrality alone dispositive should not have encouraged voucher opponents, in light of Justice O'Connor's expressed views. All that was needed to gain her vote was to present the Court with a real voucher program, allowing her to set aside her qualms about direct aid programs. *Zelman* was that case.

Zelman's constitutional doctrine has two components. Voucher programs must be "neutral with respect to religion," and they must permit recipients "to exercise genuine choice among options."[24] *Neutrality* means facial neutrality, not neutrality in impact. The opponents of Ohio's voucher program argued that the voucher program was not neutral in effect, because a substantial majority of the vouchers were used at religiously affiliated schools. The Court rejected this argument on two grounds, precedent and principle. The Chief Justice said that the Court had rejected the argument that neutrality was violated by disparate impact in *Mueller*, where parents of students attending religiously affiliated schools claimed virtually all of the tax deductions. He pointed to *Agostini v Felton*[25] to demonstrate that the Court had rejected a disparate-impact test where nonpublic schools received direct aid. That disparate impact alone would not invalidate a voucher program seems to follow a fortiori.

The Chief Justice's principled argument in *Zelman* tracked an argument he had made in *Mueller*. For him, and for the Court, courts could not reasonably administer a constitutional doctrine turning on disparate impact because the degree of impact might vary from state to state and, importantly, from year to year. In *Mueller*, Justice Rehnquist posed the hypothetical case in which

[23] Id at 842–43 (O'Connor concurring in judgment).

[24] 122 S Ct at 2473.

[25] Id at 2470, discussing *Agostini v Felton*, 521 US 203 (1997) (upholding a program providing financial assistance to schools serving children from low-income families).

nearly all parents who sent their children to nonpublic schools, most of which were religiously affiliated, claimed the tax deduction and nearly all of the parents who sent their children to public schools did not.[26] Undoubtedly there would be a disparate impact—in that year. But, imagine that the state—or some private entity—conducts a substantial public service advertising campaign the next year, informing parents of their entitlement. The disparate impact would drop—and might even disappear—if, because of the advertising campaign, parents of children enrolled in public schools claimed the deduction.[27] The Chief Justice thought it unattractive to have a rule of constitutional law under which a program constitutional in year 1 would become unconstitutional in year 2 because of decisions made not by legislatures but by private individuals. Even worse, of course, such a rule might lead a court to hold unconstitutional a program in year 1 that, if given a chance, would have become constitutional in year 2.

The Chief Justice illustrated his concerns by citing some facts about the program in *Zelman*. In the program's first year, 78 percent of the students receiving tuition aid attended religiously affiliated schools. That figure went up to 96 percent in the following year. Why? Because two private schools with no religious affiliations decided to become charter schools, continuing to receive voucher-based funds, but from a different facet of the program.[28] This sort of instability, which is inevitable in any large-scale social program, reduces the administrability of a disparate-impact test.

The Chief Justice also cited experience under one of the few voucher programs operating outside Ohio. According to a brief filed by the state of Wisconsin, the number of children enrolled in nonreligious schools accepting vouchers in that state's program

---

[26] 463 US at 401.

[27] This is true even if the amount claimed by the average parent with a child in public school was substantially smaller than the amount claimed by the average parent with a child in a private school, as was likely to be true. (Parents could claim deductions for school expenses, which include tuition for parents of children in private schools—not an expense available to parents with children in public schools, who could claim a deduction only for such things as school supplies and expenses associated with school trips.) The average claim for the public school parent might be small, but there are many more such parents than there are parents with children in private schools, so, if fully claimed, the deductions available to public school parents might be substantially greater overall than the overall deductions available to parents with children in private schools.

[28] 122 S Ct at 2470–71.

grew from 337 to 3,582, to the point where 32 percent of all students using vouchers were enrolled in nonreligious schools.[29] Citing an increased number is a bit misleading, because the Chief Justice does not say how many students were enrolled in religious schools at the outset, nor whether the percentage of students enrolled in nonreligious schools increased.

Despite this, the Chief Justice's analysis is probably sound. Consider the implications of the figures for various formulations of the disparate-impact test. The Court worked with the general formulation derived from *Lemon v Kurtzman*,[30] that a program will be unconstitutional if its primary effect is to advance (or inhibit) religion. But, of course, in any specific case the "primary effect" test must be refined.[31] One might imagine a test that would find unconstitutional disparate impact where substantially all of the students using voucher funds attend religiously affiliated schools.[32] The Ohio program might well be unconstitutional under such a test. But the more stringent the test, the more susceptible it is to the volatility that concerned the Chief Justice. The facts about the Ohio program showed that the disparate impact increased to a point where substantially all students using voucher funds did attend religiously affiliated schools, but if the two schools that became charter schools converted back to nonreligious private schools, the disparate impact would decrease below such a stringent threshold.[33]

An alternative formulation might find an impermissible disparate impact where a substantial majority of the students using voucher funds attended religiously affiliated schools. Such a test would be much less susceptible to troubling volatility, as the Chief

---

[29] Id at 2471 n 5.

[30] 403 US 602 (1971). The majority's distaste for *Lemon*, and its unwillingness to provide even inferential support for the view that *Lemon* remains controlling, is suggested by the fact that the Chief Justice cited not *Lemon* but *Agostini v Felton* for the "primary effect" test. 122 S Ct at 2465.

[31] For a general discussion of the role implementation concerns have in generating more specific versions of general doctrines, see Richard H. Fallon, Jr., *Implementing the Constitution* (Harvard, 2001).

[32] One might use a measure of money flows rather than students in attendance. The Chief Justice's figures and examples involve student attendance, and I follow his usage here.

[33] The Chief Justice suggested that the two schools changed their form in part because they were concerned that the then ongoing litigation would invalidate the voucher program and deprive them of funds were they to continue to operate as private schools. 122 S Ct at 2471 (referring to "the uncertain future of the scholarship program generated by this litigation").

Justice's own examples indicate; it would not be difficult to hold that 78 percent (the flow in the Ohio program's first year) and 68 percent (the figure cited for Milwaukee) satisfy a "substantial majority" test.

Still, the experience the Chief Justice cites may carry a broader lesson about volatility. He does not explain *why* the observed volatility might occur,[34] but there is one obvious reason: the market. That is, entrepreneurs may find the opportunity to receive voucher funds attractive and enter the market for providing education in nonpublic schools. I think it unlikely that today we can know how much education would be delivered in public and nonpublic schools, and in the latter how much in religiously affiliated schools, under a voucher program in full flower. The equilibrium level of students attending religiously affiliated schools might be around the two-thirds in the Milwaukee program, but it might be lower. Invalidating a program based on its "primary effects" before we know what the effects will actually be, in equilibrium, seems a wrong way to go about making constitutional law.

The Chief Justice was also concerned about another problem that a disparate-impact approach would create. The Chief Justice referred to it as the "denominator" problem.[35] Calculating a program's impact requires comparing the number of students using vouchers at religiously affiliated schools to some other count of students doing something else. The dissenters argued that disparate impact should be measured by comparing the number of students using voucher funds at religiously affiliated schools to the number of students using such funds at all nonpublic schools. Their rationale was that the program being challenged was not a generic voucher program covering a variety of needs, but a particular tuition-assistance program that provided vouchers for use in nonpublic schools. The 96 or 78 percent figures come from using the number of students using vouchers at nonpublic schools as the denominator. The Chief Justice had a different candidate for the denominator: the number of students receiving state funds, other than the ordinary per-pupil outlays, because they chose to attend what the Chief Justice called "nontraditional schools" such as

---

[34] Aside from his reference to uncertainty about the Ohio program's legal status.

[35] See 122 S Ct at 2471 (analyzing the disparate impact under two versions of the denominator).

charter and community schools. And, with that as the denominator, the proportion of students using vouchers to attend religiously affiliated schools drops to 20 percent.[36]

The dissenters had a rationale for their choice of denominator: the coverage of the statutory scheme itself. The Chief Justice's rationale for his competing view is at least as appealing: that the denominator should reflect the full range of choices available to parents, so that a severe disparate impact will appear only if parents' choices are severely affected by the voucher scheme. The Chief Justice asked that we take "the perspective of Cleveland parents looking to choose the best educational option for their school-age children," and said that we would then see no difference between private schools, community schools, or magnet schools.[37] As the Chief Justice put it, "The Establishment Clause question is whether Ohio is coercing parents into sending their children to religious schools, and that questions must be answered by evaluating *all* options Ohio provides Cleveland schoolchildren. . . ."[38] In arguing that Ohio's program did not skew choice in favor of religiously affiliated schools, the Chief Justice pointed out that the program "creates *dis*incentives for religious schools," because private schools, including religious schools, "receiv[e] only half the government assistance given to community schools and one-third the assistance given to magnet schools."[39] In particular, "[f]amilies have a disincentive to choose a private religious school over other schools,"[40] because parents enrolling their children in private schools will have to pay *something* as a copayment, whereas parents who enroll their children in community or charter schools do not.

The Chief Justice's argument here is that the Constitution requires only that parents have a real choice when they participate in a voucher program, and that the best measure of choice is financial: We know that parents have made a real choice when the course they pursue requires them to spend real money.[41] The mea-

---

[36] Id.

[37] Id at 2471 n 6.

[38] Id at 2469.

[39] Id at 2468.

[40] Id.

[41] The Chief Justice may have used money as a measure of choice to gain Justice O'Connor's vote. She had refrained from joining the plurality opinion in *Mitchell v Helms* (which the Chief Justice had joined) because she did not believe that neutrality alone was a sufficient test of

sure of choice is revealed preference for one package of benefits provided by schools rather than some disaggregated analysis of choice along several dimensions. It does not matter that, when questioned, a parent who sent her child to a religiously affiliated school might say that she preferred the curriculum at the public school and disliked the religious instruction that her child received at the religiously affiliated school, but found the safety provided by the latter enough to outweigh her other concerns.

This analysis has an obvious implication, which the Chief Justice appeared to recognize:[42] Nothing in it turns on the fact that parents have a choice among private schools, charter schools, magnet schools, and community schools. All that matters is that the cost to parents of participating in the voucher program is greater than zero—the cost to them of sending their children to traditional public schools. "*All* the options" Ohio provides include the public schools.[43]

Having suggested that parental choice should be the basis for choosing a denominator, I should emphasize how sweeping the implications of using that denominator are. The denominator consists of all students whose parents have a true choice about using vouchers. Justice O'Connor's formulation is that the test must consider "all reasonable educational alternatives to religious schools that are available to parents."[44] Under this test, it might make sense to exclude Cleveland's public schools from the denominator, because the Ohio program was predicated on a legislative determination that Cleveland's public schools had failed. That might be taken to mean that, in Cleveland, sending one's children to public schools was not a reasonable educational alternative.[45]

Still, Justice O'Connor's approach pretty strongly suggests that any system that creates charter, community, or magnet schools is

---

constitutionality under the Establishment Clause. See 530 US at 837–39 (O'Connor concurring in judgment). *Zelman* adds a requirement of choice to the requirement of neutrality, but making money the measure of choice adds as little to the neutrality requirement as possible.

[42] See 122 S Ct at 2468 ("Families that choose . . . a traditional public school pay nothing. . . . [a]lthough such features of the program are not necessary to its constitutionality. . . .").

[43] See id at 2493 n 9 (Souter dissenting) (noting that "once any public school is deemed a relevant object of choice, there is no stopping" the progression from community schools to public schools generally).

[44] Id at 2473 (O'Connor concurring).

[45] This interpretation of Justice O'Connor's approach is supported by the lengths she went to refute Justice Souter's contention that a number of the community schools provided inadequate education and so should be excluded from the denominator. Id at 2478–79.

going to have enough students in the denominator to ensure that any voucher program will be constitutional.[46] And systems with traditional schools that are not failing will have a very large number of students in the denominator—all those whose parents choose to send their children to public schools, and not merely those who choose to send them to nontraditional public schools. In any reasonably foreseeable future that number is going to swamp everything else. Specifically, a program providing vouchers only to students who attend religiously affiliated schools would satisfy the "choice" requirement, although it would of course fall to the Court's other requirement, that voucher programs be neutral as between religious and nonreligious entities. Or, more realistically, a program that provided vouchers to students attending private schools—with no special supplementation of the per-pupil grants to students attending charter or community schools—would certainly satisfy the Court's requirements. The Court's attention to the role of charter and community schools in Ohio's program is a distraction when we understand what principle underlies the choice of denominator.

Finally, the Court held that parental choices made under a voucher program that satisfied the neutrality and "true choice" requirements could not reasonably be attributed to the government. On this point, the Chief Justice simply quoted Justice O'Connor's opinion in *Witters:* "no reasonable observer is likely to draw from the facts . . . an inference that the State itself is endorsing a religious practice or belief."[47]

II. The Next Questions after Zelman

With the fundamental question about the constitutionality of voucher programs resolved, the courts can now turn to impor-

[46] Justice O'Connor's approach does have the peculiar implication that voucher programs for completely inadequate public school systems are more constitutionally problematic than programs for systems with some decent schools; because the inadequate public schools must be excluded from the denominator, the ratio of vouchers used in religiously affiliated schools to reasonable educational choices will be larger than when some decent public schools are in the denominator. Of course, the denominator for voucher programs for wider use—where the public schools are not failing—would include traditional public schools under Justice O'Connor's approach.

[47] 122 S Ct at 2467 (quoting *Mitchell,* 530 US at 843 (O'Connor concurring in judgment) (quoting *Witters,* 474 US at 493 (O'Connor concurring in part and concurring in judgment)).

tant collateral issues. I address three here. First, may a state create a voucher program and *exclude* religiously affiliated schools from participation? Second, are states limited in the degree of regulation they can impose on schools accepting voucher payments? In particular, may states require that schools accepting vouchers refrain from discriminating in admissions or employment on the basis of race or gender, when such discrimination is dictated by the school's religious commitments? Third, and most expansively, given the role that choice plays in structuring *Zelman*'s doctrine, must states create voucher programs to ensure that parents have real choices with respect to their children's education?

A. EXCLUDING RELIGIOUS INSTITUTIONS FROM PARTICIPATION: THE "LITTLE BLAINE AMENDMENTS" AND STATUTORY EXCLUSIONS

Zelman finds constitutional a voucher program that allows vouchers to be used at religiously affiliated schools. What of a voucher program that does not? A state might be barred by state constitutional law from making vouchers available for use at such schools, or its legislature might decide to limit the scope of a voucher program to secular private schools. Substantial federal constitutional arguments can be raised against either type of exclusion.

State legislatures and courts might find a so-called Little Blaine Amendment to stand in the way of including religiously affiliated schools in voucher programs. In 1875 Republican Representative James M. Blaine introduced a proposed constitutional amendment that provided: "[N]o money raised by taxation in any State for the support of public schools . . . shall ever be under the control of any religious sect. . . ." The Senate version provided: "No public property, and no public revenue . . . shall be appropriated to, or made or used for, the support of any school, educational or other institution, under the control of any religious or anti-religious sect, organization, or denomination. . . ."[48] Congress did not submit the Blaine Amendment to the states for ratification, but many states incorporated its provisions into their own constitutions.[49] Advo-

---

[48] For an examination of the genesis of the Blaine Amendment, see Stephen K. Green, *The Blaine Amendment Reconsidered*, 34 Am J Legal Hist 38 (1992).

[49] For an enumeration of states with constitutions whose provisions dealing with religion place substantial restrictions on the use of public money at religiously affiliated schools,

cates of including religiously affiliated schools in voucher programs would have to establish either that the Little Blaine Amendments do not require excluding such schools from those programs— probably a difficult showing to make—or that the Little Blaine Amendments are themselves unconstitutional.

On their face, the Little Blaine Amendments might seem no more than the embedding into a state constitution of a policy preference, where the losers happen to be disproportionately adherents of religion (or particular religions). And, as such, the Little Blaine Amendments might be thought unproblematic. Any state constitutional amendment does what the Little Blaine Amendments do, and *Zelman*'s neutrality test itself instructs us that the Establishment Clause is not violated by a policy that simply has a disproportionate impact on religious believers.[50]

There is, however, a fly in the ointment. Otherwise acceptable policies might become unacceptable if their adoption was improperly motivated.[51] And, as Justice Thomas wrote in *Mitchell v Helms*, the Blaine Amendment and its local variants have "a shameful pedigree," originating in what we today understand to be simple hostility to the Catholic Church.[52] Yet, it seems puzzling that a shame-

---

see Frank R. Kemmerer, *State Constitutions and School Vouchers*, 120 Educ L Rep 1, 39–40 table 1 (1997). State constitutional provisions requiring the states to maintain systems of public education might conceivably be interpreted to preclude legislatures from adopting voucher programs of any sort, but they seem unlikely vehicles for rulings against voucher programs that authorize the use of vouchers at secular schools but not at religiously affiliated ones.

[50] At least if, as the Court has consistently held, neutrality is symmetrical, meaning that policies that have disproportionate effects on religious believers or nonbelievers are to be tested against the same constitutional standard.

[51] See, for example, *Hunter v Underwood*, 421 US 222 (1985) (finding a state constitutional provision disfranchising persons convicted of crimes of moral turpitude to be a violation of the Fifteenth Amendment because it was motivated in part by a desire to disfranchise African Americans); *Romer v Evans*, 517 US 620 (1996) (finding a state constitutional provision prohibiting state and local government agencies from including gays and lesbians within the classes protected by antidiscrimination statutes to be a violation of the Equal Protection Clause because it was "inexplicable by anything but animus toward the class that it affects," id at 632).

[52] 530 US at 828. One might note that the Blaine Amendment might have been motivated, not by hostility to the *religious* dimensions of Catholicism, but by concern about *political* aspects of Catholic doctrine in the 1870s, which proponents of the amendment believed had strongly antidemocratic implications. I doubt that there could be a constitutional objection to state policies, even embedded in constitutional amendments, that do no more than take off the agenda of ordinary politics substantive policies that majorities believe to originate in antidemocratic impulses, unless, as discussed below, the policies enacted are objectionable on other grounds—such as antireligious or other class-based improper motivation, or where the policies themselves deal with free expression.

ful pedigree alone is enough to find the Little Blaine Amendments unconstitutional. The reason, simply, is that the Little Blaine Amendments are *old*. A bad motive might invalidate even an old provision if the provision was put on the books *and maintained* for bad reasons, but why should a bad motive at the outset be enough to overturn a policy that today might be supported for perfectly acceptable reasons?[53]

One possibility is that there is an asymmetry between enactment and repeal: Even if a lot of people today reject the anti-Catholic views that pervaded the movement to adopt the Little Blaine Amendments, and have no particular fondness for those amendments, still the amendments might remain on the books because a majority is indifferent to their continued existence, at least in the sense that the majority cares to devote its political energy to matters it thinks more important. One might call this a problem of selective indifference, which signals the difficulty: The Court has not accepted theories according to which selective indifference is enough to establish unconstitutionality.[54] Even more, there is some precedent in the Religion Clause context suggesting fairly strongly that bad motivation at the outset can become irrelevant over time, if eventually a law can be justified by identifying some permissible goals the legislature *might* be pursuing (today) in keeping it on the books.[55]

The bad motivations underlying the Little Blaine Amendments therefore should be put aside as we try to evaluate the argument that those amendments are unconstitutional when invoked to justify excluding religiously affiliated schools from voucher pro-

---

[53] See Toby J. Heytens, Note, *School Choice and State Constitutions*, 86 Va L Rev 117, 147–50 (2000) (arguing that the Little Blaine Amendments were unconstitutionally motivated, but that they may have been "purged" of the impermissible motivation by reenactment though not simply by the passage of time).

[54] For a discussion, see Geoffrey Stone et al, *Constitutional Law* 528 (Aspen, 4th ed 2001) (describing the problem of selective insensitivity).

[55] The cases are the Sunday Closing Cases, such as *McGowan v Maryland*, 366 US 420 (1961), where the Court upheld statutes that originated in efforts to promote church attendance (an impermissible purpose under today's views of the Establishment Clause), because in the circumstances of the early 1960s, Sunday closing laws advanced the permissible goal of creating "a uniform day of rest for all citizens." According to the Court, saying "that the States cannot prescribe Sunday as a day of rest for these [that is, for permissible] purposes solely because centuries ago such laws had their genesis in religion would give a constitutional interpretation of hostility to the public welfare rather than one of mere separation of church and State." Id at 445. Suitably adjusted, that statement seems apt with respect to the problem posed by the Little Blaine Amendments.

grams.[56] In any event, the motives behind the Little Blaine Amendments would not matter if, instead of invoking a state constitutional requirement, state legislators decided as a matter of policy to exclude religiously affiliated schools from voucher programs. What might the federal constitutional objection be to such an exclusion?[57]

Rosenberger v Rector and Visitors of University of Virginia provides a substantial basis for claiming that the exclusion of a religiously affiliated school would violate its right of free expression.[58] *Rosenberger* involved the distribution of money from a fund made up of student activities fees at the University of Virginia. The program's criteria for distributing funds excluded from participation groups that promoted religion.[59] The Court held that the exclusion violated free expression principles. It began by characterizing the fund as a limited public forum. The public finances classic public forums—streets and parks—and public forum doctrine allows speakers to take advantage of that public funding to support their own speech. The fund in *Rosenberger* was a limited public forum, the Court said, because the university gave access to such a wide range of speakers that no one could reasonably believe that the funds were supporting speech by the university itself rather than speech by the private recipients. The Court has held that government may not discriminate on the basis of viewpoint in making the public forum subsidy available. And *Rosenberger* held that exclusion of re-

---

[56] Lupu and Tuttle, 78 Notre Dame L Rev (forthcoming) (cited in Author's Note), point out that arguments against Little Blaine Amendments predicated on impermissible motivations can work only on a state-by-state basis, thereby complicating the litigation picture for voucher supporters in states with broadly construed Blaine Amendments.

[57] Heytens, 86 Va L Rev at 153–60 (cited in note 53), argues that exclusion of religiously affiliated schools violates the Equal Protection Clause by discriminating on the basis of religion, a suspect classification. See also Lupu and Tuttle, 78 Notre Dame L Rev (forthcoming) (cited in Author's Note), for a similar argument. I believe the equal protection argument works reasonably well where schools are excluded from participation solely on the ground that they are religiously affiliated, but less well where they are excluded because their curricula have religious content. To the extent that Little Blaine Amendments bar states from making funds available to religiously affiliated schools solely because of their affiliation (and not because of the content of the instruction they offer), the amendments might be inconsistent with the principles of equal protection and free exercise enforced in *McDaniel v Paty*, 435 US 618 (1978). (Marty Lederman pointed out to me the relevance of the distinction between exclusion based on affiliation and exclusion based on content.)

[58] 515 US 819 (1995).

[59] The terms, more precisely, excluded groups that "primarily promote[ ] or manifest[ ] a particular belief in or about a deity or an ultimate reality." Id at 822.

ligious groups because they were religious and sought to communicate their religion was viewpoint- rather than content-based discrimination.[60]

Rosenberger seems directly applicable to voucher programs.[61] Like the fund in *Rosenberger*, voucher programs make public money available to parents who can choose to send their children to schools whose curricula—their speech—range widely.[62] *Zelman* holds that the religious speech of institutions to which parents send their children in voucher programs that provide "true choice" and neutrality cannot reasonably be attributed to the state, just as the religious speech in *Rosenberger* could not reasonably be attributed to the university. *Rosenberger* also emphasized that the case did not involve direct aid to religious entities, pointing out that the university's checks were made out, not to the religious group, but to the company that printed the group's newspaper.[63] The Chief Justice treated *Zelman* as another case not involving direct aid to religiously affiliated institutions.

Two distinctions might be drawn between *Rosenberger* and voucher programs. First, the former involves higher education, the latter elementary and secondary education. Perhaps the inference of government endorsement is stronger with respect to what is said in the wide range of elementary and secondary schools participating in voucher programs than it is with respect to public universities. Precisely where one is to get information about what people reasonably believe is quite unclear. My own preference would be to require the presentation of evidence by those whose case turns

---

[60] Id at 830.

[61] But see Lupu and Tuttle, 78 Notre Dame L Rev (forthcoming) (cited in Author's Note), arguing that "the provision of public services—even if they have an expressive component—is conceptually distinct from the creation of a forum for debate. Unlike the context of public fora, in which the state provides resources for the very purpose of association and expression, school choice programs have the narrower and more focused purpose of delivering educational service to the young in the community." I do not think that this distinction can bear the weight Lupu and Tuttle place on it: The distinction between providing resources for association and expression and delivering educational service is thin indeed. What else is education other than association (socialization) and expression (knowledge)?

[62] Subject to the possibility, discussed below, that state-imposed curricular requirements might (constitutionally) restrict the range of offerings so substantially that the inference is strong that what the school communicates is no more than what the government wants it to say.

[63] 515 US at 843–44.

on what is essentially an empirical point—in this context, those who would defend the exclusion on the ground that a reasonable observer might attribute religious speech at an elementary school to the government. I certainly have no strong intuitions about what reasonable observers would infer, and little confidence in the intuitions of judges on that question.

Second, it might be said that the university in *Rosenberger* asserted no interest in the content of what was said by groups receiving money from the fund (except that it did not want them to engage in proselytizing speech, or perhaps religious speech more broadly understood), whereas the state does have an interest in the content of what is taught in schools receiving vouchers, as is shown by the obvious constitutionality of requirements that those schools teach English, algebra, and other subjects.[64] I question this distinction too.[65] The University of Virginia is, after all, an educational institution, and I would think that its governing board would take the position that everything it uses its money for is part of the university's educational mission. The student activities fund, for example, allows students to explore their own views through publication, gain experience in disseminating their views to a wide audience, and learn how to run an organization. I would think, that is, that the university would indeed assert that it has an interest in the content of what is said by groups receiving the funds, an interest, that is, in ensuring that what is said fits the university's pedagogical mission.[66] The difficulty in *Rosenberger* was not that the university had no interest in the content of what was said; it was that it implemented its interest in a viewpoint-discriminatory manner.

A related argument is this: The university in *Rosenberger* was *generally* indifferent about the content of what was said in the limited public forum created by the students activities fund, but restricted *some* speech because of its viewpoint. In contrast, governments operating voucher programs are *generally* interested in the content of what the money is used for, and as a result must use

---

[64] Again, subject to the possibility that some curricular requirements might be unconstitutional.

[65] It was suggested by Alan Brownstein in an e-mail to the Religionlaw listserv, and I may not be presenting the argument as Brownstein would.

[66] I seriously doubt whether the university would disclaim an interest in the publication by a magazine that printed sexually provocative (though not obscene) pictures, for example.

content-based criteria for determining who properly gets the money. In the words of two defenders of voucher programs, the government may have the right to insist that "education funds are being spent to educate, and that the public good is being well-served through sound performance and achievement. . . ."[67]

The interest in "sound performance and achievement" might support a requirement that students pass government-specified tests.[68] This general interest would not, however, justify excluding religiously affiliated schools. Perhaps one could contend that, for example, instruction in religious doctrine falls outside the scope of education (but does instruction in creationism?). I doubt, though, that the government interest in ensuring that "education funds are being spent to educate" is strong enough to justify supervision of what happens during every moment of school time to ensure that nothing other than education, as defined by the government, is occurring. That is, governments operating voucher programs have only a general interest in how the funds are used, just as the university in *Rosenberger* did.

A final variant on the same argument is that states imposing substantial conditions on the schools at which vouchers are used convert the theretofore private schools into public schools, where the speech is government speech. Or, put another way, a school that chooses to accept vouchers becomes a particular kind of public school, less regulated than charter or community schools but still a public school. Once the argument reaches this point, the only reason for saying that a school accepting vouchers under these conditions becomes a public school is to justify the conditions. That seems to me a nominalism that constitutional law ought to avoid.[69] There is, then, substantial reason for thinking that it is unconstitutional to exclude religiously affiliated schools from voucher programs.[70]

---

[67] Nicole Stelle Garnett and Richard W. Garnett, *School Choice, the First Amendment, and Social Justice*, 4 Tex Rev L & Pol 301, 341 (2000).

[68] Those tests might test for knowledge about the theory of evolution and not on creationism, which would provide schools an incentive to educate their students about the theory sufficiently to pass the tests.

[69] Particularly because the regulatory impositions, while quite important from the schools' point of view, seem to me not large enough to justify treating what is said in the schools, taken as a whole, as government speech.

[70] Cf. *Davey v Locke*, 299 F3d 748 (9th Cir 2002) (finding it unconstitutional for Washington to refuse to provide a scholarship from a program for high-achieving high school stu-

B. IMPOSING REGULATORY REQUIREMENTS

As noted earlier, the Ohio program required that private schools accepting vouchers not discriminate on the basis of race, religion, or ethnic background. Given the issues in *Zelman*, the Court had no occasion to address the constitutionality of these requirements. They and others like them will inevitably be brought into question. Here I consider two kinds of regulatory requirements. First, may a voucher program require that a school accepting vouchers teach particular subjects, or teach particular subjects in specific ways, where the curricular requirement conflicts with some religious beliefs of the school? Second, may a voucher program impose non-discrimination requirements on schools whose religious tenets require discrimination?

The structure of the answer to both questions is the same. The schools might have valid constitutional objections to the imposition of the regulatory requirements outside a voucher program. The government might not be able to insist that a religiously affiliated school teach evolution rather than creationism, or avoid discrimination when required by religious belief. Many such cases have been litigated under the Free Exercise Clause, with mixed results.[71] After *Employment Division, Department of Human Resources v Smith*,[72] the Free Exercise Clause would not seem to prohibit the imposition of these regulatory requirements, but there is a chance that it does. In addition, the right of free expression provides the basis for objecting to curricular impositions, and the right of expressive association, newly invigorated by the Court,[73] now provides ground for objecting to the nondiscrimination requirements.

---

dents to a graduate who intended to use the scholarship to pursue a degree in theology). The argument developed in the text assumes that the Court will follow through on the implications of *Rosenberger*. *Rosenberger* seems to imply, for example, that a state university must fund white supremacist organizations if it has a student activities fund, and that Ohio's statutory exclusion of racist schools from voucher programs is unconstitutional. It is not clear to me, though, how the Court could limit *Rosenberger*. The suggestion that religion offers a viewpoint, and that *Rosenberger* therefore involved viewpoint-based discrimination rather than content-based discrimination, would not seem to solve the problem posed by organizations promulgating racist views.

[71] For a brief summary, see John T. Noonan, Jr., and Edward McGlynn Gaffney, Jr., *Religious Freedom: History, Cases, and Other Materials on the Interaction of Religion and Government* 452–55 (Foundation, 2001).

[72] 494 US 872 (1990).

[73] See *Boy Scouts of America v Dale*, 530 US 640 (2000).

One might think that, whatever was true of general regulatory impositions outside the context of a voucher program, imposing such regulations as conditions for receiving vouchers would be constitutionally unproblematic. The unconstitutional conditions problem is probably intractable, but one need not confront that problem in order to conclude that states may not impose regulatory conditions on voucher recipients. The argument in the preceding section rested, not on the claim that exclusion of religiously affiliated schools from voucher programs violated some freestanding right, but rather than such exclusions amounted to unconstitutional discrimination on the basis of the schools' expression.[74] A similar discrimination-based argument is available to challenge exclusions of schools that cannot comply with general regulatory requirements because of their operators' faith commitments. My argument begins by suggesting that regulatory requirements imposed on *all* schools might violate freestanding constitutional provisions, and then turns to regulatory requirements imposed as a condition of participating in a voucher program, where the constitutional difficulty is one of discrimination.

Curricular requirements present the easier case. Consider first a state regulation that requires all schools, public or private, to teach evolution and not creationism.[75] That requirement might well violate the school's free-expression rights by coercing it into making statements—to its students, if not to the public at large—with which it disagrees. The great quotation from *West Virginia Board of Education v Barnette* seems precisely on point: "If there is any fixed star in our constitutional constellation, it is that no official, high or petty, can prescribe what shall be orthodox in politics,

---

[74] For a related argument, see Michael Stokes Paulsen, *A Funny Thing Happened on the Way to the Limited Public Forum: Unconstitutional Conditions on "Equal Access for Religious Speakers and Groups,"* 29 UC Davis L Rev 653, 713 (1996) ("Religious private schools have a First Amendment 'equal access' right to accept voucher funds from their students, if such funds could be used as secular private schools. . . . The state consequently cannot condition this right of equal access on the relinquishment of any other constitutional or statutory rights that the religious school, as a private entity, possesses.").

[75] I note at the start of this discussion that this kind of regulatory imposition can be redescribed as posing an unconstitutional conditions problem: The school must teach evolution as a condition of the state's accepting enrollment in a school as one way of satisfying the state's mandatory education requirement. My general view is that in the modern state all regulatory impositions can be similarly redescribed, so that there is no such thing as a problem of unconstitutional conditions that is distinctive from the question of whether a regulatory imposition is constitutionally permissible. But that is a larger argument that I think it possible to avoid here.

nationalism, *religion*, or other matters of opinion or force citizens
to confess by word or act their faith therein."[76] Later cases have
qualified *Barnette* by suggesting that sufficiently strong government interests might overcome the right to avoid coerced expression. But, it seems, any such interest must be "ideologically neutral."[77] The reasons a government has for imposing curricular
requirements are, almost by definition, *not* ideologically neutral:
The government wants evolution taught rather than—or perhaps
in addition to—creationism because the government thinks that
evolution is a better theory than creationism.[78] And similarly with
all curricular requirements to which some religiously affiliated
school might object.

The relevant right in connection with antidiscrimination requirements is the right of expressive association as elaborated in
Boy Scouts v Dale.[79] The prohibited discrimination might occur in
connection with admissions or employment. A religiously affiliated
school might prefer students who were already adherents of the
school's religion, or it might disfavor students who adhered to
other religions ("heathens," pejoratively). It might have religious
tenets that prohibited it from hiring as teachers married women
with children even though it would hire married men with children. The very existence of the nondiscrimination provisions in
the Ohio statute suggests that such provisions are politically attractive; it might even be that including such provisions in voucher
statutes is a necessary condition for their enactment. But are they
constitutional?

According to *Dale*, the right of expressive association protects
associations that "engage in some form of expression, whether it
be public or private."[80] Second, the courts must "defer[ ] to an
association's assertions regarding the nature of its expression."[81]
That is, the values an association seeks to transmit simply *are* what

---

[76] 319 US 624, 642 (1943) (emphasis added).

[77] *Wooley v Maynard*, 430 US 705, 717 (1977).

[78] Cf. Paulsen, 29 UC Davis L Rev at 713–14 (cited in note 74) ("A religious school's
decision to maintain a distinctive religious creed is at the absolute core of that religious
institution's collective First Amendment freedom of expression.").

[79] 530 US 640 (2000).

[80] Id at 648.

[81] Id at 653.

the association asserts them to be; the courts should not examine the values, or the views expressed, to determine whether they are "internally inconsistent" or otherwise problematic as long as they are sincerely held.[82] Third, the right of expressive association is impaired if the government's requirement "affects in a significant way the group's ability to advocate public or private viewpoints."[83] Finally, just as the courts must defer to an association's statements about its own views, so too they must defer "to an association's view of what would impair its expression."[84] In particular, some entities entitled to the protection of the right of expressive association are protected against "[t]he forced inclusion of an unwanted person" because such inclusion would "force the organization to send a message . . . to the world" that is inconsistent with the organization's own message.[85]

Probably because *Dale* is another of the Chief Justice's terse opinions, the precise scope of the right of expressive association remains to be determined.[86] But, with respect to religiously affiliated schools, the scope of the right seems reasonably clear. As the Court put it, an organization claiming a right of expressive association "must engage in *some form of expression*, whether it be public or private,"[87] which religiously affiliated schools certainly do. The right is violated when a statute has the effect of requiring an entity covered by the right of expressive association to "send a message to the world" inconsistent with the entity's own beliefs. In *Dale*, enforcing the state's antidiscrimination laws would not have required the Boy Scouts actually to send a literal message. Rather, as the Court put it, "Dale's presence" sends the message.[88] Action, not words, sends the message that impairs the Boy Scouts' own message. A person or entity covered by the right of expressive association might claim that complying with some government direc-

---

[82] Id at 651.

[83] Id at 648.

[84] Id at 653. Assertions to that effect appear to be insufficient standing alone; apparently the courts must be satisfied that the association's claim of impairment is at least reasonable in some minimal sense.

[85] Id at 648, 653.

[86] For a variety of views on *Dale*, see Symposium, *The Freedom of Association*, 85 Minn L Rev 1475–1954 (2001).

[87] 530 US at 648 (emphasis added).

[88] Id at 653.

tive would similarly send a message, for example, that the religiously affiliated school does not really believe that those who do not share its beliefs are heathens, or that it does not have strong objections when married women with children work outside the home.[89] *Dale* holds that the courts must defer to the claimant's own characterization of its beliefs, which, I would think, would have to include beliefs about what constitutes a message that the claimant does not want to send.

Suppose, then, that government cannot impose general regulatory requirements on religiously affiliated schools because of coerced expression and expressive association concerns. Can government make compliance with such requirements a condition of participating in a voucher program? I have argued that governments may not create voucher programs that exclude religiously affiliated schools from participating because of their religious character. Can they nonetheless exclude schools from participating because they fail to comply with regulatory requirements, where the noncompliance arises from the schools' religious commitments?

Even after *Smith*, the schools might be able to raise a Free Exercise objection. *Smith* noted the possibility of a "hybrid" claim, in which a Free Exercise claim that could not succeed on its own might be brigaded with some other constitutional claim, such as an objection premised on free expression or the right of expressive association.[90] The Court has not clarified precisely what this rule covers, and the rule is difficult to make sense of.[91] Religiously affiliated schools that cannot comply with regulatory requirements because of their religious commitments might have a valid hybrid claim, though.

Further, just as the exclusion of religiously affiliated schools

---

[89] Cf. Paulsen, 29 UC Davis L Rev at 714 (cited in note 74) ("'[A] religious school's decision to require its leadership—teachers, administrators, and others that the school regards as essential models of its creed to its students—to adhere to and support the religious institution's religious creed, purposes and policies, lies within the core of First Amendment expressive association. . . .'").

[90] 494 US at 882.

[91] If the statute objected to does not violate the Free Exercise Clause standing alone, and does not violate the clause with which it is brigaded, I find it difficult to explain why it would violate the Constitution nonetheless. For an expansive reading of the "hybrid" claim rule, see *Thomas v Anchorage Equal Right Comm'n*, 165 F3d 692 (1999), panel opinion vacated and district court reversed with instructions to dismiss action as unripe, 220 F3d 1134 (9th Cir 2000).

from voucher programs might constitute discrimination on the basis of expression, so might exclusion of schools whose religious commitments preclude them from complying with regulatory requirements. Curricular regulatory requirements are cast directly in expressive terms, and excluding schools that cannot teach evolution because of their religious commitments seems a straightforward case of content-based discrimination. So, for that matter, does exclusion of schools that teach race hatred.

Nondiscrimination requirements are not cast in expressive terms, and Justice Scalia suggested in *R.A.V. v City of St. Paul* that "[w]here the government does not target conduct on the basis of its expressive content, acts are not shielded from regulation merely because they express a discriminatory idea or philosophy."[92] Reconciling this dictum with *Dale*'s protection of expressive association as manifested in exclusions from association is by no means easy, although perhaps one could put a lot of weight on the word *merely* in *R.A.V.* But even if excluding schools with discriminatory policies does not amount to discrimination on the basis of the schools' exercise of their right of expressive association, an additional problem arises. The common sense behind exclusions from programs that make some government benefits available on condition that the recipients comply with the conditions the government imposes is that recipients can generally reject the benefits if they find the conditions too burdensome or intrusive.[93] Assume that schools really do have a choice about accepting vouchers. Some religiously affiliated schools will refuse to participate in programs with conditions inconsistent with their faith commitments, taking the position that adherence to their commitments to specific curricula or discriminatory policies is more important than the benefit they—and their potential students—receive from the voucher program.[94] Other religiously affiliated schools will participate. Under

---

[92] 505 US 377, 389 (1992).

[93] I mean by referring to the commonsense understanding to avoid getting into the morass of the unconstitutional conditions doctrine.

[94] I note here the traditional concern among pro-religion strict separationists that some religiously affiliated schools will be seduced away from their religious commitments by the offer of benefits from the government if only they change their beliefs. See 122 S Ct at 2499–2500 (Souter dissenting) (describing the effects of nondiscrimination requirements on the operation of religiously affiliated schools). For discussions, see Mark Tushnet, *Questioning the Value of Accommodating Religion*, in Stephen M. Feldman, ed, *Law and Religion: Critical Essays* 245 (NYU Press, 2000); Paulsen, 29 UC Davis L Rev at 664–65 (cited in note

the program as it operates, some denominations will receive more benefits than others. In short, regulatory conditions operate to create sect preferences, and sect preferences are at the heart of the prohibition against establishment of religion.

Of course, a voucher program with regulatory requirements is neutral on its face among denominations, and *Zelman* emphasizes that neutrality is an important factor in determining whether a program survives Establishment Clause review. But *Zelman* involved facial neutrality as between religiously affiliated schools and secular ones. A program whose disparate impact leads to sect preferences rather than to preferences for religiously affiliated schools as compared to secular ones might be more vulnerable to constitutional challenge. The analogy here is to the distinction in free expression law between content-based regulations and viewpoint-based ones. Review of viewpoint-based regulations is more stringent than review of content-based (or subject-matter-based) ones because viewpoint-based regulations pose a greater threat to free expression values. So too do sect preferences pose a greater threat to Establishment Clause values than preferences for religion as against nonreligion.[95]

The foregoing arguments raise an important collateral question. The politics of school voucher programs are complex, but two features of them seem fairly deeply embedded. First, there is strong public opposition to the possibility that truly repugnant ideologies will be propagated in schools accepting vouchers. The Ohio statute is exemplary. The exclusion of schools that teach race hatred rests on the fear that some schools might spring up to teach white supremacist views, or would be affiliated with the Nation of Islam and therefore (in the view of legislators and the public) also teach race hatred. Second, the public seems unlikely to be comfortable with the use of vouchers at schools that expressly discriminate, at least if the discrimination extends beyond an affirmative preference

---

74). The risk of seduction is diminished, perhaps even eliminated, if religious institutions are entitled to receive the funds without complying with the government's regulatory requirements. But see notes 75–78 above (describing how permissible regulatory requirements might give religiously affiliated schools incentives to alter their commitments).

[95] I think it useful to point out that it does not create a preference for religion as such to conclude that schools participating in voucher programs need not comply with regulatory requirements to which they have religious objections. Rather, the preference is one commanded by the Constitution's guarantees of free expression and expressive association, of which religions are incidental beneficiaries.

for coreligionists as students and faculty. Here again white supremacist and Nation of Islam schools might be examples of what the public will be troubled by. As a result, I believe, some curricular and nondiscrimination requirements are quite likely to be included in any statutes creating voucher programs.

If the arguments developed above are right, the courts will have to strike those requirements from the authorizing legislation. And, after doing so, they will have to confront another question: Is the voucher portion of the program severable from the unconstitutional regulatory portion? My sense of severability law is that, in light of the political factors I have described, most programs are probably inseverable.[96] Which means, in turn, that the combination of constitutional requirements with the politics of voucher programs may place quite severe limits on what voucher programs actually go into effect.

C. REQUIRING VOUCHERS TO PROMOTE CHOICE

One of the most potent rhetorical tropes in voucher proponents' arguments is a broad-based claim for equality in choice about education. Well-to-do parents, voucher proponents argue, can choose between sending their children to public or private schools. Vouchers simply make that choice available to everyone. Such arguments sounding in freedom and equality are natural candidates for constitutionalization. The potential constitutional argument here is of course quite expansive; it is that states that operate public schools *must* also create voucher programs to ensure that all parents have the range of choices available to well-to-do parents. Notwithstanding its breadth, the argument is not at all frivolous.

Again, *Zelman* provides a useful opening for the discussion. Recall that the Ohio program provided larger subsidies to parents who sent their children to charter or community schools (by means

---

[96] Opponents of voucher programs might take advantage of the political attractions of curricular and, in particular, nondiscrimination requirements to insist on the inclusion of an express inseverability clause in voucher legislation. Voucher opponents may find themselves the ultimate winners even if they lose in the legislature if courts accept the arguments made here about what the Constitution requires. And, strikingly, proponents of vouchers for use in religiously affiliated schools are unlikely to be comfortable arguing strongly against the free-expression and expressive-association arguments I have developed. (*Rosenberger*, after all, was brought and supported by people who support voucher programs that include religiously affiliated schools.)

of per capita payments to the schools) than it did to parents who sent their children to private schools. Put another way, the subsidy program discriminated against those who chose to send their children to private schools, relative to those who sent their children to charter or community schools. The Chief Justice emphasized the differential subsidy in explaining why the Ohio program was constitutional. Citing *Witters*, he pointed out that one constitutional concern was whether a program skewed parental choice in favor of religion. But, he wrote, "[t]he program here in fact creates financial *dis*incentives for religious schools" because of the differential subsidies, and "[f]amilies too have a financial disincentive to choose a private religious school over other schools," because of the copayment requirements.[97]

But in avoiding a skew in favor of religion, the differential subsidy might create a skew *against* religion. Neutrality might be enough to satisfy Establishment Clause concerns, but few would defend the proposition that government programs hostile to religion are constitutional. In fact, the Chief Justice misspoke: The Ohio program gave families disincentives to send their children to private schools, not (merely) to private religious schools. The program therefore was not hostile to religion as such, but only to private schools. Even so, skewing choice against private schools presents much the same constitutional issue as skewing choice against religious schools per se.[98] The problem is the obverse of the Establishment Clause issue in *Zelman*. That issue was whether the disproportionate use of vouchers at religiously affiliated schools violated the Establishment Clause. Now the issue is whether the disproportionate impact of the differential subsidy on parents who choose to send their children to religiously affiliated schools violates constitutional equality principles. Disproportionate impact alone does not violate the Constitution, but programs with a disproportionate impact on constitutionally protected interests must at least be rational.

The question then is what justification there might be for providing the differential subsidy to public schools in the Ohio pro-

---

[97] 122 S Ct at 2468.

[98] I put aside the question of whether skewing choice against private schools is inconsistent with parents' constitutional entitlement to send their children to such schools. See *Pierce v Society of Sisters*, 268 US 510 (1925).

gram. One possibility is that, while public charter and community schools and private schools all serve the public interest, the former types of schools do so better, or (in some sense) more, than private schools do. Children who attend public schools will absorb more public values than those who attend private schools even if the latter group gets "enough." This justification for the differential subsidy, though, seems pretty clearly content- or viewpoint-based. Here too *Rosenberger* seems relevant. There the Court treated the student activities fund as a limited-purpose public forum, in which viewpoint-based discrimination was impermissible. The general scope of the Ohio voucher program is broad enough to be treated similarly, as a fund to be used for expressive purposes. Discriminating in the distribution of that fund on the basis of viewpoint should also be impermissible. The Ohio program discriminates against parents who believe that religiously affiliated schools convey a better set of values than public schools do.

What of fiscal justifications? A standard baseline problem arises. The state expends less money on the voucher program when parents choose to send their children to public schools—but it does not save money by having a differential subsidy within the voucher program as compared to having no voucher program at all. This baseline problem suggests that the broader challenge to states that operate public schools and provide no voucher programs might be easier to make out than a challenge to a differential subsidy within a voucher program. Public education is a system of subsidies available to every parent in the state. But, in states without voucher systems, education subsidies are not provided to parents who choose to send their children to private schools.[99] As a result, there is a disparate impact on parents who send their children to religiously affiliated schools out of religious conviction. The only way a state could save money by subsidizing public but not private education is in the unlikely case that operating public schools is more efficient than operating private schools. Otherwise, subsidizing both simply transfers the expenditure from one line—"public education"—to another, the voucher program.

Prior to *Zelman*, the justification for refusing to adopt a voucher

---

[99] Everyone in the state benefits from the public good aspects of education, but that seems to me insufficient to provide a reasonable basis for providing a differential subsidy to public and private education.

program might have been to avoid violating the Constitution. Now that reason is unavailable.[100] It may be that no other reason is available either.

D. CONCLUSION

The arguments developed here are of course not unassailable. The argument against excluding religiously affiliated schools from voucher programs is the strongest, the argument that the Constitution requires vouchers for private education (in any state with a public school system) is the weakest. I do not believe that the Supreme Court will accept the latter argument any time soon.[101] It bears emphasizing, though, that *Zelman* was decided by a vote of five to four. That is, even in today's legal culture, the arguments *against* voucher programs were strong—but ultimately unsuccessful. That might be true of the arguments against the positions I have laid out in this section as well. What will matter, I think, is whether proponents of vouchers are in a position to develop a legislative-and-litigation campaign that would extend the scope of voucher programs, as they did in developing the strategy that led to *Zelman*. The next section addresses that question.

III. Zelman and Movement Conservatism

As noted at the outset, voucher proponents linked *Zelman* to *Brown v Board of Education*. This section explores two ways in which the linkage is apt: the connection between *Zelman* and broader social forces, including strategic litigation, and the extent to which the social benefits claimed for vouchers are likely to occur. The discussion highlights only a few aspects of the complex political setting of the school voucher debate.

---

[100] One could defend a complete absence of a voucher program on the ground that a fund dedicated solely to public education is not a public forum at all, not even a limited purpose public forum, but a means through which the state itself speaks. Even viewpoint discrimination is permissible with respect to the state's speech, so refusing to subsidize private schools would not be unconstitutional. I think this argument correct, but note that it leads to states having something like an all-or-nothing choice: Either operate a public school system with no vouchers for private education at all, or provide equal subsidies for public and private education.

[101] Cf. Paulsen, 29 UC Davis L Rev at 717 (cited in note 74) ("It may take some time for these points to gain acceptance (if indeed they ever do). . . .").

A. VOUCHERS, SOCIAL MOVEMENTS, AND STRATEGIC LITIGATION

As John Jeffries and James Ryan have shown, we cannot understand the doctrinal development of Establishment Clause law without appreciating the connection between doctrine and social change.[102] Jeffries and Ryan argue that the more or less strict separationist doctrine that prevailed from the 1940s through the early 1970s reflected the secularist views of legal elites allied with politicians who drew their electoral support from mainline Protestant denominations. And, they continue, that doctrine lost support in the courts as the alliance crumbled. As they put it, "Old coalitions have collapsed, and new alliances are demanding change."[103] The anti-Catholicism that animated much strict separationism has weakened among legal elites, though it has not disappeared. Mainline Protestant denominations have lost members and—as a result—political influence, and evangelical religious groups have increased in numbers and political influence, particularly as evangelicals became less firmly attached to their traditional posture toward politics: Rather than viewing political participation as at best a matter of indifference to the faithful, evangelicals began to see participation as one of the obligations of people of faith.

Historically, evangelical groups focused on spiritual matters, taking the phenomena of this world as essentially insignificant to salvation (or, in some denominations, to conforming one's conduct to the demands of the deity). Evangelicals were political quietists, basically indifferent to the ordering of the material world. To the extent that Protestant evangelicals mobilized politically, they opposed policies they believed would assist the Catholic Church, such as public assistance to religiously affiliated schools, which they correctly understood to be predominantly Catholic schools. Jeffries and Ryan explain how the political commitments of Protestant evangelicals changed with the rise of Christian academies in the South. Schools initially founded as secular ones for white parents seeking to avoid sending their children to integrated schools morphed into Christian academies.[104] The Christian commitments

---

[102] John C. Jeffries, Jr., and James E. Ryan, *A Political History of the Establishment Clause*, 100 Mich L Rev 279 (2001).

[103] Id at 283.

[104] Id at 330–34.

of these schools gradually deepened as their sponsors came more and more to "disdain . . . public schools."[105]

The Republican party's so-called Southern strategy took advantage of the fact that the roots of Christian academies were in opposition to desegregation. Proposals to support private education were consistent with the conservative ideology that fueled the modern Republican party and plainly made sense to Republican supporters who were sending their children to private schools. More broadly, the Religious Right found the Republican party an important vehicle for advancing its general political agenda, of which school vouchers were a significant part.

Like other analysts, Jeffries and Ryan emphasize that constitutional doctrine tracks, with varying degrees of accuracy, the prevailing political winds. The Supreme Court's rulings on the rights of African Americans in the 1950s and, particularly, 1960s responded to the political support the civil rights movement then had in national politics. And, as Jeffries and Ryan point out, the Court's hostility to government interactions with religion responded to the political support that position had among legal elites and dominant political majorities. When politics changed, so did constitutional doctrine. That the Court found vouchers to be constitutionally permissible should surprise no one who observed the growth of a conservative movement that gave vouchers an important place on its policy agenda.

The arguments for school vouchers underwent an important transformation as the campaign for vouchers developed. At first the arguments were predicated on choice as such: Libertarians and supporters of the Religious Right supported vouchers because vouchers would give parents choices between public and private schools. Some in the Religious Right argued that choice was particularly important to them because the public schools had failed, in the sense that the public schools no longer were reliable vehicles for transmitting the values that these proponents thought particularly important. Gradually the concept of failure changed. It became a way of describing the lackluster performance of public schools with respect to standard educational goals such as the transmission of knowledge. Voucher programs gained support,

[105] Id at 335.

particularly among the urban African American community, because they were seen as ways of addressing the problem of failing
schools. The Ohio program in *Zelman* exemplifies the modern version of voucher programs.

Vouchers, then, were a part of a broader political agenda associated with the modern conservative movement, which took advantage of the interests of nonconservatives in some aspects of
voucher programs to build support for such programs. The conservative movement began to develop the standard organizational ac-
coutrements of other political movements. Among these were politically oriented litigating groups such as the Institute for Justice.
Founded in 1991, the Institute describes itself as a "libertarian
public interest law firm."[106] Its litigation has had two focal points,
the defense of small entrepreneurs against regulations said to violate principles of economic liberties, and defense of school vouchers, which the Institute sees as a mechanism for promoting parental choice in a world of public subsidies for education.

The Institute's self-description suggests that its organizers see
it as the litigating arm of a broader social movement, just as liberal
public interest groups see themselves as assisting liberal social
movements.[107] Two differences between litigation supporting
voucher programs and liberal public interest litigation deserve
note. First, and probably more important, liberal public interest
litigation traditionally aimed at using the courts to overturn policies adopted by governments under the control of the movements'
opponents.[108] Liberal public interest litigation, that is, aimed at obtaining through the courts policy objectives that liberal social
movements could not obtain through legislation. Litigation supporting voucher programs, in contrast, aims at *defending* in the
courts victories already won in legislatures.

Second, liberal public interest litigation took as a model the strategic litigation campaign the National Association for the Ad-
vancement of Colored People (NAACP) conducted against segregated education. As liberal public interest litigators understood the

---

[106] For this description, see <http://www.ij.org/profile/body.shtml>.

[107] The classic discussions of the connection between liberal social movements and public
interest litigation are in Symposium, *The New Public Interest Law*, 79 Yale L J 1005 (1970).

[108] Recent liberal litigation supporting affirmative action departs from this tradition, and
resembles the litigation supporting voucher programs.

NAACP's campaign, NAACP litigators carefully staged their attack, choosing easy targets first to obtain favorable precedents that could be used to extend the campaign into more difficult territory.[109] Pursuing strategic litigation required a combination of control over the cases to be brought and cooperation from the courts, particularly the Supreme Court, in choosing which cases to hear. The litigation supporting vouchers differed in both dimensions. Precisely because the litigators were defending programs already adopted, they could not—in their capacity as litigators—control the challenges to vouchers they had to fend off.[110] And, as the voucher cases developed, the Supreme Court, not the litigators, structured doctrinal development as the Justices picked out cases they saw as good vehicles for developing constitutional doctrine.

These differences between the old model and the new conservative model of public interest litigation matter. The politics of vouchers shaped the programs that were actually adopted, thereby shaping the ensuing litigation. The litigators defending voucher programs had to defend what was enacted, in the hope of creating doctrine that would allow them to move forward. The liberal public interest litigators could move forward *in the courts*, taking their initial victories and extending them. The conservative public interest litigators can only use their victories in courts defensively, to show that legislatures can adopt voucher programs if they want. Until the courts accept the arguments developed in Section II, politics imposes substantial limits on what the conservative public interest litigators can achieve.

B. THE PROSPECT FOR VOUCHER PROGRAMS

Zelman eliminates federal constitutional objections to the voucher programs that have gained enough support to be enacted—that is, to voucher programs keyed to the educational failures of some (or many) public schools. Those schools are disproportionately located in America's inner cities, and provide what

---

[109] For my argument that this understanding of the NAACP's campaign did not in fact reflect the actual course of the NAACP litigation, see Mark Tushnet, *The NAACP's Legal Strategy Against Segregated Education, 1925–1950* (University of North Carolina Press, 1987).

[110] The qualification in the text is important because the litigators might attempt to influence the shape of the programs before they were adopted, to reduce the risk that the programs would be vulnerable to successful legal challenges.

education they do to African American and other minority children. Justice Thomas, articulating one element in his personal brand of black nationalism,[111] opened and closed his concurring opinion in *Zelman* by invoking Frederick Douglass.[112] Douglass described education as "emancipation," and, Justice Thomas wrote, "[t]oday many of our inner-city public schools deny emancipation to urban minority students." He cited *Brown* and described Ohio's voucher program as an attempt "to provide greater educational opportunity for underprivileged minority students."[113]

Voucher proponents' analogy between *Zelman* and *Brown* suggests that the proponents see vouchers as a means of accomplishing the educational goals that *Brown*'s supporters mistakenly thought would flow from that decision. Yet, the politics of vouchers may limit what *Zelman* can actually achieve for minority children in inner-city schools, just as the politics of desegregation limited what *Brown* achieved for the education of African American children. The political coalition that supports voucher programs, and that provides the political backdrop for the Court's decision, has more ambitious goals than remedying the ills of inner-city schools. Adherents of the Religious Right may have sincere faith commitments to the improvement of inner-city education, but they also have faith commitments to the religious education of their own children, and they hope to design voucher programs that allow support for alternatives to public schools that fail not in the ordinary educational sense but in the spiritual sense that most concerns them. Ryan and Michael Heise have recently developed an argument that, suitably adapted, suggests strongly that in the foreseeable future, that coalition will be unable to achieve its broader goals.[114]

Vouchers have not fared well in the political arena. Ryan and Heise point out that "[m]ore voucher plans have been rejected than passed," and—important for my argument—that "[e]very proposal to provide for vouchers on a large scale has failed."[115]

---

[111] See also *United States v Fordice*, 505 US 717, 745–49 (1992) (Thomas concurring); *Jenkins v Missouri*, 515 US 70, 114–23 (1995) (Thomas concurring).

[112] 122 S Ct at 2480, 2484 (Thomas concurring).

[113] Id at 2480.

[114] James E. Ryan and Michael Heise, *The Political Economy of School Choice*, 111 Yale L J 2043 (2002).

[115] Id at 2079.

The usual accounts of the politics of vouchers lay blame for this fact at the foot of teachers' unions aided by what Jeffries and Ryan call "ideological secularists," exemplified by the American Civil Liberties Union and People for the American Way.[116] Ryan and Heise direct attention to another reason for the failure of the voucher proposal: opposition, or at most lukewarm support, from suburban voters.[117] A large-scale voucher program whose benefits are available to suburban parents will almost inevitably reduce public expenditures on public schools. But, Ryan and Heise note, suburban parents typically pay a premium in the price of their homes for the quality of education their children will receive in the local public schools. Anything that takes money away from those schools reduces the value of their houses. Suburban parents also fear the educational and social effects of an influx of minority children into suburban schools. It is no surprise that no public school in Cleveland's suburbs accepted the vouchers created by Ohio's programs: The parents in those suburbs feared that accepting students from Cleveland's inner-city schools would reduce the quality of education in the suburban schools.[118]

Suburban indifference or opposition to large-scale voucher programs means that voucher programs are likely to be confined to failing inner-city schools. As Ryan and Heise put it, "Urban vouchers allow Republican leaders to push a policy that is ideologically attractive and politically low-risk, as it leaves suburbanites alone."[119] Yet, this strategy may not be sustainable in the long run. The Religious Right in the Republican party wants more than urban vouchers. A political strategy that always holds out the promise that vouchers for all are just around the corner, and then never delivers, may reduce the Religious Right's enthusiasm for the Republican leadership—and, perhaps more important, for voucher programs confined to failing inner-city schools.[120]

In this scenario, the initial success of urban vouchers may resem-

---

[116] Jeffries and Ryan, 100 Mich L Rev at 361 (cited in note 102).

[117] Ryan and Heise, 111 Yale L J at 2080–82 (cited in note 114).

[118] Ryan and Heise note suburban objections to funding mechanisms for voucher programs that reduce state aid to districts not in the inner city. Id at 2084.

[119] Id at 2085.

[120] Not necessarily, though: Republican leaders might hold on to Religious Right support by blaming teachers' unions for the failures of large-scale voucher programs, hoping that the Religious Right will not notice the role suburban voters are playing.

ble the immediate aftermath of *Brown v Board of Education*. Desegregation did occur in a number of cities in border states immediately after *Brown*. But then desegregation came to an end for about a decade. By the time it started up again in the 1960s, after the passage of the Civil Rights Act of 1964 and threats to deprive school districts of newly available federal funds for education, the possibility that desegregation would produce integrated schools—and, in particular, schools attended by African American children in which white parents had real investments—had faded because of white flight to suburbs. The limited voucher programs on the books today may be the parallel to desegregation just after *Brown*, and the hope of real improvements in the educational opportunities available to minority children proffered by voucher supporters and Justice Thomas may fade as well.

IV. CONCLUSION

The first round in the constitutional battle over vouchers is now over. The courts, though, are not the only terrain on which battles over social and constitutional policy are fought. The political constraints on enacting voucher programs of sufficient scale to satisfy important components of those programs' constituencies are substantial. The heart may go out of the struggle for vouchers unless those constituencies can be satisfied. I suspect that the only way to do so will be to persuade the courts that religiously affiliated schools must be included in voucher programs—perhaps not too difficult a task—and that such schools must be free from regulatory impositions if they accept vouchers, a much more difficult task. The conservative public interest litigators who celebrated *Zelman* have their work cut out for them.

DOUGLAS LICHTMAN AND
RANDAL C. PICKER

ENTRY POLICY IN LOCAL
TELECOMMUNICATIONS:
IOWA UTILITIES AND VERIZON

The Telecommunications Act of 1996 requires, among other things, that incumbent local telephone carriers lease parts of their telephone networks to would-be rivals.[1] If you have children, you can easily imagine the difficulties inherent in this approach; mandated sharing is often contentious when forced upon young kids and is no easier as applied to firms with strong, contradictory interests. These problems are exacerbated in the telecommunications setting by imprecision in the rules of the game. As Justice Scalia put it in *AT&T Corp. v Iowa Utilities Board*,[2] "[i]t would be gross understatement to say that the Telecommunications Act of 1996

Authors' note: Douglas Lichtman is Professor of Law, The University of Chicago Law School, and Randal C. Picker is Paul and Theo Leffmann Professor of Commercial Law, The University of Chicago Law School, and Senior Fellow, The Computation Institute of the University of Chicago and Argonne National Laboratory. We thank the John M. Olin Program in Law and Economics at The University of Chicago Law School for its generous research support, and, through their support of the Olin Program, Merck & Co., Inc.; Microsoft Corp.; and Pfizer, Inc. We also thank Stuart Benjamin, Richard Epstein, Howard Shelanski, Jim Speta, and Phil Weiser for helpful comments; Pat Curran for research assistance; and participants in a workshop sponsored by the Manhattan Institute's Center for the Digital Economy and entitled "Competition Policy in the Telecom Industry: When the Sherman Act Meets the Telecommunications Act, Who Wins?" Lastly, in the interest of full disclosure, Mr. Lichtman has provided some consulting services to Verizon but was not involved in the litigation or issues that are the subject of this article.

[1] See Telecommunications Act of 1996, Pub L No 104-104, 110 Stat 56 (1996), §§ 251–52, as codified at 47 USC §§ 251–52 (2002).

[2] 525 US 366 (1999).

is not a model of clarity. It is in many important respects a model of ambiguity or indeed even self-contradiction."[3]

However complicated the legal provisions, the intuition behind them is straightforward: the purpose of mandatory sharing is to facilitate competition. Without mandatory sharing, a competitor can enter the market only if it can either cut a deal with an existing telephone company or build its own network from the ground up. With mandatory sharing, by contrast, a competitor has a third option: it can enter the market in stages, building part of its network itself but then leasing the rest at regulated rates from existing firms. The competitor can later choose to build out its network more fully, for example, if its original offering has helped it to establish market share, to develop some relevant expertise, or to accumulate necessary financial resources. Alternatively, the competitor can continue to compete along only the narrower dimension, borrowing most network elements from the incumbent and in that way focusing its competitive energies on some small subset of the relevant infrastructure.

The mandatory sharing provisions of the 1996 Act have generated a flood of litigation in the past six years, in part because these provisions represent a sweeping change in the regulatory landscape. Prior to 1996, local telephone regulation had proceeded under the assumption that each community should be served by one and only one local telephone carrier. That carrier was subject to regulation so as to ensure that its prices remained low and the quality of its service remained high. But competition was not encouraged. It was expensive enough to have one firm build a local telephone network connecting every home and business in the community; policymakers deemed it ridiculous to encourage a second or third firm to duplicate that infrastructure.

The 1996 Act turned this conventional wisdom on its head. Gone was the assumption that regulated monopoly is the best approach to local telephone service. Replacing it was a firm commitment to competition. That commitment reveals itself throughout the 1996 Act, for example, in a provision requiring that existing telephone carriers exchange traffic with new entrants,[4] and in a provision forbidding state authorities from adopting regulations

---

[3] Id at 397.
[4] 47 USC § 251(c)(2).

that favor one local telephone company at the expense of another.[5] But the central and most controversial pro-competitive provisions of the 1996 Act are those that create the above-described regime of mandatory shared infrastructure. Insiders term these the "un-bundled network element" (UNE) provisions; and twice already these provisions have been subject to Supreme Court review.

In the first case, the aforementioned *Iowa Utilities*, the Court considered whether the Federal Communications Commission (FCC) had been faithful to the 1996 Act when it promulgated a regulation identifying the specific network elements that an in-cumbent telephone company has to share with rival firms.[6] The incumbent firms argued that the Commission had applied too lax a standard. According to them, the right standard would have re-quired sharing only if a given element was an "essential facility" as that phrase is used in antitrust law.[7] The Court rejected this argument on grounds that a telecom-specific standard might better accomplish the 1996 Act's goals. But the Court did find that "the Act requires the FCC to apply *some* limiting standard"—some-thing the Commission, in the eyes of the Court, had "simply failed to do."[8]

The Court's specific criticisms centered on the Commission's interpretation of section 251(d)(2), a provision that instructs the Commission to "consider, at a minimum, whether (A) access to such network elements as are proprietary in nature is necessary; and (B) the failure to provide access to such network elements would impair the ability of the telecommunications carrier seeking access to provide the services that it seeks to offer."[9] According to the Court, the Commission eviscerated the first of these criteria by interpreting it "as having been met regardless of whether 're-questing carriers can obtain the requested proprietary element

[5] 47 USC § 253 (2002).

[6] *Iowa Utilities* addressed other issues as well, including jurisdictional questions about whether the Act empowers the federal government, through the Federal Communications Commission, or state government, through local public utilities commissions, to take the lead in coordinating various aspects of mandatory sharing. We do not focus on the jurisdic-tional issues in this article, but interested readers are invited to consult Stuart Benjamin, Douglas Lichtman, and Howard Shelanski, *Telecommunications Law and Policy* 731–35 (Caro-lina, 2001) (*"Telecommunications Law & Policy"*).

[7] 525 US at 388.

[8] Id.

[9] 47 USC § 251(d)(2).

from a source other than the incumbent' "[10] and similarly eviscerated the second by deeming competition impaired if "the failure of an incumbent to provide access to [some specific] network element would decrease the quality, or increase the financial or administrative cost of the service a requesting carrier seeks to offer, compared with providing that service over other unbundled elements."[11] The Court therefore vacated the Commission's rule as unreasonable under even the generous standards of *Chevron* deference.[12]

The second case, last Term's *Verizon Communications v Federal Communications Commission*,[13] raised two primary objections to the procedure that the Commission had established for determining the price at which various network elements would be made available for mandatory sharing. The first objection was that the Commission's procedure did not sufficiently track the relevant statutory language. The 1996 Act does not say much about prices, but it does say that a "just and reasonable rate" should be "based on the cost" of the shared facility, should be "nondiscriminatory," and "may include a reasonable profit."[14] The incumbent local telephone carriers argued that the Commission's rule did not satisfy these commands, the objection being that the Commission's approach—a forward-looking cost methodology known as "total element long-run incremental cost," or TELRIC—was not "based on cost" because, among other things, it defined cost to mean the expense that would be incurred were an equivalent network built today instead of adopting the arguably more conventional definition that cost means actual monies spent.[15] The Court ultimately found that the Commission's interpretation was reasonable on this score, or, less enthusiastically, that it was "reasonably within the pale of statutory possibility."[16]

---

[10] 525 US at 389, quoting FCC, *In re Implementation of the Local Competition Provisions in the Telecommunications Act of 1996*, 11 FCC Rcd 15499 (1996) ("First Report & Order") at ¶ 283.

[11] 525 US at 389 (italics omitted), quoting First Report & Order at ¶ 285 (cited in note 10).

[12] *Chevron USA, Inc. v Natural Resources Defense Council, Inc.*, 467 US 837 (1984). The Commission rewrote its rules after the remand, with no more success. See *United States Telecom Ass'n v FCC*, 290 F3d 415 (DC Cir 2002).

[13] 122 S Ct 1646 (2002).

[14] 47 USC § 252(d).

[15] 47 CFR § 51.505 (1997).

[16] 122 S Ct at 1687.

The incumbents' second objection was that the Commission's pricing methodology, if deemed permissible under the statute, would result in regulated prices so low as to constitute a taking of the incumbents' property without just compensation, a violation of the Fifth and Fourteenth Amendments. This, the incumbents argued, justified application of the rule of constitutional avoidance; in essence, the Court should interpret the 1996 Act to preclude the Commission's pricing methodology in order to avoid a serious constitutional question. The Court was not convinced that a serious constitutional question was in the offing, however, mainly because the Commission's pricing methodology is so flexible that, even knowing what it is, it is still almost impossible to guess whether the resulting prices will be high or low, let alone so unconstitutionally low as to set up a possible takings argument.[17] The Court noted that this conclusion was consistent with its "general rule" of not considering "a taking challenge on ratesetting methodology without being presented with specific rate orders alleged to be confiscatory."[18]

This account covers a great deal of law and policy, and obviously we will unpack it with care below. But before we delve too deeply into that analysis, we should make clear that we think the Commission in promulgating the regulations at issue in these two cases, and the Court in analyzing those regulations in light of both the 1996 Act and the Constitution, performed admirably. The 1996 Act gave the Commission only six months to promulgate all of the regulations needed to implement network element unbundling.[19] Viewed in that light, the rules that the Commission produced[20] and the document that attempts to explain and justify them[21] represent a substantial accomplishment. Similarly, while we think that the Court made some missteps in *Iowa Utilities* and *Verizon*, overall the Court's analysis in both of these cases strikes us as reasonable and likely even right. The economic issues at the core of these cases were complicated and at times ambiguous, and the Court in

---

[17] Id at 1679.

[18] Id.

[19] 47 USC § 251(d)(1).

[20] See, in particular, 47 CFR § 51.317 (1997) (standards for identifying network elements to be made available); 47 CFR § 51.319 (1997) (specific unbundling requirements); 47 CFR §§ 51.501–51.515 (2002) (establishing pricing rules for unbundled network elements).

[21] First Report & Order (cited in note 10).

our view exercised good judgment in deciding when to wade into the morass and when to defer technical issues to the Commission.

Our purpose in this article, then, is not to criticize either the Commission or the Court. Instead, we set out here to move the analysis forward by highlighting some possible mistakes, raising some overlooked issues, and along the way clarifying exactly what is at stake in these battles over the form and substance of the 1996 Act's unbundling regime. Our hope is that the ideas presented here will amount to more than just a postmortem on two interesting and important Supreme Court cases. Indeed, we hope that our discussion helps to inform the ongoing legal and regulatory process put in motion by these cases and still underway at the Commission and in, among others, the Second, Seventh, Eighth, and D.C. Circuits.[22]

We proceed as follows. In Section I, we explain the key sharing rules established by the 1996 Act and parse in some detail the Court's analysis of those rules in *Iowa Utilities* and *Verizon*. In Section II, we consider more conceptually the main reasons why sharing rules are sometimes imposed in markets like the market for local telephone service, focusing in particular on the problem of natural monopoly and its implications for both market entry and government regulation. In Section III, we point out the three main differences between the sharing rules promulgated under the 1996 Act and the rules that were in place prior to 1996. In Section IV, we present some data on how all this regulation has begun to unfold in practice. Finally, in Section V, we use the preceding analysis to look forward from *Iowa Utilities* and *Verizon*, offering our thoughts on how these cases will influence the regulatory and legal landscape in the coming years.

I. IOWA UTILITIES AND VERIZON

The Telecommunications Act of 1996 is wide-ranging, but among its most important provisions are those designed, in the

---

[22] See, for example, *Iowa Utilities Board v FCC*, 219 F3d 744, 757 (8th Cir 2000) (continued proceedings in light of *Iowa Utilities*); *United States Telecom Ass'n v FCC*, 290 F3d 415 (DC Cir 2002) (judicial review of the Commission's revised list of elements to be unbundled); *Goldwasser v Ameritech Corp.*, 222 F3d 390 (7th Cir 2000) (analysis of relationship between the unbundling requirements and federal antitrust law); *Law Offices of Curtis V. Trinko v Bell Atlantic Corp.*, 305 F3d 89 (2d Cir 2002) (same).

FCC's words, "to let anyone enter any communications business—to let any communications business compete in any market against any other."[23] This might sound like an obvious objective; but in the early days of telecommunications regulation, competition was in fact restricted in telecommunications markets for fear that it would mean wasteful duplication of telecommunications resources and, worse, the possibility of competing but incompatible telephone networks.[24]

Granted, that view had lost some ground even before the 1996 Act. In the 1960s, for example, the Commission embraced competition by authorizing the use of telephone handsets purchased in the marketplace, rejecting the earlier view that telephone handsets were part of the telephone network and thus had to be rented from the telephone company itself.[25] Similarly, in the 1980s, the Commission joined forces with the Department of Justice and used a combination of regulation and antitrust litigation to open the long-distance market to competition, this time by requiring local telephone companies to work with all the various long-distance firms instead of each just picking a favored partner.[26]

But the market for local telephone service had been left untouched by these and related changes. Simply put, it was expensive to build a fully functional local telephone network, and having a single network sufficed in terms of being able to provide adequate service to every interested home and business. Given that, policymakers saw little reason to encourage the construction of a second or third overlapping infrastructure. The 1996 Act thus represented a significant shift in telecommunications policy. The new

---

[23] See FCC, *Telecommunications Act of 1996*, available online at <http://www.fcc.gov/telecom.html> (visited Nov 1, 2002).

[24] See *Telecommunications Law & Policy* at 614–21 (cited in note 6). It is possible that incompatible local telephone networks would benefit society by spurring innovation and encouraging quality service. See Milton L. Mueller, Jr., *Universal Service: Competition, Interconnection, and Monopoly in the Making of the American Telephone System* (MIT & AEI, 1997).

[25] The Commission had required some convincing on this point. See *Hush-A-Phone v United States*, 238 F2d 266 (DC Cir 1956); *Use of the Carterfone Device in Message Toll Service*, 14 FCC 2d 571 (1968). For discussion, see *Telecommunications Law & Policy* at 624–28 (cited in note 6).

[26] See *United States v American Telephone & Telegraph*, 552 F Supp 131 (DC Cir 1982), aff'd, 460 US 1001 (1983); *In re MTS and WATS Market Structure Phase III*, 100 FCC 2d 860 (1985). For discussion, see Glen Robinson, *The Titanic Remembered: AT&T and the Changing World of Telecommunications*, 5 Yale J Reg 517 (1988).

goal was to encourage competition even in the local market, at least to whatever extent the economics of the industry would allow.

Some of the 1996 Act's mechanisms for encouraging competition are easy to understand. One set of provisions, for instance, obligates all existing telecommunications carriers to exchange traffic with each other and with any new entrants.[27] This is important since a new entrant—a "competitive local exchange carrier," or CLEC in telecommunications jargon—can attract customers only if it can guarantee that its subscribers will be able to communicate with existing telephone users. Another set of provisions facilitates competition by allowing a CLEC to resell under its own name services that are in fact provided by another firm.[28] This makes it easy for a new firm to enter the market, especially since services can be purchased at cheap "wholesale rates" if purchased from an "incumbent local exchange carrier" (ILEC)—telecom-speak for a local telephone company that was already in business at the time the 1996 Act took effect.[29]

The most important mechanism, however—and the one of most interest in both *Iowa Utilities* and *Verizon*—requires incumbent local telephone carriers to share, at regulated rates and with any interested firm, certain components used in their networks. For example, suppose that the existing local telephone network in a given community uses copper wires to connect local homes to some centralized automatic switch. Under the 1996 Act, the ILEC that owns those wires must allow any interested competitor to use them. The idea is to give new entrants the opportunity to enter the market without requiring that each entrant build its own entire telecom network right from the start. Using unbundled network elements, firms can enter the market gradually, providing some network elements on their own but leasing the rest from the relevant incumbent firm.

The 1996 Act only sketches the rough contours of this unbundled network element mechanism. Indeed, as we have mentioned, one critical provision sets out the standards that the Commission

---

[27] See 47 USC § 251(a)(1) (general obligation of interconnection); 47 USC § 251(c)(2) (more detailed interconnection obligation for incumbents). For discussion, see *Telecommunications Law & Policy* at 715–18 (cited in note 6).

[28] See 47 USC § 251(b)(1) (resale obligation for all firms); 47 USC § 251(c)(4) (specific obligation for incumbents).

[29] See 47 USC § 252(d)(3) (defining wholesale rates for purposes of § 251(c)(4)).

should use when deciding which network elements must be made available for lease, but that provision states only that the Commission should "consider, at a minimum, whether access to such network elements as are proprietary in nature is necessary" and also whether "the failure to provide access . . . would impair the ability of the telecommunications carrier seeking access to provide the services it seeks to offer."[30] Another central but vague provision is the pricing provision also mentioned earlier, which states in relevant part that the price should be "based on the cost" of the relevant network element and "may include a reasonable profit."[31]

All that left much of the hard work to the Federal Communications Commission, as it was to promulgate the rules that would implement these ambiguous and complicated provisions. And for all of the uncertainty about how to actually read the Act, Congress left no doubt as to *when* the FCC was to complete its work implementing the core sharing rules; the 1996 Act required that the Commission issue the relevant implementing regulations within six months of the statute's enactment.[32] Somewhat miraculously given the enormity of the task, the FCC met the deadline, issuing the relevant regulations on August 8, 1996.[33] The litigation that ultimately led to both Supreme Court challenges began shortly thereafter.

A. IOWA UTILITIES

One of the main issues in contention in *Iowa Utilities* was the question of whether the Commission exercised reasonable discretion when it promulgated a rule identifying seven specific network elements that every incumbent would have to unbundle.[34] Incumbent local exchange carriers argued that the Commission had applied too lenient a standard when identifying those seven elements. For example, the incumbents argued that the Commission had not adequately considered the possibility that entrants can purchase some elements through voluntary transactions, a consideration that

---

[30] 47 USC § 251(d)(2).

[31] 47 USC § 252(d).

[32] 47 USC § 251(d)(1).

[33] See First Report and Order (cited in note 10).

[34] 47 CFR § 51.319 (1997).

might argue against mandatory unbundling with respect to those elements. The Court was largely receptive to these challenges and ultimately vacated the challenged rule; but, before we explain why, it might be helpful to first set out and analyze the relevant legal provisions, sections 251(c)(3) and 251(d)(2) of the 1996 Act.

Section 251(c)(3) sets forth the basic requirement that incumbent local exchange carriers "provide, to any requesting telecommunications carrier . . . access to network elements on an unbundled basis at any technically feasible point on rates, terms, and conditions that are just, reasonable, and nondiscriminatory."[35] When *Iowa Utilities* was litigated in the Eighth Circuit, there was some dispute over what the phrase "at any technically feasible point" means.[36] The Commission thought that the phrase creates a presumption that every element should be unbundled so long as unbundling is technically feasible.[37] Incumbent carriers thought that the phrase merely defines *where*—at technically feasible points—unbundling should take place.[38] The Eighth Circuit ultimately sided with the incumbents[39] and the Commission did not challenge that decision in the Supreme Court,[40] and thus today the accepted reading of section 251(c)(3) is that it creates a general unbundling obligation without in any way specifying exactly what should be unbundled.[41]

Section 251(d)(2), by contrast, offers guidance as to which elements should be included in the unbundling regime. Specifically, the provision instructs the Commission to "consider, at a mini-

[35] 47 USC § 251(c)(3).

[36] *Iowa Utilities Board v FCC*, 120 F3d 753, 810 (8th Cir 1997).

[37] 525 US at 391.

[38] Id.

[39] 120 F3d at 810.

[40] 525 US at 391.

[41] Note that the Supreme Court could have vacated and remanded the Commission's unbundling rules on this ground alone. The argument would have been that the Commission's admitted error in interpreting section 251(c)(3) infected all of its regulations; in essence, the Commission had started the process with a presumption in favor of unbundling and then looked for reasons not to unbundle instead of starting with a blank slate and looking for reasons to unbundle. The Court did not vacate on this ground, however, perhaps out of a suspicion that the two approaches in the end lead to the same basic results. This conclusion is bolstered by a comparison of the Commission's original list of elements (47 CFR § 51.319 (1997)) with the nearly identical list put forward on remand (47 CFR § 51.319 (2002)).

mum, whether (A) access to such network elements as are proprietary in nature is necessary; and (B) the failure to provide access to such network elements would impair the ability of the telecommunications carrier seeking access to provide the services that it seeks to offer."[42] One way to think about this provision is to see it as setting up a two-level standard: for elements that involve some form of intellectual property, the Commission should ask whether unbundling is "necessary," whereas for nonproprietary elements the Commission should ask only whether a decision not to unbundle would somehow "impair" competition. Phrased another way, Congress in this provision seems to be telling the Commission to be especially reluctant to unbundle elements where patent, copyright, trademark, or trade secret protection is implicated—more reluctant than the Commission would be under its normal, baseline standard.

But what is that baseline? Try three different formulations, all seemingly consistent with the vague contours of section 251(d)(2). In the first, the baseline for unbundling is that we should unbundle only in instances where it is physically or economically impractical for an entrant to provide a given element itself or to acquire that element through voluntary market transactions. This would be a relatively strict standard, in that it would roughly shadow antitrust law's essential facilities doctrine and thus would favor unbundling only in extreme situations. That might make sense; and, indeed, the incumbents pushed for this interpretation in the Supreme Court.[43] However, as we will see in a moment, there are arguments in favor of mandatory access even in cases where self-provision or voluntary transactions are plausible.

Try, then, a second formulation, that we should unbundle even in cases where entry would otherwise be possible, the purpose being either to make it easier for firms to enter the market or to accelerate entry into the market. The Commission was clearly sympathetic to at least this latter idea of accelerating entry. In fact, at one point in the document explaining its unbundling regulations, the Commission explicitly stated that while "it is possible that there will be sufficient demand in some local telephone markets to support the construction of competing local exchange facil-

---

[42] 47 USC § 251(d)(2).

[43] 525 US at 388.

ities" at some point, those future competitors should "be able to use unbundled elements from the incumbent [local exchange carriers] until such time as they complete construction of their own networks."[44] Note that this articulation seems to let the entrants determine when any transition takes place, although one could easily imagine an alternative articulation where unbundling was an option only for a predefined transition period.

Consider, finally, a third formulation, that we should unbundle in instances where new entrants would otherwise provide their own elements but those duplicative elements would represent social waste. This interpretation harkens back to the old regulatory notion that it is expensive to build certain parts of the local telephone network and it is therefore ridiculous to encourage firms to duplicate that infrastructure. Unbundling on this view is necessary not because a given entrant would not build its own facility, but rather because it would be socially wasteful to have a second facility built. On this story, mandatory access—at sufficiently cheap prices—is a means by which to avoid the needless duplication of facilities.

Again, section 251(d)(2) does not on its face dictate any particular choice among these three formulations. And, in fact, the record suggests that in some form the Commission thought about each of them when crafting its unbundling rules.[45] The question in *Iowa Utilities* was therefore whether, in the end, that thought process was sufficient; or, more specifically, whether the Commission had reasonably interpreted Congress's command that it "consider" whether access to proprietary elements was necessary and whether the failure to provide access to nonproprietary elements would impair a given entrant's ability to offer a particular telecommunications service.

Focus first on the direct command issued to the Commission, that it *consider* the two factors at issue. The most natural inter-

---

[44] First Report & Order at ¶ 232 (cited in note 10).

[45] See, for example, id at ¶ 286 (refusing to hold that incumbents "must provide unbundled elements only when the failure to do so would prevent a carrier from offering a service," thus considering and rejecting the first articulation given in the text); id at ¶ 378 (noting that the failure to unbundle a given element "would likely delay market entry and postpone the benefits of local telephone competition for consumers," the issues raised in our second articulation); and id (noting that, in some instances, "preventing access to unbundled loops would . . . cause the competitor to construct unnecessarily duplicative facilities, thereby misallocating societal resources," our third concern).

pretation of "consider" is just that: were the necessity and impair factors thought about in defining the unbundling standards? So long as they were—as they almost certainly were—the regulations would pass muster. Unsurprisingly, this is exactly how the Commission understood its obligation under section 251(d)(2), concluding that "the word 'consider' means we must weigh the standards enumerated in section 251(d)(2) in evaluating whether to require the unbundling of a particular element"[46] and, later, that "the plain language of section 251(d)(2), and the standards articulated there, give us the discretion to limit the general obligation imposed by subsection 251(c)(3), but they do not require us to do so."[47]

Arguably, this was a reasonable interpretation of the law. After all, Congress does from time to time order administrative agencies to include certain considerations in their deliberations. For example, the National Environmental Policy Act requires that federal agencies give environmental concerns "appropriate consideration in decisionmaking," but that Act does not itself impose any substantive standard on actual outcomes.[48] Moreover, the "shall consider" formulation is used more than a dozen times in federal communications laws,[49] and in at least some of those instances courts have interpreted the phrase to mean exactly what the Commission says it meant here.[50]

The Commission pressed this argument—that it need only consider necessity and impairment and that it had done so—in the Supreme Court,[51] but the Court's decision does not explicitly ad-

[46] Id at ¶ 280.

[47] Id at ¶ 286.

[48] 42 USC § 4332 (2002). See *Strycker's Bay Neighborhood Council, Inc. v Karlen*, 444 US 223 (1980).

[49] See, for example, 47 USC §§ 154(a)(3), 160(b), 226(e)(2), 227(b)(2), 251(d)(2), 254(c)(1), 273(e)(1)(A), 311(b), 325(b)(3)(A), 332(a), 332(c)(1)(C), 534(g)(2), 543(c)(2), 544a(c)(1), 548(c)(4), 610(b)(3) (2002).

[50] In a dispute over cable television rates, for example, the D.C. Circuit noted that the relevant statute "by its terms merely requires the Commission to consider" several relevant factors. The court went on to say that this means only that the Commission must "reach an express and considered conclusion about the bearing of [each] factor, but is not required to give any specific weight" to those factors. *Time Warner Entertainment Co. v FCC*, 56 F3d 151, 175 (DC Cir 1995) (interpreting 47 USC § 543(c)(2)) (internal citations and quotations omitted).

[51] See *Reply Brief for the Federal Petitioners and Brief for the Federal Cross-Respondents* at 43–44 ("*Reply Brief*") (available on Lexis).

dress it. We must admit that we are a little puzzled by that. The argument seems strong enough to warrant serious discussion, especially given the fact that, if accepted, it would leave the Commission's rule fully intact, a result directly opposite the one ultimately reached in the case. The best defense of what the Court did would be to say that the Commission's interpretations of the necessary and impair standards were so misguided that the Commission cannot fairly be said to have considered these factors. That would explain why the Court went ahead and analyzed the substance of the Commission's interpretations, and it is to that substance that we now turn.

The Court raised two fundamental concerns about the Commission's interpretations. The first was that, in the Court's view, the Commission had ignored the possibility that some elements can be obtained in the market or built by would-be entrants. As we have already explained, it might make sense to unbundle even if a given element can be built anew or acquired through voluntary transactions; for instance, the purpose of unbundling might be to discourage wasteful duplication by offering entrants cheap access to existing infrastructure. But the question of whether a given element can be acquired through voluntary transactions or built anew is certainly relevant to the section 251(d)(2) inquiry. The Court was therefore troubled by what it perceived as a Commission completely insensitive to these possibilities.

In truth, the evidence on this point was mixed. Yes, when the Commission announced its interpretation of the "necessary" standard, the Commission did say that a proprietary element is necessary unless the "requesting telecommunications carrier could offer the same proposed telecommunications service *through the use of other, nonproprietary unbundled network elements*" borrowed from the incumbent's network.[52] That comparison captures what the Court

---

[52] 47 CFR § 51.317 (1997) (emphasis added). This quotation is taken from Rule 317, a rule that was promulgated alongside the rule explicitly at issue in *Iowa Utilities*, Rule 319. Rule 317 instructed state commissions in how to interpret the necessary and impair standard in the event that they were called upon to unbundle additional elements above and beyond those unbundled on the federal level by the Commission. We quote this rule because it makes clear how the Commission was interpreting the "necessary" and "impair" standard. The *Iowa Utilities* Court, by contrast, quotes similar but more ambiguous language drawn from the document wherein the Commission explains and justifies both Rule 317 and Rule 319. See 525 US at 389, quoting First Report & Order at ¶ 283 (cited in note 10). Note that, while the Supreme Court ultimately vacated only Rule 319 and left Rule 317 intact, the Eighth Circuit on remand recognized the link between these two rules, going so far

saw as the Commission's error; it compares the incumbent's unbundled proprietary elements to the incumbent's unbundled nonproprietary elements, completely ignoring elements not borrowed
from the incumbent at all. Similarly, in interpreting the statutory
language about impairment, the Commission held that a requesting carrier would be impaired in its ability to provide a given
service if "the failure of an incumbent to provide access to a network element would decrease the quality, or increase the financial
or administrative cost of the service a requesting carrier seeks to
offer, *compared with providing that service over other unbundled elements*" borrowed from the incumbent's network.[53] Again, same
problem: this articulation compares unbundled elements to unbundled elements, failing to account for elements that might be acquired outside the unbundling regime.

In the Commission's defense, however, it is unfair to read too
much into those quotations. The Commission obviously did think
about the possibility that entrants would build elements themselves
or purchase elements in voluntary transactions. A few paragraphs
back, for instance, we quote the Commission as saying that "it is
possible that there will be sufficient demand in some local telephone markets to support the construction of competing local exchange facilities,"[54] and surely that sentence recognizes that entrants can build their own networks. The Court was therefore
wrong to say that the Commission did not account for these ideas
in its analysis; the Court's actual complaint is that the Commission
did not build these ideas into the rules that were ultimately promulgated.

If that is right, however, then it must be pointed out that the
Commission was under no legal or logical obligation to build these
ideas into its final rules. Suppose, for instance, that the Commission's honest evaluation of unbundling was that, in most instances,
elements should be unbundled even if they are also available
through voluntary transactions. Suppose, further, that the Commission believed that the added costs of distinguishing situations

---

as to vacate Rule 317 on grounds that, if Rule 319 was invalid, Rule 317 also could not
stand. See *Iowa Utilities Board v FCC*, 219 F3d 744, 757 (8th Cir 2000).

[53] First Report & Order at ¶ 285 (emphasis added) (cited in note 10). Cf. 47 CFR
§ 51.317(b)(2) (1997) (similar language used in Rule 317).

[54] See note 46.

where that assumption works from situations where it does not are high—both administratively and with respect to the additional legal uncertainty imposed by a contingent rule—and thus that the public interest was better served by a rule that ignores the possibility of voluntary transactions. In such a case, the Commission would have written rules exactly like those criticized in *Iowa Utilities*, and yet the Commission would have indeed considered voluntary market transactions in formulating its rules.

Turn attention for a moment to the Court's second concern, that neither of the Commission's interpretations included an explicit requirement that harms and differences be substantial. In the above-quoted language about impairment, for instance, the Commission concluded that a carrier is impaired in its ability to provide a given service if "the failure of an incumbent to provide access to a network element would decrease the quality, or increase the financial or administrative cost of the service a requesting carrier seeks to offer." That language seems to imply that—no matter how small—any increase in cost or decrease in quality would be sufficient to justify unbundling. And that, the Court objected, is an interpretation not sufficiently "in accord with the ordinary and fair meaning" of the terms "necessary" and "impair."[55]

Again, there is room to defend the Commission. A materiality requirement was surely implicit in the Commission's analysis; after all, if the Commission really believed that even trivial harms were sufficient to justify an unbundling obligation, the Commission would have required the unbundling of a large number of elements. In fact, the Commission's rule had required that only seven elements be unbundled.[56] Those elements obviously satisfy the barely-there impairment standard that the Court ascribes to the Commission, but almost certainly they also satisfy a much higher threshold—as the Commission itself concluded when it revisited these issues on remand.[57] Moreover, the Commission's list matches up quite well with the list Congress built into section 271, a provision that more fully specifies the unbundling requirement as it applies to former Bell Operating Companies interested in offering

---

[55] 525 US at 390.

[56] See 47 CFR § 51.319 (1997).

[57] See 47 CFR § 51.319 (2002).

2]   **ENTRY POLICY IN LOCAL TELECOMMUNICATIONS**   57

in-region long-distance service.[58] That further suggests that the Commission in fact did apply some sort of materiality standard in its analysis, even if that standard was not explicitly written out.

All that said, however, the Court's real objection with respect to both market availability and materiality is that the Commission had not made sufficiently clear its assumptions, reservations, and interpretations. The document in which the Commission had explained its rules was muddled and at times seemingly inconsistent. This was understandable given that Congress had ordered the Commission to prepare the document and issue the accompanying rules no later than six months after the enactment of the 1996 Act.[59] But the Court nevertheless thought that the problems were serious enough so as to require that the Commission attempt once more to clarify and explain the scope of the unbundling requirement. Hence the Court vacated the rule in which the Commission named the specific elements that were to be unbundled and then remanded for further proceedings both in the Commission and in the Eighth Circuit.

Iowa Utilities does approve some other, less sweeping regulations that the Commission had put forward with regard to mandatory sharing. For instance, the Commission had announced in the so-called "all elements" rule that an entrant can purchase access to unbundled network elements even if that entrant does not itself own any telecommunications facilities.[60] Incumbents had argued for the opposite rule, that entrants should have to bring at least some equipment to market in order to qualify for mandatory sharing. That, of course, would have delayed entry—presumably exactly what the incumbents were seeking—but it would have had the possibly offsetting benefit of encouraging entrants to invest in their own facilities, what is called in the industry "facilities-based" competition. The Court upheld the Commission mainly on grounds that the statute said nothing explicit on the subject.[61]

Similarly, the Court sided with the Commission in its determination that incumbents should not be allowed to separate previ-

---

[58] See 47 USC § 271(c)(2)(B) (2002). For discussion, see *Telecommunications Law & Policy* at 755–67 (cited in note 6).

[59] 47 USC § 251(d)(1).

[60] See First Report and Order at ¶¶ 328–40 (cited in note 10).

[61] 525 US at 392–93.

ously joined network elements before granting access to entrants.[62]
The idea, in the Commission's words, was to stop incumbents
from "disconnecting previously connected elements, over the objection of the requesting carrier, not for any productive reason,
but just to impose wasteful reconnection costs on new entrants."[63]
Incumbents had plausibly objected to this rule on grounds that it,
especially when combined with the "all elements" rule, made it
too easy for entrants to use the unbundling provisions to purchase
complete telecommunications services. An entrant who wanted to
purchase a complete service could do so under other provisions of
the 1996 Act, but at wholesale prices, not cost.[64] The incumbents'
point was that the unbundling provisions should be kept meaningfully distinct from these resale provisions, in that way ensuring
that each entry mechanism offers a unique mix of price, risk, and
obligation.[65]

Lastly, the Court also approved the Commission's "pick-and-
choose" rule, an interpretation of section 252(i) of the Act. Section
252(i) somewhat cryptically states that an incumbent must make
any network element that it provides to one party "available to
any other requesting telecommunications carrier upon the same
terms and conditions as those provided in the agreement."[66] The
Commission took this to mean that entrants can scour agreements
previously reached between incumbents and other entrants, pull
out a provision from a deal over here and another over there—
hence the pick-and-choose denomination—and cobble them together into a single agreement.[67] But that interpretation, incumbents pointed out, undermines the "give-and-take of negotiation,"
since every concession made in one setting automatically becomes
available in all future settings.[68] Incumbents therefore favored an

---

[62] For the Commission's rule, see 47 CFR § 51.315(b) (1997). For the Court's discussion, see 525 US at 395–96.

[63] 525 US at 395, quoting *Reply Brief* (cited in note 53).

[64] Section 251(c)(4) states that an incumbent must sell to rivals, at wholesale rates, any telecommunications service it provides at retail to subscribers. Section 251(b)(1) requires nonincumbents to also offer these services for resale, but that provision says nothing about the relevant price. 47 USC §§ 251(c)(4), 251(b)(1).

[65] In essence, the incumbents were trying to stop a form of regulatory arbitrage.

[66] 47 USC § 252(i).

[67] 47 CFR § 51.809 (2002) (Commission regulation implementing the provision).

[68] 525 US at 395.

interpretation where an entrant would be allowed to use an existing agreement but only if taken as a whole. As we said, the Court in the end sided with the Commission, reasoning that the Commission's approach, while unusual, tracked the actual language of the statute.[69]

Let us pause a moment here and insure that we have not lost the forest for the trees. In addition to some jurisdictional issues,[70] *Iowa Utilities* addressed a number of important questions about how mandatory sharing would work. The Court addressed these issues narrowly, focusing as it must on its job of statutory construction. But it ultimately approved and rejected an array of regulations that have significant implications for how sharing will work in the telecommunications market. Think, for instance, about pick-and-choose. An incumbent's natural response to the Commission's interpretation will be to push toward uniformity in its agreements, thereby minimizing the opportunities for cherry-picking across agreements. That does straitjacket the incumbents, and we should be concerned about that, but a countervailing benefit is that it pushes the incumbents toward nondiscrimination in their dealings with entrants. Nondiscrimination duties are frequently imposed on regulated firms as part of sharing regimes[71] and they are normally quite difficult to enforce. The pick-and-choose rule goes at this from another angle, adopting something of a self-enforcing, decentralized approach to nondiscrimination. Give some entrant a good deal on something and later entrants will grab it as well, almost like a statutory most-favored-nation clause. This decentralized approach might very well be a superior alternative to centralized enforcement of nondiscrimination obligations and ultimately an important factor in how the 1996 Act's overall sharing regime will work in practice.

B. VERIZON

That takes us to this past Term and *Verizon*. At issue in *Verizon* was the Commission's approach to pricing shared access. Incum-

---

[69] Id at 396.

[70] See note 6.

[71] See, for example, 16 USC § 824k(a) (2002) (nondiscrimination in wheeling electricity); 47 USC § 251(b) (nondiscrimination duties of local exchange carriers); 47 USC § 251(c) (additional duties for ILECs).

bent local exchange carriers challenged the Commission's rules on two grounds: first, that they were not a reasonable interpretation of the relevant provisions of the Act; and, second, that under the rule of constitutional avoidance the Court should interpret the 1996 Act to preclude the Commission's pricing methodology and in that way avoid the possible constitutional question of whether the statute as implemented by the Commission results in a taking of property in violation of the Fifth and Fourteenth Amendments. We will return to both of these arguments immediately below; but to understand them, it is helpful to begin by getting a sense of the issues at stake when it comes to setting the price for an unbundled network element.

The first issue is whether access prices should be set at the level of marginal cost. Basic economics teaches that marginal cost pricing leads to efficient use. But marginal cost pricing does not compensate firms for their nonmarginal investments—in this case, investments in copper wires, computerized telephone switches, and other parts of the local telecommunications network. Denying incumbents any return on these investments seems unfair, and it also would distinguish this market from a well-functioning conventional market, since even conventional markets allow competing firms to earn returns on their nonmarginal investments. Worse, there is a dynamic wrinkle: if incumbents are treated unfairly in this instance, new entrants might be reluctant to enter the market for fear that future regulations will burn them, too.[72]

All this might in the end mean that the right approach is to sacrifice efficiency and build nonmarginal costs into access prices. But which costs? For example, should incumbents be allowed to

---

[72] Of course, there are ways to compensate incumbents for their nonmarginal investments while still setting access prices at the level of marginal cost. For example, the government could set prices at marginal cost—thereby maximizing efficiency—but then pay incumbents a one-time cash transfer funded by general tax revenues. If that seems too vulnerable to government error or abuse, an alternative approach would have the government set prices at marginal cost and then encourage incumbents to sue for fair compensation under the Takings Clause. This would introduce the courts as a check on the level of the transfer payment, and this is in fact one way to understand the *Verizon* litigation. For discussion of these ideas in the context of the patent system, see Michael Abramowicz, *Perfecting Patent Prizes*, Vand L Rev (forthcoming 2003); Douglas Lichtman, *Pricing Prozac: Why the Government Should Subsidize the Purchase of Patented Pharmaceuticals*, 11 Harv J L & Tech 123 (1997). Note that using the Takings Clause in this manner might be particularly attractive if our main worry here is that, in the heat of the moment, regulated parties will be mistreated. The reason is that the takings approach separates in time the decision to regulate from the decision over fair compensation.

recover the costs of an expensive computer system that was purchased even though a less expensive alternative would have sufficed? How might such a purchase be distinguished from a computer system that was wisely purchased, or a computer system that was prudent when purchased but turned out to be useless or excessive?[73] Should we think differently about that question if it turns out that regulators encouraged incumbents to choose one computer system over the other? What if regulators were more passively involved, not explicitly weighing in on the decision but approving it after it was already made by the incumbent? Does that bind the government to later build the relevant expense into access prices on some form of implicit contract theory?[74]

These concerns represent just the tip of the iceberg. How should we account for the monies that incumbents have already earned on their infrastructure investments, ensuring that regulation does not allow the incumbents to recoup their expenses twice? How should nonmarginal costs be adjusted in light of various tax and accounting issues? For instance, if an incumbent has depreciated a given infrastructure investment in a particular way in order to achieve some tax advantage, should that depreciation path be binding in this setting as well? And, realistically, how well can we expect the government to estimate any of these many figures, given that the best source for all this information is the regulated incumbent itself, but the regulated incumbent has strong incentives to distort this information in ways that increase access prices?

A second set of issues here involves the relationship between access prices and the incentives firms face to either improve the existing network or build new infrastructure. Consider the incentives facing new entrants first. If access prices are sufficiently low,

---

[73] This is not just a hypothetical difficulty. For example, telecommunications firms have spent billions of dollars in recent years laying over 100 million miles of high-capacity optical fiber, yet it is estimated that only 2.7% of that installed fiber is currently being used. See Yochi J. Dreazen, *Wildly Optimistic Data Drove Telecoms to Build Fiber Glut*, Wall Street Journal (September 26, 2002). Was this a case of imprudent investment run amok, or did these investments make sense at the time but prove unwise in hindsight? For discussion of a similar problem in the electric industry—namely, storage facilities built to accompany planned nuclear power plants where the relevant power plants were then never built—see *State of North Carolina Utilities Commission v Thornburg*, 325 NC 484 (1989), and *State of North Carolina Utilities Commission v Thornburg*, 325 NC 463 (1989).

[74] For more detailed discussion of the so-called regulatory contract, see Gregory Sidak and Daniel Spulber, *Deregulatory Takings and the Regulatory Contract* (Cambridge, 1997).

entrants have little reason to venture into the business of actually developing their own facilities. Why take on the risk of building it yourself when the existing infrastructure is available at a bargain price? That is not so troubling if we think that incumbents are better suited to build and innovate anyway—say, because they have more experience in the industry, or more financial wherewithal— but it is more likely that, when we say we want competition in the local loop, we mean that we want several firms working on new ideas about marketing, pricing, and, yes, the design of the network itself. If that is true, low prices can undermine a key objective of the Act.[75]

Of course, high prices can be just as bad. A sufficiently high price might lead entrants to build their own infrastructure even in instances where society would be better off had the entrants just shared existing equipment. Entrants would be building in this instance not because the new infrastructure was cost-justified, but instead because the regulated price was artificially high. In some of these instances, the incumbent might voluntarily offer the entrant a lower price, thereby avoiding inefficient build-around. But that seems unlikely, at least if the incumbent's main goal is to keep the costs of entry high and thereby protect its market dominance. Moreover, even if the incumbent does offer a lower price, the Act will have played no role in that outcome; a world with a mandatory sharing regime and a sufficiently high access price is roughly equivalent to a world with no mandatory sharing regime at all.

Now consider the incentives facing incumbents. If our goal is to maximize incumbents' investment incentives, it is not at all clear how best to set the access price. On the one hand, if incumbents know that their facilities will be available to rivals at low rates, they might be reluctant to invest in new infrastructure. What would be the point, since any advantage would immediately be made avail-

---

[75] Even if prices are low, entrants do still have some incentive to innovate. For instance, entrants have an incentive to innovate with respect to whatever infrastructure and services they combine with the incumbent's unbundled network elements; so, to be simple, if an entrant leases copper lines from the incumbent but is using its own computer system to provide internet access over those lines, obviously the entrant has incentive to upgrade and improve its own computer system. Similarly, entrants have some incentive to innovate with respect to leased elements, too. Staying with our simple example, if our hypothetical entrant sees a way to improve the copper lines, he might contact the relevant incumbent and offer to cut a deal, suggesting the improvement to the incumbent and in exchange demanding some sort of financial reward. Our point in the text is only that a significant incentive disappears if the regulated price of leased access is too low.

able to rivals anyway? Worse, the costs of any errors would be borne entirely by the incumbent, since a dud technology would not attract any buyers. On this story, low access prices seem likely to discourage investment in unbundled network elements, driving incumbents to invest instead in their brand names and other resources not subject to mandatory sharing.

On the other hand, low access prices can stimulate investment. Consider, for example, an investment that would slightly decrease the marginal costs of providing some network element. If access prices are high, demand is likely low, and the allure of investing in this new technology is thus also relatively low. Saving a few pennies on each of a few sales simply does not warrant a significant infrastructure expense. If access prices are low, however, demand for the network element will skyrocket, and now the analysis might shift, since saving a few pennies on each of a large number of sales might very well justify a significant infrastructure investment.[76] Thus we can say nothing definitive about the access price that maximizes an incumbent's incentive to innovate.

The Commission could not escape so easily; it had to promulgate some rule, and whatever rule it chose was going to have implications for all of the various incentives and debates outlined above. Congress had given the Commission little help in this effort. Remember, the relevant provision of the 1996 Act states only that firms should be allowed to purchase access to unbundled network elements at "just and reasonable rates" that are "non-discriminatory" and "may include a reasonable profit."[77] Good luck mapping those vague constraints to the practical issues at stake in the decision. Congress had offered one further bit of guidance, however, that being a clause in section 252 that states that rates should be "based on . . . cost" but "determined without reference to a rate-of-return or other rate-based proceeding."[78] That is a lot of lingo, but the clause seems to refer to and reject the conventional mechanisms that had previously been used to set prices in telecommuni-

---

[76] This is consistent with the literature that questions whether monopolists or competitors have a greater incentive to engage in innovation. The point there, and here, is that one important factor is the researching firm's expectations as to the number of units it will ultimately sell. For links into that literature, see Jean Tirole, *The Theory of Industrial Organization* 390–94 (MIT, 1988).

[77] 47 USC § 252(d).

[78] Id.

cations and other regulated industries. Congress did not tell the Commission what alternative to adopt; but Congress seems to be saying that the old approaches—each fraught with difficulties well known in the network industries literature[79]—were not to be applied.

Writing on this virtually blank slate, the Commission adopted the following approach. First, the Commission chose to interpret "cost" to mean "forward-looking economic cost" instead of cost defined by the actual historic investments made in the particular element at issue.[80] The FCC defined the forward-looking cost of a network element to be the sum of "the total element long-run incremental cost of the element" (TELRIC) plus "a reasonable allocation of forward-looking common costs" where common costs are "costs incurred in providing a group of elements that cannot be attributed directly to individual elements."[81] Most controversially, the Commission announced that TELRIC would "be measured based on the use of the most efficient telecommunications technology currently available and the lowest cost network configuration, given the existing location" of the incumbent's wire centers.[82]

Again, a great deal of lingo; but the key insights here are two. First, when fully unpacked, the Commission's rule adopts a middling position with respect to most of the competing factors discussed above. Forward-looking cost as defined by the Commission focuses on marginal cost but also accounts for some fixed costs, some degree of profit, some degree of depreciation over time, and so on. It is in truth a complicated balance that, for better or worse, can be applied flexibly to various specific network elements. Second, and a bit more extreme, the Commission's approach does take a firm stance on the issue of incumbent-specific costs: while access prices will account for a variety of factors, those factors will largely be calculated in the abstract instead of being specifically mapped to the actual history of the network element at issue. This avoids the problem of relying too heavily on numbers that only the in-

---

[79] For an introduction to the standard approaches and their pitfalls, see *Telecommunications Law & Policy* at 425–29 (cited in note 6).

[80] See 47 CFR § 51.505 (2002).

[81] 47 CFR § 51.505(a) (2002).

[82] 47 CFR § 51.505(b)(1) (2002).

cumbent knows, and it also matches up with how value is calculated in competitive markets, since the value of any good is determined by its benefits and costs as compared to current alternatives,
not the history of how much its seller spent in creating it. The
downsides to this approach from the incumbents' perspective are
that it might mean that some investments will never be fully re-
couped, and it almost surely means that access prices will steadily
drop over time as new alternatives erode the value of existing infrastructure.

The legal analysis in *Verizon* did not end up delving significantly
into any of the above details. The Court surveyed these issues, but
on the question of whether the Commission's interpretation was
reasonable, the Court quickly recognized that there was considerable discretion built into the statute. For instance, the incumbents
had argued that the Commission's pricing methodology was not
"based on . . . cost" because, among other things, the Commission
had defined cost to mean the expense that would be incurred were
an equivalent network built today instead of adopting the arguably
more conventional definition that cost means actual monies spent.
The Court responded that the word cost "is a virtually meaningless term" that gives "rate setting commissions broad methodolog-
ical leeway" and says "little about the method employed to determine a particular rate."[83] In short, given the vague language used
in the Act, virtually anything the Commission had put forward in
terms of its pricing methodology would have fallen within the
scope of *Chevron* deference. When it came to access pricing, Congress seems to have had only one specific detail in mind—a distrust
of the traditional approaches—and, whatever one wants to say
about the Commission's rule, it certainly is not a traditional approach.

The possible issue with respect to the Takings Clause was also
easily—albeit somewhat unsatisfactorily—resolved. Again, the incumbents had argued that the Court should interpret the 1996 Act
to preclude the Commission's pricing methodology in order to
avoid the possible constitutional question of whether the statute
as implemented by the Commission results in a taking of property
in violation of the Fifth and Fourteenth Amendments. The Court

---

[83] 122 S Ct at 1667 (internal citations and quotations omitted).

refused to do so on grounds that the takings claim as alleged by
the incumbents did not itself raise a "serious question," or at least
that it did not raise a sufficiently serious question to warrant application of the rule of constitutional avoidance. The primary reason
was that the incumbents were endeavoring to challenge a pricing
methodology as opposed to specific rates. This ran against the
Court's "general rule" that it does not consider "a taking challenge
on ratesetting methodology without being presented with specific
rate orders alleged to be confiscatory."[84] The logic is that it is
difficult to anticipate how a methodology will translate into numbers. The pricing methodology at issue in *Verizon*, for instance,
was so flexible that it was still almost impossible for the Court to
guess whether the resulting prices would be high or low, let alone
unconstitutionally low in violation of the Takings Clause. The
Court was thus reluctant to deem the constitutional issue sufficiently serious.[85]

All that strikes us as somewhat reasonable, and we do not want
to be unfairly critical; however, this decision to in effect defer the
incumbents' possible takings claim had significant implications,
and we are not convinced that the Court weighed them with care.
First, by punting on the takings claim, the Court in essence set in
motion fifty new lawsuits that will soon be filed in the federal
courts, each alleging that the pricing provisions as tailored and
implemented in a specific state violate the Takings Clause given
the regulatory history of that state's incumbents. Maybe that flood
of litigation was unavoidable, but one wonders nevertheless
whether the Court could have said something more to help shape
expectations and thus minimize the disruption those cases will ultimately cause.

Second, and more broadly, while it might sound prudent to delay any serious takings analysis until actual numbers are in hand,
the fact is that the benefits of delay are small and the costs are
substantial. Focus on the benefits first. Delay does indeed mean
that, when the claim is litigated in the future, there will be real

---

[84] Id at 1679.

[85] The Court did indicate that it might have been willing to further consider the takings
claim if there were evidence that the regulatory change had been "arbitrary, opportunistic,
or undertaken with a confiscatory purpose." Id at 1681. There was no such evidence presented, however.

numbers to work with instead of just a verbal description of the Commission's pricing methodology. But numbers really do not matter much when it comes to answering the basic questions about whether there can be a taking in a situation like this and, more specifically, how courts will ultimately calculate the extent of any such taking. These are difficult questions to be sure, but the answers are not at all tied to specific numbers. The Court was therefore in as good a position to answer them in *Verizon* as it will be in some hypothetical case down the road.

The benefits of waiting, then, seem small; but consider the costs. The Takings Clause is primed to play a central and beneficial role in the implementation of the unbundled network elements regime. For it to do so, however, both the Commission and the incumbents need to have confidence that ultimately a takings remedy will be available. Think of it this way: if the takings claim looks implausible, the Commission has to set prices with an eye toward balancing several competing factors. Specifically, the price has to promote efficient use of network elements in the short run; promote efficient investment in research and development by the incumbents in the long run; similarly promote efficient investment in research and development by new entrants in the long run; and on top of that, address the distributional implications that are the core of the takings claim. This is hard to accomplish, both because the analysis becomes complicated with all these factors in play and because these factors often push in opposite directions. For instance, to maximize short-run efficiency, the Commission should set prices at the level of marginal cost, but to address the distributional issue, prices will certainly have to be far above marginal cost.

If the Commission and the incumbents have confidence that a takings claim will ultimately be successful, by contrast, the Commission can ignore the distributional issue when setting access prices and focus exclusively on the various incentive effects. It can do this knowing all the while that any distributional issue will be fairly addressed separately. This is important because it eliminates the tension identified above. If the distributional and efficiency issues can be handled separately, then when the Commission sets its prices it does not have to compromise on efficiency in order to account for distributional concerns. Instead, it can set prices that sensibly balance all the various incentives and then, through takings litigation, help to ensure that incumbents are fairly compensated for their losses. Incumbents, meanwhile, would in these circumstances be precluded from arguing against the Commission's prices on purely distributional grounds. That would not only narrow the grounds for disagreement but perhaps also dampen incumbents' incentives to delay implementation of the Act.

Again, all this is possible only if the Commission and the incumbents can have confidence that the distributional issue will ultimately be addressed. The *Verizon* Court did nothing in support of that aim. This is not surprising given existing Takings Clause jurisprudence. The leading cases do express a general reluctance to litigate takings claims in the abstract, and the Court certainly was understandably reluctant to rewrite takings law as part of the *Verizon* litigation. That said, however, the net result here is that the Court will have slightly better information to work with if and when it finally does evaluate the takings claim, but the bulk of the value in allowing that claim will have already been sacrificed.

II. Natural Monopoly and Entry

From its infancy, federal telecommunications law has proceeded on the assumption that local telephone service is a natural monopoly. That is, it has been assumed that costs in this market are such that it is less expensive for demand to be met by one firm than it is for demand to be met by any number of competing firms. In this section, we want to explore in some detail what it means to say that something is a natural monopoly and, further, what insight that might offer in terms of understanding the issues at stake in *Iowa Utilities* and *Verizon* and, more broadly, the local competition provisions of the 1996 Act itself.

A. NATURAL MONOPOLY IN THE LOCAL TELEPHONE MARKET

Let us start by making the case that local telephone service is indeed best understood as a natural monopoly. Again, the generic definition is that natural monopoly occurs where it is less expensive for demand to be met by one firm than it would be for that same demand to be met by some number of competing firms. One reason that this might be true in local telephony is that there are significant fixed costs associated with telephone service. For example, to provide service, a firm must lay wires throughout the relevant area and install appropriate computer equipment to route telephone signals along the network. It would greatly increase the total cost of telephone service to have two firms incur those same expenses in the same geographic area, and any such added costs are pure waste if a single network could have satisfied demand. Thus, on this argument, telephone service looks like a natural monopoly.

There are other reasons as well to think that local telephone service exhibits the properties of a natural monopoly.[86] For instance, an individual's demand for telephone service varies significantly from moment to moment and day to day; yet, in order to provide adequate service, the telephone company has to be ready to serve a given user whenever that user happens to pick up the telephone. If a different firm were to serve each user, there would be significant waste since almost all of each phone system's capacity would sit idle for most of the day. By having a single firm serve a large number of users, by contrast, the costs of providing phone service can be lowered dramatically. Several users can share a given amount of capacity, putting the equipment to better use since the variance in each consumer's demand would to some degree cancel out, leaving less of the phone system's capacity to sit idle at a given time. Sometimes—say, Mother's Day—everyone will want to use the phone at the same moment, and, at that time, some customers will be denied service; but, for most of the year, users can share capacity without any degradation in service, and thus it is cheaper to have a single firm serve many customers than it is to have multiple firms serve that same number of customers.

Similarly, telephone systems are said to exhibit "network effects," which for our purposes means that the benefits of telephone ownership increase as the number of subscribers increases. A single telephone in isolation is of little value to its owner since there is no one to call. But the usefulness of that telephone grows exponentially as more and more people join the same telephone network. If there were competing telephone networks, to achieve this same level of value society would have to spend considerably greater resources. Perhaps consumers would have to purchase and maintain multiple telephones, using their WorldCom telephone to talk

---

[86] Parts of this discussion are adopted, with permission, from *Telecommunications Law & Policy* at 614–18 (cited in note 6).

to their friends on the WorldCom network and their AT&T telephone to talk to their friends on the AT&T network.[87] Or perhaps the government would have to force the networks to interconnect—an expensive proposition given that it would likely require that the government monitor compliance, oversee negotiations, and otherwise help to ensure that the various reluctant allies work together. In short, network effects increase the value of having just a single telephone network, which is the same thing as saying that having multiple telephone networks increases the costs of achieving a given quality of service. That, like the two preceding arguments, makes it likely that local telephone service is a natural monopoly.

So what? As we will explain below, characterizing local telephone service as a natural monopoly tells us very little. It does not tell us whether we should expect to see competition. It does not tell us whether, if we see competition, we should be pleased or discouraged. It does not tell us that there should be regulation, nor does it tell us that regulation is unnecessary. Instead, characterizing local telephone service as a natural monopoly tells us only that there is an important conversation to be had—a conversation about the possibility of competition in the first place, and the costs and benefits of competition should we believe it possible. It is to that conversation that we now turn.

B. IMPLICATIONS OF NATURAL MONOPOLY

Natural monopoly suggests a contrast to *unnatural* monopoly or artificial monopoly. This is in fact how Judge Learned Hand saw the issue in 1945 when—because the Supreme Court could not muster a quorum[88]—the Second Circuit was called upon to offer

---

[87] A similar set of issues is currently playing out with respect to instant messaging (IM). America Online has had the leading IM service. Entrants, including Yahoo and Microsoft, have sought to interconnect their IM programs with AOL's, in that way gaining quick access to a large pool of IM users. AOL has responded with technology walls that make it more difficult for new entrants to interconnect with the AOL IM network. Users, in turn, have responded by downloading multiple IM programs. See Philip J. Weiser, *Internet Governance, Standard Setting, and Self-Regulation*, 28 N Ky L Rev 822 (2001).

[88] See *Allen-Myland, Inc. v IBM*, 33 F3d 194, 203 n 10 (3d Cir 1996) ("In *Alcoa*, however, a sufficient number of justices were recused that a quorum could not be obtained; accordingly, the Supreme Court . . . remanded the case to the three most senior judges of the Second Circuit").

the final word as to whether Alcoa had monopolized the aluminum market in violation of Section 2 of the Sherman Act:

> It does not follow because Alcoa had . . . a monopoly, that it "monopolized" the ingot market: it may not have achieved monopoly; monopoly may have been thrust upon it. If it had been a combination of existing smelters which united the whole industry and controlled the production of all aluminum ingot, it would certainly have "monopolized" the market. In several decisions the Supreme Court has decreed the dissolution of such combinations, although they had engaged in no unlawful trade practices. . . . [P]ersons may unwittingly find themselves in possession of a monopoly, automatically so to say: that is, without having intended either to put an end to existing competition, or to prevent competition from arising when none had existed; they may become monopolists by force of accident. . . . A market may, for example, be so limited that it is impossible to produce at all and meet the cost of production except by a plant large enough to supply the whole demand. Or there may be changes in taste or in cost which drive out all but one purveyor. A single producer may be the survivor out of a group of active competitors, merely by virtue of his superior skill, foresight and industry. In such cases a strong argument can be made that, although the result may expose the public to the evils of monopoly, the [Sherman] Act does not mean to condemn the resultant of those very forces which it is its prime object to foster: *finis opus coronat*. The successful competitor, having been urged to compete, must not be turned upon when he wins.[89]

Hand's point is that artificial monopoly and natural monopoly require different sorts of legal responses. Mergers between rivals and collusion among competitors both create artificial forms of monopoly and, in Hand's view, both are rightly regulated under

---

[89] *United States v Aluminum Co. of America*, 148 F2d 416, 430 (1945). Hand wrote this against an almost nonexistent Supreme Court backdrop. The Court had used the phrase "natural monopoly" only twice, first in 1910 in a dispute over a waterworks plant, *City of Omaha v Omaha Water Co.*, 218 US 180 (1910), and then again in 1932 in a Fourteenth Amendment challenge to an Oklahoma statute restricting entry into the ice business, *New State Ice Co. v Liebmann*, 285 US 262 (1932). Neither case had offered any real sense of how to think about natural monopoly or its implications. Perhaps even more interesting, the Court had not used the phrase in any of its three key pre-*Alcoa* decisions on the constitutional limits on public utility rate regulation—*Smyth, Southwestern Bell*, and *Hope Natural Gas*—three cases that would today almost surely be analyzed as cases primarily about natural monopoly. See *Federal Power Commission v Hope Natural Gas Co.*, 320 US 591 (1944); *Missouri ex rel Southwestern Bell Telephone Co. v Public Service Commission of Missouri*, 262 US 276 (1923); *Smyth v Ames*, 169 US 466 (1898).

federal antitrust law. But "natural" monopoly—what Hand saw as monopoly thrust upon a firm either as the inevitable result of vigorous competition or because of the cost structure of the relevant market—is different. It might lead to the same evils in terms of high prices and restricted quantities, but it should be regulated, if at all, through special legislation targeted at the particular industry, not through the generic provisions of antitrust.

So far so good, but matters become significantly less clear when the question turns to what exactly that special legislation should say. Consider a core case of natural monopoly, for example, a situation where a firm has to first undertake a substantial fixed cost before any units of the relevant product can be produced, but the firm can then produce as many units as it wants at a stable per-unit cost. Computer software, for example, matches this pattern. A company spends a substantial amount of money to write, test, and debug its software, but once the product is in hand, it can produce as many CDs as it wants at a set per-unit cost.

Note why this cost structure can be thought of as a natural monopoly cost structure. The least expensive way to produce any amount of the good in question is to have one firm supply all comers. This is the conventional—perhaps even natural!—definition of natural monopoly.[90] If two firms were to produce, the fixed costs would be incurred twice; and yet there would be no benefit, since per-unit cost is the same regardless of how production is split between the two firms. That is, if the industry produces ten units, the marginal cost of producing each unit will be the same regardless of whether all ten are produced by one firm, five are produced by one firm and five by the other, or any other pattern. The only cost that changes is the amount of money invested up front. Those fixed costs rise directly with the number of firms in the industry— two times the fixed costs with two firms, fifty times with fifty firms—and, focusing just on the costs of production, we are therefore better off having only one firm produce.[91]

But does this cost structure mean that we will see only one firm

---

[90] See, for example, Dennis Carlton and Jeffrey Perloff, *Modern Industrial Organization* 101 (Addison-Wesley, 3d ed 2000).

[91] Notice that this is an argument about the costs of production; it says nothing about the price that will ultimately prevail. For discussion of other cost structures that lead to natural monopoly, see *Telecommunications Law & Policy* at 374–80 (cited in note 6).

in the market? In short, does a natural monopoly naturally lead to monopoly? And, if so, what implications flow from that conclusion? Start with the second question first. If we would naturally see only one firm producing in a natural monopoly market, we would then need to be concerned about whether that firm can exercise monopoly power. The social harm of monopoly is well known: monopolists tend to raise prices and restrict output, the net effect being both a transfer of wealth from consumers to the monopolist and pure deadweight loss in the form of efficient transactions that never take place due to the monopolist's supracompetitive price. This is an argument for regulating the monopolist's price and, if the monopolist can respond to price regulation by skimping on quality, then regulating its quality, too.

We should be careful though. Even if natural monopoly means that there will be only one firm producing, that does not at all imply that the firm will be capable of exercising market power. This is part of what had worried Hand in *Alcoa*, and the same question has been an issue in the Microsoft antitrust litigation.[92] But the theory is clear: the threat of potential entry can exert substantial pressure on prices, even in a market where everyone knows that at the end of the day only one firm will remain standing. The idea is that the producing firm will in certain instances have to cabin its price in order to discourage would-be rivals from entering the market, undercutting the prevailing price, and ultimately taking over as the new monopolist. The credibility of this threat depends on a host of issues; for instance, if the existing firm can change its price quickly, the threat of entry might not be substantial, since the moment a rival enters the existing firm will be able to match the rival's price and in that way thwart the rival's strategy. Conversely, if the existing firm cannot change its price quickly, or indeed if it can change price quickly but is slow at detecting entry by a rival, then the threat of future entry is significant and the existing firm will face strong pressure to keep prices low.[93]

That answers the second of our questions, but what of the first? All of the analysis so far has assumed that, at equilibrium, natural

[92] See Robert E. Hall, *Optimal Contracts to Defend Upstream Monopoly* 23 (January 25, 2000) (working paper on file with authors).

[93] See William J. Baumol et al, *Contestable Markets and the Theory of Industry Structure* 2 (Harcourt, 1988).

monopoly means that there will be only one firm producing in the market. But that is not necessarily right, since even in the face of natural monopoly costs there is still often a real incentive for firms to enter the market. Be clear on what that means: even if we have a cost technology such that overall production costs could be minimized by having a single firm produce, we might see more than one firm producing. When might that be true? One key issue is what the potential entrant anticipates the incumbent producer will do in response to entry. For example, if the entrant believes that the incumbent will cut prices to marginal cost, the entrant would foresee little chance of recovering its fixed costs—hardly an attractive business plan to the venture capitalists or bond-holders forking over the money to pay the fixed costs. In contrast, if the entrant believes that it and the incumbent will be able to come to terms, either through explicit collusion or implicit interactions in the marketplace, the entrant may anticipate sufficient profits so as to justify entry despite the natural monopoly cost structure.

Economists, it turns out, have said a lot about all of this. If we expect the incumbent and the entrant to compete in prices—so-called Bertand competition[94]—then the resulting Nash equilibrium would result in marginal cost pricing and hence the entrant has no incentive to enter in the first place. In that case, natural monopoly does naturally lead to monopoly. If we expect the incumbent and entrant to compete in quantities, however—Cournot competition[95]—we may have entry by some number of firms and an equilibrium with some competition. Similarly, if we expect the incumbent and the entrant to bifurcate the market, with each firm specializing in some subset of customer needs or some specific geographic area, we might again see an equilibrium with multiple firms, this time with each firm acting as a monopolist to its own smaller submarket.

Where does all this leave us? If we have natural monopoly costs and just one firm producing, but we do not have potential entrants exerting pressure on prices, natural monopoly means a market where prices are inefficiently high. That is a problem and should make clear why rate regulation has been the historical legislative response to natural monopoly situations. If, by contrast, we have

---

[94] Carlton and Perloff, *Modern Industrial Organization* at 157–61 (cited in note 92).

[95] Id at 166–68.

natural monopoly costs, one firm producing, and a real threat of potential entry, then we likely will have quasi-competitive pricing and, interestingly, no need for regulation. Lastly, if we have natural monopoly costs but nevertheless the possibility of multiple firms in the market, we have a choice to make. We can restrict competition—that is, turn away would-be competitors—and in that way force the market to revert to one of the two situations just considered. That was the traditional approach to the local telephone market adopted by federal telecommunications law in its infancy and maintained up until the 1996 Act.[96] Or we can embrace the possibility of competition but use regulation simultaneously to mitigate the economic waste it causes and to insure that prices stay well below the monopolistic level. This, as we will discuss further, is arguably the approach adopted under the 1996 Act.

Obviously this choice has implications not only for social welfare but also for would-be market participants. For instance, the first firm to enter a natural monopoly market might be reluctant to invest heavily without promises from the state that later competitors will be turned away. It is one thing to invest in a natural monopoly market where your firm will be the sole regulated entrant; quite another to invest in a natural monopoly market that might feature a revolving cast of would-be competitors. Local governments used to lure cable television providers by making just these sorts of promises.[97] Applicants would compete ex ante to be the chosen firm, but once a winner was chosen, that winner would be awarded an exclusive franchise for the term of the deal. Local officials would regulate cable prices and thus ensure that the chosen firm was not behaving as a monopolist, but in exchange the government would protect that firm from competition. Federal law changed to prohibit the practice in 1992, the fear being that the ability to grant exclusive licenses invested too much power in local government.[98]

---

[96] This parallels the long-standing approach of regulating entry by giving public utilities commissions the power to enforce certificate of convenience and necessity statutes.

[97] For discussion, see *Telecommunications Law & Policy* at 429–31 (cited in note 6).

[98] This change was made by the Cable Television Consumer Protection and Competition Act, which prohibited local government both from granting exclusive franchises and from unreasonably refusing to award additional franchises. See Cable Television Consumer Protection and Competition Act of 1992, Pub L No 102-385, 106 Stat 1460 (1992) at § 7(a)(1), codified at 47 USC § 541 (2002).

C. IMPLICATIONS FOR THE 1996 ACT, IOWA UTILITIES, AND VERIZON

The preceding analysis tells us what to expect if local telephone service turns out to exhibit the properties of a natural monopoly. Let us now connect these issues first to the 1996 Act and then to both *Iowa Utilities* and *Verizon*. We said in the introduction that the purpose of the Act's unbundling provisions is to promote competition. But how does that claim link to the discussion here about natural monopolies? There are several possible answers.

One possibility is that the Act rejects the long-standing view that the market for local telephone service exhibits the properties of a natural monopoly. On this interpretation, either regulators have been wrong all these years about how the economics of this industry play out, or they have been right but the dynamics of the market are different now thanks to new technologies like wireless telephony and the possibility of carrying voice traffic over the cable television infrastructure. Note that the purpose of the 1996 Act on this story is to guide the transition from a regulated natural monopoly to an unregulated, competitive market. Sharing provisions encourage entry during this transition period and possibly also make up for any advantages enjoyed by the incumbents by virtue of their long involvement in the local market. But on this view the sharing provisions should ultimately sunset once the transition period is complete.

A more likely interpretation of the 1996 Act is that it does not reject the notion that local telephone service is a natural monopoly, but instead simply reflects a new consensus that the costs of competition are not so high as once feared and thus a mix of competition and regulation might in the end be more attractive than an approach that relies on regulation alone. Phrased another way, it might be the case that the experience of regulating monopolist telephone carriers over the years has convinced Congress that regulation in that form is too costly, insufficiently effective, or both, and thus the 1996 Act experiments with a more competitive approach. Such an approach might mean increased economic waste, but the upside is that competition can supplement regulation and perhaps create better incentives when it comes to innovation, quality, and price. Note that this time there is no reason to believe that the 1996 Act will ever sunset; competition in this story is a supplement to, but not a replacement for, government regulation.

It is tempting to offer two other possible interpretations of the 1996 Act, but neither is correct. The first would suggest that the Act's real purpose is to help policymakers answer the question of whether and to what extent local telephone service is a natural monopoly. On this view, if entrants invoke the mandatory sharing provisions, then it can be assumed that the market has natural monopoly properties, whereas if they build their own infrastructure, the opposite implication can be drawn. That would be great, but it turns out that neither of those inferences hold. Entrants will use the shared access provisions if the regulated price of access is lower than the price of self-provision, a decision that has nothing to do with natural monopoly and everything to do with regulation. Similarly, entrants will build their own facilities if the regulated price is higher than the price of self-provision, again irrespective of any natural monopoly issues. This is one of the reasons why the pricing rules at issue in *Verizon* are so important; the government is regulating prices because of a natural monopoly problem, but it is those prices—not the underlying economics of the market—that will determine both patterns of entry and the incentive to develop new infrastructure.

The second tempting but incorrect interpretation casts the 1996 Act as an exercise in deregulation. As is surely clear by now, that is not at all right, since the Act introduces a great deal of new regulation, and much of it will powerfully influence behavior in the local telephone market. That said, the 1996 Act does promise to diminish the importance of regulation, since if competition takes hold, competitive forces will do some of the work formerly accomplished by government fiat. The 1996 Act, then, is probably best understood as regulation designed to harness competition. Regulation will still in some instances be outcome-determinative, but in most cases outcomes will be determined by some combination of regulation and competitive pressures.

Turn now to *Iowa Utilities*. We pointed out above that there is no obvious connection between a natural monopoly cost structure on the one hand and the possibility of competitive supply on the other. As applied to local telephone service, this means that network elements—even network elements that exhibit the properties of a natural monopoly—can in certain cases be competitively supplied even in the absence of regulation. The upside is that competitive supply might yield good incentives for quality, pricing, and innovation; the downside is that competitive supply in the face of natural monopoly risks wasteful duplication of resources. The 1996 Act does not specifically speak to this trade-off, and thus it does not give the Commission direct guidance in how to react to this possibility of competition. Based solely on the provisions enacted, it is possible that Congress meant to unbundle only those elements where competition is unlikely. But it is also possible that Congress meant to unbundle any element that exhibits natural monopoly properties.

This was part of what the Commission had to struggle with when interpreting the necessary and impair standards of section 251(d)(2). And, while the Commission did not issue a clear final statement on this particular question, the regulations at issue in *Iowa Utilities* certainly were broad enough to include in the unbundling regime elements where competition is possible even without mandatory unbundling. The Court did not reject this conclusion per se; as we have pointed out, the Court merely pushed for further explanation as to how the Commission had come to this conclusion and, more specifically, how the possibility of market provision affects the scope of the unbundling requirement in the Commission's view.

Verizon addressed issues a little further removed from our basic intuitions about natural monopolies. The core issue there was the price at which the government would require incumbents to sell access to their unbundled network elements; and, while an understanding of natural monopoly helps us to think about whether sharing itself makes sense, that understanding tells us very little about the optimal price at which any sharing should take place. That said, our discussion of natural monopoly does elucidate one aspect of *Verizon*, namely, the incumbents' takings claim. As we explained above, while natural monopoly can lead to any number of regulatory responses, firms in a regulated market care a great deal about which regulatory response is chosen. Indeed, firms rely on and react to the government's decision with respect to regulatory form, adjusting their pricing and investment patterns accordingly. This is the core insight behind the incumbents' takings claim. Their objection is that the government changed the rules of the market midstream, leaving incumbents holding the bag with respect to their long-term investments. The strength of that argument depends on a number of factors—including whether the incumbents should have expected the possibility of regulatory reform, and whether the incumbents have already earned sufficient returns on their investments anyway—but it is certainly true that firms working in regulated natural monopoly markets do make investment decisions that are in part contingent on which of the several plausible regulatory responses the incumbent expects.

III. SHARED ACCESS UNDER THE 1996 ACT

We are now ready to consider in more detail how regulation of the form established by the 1996 Act differs from regulation as it had previously existed in the local telephone market. We will focus on three principal changes. First, under the old approach, local telephone service was regulated under the assumption that there should be only one monopolist seller serving each community. The 1996 Act, by contrast, allows for multiple competing sellers. Second, under the old approach, the entire local loop was lumped together and regulated as an undifferentiated whole. The new approach attempts to quarantine the effects of regulation by focusing more narrowly on particular network elements. Third, and finally, the old approach relied heavily on government regulation of output prices, by which we mean regulation of the prices for goods and services sold directly to consumers. The new approach continues to rely on output price regulation but adds in addition regulation of input prices—that is, regulation of the prices incumbent local telephone companies charge new entrants for access to unbundled network elements.

A. ONE INFRASTRUCTURE, SEVERAL OWNERS

We have thus far identified as a natural monopoly any market where it is less expensive for demand to be met by one firm than it is for demand to be met by some number of competing firms. That is the standard definition of natural monopoly, but it is not quite right. A more precise variant would state that a natural monopoly exists whenever it is less expensive for demand to be met using a single *infrastructure* than it is for demand to be met using multiple, uncoordinated infrastructures. To see what we mean, and why this point is so important to understanding the 1996 Act, consider two examples.

Start with cable television. It is easy to see that cable television likely exhibits the properties of a natural monopoly. The main cost incurred in providing cable television comes in laying the cable grid. Once that cost has been incurred and there are wires running along all the major streets, the cost of supplying cable to an additional home is relatively small. A single cable grid can typically serve all customers who are willing to pay the marginal cost of cable service, and thus cable television is likely a natural monopoly: costs are minimized by having only one cable grid in each geographic area.

Natural monopoly thus implies that there should be only one cable infrastructure. It tells us nothing, however, about how many firms should own that single infrastructure. Suppose, for example, that two firms were ordered to share ownership of a given community's cable grid, with one firm programming fifty channels and a competing firm programming a different fifty channels. That sort of competition would not be wasteful since there would be no duplication of the natural monopoly infrastructure. Moreover, it would offer some benefits, for example, ensuring some diversity in terms of content and viewpoint. It would thus be fully consistent to say that cable television exhibits the properties of a natural monopoly, and that cable regulation should ensure that each community has one cable grid but several firms using that grid to offer cable television.

Consider now a second example, this one drawn from the 1912 Supreme Court decision in *Terminal Railroad*.[99] At issue was an organization called the Terminal Railroad Association. Jay Gould—one of the great figures in late nineteenth-century railroading and telegraphy—had combined into the Terminal Railroad Association the three main routes by which railroads crossed the Mississippi River at St. Louis. These were the ferry system run by Wiggins Ferry Company, a bridge called Eads Railroad Bridge, and another bridge called the Merchants Bridge. The United States challenged the three-way combination under the Sherman Act, apparently afraid that competition in the railroad industry would suffer in a world where a single entity controlled every plausible means for crossing the Mississippi at St. Louis.

---

[99] *United States v Terminal Railroad Ass'n of St Louis*, 224 US 383 (1912).

The government's case was not particularly strong, as there was no obvious discrimination by the railroad association in favor of insiders and against outsiders. That is, Gould's railroads used the terminal facilities on the same terms that nonaffiliated railroads used the facilities. Of course, given our concern about monopoly pricing, that could just mean that all of the railroads were being gouged by the terminal association. But the association was operated on a nonprofit basis, just covering costs and never paying dividends, and so it seems unlikely that monopoly prices were being charged.[100] The terminal association had also expanded over time—moving from six members to fourteen—turning outsiders into insiders and thus further undermining any claim that Gould was using his position to favor his own railroads over competing ones.

The Court saw much of this, recognizing that there was no real problem with respect to equal access—at least, not yet—and also that operating the three facilities together had some likely efficiency benefits. But the Court still found that Gould had violated the Sherman Act. The problem was not unequal access. It was unequal ownership. This is apparent from the Court's ultimate remedy. The Court did not require that the three means for crossing the river be operated separately. Instead, the Court simply required that Gould offer all existing and future railroads the opportunity to join his Terminal Railroad Association on "just and reasonable terms."[101] This would make the terminal association "the agent of all" and would legitimate Gould's unification of the facilities.[102]

We can quibble with this result. For instance, it is far from obvious that the Court's solution actually accomplished anything. Prior to its ruling, fourteen insiders made decisions for the group of twenty-four users, and ten outsiders had no say. After the ruling, if internal decisions are made by majority vote, the same fourteen can continue to set policy. It is true that if there were direct bene-

---

[100] This is somewhat tricky, as the Court recognized. Understanding who was making money on nineteenth-century railroads requires close tracking of the cash. You might lose money on the railroad proper and make it up by owning the construction company doing the building. In *Terminal Railroad* itself, it is possible that Gould and his compatriots were making money from the bonds of the association rather than the stock. See id at 401.

[101] Id at 411.

[102] Id at 405.

fits flowing to the owners as such—returns on equity—those presumably would have to be shared with the now larger group, but there is nothing in the case to suggest that special returns were flowing to the equity holders. But the big picture here is that the concern in this case was not the existence of a single infrastructure for crossing the Mississippi, but was instead the fact that the single infrastructure was controlled by a single entity, Gould's Terminal Railroad Association.

How does all this tie into the 1996 Act? Prior to the 1996 Act, local telephone regulation had proceeded under the implicit assumption that, if there were going to be only one local telecommunications network, it should be owned and operated by only one local telecommunications firm. The 1996 Act rejects that assumption, following the lesson of *Terminal Railroad* and thus opting for what is in essence shared ownership of the local network. It is possible that, years from now, there will still be only one infrastructure. But, even if that happens, under the 1996 Act there will at least be competition over the use of that infrastructure. Any firm can use the shared infrastructure to offer its own unique mix of services and products, and each firm can add to that shared infrastructure its own additional proprietary elements. Rejection of the old approach—one infrastructure, one firm, one array of product offerings—is thus the first significant difference between telephone regulation before and after 1996.

B. NATURAL MONOPOLY AND THE QUARANTINE

Now for the second big change: from a regime where the entire local market was regulated as a cohesive whole to a regime where regulations attempt to target more narrowly specific network elements. In the pre-1996 Act world, even though a would-be entrant had no right to enter the market, potential entrants did have a strong incentive to innovate with respect to local telephone infrastructure, products, and services. After all, if an entrant were to come up with some new innovation—say, caller ID—the incumbent might want to purchase it, since in the incumbent's hands the new technology could be lucrative. Granted, the incumbent would likely be somewhat miserly in the negotiation, knowing that the entrant has few other potential buyers. At the same time, however, the incumbent would not want to be too miserly, since a reputation for paying well would encourage other entrants to develop new technologies, and those technologies might also be profitable in the incumbent's hands. Voluntary transactions, then, themselves created a real incentive for would-be entrants to innovate, even prior to the 1996 Act.

So why did Congress intervene? Mainly because those voluntary transactions served to benefit the incumbent at the expense of both consumers and the entrant. Focus first on consumers. Prior to the 1996 Act, an incumbent might purchase new technologies, yes, but it would not share its monopoly position with another firm. So while consumers did enjoy some benefit from innovation in terms of getting access to new products and services, consumers did not get one important possible benefit: competition. If entrants had been allowed to use their innovations to enter the market, by contrast, innovation would have meant new products and also lower prices. Now turn to the entrants. If a would-be entrant came up with a new technology that created $200 in value, the entrant would not keep the full $200. It would keep some, sure; but the incumbent would capture some of that upside as well, since without that there would be no reason for the incumbent to purchase the invention. Thus entrants earned less of a reward—and therefore had less of an incentive to innovate—than they might have otherwise had.

Now consider the world after the 1996 Act. Entrants who develop new infrastructure, products, or services can enter the market without the incumbent's permission. The entrant might have to pay a regulated fee to the incumbent for access to some UNEs; but, beyond that, the entrant is free to use any new invention to compete with the incumbent. That might mean that the entrant will earn more from its innovation than it did under prior law, since this time the returns are not shared with the incumbent. Or it might mean that the entrant earns less, since competition between the incumbent and the entrant might drive prices down. But, either way, the benefits of innovation now go to either the entrant/innovator or consumers, instead of going in large proportion to the incumbent.

Interestingly, the entrant's incentive to innovate might be even greater than the above analysis suggests. To see why, think about inferior technology. In the pre-1996 Act world, an entrant who came up with some inferior technology had nothing to offer.

There was no point in reaching out to the incumbent and asking about a deal; the incumbent was not interested in buying technology that was inferior to its own. For the entrant, this meant that investments in research paid off only if the result was an actual improvement over existing technology. Now jump to the world made possible by the 1996 Act. In this world, an entrant who develops a technology superior to the incumbent's clearly has something of value. The entrant can sell it to the incumbent, or the entrant can use it to enter the market. But—and here is the interesting part—an entrant who develops an inferior technology can also in certain settings enter the market. Yes, the incumbent will have a better product or lower costs; but the entrant might still be able to compete, for example, if market prices are far enough above both the incumbent's and the entrant's total marginal costs. This artificially increases the entrant's incentive to engage in research. Whereas before the only good outcomes to research were ones where the resulting technology was superior to the incumbent's technology, now the entrant can benefit both when research "succeeds" and, albeit to a lesser extent, even when research "fails."

So far, we have focused on reasons why the approach to natural monopoly under the 1996 Act is an improvement over prior law. But there are obviously drawbacks, too. Consider, for instance, the difficulties that will arise every time the incumbent decides to change some basic element of the telephone network. If the incumbent owned the entire network—UNEs plus all other components—it could coordinate change. It would have a sense of the full system-wide costs and benefits associated with any upgrade, and it would be able implement any desirable upgrade in a consistent manner. When components of the network are separately owned, by contrast, change becomes more difficult. A company that sells only end-user equipment, for example, will fight tooth and nail against any network change that might decrease the value of its equipment, regardless of the overall costs and benefits to the system.[103] Even if that firm were to agree to a change, the costs of

---

[103] But see *In re Use of the Carterfone Device in Message Toll Telephone Service*, 13 FCC 2d 420, 424 (1968) (rejecting this same argument in a dispute over whether telephone handsets had to be approved by the telephone company or could instead be supplied competitively).

passing information and otherwise coordinating an improvement would certainly be higher. In short, bifurcated ownership creates bifurcated information and incentives; and there is something to be said for a market structure where, instead, the telephone network is maintained and analyzed as a coherent whole.

C. NATURAL MONOPOLY, INPUT PRICES, AND OUTPUT PRICES

The third big change—in essence, the introduction of network element pricing—is in many ways just a necessary ramification of the second. That is, given that the 1996 Act regulates UNE by UNE instead of lumping together the entire local telephone infrastructure, the government had to set prices for UNEs. This is actually the link between *Iowa Utilities* and *Verizon*. *Iowa Utilities* is a fight over the scope of access; *Verizon* is a challenge to the pricing rules that will apply however the access issue shakes out. For better or worse, then, regulating "input" prices was foreordained, at least if the narrower quarantine was going to be meaningfully accomplished.

That said, there is no reason to either celebrate or lament this change. Regulating input prices does not seem likely to be substantially harder or easier than regulating output prices; both, it turns out, are complicated and difficult to accomplish. The first problem is information. In *United States v American Telephone & Telegraph*,[104] the government argued that one reason to break up the then-dominant Bell Telephone Company was that it was impossible for the government to regulate Bell effectively. Bell had all the information about the costs of providing various telephone services. The government was thus in the uncomfortable situation of setting policy and prices based on information provided by the very firm it was trying to regulate. Worse, the government argued that Bell would intentionally keep itself in the dark about some information, not gathering it so as to ensure that the government could not use that information against Bell in regulatory proceedings. The resulting argument was thus not the conventional claim that a monopolist was pricing excessively above cost or even predatorily below cost; the government's claim was that Bell was pricing *without regard to* cost, and the government did not know enough about

---

[104] 552 F Supp 131 (DC Cir 1982).

costs to intervene effectively.[105] That problem to some extent continues today, and it seems to apply equally to both input and output prices.

A second and more significant problem stems from the complicated relationship between prices and innovation incentives. If price regulation were merely designed to keep prices low, regulation would be relatively straightforward; the government can gather good information about consumers' willingness to pay for various telecom services, and the government would therefore be able to adopt relatively effective, aggressive pricing measures if the only goal were to ensure that most consumers can afford most telephone services. But the goal of price regulation is significantly more complicated, as it is designed not only to keep prices low for existing services but also to encourage firms to maintain quality, minimize costs, and invest in new infrastructure. Accomplishing all that is no easy task, even if price regulation just focuses on the output market.

Take one example: price cap regulation. Under this approach, the government announces a maximum price that can be charged for some service and further specifies how that price will change over time to account for expected efficiency gains, inflation, and so on. The idea is to give the regulated party a strong incentive to minimize costs. If the regulated firm can lower its costs, it can keep the extra profits for itself. The government, meanwhile, can regulate in this fashion even without knowing very much about the regulated firm's cost structure. The government just sets a price that seems reasonable given past prices and expected consumer demand, and the rest takes care of itself.

So far, so good. In practice, however, there are problems. First, price cap regulation tempts firms to slash costs not only by increasing efficiency but also by skimping on quality. That is, there are two ways to increase profits under a price cap: one is to provide the same service at lower cost, but the other is to provide worse service. Price cap regulation might therefore ironically encourage firms to offer cheap, low-quality service instead of more expensive, higher-quality service. Second, because the government cannot

[105] Roger Noll and Bruce Owen, *The Anticompetitive Uses of Regulation: United States v AT&T*, in J. Kwoka and L. White, eds, *The Antitrust Revolution* 290, 295–326 (Scott, 1989).

credibly commit not to change the price cap, the incentive to lower costs is in fact significantly weaker than at first appears. If the regulated firm does a great job at cutting costs, there is some chance that the government will renege on the deal and lower the price cap. A regulated firm making a large profit and charging high prices is just too easy a target.[106] Conversely, if the regulated firm sees its costs skyrocket, it is likely that the government will bail the firm out by raising the price cap instead of, say, allowing the lone local telephone provider to go bankrupt. Both of these responses undermine the incentive to cut costs. The upside to cost reductions is reduced since the government might recapture some of that savings for consumers, and the downside to waste is also reduced since the government might allow the firm to raise its prices if costs are overwhelming revenue.

Moreover, the details of the price cap regime alter these dynamics in important ways. Consider again the possibility that firms will make "too much" money under a price cap regime and that regulators will seek to re-cut the deal afterward. Individual firms would anticipate that and would seek to avoid "excess" profits by spending more excessively. This might lead to nice cars for firm executives, fancy offices, and so on. But the incentive of individual firms to pull back on the profits throttle depends critically on whether the regulator sets policy at the firm level or the industry level. If the price cap is altered at the firm level, the dynamics play out as we have indicated. If instead the price cap is based on overall industry profits, individual firms may lack the incentive to cut back. The firms in the industry face a collective action problem: their individual decisions matter only at the margin for the industry outcome, and, given that, they may as well make as much money as they can. Doing so, however, ends up hurting them all, because the regulator will see those profits and react accordingly.

Overall, the point here is simply that price regulation is complicated even when applied to outputs. It is therefore not the case that the 1996 Act moves regulation away from a type of regulation

---

[106] To see the enormous instability associated with price cap regulation in practice, consider the cases on price cap regulation as it applied to the interstate services of local telephone exchange companies: *U.S. Telephone Ass'n v FCC*, 188 F3d 521 (DC Cir 1999); *Bell Atlantic Telephone Companies v FCC*, 79 F3d 1195 (DC Cir 1996); and *National Rural Telecom Association v FCC*, 988 F2d 174 (DC Cir 1993).

that has been very successful and toward one that is more precarious. Price regulation is difficult no matter whether it applies to inputs or outputs, mainly because both require the government to make educated guesses about costs and incentives, two things about which the government understandably knows very little. The main policy concern, then, might just be transition costs. That is, the strongest argument against the new pricing regime might simply be the cost of designing—and litigating over—a new system. Beyond that, price regulation for inputs presents different complexities than those already familiar under price regulation for outputs, but there is no reason to think that the one is any more difficult than the other.

IV. The State of Entry in Local Telecommunications

We have covered a great deal of theory; it is thus here a good time to pause and look at practical consequences, specifically, some data relating to the state of entry in local telecommunications. When a good business can be made out of melting down millions of dollars in redundant telecommunications equipment to recover precious metals,[107] we know that serious mistakes have been made, though not necessarily that we could have done any better. And so let us ask: What has entry looked like in local telecommunications? Has the 1996 Act resulted in overinvestment in local telecommunications, underinvestment, or, in Goldilocks fashion, did it get it just right?

As of December, 1999—roughly three years after the 1996 Act went into effect—CLECs held roughly 4.3% of the market in end-user switched access lines.[108] By June 30, 2002, total lines had drifted down slightly from roughly 189.5 million to 189.1 million, after peaking at 192.6 million at the end of 2000. Since December 1999, CLEC market share has grown steadily, reaching 11.4% as of June 30, 2002. This entry disproportionately targets medium and large businesses, institutions, and the government. As of mid-

---

[107] See Dan Roberts, *Glorious Hopes on a Trillion-Dollar Scrapheap*, Financial Times (Sept 5, 2001). For more detail, visit the Shields Environmental website at <http://www.shields-e.com> (visited Nov 1, 2002).

[108] See FCC, Industry Analysis Division, *Local Telephone Competition: Status as of June 30, 2002* at Table 1 (2002) (available online at <http://www.fcc.gov/Bureaus/Common_Carrier/Reports/FCC-State_Link/IAD/lcom1202.pdf>).

year 2002, incumbents had 78.3% of their lines with residential and small business customers, while CLECs had only 51.2% of their lines with these end-users.[109]

Of the roughly 21.6 million CLEC lines with end-users as of mid-2002, 28.8%, or about 6.2 million, were CLEC owned; 50.5%, or about 10.9 million, were provided through UNE access; and 20.7%, or about 4.5 million, were provided through the resale provisions of the Act. The resale provisions, as you might recall, basically mean that the entrant is buying service from the incumbent at regulated, wholesale rates and then rebranding it for sale to end-users. Between December 1999 and June 2002, the number of CLEC-owned lines more than doubled, but actually dropped as a percentage of the total number of CLEC end-user lines (from 33.2% to 28.8%).[110]

From the perspective of the incumbents, the direct burden of CLEC access is growing. The number of resold lines purchased by CLECs rose from roughly 1.7 million in December 1997 to 5.4 million in December 2000 and then fell to 3.5 million as of June 2002.[111] This suggests that resale has become relatively less attractive. UNE access, meanwhile, is growing rapidly. CLECs have gone from 133,000 UNE-accessed lines in December 1997 to 1.5 million in December 1999 to 11.5 million in June 2002. Still, the overall presence of CLECs on ILEC premises is small: only 8.3% of all ILEC lines were being either resold or accessed under the UNE provisions as of June 2002.[112]

Not only is CLEC entry targeted on heavy users—large businesses and the government—but, unsurprisingly, it focuses on dense population areas. As of June 2002, 33% of U.S. zip codes had no CLECs and another 19.5% had only one. Only 6.6% of U.S. households actually live in the zip codes without a CLEC, however, and another 9.1% of U.S. households live in zip codes with only a single CLEC entrant.[113] This is somewhat interesting,

---

[109] Id at Table 2.

[110] Id at Table 3.

[111] For those reading carefully, note that as of June 2002, while CLECs resell 3.5 million lines from ILECs, total CLEC resales are at 4.5 million lines. The 1 million difference presumably reflects lines resold from sources other than ILECs.

[112] Id at Table 4.

[113] Id at Table 12.

as it offers some sense of the costs of entry. Remember that CLECs were using their own lines only 29% of the time as of June 2002, though, to be sure, they could have been using some of their own facilities in conjunction with ILEC lines in the other 71% of the cases. Still, the CLECs are not choosing to enter rural areas using just the ILEC's equipment, even though they obviously do a fair amount of this in densely populated areas. This suggests that some costs, such as advertising costs and other brand-building expenditures, are best spread over dense areas and that these costs are important in explaining the pattern of CLEC entry.

In sum, after nearly seven years under the 1996 Act, CLECs have about 11% of the end-user lines market, and, of that, roughly 71% of the lines are owned by other carriers. Put differently, at least over the so-called last mile, CLECs provide service over their own lines for only 3% of the market. The 7% of the market covered by CLECs using the lines of others should be counted as at least a partial success for the Act, as in some of those situations the CLEC may be using some of its own facilities to provide telecommunications service.

All of this confirms what we instinctively knew: that the real hot spot for consumers is not landlines, but cell phones. The competition in local markets that was to come from CLECs really seems instead to be coming through wireless. Mobile wireless telephone subscribers have jumped from roughly 79.7 million in December 1999 to 128.8 million in June 2002.[114] In that same period, end-user switched access landlines declined slightly, dropping from 189.5 million to 189.1 million. That looks like a declining market, especially as measured against the December 2000 peak of 192.6 million lines. Market shares have moved around during that period: CLECs added about 13.4 million lines and ILECs lost about 13.8 million lines. But, obviously, the major action is in cell phones, where carriers added 49.1 million cell phone users during the same period.[115] Now lines are a crude measure; we might care more about market share as defined by the number of minutes used—that would be true for evaluating CLECs as well—but in-

---

[114] Id at Table 11.
[115] Id at Tables 1, 11.

dustry analysts believe that as many as 10 million landlines have been displaced by wireless lines.[116]

What do these numbers mean for our questions? We said before that we cannot assess how competitive a market is by the number of participants, so the fact that CLECs have an 11% market share tells us nothing directly. The threat of entry itself might be significantly altering incumbent incentives and market prices. Similarly, the fact that many CLECs have entered and failed—more than 50 CLECs are reported to have filed for bankruptcy[117]—does not tell us much either. It would make no more sense to say that a drug company wasted the first ninety-nine petri dishes when it turned out that the new blockbuster drug was in the hundredth dish. The nature of research and development is substantial failure, and failure alone cannot be seen as equivalent to waste. What of missing investment? It is almost impossible to quantify the extent to which incumbents may have been discouraged from either making new investments or repairing old investments, just as it is hard to quantify how much new research is being done by entrants. It might also be somewhat unfair to evaluate any of these numbers at this stage, since entry and competition in the local market have throughout this period taken place under the shadow of considerable legal uncertainty. That uncertainty has been partially diminished, but as we will explain below, even now there are clouds on the horizon.

V. Conclusion

The data presented in the previous section offer at least a partial answer to the question of what the 1996 Act has actually accomplished thus far. Here, let us conclude by asking the same question about the Court: After millions of dollars and several years of litigation, what have the Court decisions in *Iowa Utilities* and *Verizon* actually accomplished?

The Court in *Iowa Utilities* accomplished a great deal, in that

---

[116] FCC, Seventh Report, *In the Matter of Implementation of Section 6002(b) of the Omnibus Budget Reconciliation Act of 1993; Annual Report and Analysis of Competitive Market Conditions with Respect to Commercial Mobile Services*, 17 FCC Rcd 12985 (2002).

[117] Jeffrey A. Eisenach, *The Real Telecom Scandal*, Wall Street Journal (Sept 30, 2002).

the opinion both resolved many of the jurisdictional issues related to the implementation of the Act and forced the Commission to more carefully articulate its understanding of the unbundled network element regime. Results followed quickly. In 1999, the Commission released new regulations specifically designed to respond to the Court's objections. These new regulations "take into consideration alternatives outside the [incumbent's] network" and also consider "whether those alternatives are actually available to the requesting carrier as a practical, economic, and operational matter."[118] The new regulations unbundle only in instances where a "lack of access" to the requested element "materially diminishes a requesting carrier's ability to provide the services it seeks to offer"[119] and they emphasize in addition five relevant factors: the rapid introduction of competition in all markets, the deployment of new telecommunications infrastructure, reduced regulation, certainty in the marketplace, and administrative practicality.[120] In short, the new regulations respond to all of the issues raised in *Iowa Utilities*.

Unfortunately, things have not gone well from there. In May 2002, the D.C. Circuit vacated the Commission's revised regulations.[121] The problem this time was that, except for two elements, the Commission's rules applied "uniformly to all elements in every geographic or customer market."[122] The D.C. Circuit found this inadequately justified, with the court wondering why differences between the various markets—the court's main example is differences in state regulations, though there are obviously economic differences as well—were not being accounted for in the unbundling rules. Interestingly, this question mirrors one of the core issues raised in *Iowa Utilities*, the question whether the Commission's rules have to account for the possibility of voluntary market transactions. The similarity is that, in both instances, the basic dispute is over the extent to which unbundling rules need to be sensitive to actual market conditions; the Supreme Court wanted more

---

[118] FCC, Third Report and Order, *In re Implementation of the Local Competition Provisions of the Telecommunications Act of 1996*, 15 FCC Rcd 3696, at ¶ 8 (1999).

[119] Id at ¶ 51.

[120] Id at ¶¶ 103–16.

[121] *United States Telecom Ass'n v FCC*, 290 F3d 415 (DC Cir 2002).

[122] Id at 419.

sensitivity to the scope of available voluntary transactions and self-provisioning, while the D.C. Circuit now wants more sensitivity to any differences in each state's economic and legal terrain.

In any event, the Commission is as of this writing back at work on its rules. This is unfortunate in the sense that these continued iterations have prolonged the process of implementing the 1996 Act and have increased the underlying legal uncertainty, two effects that have likely reduced overall investment in the local telecommunications market. But it would be unreasonable to expect that the Court would anticipate all possible interpretive issues related to the "necessary" and "impair" standard, and so it is hard to fault the Court for not spotting this issue back in *Iowa Utilities*.

As for *Verizon*, the Court did resolve the dispute over TELRIC, thus paving the way for the Commission's pricing methodology to be implemented in the states. Feedback from that process should help the Commission adjust its methodology to better serve the goals of the 1996 Act, and of course implementation at the state level is the next big step in terms of bringing the 1996 Act into full effect. Our concerns with respect to the Takings Clause, by contrast, were left largely unresolved. As we have pointed out, that is unfortunate; delaying the takings analysis likely means that the Takings Clause cannot serve what would have been a valuable purpose, namely, allowing the Commission to address separately the distributional and efficiency issues implicated by access pricing.

Ironically, then, while *Iowa Utilities* will for the next many years be an important window through which regulators and industry participants will understand and evaluate both the 1996 Act and access rules more generally, it is possible that *Verizon* is destined to quickly become a footnote in the history of telecommunications regulation. The case seems likely to have legs, if at all, as part of Takings Clause jurisprudence—not yet, and not for what it says or does, but for what it failed to do and for the series of events implicitly put into motion by virtue of the Court's decision to postpone the takings issue.

ELIZABETH GARRETT

IS THE PARTY OVER? COURTS AND THE POLITICAL PROCESS

Political parties organize and rationalize politics. Decisions about elections, government structure, the relationship among states and between the federal and subnational governments, and the ability of Congress and the President to pursue their legislative agendas are affected by and affect political parties. But the legal community, in particular the judiciary, has failed to develop sophisticated positive and normative views of political parties, resulting in a jurisprudence of the political process that is inconsistent and unsatisfying. The reluctance to think seriously about political parties may be a lingering effect both of the Founders' distaste for them and of the unsavory reputation they developed during the era of party machines. Increasingly, legal academics, often in collaboration with political scientists, are acknowledging the constructive role of political parties in our constitutional structure.[1] This aca-

Elizabeth Garrett is Professor of Law, University of Chicago; Visiting Professor of Law, University of Southern California.

AUTHOR'S NOTE: I appreciate comments from Scott Altman, Bill Crotty, Phil Frickey, Barry Friedman, Paul Frymer, Howard Gillman, Rick Hasen, Sam Issacharoff, Pam Karlan, Andrei Marmor, Dan Ortiz, Nate Persily, Rick Pildes, Eric Posner, Michael Shapiro, Larry Simon, Geof Stone, Mark Tushnet, Adrian Vermeule, Albert Yoon, and participants in a USC Law School workshop, especially Ed McCaffery, who served as commentator and has provided invaluable help; a helpful suggestion from Efton Park; assistance from Connie Fleischer and Margaret Smith at the University of Chicago law library; preliminary research assistance by Peggy Cusack (Virginia '02) and exceptional research assistance by Colin McNary (Chicago '04); and the financial support of the James H. Douglas, Jr. Fund for the Study of Law and Government and the Law and Government Faculty Fund, both at the University of Chicago Law School.

[1] For a general discussion, see *Symposium: Law and Political Parties*, 100 Colum L Rev 593–899 (2000); Samuel Issacharoff, *Private Parties with Public Purposes: Political Parties, Associational Freedoms, and Partisan Competition*, 101 Colum L Rev 274 (2001); Larry D. Kramer, *Putting the Politics Back into the Political Safeguards of Federalism*, 100 Colum L Rev 215 (2000).

demic trend may encourage the judiciary to overcome its tendency to slight parties, but this seems unlikely. Courts are ill equipped to develop and evaluate regulatory strategies affecting political parties.

In the first part of this article, I will describe and analyze five features of political parties that place them among the most complex and dynamic of any modern political institution and therefore among the most difficult to regulate effectively. These features ensure considerable competition for control within a political party and among different political parties, thereby allowing for change in the political process without judicial involvement. In Part II, I will demonstrate how these characteristics of political parties challenge the judiciary's capacity to understand the effect of regulation on parties, their members, and others by describing controversies that resulted in three Supreme Court cases. In Part III, I will question the propriety of judicial involvement in this area. I conclude that courts have only a narrow role to play in ensuring a sufficiently dynamic and competitive political environment to protect the interests of major and minor parties and their members. The judicial role should be limited to extreme and obvious cases of anticompetitive laws designed to entrench a particular interest's position, leaving most disputes to be worked out in the politically accountable branches.

I. The Dynamic Nature of Political Parties

The unique characteristics of political parties pose a challenge for any institution seeking to regulate them. This challenge is especially formidable for the judiciary, given its institutional design. Because of the structure of political parties, however, regulations affecting them are subject to intense debate and scrutiny within the political branches, and the dynamic nature of parties ensures that reforms can occur naturally over time without significant judicial involvement. What are the distinctive features of political parties that justify characterizing them as complex, competitive, dynamic, and endogenous?

A. DECENTRALIZED AND MULTILAYERED ENTITIES

The most evident complexity of the modern political party, the division into national entities, state parties, and local organizations, is mainly a function of the constitutional scheme of federalism. Thus, the national party is an amalgam of fifty state parties, and it includes as well several strong local parties whose leaders do not always work closely with leaders on the state or national levels. The state and local parties are not branches of a cohesive national entity, nor are they the members of a national party that control its actions. Instead, political parties are noncentralized "confederations of national, state, and local cadres whose most conspicuous features are flabby organization and slack discipline."[2] Minor parties often can be even less subject to top-down control than major parties because of their grassroots character, limited national resources, and inability to use governmental positions to enhance party organization.[3]

Over time, the power of one level may change in relation to the others. For example, during the era of political machines and patronage, local political organizations wielded more clout than they do now. Political parties today are increasingly centralized, and national parties are more powerful relative to their state and local counterparts.[4] Nonetheless, political parties remain resistant to hierarchical control. National parties may be more expert in raising money and providing campaign services, but they must rely on state and local organizations in order to deploy their resources to best effect.[5]

---

[2] Kramer, *Putting the Politics Back* at 279 (cited in note 1). See also Richard S. Katz and Robin Kolodny, *Party Organization as an Empty Vessel: Parties in American Politics*, in Richard S. Katz and Peter Mair, eds, *How Parties Organize: Change and Adaptation in Party Organizations in Western Democracies* 23, 24–29 (Sage, 1994) (discussing effects of federalism and separation of powers on organization of political parties).

[3] Rifts in some of the layers of the larger minor parties demonstrate that they also are decentralized entities. See, for example, Cathy Newman and Ben White, *States Left to Pick Reform Ticket: For Party Nominees, Ballot Access Is Key to Federal Funds*, Wash Post A5 (Aug 27, 2000) (describing the 2000 legal battle between leadership and activists within the Reform Party over whether Pat Buchanan or John Hagelin was presidential nominee).

[4] Paul Frymer and Albert Yoon, *Political Parties, Representation, and Federal Safeguards*, 96 Nw U L Rev 977, 980 (2002) (arguing that state and local parties are not strong enough vis-à-vis national organizations to protect federalism values sufficiently but not claiming that they are entirely powerless). Compare with Marjorie Randon Hershey and Paul A. Beck, *Party Politics in America* 82 (Longman, 10th ed 2003) (concluding that even with modern changes in the relative strength of the levels of the major parties, they are still largely decentralized entities).

[5] See Hershey and Beck, *Party Politics in America* at 62–64 (cited in note 4) (discussing rise in strength of state party organizations and interaction in fundraising efforts between national and state party organs). The reliance on state parties will only increase if the provisions banning soft money in the new campaign finance law survive judicial review. See Bipartisan Campaign Reform Act of 2002, PL No 107-155, 116 Stat 81, § 101.

Moreover, national party organizations consist of relatively in-dependent entities that sometimes work together and sometimes pursue their own objectives. This is largely the result of separation of powers at the federal level. In recent years, the major parties have organized separate congressional campaign committees for the House and Senate, and the national party organizations have focused on the presidential election and state elections for gover-nors and state legislatures.[6] Similar developments are occurring within some states as state legislative parties have organized them-selves to assist in maintaining or gaining control of each legislative house, separate from the traditional state party organization.[7]

Although these national organizations coordinate with each other and with state parties, they also compete and check each other, with no layer possessing enough disciplinary power to en-force its will in all cases. Often their interests will run parallel, but occasionally they will clash as politicians make strategic decisions in their own interests. The national congressional committees must target their resources to maximize their chances of winning a majority in each house, which may mean that some state races are ignored or slighted, to the dismay of local and state partisans. Or a state candidate may wish to distance herself from an unpopu-lar presidential candidate running on a platform different from the ideology espoused by the state and local parties. The congressional campaign committees are run by incumbent members of the House and Senate, while the national party committees are run by political operatives, who may have held office in the past or may hold it currently, perhaps at the state level. These individuals will approach a campaign with different perspectives and objectives, not all of which are compatible.

B. THE TRIPARTITE NATURE OF POLITICAL PARTIES

V. O. Key divided political parties into three elements: the party-in-the-electorate, people who identify themselves as mem-bers of a political party and use the party label as a way to choose

---

[6] For a general discussion, see Robin Kolodny, *Pursuing Majorities: Congressional Campaign Committees in American Politics* 3–14 (Oklahoma, 1998).

[7] See Alan Rosenthal, *The Decline of Representative Democracy: Process, Participation and Power in the State Legislatures* 177 (CQ, 1998).

candidates; the party-organization, party leaders and professionals who provide campaign services through the party; and the party-in-government, people in elected and appointed offices who affiliate with a political party.[8] There are subparts within each of these elements, further complicating the analysis and providing additional, occasionally contending forces. Take, for example, the party organization. Not only are there layers of organizations because of federalism and separation of powers, but party leaders are a different group from professional campaign consultants, who may affiliate with a party or an ideology but are, in the end, paid political guns who may also work for candidates affiliated with other parties. Separate from both these groups are political activists, whose volunteered time and energy are important to the party organization, but who may be more committed to specific ideological goals than to the overriding objective of party leaders: gaining party control of government.

The tripartite framework vividly emphasizes that any regulation of political parties enacted by the democratic branches is drafted, advocated or opposed, and ultimately adopted by different elements of political parties. Indeed, there are elements of political parties on both sides of every case concerning parties that comes to the courts. The state consists of elected or appointed partisans, whose views will inevitably be influenced by their party affiliation. The party-organization is often also an active participant in such litigation. The segment of the party that is usually unrepresented in judicial disputes, or that must rely on virtual representation, is the party-in-the-electorate.[9] The key point is that these controversies inevitably involve conflicts between elements of different parties or elements of the same party or both.

---

[8] See V. O. Key, *Politics, Parties, and Pressure Groups* 163–64 (Crowell, 5th ed 1964). Issacharoff describes these three elements somewhat differently: "[P]arties are an unstable amalgam of voter preferences, an internal apparatus driven by activists and a structure through which party affiliates participate in government." See Issacharoff, *Private Parties* at 279 (cited in note 1).

[9] In the blanket primary case, for example, the interests of the party-in-the-electorate were supposedly represented by state officials, but such officials had (at least) divided loyalties because they were associated with the party organizations opposing the reform. In other cases, such as the fusion case, it is not clear who represents the party-in-the-electorate. Perhaps minor parties advocating fusion represent them in some sense, or perhaps state officials, opposed to fusion partly because of possible voter confusion, acted as their representatives.

C. DEFINING THE MEMBERS OF A POLITICAL PARTY

Although political parties are often referred to as membership groups,[10] it is often not possible to determine who their members actually are. The definitions of "political party" in state statutes and party rules reflect the absence of any clear idea of the precise contours of party membership. Hawaii defines political party as "an association of voters united for the purpose of promoting a common political end or carrying out a particular line of political policy, and which maintains a general organization throughout the State."[11] The Virginia Democratic Party declares in its Party Plan that "[e]very resident . . . who believes in the principles of the Democratic Party is hereby declared to be a member of the Democratic Party of Virginia."[12]

There are at least four ways of thinking about party membership, with each of the four groups containing subgroups that further contribute to internal tensions and divisions. Membership might consist of (1) voters who identify themselves as partisans, (2) party leaders and activists, (3) officeholders and office seekers using the party label, or (4) interest groups that contribute to and

---

[10] For a general discussion, see Nancy L. Rosenblum, *Political Parties as Membership Groups*, 100 Colum L Rev 813 (2000) (but also discussing how they differ from traditional membership groups). Although the Court and others seek to evaluate the constitutional and legal interests of parties by assessing the interests of their members, some scholars have suggested that a better approach would consider parties as producing a product for various consumers. See, for example, Daniel R. Ortiz, *Duopoly versus Autonomy: How the Two-Party System Harms the Major Parties*, 100 Colum L Rev 753, 754 (2000). See also Gerald M. Pomper, *The Alleged Decline of American Parties*, in John G. Geer, ed, *Politicians and Party Politics* 14, 17 (Johns Hopkins, 1998) (arguing that voters are the "clientele" of a party, not its members). Although this perspective might lead to different conclusions about appropriate regulatory policies, it still demands the sort of analysis provided in the text. It is necessary to determine what people or groups are the consumers of the product that parties provide before assessing proposed reforms. Just as the several groups that might be considered as "members" of parties have different and sometimes competing interests, these same groups would have different tastes and preferences as consumers.

[11] Hawaii Rev Stat § 11-61(a) (1993). See also Alaska Stat § 15.60.010(15) (Michie 2001) (defining a member of a political party to be "a person who supports the political program of a party"). For a general discussion, see Nathaniel Persily, *Candidates v. Parties: The Constitutional Constraints on Primary Ballot Access Laws*, 89 Georgetown L J 2181, 2185 (2001) (noting that "a court will search the statutes and casebooks in vain for a clear articulation of exactly which particular personnel share in a political party's rights or obligations").

[12] Party Plan of the Democratic Party of Virginia, Art 2, § 2.1 (June 22, 2001) (available online at ⟨http://www.vademocrats.org/public/plan/plan.cfm⟩). See also Missouri Democratic Party Platform, Introduction (available online at ⟨http://www.missouridems.org/talking/platform.htm⟩) ("We are a party of the people, all people, and our only qualification for membership is a genuine concern for the welfare of our nation and its citizens.").

interact with the larger intermediaries of political parties. The first three categories correspond roughly to Key's tripartite division; the final responds to current scholarship that views political parties as organizations mediating among other groups, individuals, and the government.[13] All four of these groups are affiliated in some sense with political parties and all of their interests are relevant in determining the best way to regulate the political process. Their interests are not always parallel, however, but often point in different regulatory directions. Moreover, none of these groups or individuals can be considered "members" of a political party in the same way that people usually are considered members of other private groups.

1. *Voters as members.* When judges and others use the term "member" with respect to a political party, they generally mean the mass of citizens who think of themselves as adherents to the party. Such party identification in the electorate is a meaningful concept. The party cue is the most important influence on voting behavior. Indeed, "one's party identification is not likely to undergo frequent changes in response to changing events or life circumstances."[14]

Nonetheless, the connection of most voters to a political party is attenuated relative to their attachments to other membership groups. In states that use a convention to select party nominees, membership requirements are minimal. In Virginia, for example, the only requirement to participate in the state convention is willingness to sign a form endorsing the principles of the party and agreeing to support the party's nominee in subsequent elections.[15] In open primaries, no evidence of party membership is required for a voter to participate in a party's primary. The only limitation is that the voter cannot also vote in another primary in that election. In states with closed primaries, voters can switch their party

---

[13] See, for example, Samuel Issacharoff and Daniel R. Ortiz, *Governing Through Intermediaries*, 85 Va L Rev 1627 (1999).

[14] John F. Bibby, *Politics, Parties, and Elections in America* 322 (Wadsworth, 4th ed 2000). See also Paul A. Beck and Marjorie Randon Hershey, *Party Politics in America* 8 (Longman, 9th ed 2001) (arguing that ordinary voters do have "strong and enduring attachments" to a particular party evidenced by their registration as members, a "strong measure of belonging" in a system without membership dues).

[15] Since *Morse v Republican Party of Virginia*, 517 US 186 (1996), a financial contribution is voluntary.

affiliation frequently, although in some states they must declare their affiliation well before the election.[16] Parties do not reject voters who register as affiliated with them, even if a voter has been switching among parties frequently, demonstrating no durable commitment to any, or if other party members do not wish to associate with her for some reason.[17] Parties do not expel members for disloyal behavior or for failure to meet ideological litmus tests.[18]

Many minor parties are no different from major parties in this respect. They do not require much affirmative action as a prerequisite for membership, although the decision to register as a minor-party member or even to declare oneself an adherent may represent a relatively serious feeling of affiliation because it is a decision out of the political mainstream.[19] It is not surprising that

---

[16] States have different requirements regulating when voters must declare their affiliation to participate in a closed primary. The time periods vary, from as late as a few days before the primary to several months before the election. See Federal Election Commission, *Party Affiliation and Primary Voting 2000* (available online at ⟨www.fec.gov/votregis/primaryvoting.htm⟩).

[17] Although in some states a voter's affiliation can be challenged by a party observer and the voter required to take a loyalty oath, such challenges never occur now. See Samuel Issacharoff, Pamela S. Karlan, and Richard H. Pildes, *The Law of Democracy: Legal Structure of the Political Process* 377 (Foundation, 2d ed 2001). See also Adam Winkler, *Voters' Rights and Parties' Wrongs: Early Political Party Regulation in the State Courts, 1886–1915*, 100 Colum L Rev 873, 888–89 (2000) (explaining that loyalty oaths sometimes required in the past before allowing participation in a party primary were not effective in protecting associational character of political parties).

[18] See Katz and Kolodny, *Party Organization as an Empty Vessel* at 31 (cited in note 2). Although the text describes the current political climate, some parties have adopted exclusionary practices in the past. The *White Primary Cases* involved decisions by the Democratic Party in Texas to exclude blacks from voting in party primaries, first by state law, then by internal party rule (which also affected membership requirements), and finally by the endorsement practices of influential political actors. See Issacharoff, Karlan, and Pildes, *The Law of Democracy* at 103–17 (cited in note 17). In today's political environment, where politicians vie for minority votes and major parties work to attract ethnic and minority groups, it is inconceivable that major parties would adopt rules excluding any group of voters from participation. For example, although the Texas Republican Party denied permission for a group of gay party members to operate a booth at its convention, *Republican Party of Texas v Dietz*, 40 Tex 384, 940 SW2d 86 (1997), the state party does not deny membership on the basis of sexual orientation nor does it require primary voters to demonstrate allegiance to a particular platform. It is possible that a minor party might espouse an ideology that would lead it to exclude certain groups from membership, although candidates with intolerant views are often willing to accept the votes of groups they dislike, even though they are unlikely to receive many.

[19] The Reform Party requires only that members fill in a membership form, which can be obtained via e-mail, and it prohibits local parties from imposing fees on members who serve as convention delegates. Bylaws and Constitution of the Reform Party, Art III, § 4(c) (available online at ⟨http://reformparty.org/PrinciplesIssues/constitution.html⟩). The Libertarian Party requires a small donation, as well as written certification that the member

major political parties and larger minor parties do not require more costly indications of membership than just signing up or showing up to vote. Their success is not measured by number of members; it is measured by the number of adherents elected to government office.

Perhaps one can distinguish among nonactivist voters on the basis of additional indices of affiliation that would identify them as "members" in a meaningful sense. For example, some people, in addition to voting, contribute money to political campaigns. Certainly, the act of contributing is more than a "bare affiliation lacking civic or expressive significance."[20] But it is not an unambiguous signal of party affiliation. Contributing to a campaign may be more an expression of support for a particular candidate than an expression of support for her party. Contributions directly to a party organ might be a better indication of party membership, but some contributions to a political party are solely intended to circumvent restrictions on contributions made directly to candidates. Moreover, some groups and individuals contribute to both parties as a way to maintain influence regardless of who is in power rather than as a way to demonstrate affiliation with any specific platform or ideology.[21]

Thus, although it is important to keep in mind those in the mass electorate who have strong feelings of attachment to a particular party, tend to vote consistently over time, and are influenced by the party label, it seems a stretch to consider them as "members" of political parties in the same way that people are members of other political, social, or civic groups. Their affiliation with a political party may more closely resemble an affiliation with a professional sports team, although the party attachment generally lacks the passion of the average sports fan's commitment to a team of players.

---

opposes "the initiation of force to achieve political or social goals." Bylaws of the National Libertarian Party, Art VII, §§ 1–3 (available online at ⟨http://www.lp.org/organization/bylaws/b07.html⟩).

[20] Nancy L. Rosenblum, *Primus Inter Pares: Political Parties and Civil Society*, 75 Chi Kent L Rev 493, 505 (2000) (describing this as the general view of voting with respect to membership in a party). See also Rosenblum, *Political Parties as Membership Groups* at 821 (cited at in note 10) (suggesting the distinction based on campaign contributions).

[21] See Victoria A. Farrar-Myers and Diana Dwyre, *Parties and Campaign Finance*, in Jeffrey E. Cohen, Richard Fleisher, and Paul Kantor, eds, *American Political Parties: Decline or Resurgence?* 138, 160 (CQ, 2001) (discussing double giving).

2. *Party leaders and activists as members.* Those who make up the party organization have made a greater commitment to the party than ordinary voters, including those who are registered party members. The major parties require more than 200,000 people to operate effectively.[22] The party-organization includes at least two subgroups: party leaders and party activists. These subgroups sometimes have conflicting interests, and each subgroup may have internal tensions. Party leaders at the state and local levels, for example, do not always share the objectives of national party leaders. More intractable disagreements tend to occur between party leaders, who are often professional and pragmatic politicians, and the scores of party workers without whom political parties could not survive.

Most party activists are volunteers who hold no official position in the party organization; their commitment of time, energy, and money differentiates them from those who merely identify with a party and vote for its candidates. It is from this activist group that party leaders are recruited, and some party activists see their involvement as the first step toward elected office. Others may seek patronage jobs or contracts. The vast majority of party activists, however, become involved because of the solidary and ideological benefits of active political participation. In short, they enjoy working with other people in collective action to pursue their own ideological objectives.[23]

Party activists tend to be more extreme in their positions than mere voters.[24] Activists are more likely to vote in party primaries, thus contributing to the tendency of candidates to take more extreme positions during primaries and then to move to more moderate positions during the general election. The pull to the center is countered, however, by the candidates' awareness that "activist-fueled get-out-the-vote drives may prove as effective in pulling out

---

[22] See Rosenblum, *Primus inter Pares* at 506 (cited in note 20) (citing Paul A. Beck and Frank J. Sorauf, *Party Politics in America* 75 (HarperCollins, 7th ed 1992)).

[23] See Beck and Hershey, *Party Politics in America* at 99 (cited in note 14).

[24] See Issacharoff, *Private Parties* at 306 (cited in note 1). But see John R. Petrocik, *Candidate Strategy, Voter Response, and Party Cohesion*, in Bruce E. Cain and Elisabeth R. Gerber, eds, *Voting at the Political Fault Line: California's Experiment with the Blanket Primary* 270, 273–74 (California, 2002) (presenting findings that cast into doubt conventional wisdom that voters in primaries are systematically different from average voter).

a close election as concerted appeals to the center."[25] Thus, activists may provide the margin of victory because of the intensity of their preferences.

Commitment to ideology is particularly strong among nonprofessional activists; professional party leaders and consultants are more pragmatic and more willing to compromise in order to achieve electoral success. Placed along a continuum of ideological purity, activists would be found at the far end, pursuing electoral goals as a way to implement policies important to them but unwilling to compromise significantly to win elections. Party leaders are somewhat committed to ideology,[26] both because they generally come from activist backgrounds but also because they understand the need for a clear partisan message to preserve the party label. These two groups will often prefer different organizational structures, with leaders preferring hierarchical arrangements and activists seeking greater voice. They may also favor different primary structures, although both groups usually oppose blanket primaries.

Activists who become frustrated with the party because its leaders and candidates do not meet their ideological expectations may first seek to influence party policy from within. If that fails, they may leave the party to join a more ideologically focused minor party.[27] The option of exit is not very attractive in the American system, however, because minor parties are unlikely to offer a real opportunity to translate a platform into policies adopted by government. This suggests a possible affinity between nonprofessional activists in the major and minor parties; they may have similar ideological preferences, with the minor-party activists representing a more extreme version.

3. *Officeholders and office seekers as members.* A third group that

<hr>

[25] Issacharoff, *Private Parties* at 307 (cited in note 1). See also Larry M. Bartels, *Where the Ducks Are: Voting Power in a Party System*, in Geer, *Politicians and Party Politics* at 43, 68 (cited in note 10) (noting that candidates have to appeal to two groups with different views: prospective voters who are likely to vote and reliable supporters "susceptible to mobilization").

[26] See William Crotty, *Democracy and the Future of Political Parties in America*, in Gerald M. Pomper and Mark Weiner, eds, *The Future of Democratic Politics: Principles and Practices* (forthcoming Rutgers, 2003) (noting differences in elites' ideological commitments across parties and segments of the party-organization).

[27] See Albert O. Hirschman, *Exit, Voice, and Loyalty: Responses to Decline in Firms, Organizations, and States* 4, 82–83 (Harvard, 1970).

might be considered as the "members" of a political party are those who seek office using the party label. There is some overlap between this group and the others. Candidates are often recruited from the ranks of party activists, and party leaders may hold political office either concurrently or at some point in their careers. The party's candidate is crucial to establishing the party's character. Candidates define the party's message because they are the means through which a party implements its platform. All of the other groups want to influence the identity of the party's candidates: voters want candidates who reflect their preferences, party leaders want candidates they can influence in office, and party activists want candidates with whom they are ideologically compatible. They all want candidates who are electable. Candidates seek to satisfy these groups in order to gain the advantage of a major-party label.

Several institutional features give potential candidates a degree of independence and enable them to use political parties for their own ends. The direct primary, for example, which is now the predominant method by which parties choose their nominees, has reduced the influence of party leaders in the selection of nominees.[28] Although party organizations do not necessarily oppose the direct primary, this institution is typically imposed on the electoral process by state law. Depending on the rules governing access to the primary ballot, some party organizations today have little say over the slate of candidates presented to voters.[29] In the context of a

---

[28] See Leon D. Epstein, *Political Parties in the American Mold* 70 (Wisconsin, 1986). See also L. Sandy Maisel, *American Political Parties: Still Central to a Functioning Democracy?* in Cohen, Fleisher, and Kantor, *American Political Parties* at 103, 108 (cited in note 21) (arguing that the parties have extremely limited "minor and informal" control over the selection of their nominees); Frymer and Yoon, *Political Parties, Representation, and Federal Safeguards* at 990 (cited in note 4) (describing debilitating effect of primary access rules on parties). But see Maisel, *American Political Parties* at 118 (noting that some states allow parties a formal, but limited, role in nominating contests); Roger H. Davidson, *Congressional Parties, Leaders, and Committees: 1900, 2000, and Beyond,* in Cohen, Fleisher, and Kantor, *American Political Parties* at 187, 199 (arguing that parties still exert important influence over the selection of nominees and describing tactics used).

[29] This is certainly true when one compares the party's role today to its power in caucuses or during the era of machine politics and bosses. See Katz and Kolodny, *Party Organization as an Empty Vessel* at 31 (cited in note 2). For an example of possible extreme consequences of this system, see Amy Franklin, *Michigan Democratic Party Files Complaint Claiming Eight Senate Candidates Not Really Democrats,* AP (May 22, 2002) (Michigan Democrats accused Republicans of "planting fake Democratic candidates" in state Senate primaries to force run-offs).

direct primary, candidates often bypass traditional party leaders and appeal directly to activists and voters for money, support, and votes.[30] Party leaders may be limited to endorsing a particular candidate in the primary; such endorsements sometimes guarantee automatic access to the primary ballot or the right to be listed first.[31]

Not only does the direct primary empower candidates relative to party leaders, it also strengthens party activists. If party leaders stray too far from the ideological objectives of the party faithful, activists can use the direct primary to nominate a candidate who supports their ideology. If their candidate wins the office, then they have influence in government; if their candidate loses, they have nonetheless forced party leaders to take them into account in the future. The direct primary, particularly a closed one, can amplify the voice of dissident members and reduce the need for insurgents to exit and form minor parties.[32] Although in this respect the interests of some office seekers and activists can be aligned, the interests of these groups can clash as well. Once in office, most politicians discover the need for compromise. Ideological purity generally cannot be maintained if they are to be effective. Thus, they may rely on party organs in government to structure votes in ways that shield them from retribution by disappointed supporters or to draft omnibus bills with provisions that satisfy the preferences of extreme supporters who may then accept the simultaneous enactment of policies they oppose.

4. *Interest groups as members.* Parties may best be seen as intermediary groups, mediating the relationships among government, interest groups, and citizens.[33] In this view, interest groups might be considered the key constituent parts of the major parties. Some interest groups may affiliate with one party consistently;[34] others

---

[30] See John H. Aldrich, *Why Parties? The Origin and Transformation of Political Parties in America* 291 (Chicago, 1995) (describing the importance of ideologically motivated activists in modern American political parties).

[31] See Bibby, *Politics, Parties and Elections* at 178–81 (cited in note 14) (describing rules concerning preprimary endorsements by party organizations).

[32] See Epstein, *Political Parties in the American Mold* at 173 (cited in note 28).

[33] For a general discussion, see Issacharoff and Ortiz, *Governing Through Intermediaries* (cited in note 13); Kramer, *Putting the Politics Back* at 267, 272–73 (cited in note 1). See also Jonathan R. Macey, *The Role of Democratic and Republican Parties as Organizers of Shadow Interest Groups*, 89 Mich L Rev 1 (1990) (arguing that latent groups that do not want to incur the costs of organizing use political parties to achieve their objectives).

[34] See Daniel J. Tichenor, *Contentious Elites: Presidents, Interest Groups and Programmatic Ambitions*, in Pomper and Weiner, *The Future of Democratic Politics* (cited in note 26).

may shift allegiance according to changes in power and substantive positions. Increasingly, political parties help form interest groups to achieve their objectives; Nathaniel Persily identifies these groups as the informal manifestation of political parties.[35] The model of interest groups as "members" is less helpful in the context of minor parties, which often are committed to a single issue and thus do not provide an environment of robust interaction among different interest groups. In addition, most minor parties lack the connection to government that allows major parties to play the role of a buffer between the power of the government and the rights of individuals engaged in collective action.

The perspective that political parties serve as forums for interest group activity and may mediate between that activity and governing bodies provides another wrinkle for those determining appropriate regulation. The view of parties as organized coalitions of more focused interests provides a different dimension along which intraparty conflict and competition can take place.[36] In addition, this perspective emphasizes structural questions over issues of individual rights and underscores the collective nature of political activity. It also illustrates an important difference between major parties and other interest groups. Parties work toward compromise among competing interest groups as they discharge their governance function, raise money, garner votes, and construct and prioritize their agendas.[37] Because their overriding objective is governance, rather than implementing policies concerning only one issue, political parties must balance short- and long-term consider-

[35] See Nathaniel Persily, *Parties, Money, and Corruption* [25–28] (unpublished manuscript prepared for the Annual Meeting of American Political Science Association, 2002) (noting possibility of shift of power to such groups because of provisions in the 2002 Bipartisan Campaign Reform Act).

[36] For an example of how this kind of analysis might affect regulatory decisions, see the opinions in *Fed Election Commission v Colo Republican Fed Campaign Committee*, 533 US 431 (2001). I do not apply the analysis offered in this article to the campaign finance cases, although it is my sense that the appropriate judicial approach is the same, at least with respect to regulations that affect political parties and probably with respect to all campaign finance rules. It remains for a future project to extend the framework advocated in this article to such laws. Compare with Elizabeth Garrett, *The William J. Brennan Lecture in Constitutional Law: The Future of Campaign Finance Laws in the Courts and in Congress*, 27 OCU L Rev (forthcoming 2002) (discussing institutional limitations of the judiciary in campaign finance cases).

[37] Michael A. Fitts, *Back to the Future: The Enduring Dilemmas Revealed in the Supreme Court's Treatment of Political Parties*, in David K. Ryden, ed, *The U.S. Supreme Court and the Electoral Process* 95, 97 (Georgetown, 2000).

ations and moderate extreme positions to construct an agenda that appeals to a majority of voters. Parties are durable, whereas many interest groups are ad hoc, brought into being by a particular issue and disappearing when that issue fades. Major parties cannot afford to be dominated by a single issue or by a small segment of society—although elements in the party, particularly activists, may resist compromise and balance.

In short, the ease with which courts and others refer to political parties as "membership organizations" masks the difficulties involved in figuring out whether there are any individuals or groups that are properly characterized as "members" in the usual sense of that word. Political parties are aggregations of many different kinds of interests, some individual and many collective. The concept of party "membership" is either not useful, or, at the least, we must be scrupulously careful to identify which people or groups we are considering as "members" and what their relevant interests are.

D. MAJOR POLITICAL PARTIES, MINOR POLITICAL PARTIES, AND OTHER ORGANIZATIONS

Distinguishing political parties from interest groups has long been a challenge for those who study the political process. One modern definition of interest group is "any group that pursues contested political or policy goals, and that is widely regarded by the public as being one contending interest among others."[38] This could include political parties. On the other hand, major parties provide forums in which other interest groups compete and interact, and the notion of narrowly focused "special" interests would seem not to include broadly based, programmatic parties.

Policymakers who want to distinguish between political parties and other political organizations must devise a test to separate the two groups. Developing such a test is particularly difficult in the case of minor parties, which often share more characteristics with

---

[38] Peter H. Schuck, *Against (and For) Madison: An Essay in Praise of Factions*, 15 Yale L & Policy Rev 553, 558 (1997). Schuck views his definition as "capacious enough to encompass the political parties themselves," although he accepts that political parties are also coalitions of other interest groups. Id at 558. See also William N. Eskridge, Jr., Philip P. Frickey, and Elizabeth Garrett, *Cases and Materials on Legislation: Statutes and the Creation of Public Policy* 48–49 (West, 3d ed 2001) (providing definitions and noting that parties are sometimes considered as interest groups and sometimes not).

private organizations than with major parties. One approach asserts that "the right to be on the election ballot is . . . what separates a political party from any other interest group."[39] But that distinction is either unnecessary or circular. Major parties generally receive automatic access to the ballot, but one does not need this "test" to distinguish the Republican Party from the Christian Coalition. Entities other than major parties must seek ballot access through petitioning, paying a fee, or using other methods usually intended to demonstrate broad-based support. Moreover, most minor parties never expect their candidates to win. Fielding candidates is merely one way to advance their agendas and to communicate with the public. In states where ballot access is easy and groups believe a strong showing at the polls and the publicity of a campaign further their objectives, more political organizations act like "political parties" than in states where ballot access is more difficult.[40]

It could be that the distinction based on ballot access suggests that political parties are those groups that have demonstrated widespread support because they pursue broader agendas than single-issue special interests.[41] Perhaps this explains why major parties are different from other political organizations, but it seems insufficient to explain why some minor parties are different. Is the Right to Life Party[42] an organization with broader support than a pro-life interest group? Is the Sierra Club, with its broad environmental agenda, fundamentally different from the Green Party? Perhaps they are different because political parties seek to control

---

[39] *Timmons v Twin Cities Area New Party*, 520 US 351, 373 (1997) (Stevens dissenting).

[40] See, for example, Howard A. Scarrow, *Parties, Elections, and Representation in the State of New York* 61 (NYU, 1983) (arguing that fusion ballot laws among other features of the legal landscape explain why the right-to-life forces in New York have formed a party but have not pursued this strategy elsewhere).

[41] Nancy Rosenblum uses the same distinction—the right to appear on the ballot—to illustrate that parties, unlike private organizations, exercise power from within the government and achieve their objectives by running serious candidates. See Rosenblum, *Political Parties as Membership Groups* at 814–15 (cited in note 10). This separates major parties from other political organizations, but it is less helpful with respect to minor ones. Her discussion appears to center primarily on broad-based parties that "have the publicly-affirmed affiliation and participation of significant numbers of active members [and that] can field candidates and hire experts." Id at 817.

[42] The Right to Life Party, which is affiliated with the National Right to Life Committee, is currently on the ballot in New York. See New York State Board of Elections 2002 Candidate List (available online at ⟨http://www.elections.state.ny.us/⟩).

the instruments of governance and not merely to influence policy. But, in reality, only the two major parties have any real hope of controlling government at the national level. Other parties and organizations seek to influence the policy agenda through various tools, including, in some cases, running candidates in political races.

Using ballot access to separate political parties from other political groups could also reflect the view that major political parties are different because they organize government. The major parties make up government and provide a structure to mediate among citizens, interest groups, and government officials. Relying on this type of analysis, the Court in the *White Primary Cases* held that the internal decisions of party organizations can constitute state action for purposes of the Fourteenth Amendment.[43] But this insight is not as helpful as might first appear. As commentators have noted, the Court's reasoning in the *White Primary Cases* does not have a logical stopping-place that would allow courts to differentiate among political actors.[44] In the most controversial of these decisions, a splintered Court found state action when a political organization with loose ties to the official party structure endorsed only white candidates in the Democratic primaries.[45] Moreover, the ability of major parties to organize government and serve as intermediaries is the result of the rules governing the political process, few of which are constitutionally mandated. Had the states and the federal government chosen different ways to organize politics and elections, minor parties might have more public characteristics than they have now.

In the end, the best way to think about the differences between political parties and other groups is to envision a continuum that represents the degree of involvement in public governance. There is no sharp dividing line, but there is a spectrum that can be rationally organized and that can enable policymakers to construct appropriate regulations. At one end, with substantial influence on governance and other public functions, are major parties. At the

---

[43] See *Nixon v Condon*, 286 US 73, 93–94 (1932), and *Smith v Allwright*, 321 US 649, 658, 663–64 (1944).

[44] For a general discussion, see Samuel Issacharoff and Richard H. Pildes, *Politics as Markets: Partisan Lockups of the Democratic Process*, 50 Stan L Rev 643, 659–60 (1998).

[45] *Terry v Adams*, 345 US 461 (1953).

other end are organizations that seek no direct influence in government and work toward purely private goals (although even these have some involvement in the public sphere and thus may be subject to some legal intrusions). Minor parties with a chance of gaining elected or appointed political office, such as the Libertarian or Green Parties, are closer to the major parties. Fringe parties that pursue single issues for a limited time resemble private organizations. Some political interest groups have broad-based agendas and a great deal in common with parties that subscribe to broader agendas. Paul Beck and Marjorie Hershey note that major political parties may have more in common with the Chamber of Commerce or a large labor organization then with many minor political parties.[46] Perhaps the best way to determine where an organization lies on the continuum is not to apply specified criteria, but rather to rely on family-resemblance concepts[47] which defy definition but can support distinctions. In short, there are no clear rules that separate political parties from other political groups.

E. POLITICAL PARTIES WILL CHANGE OVER TIME

John Aldrich has described political parties as "the most highly endogenous institutions of any substantial and sustained political importance in American history."[48] Political parties, with all their various parts and subparts, are instrumental institutions, used by goal-oriented actors to achieve their objectives. Any current configuration of a political party is likely to change, sometimes substantially, as the preferences of voters, leaders, activists, and interest groups change and as the rules governing them change. For example, over time the party-organization has ceased to function as a machine led by bosses earning loyalty through patronage and

---

[46] Beck and Hershey, *Party Politics in America* at 16 (cited in note 14).

[47] See Andrei Marmor, *Interpretation and Legal Theory* 133 (Clarendon, 1992) (describing Wittgenstein's metaphor of family resemblance for words describing things that are related but have no one thing in common that explains the use of the word for all).

[48] Aldrich, *Why Parties?* at 19 (cited in note 39). See also Crotty, *Democracy and the Future of Political Parties* (cited in note 26) ("[P]olitical parties are not static. They are 'living' organisms, which have evolved over time and are continuing to evolve to meet the demands that society places upon them."); Frymer and Yoon, *Political Parties, Representation, and Federal Safeguards* at 981 (cited in note 4) (describing parties as "pliable organizations that leaders and elites use over time to advance their own interests and as such, lack any fundamental, enduring, and essential nature").

other benefits for committed members. As legal, technological, and social changes made that model impossible to sustain, the party-organization evolved into a service organization, providing expertise, money, and a party label to candidates seeking public office. Aldrich identified the "critical era of the 1960s" as a turning point for party-organizations as they changed to accommodate a new environment in which ambitious politicians could realize their goals through personal campaign organizations rather than through a party monopoly.[49]

The challenges posed by the endogeneity of political parties are especially serious for the judiciary, which makes decisions in the context of isolated cases often without the benefit of historical or political context. Party endogeneity also suggests that rules adopted at one time will have counterproductive, inefficient, or at least unexpected consequences at later times as political parties alter their structure, in part as a response to the rules applied to them and in part as a reaction to other changes in the political landscape.

Consider, for example, the varied reactions of segments of political parties to the blanket primary.[50] Unlike California, where both major party-organizations and some minor parties opposed the blanket primary, in Alaska the Democratic Party did not oppose the blanket primary in a recent lawsuit challenging it, and the Alaskan Independence Party, a minor party that sometimes elects members to statewide office, supported it.[51] When it was first enacted in Alaska, the Republicans were its main advocates (although it received support from many Democratic officeholders).[52] By

---

[49] Aldrich, *Why Parties?* at 241–74 (cited in note 30).

[50] In a blanket primary, voters can vote in the primary of more than one party because each voter receives a ballot listing every candidate in each race, regardless of the voter's party affiliation. So, for example, a voter can choose among Democrats for governor, among Republicans for attorney general, and among Libertarians for secretary of state.

[51] See *O'Callaghan v State*, 914 P2d 1250 (Alaska 1996) (case challenging blanket primary brought by the Alaskan Republican Party, in which the Democratic Party did not intervene and the Independence Party submitted a brief in support of the primary's constitutionality). See also id at 1255, n 8 (describing the Independence Party).

[52] Id at 1255–56. The history of the blanket primary in Washington is more consistent with the California story. The legislature adopted it after a successful petition drive suggested that proponents would enact the blanket primary by popular vote. The major-party leadership challenged the primary twice, but it was upheld by the state supreme court. Another challenge was mounted, in light of the Supreme Court's decision in *California Democratic Party v Jones*, 530 US 567 (2000), by both major parties and some minor parties. The District Court granted the state's motion for summary judgment upholding the blanket

1996, however, the Republican Party had switched its position, challenging the constitutionality of the blanket primary and adopting a party rule in favor of semiclosed primaries.[53] Thus, as long as Alaska used the blanket primary, the party leadership of at least one major party did not view the format as a threat to its ability to formulate and communicate a clear message, and not all minor parties viewed it as a threat to their existence.

Not only do political parties adapt to new circumstances, but most other aspects of the political environment also change over time. These changes then further affect political parties. The interactions and feedback effects increase the dynamic complexity facing courts and virtually guarantee that judicial decisions in this arena will have unforeseen consequences for all facets of government. Adjudication is a blunt and often counterproductive tool. Courts do not have the resources to gather reliable information about the political environment or to make accurate predictions about the likely effects of their rulings on parties and other institutions. Courts are presented only with a partial picture and often cannot grasp the entirety of a problem.[54] Moreover, if the system adapts to a particular ruling in unexpected ways, courts do not have the ability to modify the law unless someone brings a case that allows adjustment. In an area of rapidly changing institutions and complex relationships among entities, the ability to revise policy

---

primary, finding that Washington's primary was relevantly different from California's. See *Democratic Party Wash State v Reed*, No C00-5419FDB (WD Wash, Mar 27, 2002) (available online at ⟨http://www.secstate.wa.gov/office/bp/bpopinion_full.pdf⟩), appeal docketed, No 02-35422 (9th Cir Apr 30, 2002).

[53] That challenge was unsuccessful, but in the wake of the Supreme Court's decision invalidating the California blanket primary, the Alaska Supreme Court has held the format to violate the Constitution. See *O'Callaghan v Kowalski*, 6 P3d 728, 730 (Alaska 2000) (finding no "constitutionally significant differences" between the two states' primary election laws). Alaska now has a semiclosed primary system, in which registered party members can vote in a party's primary along with unaffiliated voters if the party's rules permit. See Alaska Stat §§ 15-25-010, 15-25-014 (Michie 2001).

[54] For example, both *Colorado Republican* cases dealt only with hard money contributions and expenditures. See *Colo Republican Fed Campaign Committee v Fed Election Commission*, 518 US 604 (1996), and *Fed Election Commission v Colo Republican Fed Campaign Commission*, 533 US 431 (2001). The advocates of the recently enacted Bipartisan Campaign Reform Act, PL No 107-155, 116 Stat 81 (Mar 27, 2002), argue that soft money expenditures present more opportunities for corruption or undue influence. The lower appellate court in *Colorado Republican II* discussed the threat posed by soft money when it questioned whether the FEC regulations of hard money expenditures by political parties were "closely-drawn" to match important government interests. *Fed Election Commission v Colo Republican Fed Campaign Committee*, 213 F3d 1221, 1229–30 (2000).

over time, engage in new and expanded fact-finding, and make decisions incrementally can be crucial to success. None of these features plays to the strengths of the courts; yet all of them lead to a dynamic environment full of contending forces.

II. THREE CASES CONCERNING THE REGULATION OF POLITICAL PARTIES

Political parties are complex and dynamic, full of competing interests. Analysis of three Supreme Court decisions will make these observations more concrete and reveal how conflicting forces within and among political parties balance rival interests and enable change over time as politicians and voters develop new structures of democracy. I do not argue that the results reached in all these decisions were wrong; after all, when a court upholds a law against constitutional attack, it reaches the same result as it does when it declines to decide the merits. My concern is not with the immediate results of judicial review, but with the fact of review itself and the broader effects of the reasoning that courts use either to uphold or strike down a regulation. By too readily addressing the constitutionality of political institutions devised through the dynamic interactions of political parties and other actors, the Court undermines the political branches and impedes the development of institutions that might better serve the democratic aspirations of the day. I will return to this theme in Part III.

A. TASHJIAN V CONNECTICUT[55]

From 1955 to 1984, Connecticut required major parties to select their nominees through conventions of party delegates.[56] The party convention could endorse any candidate receiving more than 20 percent of votes cast in a roll call vote at the convention. Any nonendorsed candidate who received more than 20 percent of the vote could challenge the party-endorsed candidate in a closed primary. The candidate selected at the convention or through the

---

[55] 479 US 208 (1986).

[56] See *Republican Party of Conn v Tashjian*, 770 F2d 265, 268 (2d Cir 1985). This system applied to multitown districts, which included all statewide offices, federal legislative offices, and many state legislative offices. Compare Conn Gen Stat §§ 9-390, 9-405, 9-406 (applying to one-town districts) with §§ 9-400, 9-416 (applying to multitown districts).

primary was placed on the general election ballot. In 1976, this system was challenged by an independent voter who sought to vote in the Republican primary without formally affiliating with the party. His lawsuit was opposed by both major party-organizations, as well as by the parties-in-government that had adopted the law. The voter lost.[57] The Supreme Court explained that it viewed the case as one brought by a "nonmember" seeking to participate in a crucial activity of a party, rather than by a party member seeking to define who could participate in the party's activities.[58] The electoral laws in Connecticut, however, gave little weight to the concept of "membership," which the Court saw as determining the decision. Under state law, a voter could register with a party as late as noon on the last business day preceding the primary and still participate as a full member in the election.[59]

In 1984, the Republican Party leadership and its partisans in government determined that they needed to appeal to independent voters in Connecticut to increase their electoral strength.[60] This shift illustrates how parties can change over time to account for developments in the electorate. Accordingly, the party convention adopted a rule that would open the party primary for federal and statewide offices to independents as well as registered Republicans. The Republicans in the state legislature, a minority in both houses, sought to repeal the law requiring closed primaries, but they were defeated in party-line votes. The state party, Republicans holding federal office, and the Republican state chairman then brought suit challenging the law. In a 5–4 decision, the Court struck it down as an impermissible burden on party members' associational rights.

Tashjian implicates many of the characteristics of political parties described above, some of which members of the Court explicitly acknowledged. The Justices discussed, for example, what it means to be a "member" of a political party. The majority discounted the extent of the affiliation between a political party and ordinary voters who register as partisans. Justice Marshall explained:

---

[57] *Nader v Schaffer*, 417 F Supp 837 (D Conn), summarily aff'd, 429 US 989 (1976).

[58] *Tashjian*, 479 US at 215 n 6.

[59] See id at 216 n 7.

[60] Independent support was a demographic necessity: there were 659,268 registered Democrats, 425,695 registered Republicans, and 532,723 registered but unaffiliated voters in the state. Id at 212 n 3.

A major state political party necessarily includes individuals
playing a broad spectrum of roles in the organization's activities. Some of the Party's members devote substantial portions
of their lives to furthering its political and organizational goals,
others provide substantial financial support, while still others
limit their participation to casting their votes for some or all
of the Party's candidates. Considered from the standpoint of
the Party itself, the act of formal enrollment or public affiliation with the Party is merely one element in the continuum
of participation in Party affairs, and need not be in any sense
the most important.[61]

Justice Scalia, in dissent, viewed formal affiliation as more meaningful, observing that "[t]he Connecticut voter who, while stead-
fastly refusing to register as a Republican, casts a vote in the Republican primary, forms no more meaningful an 'association' with
the Party than does the independent or the registered Democrat
who responds to questions by a Republican Party pollster."[62]

In both opinions, the mass of voters who register as partisans
were seen, in at least some sense, as members of the party. Yet,
it is difficult to discover what their interests were and who was
asserting those interests on their behalf. An absence of discussion
of their interests is not surprising for the majority because it down-
played the importance of formal affiliation. Justice Scalia, who had
a thicker concept of membership, focused more on party activists,
whom he called the "rank and file"[63] of the party, than on ordinary
voters. It is possible to view the interests articulated by the state
to support closed primaries as vindicating the interests of the mass
electorate. But because the state consisted primarily of Democratic
officeholders, one suspects that its claim about protecting the interests of the ordinary voters was as strategic as it was sincere.

For example, the state argued that voters would be confused
about the ideology of a candidate in the general election if the
candidate had been selected by independents as well as partisans.
This argument depends on a conclusion that the involvement of
independents in primaries dilutes the party label. Dilution is possible if independents who vote in party primaries have preferences
that systematically diverge from partisans. Certainly, the Republi-

---

[61] Id at 215.

[62] Id at 235 (Scalia dissenting).

[63] Id at 236.

can Party believed that independents have different perspectives than partisans because it hoped that the involvement of independents would produce more moderate nominees. The Court's analysis of this interest is unsatisfactory because it dismissed the importance of the information contained in the party label. Although Justice Marshall acknowledged that party labels act as voting cues and "play[ ] a role in the process by which voters inform themselves in the exercise of the franchise," he concluded that voters can be expected to seek out better and more complete information.[64]

The more convincing argument made by the Court in rejecting the claim of voter confusion was that other aspects of the nomination process guaranteed the vitality of the party label. Only candidates receiving the votes of more than 20 percent of the delegates at the party convention were eligible to appear on the primary ballot.[65] The Court reasoned that this control over the identity of the candidates by committed party members was sufficient to preserve the integrity of the party label. Of course, the Court's reliance on rules maintaining the party-organization's influence over the identity of its nominees seems discordant in an opinion that also affirmed the authority of the state to require direct primaries[66] because the direct primary is the principal mechanism used to limit the party's power to freely select its nominees.

Perhaps the most interesting feature of political parties relevant to *Tashjian* is how the competing interests of segments of the political parties other than the mass electorate were affected by the Republican rule change. First, the "state" was for all practical purposes the Democratic Party, which competed against the Republican Party and, at the time of the case, enjoyed substantial control over elected offices. The Court in *Tashjian* explicitly viewed that fact as pertinent to its analysis. For example, the Court dismissed the state's claim that closed primaries protect parties from raiding

---

[64] Id at 220. This faith in the dedication of voters to spend a great deal of time gathering information about candidates will often be unwarranted, given the competing demands on people's time and attention. For a general discussion, see Garrett, *Future of Campaign Finance Laws* (cited in note 36) (discussing importance of voting cues for voter competence).

[65] See *Tashjian*, 479 US at 221 (requirement that all candidates in the primary have received substantial support at the convention attenuates concern that the relationship between party and nominee is merely a "marriage of convenience").

[66] See id at 237 (Scalia dissenting) (making similar point: "It is beyond my understanding why the Republican Party's delegation of its democratic choice to a Republican Convention can be proscribed, but its delegation of that choice to nonmembers of the Party cannot.").

and disintegration because the state "to some extent represent[s] the views of the one political party transiently enjoying majority party power."[67] Claims by Democratic officeholders that they knew what was best for their Republican competitors rang false to the Court. In this respect, *Tashjian* involved one party imposing a regulation on its competitor in order to retain majority status. Such a circumstance is arguably a compelling justification for judicial action.[68]

But, as usual in the case of political parties, the circumstances were more complicated. It is also possible that this was an intraparty dispute. Justice Scalia's dissent argued that the decision to allow independents to vote in Republican primaries could have been a decision made by party elites and officeholders and imposed on party activists without their consent. Party leaders and ambitious office seekers wanted to enhance candidates' electability, even at the price of compromising ideological commitments. As Justice Scalia noted:

> We have no way of knowing that a majority of the Party's members is in favor of allowing ultimate selection of its candidates for federal and statewide office to be determined by persons outside the Party. That decision was not made by democratic ballot, but by the Party's state convention—which, for all we know, may have been dominated by office holders and office seekers whose evaluation of the merits of assuring election of the Party's candidates, vis-à-vis the merits of proposing candidates faithful to the Party's political philosophy, diverged significantly from the views of the Party's rank and file.[69]

At the least, it is not clear that the *only* group supporting a closed primary in Connecticut was the Democratic Party in a move to disadvantage its opposition.

Moreover, the political situation might have changed without judicial involvement. The dynamism that characterizes political

---

[67] Id at 224.

[68] For a general discussion, see Richard L. Hasen, *Do the Parties or the People Own the Electoral Process?* 149 U Pa L Rev 815, 836 (2001). See also Daniel Lowenstein, *Associational Rights of Major Political Parties: A Skeptical Inquiry*, 71 Tex L Rev 1741, 1788 (1993) (noting that an interparty dispute is more appropriate for judicial resolution when the minority party has worked to achieve its objective legislatively and most of its partisans in government supported the change). But see id at 1790 (nonetheless providing reasons in favor of judicial restraint in *Tashjian*).

[69] *Tashjian*, 479 US at 236 (Scalia dissenting).

parties provides significant opportunities to revisit and revise decisions about primary format. Perhaps party activists would have succeeded in repealing the rule at the next convention. Perhaps the Democratic leadership would have decided that more open primaries were in its electoral interests as Connecticut, along with the rest of the nation, became more competitive. Perhaps the Republicans would have gained control of the state legislature and changed the law.[70] Indeed, notwithstanding the system of closed primaries, the Republican Party took control of both state houses after the 1984 election and passed a law allowing independents to vote in primaries when authorized by party rule. The law was vetoed by the Democratic governor.[71] Currently, both major parties restrict voting in their primaries to registered members, although state law allows them to open their primaries to nonmembers if they choose to do so.[72]

The Connecticut primary system continues to provide opportunities for judicial intervention into the political process. The laws allowing party control over access to primary ballots were retained after *Tashjian*, although the amount of support at the convention required for a nonendorsed candidate to appear on the primary ballot was reduced from 20 percent to 15 percent. This law has been attacked; for example, in 2001, the governor supported a law implementing a typical direct primary, and it passed the General Assembly but narrowly lost in the Senate.[73] Even with the Court's implicit acceptance of the current arrangement in *Tashjian* and the possibility of change through the political branches, a federal district court recently ruled the law is likely unconstitutional because it places too great a burden on nonendorsed (and usually nonin-

[70] This possibility was a real one when *Tashjian* was decided. Although the Republican Party in Connecticut tended to be in the minority in the legislature more than it controlled one or both of the houses, Connecticut was not a one-party state. During the period between 1955 and 1984, the Republicans had controlled the Senate twice and the General Assembly six times, and they were often a sizable minority in Democratic-controlled legislatures. See Connecticut Register and Manual (available online at ⟨http://www.sots.state.ct.us/RegisterManual/SectionIII/Leg3.htm⟩).

[71] *Tashjian*, 479 US at 212–13 n 4.

[72] See Conn Gen Stat § 9-431(a); Party Rules for Connecticut Democratic Party and Connecticut Republican Party (available online at ⟨http://www.sots.state.ct.us/ElectionsDivision/TCRules/PartyRules.html⟩). The law states that if the parties choose semi-open primaries, unaffiliated voters can vote in only one such primary.

[73] See Carrie Budoff and Michael Grynbaum, *Judge Voids Ballot Law, Ruling Meant to Open Up Primaries; State Seeks Stay*, Hartford Courant A1 (July 24, 2002).

cumbent) candidates seeking access to the primary.[74] At least one party to the lawsuit, Common Cause of Connecticut, hailed its court victory as a way to leverage its legislative proposals,[75] demonstrating that political losers turn to the courts notwithstanding available political channels for change if aggressive judicial review is available.

B. TIMMONS V TWIN CITIES AREA NEW PARTY[76]

Minnesota formally banned fusion candidacies in 1901. Fusion allows an individual to appear on the ballot as a candidate of more than one party. Multiparty endorsements generally strengthen the influence of minor parties, which cannot ordinarily hope to elect their own candidates but might be able to demonstrate electoral influence. In 1994, State Representative Andy Dawkins was nominated by one of the two major parties, the Democratic-Farmer-Labor (DFL) Party, and then by a minor party, the Twin Cities chapter of the national New Party. Dawkins welcomed the New Party nomination and supported the effort to legalize fusion.[77] Nonetheless, state officials, including the Secretary of State, who was a member of the DFL Party,[78] refused to accept the New Par-

---

[74] *Campbell v Bysiewicz*, Ruling on Defendant's Motion to Stay and on Plaintiff's Motion for Reconsideration, Civ No 3:02cv488(PCD) (D Conn Aug 5, 2002) (enjoining state from enforcing laws regarding multicity district primaries and allowing access to the primary ballot to candidates who are members of the party and file appropriate forms). The Second Circuit Court of Appeals stayed the district court's injunction changing the rules for the 2002 primaries, see *Campbell v Bysiewicz*, Order No 02-7819 (2d Cir Aug 9, 2002), and the case is now again before the district court for a full trial. In addition, the appellate court indicated that the political parties should be added as parties to the lawsuit.

[75] See Connecticut Common Cause, *Important Victory for Democracy in CT* (July 24, 2002) (available online at ⟨http://www.commoncause.org/states/connecticut/072402.htm⟩). One gets the impression from the district court opinion that the federal judge in that case had lost patience with the legislature, which has "over the years, . . . rebuffed multiple attempts to reform the system." *Campbell*, Ruling on Defendant's Motion to Stay and on Plaintiff's Motion for Reconsideration at 5 (cited in note 74). However, there have been continuing efforts in the Connecticut legislature to establish a direct primary, which presumably would look different from the system that would have been established by district court's decision and that would have allowed virtually anyone ballot access.

[76] 520 US 351 (1997).

[77] For a description of Dawkins's motivations, see Lisa Jane Disch, *The Tyranny of the Two-Party System* 17–18 (Columbia, 2002). For a description of the New Party's fusion strategy, see Micah L. Sifry, *Spoiling for a Fight: Third-Party Politics in America* 231–35 (Routledge, 2002).

[78] Joan Anderson-Growe, the elected secretary of state, had previously served in the Minnesota House of Representatives. See Minnesota Secretary of State, Joan Anderson Growe, MinnesotaPolitics.net (available online at ⟨http://minnesotapolitics.net/ConstitutionalOfficers/SOS.htm⟩). Dawkins's decision to accept the New Party's nomina-

ty's nominating petition or to list Dawkins as the New Party nominee on the ballot because state law prohibited multiple-party nominations.[79] The New Party, which was pursuing a multistate strategy of nominating or endorsing major-party candidates to increase its influence, filed suit. The Supreme Court upheld the state law.

In reaching this result, the Court failed to take account of many of the unique features of political parties described above. Unlike the opinion in *Tashjian*, the Court in *Timmons* did not acknowledge that the antifusion law was enacted by partisans in government, rather than by some neutral entity called the "state." The Court held that the "Minnesota Legislature," without any reference to its partisan makeup, could justify the fusion ban on the ground that "political stability is best served through a healthy two-party system."[80] The Court reasoned that the state could favor the two-party system, although it could not "completely insulate the two-party system from minor parties' or independent candidates' competition and influence."[81] Because the Court failed to recognize that the government officials who enacted these rules were also members of the two major parties, it did not ask whether these partisans-in-government were likely to construct rules to entrench themselves and their copartisans in office.

As some scholars have observed, however, fusion bans can be examples of "partisan lockup" of the government by the two major parties[82] or of duopolistic behavior that may reduce competition.[83] In general, major parties will be strengthened and better able to resist dissident voices if minor parties remain weak and unable to exert significant influence on electoral outcomes; thus, the two parties have an incentive to cooperate to pass laws that disadvantage minor parties. On the other hand, antifusion laws illustrate that explanations for laws regulating political parties are seldom

---

tion was not opposed by DFC party leaders. Sifry, *Spoiling for a Fight* at 245 (cited in note 77).

[79] *Timmons*, 520 US at 354 nn 3–4.

[80] Id at 367.

[81] Id.

[82] See Issacharoff and Pildes, *Politics as Markets* at 684 (cited in note 44).

[83] See Richard L. Hasen, *Entrenching the Duopoly: Why the Supreme Court Should Not Allow the States to Protect the Democrats and Republicans from Political Competition*, 1997 Supreme Court Review 331, 337–41.

simple, and regulations are not always the result of partisan lockup. In some cases, the major parties may cooperate to oppose fusion; in other cases the prohibition may be supported only by the dominant major party as a way to prevent the other major party from garnering support.[84] In the early days of antifusion laws, the Republican Party, dominant in many western states, passed such laws to ensure its preeminence over the Democratic Party, although it often received help from conservative Democrats. The Republicans also found support for the bans from some third parties who hoped to become more significant electoral forces in their own right and thought fusion politics maintained their position as peripheral players.[85]

Often, not all the elements of the party (or parties) working to ban fusion are in agreement. *Timmons* itself provides evidence of the disagreement about fusion within a major party: Dawkins, an incumbent candidate of a major party, did not object to his nomination by the New Party, even though the law had been supported by some members of his party and was enforced by officials affiliated with his party. Laws regulating fusion candidacies and cross-nominations can change over time as circumstances and alignments change. Moreover, depending on the constellation of forces within the state electoral system and the party itself, political parties can enforce antifusion policies internally. For example, they can prohibit their nominees from accepting the nomination of other parties.[86] Thus, striking down antifusion laws may not allow

---

[84] See Peter H. Argersinger, *"A Place on the Ballot": Fusion Politics and Antifusion Laws*, 85 Am Hist Rev 287 (1980) (discussing history of antifusion and finding that the laws were often the tool of the Republican Party to maintain superiority over its rival Democratic Party). During the 1890s, Democrats, including the national party, hoped to use fusion to increase their strength. See Disch, *Tyranny of the Two Party System* at 52–53 (cited in note 77).

[85] Argersinger, *Place on the Ballot* at 290 (cited in note 84).

[86] See Nathaniel Persily and Bruce E. Cain, *The Legal Status of Political Parties: A Reassessment of Competing Paradigms*, 100 Colum L Rev 775, 803–04 (2000). Following the lower court's decision in *Timmons* that the antifusion law was unconstitutional, Minnesota amended its law to allow fusion candidacies only if the state chairs of the nominating parties provided their consent in writing. It also punished a candidate who sought the nomination of both a minor and major party but who did not receive the major-party nomination by requiring her also to forfeit the minor-party nomination. See Act of April 2, 1996, 1996 Minn Sess Law Serv 419 (expired 1997). The amendment states that the law was intended "to provide an orderly procedure for complying with the [Eighth Circuit's] decision while retaining the prior law prohibiting simultaneous nominations to the extent permitted by the United States Constitution." Under the terms of the amendment, it was suspended as soon as the Eighth Circuit's ruling was overturned.

multiparty endorsements if the parties themselves discipline candidates who accept such endorsements.

Another omission in the Court's analysis in *Timmons* is the absence of sophisticated consideration of the role of minor parties, an issue that the dissent addressed more usefully. The Court failed to discuss the relationship between voice and exit or to respond to the dissent's observation that fusion candidacies allow minor parties vitality while preserving political stability.[87] Although both the Court and the dissent speculate about the effect of fusion on minor and major parties, they offer little empirical proof to support their claims. Instead, "the Court moved in dramatic fashion to wrap the two-party system in the shroud of constitutional legitimacy" on the basis of "assumptions about the effects of various party systems and electoral systems [that] were outdated, misleading, and often simply mistaken."[88] Furthermore, the Court viewed minor parties as seeking the same objectives as major parties: to elect their own nominees to office. The Court situated the New Party at the wrong end of the continuum, placing it closer to major parties than to political organizations that primarily seek to express political viewpoints and to influence government actors.

The Court's real difficulty with fusion candidacies was its concern that this particular tool, ballot labels, is an inappropriate means to influence voters. As Chief Justice Rehnquist put it succinctly: "Ballots serve primarily to elect candidates, not as forums for political expression."[89] The majority was worried that multiple endorsements from single-issue parties (which I have described as essentially interest groups using the ballot as a tool) would transform the ballot into "a billboard for political advertising." This would occur, he argued, if minor parties endorsing major-party candidates had names that indicated their policies, such as "No New Taxes" or "Healthy Planet" Party.[90] Major-party candidates might encourage this practice to provide voters with more information about their positions (or to mislead voters) at the crucial

---

[87] *Timmons*, 520 US at 380–81 (Stevens dissenting) (noting that fusion candidacies "[i]n some respects" are "the best marriage of the virtues of the minor party challenge to entrenched viewpoints and the political stability that the two-party system provides").

[88] Douglas J. Amy, *Entrenching the Two-Party System: The Supreme Court's Fusion Decision*, in Ryden, *The U.S. Supreme Court and the Electoral Process* at 142, 160 (cited in note 37).

[89] *Timmons*, 520 US at 363.

[90] Id at 365.

moment of voting. The Court provided no evidence to support this concern, and the dissent pointed out that experience with fusion candidacies is not consistent with this claim.[91]

Timmons is unsatisfactory because the Court's analysis is simplistic and full of unsupported, and intuitively unpersuasive, assertions. The Court premised its analysis on an erroneous view of fusion and ignored the existence of dynamic forces that enable laws affecting fusion to be changed over time through formal and informal mechanisms. Perhaps one way to rationalize these decisions is to focus on the Court's unarticulated concept of membership. In *Tashjian*, the Court protected the party's ability to define the people it wanted to participate in its primary, although it was unwilling in an earlier case to let a nonmember force his way into the primary. In *Timmons*, the Court was not concerned with the limitation on the New Party's power to nominate Andy Dawkins because Dawkins was an active member of the DFL party, and not a member of the New Party (although he was willing to affiliate with them through a fusion nomination). In *California Democratic Party v Jones*,[92] the Court was explicitly concerned that the participation of nonmembers in a blanket primary could overwhelm political parties and render them ineffective in the political process.

C. CALIFORNIA DEMOCRATIC PARTY V JONES

Until 1996, California required closed primaries. Pursuant to state law and party rules, only registered members of a political party could select that party's nominees.[93] In 1996, California voters passed an initiative that amended the election laws to require a blanket primary. Supporters of the initiative explicitly intended to compel changes in the nomination decisions of the political parties and to alter the messages that the parties promoted. A blanket primary format, in which voters can vote in different party pri-

---

[91] See id at 375 n 3 (Stevens dissenting). Furthermore, the majority did not tie its analysis of ballot cues to voter competence, the primary objective served by party labels and other ballot information. Chief Justice Rehnquist did not discuss whether fusion candidacies would either dilute the party cue (thereby decreasing voter competence) or enhance it by providing more particularized information (thereby improving voter competence).

[92] 530 US 567 (2000).

[93] The deadline for registering to vote in the party primary in California was twenty-nine days before the primary. See Cal Elec Code § 2102(a), 2000 Cal Legis Serv 899 (West), 1996 Cal Legis Serv 1123 (West).

maries for different offices and thus avoid both formal affiliation with a party and the necessity of voting in only one party's primary, is likely to result in candidates who appeal more to the median voter than to activists. Blanket primaries are moderating devices designed to move political parties closer to the center, or, in the words of the California ballot pamphlet, to "weaken" party "hard-liners" and empower "moderate problem-solvers."[94] In holding the initiative unconstitutional because it infringed on the First Amendment rights of party members, the Court placed great emphasis on the significant outside influence on internal party decisions about its message and its candidates that occurs under a blanket primary system.

The Court reasoned that the state's decision to compel party members to associate with nonmembers during a primary had the intended effect of changing the party's ideological message, and "[w]e can think of no heavier burden on a political party's associational freedom."[95] It is difficult to reconcile the strongly worded protection of this aspect of party activity with the Court's unquestioning acceptance of laws that require parties to select their candidates though a direct primary rather than a convention or caucus.[96] The Court left open the constitutionality of the state-mandated open primary, although it cited, apparently approvingly, a passage from a prior dissent that the mere act of voting in a party primary "fairly can be described as an act of affiliation" with that party.[97] The blanket primary, in contrast, raises the possibility that a par-

---

[94] 530 US at 570.

[95] Id at 582. It is not clear that blanket primaries inevitably weaken political parties. The Washington Republican Party is one of the strongest state parties. See Hasen, *Parties or the People* at 834 (cited in note 68). The court which upheld Washington's blanket primary relied on expert testimony that the strength of the segments of political parties in Washington were very similar to the strength of those throughout the nation. *Reed* at 24–26 (cited in note 52).

[96] See 530 US at 572 (finding it "'too plain for argument' . . . that a State may require parties to use the primary format for selecting their nominees, in order to assure that intraparty competition is resolved in a democratic fashion.") (quoting *American Party of Tex v White*, 415 US 767, 781 (1974)).

[97] See 530 US at 577 n 8 (quoting *Democratic Party of the United States v La Follette*, 450 US 107, 130 n 2 (Powell dissenting)). See also Nathaniel Persily, *The Blanket Primary in the Courts: The Precedent and Implications in California Democratic Party v. Jones*, in Cain and Gerber, *Voting at the Political Fault Line* at 303, 315 (cited in note 24) (noting that while the line between open and blanket primaries may be "arbitrary" it is "easier to specify than others").

ty's nominee will be selected primarily by nonmembers who are unwilling to associate even briefly with the party. Nevertheless, a recent primary election in Georgia demonstrates the possibility of crossover voting in open primaries, which can dilute the party membership's influence in selecting their standard-bearer.[98] Predictably, given the Court's analysis in *California Democratic Party*, other courts have begun to use this rationale to invalidate laws that impose direct primaries on political parties that would prefer a closed format.[99]

But the Court's analysis is more than incomplete; it inaccurately describes the significance of membership in a political party. The Court's opinion is grounded in the right of association, which includes not only the right to determine who can associate with a group but also the right to exclude others from the association.[100] The Court distinguished between the interests of party leaders, which might be sufficiently served by the ability to endorse primary candidates in a blanket primary format, and the interests of "party members" in choosing their own nominee.[101] The former, the Court held, is no substitute for the latter. The Court saw forced association—that is, opening the party's candidate selection process "to persons wholly unaffiliated with the party"[102]—as a heavy burden on associational rights. Although "affiliation" is the term often used by the Court rather than "membership," membership is clearly an important concept for the majority. For example, the Court distinguished the blanket primary from the closed primary because a voter must "formally *become a member of the party*"[103] in the latter, and it distinguished the blanket primary from

[98] See Thomas B. Edsall, *Impact of McKinney Loss Worries Some Democrats; Tension Between Blacks and Jews a Concern*, Wash Post A4 (Aug 22, 2002) (noting that many Republicans took advantage of open primary laws to vote for a moderate Democratic challenger to incumbent Cynthia McKinney).

[99] See, for example, *Ariz Libertarian Party, Inc. v Bd of Supervisors of Pima County*, 216 F Supp 2d 1007, 1010 (D Ariz 2002), appeal docketed, No 02-16535 (9th Cir Aug 7, 2002). The Ninth Circuit issued a stay that allowed the open primaries to be held as usual in the 2002 elections. *Ariz Libertarian Party, Inc. v Bd of Supervisors of Pima County*, No 02-16535 (9th Cir Aug 7, 2002).

[100] *Cal Democratic Party*, 530 US at 574–75.

[101] Id at 580.

[102] Id at 581.

[103] Id at 577.

the open primary, where the act of voting remains an "act of affil-iation" with a particular party.[104]

Despite its emphasis on membership, the Court's use of the term is inconsistent. Moreover, the Court failed to appreciate that there are many groups that might be considered as party "mem-bers," and its holding favors the interests of some of these groups—members of the party-organization and partisans in gov-ernment—over others—members in the electorate and some of-fice seekers. Much of the time the Court used the term "member" in its broadest sense to include voters who are qualified to vote in the closed primary. The dictum about open primaries suggested that the mere act of voting in a party primary results in some sort of constitutionally meaningful affiliation between voter and party. But these party members (i.e., voters who register as partisans) supported the initiative, signaling their desire to allow unaffiliated voters the opportunity to vote in some of the party's primary races. The majority of the party-in-the-electorate of all the parties voted in favor of the blanket primary,[105] imposing this structure on the party-organizations and the parties-in-the-[traditional]-government. Joining the voters in their support of the initiative were some major- and minor-party candidates and officeholders.[106] If the problem is that the blanket primary imposes unwanted par-ticipants on these members of political parties, the facts suggest that a majority of these members welcomed the broader involve-ment.

---

[104] Id n 8 (quoting *La Follette*, 450 US at 130 n 2 (Powell dissenting)).

[105] See id at 601 (Stevens dissenting).

[106] Two Republicans, moderate Tom Campbell and maverick Becky Morgan, endorsed the initiative, as did a prominent independent and former Democrat, Lucy Killea. See Brian J. Gaines and Wendy K. Tam Cho, *Crossover Voting before the Blanket: Primaries versus Parties in California History*, in Cain and Gerber, *Voting at the Political Fault Line* at 12, 30 (cited in note 24). In addition, Governor Davis, elected in part because of the blanket primary, filed an amicus brief arguing for its constitutionality. See Brief of Amicus Curiae California Governor Gray Davis, *Cal Democratic Party v Jones*, No 99-401, United States Supreme Court (filed March 31, 2000) (2000 WL 340234). See also Christian Collet, *Open-ness Begets Opportunity: Minor Parties and California's Blanket Primary*, in Cain and Gerber, *Voting at the Political Fault Line* at 214, 227 (cited in note 24) ("Minor-party candidates seemed to sense the potential benefits of the primary and, as a result, supported it."). Bruce Cain observes that the blanket primary fight might be seen as an attempt by one faction in the Republican party (led by moderates like Tom Campbell) to impose rules on another faction of the party (more extreme conservatives) using the initiative process. Bruce E. Cain, *Party Autonomy and Two-Party Electoral Competition*, 149 U Pa L Rev 793, 800 (2001).

In other passages, however, the Court's definition of "members" seemed more limited, focusing on party leaders and party activists.[107] But the treatment of this group is inconsistent. For example, party leaders and activists may prefer to use party conventions to choose nominees rather than a direct primary which involves individuals who are not really committed members of the party; however, that is an option they can constitutionally be denied. At the least, there is some limit to the Court's protection of this group, even though they won the battle of the blanket primary.

The other aspect of the blanket primary decision that reveals the Court's indifference to the dynamic complexity of political parties is its failure to mention as significant the collection of plaintiffs challenging the law. The blanket primary did not present the usual constellation of major parties opposing minor parties, or of one major party opposing the other. Instead, the challenge was brought by an alliance of the two major-party organizations, the Libertarian Party, and the Peace and Freedom Party.[108] In short, there were representatives of the range of organizations that use the political party format and the ballot, from those that also have significant governance roles, to a well-established, durable, minor party that occasionally places its candidates in government positions, to a little-known organization that is essentially an expressive organization with no hope of electoral success.[109] The Court's only mention of minor parties is its observation that for many such parties, the

---

[107] I am assuming that Justice Scalia is referring to activists when he talks about "rank and file." That is the phrase used in his *Tashjian* dissent to describe committed party members who do not hold official party positions. *Tashjian*, 479 US at 234–37. And that group is suggested by the passage in *California Democratic Party* in which the Court worries that "the party rank and file, who may themselves not agree with the party leadership, . . . do not want the party's choice decided by outsiders." 530 US at 581.

[108] Not all minor parties joined in the challenge, however. See Collet, *Openness Begets Opportunity* at 224–25 (cited in note 106) (describing reasons that the Reform Party, although it did not have an official position, "gave lukewarm backing to the blanket primary").

[109] In California, the Libertarian Party has placed some of its candidates in local offices, often in nonpartisan positions. It claims fifty officeholders as members, including members of planning commissions, city council persons, and a district attorney. See ⟨http://www.ca.lp.org/⟩. The Peace and Freedom Party, which appears to exist only in California, is a feminist socialist party which calls for the public ownership of industries, financial institutions, and natural resources, as well as a change to a "peace economy." See ⟨http://www.peaceandfreedom.org⟩. It may have some members who serve in local offices. Unlike the Libertarian Party, it no longer appears on the ballot for statewide elections because of its poor showing in 1998.

party itself is "virtually inseparable from [its] nominees (and tends not to outlast them)."[110] Not only is the concept of membership different in the case of minor parties, making some of them more like private organizations to which the Court's framework of associational rights more properly applies, but they are also affected differently by the blanket primary. An amicus brief argued to the Court that crossover voting, which has not been a problem in major-party races, could swamp minor-party primaries and "make the participation by minor party members irrelevant."[111]

In the end, whatever one thinks of these decisions, one is left with the impression that the Court has not come to grips with the complexity of political parties, how quickly they and their environment change (in part as a consequence of judicial decisions), and how these characteristics of parties affect the policies that partisans in government (or in the electorate) devise. Of course, many equally complicated matters are left to judicial resolution. But such matters may necessarily require that courts render decisions on the merits either because judicial decision making is better than the alternatives or because there are no alternatives. But, as these political party decisions suggest, the dynamic and competitive aspects of political parties that make them a challenge for policymakers and courts may also ensure sufficient conflict and change over time to provide ample protection for fundamental constitutional values without judicial involvement.

III. The Role of the Judiciary in Cases Concerning Political Parties

There is scant constitutional basis on which to determine the appropriate role of political parties or what political arrange-

---

[110] 530 US at 575 (listing as examples the Theodore Roosevelt Bull Moose Party, the La Follette Progressives, the Henry Wallace Progressives, and the George Wallace American Independent Party).

[111] See Brief for the Brennan Center for Justice at New York University School of Law as *Amicus Curiae* In Support of Neither Party, *Cal Democratic Party v Jones*, No 99-401, United States Supreme Court, at 26, Tables 1 and 2 (filed March 2, 2000) (available on Westlaw at 2000 WL 245529). Compare with Collet, *Openness Begets Opportunity* at 225 (cited in note 106) (arguing that minor parties would benefit from blanket primary). Perhaps because of the blanket primary, traditionally minor parties in Washington have sometimes qualified for major-party treatment. See *Reed* at 5 (cited in note 52) (describing the Libertarian Party as a "fledgling major party").

ments are consistent with the democratic design of the Constitution. For example, although courts often rely on the First Amendment's protection of speech or association to decide these cases, this constitutional provision does not lead to clear conclusions because of the conflicting interests of "members" of political parties. Rulings vindicate the interests of one group of people involved in political parties at the expense of others, and the Constitution provides no guidance about how to resolve these conflicts. Moreover, several different outcomes are often consistent with plausible visions of democratic institutions. Thus, to decide political party cases, judges are very likely to rely on their own views of the best governance structures for a stable democracy. This means that one contested view of the role of political parties in a democracy is constitutionalized, thereby eliminating the opportunity for states and the federal government to experiment over time with other democratic forms. As Justice Frankfurter observed in a similar context, "What is actually asked of the Court in [these cases] is to choose among competing bases of representation—ultimately, really, among competing theories of political philosophy—in order to establish an appropriate frame of government" for the states and finally the United States.[112] In the case of the blanket primary, for example, the Court determined that the Constitution does not allow states to establish, without the permission of party organizations, democratic structures that empower the median voter over citizens with more extreme partisan preferences, even though such an electoral structure is consistent with a reasonable vision of democracy and may be supported by a majority of citizens.

Of course, other areas of law in which judicial review is accepted may also reflect some of these characteristics.[113] In those areas, the disadvantages of constitutionalizing decision making may be outweighed by other advantages of judicial review. In addition, it is the dynamic nature of political parties that makes them especially unsuitable for judicial review. Even minor parties are better pro-

---

[112] *Baker v Carr*, 369 US 186, 300 (1962) (Frankfurter dissenting).

[113] This article is limited to an analysis of the political process cases. My conclusions about judicial review are thus limited to such cases; however, if other contexts exhibit similar characteristics—scant constitutional guidance and the existence of institutional features that provide extrajudicial protection of fundamental interests—more modest judicial review in those contexts may also be appropriate. I leave extension of my approach to other aspects of the political process to another day.

tected by the political process, where they can bargain with some segment of the major parties, than they are by the courts. Judicial review in political party cases should be limited to only the most extreme cases in which one segment of a party works success-fully, perhaps with other party entities, to impose anticompeti-tive structures.[114]

A. ASPECTS OF POLITICAL PARTY CASES THAT MILITATE AGAINST JUDICIAL REVIEW

Decisions in cases concerning political parties tend to institu-tionalize—and constitutionalize—one vision of democracy and of political parties. Not surprisingly, it is a vision that reflects the backgrounds and preferences of the judiciary, a group "grossly un-representative of the population."[115] Judges are not politically na-ive; after all, they have developed enough connections with politi-cians and other political actors to win election or appointment to the bench. Some judges have experience in government, in either elected or appointed positions. They overwhelmingly come from the ranks of major parties—a fact that perhaps explains their lack of concern for minor parties—and they have chosen careers on the sidelines of politics, perhaps indicating a preference for order and stability that is reflected in the law. These experiences may explain why judges tend to accept preservation of the two-party system as a compelling justification for certain regulations, and why they tend to view parties and voting in instrumental, rather than expressive, terms. In addition, their active involvement in po-litical parties may explain their assumption that the concept of "party membership" has some widely understood meaning.

Richard Pildes has argued convincingly that the Court exhibits a "cultural conservatism" toward democracy. He describes this worldview:

[114] Although this solution relies on a number of scholars who use theories of competition to analyze political parties, see, for example, Issacharoff and Pildes, *Politics as Market* (cited in note 44), there are important differences in our approaches. First, I conclude that the political marketplace is relatively competitive and not plagued by the partisan lockups that they identify. Second, my approach would justify judicial intervention in far fewer situations than theirs appears to support.

[115] Michael W. McConnell, *A Moral Realist Defense of Constitutional Democracy*, 64 Chi Kent L Rev 89, 105 (1988) (concluding from this and other reasons that the judiciary ought not to be the institution solely responsible for constitutional decision making).

> To ensure "political stability" and avoid "ruinous competi-
> tion," American democracy required regular organizations, a
> highly ordered two-party system, a style of politics that was
> channeled and contained, lest too much politics undermine de-
> mocracy itself. Perhaps it also required, or came to be seen
> as requiring, an active judicial role to ensure that too much
> democratically-adopted restructuring did not undermine the
> stability of democracy itself.[116]

Such a culturally conservative vision of democracy is only one
of many possible frameworks through which to organize institutions of governance. The Constitution contains few design details,
and those it provides are compatible with a variety of institutional
arrangements.[117] To the extent that the Constitution permits various forms of democracy, it should be left to the politically accountable branches and the voters to determine which model will govern. Furthermore, because political parties are endogenous, the
rules set by courts play a significant role in shaping political parties, both directly and indirectly, as political actors make changes
in party structures in response to judicial decisions. Judicial review
empowers judges to rule some arrangements out of bounds, such
as the blanket primary, and denies the democratic process some
of the critical advantages of a federal system. Moreover, if courts
uphold regulations but do so after a review on the merits, opinions
are often full of heavy-handed hints about the "appropriate" political structures so that they influence future political developments.
For example, the *Timmons* Court did not rule that fusion was unconstitutional, but its disparaging description of a world with wide-

---

[116] Richard H. Pildes, *Democracy and Disorder*, in Cass R. Sunstein and Richard A. Epstein,
eds, *The Vote: Bush, Gore, and the Supreme Court* 140, 164 (Chicago, 2001) (arguing that
several recent political process cases underscore the judicial culture that is leery of political
developments that appear chaotic or unfamiliar); Richard H. Pildes, *Constitutionalizing Democratic Politics*, in Ronald Dworkin, ed, *A Badly Flawed Election: Debating Bush v. Gore, the
Supreme Court, and American Democracy* 155 (New Press, 2002) ("[T]he Court has invalidated experiments with new forms of democracy while refusing to require that the system
be open to emerging sources of challenge. . . . The Court has done so because it believes,
or fears, or assumes that American democracy requires judicial constraint to ensure that
stability and order are maintained").

[117] Issacharoff, *Private Parties* at 310 (cited in note 1) (noting that "the initial federal
Constitution is conspicuously silent on the actual conduct of democracy"); id at 311
("[B]road-gauged constitutional principles turn out to be exceptionally difficult to apply to
limit the potential range of institutional arrangements consistent with republican governance."). For a general discussion, see also Dan M. Kahan, *Democracy Schmemocracy*, 20
Cardozo L Rev 795 (1999) (arguing that democracy is a contested concept instantiated by
various institutional arrangements).

spread fusion candidacies makes clear that a majority of the Justices found this political arrangement dubious and potentially destabilizing. Thus, judicial review, whether it results in the law being struck down or upheld, entrenches a judicial perspective that is not compelled by the Constitution and is only one of many contending perspectives.

In contrast, judicial restraint allows voters to make choices among plausible electoral and political structures and to change institutions as their views of democracy evolve as a result of their own experience and of observing practices in other states. Certainly, some arrangements are clearly out of bounds, but judicial review to prevent only clear constitutional violations would look very different from the current situation. When elected officials enact a particular set of regulations, they act on their own theories of democratic governance, knowing that they are subject to accountability at the ballot box. As long as such an approach is reasonable, the Court should not rule it out as unconstitutional simply because it is not the reasonable theory that a majority of the Justices would select.[118]

Thus, Bruce Cain misses the real problem of the decision striking down the blanket primary. He argues that upholding the blanket primary would have made the Court "party to yet another, unnecessary lock-in of one particular representational theory (i.e., hypercentrism)."[119] But the Court's decision locked out a choice made by the people of California about their election process, requiring this segment of the party to obtain the permission of party organizations before they could implement a blanket primary. Moreover, the Court eliminated a choice that is consistent with a reasonable vision of democracy that emphasizes the views of voters in the center of the ideological spectrum and moderates an increasingly partisan system.[120] One may argue that this is not the best

---

[118] Compare Frank I. Michelman, *Brennan and Democracy* 28–29 (Princeton, 1999) ("[I]f someone is going to use 'moral readings' of highly interpretable constitutional texts to resolve for the country such basic and contested issues of morality and prudence, . . . it ought to be the people acting democratically who do that and not any cadre of independent judges."). See also id at 55–57 (noting fact of disagreement on correct lawmaking procedures in a democracy and arguing that respect is due to reasonable decisions even when there is disagreement as to correctness, but still approving of far-reaching judicial review).

[119] Cain, *Party Autonomy* at 795 (cited in note 106).

[120] For a theory of democracy preferring structures that favor the median voter, see Robert Cooter, *Constitutional Consequentialism: Bargain Democracy versus Median Democracy*, 3 Theo-

vision of democracy, but nothing in the Constitution mandates that it be rejected.

Cain is right, however, that legislative decisions entrench one vision of democracy. In a way, the choice presented by political party cases is between judicial entrenchment of a contested view of democracy versus legislative entrenchment of a different view. The key difference is that courts constitutionalize their vision, making subsequent change more difficult. Had the Court not become involved, California's decision to adopt a blanket primary would not have been the last word about the state's electoral institutions. If voters in California became dissatisfied with blanket primaries, they could have changed the system through the initiative process. Even without repealing the initiative, partisan lawmakers could have adopted laws that would have compensated for the parties' loss of influence.[121] For example, party leaders could have worked to convince legislators to adopt a different system of determining access to a party's primary ballot, perhaps similar to the system used by Connecticut where party conventions play an essential role in deciding who can run in primaries.[122]

---

retical Inq in Law 1 (2002). See also Dennis F. Thompson, *Just Elections: Creating a Fair Electoral Process in the United States* 84–87 (Chicago, 2002) (discussing the various forms of primaries and how they further particular conceptions of representation and choice and concluding that the answers to these questions are "surprisingly complex").

[121] Although only another initiative can repeal or modify a law passed through a popular election, see Cal Const Art 2, § 10(c); Prop 198, § 11(a), the legislature has the power to pass related laws as long as they are not inconsistent with the initiative's purpose.

[122] See notes 56, 65, and 66. If the district court continues to adhere to its view that this system is unconstitutional and its ruling survives appeal, this option would be eliminated at least in Connecticut. See notes 74 and 75. Currently, parties in California have little control over who can run in a party's primary. A candidate seeking access to the primary ballot need only be a registered member of the party for at least three months, not have recently been a registered member of another party, and submit a petition with 100 or fewer signatures, depending on the race. See Cal Elec Code §§ 8001(a), 8062. Similarly, in Alaska, political parties had virtually no role in the candidate selection process for the blanket primary. Any person could declare herself to be a candidate of a political party merely by registering as a member of the party, an action that could take place on the same day she declared her candidacy. Alaska Stat §§ 15.25.030(a)(16), 15.07.040 (Michie 2001). Although parties can endorse candidates in a primary, the Court in *California Democratic Party* properly refused to equate the ability of parties to endorse particular candidates with other mechanisms, like closed primaries, that provide stronger control to party members over the selection of their candidates. 530 US at 580. Until recently, some states had laws prohibiting parties from endorsing candidates in elections, but the Supreme Court ruled those laws unconstitutional. See *Eu v San Francisco County Democratic Central Committee*, 489 US 214 (1989). Had the Court not intervened in *Eu* but let the matter be determined by the interplay of political forces, it seems very likely that party leaders and officeholders would have repealed or modified the California law banning party endorsements as a response to adoption of the blanket primary.

Thus, the adoption of the blanket primary did not lock in a single vision of democracy to the same extent that the Court locked this particular primary format out. Of course, even judicial entrenchment is not absolute in the dynamic world of political parties, although modification and self-correction are more difficult. For example, the party-in-the-electorate can now seek to convince the party-organizations to accept blanket primaries, which the experience in Alaska demonstrates is not impossible. As the Court noted in *California Democratic Party*, California can move to non-partisan primaries.[123] The presence of a few ways to circumvent the Court's decision about the appropriate structures of governance, however, does not justify a judicial decision to deny supporters of a reasonable vision of democracy one effective means to implement it. In short, *California Democratic Party* and its language of constitutionality entrench the judicial view of democracy much more deeply than the initiative entrenched the people's preference for a structure that privileged the median voter.

Perhaps judicial review can be justified in this context because it provides a necessary element of stability in the political process. This argument overestimates the danger of instability in the absence of judicial involvement and underappreciates the institutional features of the political process that make significant instability unlikely in the United States. Legislative procedures favor the status quo. Because there are high procedural hurdles to enacting legislation at all levels of government, any radical change in political structures is difficult. The argument that judicial review is necessary because the political branches are likely to implement policies so radical that they would destabilize or undermine de-

---

[123] See *Cal Democratic Party*, 530 US at 585–86. This format involves trade-offs and policy decisions that supporters of the blanket primary may not embrace. See Daniel H. Lowenstein and Richard L. Hasen, *Election Law: Cases and Materials* 493 (Carolina Academic, 2d ed 2001) (describing nonpartisan primary in Louisiana and noting one constitutional problem with using the format in congressional elections). The California Chamber of Commerce recently announced that it would seek to qualify an initiative for the 2004 ballot implementing a nonpartisan primary. The chamber proposes listing the party affiliation of the candidates on the primary ballot, and the two top vote getters would run in the runoff election, even if they were from the same party. Dan Morain, *Bid Launched to Bring Back Open Primary*, LA Times B6 (Nov 13, 2002). Since *California Democratic Party*, both major parties have opened their primaries to independents. See California Democratic Party, State Central Committee By-Laws, Art X, § 8 (Mar 2001) (available online at ⟨http://www.ca-dem.org/files/ByLaws AndRules.pdf⟩); Standing Rules and Bylaws of the California Republican Party, § 1.04(A) (Oct 27, 2001) (available online at ⟨http://www.cagop.org/images/pdf/bylaws.pdf⟩).

mocracy does not correspond to the inherently conservative legislative process that has been put in place by the federal and state constitutions.

Moreover, judicial review is largely unnecessary in the context of political parties given the ample protections provided in the tumultuous and competitive realm of politics. This feature of these cases distinguishes them from other complex areas where judicial review is commonplace and accepted. Cases involving the major parties are often merely disputes between different segments of the party. The party-organization opposes a regulation passed by the party-in-government, or the national party dislikes a law supported by parts, but perhaps not all, of the state party. In these cases, courts should decline to referee an internal dispute. Just as courts often instruct disgruntled legislators who have lost in the political process that their redress lies in political remedies,[124] so too should courts declare that internal party disputes should be resolved without resort to the courts. No segment of the party is powerless in such a dispute. The party-in-government is dependent on the party-organization to help elect more copartisans and ensure control of the government, party activists are crucial to a winning electoral strategy, and the unorganized party-in-the-electorate actually elects candidates.

Party-organizations can protect themselves from regulation by legislatures because of their intimate connection with and influence over legislators.[125] There is competition between these two segments of the party, thus ensuring that many interests will be heard and that change over time is possible as those losing in the political process today may emerge victorious tomorrow. Consider campaign spending. Political parties, at the local, state, and national levels, play vital roles in raising money, providing expertise to candidates, and encouraging interest groups to contribute. Although recent changes in campaign laws will force a restructuring

---

[124] See, for example, *Raines v Byrd*, 521 US 811, 829 (1997).

[125] In contrast, some commentators have concluded that courts should step in to invalidate legislation that regulates "purely" internal party decisions, such as the ability to endorse candidates in primaries and rules concerning election of party leaders. For example, see Hasen, *Parties or the People* at 826–27 (cited in note 68) (although generally concluding that the two parties can protect their own interests, viewing as correct the Court's decision in *Eu*). Like Lowenstein, I favor judicial restraint even in these cases because the party-organization has effective political channels that will allow it to prevail at some point (or to force a compromise) without recourse to the judiciary. See Lowenstein, *Associational Rights of Major Parties* at 1786 (cited in note 68).

of this relationship, probably giving more influence to state and local organizations, the expertise provided by parties will still be valuable to office seekers. The intertwining of the party-in-government and the party-organization is evident in the growth of congressional campaign committees and the explosion of leadership PACs to facilitate contributions from influential members of Congress to the campaigns of other candidates. For example, Newt Gingrich's efforts to raise money for other House members were partly responsible for the success of the "Contract with America" in the 104th Congress.[126]

Of course, not all members of Congress with excess funds will contribute to others in order to enhance party government. Some, like John McCain, hope to forge personal bonds with other legislators so they can succeed in a maverick agenda to undermine party discipline on matters like campaign finance reform.[127] Others work to further personal objectives, such as improving the chances for a successful run for the presidency by earning the gratitude of influential lawmakers.[128] In other cases, a powerful committee chair may seek to increase her influence at the expense of party leaders. Although almost all government officials are members of a major political party, they have different views about the appropriate strength of the party-in-government and the party-organization and may favor different regulatory schemes depending on those views. It is this group of people who enact the vast majority of laws regulating political parties, and this competitive environment allows protection for a variety of interests, as well as guaranteeing that no outcome is permanent.

In addition, the party-organization and party-in-government are able to combat efforts by the electorate to regulate the electoral

---

[126] See Barbara Sinclair, *Evolution or Revolution? Policy-Oriented Congressional Parties in the 1990s*, in L. Sandy Maisel, ed, *The Parties Respond: Changes in American Parties and Campaigns* 263, 274 (Westview, 3d ed 1998). See also Juliet Eilperin, *House Whip Race Seen as Indicator of Democrats' Future*, Wash Post A1 (Sept 8, 2001) (detailing use of fundraising by members of the House running for leadership positions to gain support from rank-and-file).

[127] See Philip Shenon, *House Critics Call McCain a Bully on Campaign Bill*, NY Times A8 (July 9, 2001).

[128] See, for example, John F. Harris, *Democrats Vie to Stand Out in the 2004 Crowd; McCain's Limelight is a Magnet for Opposition Senators Seeking Notice as Future Contenders*, Wash Post A1 (May 14, 2001); Dan Balz and Ruth Marcus, *As Gore Plans His Next Move, a Debate Brews; Democrats' Split Underscores Obstacles to Presidential Bid*, Wash Post A1 (Aug 12, 2001).

process through ballot initiative. Not surprisingly, given their expertise, parties are influential players in initiative campaigns and can often defeat ballot propositions that would impair their interests.[129] They also control the executive branch, which implements any proposal, and the legislative branch, which controls funding.[130] They can thus protect their interests at later stages of the process even if they lose in the campaign. At first glance, one of the mysteries about the blanket primary campaign in California is that the major parties were not active opponents of the ballot question.[131] The mystery disappears, however, when we understand that the parties were merely waiting to mount a judicial challenge after the election because they thought their chances of victory were good and that any victory through a court decision would firmly entrench the result by constitutionalizing it. If the parties had believed that judicial intervention was unavailable, they would have adopted different strategies in order to prevail at an earlier stage.[132]

Disputes between the major parties, rather than within one party, present a different, more difficult situation. Again, however, the major parties are powerful political agents able to protect themselves in the political process. Even in jurisdictions that are

---

[129] For a general discussion, see Richard L. Hasen, *Parties Take the Initiative (and Vice Versa)*, 100 Colum L Rev 731 (2000); Daniel A. Smith and Caroline J. Tolbert, *The Initiative to Party*, 7 Party Pol 781 (2001).

[130] For a discussion of effective techniques employed by partisans in government to undermine ballot initiatives that succeed at the polls, see Elisabeth R. Gerber, Arthur Lupia, Mathew D. McCubbins, and D. Roderick Kiewiet, *Stealing the Initiative: How State Government Responds to Direct Democracy* (Prentice-Hall, 2001).

[131] See Hasen, *Parties or the People* at 836–37 (cited in note 68) (noting that parties did not aggressively work to defeat the blanket primary proposition); Thompson, *Just Elections* at 81 (cited in note 120) (discussing parties' strategic decision not to campaign against initiative).

[132] This discussion necessarily underestimates the level of protection that conflict within and among the parties could provide and the outcomes it would produce because the current level of conflict takes place in a world where all the actors know that judicial intervention is possible and likely. In other words, a loser in the political process now might not continue to fight in the political realm but instead choose to move the battle into the courts, perhaps because it believes that success would be less costly (given the state of the precedents) and more permanent (because the outcome may be characterized as constitutionally mandated thus eliminating further political development). See, in a related context, Howard Gillman, *How Political Parties Can Use the Courts to Advance Their Agendas: Federal Courts in the United States, 1875–1891*, 96 Am Pol Sci Rev 511 (2002) (arguing that politicians have used courts and judicial appointments to entrench their policy preferences by constitutionalizing them). If the courts adopted a much more modest role in these cases, then the political conflict would only increase and continue into the future as players sought to mold the ever-changing institutions of political parties to better serve their objectives.

largely dominated by one party, the opposition party is not without resources. For example, a party-organization at the national level may devote resources to empower a faltering state party organization. In recent years, competition between the two parties has become more robust not only at the national level but also at the state level. By the mid-1990s, a majority of states were considered competitive, and there were no longer any one-party states, a significant change from the 1960s and earlier.[133] This change to greater interparty competition occurred despite the fact that governments in one-party states presumably were able to pass laws that handicapped the other major party and entrenched a noncompetitive environment for as long as possible.

Furthermore, the political landscape changes rapidly, so a law that seems to favor one party today may work to its disadvantage in the near future. This appears to have been the case with the blanket primary in Alaska, where the major parties' support for different forms of primaries has changed over time. And in Connecticut, the Republican Party's position on the type of primary that best serves its interests—closed or semi-open—has changed several times over the last few decades. Although it fought all the way to the Supreme Court in the 1980s for the right to have independents participate in its primaries, it now prefers closed primaries, as is its option under current law. The likelihood that the dominant party today will be the opposition party in the future may encourage moderate policies, especially if party leaders have relatively long time horizons.

Finally, it can be challenging to diagnose an interparty dispute. Justice Scalia plausibly saw *Tashjian*, which is usually cited as the classic example of one party in power attempting to disadvantage its rival, as an intraparty dispute between party leaders and party activists. His analysis also suggests that an aggrieved opposition

---

[133] See Bibby, *Politics, Parties and Elections* at 70–71, 72, fig 3-1 (cited in note 14). See also Hershey and Beck, *Party Politics in America* at 30, table 2.2 (cited in note 4) (showing twenty-eight states as competitive and the rest either modified one-party Democratic or Republican). One of the most important changes leading to greater major-party competition has been the rise of the Republican Party in the South. See generally Earl Black and Merle Black, *The Rise of Southern Republicans* (Belknap, 2002). Compare with Richard H. Pildes, *Is Voting-Rights Law Now at War with Itself? Social Science and Voting Rights in the 2000s*, 80 NC L Rev 1517 (2002) (discussing how change in levels of political competition throughout the country, and particularly in the South, may require a reexamination of the Voting Rights Act and associated law).

party may have allies within the dominant party, providing it with additional tools to fight off, delay, or reverse "oppressive" regulation.

My conclusion with respect to major parties is consistent with the judgment Daniel Lowenstein reached a decade ago with respect to intraparty and interparty disputes,[134] and it is supported by recent evidence that the major parties are increasingly competitive at all levels of government. I would go further, however, and argue that minor parties are also amply protected through the political process and do not need the protection of judicial review.

Some scholars have argued that courts should be particularly solicitous of the interests of minor-party members.[135] The case for special constitutional protection of minor parties is unpersuasive, in part because courts are not willing to protect minor parties. The pervasive judicial vision of democracy assumes a stable, two-party system, without the chaos and uncertainty associated in judges' minds with strong and independent dissident voices and the prospect of candidates winning regularly by slim pluralities. This vision is necessarily unsympathetic to third parties. Indeed, minor parties have lost almost every Supreme Court decision implicating their rights in the last quarter-century (unless their interests coincided with those of the major parties). In most of these cases, the Court has not appreciated the unique role of minor parties in our political process, misconceiving them as entities designed primarily to elect their own candidates rather than as instruments for debate and dissent.[136] Because of this fundamental misunderstanding, the Court consistently undervalues the interests of minor parties.

Moreover, those who argue for special judicial solicitude for

---

[134] See Lowenstein, *Associational Rights of Major Parties* at 1786–87 (cited in note 68). But see id at 1744 (limiting his consideration to major parties).

[135] See, for example, Hasen, *Parties or the People* at 839 (cited in note 68) ("[M]inor parties are in much greater need of protection than the major parties. Minor parties do not have easy recourse to the legislature or the executive, for example, when the people act by initiative. Minor parties are likely to be ideologically driven groups, and sometimes their ideologies are unpopular."). An amicus brief in *California Democratic Party* tried to convince the Court to provide more protection for minor parties, thereby explicitly recognizing that minor parties are often more like private political organizations than like major parties. See Brief for the Brennan Center as *Amicus Curiae, Cal Democratic Party* (cited in note 111).

[136] See, for example, *Timmons*, 520 US at 363. But see *Munro v Socialist Workers Party*, 479 US 189, 201, 202–03 (1986) (Marshall dissenting) (characterizing as a major contribution of minor parties their objective of adding new voices and changing the substance of political debate).

minor parties underestimate the protections for these parties that
are already built into the political process. Dissident voices do
not need to use minor parties to influence political outcomes. As
Hirschman's work suggests, some dissidents, perhaps most, can influence the major parties from within. The direct primary enables
activist groups to support their own candidates in the nomination
process, capturing the party label and influencing the direction of
the party. Decentralization and the advent of new technologies like
the Internet help third parties and other outsiders play a more
significant role.[137] Minor parties sometimes find allies within the
major parties. If a major party-organization believes that minor-
party candidates will draw votes from the opposing party's candidates, it may favor easier ballot access for third parties.[138] More
generally, major-party activists who want to maximize their influence may oppose laws that would eliminate third parties because
they know that the existence of relatively credible minor parties
is strategically helpful to them. Perhaps because segments of major
parties understand that credible third parties and independent
candidacies may sometimes serve their own purposes, few states

---

[137] See Steven J. Rosenstone, Roy L. Behr, and Edward H. Lazarus, *Third Parties in
America: Citizen Response to Major Party Failure* 226 (Princeton, 2d ed 1996).

[138] This possibility is not fanciful. A Republican Party operative in Washington recently
supported a Green Party candidate, providing expertise and money, because he expected
the third-party candidate would harm the Democratic contender and improve the chances
of a plurality win for the Republican. See Sam Howe Verhovek, *Green Party Candidate Finds
He's a Republican Pawn*, NY Times A10 (Aug 8, 2001). The Green Party in New Mexico
has become a significant player in state politics as both parties use it to siphon off support
from their opposing major party in various races. See Michael Janofsky, *New Mexico Greens
Go from Gadflies to Players*, NY Times A18 (July 21, 2002). The analysis of *Timmons* suggests
that elements of major parties may sometimes work with minor parties and thus can be
counted on sometimes to oppose laws that impose substantial burdens on third parties.
Although party leaders of both major parties in government may have believed that multiple
endorsements diluted party discipline, some major-party incumbent candidates believed that
they would benefit from multiple nominations. See Disch, *Tyranny of the Two Party System*
at 21, 146 n 10 (cited in note 77) (describing major-party candidates other than Dawkins
who supported fusion candidacies). Moreover, despite the majority's unsubstantiated concerns about voter confusion, the party-in-the-electorate may have been helpfully informed
by the additional ballot notations. In some states with robust direct democracy, voters have
been supportive of ballot notations that would provide additional information about candidates' positions on certain issues, a movement abruptly halted by the Supreme Court's decision in *Cook v Gralike*, 531 US 510 (2001). These voters may be interested in reconsidering
fusion laws as a way to use third-party endorsements to improve voter competence. See
also Elizabeth Garrett, *The Law and Economics of "Informed Voter" Ballot Notations*, 85 Va L
Rev 1533 (1999) (discussing the benefits of ballot notations and their relationship to fusion).

have adopted all the constitutionally permissible devices that can be used to silence minor parties.[139]

B. JUDICIAL RESTRAINT IN POLITICAL PARTY CASES

Given the competitive political process, how should courts deal with a dispute involving elements of political parties? By and large, they should decline to intervene, letting the parties, major and minor, fight it out in the political realm. Thus, my proposal would alter the general presumption that judicial review is available and appropriate to a nearly conclusive presumption in political party cases that courts should decline to become involved. As a prudential matter, judicial review should be limited to extreme examples of anticompetitive laws and regulations designed to ensure the success of one party over the other or of the major over the minor parties. Judicial intervention should be rare because competition is possible not only among parties but also within parties.

This shift would require courts to determine which cases primarily concern the regulation of political parties and which primarily concern other matters that only indirectly involve political parties. In making that determination, courts should be guided by the reasons for judicial restraint in political party cases: such disputes concern decisions about structures of governance that are not dictated by the Constitution or by larger democratic principles and occur in contexts where dynamic political forces can be summoned by contending parties. In some cases, this determination will be easy. Ballot access cases, for example, primarily concern political parties and should trigger judicial restraint. A criminal prosecution accusing the leader of a political party of corruption, on the other hand, is not primarily about the structure of political parties.[140]

Other cases are closer to the margin. Consider, for example, a challenge to patronage. Such a challenge implicates the ways in which political parties mediate between individuals and govern-

---

[139] See, for example, Daniel H. Lowenstein, *The Supreme Court Has No Theory of Politics— and Be Thankful for Small Favors*, in Ryden, *The U.S. Supreme Court and the Electoral Process* at 245, 262 (cited in note 37).

[140] However, the possibility that such prosecutions may be politically motivated and that vague statutes dealing with corruption can be used by ambitious prosecutors to achieve personal objectives may play a role in how courts interpret such statutes and apply principles like the rule of lenity.

ment, as well as the right of individuals to be judged on merit
rather than on political affiliation.[141] Such cases are appropriately
characterized as political party cases, with a presumption of judicial
restraint, because the political process has provided an effective av-
enue for opponents of patronage to adopt civil service protections.
Such rules are modified over time as our sense of the appropriate
mix of political considerations and merit changes, and no particular
mix is required by constitutional or democratic principles. Although the presumption against judicial review would generally
apply in such cases, there may be extreme cases where employees
who advocate unpopular political views are treated inappropriately
for exercising their First Amendment rights. Those cases should
be examined through the prism of individual rights analysis.

Because classifying a case as a "political party case" would trigger a presumption against judicial review, this approach could invite strategic behavior by both parties and judges. Plaintiffs would
have an incentive, for example, to frame cases so that they appear
not to concern the structure and regulation of political parties.[142]
The problem of dealing with such strategic behavior is a familiar
one to lawyers. There is no reason to believe that it will be more
acute in this context than in others. The key question should be
whether the case should be considered in terms of individual rights
or as a disagreement about which structures are best suited to vindicate those rights. Of course, judges might be reluctant to reframe
a case brought as one vindicating individual rights as one determining the structure of political institutions if that decision
would then require them to defer to the political process. There

---

[141] See William N. Eskridge, Jr., Philip P. Frickey, and Elizabeth Garrett, *Legislation and
Statutory Interpretation* 137–39 (Foundation, 2000) (discussing patronage cases in Supreme
Court). See also Hasen, *Parties or the People* at 834 (cited in note 68) (also viewing patronage
cases as primarily raising structural concerns about political parties and not primarily concerning First Amendment issues).

[142] Of course, plaintiffs often frame their cases in these terms now because the judicial
analysis in political process cases is usually a traditional rights perspective rather than a
structural assessment. For example, the current case challenging the Connecticut law restricting candidate access to primary ballots has been brought by a collection of individuals
seeking ballot access and of voters seeking more choice in the primary (as well as by two
organizations representing such individuals). They claim that their First and Fourteenth
Amendment rights have been violated. The state official named as defendant is sued in
her official capacity as secretary of state, not as a representative of a major political party.
Nonetheless, in its decision staying the lower court's ruling, the Court of Appeals for the
Second Circuit has required that the party-organizations be joined in the lawsuit, clearly
understanding that this is a political party case. See note 74.

is little that can be done about this sort of strategic behavior by the courts; the justifications for the presumption should, over time, persuade judges that restraint in this context is the better policy.

It is important to understand the relationship between my approach and the approach urged by those who advocate a political markets perspective. Such scholars argue that the courts should work to promote robust competition in the electoral arena.[143] As they do in the corporate context, judges should guard against regulations and institutions that lock up the electoral system in favor of a dominant party or in favor of the two major parties. By guarding against rules that entrench the duopoly of the major parties, judges can construct an environment more conducive to competition, thereby allowing voters to rely on political processes to protect their other interests. Thus, these theorists argue for judicial intervention based on structural concerns and an awareness of the inherently collective nature of political activity, rather than intervention grounded on theories of individual rights. Their approach might or might not lead to less judicial involvement.[144]

---

[143] For leading presentations of the political markets theory, see Issacharoff and Pildes, *Politics as Market* (cited in note 44); Richard H. Pildes, *The Theory of Political Competition*, 85 Va L Rev 1605 (1999); and Ortiz, *Duopoly versus Autonomy* (cited in note 10). Hasen often uses economic language to describe the judicial approach that he advocates, although he has expressed doubt about using competition as the objective of judicial review. For example, see Hasen, *Entrenching the Duopoly* (cited in note 83); Richard L. Hasen, *The "Political Market" Metaphor and Election Law: A Comment on Issacharoff and Pildes*, 50 Stan L Rev 719 (1998). Theorists other than those identified as political market scholars also believe that competition is a key component of a healthy system and should be part of any judicial analysis of political process cases. For example, the advocates of the party-autonomy perspective contend that only by ensuring that there are two strong major parties can the Court serve the objectives of political competition and minority representation. See, e.g., Persily and Cain, *Legal Status of Political Parties* (cited in note 86); Nathaniel Persily, *Toward a Functional Defense of Political Party Autonomy*, 76 NYU L Rev 750, 793 (2001). In addition, Richard Briffault has argued that preserving and enhancing political competition should be considered a compelling state interest by the Court in its campaign finance cases. See Richard Briffault, *Nixon v. Shrink Missouri Government PAC: The Beginning of the End of the Buckley Era?* 85 Minn L Rev 1729 (2001).

[144] For example, see Issacharoff and Pildes, *Politics as Markets* at 644 (cited in note 44) (noting that "judicial oversight over the political process has expanded to a level unimaginable when the Supreme Court first entered the political thicket" but mainly critiquing the Court for failure to develop a sophisticated and workable framework to use in its review); Pildes, *Theory of Political Competition* at 1607 (cited in note 143) (intimating that the logic of rights perspective that he rejects means such claims "will always demand an increasingly aggressive judicial role"). In some work, their approach appears relatively agnostic as to the right level of judicial intrusion. Id at 1611 ("Our principal aim is to provide a theoretical perspective on legal issues surrounding democratic politics, rather than to defend a specific role for courts or for constitutional law."). However, Issacharoff's recent application of a political markets perspective to political gerrymandering cases suggests that he is comfort-

Although I also focus on structural considerations and the competitive and dynamic nature of the political process, my approach differs from the political markets theorists in two ways. First, I am less optimistic than they are that courts will be able to police competition competently using the political markets approach. Skeptics of this literature have noted a problem of baseline that makes adjudication under market-based theories difficult, if not impossible.[145] How much competition is necessary for a healthy system? What is the appropriate level of state protection for the two-party system as a stabilizing influence? How much room should be left for third parties and alternative players? Are all structures that favor the current duopoly invalid, including plurality voting in single-member districts? How does a court determine the appropriate baseline—by reference to historic levels of competition, political science, or analogies from the corporate context? Recent scholarship reaches different conclusions about how much judicial intervention is appropriate and what is required for well-functioning political competition,[146] perhaps demonstrating the indeterminacy of this approach.

Second, even under a political markets approach, judicial review is largely unnecessary because the political process *is* competitive. These theorists have underestimated the degree of dynamism in the system and the extent of protection afforded by the political process and thus have too readily accepted judicial review, albeit on different terms than courts use now. In part, they miscalculated the level of conflict within and among political parties because determining the background level of actual competition is tricky.

---

able with relatively aggressive judicial intervention. Samuel Issacharoff, *Gerrymandering and Political Cartels*, 116 Harv L Rev 594 (2002).

[145] For example, see Bruce E. Cain, *Garrett's Temptation*, 85 Va L Rev 1589, 1600–03 (1999); Persily, *Toward a Functional Defense* at 794–95 n 179 (cited in note 143); Hasen, *Political Market Metaphor* at 724–28 (cited in note 143) (arguing that the problem is particularly acute with respect to claims of two-party partisan lockup). Issacharoff and Pildes recognize the problem when they acknowledge that they "do not have a comprehensive and complete theory that offers necessary and sufficient conditions for identifying" anticompetitive regulations. Issacharoff and Pildes, *Politics as Markets* at 680 (cited in note 44) (also acknowledging that "it is far easier to identify dramatically anticompetitive practices than it is to specify precisely what optimal competition would look like"). Pildes provides a more complete response in *Theory of Political Competition* at 1611–15 (cited in note 143).

[146] Compare Issacharoff and Pildes, *Politics as Markets* (cited in note 44), and Pildes, *Theory of Political Competition* (cited in note 143), with Frymer and Yoon, *Political Parties, Representation and Federal Safeguards* (cited in note 4) (the latter arguing for aggressive judicial intervention along the lines of recent federalism cases and focusing on state and local actors).

Even in jurisdictions with a dominant political party,[147] the opposition party can compete by electing some state legislators or occasionally sending a partisan to the governor's mansion. It is not enough to know that one party wins most elections; to develop a sophisticated sense of the level of competition, one must understand both the opposition party's power to influence campaigns and policies,[148] and the degree of competition within the parties themselves.[149] Electoral competitiveness may look quite different when one examines different levels of government or different political races.[150] Moreover, competition within a particular region can be affected by national political conditions or by trends in other states. Thus, the South, locked up by one party for decades, is now an area where both parties are competitive. This shift occurred despite regulations crafted by Democrats-in-government designed to entrench themselves and their copartisans.

Measuring the strength of the duopoly in states with strong major parties but weak minor ones is also difficult. One cannot simply count up the number of parties and candidates on the ballot. The number of third parties regularly on the ballot may not alter the fundamental nature of the competition. When minor parties were more powerful in some states than they are now, the two major parties still controlled the political system.[151] More importantly, the formation of minor parties and their appearance on the ballot is not the only way to measure the strength of alternative voices in politics. Not only may major-party activists have an interest in some credible system of third parties, but major parties, incumbent lawmakers, office seekers, and voters may sometimes have interests that align with third parties.

My approach benefits from the insights of the political markets theorists, but it minimizes the problems they face because it allows

---

[147] See Issacharoff and Pildes, *Politics as Markets* at 667 (cited in note 44) (noting that courts would find measuring level of competition easier in cases from states with only one real political party).

[148] See Epstein, *Political Parties in the American Mold* at 128 (cited in note 28) (observing that even if one party routinely wins all elections, if the races are contested and close, then competition is not meaningless and the second party remains a plausible electoral alternative).

[149] See Nathaniel Persily, *In Defense of Foxes Guarding Henhouses: The Case for Judicial Acquiescence to Incumbent-Protecting Gerrymanders*, 116 Harv L Rev 649, 662 (2002).

[150] Id at 656–57.

[151] See Winkler, *Voters' Rights and Parties' Wrongs* at 885 (cited in note 17).

only a modest role for the courts. Political markets theorist Michael Klarman observes correctly that any judicial concern about entrenchment, or partisan lockup, must be calibrated to take account of "the extent to which it is self-correcting."[152] In that I agree with the political markets approach; our disagreement lies in our differing confidence both in the ability of the courts to address questions about competition and in the ability of the political market to self-correct. Given the multiplicity of interests and the change that is possible over relatively short periods of time, we should assume that self-correction is possible and allow judicial intervention only when it is patently clear that no political redress is likely. For example, a political markets rationale apparently would overturn the fusion ban in Minnesota,[153] but under my approach the Court should have exercised judicial restraint. A prohibition on fusion candidacies is not sufficiently egregious to justify judicial intervention, particularly because there are alternate ways for the losers to prevail in the future. Moreover, a law allowing fusion candidacies would not significantly diminish the strength of the major parties because they can effectively encourage their candidates to forgo such endorsements if they wish to.

C. WHEN IS RESTRAINT INAPPROPRIATE?

There are at least three circumstances in which judicial restraint in these cases might be inappropriate under my approach.[154] These

---

[152] Michael J. Klarman, *Majoritarian Judicial Review: The Entrenchment Problem*, 85 Georgetown L J 491, 541 (1997).

[153] This conclusion seems to follow from the work of political markets theorists Issacharoff and Pildes. See *Politics as Markets* at 685 (cited in note 44) (arguing that fusion bans should trigger strict scrutiny). Demonstrating his disagreement with the political markets theorists notwithstanding the use of similar language, Hasen concludes that the question of the benefits of the two-party system is sufficiently unresolved that courts should refuse to intervene, allowing states either to permit or to ban fusion. See Hasen, *Entrenching the Duopoly* at 341–43 (cited in note 83).

[154] One possible exception would turn on the age of the law in question. The three case studies provide interesting contrasts in this respect: *Tashjian* involved a relatively old law, but one that the legislature had recently considered and declined to repeal; *Timmons* involved a law passed decades earlier in a very different political climate and not reconsidered by the legislature; and *California Democratic Party* involved a recently enacted initiative. Given the dynamic nature of political parties, one might argue that the courts should be more willing to intervene with respect to old laws that have not been the subject of recent consideration by the political branches. I am not convinced that age of a regulation is a valid reason to reject the presumption of judicial restraint, however. Any possibility that courts would intervene in the context of old laws would make it more likely that entities hoping to change such laws would turn to the courts rather than trigger contemporary reassessment by the political branches. Moreover, if an old law no longer fits the needs of

possible exceptions to the general presumption follow from the focus on competition and the concerns about entrenchment. In formulating them, I have tried to identify circumstances where the usual dynamism of the political process has been so impaired that interests opposing the status quo have been effectively silenced and are not likely to regain influence in the future. I have also drawn from literature that seeks to identify features of institutional design that work to impede the incentive of lawmakers to behave in self-interested ways.[155] If laws do not exhibit these features, then legislative entrenchment is more likely and it will be more difficult to change regulations though conflict and dynamic interaction.

First, timing is relevant. Rules that are adopted after a problem develops and are applied retroactively should be presumptively illegitimate. In the context of elections, rules should be specified well in advance so combatants can play by the rules and develop informal strategies. Rules that set forth clearly and in relatively objective terms the requirements for people seeking to obtain the party label in a primary are superior to ad hoc proceedings where party leaders determine that a particular candidate, such as Lyndon LaRouche or Patrick Buchanan, does not share the ideological commitments of the party. If open textured tests are adopted, then the procedures for applying those tests should be clearly specified in advance.[156]

Rules developed immediately after a new element of political competition has emerged and targeted at that development should be suspect but not necessarily struck down.[157] Antifusion laws might well raise this concern because many were passed after fusion candidates had allowed the weaker major party to make electoral gains and empowered some third-party candidates in several

---

segments of political parties, they have the ability to change the regulations to accord with modern reality. Of course, modifying or repealing laws and party rules is costly because of the status quo bias of any system, but these actors are sophisticated political players with substantial influence in lawmaking and law-implementing arenas.

[155] For a general discussion, see Elizabeth Garrett, *The Impact of Bush v. Gore on Future Democratic Politics*, in Pomper and Weiner, *Future of Democratic Politics* (cited in note 26); Adrian Vermeule, *Veil of Ignorance Rules in Constitutional Law*, 111 Yale L J 399 (2001).

[156] For a general discussion, see Persily, *Candidates v Parties* at 2211–12 (cited in note 11).

[157] Klarman makes this point and provides examples of ballot access requirements adopted to combat an unexpectedly strong third party. Klarman, *Majoritarian Judicial Review* at 536, n 207 (cited in note 152).

states. This consideration should not necessarily lead courts to abandon judicial restraint, however, because opponents of such a new rule may be able to overturn or modify it in the political process, particularly if they are denied access to the courts and thus have an incentive to wage a political rather than judicial battle. Thus, judicial restraint is still warranted in these cases unless they exhibit other suspect characteristics.

Second, laws that are not relatively durable should be suspect. Because political fortunes change quickly, self-interested actors are less likely to pass restrictive laws if the regulations may work against them in the future. Thus, a law that applies only to the next election is much more likely to serve anticompetitive goals than a law that must be repealed through the ordinary legislative process or a constitutional amendment that can only be repealed through supermajority and popular votes. This concern is heightened in the context of internal party rules that might be adopted to defeat a faction in the short run, but not to bind party leaders or other currently powerful segments of the party in the long term. Of course, no law is permanent in the political process, nor should it be, because the ability to deal with problems incrementally over time is one of the advantages of legislative institutions. However, a relatively temporary law that also exhibits suspicious timing might be sufficient to convince a court that it faces an extreme case of anticompetitive behavior.

Third, rules that apply generally are less suspect than laws targeted at one party or only at minor parties.[158] In some cases, this consideration is relatively easy to apply, as where rules provide rebates of filing fees only to candidates of major parties.[159] In cases where identical treatment of parties and candidates is impossible, the law should provide equivalent treatment. This can be tricky. How does one determine, for example, how many signatures on a petition for an independent candidate or a new party are equivalent to the automatic ballot access provided to major parties? Be-

---

[158] Cain and Persily identify a similar principle in their recommendations to guide judicial intervention: The Principle of Equal Treatment, which encourages courts to invalidate "[s]tate laws that impose unique and disproportionate burdens of ballot access on minor parties." Persily and Cain, *Legal Status of Political Parties* at 804 (cited in note 86).

[159] See, for example, *Libertarian Party of Fla v Smith*, 687 So2d 1292, 1295 (Fla 1996) (upholding such a statute because it strengthened major parties and reduced factionalism, both appropriate state interests in the court's view).

cause this inquiry is fraught with difficulty and differing treatment is problematic, courts are justified in invalidating laws allowing only some parties automatic ballot access and instead requiring uniform treatment.

Application of this exception to judicial restraint is problematic in some circumstances, however, even when it requires uniform treatment. For example, in the ballot-access context, major-party legislators could set signature requirements at such a high level that no minor party or independent candidate could realistically hope to meet them. Although the major parties would face the same costs, they have substantial resources and may be willing to bear the costs if the system would eliminate the threat of third-party competition. Moreover, one major party may have different interests than the other, and those differences might legitimately support different regimes for the two major parties. In *Tashjian*, the Republican Party may have been better served by an open primary, and the Democrats by a closed primary, given their different strengths and the particular demographics of the state. Nonetheless, that the law required closed primaries by all parties was a factor in its favor, justifying judicial restraint.[160] One way to balance the competing needs for uniformity and flexibility is for legislatures to enact uniform laws that allow parties to opt out voluntarily through party rules. Such a law might require closed primaries unless a party decides to open its primary to independent voters or even to members of other parties.

The identification of these factors is only a starting point in deciding when courts may depart from the presumption of judicial restraint.[161] Any decision to depart from that presumption should

[160] For a general discussion of uniformity's virtues, see Lowenstein, *Associational Rights of Major Political Parties* at 1790 (cited in note 68) ("[T]here is some advantage in uniformity for its own sake. When both parties operate under the same rules and procedures, the overall system is likely to seem fairer and more natural to voters. . . . [S]pecific reasons for uniformity may be subtle and escape the attention of state deputy attorneys general and judges, neither of whom are necessarily attuned to the workings of party politics.").

[161] A frequent question regarding my approach concerns its application to the *White Primary Cases*. Of course, the political situation in Texas at that time was not at all competitive. Not only was Democratic-controlled Texas a one-party state, but a plethora of laws disenfranchised blacks. See Michael J. Klarman, *The White Primary Rulings: A Case Study in the Consequences of Supreme Court Decisionmaking*, 29 Fla St U L Rev 55 (2001) (discussing social, legal, and political forces in Texas at that time); see also Issacharoff and Pildes, *Politics as Markets* at 665–66 (cited in note 44) (noting that in a world where blacks in Fort Bend County could vote, the Jaybird endorsement strategy at issue in *Terry v Adams* would not have been successful as some white candidates would have sought black votes to gain office). Given the relationship between major parties and institutions of governance, courts should

be narrowly drawn and should leave ample room for the political process to construct alternative approaches.[162]

IV. Conclusion

Within the very broad outlines provided by the Constitution, courts should permit the political processes of local, state, and federal governments to work out their own precise forms of representative (and direct) democracy. These forms will doubtless vary from jurisdiction to jurisdiction and change over time. The arguments that political scientists, legal scholars, and others offer about the merits of any particular form should be made in the political rather than the judicial arena. A regime of judicial restraint may mean that courts will leave in place regulations that some people will find objectionable. But except in exceptional circumstances, these battles are best left to the legislative debate or the initiative campaign. A greater sense of modesty about the capacities of the judiciary and a greater faith in the rough-and-tumble of the political process will produce a more satisfactory jurisprudence and perhaps even enhance the vitality of political institutions.

---

continue to find state action with respect to their internal party rules, as well as state laws, while minor parties should be treated as other organizations are with respect to claims of racial discrimination. A harder question concerns the appropriate judicial response if a minor party adopts other sorts of exclusionary membership policies. (Such a strategy is inconceivable in the context of major parties. See note 18.) For example, what should a court do if gay and lesbian voters are denied membership in a newly formed Heterosexual Party that seeks ballot access? My tentative conclusion is that such a policy, although morally repugnant, ought not to be struck down by courts. Instead, voters can evaluate the parties on the basis of their ideology and membership practices. If, however, the state or federal government has passed laws requiring all political parties to accept any citizen who registers as a member and prohibiting a consideration of sexual orientation, then such a law should not be invalidated by a court as an impermissible burden on political parties, including minor ones. In such a case, the parties-in-government, accountable to the electorate, have made their regulatory decisions, just as they do when they impose an open or blanket primary format on parties that prefer a more exclusionary process. In all these examples, courts should let the political process take its course.

[162] See Cass R. Sunstein, *One Case at a Time: Judicial Minimalism on the Supreme Court* xiv, 24–45 (Harvard, 1999) (advocating such an approach in many cases and terming it "judicial minimalism" that allows the democratic branches more room in responding to judicial decisions).

JANICE NADLER

NO NEED TO SHOUT: BUS SWEEPS
AND THE PSYCHOLOGY OF COERCION

In the last two decades, the Supreme Court repeatedly has examined consensual encounters between citizens and police that lead to
searches. Law enforcement agencies rely heavily on the consensual
encounter technique to discover evidence of ordinary criminal
wrongdoing, especially narcotics trafficking. But police-citizen encounters and requests to search pose challenges to the boundaries
of the Fourth Amendment. When is an encounter between a citizen and a police officer a consensual one, and when does such an
encounter rise to the level of a seizure? When a citizen gives a
police officer permission to search his or her bags or person, under
what circumstances is such permission considered voluntary, and
under what circumstances is such grant of permission no longer
voluntary but instead mere acquiescence to legitimate authority?

The police tactic of approaching and requesting to search in the
absence of individualized suspicion is reportedly an important law
enforcement tool,[1] and in some localities it is used quite frequently.[2] These encounters typically take place in one of a few

Janice Nadler is Assistant Professor, Northwestern University School of Law, and Research Fellow, American Bar Foundation.

AUTHOR'S NOTE: I am grateful to the following people for conversations and comments:
Ron Allen, Leigh Bienen, Shari Diamond, Adam Galinsky, Jen Hay, Lauren Kanter, Richard McAdams, Tracey Meares, Tom Merrill, Don Moore, Michael Roloff, and Mary Rose.
Thanks to Amanda Dykema-Engblade, Cristina Lane, David Hazan, Justin Ruaysamran,
and Emily Solberg for research assistance, and to the American Bar Foundation for financial
support.

[1] Amicus Brief of Washington Legal Foundation and the Allied Educational Foundation
as Amici Curiae in Support of Petitioner, *United States v Drayton*, 122 S Ct 2105 (2002).

[2] For example, one officer testified that he searched more than 3,000 bags over the course
of nine months. *Florida v Kerwick*, 512 So2d 347, 349 (1987) (noting that in the Florida

settings: during the course of a traffic stop, in the waiting rooms of airports or train stations, or on board intercity (Greyhound) buses. In the last decade the Court has focused its attention twice on the last category, otherwise known as "bus sweeps," in which the police conduct suspicionless searches of bus passengers and their possessions pursuant to the passengers' consent. Typically, the police board a Greyhound bus during a scheduled stopover,[3] and make known to passengers their mission of conducting "drug interdiction."[4] While on the bus, police approach individual passengers, sometimes ask for information about destination and ask to see identification, and then ask the passenger to identify his or her carry-on baggage. The officers then sometimes ask the passenger for consent to search the passenger's bag or person or both.

In bus sweep cases there are commonly two Fourth Amendment issues. The first is whether the passenger has been seized within the meaning of the Fourth Amendment. The second is whether the passenger's consent to the officers' request to search was voluntary. In the bus sweep situation, these two questions are often intertwined, as I will discuss in more detail below.

The Court's most recent pronouncement about the bounds of seizure and consent came this past term in a bus sweep case, *United States v Drayton*.[5] Eleven years earlier, in *Florida v Bostick*[6]—a case with very similar facts—the Court ruled that police requests to search bus passengers are not coercive per se. In *Bostick*, however, the police had informed passengers of their right to refuse the search request; in *Drayton* the police gave no such warnings. Nonetheless, *Drayton*'s holding—that despite the failure of police to advise passengers of their right to refuse, there was no seizure and

---

county in question, police officers approach every person on board buses and trains ("that time permits") and ask for consent to search luggage). Id. An appellate court in Ohio noted that police requests for consent to search during routine traffic stops had become standard practice in Ohio. *Ohio v Retherferd*, 639 NE2d 498, 503 (Ohio 1994).

[3] This is typically arranged in advance with the driver or done pursuant to an ongoing agreement. Sometimes, police pay cash to the bus driver in exchange for permitting the search. See Tom Gibb, *Bus Stop Drug Searches Getting Mixed Reviews*, Pittsburgh Post-Gazette B1 (Apr 19, 2000) (reporting that one officer testified that he had paid the bus driver $50 after a search uncovered illegal drugs).

[4] Police make their mission known to passengers either by way of a general announcement or during the course of conversation with individual passengers.

[5] 122 S Ct 2105 (2002).

[6] 501 US 429 (1991).

that the search in question was reasonable—is not particularly surprising, given *Bostick* and the Court's prior consent search decisions.

What is remarkable, however, is the ever-widening gap between
Fourth Amendment consent jurisprudence, on the one hand, and
scientific findings about the psychology of compliance and consent
on the other. Ever since the Court first applied the "totality of
the circumstances" standard to consent search issues in *Schneckloth
v Bustamonte*[7] in 1973, it has held in case after case, with only a
few exceptions, that a reasonable person in the situation in question either would feel free to terminate the encounter with police,
or would feel free to refuse the police request to search. By contrast, empirical studies over the last several decades on the social
psychology of compliance, conformity, social influence, and politeness have all converged on a single conclusion: the extent to which
people feel free to refuse to comply is extremely limited under
situationally induced pressures. These situational pressures often
are imperceptible to a person experiencing them; at the same time,
they can be so overwhelming that attempts to reduce them with
prophylactic warnings are insufficient.

The question of whether a citizen feels free to terminate a police
encounter depends crucially on certain empirical claims, as does
the question of whether a citizen's grant of permission to search
is voluntary. These questions cannot reliably be answered solely
from the comfort of one's armchair, while reflecting only on one's
own experience. An examination of the existing empirical evidence
on the psychology of coercion suggests that in many situations
where citizens find themselves in an encounter with the police, the
encounter is not consensual because a reasonable person would not
feel free to terminate the encounter. Furthermore, such evidence
suggests that often the subsequent search is not in fact voluntary,
because a reasonable person would not be, under the totality of
the circumstances, in a position to make a voluntary decision about
consent. This is especially true in the bus sweep situation, as I will
demonstrate in detail.

Even worse, the existing empirical evidence also suggests that
observers outside of the situation systematically overestimate the

---

[7] 412 US 218 (1973).

extent to which citizens in police encounters feel free to refuse. Members of the Court are themselves such outside observers, and this partly explains why the Court repeatedly has held that police-citizen encounters are consensual and that consent to search was freely given. In fact, the Court's focus in *Drayton* on the desirability of *Miranda*-type warnings in situations potentially implicating the Fourth Amendment is misplaced, because it is likely that citizens attach virtually no meaning whatever to these warnings.

In light of mounting empirical evidence, it is remarkable that the "totality of the circumstances" standard has nearly always led the Court to the conclusion that a reasonable person would feel free to refuse the police request to search. Fourth Amendment consent jurisprudence is now at a point where the Court's reasoning must struggle against scientific findings about compliance. The majority opinion in *Drayton* is filled with assertions that are implausible in light of research on social influence (e.g., "the presence of a holstered firearm thus is unlikely to contribute to the coerciveness of the encounter absent active brandishing of the weapon").[8] Thus, the Court's Fourth Amendment consent jurisprudence is either based on serious errors about human behavior and judgment, or else has devolved into a fiction of the crudest sort—a mere device for attaining the desired legal consequence.

The direction the Court has taken in this area is likely to lead to several unwelcome consequences. First, the fiction of consent in Fourth Amendment jurisprudence has led to suspicionless searches of many thousands of innocent citizens who "consent" to searches under coercive circumstances. Perhaps the systematic suspicionless searching of innocent citizens is a worthwhile price to pay in exchange for effective law enforcement, but the Court has not engaged in this analysis in any of its Fourth Amendment consent search or seizure cases. Second, the Court's repeated insistence that citizens feel free to refuse law enforcement officers' requests to search creates a confusing standard for lower courts, because it is unclear in new cases how to weigh the "totality of the circumstances" if the "correct" result is virtually always that the encounter and search were consensual. Incorporation of empirical findings on compliance and social influence into Fourth Amend-

---

[8] *Drayton*, 122 S Ct at 2112.

ment consent jurisprudence would help to dispel the "air of unreality"[9] that characterizes current doctrine.

I. Drayton and Fourth Amendment Consent Jurisprudence

Christopher Drayton and Clifton Brown, two young African-American men, boarded a Greyhound bus in Fort Lauderdale, Florida, intending to go to Indianapolis. About 10 hours into the trip, the bus made a scheduled stop in Tallahassee, Florida, where the passengers disembarked from the bus during the 45-minute stopover. About five minutes prior to the scheduled departure, after the passengers had reboarded, the driver took the passengers' tickets and went inside the bus terminal building to complete paperwork. At that point, three plainclothes police officers from the Tallahassee Police Department Drug Interdiction Team boarded the bus. One officer knelt backward in the driver's seat, where he could observe everyone on the bus. Another officer stood at the back of the bus. A third officer, Officer Lang, began questioning passengers individually. Officer Lang approached individual passengers from the rear, leaned over their shoulder, placed his face 12–18 inches from theirs, and held up his badge. He introduced himself as Investigator Lang from the Tallahassee Police Department and informed them that he was conducting bus interdiction to make sure there were no drugs or weapons on the bus. He told them that he would like their cooperation and asked them to identify their carry-on baggage. Sometimes he asked permission to search a passenger's baggage.

After speaking with three passengers, and searching the bag of one of those passengers, Officer Lang approached Drayton and Brown. In response to Officer Lang's request to identify their baggage, Drayton and Brown pointed to a bag in the overhead compartment. Officer Lang asked for permission to search it, and Brown agreed. The bag was searched and no contraband was found. The officer then asked Brown for permission to check his person for weapons, which Brown gave. Officer Lang noticed hard objects in Brown's upper thigh area that were "inconsistent with the human anatomy."[10] Those objects turned out to be two pack-

---

[9] Id at 2114 (Souter dissenting).

[10] *United States v Drayton*, 231 F3d 787, 789 (11th Cir 2001).

ages of cocaine taped to Brown's thighs. After handcuffing Brown and escorting him off the bus, police then asked Drayton's permission to search his person, and similar cocaine packages were found on Drayton's person. The two men were convicted in federal court of narcotics offenses.

Prior to trial, Drayton and Brown moved to suppress the cocaine on two grounds. First they claimed that they had been unlawfully seized by police and the search was a fruit of the unlawful seizure. Second, they claimed that even if they had not been seized, they had not consented voluntarily to the search. The trial judge denied the defendants' motion to suppress, ruling that they had not been seized, and that their consent was voluntarily given. The Eleventh Circuit reversed the convictions. It held that when Drayton and Brown consented to the search of their persons, that consent was coerced and not voluntary, and as a result the cocaine should have been suppressed. In finding that the defendants' consent had been coerced, the Eleventh Circuit noted several facts. These included the officers' show of authority in approaching passengers at a distance of 12–18 inches with badge displayed, the intimidating presence of the officer in the driver's seat of the bus, and, notably, the absence of "some positive indication that consent could have been refused."[11] The Eleventh Circuit did not address the issue of whether the defendants had been unlawfully seized.

The Supreme Court granted certiorari and reversed. Two issues were before the Court: whether Drayton and Brown were seized within the meaning of the Fourth Amendment, and whether Drayton and Brown voluntarily consented to the search that uncovered the narcotics taped to their bodies. Justice Kennedy, writing for the majority, held that Drayton and Brown had not been seized because a reasonable person in the situation would have felt free to terminate the encounter with the police. Further, the Court concluded that Drayton and Brown's permission to search their persons had been voluntarily given under the totality of the circumstances. The Court noted that the police officers did not command passengers to answer their questions; instead they spoke in polite, quiet voices, and asked permission first before searching bags or persons. The Court concluded that the passengers cooper-

---

[11] Id at 790.

ated not because they were coerced but because they knew that doing so would enhance their own safety.

Justice Souter, who was joined by Justices Stevens and Ginsburg, dissented. The dissent concluded that the two men had indeed been seized for purposes of the Fourth Amendment, that the seizure was unreasonable in light of the absence of individualized suspicion of wrongdoing, and that the cocaine discovered should have been suppressed as the fruit of an unlawful seizure. The dissent argued that the three police officers had established an "atmosphere of obligatory participation" so that a reasonable person would not have felt free to end the encounter with the officers. (The dissent did not reach the issue of whether Drayton and Brown consented voluntarily to the search.)

The stage had been set for the decision in *Drayton* by *Florida v Bostick*, a remarkably similar case decided 11 years earlier. In *Bostick*, the defendant was on board a bus during a stopover when police officers boarded the bus and asked him for his ticket and identification. After inspecting the documents, the police asked Bostick for permission to search his bag and advised him that he had a right to refuse. A search of the bag revealed cocaine. The Supreme Court, although refraining from deciding whether a seizure had actually occurred, held that the standard is whether, considering all of the circumstances surrounding the encounter, a reasonable person would feel free to decline the officers' requests or otherwise terminate the encounter. One of the surrounding circumstances in *Bostick* was that the police advised Bostick that he need not agree to the search. The Florida courts took the Court's hint and found on remand that no seizure had occurred, and that the subsequent consent to search was voluntary.

With the war on drugs well under way, law enforcement agencies capitalized on the *Bostick* decision by stepping up their efforts to root out drug trafficking on interstate buses. But confusion ensued among lower courts in deciding similar bus sweep cases. Some courts ruled that the bus sweep encounter in question was consensual, following the *Bostick* Court's warning that there is no seizure "so long as the officers do not convey as message that compliance with their requests is required."[12] Other lower courts, however,

---

[12] *Bostick*, 501 US at 437.

attached significance to the absence, in some subsequent cases, of police advice to bus passengers of their right not to cooperate, and held that under these circumstances the encounter cannot be deemed consensual.

The confusion in the lower courts following *Bostick* arose from differing interpretations of the totality of the circumstances standard. The *Bostick* majority accused the Florida courts of finding all police-citizen encounters on buses nonconsensual by positing inherent coercion in the bus setting. Whether the Florida courts actually had adopted a per se rule was the subject of considerable debate among members of the Court in *Bostick*. Justice Marshall, writing for himself as well as Justices Blackmun and Stevens, argued that the Florida courts had done no such thing, but had instead considered all of the details of the encounter, just as the standard requires. In the end, the dissent agreed with the standard set out by the majority (under the totality of the circumstances, whether a reasonable person would feel free to decline the officers' requests or otherwise terminate the encounter). "What I cannot understand," Justice Marshall said, "is how the majority could possibly suggest an affirmative answer to this question."[13]

The "free to terminate the encounter" test evolved from the basic proposition that the Fourth Amendment does not prohibit law enforcement officers from approaching citizens on the street and asking questions, even in the absence of individualized suspicion.[14] So long as the encounter remains consensual, then no Fourth Amendment interests are implicated.[15] Both *Bostick* and

---

[13] Id at 445 (Marshall dissenting).

[14] See *Terry v Ohio*, 392 US 1, 19 n 16 (1968); *United States v Mendenhall*, 446 US 544, 557–58 (1980); *Florida v Royer*, 460 US 491, 501 (1983); *INS v Delgado*, 466 US 210, 216 (1984).

[15] See *Florida v Rodriguez*, 469 US 1, 5–6 (1984). In *Terry v Ohio*, the Court noted that "not all personal intercourse between policemen and citizens involves 'seizures' of persons," and that a seizure has occurred "[o]nly when the officer, by means of physical force or show of authority, has in some way restrained the liberty of a citizen." 392 US at 19 n 16. The Court later clarified this standard by declaring that a person has been seized within the meaning of the Fourth Amendment if a reasonable person in the totality of the circumstances would believe "he was not free to leave." *United States v Mendenhall*, 446 US at 554–55. Though this test was articulated in a plurality opinion, it was later endorsed by a majority in *INS v Delgado*, 466 US at 216. Subsequently, in *Bostick*, the Court held that the "free to leave" standard is "inapplicable" to a bus passenger (who does not desire to leave), and that "the appropriate inquiry is whether a reasonable person would feel free to decline the officers' requests or otherwise terminate the encounter." *Bostick*, 501 US at 436–37.

Drayton concluded that there is no real difference between police-citizen encounters that take place on buses and those that take place on the street, and so the fact that an encounter occurs on a bus does not transform police questioning into an illegal seizure.

Beyond the question of whether a seizure occurred, there is a separate, related question of whether the citizen's subsequent consent to search was voluntary. The voluntariness of consent analysis is very similar to the seizure analysis, and ultimately turns on similar (if not identical) facts. As originally articulated in *Schneckloth v Bustamonte*,[16] the question of whether a citizen's consent to search was voluntary, or instead was the product of duress, must be determined from the totality of the circumstances. In *Schneckloth*, the Court modeled its Fourth Amendment definition of voluntariness on the Court's earlier (pre-*Miranda*) analysis of voluntariness of confessions under the Fifth Amendment. The Court said in *Schneckloth* that the voluntariness analysis must balance "the legitimate need for such searches and the equally important requirement of assuring the absence of coercion."[17] Whether coercion was present must be determined from the totality of the circumstances, including the nature of police questions as well as the vulnerability of the citizen who is the target of police attention, and whether the citizen knows that he has a right to refuse the officer's request. Unlike the Fifth Amendment analysis, however, *Schneckloth* stopped short of holding that the police are required to advise citizens of their right to refuse a request for consent to search. Instead, whether the citizen knew his right to refuse is simply one factor to be considered in the totality of circumstances analysis. Unfortunately, aside from specifying that the voluntariness analysis should consider the totality of the circumstances, the Court did not further illuminate the terms "voluntariness" or "coercion," so lower courts were left to their own devices.

Over the years, lower courts applying *Schneckloth* tended to focus their inquiry about the voluntariness of consent to search on police misconduct, rather than on characteristics of the suspect that might increase the likelihood that consent was involuntary.[18]

---

[16] 412 US 218 (1973).

[17] Id at 227.

[18] See Marcy Strauss, *Reconstructing Consent*, 92 J Crim L & Criminol 211, 221–22 (2002). *Schneckloth* listed several potential relevant "subjective" factors that might be considered in

Bostick and *Drayton* continued in this vein. *Bostick* emphasized that for consent to be voluntary it must not be the product of official intimidation. "Citizens do not forfeit their constitutional rights when they are coerced to comply with a request that they would prefer to refuse."[19] Thus, a citizen who prefers to refuse a police request to consent but is intimidated into saying yes will be deemed to have been coerced and the consent involuntary.[20] *Drayton* ultimately concluded that Drayton and Brown's consent to search their persons was voluntary because the manner in which the police requested consent "indicat[ed] to a reasonable person that he or she was free to refuse." Thus, in *Drayton* the Court implicitly adopted the same "free to refuse/terminate" test for deciding voluntariness of consent to search that has been used since *Bostick* for deciding the seizure question. These two questions— seizure and voluntariness of search—have essentially merged in *Bostick* and *Drayton*. The *Schneckloth* Court's emphasis on balancing order and liberty has receded into the background. The test is now stated in much more definite terms: free to refuse or terminate.[21]

This standard demands both consideration of the totality of the circumstances and a determination of the citizen's voluntary con-

---

determining voluntariness, including the suspect's age, intelligence, and amount of schooling. Even when lower courts do consider an individual suspect's characteristics, they generally still find that the consent was given voluntarily. And where consent was found to be involuntary it was usually because there was egregious police misconduct, such as threats or an extreme show of force. Id at 223.

[19] *Bostick*, 501 US at 438.

[20] Though both *Bostick* and *Drayton* focused mostly on the question of whether the defendants had been seized, the majority opinions in each case also briefly addressed the question of whether defendant's consent to search was voluntary. The Court applied essentially the same standard to both inquiries. "Where the question of voluntariness pervades both the search and seizure inquiries, the respective analyses turn on very similar facts." *Drayton*, 122 S Ct at 2113.

[21] It may be that the Court is still implicitly engaging in a balancing of "the legitimate need for such searches and the equally important requirement of assuring the absence of coercion" when it decides consent search issues in cases like *Bostick* and *Drayton*. *Schneckloth*, 412 US at 227. Indeed, some commentators argue that *Schneckloth* used the term "voluntariness" as a term of art—that is, as a "placeholder for an analysis of the competing interests of order and liberty." Tracey L. Meares and Bernard E. Harcourt, *Foreword: Transparent Adjudication and Social Science Research in Constitutional Criminal Procedure*, 90 J Crim L & Criminol 733, 738 (2000). While this may be true, the Court certainly speaks in its opinions as if it is engaging in a completely different kind of analysis when it decides consent search issues. If it is true that the Court is implicitly using an analysis that is at odds with its announced rationale, we must examine the possible implications of such a discrepancy. As I argue later (in Section IV), this incongruity in Fourth Amendment consent jurisprudence is both undesirable and unnecessary.

sent: either consent to engage in the encounter or consent to have
the police search. The standard thus requires an examination of
the following question: How would a reasonable person in these
circumstances feel? Would a reasonable person, seeing what the
bus passengers saw, hearing what the bus passengers heard, and
knowing what the bus passengers knew, feel free to terminate the
encounter, or to say no to the request to search? Note that the
question of whether a reasonable person would feel free to terminate the encounter, or refuse the request to search, must necessarily be answered from the perspective of the citizen. By necessity,
to answer the "free to refuse" question, the focus cannot be on
the police perspective, and what the police did or could have done
differently, and whether what the police did seems reasonable. The
police could honestly view their actions as restrained and discreet
in a situation where, at the same time, a reasonable person would
feel coerced.

This distinction between citizen perspective and police perspective is a crucial one. As I shall demonstrate later, the Court's analysis in *Bostick* and in *Drayton* is at bottom based on a judgment about
the reasonableness of police conduct under the circumstances. In
both cases, the Court's real (but unstated) concern was whether
the police conduct was acceptable (in a general policy sense) under
the circumstances (no guns drawn, no explicit threats uttered).
Having been satisfied implicitly that the police did not engage in
abusive conduct, the Court then directly concluded that there must
have been no seizure and no unconsented search.

Although the police conduct in *Bostick* and *Drayton* may have
been reasonable under the circumstances, it does not follow that
there was no seizure and no unconsented search for Fourth
Amendment purposes. The standard for determining whether a
citizen has been seized or subjected to an involuntary search focuses on whether a reasonable person in the situation would feel
free to refuse the police requests. As I argue later, empirical evidence suggests that reasonable citizens in the same situation in
which Drayton and Brown found themselves would not, in fact,
feel free to refuse the police requests. Thus, the Court's unstated
concern—that the police be permitted to engage in suspicionless
seizures and consentless searches so long as they avoid abusive or
overly coercive tactics—is masked by its stated holding that citizens are not seized or involuntarily searched within the meaning

of the Fourth Amendment if they feel free to refuse police requests. The Court's conclusion that a reasonable person in Drayton and Brown's position would have in fact felt free to refuse
police requests is implausible in the face of empirical findings that
I discuss later.[22] This implausible conclusion makes more sense,
however, if we understand the Court to be doing something other
than what it says it is doing. Specifically, instead of analyzing the
voluntariness of the encounter and of the consent to search, the
Court is simply passing judgment on the reasonableness of the
police conduct under the circumstances. The problem here, of
course, is that in the absence of voluntary consent given by the
bus passengers, the police search of those passengers violated
the Fourth Amendment, however pleasant the police officers' de-
meanor and however reasonable the nature of their requests.[23]
Similarly, if the police effected a suspicionless seizure of the bus
passengers, such a seizure violated the Fourth Amendment, regardless of whether the police conduct seems otherwise reasonable.
Unfortunately, the Court's failure to acknowledge explicitly its
true concern is likely to exacerbate the confusion that *Bostick* trig-
gered in the lower courts 11 years earlier.

Observers generally have viewed *Drayton*'s ruling that police
warnings are not necessary to initiate consensual bus passenger
searches as the crucial aspect of the Court's decision.[24] In some
respects, the Court's explicit refusal to require a *Miranda*-type
warning in Fourth Amendment situations is indeed significant, especially after *Dickerson v United States*.[25] Nevertheless, I will argue
that *Drayton*'s holding regarding police warnings is a red herring
that only serves to distract attention from the real issue: the fiction
of consensual encounters and consensual searches. The disagreement between the majority and the dissent in both *Drayton* and

---

[22] A few of these findings were brought to the attention of the Court in the Respondents'
brief. Brief of Respondents at 42 n 4.

[23] See *Indianapolis v Edmond*, 531 US 32 (2000) ("A search or seizure is ordinarily unreasonable in the absence of individualized suspicion of wrongdoing.").

[24] See *Civil Rights on a Greyhound*, New York Times A22 (June 18, 2002); Jan Crawford
Greenberg, *Justices Strengthen Police Search Power*, Chicago Tribune 1 (June 18, 2002); Patty
Reinert, *Court: Warnings Unnecessary in Searches of Buses and Trains*, Houston Chronicle A10
(June 18, 2002); Lyle Denniston, *Justices Broaden the Right to Search*, Boston Globe A1 (June
18, 2002).

[25] 530 US 428 (2000) (holding that *Miranda*'s warning regime arises from constitutional
requirements).

Bostick was whether a reasonable bus passenger approached by police feels free to say, "I don't want to talk, and you may not search
me." Members of the Court have had difficulty agreeing on an
answer to this question because they are approaching the question
incorrectly. They are trying to answer a question with a crucial
empirical component[26] using only intuitive reflections on their own
experience and about the imagined experience of other citizens.
But people's intuitions differ about the question of whether a bus
passenger feels free to say no to a police officer; these differences
in intuitions are not particularly surprising, or important. The important point is that casual intuitions are, at best, irrelevant in answering this question. In fact, as I will argue, attempts to address
this question from intuition alone will produce answers that are
skewed in the direction of inferring more voluntariness on the part
of the citizen than is warranted.

II. Feeling Free to Refuse and the Reasonable Person: The Evidence from Social Science

The two issues that were decided in *Drayton* were, first,
whether the encounter between the defendants and the officers was
consensual, and second, whether the defendants' consent to search
was given voluntarily. The standards for resolving these issues re-
volve around what a reasonable person[27] would feel free to do in

---

[26] The question of whether a bus passenger feels free to refuse police requests is arguably
itself an empirical question. That is, the extent to which a person feels free to refuse is a
psychological state that is, at least in principle, measurable in the same way that questions
about the extent to which someone feels hungry or feels happy or feels anxious are measurable. The Court's test (whether a reasonable person would *feel* free to refuse police requests)
thus turns only on how a reasonable person would react psychologically under the totality
of the circumstances. If a reasonable person would not feel free to refuse, then that person
has been seized (or has given consent involuntarily). But what does it mean to feel free to
refuse? Interestingly, the language of the *Bostick* opinion provides some guidance: "Citizens
do not forfeit their constitutional rights when they are coerced to comply with a request
that they would prefer to refuse." *Bostick*, 501 US at 438. Thus, if a reasonable person feels
constrained to cooperate with police because of a strong internal sense of civic duty, that
person has not been subjected to an involuntary search because they are not complying
with a request that they would prefer to refuse. But if a reasonable person feels constrained
to cooperate with police because the situation makes them feel intimidated, that person's
consent indeed has been vitiated because they have complied with a request that they would
prefer to refuse.

[27] The Court has emphasized that this standard presumes a "reasonable innocent person."
Florida v Bostick, 501 US at 437–38. This standard thus rules out the argument that the
search was coercive because coercion is the only explanation for why a person carrying
enough illegal drugs to send them to prison for decades would voluntarily consent to a

the situation. Specifically, as to the seizure question, *Bostick* set out a very simple, specific test for determining whether a seizure has occurred in the course of a citizen-police encounter: would a reasonable person in this situation feel free to terminate the encounter? As to the search question, the standard (as articulated in *Bostick* and *Drayton*) is similar: was the consent involuntary, in the sense that the citizen was forced to comply when he or she would have preferred to refuse?[28] Notably, the *Drayton* Court attempted to discern whether a reasonable person would feel free to terminate the encounter in the circumstances in the case at hand simply by thinking hard about each specific circumstance that characterized the encounter and then answering, based on the Justices' own imagined thoughts and feelings of a reasonable person.[29]

---

search. The argument is that no rational (guilty) person in that position would voluntarily consent to a search, and therefore the consent must have been coerced. Of course, there are a number of explanations, other than coercion, for why a person carrying large amounts of unlawful contraband would consent to a search that is certain to result in devastating personal consequences. These include convincing oneself (for the moment) that the contraband is so well hidden that police won't find it, hoping that the grant of permission to search will signal to police that they need not bother doing so, or reasoning that they have already been caught and refusal will only make things worse. For the purpose of the analysis in this essay, I follow the Court's standard and assume that reasonable person means reasonable innocent person.

[28] *Bostick*, 501 US at 438; *Drayton*, 122 S Ct at 2113. I note that the term "voluntary" here appears to mean whether a reasonable person would feel that he or she had a choice. This term therefore raises a question about a psychological state (how a reasonable person would *feel*), rather than a philosophical question about free will.

[29] See, for example, *Drayton*, 122 S Ct at 2112 ("Indeed, because many fellow passengers are present to witness officers' conduct, a reasonable person may feel even more secure in his or her decision not to cooperate with police on a bus than in other circumstances."); id at 2112 ("Officers are often required to wear uniforms and in many circumstances this is cause for assurance, not discomfort. The same can be said for wearing sidearms. . . . The presence of a holstered firearm thus is unlikely to contribute to the coerciveness of the encounter absent active brandishing of the weapon."); id at 2113 ("[B]us passengers answer officers' questions and otherwise cooperate not because of coercion but because the passengers know that their participation enhances their own safety and the safety of those around them."); id at 2113 ("[W]hen Lang requested to search Brown and Drayton's persons, he asked first if they objected, thus indicating to a reasonable person that he or she was free to refuse.").

Drayton is by no means the only case in which members of the Court used their own thoughts and feelings that they imagine they would experience in a particular set of circumstances to determine reasonableness. In oral argument in *Bond v United States*, 529 US 334 (2000), which considered the question of whether an officer's manual squeezing of a bus passenger's luggage amounts to a search, one Justice commented on his own personal, individual expectation of privacy regarding his own luggage: "QUESTION: . . . I fly quite a lot up to Boston and so forth, and I put bags all the time in the upper thing, and people are always moving them around. They push them, they lift them up, they move them to other places, and if they're soft they would feel just what was on the inside. Now, that happens all the time, and I do it myself, frankly. I move somebody else's bag and push

In using this method for determining whether a seizure has occurred, and whether the consent to search was voluntarily given,
the Court assumed these questions can be answered from intuition
alone. In fact, these are questions that depend crucially on empirical inquiries. Would a reasonable person in Drayton's situation
feel free to terminate the encounter with the police? This question
concerns facts about the world that we can observe. A question is
empirical if any answer to that question could be either confirmed
or disconfirmed by observation.[30] The question the Court asks is
a question about the actual behavior of real people—about what
a reasonable person would do and feel under a specific set of circumstances.

One might respond that even if these questions turn on empirical inquiries, perhaps it is still appropriate to answer them based
on intuition alone, especially in light of the fact that there is no
direct evidence testing this specific situation. But this is an enter-
prise fraught with danger. The reason is that relying on casual
intuition to infer why someone acted the way they did in a situation where *all* of the details and circumstances are important and
must be taken into account (as the Court has emphasized repeatedly) almost always leads to mistaken and erroneous judgments.
In the next section I will explain why. While it is true that there
is no single study providing direct empirical evidence addressing
all the specific circumstances of bus passengers, there is abundant
evidence addressing almost all of the individual factors present on
the bus (the authority of the officers, the politeness of the request,
the physical proximity, the surprise nature of the request, etc.),
and all of these factors point to the same conclusion: a reasonable
passenger on the bus would have felt compelled to comply even
if he or she would have preferred to refuse.

The empirical studies I describe below differ in their method
from the method used by the Court to determine whether citizens
in particular circumstances feel free to refuse police requests. Each
of the empirical studies I describe is governed by rigorous scientific

---

mine in, and I imagine the interstate bus here was no different. So if that happens all the
time, how can I say that your client has some kind of special expectation, since in my own
experience, people are always handling this soft luggage?" Oral argument transcript at 6–
7 (Feb 29, 2000).

   [30] See Roderick Chisholm, *Theory of Knowledge* 36 (Prentice-Hall, 2d ed 1977); Michael
Williams, *Problems of Knowledge: A Critical Introduction to Epistemology* 2 (Oxford, 2001).

methods that are generally accepted in the field to which they belong. Some of the results described below are based upon laboratory experiments in which all relevant variables are tightly controlled to isolate and examine factors of interest. Other results I describe are based upon field experiments in which the behavior of interest is observed in its natural context. Some of the studies are based upon observations of college students; others are based upon observations of other adults who differ widely in age and other demographic characteristics. The studies I will discuss present well-established findings that are not particularly controversial. Many of the findings I describe have been replicated, in various forms, many different times in many different contexts. Strikingly, despite their diverse methods and topics, all of the different studies I describe point to the same conclusion: bus passengers confronting the same situation as Drayton and Brown are extremely unlikely to feel free to refuse the police officers' requests and terminate the encounter.

In this section, I will consider each feature of the situation in which the passengers in *Drayton* found themselves and examine the empirical evidence, if any exists, regarding whether and how that feature affects the extent to which a reasonable person feels free to refuse the requests of the officers. These features include the authority of the police, the politeness and pragmatic implications of their requests, the presence and behavior of other passengers on the bus, the close physical quarters of the officers' approach and the bus itself, and the time constraints of the situation. Before examining these individual factors that characterize the environment on the bus, I review other evidence that suggests that close attention to empirical evidence in the totality of the circumstances analysis is crucial because of the general human inability to discern coercion in a particular set of circumstances from the perspective of outside of the situation in question.

A. THE ACTOR-OBSERVER BIAS

Accurately predicting what a reasonable person would do and feel under a specific set of complex circumstances using one's intuition alone (as the Court has tried to do in *Bostick* and *Drayton*) is nearly impossible. This is because, as a general matter, people tend to grossly overestimate the voluntariness of others' actions. A vast scientific literature has established that although situational forces systematically pull and push behavior, our ability to recognize these forces depends on whether we are explaining our own behavior or someone else's behavior. As a general matter, people are strongly inclined toward explaining another person's behavior in terms of internal causes (their intentions and dispositions), while ignoring aspects of the situation that could account for the person's actions.[31] For this reason, behavior that looks voluntary from the outside can feel constrained by the situation from the perspective of the actor. "It may be, for example, that a gentle request in a particular setting is just as constraining, as 'motivating,' as a large bribe" even though, from the outside, it is difficult to perceive the constraining features of a particular setting.[32] In a now-classic experiment, subjects observed part of a debate in which the speakers took positions defending or opposing Fidel Castro. Even though the subjects were told that the positions in the debate had been assigned and the speakers had no choice about which position they were presenting, subjects assumed that the speakers had attitudes corresponding to their speech: the speakers who presented the pro-Castro position were perceived to be more pro-Castro than the speakers who took the anti-Castro position.[33] In spite of the fact that subjects understood that the debate position had been assigned, they still could not shake the intuition that the speakers personally believed what they said, because they failed to appreciate the strength of the situational constraints the speaker was under.

There are a number of reasons why people interpret situationally induced behavior as being caused by internal, dispositional factors. Sometimes the situational factors are "invisible"[34]—that is, difficult to pinpoint from the perspective of an observer. For example, in one study, subjects observed people being randomly assigned to the roles of "quizmaster" and "contestant" in a mock game show.[35] Quizmasters created questions from their own men-

---

[31] See, for example, Daniel T. Gilbert and Patrick S. Malone, *The Correspondence Bias*, 117 Psychol Bulletin 21 (1995).

[32] Edward E. Jones, *Interpersonal Perception* 122 (Freeman, 1990).

[33] Edward E. Jones amd V. A. Harris, *The Attribution of Attitudes*, 3 J Exp Soc Psychol 1 (1967).

[34] Gilbert and Malone, 117 Psychol Bulletin at 25 (cited in note 31).

[35] Lee D. Ross, Teresa M. Amabile, and Julia L. Steinmetz, *Social Roles, Social Control, and Biases in Social-Perception Processes*, 35 J Personality & Soc Psychol 485 (1977).

tal inventory of favorite trivia, and because the deck was "stacked" in this manner, contestants had trouble answering the questions. Despite the obvious fact that contestants had a much more difficult task than quizmasters, observers rated the quizmasters as genuinely smarter than the contestants. Without the benefit of actually being in the contestants' shoes, observers could not appreciate the strength of the situational constraints on the contestants' ability to answer the questions.

The general finding that observers do not reliably appreciate the strength and consequences of situational constraints on an actor's behavior is robust and has been demonstrated in many different settings, including police-citizen encounters. In police interrogation contexts, observers perceive confessions as more voluntary from the police's perspective compared to the suspects' perspective.[36] To demonstrate this, Daniel Lassiter videotaped a single confession with two cameras. When the camera angle depicted the suspect from the interrogator's perspective (so that the audience saw everything the interrogator saw), the very same confession was perceived as more voluntary than when the camera angle depicted the interrogator from the suspect's perspective (so that the audience saw everything the suspect saw). This robust result has been replicated in no fewer than 15 different studies, using both students and nonstudents, both old and young people, and with whites, blacks, and Hispanics. When the camera is focused on the suspect, observers infer only a small degree of coercion because they attribute the act of confessing largely to the most salient object on the screen: the suspect. On the other hand, when the camera is focused on the interrogator, observers infer a large degree of coercion because they again attribute the act of confessing largely to the most salient object on the screen: this time that is the interrogator. Thus, when the camera is placed so that it shows exactly what the suspect saw, the external forces on the suspect's behavior (notably, the pressure from the interrogator) become more apparent.

It is tempting to conclude that perhaps we can overcome the exaggerated perception of voluntariness by simply imagining the suspect's perspective and then imagining how coercive the situa-

---

[36] Daniel G. Lassiter et al, *Videotaped Confessions: Is Guilt in the Eye of the Camera?* in Mark P. Zanna, ed, 33 *Advances in Experimental Social Psychology* 189 (Academic, 2001).

tional constraints would feel. So, for example, we can try to predict what a reasonable person would do in the circumstances present on the bus on which Drayton and Brown were riding by simply imagining ourselves in those circumstances. By imagining oneself in the shoes of the citizen whom the police are targeting, perhaps we can understand the situational pressures that the person feels, and thus more accurately determine whether they are in a position freely to choose whether to consent to the police officers' requests.

But this task is not as easy as it sounds. Because people have difficulty imagining situational influences that constrain choice when such imagining takes place outside of the situation, people tend to grossly overestimate the voluntariness of even their own hypothetical actions. For example, people listening to special beeps tend in a laboratory to overestimate the number of beeps they heard if other people who answer first also overestimate—in this sense, we conform with the decisions of others.[37] But more importantly, observers secretly watching the laboratory session predict that they themselves would be more accurate than the participants.[38] The researchers concluded, "Thus, when the degree of influence shown by others is noted, we see this as relatively large and excessive (even though we might have been influenced an equal amount). We are thus likely to make rather hard moral judgments about those who are 'easily' influenced on the rationale that we wouldn't have given in to such pressure."[39]

Other research confirms the difficulty of accurately imagining the extent to which situational constraints shape our behavior. For example, when participants were asked to write an essay that advocated a position with which they disagreed, compliance rates were high.[40] However, when outsiders are asked hypothetically whether they would engage in the same counterattitudinal essay writing, almost three-quarters said they would not.[41] In another study, ob-

---

[37] Robert J. Wolosin, Steven J. Sherman, and Arnie Cann, *Predictions of Own and Other's Conformity*, 43 J Personality 357 (1975).

[38] Id.

[39] Id at 374.

[40] See Gilbert and Malone, 117 Psychol Bulletin at 27 (cited in note 31) (compliance rates with essay-writing request over "decades of research" are "exceptionally high").

[41] Steven J. Sherman, *On the Self-Erasing Nature of Errors of Prediction*, 39 J Personality & Soc Psychol 211 (1980) (three-quarters of those asked to forecast their own compliance predicted they would refuse).

servers who read about a job candidate who is asked inappropriate interview questions predicted that if they were in that situation themselves, they would confront the interviewer directly; however, actual candidates who were placed in the very same situation capitulated and answered the question.[42] There is a gap between what people predict they would do in a situation, and what they actually do. Because of this, it is not enough to try simply to imagine how free a reasonable bus passenger would feel upon being approached by the police with a request to search. Instead, it is important to gain a more systematic and methodical understanding of the influence of each situational factor that might influence how free a citizen feels to refuse police request to search.

B. COMPLIANCE

The Court's analysis of the seizure and consent to search issues has led to highly consistent results. In nearly every case involving police-citizen encounters where the consensual nature of the encounter was at issue, the Court held there was no seizure.[43] Similarly, in cases where the issue of voluntariness of consent to search arose, the Court has held that the search was consensual.[44] We have seen that observers often grossly and systematically overestimate the voluntariness of others' actions, and this is reflected in the Court's consensual police-citizen encounter decisions. By contrast,

---

[42] Julie A. Woodzicka and Marianne LaFrance, *Real versus Imagined Gender Harassment*, 57 J Soc Issues 15 (2001).

[43] See *United States v Mendenhall*, 446 US 544, 557–58 (1980) (no seizure where federal drug agents approached a woman walking through an airport concourse and asked to see her ticket and identification); *INS v Delgado*, 466 US 210, 216 (1984) (no seizure where immigration agents questioned factory workers while other agents were positioned at building exits); *Florida v Rodriguez*, 469 US 1 (1984) (no seizure in an airport concourse where police approached and questioned a man who briefly attempted to run away); *Michigan v Chesternut*, 486 US 567 (1988) (no seizure where man fled at sight of police and police drove alongside him for a short distance); *California v Hodari D.*, 499 US 621 (1991) (no seizure where youth fled at sight of police and police gave chase). One exception in this line of no-seizure findings was *Florida v Royer*, 460 US 491, 501 (1983), in which the Court held, in a plurality opinion, that a seizure occurred when police approached and questioned a man in an airport and subsequently held his ticket and identification. In a fractured set of concurring and dissenting opinions, there was no agreement among the Justices on precisely when the seizure began, or whether there was *Terry*-level suspicion to justify it. In another seizure case, *Florida v Bostick*, the Court remanded the seizure question back to the lower courts. However, as I explain in Section IV.B., *Bostick*'s implicit message was that there was no seizure.

[44] See *Schneckloth v Bustamonte*, 412 US 218 (1973); *Ohio v Robinette*, 519 US 33 (1996).

empirical research over the last several decades paints a very different picture—the extent to which we feel free to refuse to comply under situationally induced pressures to do so is extremely limited. Evidence from several different disciplines and research areas all converges on the same general finding regarding limited decision freedom.

The social psychology of compliance is the study of the conditions under which people accede to requests made by others.[45] Thus, empirical evidence on the social psychology of compliance can assist in determining when a citizen's response to a police officer's request to search is voluntary and when it is "no more than acquiescence to a claim of lawful authority."[46] Systematic study of the social psychology of compliance has been advancing for more than 50 years,[47] and social scientists have successfully identified a variety of factors that lead people to consent involuntarily, or, in the language of the majority in *Bostick*, to feel "coerced to comply with a request that they would prefer to refuse."[48] In the discussion that follows, I shall consider two of the most important principles of the social psychology of compliance—authority and social validation[49]—and I will illustrate how the presence of each of these factors makes it more likely that a citizen will "comply with a request they would prefer to refuse."

1. *Compliance with authority.* Whether a request results in acquiescence depends a great deal on whether the requester is a legitimately constituted authority. As a general matter, persons with such authority exert an enormous amount of influence over our decisions.[50] In many ways, it is logical that this is the case: the reason for their inordinate influence is that their position of authority signals that they possess information and power that is greater than our own. Throughout the course of our lives we learn that taking the advice of people like parents, teachers, supervisors,

---

[45] See Robert B. Cialdini and Melanie R. Trost, *Social Influence: Social Norms, Conformity and Compliance*, in Daniel T. Gilbert, Susan T. Fiske, and Gardner Lindzey, eds, 2 *The Handbook of Social Psychology* 151, 168 (McGraw-Hill, 4th ed 1998).

[46] *Bumper v North Carolina*, 391 US 543, 548–49 (1968).

[47] See Cialdini and Trost, 2 *The Handbook of Social Psychology* at 168 (cited in note 45).

[48] *Bostick*, 501 US at 438.

[49] See Cialdini and Trost, 2 *The Handbook of Social Psychology* at 170 (cited in note 45).

[50] See, for example, Stanley Milgram, *Obedience to Authority* 104 (Harper & Row, 1983).

oncologists, and plumbers is beneficial for us, both because of their ability to enlighten us and because we depend on their good graces.[51] For example, patients are in the habit of following the advice of their doctors because that advice usually turns out well; employees adopt a general strategy of abiding by the wishes of their supervisor, because in the long run that strategy is good for their career. For most people, most of the time, conforming to the wishes of persons with authority makes a great deal of sense. "It makes so much sense, in fact, that people often do so when it makes no sense at all."[52]

One example of complying with the wishes of an authority even when compliance makes little sense is a phenomenon that airline industry officials have dubbed "captainitis."[53] Like all humans, flight captains in the airplane cockpit sometimes make errors. These errors often go uncorrected, even when they are detected by other crew members, and these uncorrected errors lead to crashes. Despite the obviously serious consequences, crew members go along with the captain's mistake, because they convince themselves that if the captain has decided to do it, it must be right.

Why do we so readily comply with the wishes of authority? One critical piece of this puzzle is the nature of the cognitive mechanisms involved: the processes that lead to compliance with an authority when we are under pressure to make a decision are fast, automatic, and unconscious.[54] Complying with authorities is something that we do quickly, on the spot, without conscious deliberation. We do not always make decisions this way. Sometimes, when

---

[51] See Cialdini and Trost, 2 *The Handbook of Social Psychology* at 170 (cited in note 45).

[52] Id.

[53] H. Clayton Foushee, *Dyads and Triads at 35,000 Feet: Factors Affecting Group Process and Aircrew Performance*, 39 Am Psychologist 885 (1984); Robert B. Cialdini, *Influence: Science and Practice* 9–10 (Allyn & Bacon, 4th ed 2001).

[54] See Eric S. Knowles and Christopher A. Condon, *Why People Say "Yes": A Dual-Process Theory of Acquiescence*, 77 J Personality & Soc Psychol 379, 385 (1999) (presenting evidence for a two-stage model of belief process, in which a request is first tacitly and automatically accepted, and then later reconsidered; because the reconsideration stage can require effort, it is easily disrupted, leading to acquiescence); Marco Iacoboni et al, *Watching People Interact: The Neural Bases of Understanding Social Relations*, unpublished manuscript (2002) (observing a person in authority giving an order to another person does not activate brain regions associated with conscious, effortful, cognitive tasks, but does activate brain regions associated with automatic, unconscious processes); Edward E. Jones, *Interpersonal Perception* 124 (Freeman, 1990) (remarking that social roles, such as authority-subordinate roles, are so ingrained that we comply with authorities' requests automatically and mindlessly).

we have the ability and the motivation to engage in careful analysis, we do so. But we do not always have the luxury of careful processing. The world is complicated, and we are often under time pressure, distracted, emotionally aroused, or mentally fatigued.[55] Many times we respond automatically, rather than thoughtfully, because many of our behaviors are situation-specific, so that we respond the same way to certain situation-specific cues. One example of a situation-specific cue that leads to automatic responses is the social role. Certain social roles, such as authority-subordinate roles, give rise to overlearned patterns of responses. We follow the leader, we stop at red lights, and we comply with the police not because we make a deliberate conscious choice to respond in a particular way, but rather because we mindlessly respond in a manner consistent with social roles.[56] As a general matter, we do not always need to make careful, sophisticated, informed decisions; as a result, much of our daily behavior relies on mental shortcuts. Engaging in automatic behavior makes room for elaborate, conscious decisions when we have the opportunity and the need to make them. Usually automatic processing serves us well.[57] But it sometimes leads us astray.

Perhaps the most well-known scientific study of compliance with authority is the set of obedience studies conducted by Stanley Milgram, who investigated the extent to which people would comply with a request to perform an apparently harmful action. Milgram's subjects, who were adults from all walks of life, were informed that they would be participating in an experiment on the effects of punishment on learning. Upon arrival in the laboratory, the subject was assigned (through an apparently random procedure) to assume the role of "teacher," while the other "subject" (actually a confederate of the experimenter) was assigned to be the "learner." The subject was informed that it is his or her job to teach a series of word pairs to the learner. In full view of the subject, the learner was then strapped into a chair, and an electrode

---

[55] See Cialdini, *Influence: Science and Practice* at 9 (cited in note 53).

[56] See Jones, 122 *Interpersonal Perception* at 124 (cited in note 32).

[57] See Gerd Gigerenzer and Reinhard Selton, *Rethinking Rationality*, in Gerd Gigerenzer, *Bounded Rationality* 1, 7 (MIT, 2001). For example, when a player runs to catch a ball, she does not calculate the distance between her current position and where she expects the ball to land, then run that distance, and then wait for the ball. Instead, she catches the ball by running just fast enough to maintain a constant angle between her eye and the ball.

was taped to his wrist. As teacher, the subject's job was to administer shocks to the learner, by pressing switches on a shock generator, each time the learner made an error in recalling a word. Before
beginning the learning task, the experimenter asked the subject to
press the electrode to his or her own arm to experience a mild
(but real) shock such as the one the learner would receive.

The subject was then led to an adjacent room where he or she
could hear, but not see, the learner. The subject was seated in
front of the shock generator, which was a box with 30 lever
switches, labeled in 15-volt increments from 15 to 450 volts. The
levers were also labeled with accompanying descriptions of the
shock intensities, ranging from "slight shock" to "danger: severe
shock." The last two switches were labeled "XXX." The experimenter informed the subject that he or she was to increase the
shock level by 15 volts with each incorrect answer given by the
learner.

After administering the first few shocks, the subject hears the
learner protest about the painfulness of the shocks. When the
shock level reaches 300 volts, the learner pounds on the wall in
protest and stops participating in the word-recall task. The learner
protests that his heart is bothering him, and his verbal protests
become agonizing screams. Eventually, there is complete silence
after each shock. Throughout the experiment, if the subject questions the procedure because of the learner's reaction, the experimenter responds by saying, "Please continue." If the subject expresses reluctance to continue, the experimenter says, "The
experiment requires that you continue." If the subject becomes
very insistent, the experimenter says, "You have no choice; you
must go on."

Unbeknownst to the subjects, the shocks delivered to the learner
are not real. Even though they believed they were delivering real
shocks, most people participating in this experiment (over 65%)
continued on until the very end, beyond the "danger: severe
shock" level and all the way to "XXX." One hundred percent of
all participants continued shocking the learner even after he pro-
tested that he was in pain.

There are obvious differences between the situation in which
Milgram's subjects found themselves and the situation of the passengers on Drayton and Brown's bus. Most prominently, unlike
in the Milgram experiments, no one was telling the bus passengers

"you must continue." But there are similarities also. Instead of an experimenter in a white lab coat expecting cooperation, the bus passengers faced a police officer with a badge (and a gun) expecting cooperation. Like the role of the white lab coat in the Milgram experiments, the role of the police officer's displayed badge in *Drayton* should not be underestimated. In *Drayton*, Officer Lang leaned in at close range and held up his badge. Despite Milgram's empirical demonstration of the power of authorities to command compliance, the Court flatly rejected the notion that a police badge exerts pressure on passengers, holding that factors such as the presence of badges, uniforms, or guns "should have little weight in the analysis."[58] At the same time that one officer leaned in close to passengers and displayed his badge, another officer had taken the driver's seat. With one officer in the back, one in the driver's seat, and another displaying his badge, the officers had essentially commandeered the bus. From the passengers' perspective, the message was clear that the bus was going nowhere until the officers were satisfied that they had received cooperation.[59] Aside from the obvious message that the continuation of the trip was dependent on the officers achieving their goal of receiving passenger cooperation, the more subtle message was conveyed through symbols of authority such as the officers' positioning on the bus and the display of the badge 12–18 inches from each passenger's face. Even though the police were not in uniform, the symbols of authority were quite strong. The main point here is that in both situations, people are coerced to comply when they would prefer to refuse.[60]

There is a parallel here to the phenomenon of "false confession," in which an innocent person confesses to a crime that he or she did not, in fact, commit.[61] Because of the situational pressures

---

[58] *Drayton*, 122 S Ct at 2112.

[59] "[T]he customary course of events was stopped flat. The bus was going nowhere, and with one officer in the driver's seat, it was reasonable to suppose no passenger would tend to his own business until the officers were ready to let him." *Drayton*, 122 S Ct at 2117 (Souter dissenting). There was also evidence in *Drayton* that, just prior to the officers boarding the bus, the driver had collected all passengers' tickets and brought them inside the terminal.

[60] "[T]here was no reason for any passenger to believe that the driver would return and the trip resume until the police were satisfied. The scene was set and an atmosphere of obligatory participation was established . . . ." *Drayton*, 122 S Ct at 2116 (Souter dissenting).

[61] See Saul M. Kassin and Katherine L. Kiechel, *The Social Psychology of False Confessions: Compliance, Internalization, and Confabulation*, 7 Psychol Sci 125 (1996). For discussions of actual false confession cases, see Hugo Bedau and M. Radelet, *Miscarriages of Justice in*

brought to bear by police, the false confessor is coerced to comply with the request to confess, when he or she would prefer to refuse.[62] Similarly, because of situational pressures brought to bear upon bus passengers, they also can be coerced to comply with the request to consent to a search of their luggage when they would prefer to refuse. Admittedly, the tactics that police typically use in false confession situations (lengthy interrogation, isolation, presentation of false evidence) are much more coercive than tactics used by members of drug interdiction police squads in bus sweeps. On the other hand, innocent bus passengers have much less to lose by complying with the police request to consent to search than do innocent suspects by complying with the police request to confess. Less pressure is used in the former situation, but less is also needed to gain compliance.

Additionally, in some situations very little pressure is needed to induce innocent people to confess to a transgression they did not commit. In a dramatic demonstration of false confession under minimal pressure, researchers brought individual subjects into the laboratory and asked them to perform a computer task. Subjects were warned not to press the "Alt" key or the computer would crash. At a preprogrammed moment, the computer did in fact crash, and the experimenter accused the subject of having hit the forbidden key. The experimenter then asked the subject to sign a written confession stating, "I hit the 'Alt' key and caused the program to crash. Data were lost." The consequence of this confession would be a phone call to the subject from the principal investigator of the experiment. A total of 69% of subjects signed the confession, admitting to a transgression that they did not in fact commit.[63] Sometimes the subject was confronted with false evidence in the form of a witness who said she saw the subject hit the forbidden key. When faced with false evidence, between 89% and 100% of all subjects confessed even though they were inno-

---

Potentially Capital Cases, 40 Stan L Rev 21 (1987); Richard A. Leo and Richard J. Ofshe, The Consequences of False Confessions: Deprivations of Liberty and Miscarriages of Justice in the Age of Psychological Interrogation, 88 J Crim L & Criminol 429 (1998).

[62] Not all false confessions involve coercion. A "voluntary" false confession is defined as one in which a person confesses in the absence of external pressure to do so. Kassin and Kiechel, 7 Psychol Sci at 125 (cited in note 61).

[63] See Kassin and Kiechel, 7 Psychol Sci at 127 (cited in note 61).

cent.[64] But even in the absence of false evidence, when the only pressure brought to bear was the experimenter asking the subject to sign the written confession, between 35% and 65% of subjects confessed even though they were innocent.[65]

In the experiment, in all instances when subjects signed the confession, they had been coerced to comply with a request that they (presumably) would have preferred to refuse. In the bus sweep situation, it is difficult to estimate how many passengers who in fact cooperated would have preferred to refuse. The *Drayton* majority implied that the number of bus passengers who would have preferred to refuse to consent to the police request to search was zero: "[B]us passengers answer officers' questions and otherwise cooperate not because of coercion but because the passengers know that their participation enhances their own safety and the safety of those around them."[66] The *Drayton* Court also decided, seemingly as a matter of law, that when a police officer asks a citizen for consent to search, and the citizen responds positively, such consent is voluntary. "When this exchange takes place, it dispels inferences of coercion."[67] Although it is difficult to estimate how many bus passengers who find themselves targets of a bus sweep would prefer to refuse the police officers' requests, evidence from the social psychology of compliance with authority discussed earlier strongly suggests that the Court is mistaken in inferring, as a matter of law, that no coercion exists so long as law enforcement asks passengers for consent. As for the question of whether citizens ever prefer to refuse a police request for consent to search, there is indeed evidence that some citizens do hold such preferences. I return to this topic in Section IV.A.

2. *Social validation.* In new or ambiguous situations, people often decide upon the correct course of action for themselves by following other people's actions.[68] The rule of thumb of "consensus

---

[64] The confession rate in the false-evidence (witness) condition was 89% when the task had required that subjects type slowly, and 100% when the task had required that subjects type quickly. Id at 127.

[65] The confession rate in the no-false-evidence (no witness) condition was 35% when the task had required that subjects type slowly, and 65% when the task had required that subjects type quickly. Id at 127.

[66] *Drayton*, 122 S Ct at 2113.

[67] Id at 2114.

[68] Cialdini and Trost, 2 *The Handbook of Social Psychology* at 155 (cited in note 45).

equals correctness" has been shown to influence behavior across a wide array of contexts. For example, amusement park visitors use this rule of thumb when deciding whether to litter;[69] pedestrians use it when deciding whether to stop and look up at an empty spot in the sky;[70] college students use it when deciding whether to donate blood;[71] and, sadly, troubled individuals use it when deciding whether to end their own lives.[72] In many situations, this rule of thumb makes a great deal of sense. For example, sometimes, to determine what to do, we need to first make sense of and attach meaning to the situation in which we find ourselves. For example, is that woman across the street in trouble, or is she engaging in horseplay with two male friends? To assess what is happening, we look around at others' reactions. If no one else seems concerned, then others have probably concluded it is horseplay. Therefore, when we decide that no action is necessary, this decision is based in part on the actions of others.

Obviously, the "consensus equals correctness" rule of thumb does not determine all of our behavior at all times. The extent to which we follow the decisions of other people depends, among other things, on the ambiguity of the situation, the number of other people present, and whether those other people are similar to oneself. People are especially likely to comply with a request when it appears that other people like themselves have already done so.[73] It is for this reason that bartenders often "salt" their tip jars at the beginning of their shift, and that political activists often display a long list of other people who have already signed onto the cause.

The socially validating effects of the decisions of similar others also explain why an onlooker in an emergency is unlikely to give

---

[69] See Robert Cialdini, Carl Kallgren, and Raymond Reno, *A Focus Theory of Normative Conduct: A Theoretical Refinement and Reevaluation of the Role of Norms in Human Behavior*, 24 Advances in Exp Soc Psychol 201, 203 (1991).

[70] Stanley Milgram, Leonard Bickman, and Lawrence Berkowitz, *Note on the Drawing Power of Crowds of Different Size*, 31 J Personality & Soc Psych 79 (1969).

[71] Peter H. Reingen, *Test of a List Procedure for Inducing Compliance with a Request to Donate Money*, 9 J Appl Psychol 110 (1982).

[72] There is evidence that news stories about suicide trigger additional suicides. See David P. Phillips and Laura L. Carstensen, *Clustering of Teenage Suicides After Television Stories About Suicide*, 315 New Engl J Med 685 (1986); David P. Phillips, *The Influence of Suggestion on Suicide: Substantive and Theoretical Implications of the Werther Effect*, 39 Am Soc Rev 340 (1979).

[73] Cialdini and Trost, 2 *The Handbook of Social Psychology* at 172 (cited in note 45).

aid when other bystanders are present. We try to infer from the way other people are acting whether what we are witnessing is a genuine emergency, or something else. Is that kid who is scream- ing "no!" being kidnapped or is he just having a tantrum outside his parents' car? Does the man lying across the sidewalk need help or is he just sleeping? Genuine emergencies are often not recog- nized as such when there are several bystanders; each person pres- ent decides that because nobody else looks worried, there must be nothing wrong. Ironically, often nobody else looks worried be- cause everyone is looking surreptitiously at the reactions of others to decide the seriousness of the situation.

Research on the automatic nature of social perception suggests that sometimes behavior can follow social perception quite auto- matically, without any conscious thought at all.[74] We often do what we see others doing not because we have consciously decided to do it, but rather as a natural consequence of the automatic activa- tion of behavioral representations that follow perceptions.[75] The simplest examples include yawning when we see someone else yawn, or scratching our head when we see someone else scratching their head.[76] We are not motivated to yawn or head scratch; we just do it because seeing someone else doing it activated the behavioral representation of the act, which in turn led, unthinkingly, to the behavior.[77] We also unconsciously imitate other people's posture[78] and tone of voice,[79] not because we are motivated to do so, but

[74] See Ap Dijksterhuis and John A. Bargh, *The Perception-Behavior Expressway: Automatic Effects of Social Perception on Social Behavior*, in Mark P. Zanna, ed, *Advances in Experimental Social Psychology* 1 (Academic, 2001).

[75] Id. This direct relation between perception and behavior is supported by neurophysio- logical evidence, which shows that thinking about a word, gesture, or complex action such as running or weightlifting leads to activation of the same neural pathways in the brain as actually uttering the word, making the gesture, or performing the action. See T. Paus, M. Petrides, A. C. Evans, and E. Meyer, *Role of Human Anterior Cingaluate Cortex in the Control of Oculomotor, Manual and Speech Responses*, 70 J Neurophysiol 453 (1993); M. Jeannerod, *The Representing Brain: Neural Correlates of Motor Intention and Imagery*, 17 Behavioral & Brain Sci 187 (1994).

[76] See, for example, Robert R. Provine, *Yawning as a Stereotypical Action Pattern and Releas- ing Stimulus*, 71 Ethology 109 (1986).

[77] Facial expression imitation can be observed in babies as young as one month old. See, for example, Andrew N. Meltzoff and Keith M. Moore, *Imitation of Facial and Manual Gestures by Human Neonates*, 198 Science 75 (1977).

[78] See Frank Bernieri, *Coordinated Movement and Rapport in Teacher-Student Interactions*, 12 J Nonverbal Behav 120 (1988).

[79] Roland Neumann and Fritz Strack, *"Mood Contagion": The Automatic Transfer of Mood Between Persons*, 79 J Personality & Soc Psychol 211 (2000).

rather because these processes are automatic and unintentional.[80] Interestingly, it is not always necessary actually to observe other people engaging in behavior for the automatic perception-behavior link to emerge. Sometimes it is enough for a stereotype of behavior to become activated in order to produce actual behavior associated with that stereotype. For example, people asked to write down all the typical attributes of college professors that they could think of performed better in a subsequent "Trivial Pursuit" game than those who were not asked to think about college professors; conversely, people (Europeans) asked to write down the typical attributes of soccer hooligans performed worse on a "Trivial Pursuit" task than those who were not.[81] Further, people asked to unscramble sentences containing some words (among other words) relating to the elderly (gray, Florida, bingo) subsequently walked more slowly when leaving the experiment (without realizing it) than people who unscrambled sentences without words relating to the elderly.[82] Finally, people asked to think about fast animals (cheetah, antelope) walked faster (without realizing it) to pick up a questionnaire in an adjacent room than did people asked to think about slow animals (snail, turtle).[83] In sum, observing others or even thinking about others doing an act can automatically lead to doing that act ourselves, even if we do not intend to, are not aware of doing so, or would prefer to do otherwise.

The influence of the behavior of others can be so great that people end up responding in a way that every bone in their body is telling them is wrong, but they do it anyway. The classic demonstration of the immense pressure exerted by social validation is Solomon Asch's 1950s studies on conformity.[84] The task in the experiment was simple. A board at the front of the room depicted several straight lines. On the left side of the board was a single

---

[80] Dijksterhuis and Bargh, 33 *Advances in Experimental Social Psychology* at 1 (cited in note 74).

[81] Ap Dijksterhuis and Ad van Knippenberg, *The Relation Between Perception and Behavior, or How to Win a Game of Trivial Pursuit*, 74 J Personality & Soc Psychol 865 (1998).

[82] John A. Bargh, Mark Chen, and L. Burrows, *Automaticity of Social Behavior: Direct Effects of Trait Construct and Stereotype Activation on Action* 71 J Personality & Soc Psychol 230 (1996).

[83] Henk Aarts and Ap Dijksterhuis, *Category Activation Effects in Judgment and Behaviour: The Moderating Role of Perceived Comparability*, 41 Brit J Soc Psychol 123 (2002).

[84] Solomon E. Asch, *Opinions and Social Pressure*, 193 Scientific Am 31 (1955).

"target" line. On the right side were three "comparison" lines. The subject was asked to choose the one comparison line that was the same length as the target line. The task was quite easy—participants working on their own chose the correct comparison line 98% of the time. This high accuracy rate decreased dramatically, however, when the subject publicly stated his or her judgment in the presence of several other "subjects,"[85] each of whom stated that the matching line was line B (rather than the correct answer, line A). In this situation, accuracy dropped precipitously, with over 75% of subjects giving wrong answers. In interviews after the experiment, subjects mentioned that they went along with the majority because they believed that the majority must have been right: either their own eyesight was failing them, or they misunderstood the instructions (maybe they were to judge line width, not length).[86] In this way, "the judgments of others are taken to be a more or less trustworthy source of information about the objective reality."[87] The appropriate response is powerfully dictated by the responses of others who went before.

At the same time, people doubt that they would succumb to social influence if they themselves were placed in the Asch experiment. When people are asked to predict what they themselves would do in a version of the Asch experiment, people predict that they would give a response contrary to everyone else in the group a much higher percentage of the time than is actually observed.[88] People are, of course, mistaken about this, but this mistake is the same mistake made by the Court when it asserted that a reasonable person would feel free to terminate the encounter with police once the cascade of acquiescence is under way.

Extreme examples of the powerful influence of the decisions and actions of other people who are similar to ourselves are not confined exclusively to artificially constructed laboratory situations. The immense power of social influence is illustrated in what has been called "perhaps the most spectacular act of compliance of our

---

[85] These other "subjects" were actually confederates who had been instructed in advance to answer incorrectly.

[86] Solomon E. Asch, *Studies of Independence and Conformity: I. A Minority of One Against a Unanimous Majority*, 70 Psychol Monogr 1 (1956).

[87] Morton Deutsch and Harold B. Gerard, *A Study of Normative and Informational Social Influences upon Individual Judgment*, 51 J Abnormal & Soc Psychol 629, 634 (1955).

[88] Wolosin, Sherman, and Cann, 43 J Personality at 372–76 (cited in note 37).

time"[89]—the mass suicide of over 900 people in Jonestown, Guyana, in 1978. The leader of the People's Temple, Jim Jones, had moved the group from San Francisco to a jungle settlement in South America about a year before the tragedy.[90] When Congressman Leo R. Ryan went to Guyana on a fact-finding mission, he was murdered, along with several others. Within hours of the murders, Jones assembled the entire group for a final gathering and called on everyone in the community to commit suicide en masse. Amazingly, nearly everyone—over 900 people—did so.[91] The first volunteer was a young woman who administered the now-famous cyanide-laced drink to her baby and to herself. According to the few people who escaped and survived, the vast majority of the people who followed did so calmly, willfully, and with no evidence of panic.[92]

Undoubtedly, many factors led to this act of mass suicide, including the charisma of the leader and the religious nature of the group, among other things. The scale of the mass suicide was so enormous that it is tempting to posit overly simple explanations such as "they did it because they were brainwashed cult members." But this "explanation" begs the question of what led to such an unthinkable event. It is improbable that all 900 otherwise mentally healthy, normal people had been transformed into automatons, so each act in their daily lives was dictated by the groups' leaders. Perhaps this is plausible for a handful of intensely loyal followers. But it is hard to imagine that it was true for 900 people.

An explanation based on social validation suggests that at the crucial moment of decision about whether to end their lives, the isolated, unfamiliar, jungle environment that group members found themselves in left them ready to follow the lead of others.[93]

---

[89] Cialdini, *Influence: Science and Practice* at 130 (cited in note 53).

[90] Id.

[91] Over 200 children died. The children were made to swallow the poison by adults. See Marc Galanter, *Cults: Faith, Healing, and Coercion* at 114 (Oxford, 2d ed 1999).

[92] Cialdini, *Influence: Science and Practice* at 132 (cited in note 53); see also Galanter, *Cults* at 114 (cited in note 91) ("The amount of force exerted to complete the mass suicide varied among the members. For most, no coercion was necessary; only a small minority acted under overt threats from Jones's henchmen, who were brandishing firearms.").

[93] Id at 132–33.

The only other similar people for miles around were other group members. Upon receiving Jones's fatal command, they looked around at their fellow community members. The few who were fanatically obedient willingly took the poison—a strong signal to the rest of the group that this was the right thing to do. The reaction of the rest of the group—that of assessing the situation—was interpreted as patient turn-taking. The genius of Jim Jones, then, was not necessarily his charisma and dynamic personal style, but his arranging of environmental conditions so that the isolation and unfamiliarity of the surroundings would prompt the vast majority of the group to be entirely dependent on observing similar others to decide how they themselves should act.[94]

At the point when the officers had approached Drayton and Brown, they had already addressed three other passengers, none of whom attempted to terminate the encounter. In addition, the officers had already requested consent to search from one of the other passengers, which was granted. Using the rule of thumb that consensus equals correctness, a reasonable innocent person in Drayton's and Brown's shoes would have concluded that consenting was the correct thing to do. There were 25–30 passengers on the bus. No one asked the officers why they were doing what they were doing or questioned them. All passengers they addressed did what was asked unquestioningly. No one tried to get up and leave. No one tried to interfere or even politely intervene. All signals pointed to polite cooperation as the rule of the day. In a totality of the circumstances analysis of whether a reasonable person would have felt free to refuse the officer's requests or terminate the encounter, the influence of the "consensus equals correctness" heuristic on decisions to comply is a factor that must be considered, and one that law enforcement conducting bus sweeps use to their advantage.[95]

---

[94] Id.

[95] As Drayton's and Brown's attorneys point out, "the Tallahassee Police Department's bus interdictions are routinized, scripted events." See *Drayton*, Respondent's Brief at 26. The police appeared to have made a conscious decision to question passengers on the bus, where they could expect (based on hundreds of prior bus sweeps) each passenger to observe other passengers' compliance with requests for information and for consent to search. Drayton, Brown, and all other passengers on the bus were required to exit the bus during the stopover in Tallahassee. The police began watching Drayton and Brown inside the bus terminal at noon, but waited until they had reboarded the bus some 40 minutes later to

C. SOCIAL CONTEXT, POLITENESS, AND THE LOGIC
OF CONVERSATION

In its analysis of the totality of the circumstances, the *Drayton* opinion focused heavily on the tone of the conversation between the police officer and the citizens. The Court pointed to the officer's quiet and polite tone of voice, the fact that he did not state or suggest that citizens he spoke with were required to answer, that he talked to passengers one by one, and that he did not say or suggest that passengers could not leave the bus or could not terminate the encounter. The Court noted that the encounter contained "no threat, no command, not even an authoritative tone of voice." Focusing on the officer who kneeled backward in the driver's seat to observe the passengers, the Court noted that he "did nothing to intimidate passengers, and he said nothing to suggest that people could not exit and indeed he left the aisle clear."

Similarly, in analyzing the consent to search issue, the Court pointed out that "[n]othing Officer Lang said indicated a command to consent to the search. . . . Rather he asked for . . . permission . . ." and that when the officer first requested to search their persons "he asked first if they objected thus indicating to a reasonable person that they were free to refuse." Even after arresting Brown, the officer "provided no indication [to Drayton] that he was required to consent to a search." To the contrary, Lang asked for Drayton's permission to search him ("Mind if I check you?"). After dismissing the notion that the officer must warn the citizen that he has a right to refuse the request to search, the Court concluded: "[a]lthough Officer Lang did not inform respondents of their right to refuse the search, he did request permission to search, and the totality of the circumstances indicates that their consent was voluntary, so the searches were reasonable."

Focusing narrowly on the tone and language used by the police makes plausible the notion that voluntary cooperation and consent were the only thoughts on the minds of passengers on the bus that day. But the Court's intense focus on precisely what Officer Lang did and did not say is problematic, because in doing so it neglected

---

question them. See *Drayton*, Joint Appendix at 108, 139. Instead of questioning Drayton and Brown privately in the relatively open confines of the terminal, the police questioned them in the close confines of a cramped bus seat, in an atmosphere where each passenger sees and hears that others are cooperating with police.

what the passengers actually experienced when they listened to the officers' polite tone and requests for permission. As Herbert Clark, widely recognized as a prominent scientific psychologist in the area of pragmatics,[96] has stated:

> [It is a] common misperception that language use has primarily to do with words and what they mean. It doesn't. It has primarily to do with people and what they mean. It is essentially about speakers' intentions.[97]

Therefore, any analysis of the conversations that took place between the officers and the passengers on the bus that Drayton and Brown rode on should not focus on the precise words that were spoken or not spoken in light of what those words generally mean and how we (as people outside the context of the bus) understand them. Instead, the analysis should focus on what the officers meant and intended and, more importantly, on the bus passengers' understanding of the officers' meaning and intention.

From the passengers' perspective, the officers appeared to board the bus with a specific goal in mind. The fact that a police officer was occupying the driver's seat in the absence of the driver gives rise to the natural inference that the officers intend to achieve their goal before the bus would continue on its regular route. Officer Lang testified that he approached each individual passenger, introduced himself while holding his badge, and told the passenger that he was looking for illegal drugs and weapons. Officer Lang announced his goal at the outset, and the meaning of the speaker's intentions was therefore clear to the passenger: he is a police officer (an authority) and intends to look for illegal contraband.

Having understood the speaker's meaning and intentions, the next thing that the passengers heard was an indirect request: "Would you mind if I searched your bag?"[98] Phrased directly, the

---

[96] Pragmatics is the study of how context influences how we interpret the meaning of language. See Victoria Fromkin and Robert Rodman, *An Introduction to Language* 189 (Holt, Rinehart & Winston, 3d ed 1983); Steven Pinker, *The Language Instinct* 480 (Harper Perennial, 1994).

[97] Herbert H. Clark and Michael F. Schober, *Asking Questions and Influencing Answers*, in J. M. Tanur, ed, *Questions About Questions* 15, 15 (Russell Sage Foundation, 1992).

[98] An indirect request ("Could you tell me what time it is?") is a polite way of uttering a command ("Tell me the time."). See Herbert H. Clark and Eve V. Clark, *Psychology and Language* 244–45, 563 (Harcourt Brace Jovanovich, 1977). The way in which an utterance is interpreted can vary drastically depending on the context. For example, if I say to a friend, "Would you like to go to the movies?" this generally will be interpreted as a question. But

request would be something like: "Let me search your bag." The question "Would you mind if . . ." is interpreted as the same thing as the direct request, but phrased more politely. The indirect request is more polite because it threatens the listener's status less than the direct request. So in all likelihood, this statement was interpreted by passengers as the officers informing the passenger what he would do, albeit in a polite fashion.[99]

The context of discourse is crucial in the understanding of it;[100] this is especially true when the speaker is making a request.[101] Perceived coercion is determined by the speaker's authority and the speaker's language working together. Because authorities such as police officers direct the actions of others, the listener is likely to conclude that an utterance is in fact a directive, or an order to be followed.[102] For example, citizens generally do not interpret "Can I please see your license and registration?" as spoken by a police officer as a genuine request; it is a command, and everyone understands this. Furthermore, certain contextual features are taken as cues as to the overall understanding of an event. Importantly, authority figures do not need to employ highly face-threatening language to achieve their goal.[103] In fact, a polite request is usually perceived by the listener as being face-maintaining because the listener understands that coercion may be used. Thus, a police officer who says, "Do you mind if I search your bags?" is perceived as being more face-sensitive than one who says, "I am going to search your bags"; at the same time, the listener in both situations

---

if I say to my son, "Would you like to wash the dishes?" this is actually a command, even though phrased in the form of a question. See Peter Meijes Tiersma, *The Language of Offer and Acceptance: Speech Acts and the Question of Intent*, 74 Cal L Rev 189, 194 (1986).

[99] See Tiersma, 74 Cal L Rev at 194 (cited in note 98) ("[a] familiar convention allows one to make a command more polite by superficially offering a choice, as in 'How would you like to do me a favor and open the door?'").

[100] See, for example, Johnny I. Murdock, James J. Bradac, and John W. Bowers, *Effects of Power on the Perception of Explicit and Implicit Threats, Promises, and Thromises: A Rule-Governed Perspective*, 48 Western J Speech Comm 344, 356 (1984).

[101] Judith A. Becker, Herbert Kimmel, and Michael J. Bevill, *The Interactive Effects of Request Form and Speaker Status on Judgments of Requests*, 18 J Psycholinguistic Res 521, 529 (1989).

[102] Thomas Holtgraves, *Communication in Context: Effects of Speaker Status on the Comprehension of Indirect Requests*, 20 J Exp Psychol: Learning, Memory, & Cognition 1205 (1994).

[103] In communication, maintaining face means preserving a person's positive personal and social identity (positive face) as well as maintaining freedom from constraint and avoiding violations of autonomy (negative face). See Penelope Brown and Stephen C. Levinson, *Politeness: Some Universals in Language Usage* 62 (Cambridge, 1987). In conversation, people try to maintain the face of the person to whom they are speaking (as well as their own). Id.

realizes he or she must comply with the message. Thus, because a police officer is perceived as an authority, he need not rely on coercive statements to achieve a goal—his role is adequate, and a polite request can increase face-sensitivity without reducing coercive power.[104] Because a coercive threat underlies any kind of confrontation regarding a potential rule violation,[105] the possibility of the officer's exercising the authority of the government influences the listener's understanding of the episode. Because people perceive discourse originating from an authority to be coercive regardless of assertive linguistic cues, authority figures need not use highly face-threatening language—part of that burden is carried by the badge and gun.[106] When discourse is framed as a suggestion (rather than imperative), and when the listener believes that he or she must comply anyway (due to the authority of the speaker), the suggestion is taken as a sign that the authority is being sensitive to face.[107]

The influence of the speaker's authority on perceived meaning has been demonstrated empirically. In one study, participants assumed the role of an employee who was late for work.[108] The employee was advised, either by her boss or by her co-worker, not to be late anymore. The results revealed that when a peer is speaking, the listener perceives imperatives ("don't be late again") as more coercive than suggestions ("try not to be late again"). But when an authority (such as the boss) is speaking, there is no such difference in perceived coercion—forcefulness of language does not matter. The authors conclude, "those who have authority apparently need not activate coercive potential through their discourse. Their roles are sufficient to do so."[109] So, when authorities

---

[104] Jennifer L. Vollbrecht, Michael E. Roloff, and Gaylen D. Paulson, *Coercive Potential and Face Threatening Sensitivity: The Effects of Authority and Directives in Social Confrontations*, 8 Intl J Conflict Mgmt 235, 236 (1997).

[105] Here, the rule violation is the carrying of illegal contraband. The authorities are police officers. So the rule violation is also a formal violation of the law.

[106] This point was understood by Justice Souter, who, in his dissent in *Drayton*, wrote that "a police officer who is certain to get his way has no need to shout." *Drayton*, 122 S Ct at 2116–17.

[107] See Peter Tiersma, *The Judge as Linguist*, 27 Loyola LA L Rev 269, 282 (1993) (arguing that the power relationship between police and citizen suggests that when police make a request that they could apparently compel, the request will be viewed as a command).

[108] Vollbrecht, Roloff, and Gaylen, 8 Intl J Conflict Mgmt at 244 (cited in note 104).

[109] Id.

use softened discourse—suggestions rather than imperatives—they can exert control without being face-threatening.

In *Drayton*, the Court apparently ignored the empirical evidence demonstrating the powerful influence of contextual factors (such as the authority of the speaker) in how listeners interpret the coerciveness of language.[110] Instead, the *Drayton* majority appears to have simply substituted the intuitive judgment of its members regarding how they would interpret a police officer's request to search had they been passengers on the bus. For example, during oral argument in *Drayton*, Justice Scalia made clear that his own personal intuition is that the literal meaning of the words of the police officer would "counteract" contextual cues suggesting compulsion, such as the placement of one of the officers in the driver's seat of the bus.[111] The majority's opinion also reflects this intuition in its emphasis on the literal meaning of the words spoken by the officer: "[n]othing Officer Lang said indicated a command to consent to the search. . . . Rather he asked for . . . permission. . . ." Again, the intuition expressed by the Court is that literal meaning overpowers contextual meaning. Unfortunately, these intuitions are not supported by the data. Rather, the available data strongly suggest that quite the opposite is the case: the meaning of the police officer's words was strongly influenced by context, so that the police officer's statement to bus passengers, "Do you mind if I search?" was interpreted in these circumstances as a command, not a request for permission. In sum, the politeness of the officer's words, so heavily emphasized by the Court, does not give rise to the inference that passengers thereby felt free to refuse the officers' requests or terminate the encounter.

D. PERSONAL SPACE, STATUS, AND COMPLIANCE

Studies of interpersonal distance and compliance have demonstrated that people feel more pressure to comply with a request when the requester speaks to them from a close physical distance

---

[110] The Court was informed of this empirical evidence in the Brief for the Respondents. Brief of Respondents at 42 n 4.

[111] Official Transcript of Oral Argument, *Drayton* at 46. Specifically, Justice Scalia asked, "Why . . . is it that the most immediate expression of the police officers does not counteract whatever other indications of compulsion might exist under the circumstances? . . . [T]here's a policeman in the front of the bus. Who cares? He . . . has made it very clear that he's asking for your permission."

(1–2 feet).[112] For example, in one study, students sitting alone in a cafeteria were approached and asked whether they would be willing to participate in a study for no compensation.[113] Students who were approached at a close distance (12–18 inches) were more likely to comply with the request than students approached from a further distance (36–48 inches). Interestingly, the experimenters chose a distance of 12–18 inches—the same distance chosen by Officer Lang in *Drayton*—specifically to ensure that participants' sense of personal space was violated. (It was.)[114] In other studies, invasion of personal space led to higher rates of compliance when adults were approached on the street with a request to make change,[115] and when college students were approached by other students on campus with a request to sign a petition.[116]

Personal space can be defined as "the area individuals maintain around themselves into which others cannot intrude without arousing discomfort."[117] This zone of discomfort varies to some extent across individuals and situations. But, generally speaking, the degree of discomfort experienced is proportional to the degree of intrusion into one's personal space.[118] Thus, in one study, subjects approached by another person reported feeling "slightly uncomfortable" at about 27 inches, "moderately uncomfortable" at about 20 inches, and "very uncomfortable" at about 12 inches.[119] People who feel that their personal space is being invaded display reactions of stress and physiological arousal,[120] which are experi-

[112] Chris Segrin, *The Influence of Nonverbal Behaviors in Compliance-Gaining Processes*, in Laura K. Guerrero, Joseph A. DeVito, and Michael L. Hecht, eds, *The Nonverbal Communication Reader: Classic and Contemporary Readings* (Waveland, 1990).

[113] Robert A. Baron and Paul A. Bell, *Physical Distance and Helping: Some Unexpected Benefits of "Crowding In" on Others*, 6 J Appl Soc Psychol 95 (1976).

[114] A questionnaire administered after the experiment revealed that students approached at a distance of 12–18 inches felt more tense and uncomfortable than students approached at a distance of 36–48 inches. Id.

[115] Robert C. Ernest and Ralph E. Cooper, *"Hey Mister, Do You Have Any Change?" Two Real World Studies of Proxemic Effects on Compliance with a Mundane Request*, 1 Personality & Soc Psychol Bulletin 158 (1974).

[116] David B. Buller, *Communication Apprehension and Reactions to Proxemic Violations*, 11 J Nonverbal Behav 13 (1987).

[117] Leslie A. Hayduk, *Personal Space: Where We Now Stand*, 94 Psychol Bulletin 293, 293 (1983).

[118] Id at 298.

[119] Id.

[120] Id at 319.

enced subjectively as bewilderment and embarrassment.[121] They may assume a defensive posture, or try to move away.[122] If these initial acts are ignored they may try to flee from the "space invader."[123] Most of these "coping tactics," of course, were not possible on the bus.

When deciding how close is too close, authority roles matter. People naturally provide high-status individuals with more personal space than low-status individuals.[124] Even though we are not usually aware of it, we show special deference to high-status people by keeping a distance from them. The prerogative to invade others' space resides with people who have higher status and power.[125] Law enforcement officials are well aware of this phenomenon and exercise their prerogative to their advantage. For example, one widely used police textbook recommends that the interrogator should begin the interrogation by sitting a few feet from the suspect, with no table or desk in between because an obstruction of any sort "affords a guilty suspect a certain degree of relief and confidence not otherwise attainable."[126] The authors recommend that the interrogator gradually move his chair closer so that the suspect's knees are almost between the interrogator's knees.[127] This technique was also used successfully by the officers on the bus in *Drayton*, where Officer Lang placed his face 12–18 inches away from each passenger he addressed.

Also relevant here is the finding that in particular physical environments people prefer more space, including when they are in a corner (as was defendant Brown in *Drayton*; he was sitting in the window seat), under a low ceiling (as were all bus passengers—the overhead rack was only 19 inches above them), in a stressful

---

[121] Nancy J. Felipe and Robert Sommer, *Invasions of Personal Space*, 14 Soc Problems 206 (1966).

[122] Robert Sommer, *Personal Space: The Behavioral Basis of Design* at 35 (Prentice-Hall, 1969).

[123] Id.

[124] Peter A. Anderson and Linda L. Bowman, *Positions on Power: Nonverbal Influence in Organizational Communication*, in Laura K. Guerrero, Joseph A. DeVito, and Michael L. Hecht, eds, *The Nonverbal Communication Reader: Classic and Contemporary Readings* (Waveland, 1990).

[125] Id.

[126] Frederick E. Inbau and John E. Reid, *Criminal Interrogation and Confessions* 80 (Aspen, 4th ed 2001).

[127] Id at 339–40.

situation (as were, presumably, all passengers approached and addressed by the police), or expecting a hostile encounter (as some
might have been when approached by a police officer whose announced intention was to investigate his suspicion that passengers
are carrying drugs or weapons).[128]

In sum, people approached at a close distance by an authority
in a tightly enclosed space with no opportunity to move further
away or leave feel discomfort and tension; at the same time, people
who find their space invaded in this manner are more willing to
comply with the request of the person making them feel uncomfortable. Compliance in the face of discomfort, anxiety, and tension strongly suggests that in bus sweep situations, passengers are
coerced to comply with a request that they would prefer to refuse—the *Bostick* Court's very definition of involuntary consent.

E. TIME PRESSURE, SCRIPTED CONFORMITY, AND MINDLESSNESS

Bus passengers like Drayton and Brown who are approached by
police and asked to submit to a search are necessarily under time
pressure to provide an immediate answer. Requesting a few days
or even a few minutes to think it over is not a viable option because the bus is in a temporary stopover city and police typically
begin their "sweep" minutes before the bus is scheduled to depart.
Also, the pragmatics of conversation demand that pauses or silence
not last more than a few seconds, lest they be interpreted as evasive
or otherwise uncooperative.

Given this time pressure, there is a question whether passengers
say yes when they would prefer to say no, and would have said no
had they been given more time to decide. This might be the case.
As an illustrative example, consider one town's effort to curb unsupervised underage drinking in private homes. The local police
in Ridgewood, New Jersey, mailed out 2,700 consent forms to
households with teenage children, requesting permission from the
homeowners to allow police to enter and search their home if the

---

[128] Hayduk, 94 Psychol Bulletin at 318 (cited in note 117). Note that, depending on one's
race, socioeconomic status, or prior personal contact with the police, some citizens might
be more likely than others to expect a hostile encounter. Demographic differences in police-
citizen interactions become relevant in the context of intercity bus travel because passengers
are disproportionately poor, nonwhite, and less educated. See note 194.

police receive a report of teenage drinking in their home.[129] Only 20 forms were signed and returned. This minuscule positive response rate stands in stark contrast to the very large percentage of bus passengers that consent to the police request to search.[130] As pointed out earlier, the large percentage of passengers who agree to a search is not, in itself, evidence of coercion. But the large difference in consent rates between citizens under severe time pressure and citizens under no time pressure to make a decision suggests that time pressure might be a factor causing passengers to say yes when they would prefer to say no.

Empirical research does suggest that time pressure affects decisions. Decisions made under time pressure use different processes from decisions made without time stress. Many studies have documented that time pressure reduces the effectiveness of decision making.[131] People making decisions under time pressure engage in what has been termed "premature closure": they end their decision process prior to considering all the relevant information and alternatives.[132] For example, people solving problems under time pressure fail to consider relevant information that people not under time pressure successfully do consider.[133] They also engage in defensive reactions, such as denying the importance of pieces of information.[134] People making decisions under time pressure tend to rely on "accessible constructs"[135] like stereotypes. For example, people who are asked to make a judgment about what another person does for a living are more likely to rely on stereotypical infor-

---

[129] Robert Hanley, *An Anti-Drinking Campaign and How It Flopped*, NY Times B1 (Sept 28, 1994). Cited in Strauss, 92 J Crim L & Criminol at 266 n 195 (cited in note 18).

[130] Of course, any given face-to-face request may be more effective than a corresponding mailed request simply because mailed requests are more easily discarded or ignored. But the low compliance rate in this example is nonetheless illustrative.

[131] See, for example, Dan Ariely and Dan Zakay, *A Timely Account of the Role of Duration in Decision Making*, 108 Acta Psychologica 187, 197 (2001); Irving L. Janis, *Stress, Attitude, and Decisions* (Praeger, 1982).

[132] See Irving L. Janis, *Decision Making Under Stress*, in L. Goldberger and S. Breznitz, eds, *Handbook of Stress* (Free Press, 1982); Jay J. J. Christiansen-Szalanski, *A Further Examination of the Selection of Problem-Solving Strategies: The Effects of Deadlines and Analytic Aptitudes*, 25 Organizational Behav & Human Decision Processes 107 (1980).

[133] See Edward M. Bowden, *Accessing Relevant Information During Problem Solving: Time Constraints on Search in the Problem Space*, 13 Memory & Cognition 280, 284 (1985).

[134] See Ariely and Zakay, 108 Acta Psychologica at 197 (cited in note 131).

[135] See Chi-yue Chiu, Michael W. Morris, Ying-yi Hong, and Tanya Menon, *Motivated Cultural Cognition: The Impact of Implicit Cultural Theories on Dispositional Attribution Varies as a Function of Need for Closure*, 78 J Personality & Soc Psychol 247, 255–56 (2000).

mation if their judgment is made under time pressure, and to fail to consider alternatives compared to decisions not made under time pressure.[136] People under time pressure immediately seize onto the first information that grabs their attention and will ignore other more diagnostic information.[137] So, people deciding whether a target person is a painter focus on information stereotypical of painters and ignore information that would rule out other related professions such as architects.

In most of the research on decision making under time pressure, the decision tasks used are ones where there is an objectively correct answer; these studies show that time pressure can cause people to be less accurate or to choose the wrong answer.[138] This is because cognitive functioning, as a general matter, declines under stresses like time pressure.[139] But even when decisions involve choosing the best alternative for oneself, as opposed to choosing an objectively correct answer, the effects of time pressure operate in the same way. This suggests that because the passengers on the bus on which Drayton and Brown were riding were faced with a police officer demanding an immediate response, the passengers may have engaged in "premature closure" when they consented to converse with the officers and to allow them to search their baggage. Even seemingly small stresses, such as the presence of other people in the same room when we are responding to an unfamiliar problem, can lead to physiological responses that make us feel threatened and compromise our ability to reason and think.[140] The decision processes used by passengers who were confronted in a public place, and who were feeling pressure to respond imme-

[136] See Arie W. Kruglanski and Ofra Mayseless, *Contextual Effects in Hypothesis Testing: The Rule of Competing Alternatives and Epistemic Motivations*, 6 Soc Cognition 1, 12–17 (1988).

[137] Id.

[138] See, for example, John W. Payne, James R. Bettman, and Mary Frances Luce, *When Time Is Money: Decision Behavior Under Opportunity-Cost Time Pressure*, 66 Organizational Behav & Human Decision Processes 131 (1996); Jose H. Kerstholt, *The Effect of Time Pressure on Decision-Making Behaviour in a Dynamic Task Environment*, 86 Acta Psychologica 89 (1994); Edward M. Bowden, *Accessing Relevant Information During Problem Solving: Time Constraints on Search in the Problem Space*, 13 Memory & Cognition 280 (1985); Dan Zakay and Stuart Wooler, *Time Pressure, Training and Decision Effectiveness*, 27 Ergonomics 273 (1984).

[139] See Ariely and Zakay, 108 Acta Psychologica at 197 (cited in note 131).

[140] See Jim Blascovich and Joe Tomaka, *The Biopsychosocial Model of Arousal Regulation*, 28 Advances in Exp Soc Psychol 1, 23–24 (1996) (reporting that people asked to solve math problems in the presence of a friend experience increased physiological responses (heart rate and blood pressure) and worse math performance compared to those solving math problems in the absence of a friend).

diately to police requests, were likely to be characterized by reliance on implicit cultural theories and norms[141] (such as "police officers must be obeyed") and by a failure to consider information that might have counseled against agreeing to be searched.

Such failure to consider all relevant information is predictable in light of the fact that human understanding of the social world is largely dependent on scripts.[142] A script is a "mental representation of a social situation as it unfolds over time."[143] Once a script is activated, it allows us more easily to interpret our perceptions and observations in a given situation. Events that always follow the same order become chronically associated, so that when we experience the first event we expect the next one to follow.[144] In fact, when we are mentally ready to perceive an event in a standard situation, we often carry out what would be the next event in the script even when the prior event did not occur, simply because the superficial features of the situation had followed the same form as the script.[145]

Ordinary people have numerous event scripts at their disposal—for restaurants, funerals, weddings, the classroom, and so on. For instance, the student script for a classroom involves finding one's seat, facing the front of the classroom, and speaking only when it is appropriate to do so. Deviations from the script (standing up, speaking out of turn, clipping one's toenails, etc.) are bound to elicit looks of surprise from others. In fact, flouting of event scripts is often the premise for humor.[146] Scripts are used so often that we rely on them without ever thinking about it—scripts are both automatic and pervasive.[147] Early use of scripts (such as the first

---

[141] See Chiu et al, 78 J Personality & Soc Psychol at 256 (cited in note 135).

[142] Roger C. Schank and Robert P. Abelson, *Scripts, Plans, Goals, and Understanding* 36–68 (Erlbaum, 1977).

[143] John A. Bargh, *Automaticity in Social Psychology*, in Tory Higgins and Arie W. Kruglanski, eds, *Social Psychology: Handbook of Basic Principles* 169, 179 (Erlbaum, 1996).

[144] Id.

[145] Ellen J. Langer, Arthur Blank, and Benzion Chanowitz, *The Mindlessness of Ostensibly Thoughtful Action: The Role of "Placebic" Information in Interpersonal Interaction*, 36 J Personality & Soc Psychol 635, 641 (1978).

[146] Consider a recent television show (called "Spy TV"), the humorous premise of which is based on the incongruence of social scripts (such as a man shaving at his lunch table) and the reactions of others that ensue. The final product is considered humorous because we so rarely see people flout implicitly agreed-upon scripts.

[147] Ellen J. Langer and Allison I. Piper, *The Prevention of Mindlessness*, 53 J Personality & Soc Psychol 280, 280 (1987).

time in a restaurant) requires thoughtful and conscious attention.[148] But once we become accustomed to relying on a particular script, it no longer requires the same level of conscious deliberation. This automatic activation and use of scripts is fortunate because without them we would suffer from cognitive overload.

Even though interacting with police is not something most people do on a daily basis, we are exposed to depictions of such interactions frequently in the popular press and other forms of popular culture—television, movies, and novels. As a result of these depictions, our script for interacting with police officers undoubtedly involves ready cooperation and compliance with requests.[149] Automatic processing of scripts is intensified when the script involves interacting with an authority. In making an on-the-spot decision about whether to comply with the request of an authority, people's actions are best characterized by "reacting, not thinking"—in other words, people often react and respond to legitimate authority in a mindless, automatic, thoughtless, fast, and shallow manner with little processing.[150] Similarly, complying with an officer's request to search may fit into a well-learned script of cooperating with legitimate authorities. Such compliance occurs automatically once a script is engaged, so that bus passengers, for example, regularly and uniformly relinquish control of their personal belongings to police officers, even if, had they been asked the question, "Would you voluntarily agree to allow a police officer looking for drugs to search your luggage?" they may, given a different context that allows opportunity for reflection, answer "no."

III. Applying the Evidence: Perspective Is Everything

A. PERCEIVING COERCION

From the earlier discussion, we know that some of the factors that have been reliably shown to lead to coercion (authority, social validation, pragmatics of politeness, time pressure, personal space,

[148] John A. Bargh, *The Automaticity of Everyday Life*, in R. Wyer, ed, 10 *The Automaticity of Everyday Life: Advances in Social Cognition* 1, 29 (Erlbaum, 1997).

[149] See Jones, 122 *Interpersonal Perception* at 50 (cited in note 32).

[150] Cialdini, *Influence: Science and Practice* at 186 (cited in note 53); see, for example, Roger Schank and Robert P. Abelson, *Scripts, Plans, Goals, and Understanding: An Inquiry into Human Knowledge Structures* (Erlbaum, 1977); Bargh, *Automaticity in Social Psychology* at 170 (cited in note 143).

and scripted conformity) were present in the situation in which Drayton and Brown (and the other bus passengers) found themselves. But how do we know that the passengers acquiesced to the search because they were coerced, rather than for other reasons? In this sense, the bus situation is unlike the situation in some of the studies discussed above, where coercion can be safely inferred solely from the person's behavior. For example, in the Milgram studies, (most) people clearly had a preference to refrain from hurting another human being. If only a small proportion of subjects had complied, we would have to consider the possibility that those subjects were actually acting consistently with their preferences—these are the few sadists who actually prefer to harm another human. But, in fact, 100% of subjects in Milgram's experiments administered shocks at the point when the subject was apparently being harmed. Assuming that most people prefer not to harm others without justification, we can infer that most (if not all) subjects were coerced into complying with the experimenter and did an act that they preferred not to do.

In *Drayton*, the preference not to engage with the officers or consent to the search cannot be inferred so readily. It is plausible that a sizable proportion of citizens approached actually preferred to engage with the officer and consent to the search, out of a sense of good citizenship, civic virtue, or some similar sentiment. If, however, a certain proportion of people that the police approached preferred not to consent, but did so because they felt coerced, how would we know this? The fact that no one says "no" is certainly consistent with coercion, but it does not prove coercion, because it could be the case that the low refusal rate is most accurately explained by people's strong sense of good citizenship and civic virtue. One way to find out is to ask people. The study described next did just that. We have no direct evidence to address whether a reasonable person present on Drayton and Brown's bus that day would have felt free to terminate the encounter or refuse consent. No one did a poll of that bus or (apparently) any other bus: there appear to be no studies examining coercion in the bus sweep situation. But there is a study examining another voluntary consent situation: the highway stop.

From the perspective of the police officers, their interactions with citizens on the bus during the sweeps are completely noncoercive. They simply board the bus and engage in friendly conversation. As Officer Lang put it, "I [was] being friendly and courteous. . . . I [was] just talking to them in a nice tone of voice."[151] The majority in *Drayton* apparently was deeply impressed with the lack of coercion that was plain from the police perspective. In its analysis of whether a seizure took place, the majority focused exclusively on the behavior of the police—what they did and, even more, what they did not do. The majority asserted that the police gave the passengers no reason to believe that they were required to answer the officers' questions.[152] Specifically, the Court noted that the officers did not brandish their weapons or make any intimidating movements.[153] They did not block the aisle. They spoke to each passenger individually in a polite, quiet voice. They said nothing to suggest passengers were prohibited from leaving or otherwise ending the conversation. The police did not use force, nor did they make "an overwhelming show of force." They did not make threats. They did not use commands. They did not even use an authoritative tone of voice. Thus, from the perspective of the police, the encounter with each passenger was far from coercive, but was instead polite, friendly, and informal.

Perspective, however, is everything. It is extremely unlikely that the targets of the police inquiry and search—the bus passengers—experienced the encounter in the same way as the police. An atmosphere interpreted as noncoercive and voluntary from the perspective of the police can at the same time be experienced as coercive and nonvoluntary from the perspective of a reasonable (innocent) person who is the target of police suspicion.[154] This crucial difference in perceived voluntariness arising from differences in perspec-

---

[151] *Drayton*, Joint Appendix at 58.

[152] *Drayton*, 122 S Ct at 2112

[153] Officer Lang's display of his badge and simultaneous placement of his face 12–18 inches from the face of each passenger was likely to have been experienced by the passengers as intimidating. But because Officer Lang was "trying to be friendly" and because the Court adopted the perspective of the police, an action experienced by passengers as intimidating was interpreted as not intimidating.

[154] In fact, citizen ratings of the intrusiveness of many different police search and seizure scenarios reveal that a scenario involving the police "boarding a bus and asking to search luggage" is perceived as among the most intrusive of all police actions, on a par with the searching of residences. See Christopher Slobogin and Joseph E. Schumacher, *Reasonable Expectations of Privacy and Autonomy in Fourth Amendment Cases: An Empirical Look at "Understandings Recognized and Permitted by Society,"* 42 Duke L J 727, 735–42 (1993). Out of 50 different scenarios, citizens ranked the bus sweep scenario as the seventh most intrusive invasion of privacy or autonomy; average ratings of the bus sweep scenario placed it as even more intrusive than police "questioning on a public sidewalk for ten minutes." Id.

tive has been firmly demonstrated as an empirical matter, as I discussed earlier. In the next section, I review survey evidence that suggests that citizens confronted by police requesting consent to search accede to those requests because of the situational constraints examined in the various empirical studies reviewed earlier.

At this point, however, a discrepancy between the Court's stated rationale and its actual analysis begins to emerge. In both *Bostick* and *Drayton*, despite announcing a rule that requires the decision maker to adopt the perspective of the citizen (whether a reasonable person would feel free to decline the officers' requests or otherwise terminate the encounter), the Court nonetheless has taken the perspective of the police and ignored the perspective of the citizen. As a result, encounters that the Court characterizes as noncoercive and consensual were likely experienced by the citizen (and the reasonable person) as coercive and nonconsensual. In *Bostick* and in *Drayton*, the Court claimed to analyze whether a seizure took place (i.e., whether a reasonable person felt free to terminate the encounter) and whether consent to search was freely given (i.e., whether the defendant was coerced to comply when he would prefer to refuse). In fact, because the Court adopted the narrow perspective of the police, the true basis of its holding in *Bostick* and in *Drayton* was that the conduct of the police was reasonable under the circumstances in the sense that it was not abusive.[155] Although it may be true that the conduct of the police in these cases was not abusive, the Court announced a holding in both of these cases that was based on a very different footing—that there was no seizure and there was no unconsented search. If the police did, in fact, effect a suspicionless seizure of the bus passengers, such a seizure violated the Fourth Amendment, even though one could argue that the officers' conduct was not abusive. Similarly, if the police failed to secure voluntary consent from the passengers they searched, such searches violated the Fourth Amendment.[156] In Section II, I discussed general evidence that pressures to comply were especially strong in the situation in which Drayton and Brown

---

[155] See William J. Stuntz, *Local Policing After the Terror*, 111 Yale L J 2137, 2170 n 102 (2002).

[156] In both *Bostick* and in *Drayton*, consent was the sole justification proffered by the prosecution for the warrantless police search. Similarly, the only seizure issue was whether the passengers had been seized at all; there was no Fourth Amendment justification for a seizure. See *Bostick*, 501 US at 433–34 ("The State concedes . . . that the officers lacked the reasonable suspicion required to justify a seizure . . .").

found themselves. Next, I discuss evidence specific to police-citizen encounters that tends to undermine the plausibility of the Court's holding that reasonable citizens feel free to refuse police requests. At the same time, this same evidence undermines the notion that requiring the police to caution citizens that they have a right to refuse to consent will enable citizens to avoid situations in which they are pressured to consent.

B. CITIZENS' FEELINGS OF INVOLUNTARINESS IN POLICE ENCOUNTERS—SURVEY EVIDENCE

The robust findings from the compliance, pragmatics, personal space, time pressure, and scripted conformity studies reviewed earlier make a strong case for doubting that reasonable passengers involved in bus sweeps actually feel free to terminate their conversations with the police or deny the request to search. The powerful findings from the confession studies show that a confession that looks voluntary to the police might feel coerced by the suspect. Analogously, what looks like a friendly conversation to the police officers boarding the bus, at the same time feels like a coerced encounter and search to the passengers. And how it feels to the passengers is the crux of the Court's test: there is no seizure if a reasonable person would feel free to terminate the encounter, and consent is voluntary if a reasonable person would feel free to refuse. How free one feels determines whether one has been seized and whether permission to search is given voluntarily.

But there is another piece of empirical evidence that also strongly suggests that reasonable bus passengers generally do not feel free to decline the officer's request to search or otherwise terminate the encounter. The simplest way to determine whether a reasonable person voluntarily consented to a police search is simply to ask them, "To what extent did you feel free to decline the officer's request?" While there is no direct evidence available about the subjective experience of the reasonable bus passenger during a bus sweep (it appears that no one has asked this question of bus passengers), there is an existing survey of motorists who had been asked to consent to a search of their car after being stopped by police for a traffic violation.[157] Some police depart-

---

[157] Illya D. Lichtenberg, *Voluntary Consent or Obedience to Authority: An Inquiry into the "Consensual" Police-Citizen Encounter*, unpublished doctoral dissertation, on file with author.

ments, including the Ohio Highway Patrol, keep records of requests for consent searches.[158] Illya Lichtenberg randomly sampled a group of citizens who had been asked for their consent to search their car after they were stopped for traffic violations on Ohio interstates between 1995 and 1997 and interviewed them about their experiences.[159] An overwhelming majority (49 out of the 54 respondents) agreed to let the police the search; five refused.[160] There are a number possible explanations for why such a large proportion of motorists agreed to have the police search their cars. As with bus passengers, it is possible that the large number of motorists consenting to the search did so because they felt that the police were doing important work and that good citizens ought to cooperate when the police request cooperation. On the other hand, it is also possible that many of the motorists felt that they did not have a choice, and agreed involuntarily. Lichtenberg's interview data suggest that the latter interpretation is more plausible. Of the 49 motorists who agreed to let police search their cars, all but two said that they were afraid of what would happen to them if they did not consent.[161] Their fears included having their trip unduly delayed, being searched anyway, incurring property damage to their car if they refused and police searched anyway, being arrested, being beaten, or being killed.[162] Some representative responses include:

> I knew legally I didn't have to, but I kind of felt that I had to.[163]

See also Illya D. Lichtenberg, *Miranda in Ohio: The Effects of Robinette on the "Voluntary" Waiver of Fourth Amendment Rights*, 44 Howard L J 349 (2001).

[158] Pursuant to standard departmental procedure, the Ohio State Police maintained a record for every traffic stop in which police requested consent to search during the period reported. Lichtenberg, *Voluntary Consent* at 163–64 (cited in note 157).

[159] Id at 241, 246.

[160] Id at 251. The rate of refusal to consent in the sample was therefore about 9%. The sample was drawn from a population consisting of all traffic stops conducted between January 1995 and May 1997 by the Ohio Highway Patrol where consent was requested ($N = 699$). The rate of refusal in the sample (about 9%) was similar to the rate of refusal in the population (about 8%). Note that the sample size of the survey described here is small ($N = 54$). Nevertheless, the sample well represented the population in terms of refusal rate, gender, and age. The race/ethnicity of the sample subjects resembled that of the population fairly well, except that Hispanic subjects were underrepresented in the sample.

[161] Id at 268.

[162] Id at 261–63.

[163] Id at 264, subject #15373.

I felt a little pressured that I didn't have much choice, due to the circumstances surrounding the incident it would have been very, very inconvenient to be locked up for the night. I didn't know if that was an option, and I didn't want to find out.[164]

. . . at first I didn't think there was any reason to [consent] and then I realized that if I didn't they would do it anyway.[165]

. . . to this day I do not know what would have happened if I had said, "No, absolutely not." . . . I really didn't know how else to respond. . . .[166]

Many emphasized that they felt pressure to consent because they were far from home and had no one to call if they angered police and ended up in jail for refusing. When asked if they felt the police would have honored their request if they had refused, only one citizen answered "yes," and one did not know.[167] All of the remaining respondents (96%) felt that police would not have honored their refusal and would have searched them anyway.[168] Their concerns were apparently well founded: of the five motorists who declined to consent to the search, two reported being searched despite their explicit refusal to consent.[169] Another motorist who refused to consent was not searched but was threatened with future retaliation.[170]

C. THE FUTILITY OF MIRANDA-LIKE WARNINGS IN
  CONSENT SEARCH SITUATIONS

The *Drayton* Court took as its main mission to "determine whether officers must advise bus passengers . . . of their right not to cooperate."[171] This is not the first time the "warning" issue has arisen in consent search cases. In *Schneckloth*, the Court rejected the possibility of requiring police seeking consent to search to issue

---

[164] Id at 261, subject #3371.

[165] Id at 261, subject #4337.

[166] Id at 263, subject #16633.

[167] Id at 271–72.

[168] Id.

[169] Id at 280–81.

[170] Id at 279–80. This motorist was apparently so shaken that he reported that he avoids driving on the interstate near his home (where the stop occurred) even though he now drives a different car than the one he drove on the day he was stopped.

[171] *Drayton*, 122 S Ct at 2108.

a warning regarding the right to refuse, akin to *Miranda*'s requirement that police interrogators warn a suspect in custody of the
right to remain silent. The *Schneckloth* majority did, however, acknowledge that whether the suspect was aware of the right to refuse is a relevant factor in the analysis of whether the consent was
voluntary. The issue of mandatory police warnings in consent
search situations arose again in *Ohio v Robinette*,[172] a case involving
a police request for consent to search during the course of a traffic
stop.[173] In *Robinette*, the Court rejected the notion that police must
inform motorists that they are "legally free to go" before requesting consent to search.

Several commentators have supported a requirement that the
police warn citizens of their right to refuse a request to search.[174]
They argue that the coercion citizens feel arises, at least in part,
from the lack of knowledge of their right to refuse the request.
One cannot refuse if one is not aware that refusal is an option. By
requiring police to advise suspects that they can refuse to cooperate with the request to search, the argument goes, we remove the
coercive aspect of the request and allow citizens to make a free
and informed choice. The assumption is that if police are required
to issue *Miranda*-type warnings in consent search cases, the compliance rate will necessarily decrease because, armed with the
knowledge that refusal is an option, some people will choose to
refuse. In fact, the majority in *Schneckloth* appears to have assumed
that if warnings were required, virtually all citizens would refuse
to consent to a search.[175]

---

[172] *Robinette*, 519 US 33 (1996).

[173] In *Robinette*, a police officer stopped a motorist for speeding and ordered him out of
the car. After checking for outstanding warrants, the officer issued an oral warning and
returned the driver's license. The officer then asked the motorist for consent to search the
car. The Court rejected the motorist's claim that because the traffic stop had concluded,
he was unlawfully seized during the request for consent. Instead, the Court held that the
Constitution does not require that the officer inform the motorist that he is free to go
before a consent search may be deemed voluntary. Id at 40.

[174] See Devon W. Carbado, *Erasing the Fourth Amendment*, 100 Mich L Rev 946, 1030
(2002); Carol S. Steiker, *How Much Justice Can You Afford? A Response to Stuntz*, 67 Geo
Wash L Rev 1290, 1294 (1999); Rebecca A. Stack, *Airport Drug Searches: Giving Content
to the Concept of Free and Voluntary Consent*, 77 Va L Rev 183, 205–08 (1991). Other commentators question whether police issuance of *Miranda*-type warnings in the consent search
context is likely to dissipate coercion. See Strauss, 92 J Crim L & Criminol at 254 (cited
in note 18).

[175] *Schneckloth*, 412 US at 229. The Court worried that adding a warning requirement
would "in practice, create serious doubt whether consent searches could continue to be
conducted." Id.

That assumption turns out to be mistaken, at least in instances where it has been explicitly examined. A study of all Ohio highway stops conducted between 1995 and 1997 found no decrease in consent rates after police were required to advise motorists of their right to refuse to cooperate with a request for consent to search.[176] In fact, the same number of citizens consent with the warnings as without the warnings. Apparently, people are unaffected by the warnings because they do not believe them—they feel that they will be searched regardless of whether or not they consent.[177] Why would people who are told by police that they have a right to refuse to consent to search persist in believing that they have no choice and will be searched anyway? Many of the factors discussed earlier in Section II come into play here: we comply with the police not because we make a deliberate conscious choice to respond in a particular way, but rather because we mindlessly respond in a manner consistent with social roles; just as we do not hear "May I see your license and registration please?" as a genuine question, we do not hear "You have the right to refuse to consent" as a genuine option; under time pressure we respond to requests of authorities in the same way we usually do, by automatically complying. In this way, the experimental research suggests generally what the survey of motorists finds explicitly: people who are targeted for a search by police and informed that they have a right to refuse nonetheless feel intense pressure to comply and feel that refusal is not a genuine option.

Given the magnitude of situational pressures brought to bear on citizens in bus sweeps and similar situations, there is no reason to think that police advising citizens that they have a right not to cooperate with their request for consent to search will significantly reduce coercion experienced by citizens in this situation. In this

---

[176] Lichtenberg, 44 Howard L J at 349 (cited in note 157). Lichtenberg examined Ohio State Police consent search data both before and after the Ohio Supreme Court ruled in *Robinette* that motorists who are stopped for traffic violations must be warned that they are free to leave prior to being asked by police for consent to search their vehicle. *Ohio v Robinette*, 653 NE2d 695 (Ohio 1995) (the U.S. Supreme Court subsequently reversed and held that no such warning was necessary. *Robinette*, 519 US 33 (1996)). This comparison revealed that the rate at which motorists consented to searches actually increased nominally after the institution of warnings. Id at 367. An examination of data from a control group (Maryland, in which warnings were never instituted) reveals that a similar nominal increase occurred there during the same time period, suggesting that the Ohio warnings had no effect whatever on rates of consent to searches. Id at 372–73.

[177] See text accompanying notes 161–70.

sense the issue of police warnings in consensual search situations—considered by the Court twice in the last 10 years—is something of a red herring and should be put aside. This issue simply diverts attention away from the real question—whether citizens who are approached and searched in these situations have consented freely or perceived themselves as having no choice.

D. THE SECURITY FICTION

In concluding that a reasonable bus passenger would have felt free to decline the police officers' requests and terminate the encounter, the *Drayton* Court asserted that passengers did not experience the situation as coercive because they were concerned about security and felt that the officers' search of bags and persons on the bus "enhance[d] their own safety and the safety of those around them."[178] But the notion that the police were rifling through passengers' bags and patting down passengers' groin areas for the passengers' own protection has an "air of unreality"[179] when considered from the perspective of the passenger.

It is undoubtedly true that after the terrorist attacks of September 11, 2001, citizens feel a greater need to rely on police for safety and security. As a result, citizens and their elected representatives now may be more willing to give police wider latitude to intrude upon individual privacy interests to further the purposes of rooting out terrorism and enhancing our safety.[180] The majority in *Drayton* was keenly aware of this: a large part of the opinion in *Drayton* was devoted to showing that the police officers' actions were designed to make the bus more safe and secure, and that the innocent citizens on the bus very much appreciated what the police were doing to enhance their security. For example, the Court noted that

---

[178] *Drayton*, 122 S Ct at 2113.

[179] Id at 2114 (Souter dissenting).

[180] See Robin Toner and Janet Elder, *A Nation Challenged: Attitudes; Public Is Wary but Supportive on Rights Curbs*, NY Times A1 (Dec 12, 2001) (a NY Times/CBS News poll revealed that 64% feel that it is a good idea for the president to have the authority to make changes in rights usually guaranteed by the constitution; 90% approve of the way the president is handling the campaign against terrorism); Brad Smith, *Critics Alarmed Over Post-9/11 Crackdown*, Tampa Tribune 12 (Sept 2, 2002) (a National Public Radio/Harvard Kennedy School poll revealed that 51% said it was necessary to surrender some civil liberties to curb terrorism; a *Los Angeles Times* poll reported that 59% were in support of wider government powers to tap telephone lines and monitor wireless communications). See also Stuntz, 111 Yale L J at 2138 (cited in note 155).

in the experience of police officers who conduct daily bus sweeps, the vast majority of all bus passengers cooperate. "Bus passengers answer officers' questions and otherwise cooperate not because of coercion but because the passengers know that their participation enhances their own safety."[181] The Court also noted that the fact that officers are armed and in uniform is a source of "assurance, not discomfort."[182] Again, the assumption is that bus passengers view the police as there to help them feel safe and secure.

This is implausible for a number of reasons. First, the purpose of "bus sweeps" as they are conducted on intercity buses is to intercept illegal narcotics. The bus sweeps are conducted by officers assigned to "narcotics interdiction" teams.[183] They choose to board only certain buses, coming from certain cities, precisely to increase the probability of finding illegal drugs.[184] Florida is a major corridor in the illicit drug trade, and this is why so many sweeps are conducted there.[185] *Drayton* is not about weapons,[186] bombs, or terrorism. Because of the risk of terrorism, there may come a time when all intercity bus passengers are subject to search as a condition of boarding the bus. Such routine searches as a condition for certain travel are now familiar and are widely accepted as being justified in light of current terrorism risks.[187]

But such was not the state of affairs in *Drayton*. The police officers' business was intercepting illegal drugs, and everyone on the bus knew why the police were there and what they were looking for (indeed, they announced this as their purpose). As a general matter, it is far from obvious that even innocent passengers generally felt relieved or assured to see police, knowing that they were

---

[181] *Drayton*, 122 S Ct at 2113.

[182] Id at 2112.

[183] *Drayton*, Joint Appendix at 69.

[184] Id.

[185] The federal government recently designated eight Florida counties as a "High Intensity Drug Trafficking Area." See Dana Treen, *Medicine Cabinets, Mailrooms Figure in Drug Trade Trafficking Hides Behind a New Face, Experts Say*, Fla Times Union (Jacksonville) B3 (Sept 26, 2001).

[186] There was testimony at the suppression hearing in *Drayton* that Officer Lang asked Brown's permission to check him for weapons. *Drayton*, Joint Appendix at 92. Brown's attorney argued that this was a ploy to convince Brown to agree to a search that Brown assumed would be limited for those purposes. Respondent's Brief at 38 n 32. The *Drayton* opinion does not address this argument.

[187] The dissent's argument in *Drayton* begins with this point. *Drayton*, 122 S Ct at 2114.

looking for drugs secreted in baggage or on persons.[188] Second, passengers who were targeted for questioning and searches likely did not feel assured or safe once they became targets. From the perspective of the bus passenger to whom the police turn their attention, the police uniform and gun were indeed sources of discomfort, not assurance—just the opposite of the majority's assertion. At the moment the police officer approaches, holds up his badge, and begins introducing himself, it is quite clear that the police are motivated by suspicion, not benevolence. The police have boarded the bus to catch criminals, and they are now trying to determine whether you are one of them.

There is an additional reason to suspect that the *Drayton* majority is mistaken in its assertion that bus passengers welcome police requests to search their belongings and their persons. As discussed earlier, ordinary citizens who are asked to rate various police search and seizure scenarios report that they perceive police boarding a bus and asking to search luggage as among the most intrusive of all 50 scenarios evaluated, representing a greater "invasion of privacy or autonomy" than police questioning on the sidewalk for 10 minutes.[189] Considering that the goal of the police in *Drayton* was to identify people who were transporting illegal drugs, and that police requests to search bus passengers are perceived by ordinary citizens to be quite intrusive and invasive, it is unlikely that the specific manner in which police carried out their searches dispelled any inference of coercion, as the *Drayton* majority held.

IV. The Social Significance of Fourth Amendment Consent Jurisprudence

A. THE COST TO INNOCENT PEOPLE SUBJECTED TO "CONSENT" SEARCHES

The sheer number of innocent people affected by the police practice of consent searches suggests that this is an issue that deserves attention. Consent searches are now a routine method of

---

[188] There are a multitude of reasons why an innocent person would not want police rifling through his or her belongings or searching his or her person. A law-abiding citizen might possess items that he or she simply would prefer to keep private, such as personal grooming items, medications, sexual aids, or controversial printed matter, to name just a few.

[189] See Slobogin and Schumacher, 42 Duke L J at 735–42 (cited in note 154).

crime control in many jurisdictions,[190] and there has been a recent proliferation of routinized, suspicionless searches.[191] The Fourth Amendment requires no justification for consent searches: they may be done pursuant to slight suspicion, a hunch, or nothing at all. In some localities, law enforcement officers have adopted a practice of requesting consent to search during every traffic stop.[192] Because many (if not most) police departments do not keep track of every instance in which they request consent to search in the absence of probable cause, it is very difficult to estimate the actual number of consent searches that are conducted across the United States or the percentage of searches conducted pursuant to consent in the absence of probable cause. But the small amount of scattered evidence that exists suggests that the absolute number of consent searches is quite high, as is the proportion of consent searches of all searches conducted.[193] And their number seems to be increasing. For example, in just one city in Florida (Tallahassee), the local police have routinized bus sweeps to such an extent that a special squad of officers is assigned to conduct daily consent searches on intercity buses.[194] Over the course of just one typical year, it is

---

[190] See Wayne R. LaFave, 3 *Search & Seizure* § 8.1 (West, 3d ed 1996).

[191] See *Minnesota v George*, 557 NW2d 575, 581–82 (Tomljanovich concurring) (noting the increasing use by police of subtle tactics to obtain citizens' consent to search, and remarking that officers have recently begun to receive training on obtaining consent, making use of tactics similar to "the training sales people receive in getting people to agree to buy things they do not want").

[192] *Robinette*, 519 US at 40.

[193] There is no single reliable estimate for the number of consent searches conducted in any given year nationwide (or even statewide). In some cases, police officers have testified that they ask for consent to search every motorist they stop. See *Harris v State*, 994 SW2d 927, 932 n 1 (Tex Crim App 1999). In one city, it was estimated anecdotally that 98% of the searches were consent searches. Paul Sutton, *The Fourth Amendment in Action: An Empirical View of the Search Warrant Process*, 22 Crim L Bull 405, 415 (1986).

[194] *Drayton*, Joint Appendix at 69. As others have observed, the targeting of intercity buses for consent searches gives law enforcement access to a segment of the population that is arguably especially vulnerable to coercive practices. Intercity bus passengers are disproportionately poor, nonwhite, and less educated. See William R. O'Shields, Note, *The Exodus of Minorities' Fourth Amendment Rights into Oblivion*, 77 Iowa L Rev 1875, 1899, n 211 (1992). Others have argued that the demographic characteristics of intercity bus passengers make it more likely that they will acquiesce to authority because they do not know how to object, or because they have more reason to be intimidated. See Dennis J. Callahan, *The Long Distance Remand: Florida v. Bostick and the Re-Awakened Bus Search Battlefront in the War on Drugs*, 43 Wm & Mary L Rev 365, 401 n 171 (2001); see also *United States v Lewis*, 728 F Supp 784, 789 (DC Cir 1990) (intercity buses "are utilized largely by the underclass of this nation who, because of greater concerns (such as being able to survive), do not often complain about [bus sweeps]").

estimated that these particular officers board and search buses carrying over 26,000 passengers, all of whom become potential search targets when police interrupt their trip to scrutinize passengers and baggage.[195] In another Florida city (Fort Lauderdale), one police officer testified that in the previous nine months he had personally conducted consent searches of over 3,000 bags.[196] One officer in Ohio testified that during the course of the past year he made 786 requests for consent to search of motorists whom he had stopped for routine traffic violations.[197]

The vast majority of people subjected to consent searches are innocent.[198] This is a fact that is easily forgotten because consent searches often come to our attention via published exclusionary rule cases, in which the defendant was (presumably) factually guilty. How do consent searches affect the lives of innocent people—that is, people who possess no illegal drugs or guns, are not engaged in illegal activity, yet find themselves in a situation where a police officer has approached them and wants them to submit to a search? In the Court's view, the citizen in this situation makes a rather simple decision, and the citizen ordinarily (absent a gun pointed at them, for example) would feel free to decline the officer's request to search, or even decline to engage in conversation at all with the officer, and to simply "terminate the encounter." In fact, the view of the *Drayton* majority appears to be that consent searches ought to be encouraged (or at least not discouraged) because they reinforce the rule of law.[199] Specifically, the Court said

---

[195] *Drayton*, Joint Appendix at 80. Officer Lang testified that over a three-year period he conducted bus sweeps of four to six buses per day, four to five days per week, with each bus containing an average of 25–30 passengers.

[196] *Florida v Kerwick*, 512 So2d 347, 349 (1987).

[197] *State v Retherford*, 93 Ohio App 3d 586, 591–92 (1994). This same officer who requested consent 786 times in one year also claimed that the main reason he requested consent to search in the instant case was that "I need the practice, to be quite honest." Id.

[198] Because of the absence of systematic record keeping, it is difficult to calculate the proportion of consent searches in which the target is innocent of any crime. There are, however, scattered statistics for individual localities. For example, the Sheriff in one Florida county arrested only 55 of the 507 motorists subjected to consent searches over a three-year period. Jeff Brazil and Steve Berry, *Color of Driver Is Key to Stops in I-95 Video*, Orlando Sentinel Tribune A1 (Aug 23, 1992). An analysis of over 1,900 consent searches of motorists concluded that illegal drugs are discovered in about one of every eight searches. Lichtenberg, *Voluntary Consent* at 171 (cited in note 157).

[199] *Drayton*, 122 S Ct at 2114.

that a citizen-police interaction in which the police request consent to search and the citizen "advise[s] the police of his or her wishes" reinforces the rule of law, and ought to be "given a weight and dignity of its own."[200]

As I have already discussed, a more plausible interpretation of these encounters—one that is based on established empirical findings—is that in many consent search situations, citizens do not feel free to decline the search request, much less to terminate the encounter at the outset. Instead, the citizen develops a clear understanding from the context of the encounter that any attempt to decline the request or terminate the encounter would be construed by the officer as refusal to cooperate, and such refusal will be met with negative consequences for the citizen (even though it is typically unclear at the time precisely what those negative consequences would be).[201] In addition, citizens anticipate that part of the set of negative consequences would be a decidedly negative affective reaction on the part of the officer.[202] The officer's request for consent to search therefore places the citizen on the horns of a dilemma: either accede to a request that you would prefer to refuse, or refuse the request and incur the (unknown) consequences of being "uncooperative."[203]

The lasting impact that consent searches have on citizens is potentially important in the aggregate because of the sheer numbers of citizens who find themselves in the position of being asked by a police officer to submit to a search. The Lichtenberg survey provides strong evidence that a substantial portion of citizens whose consent was requested from the Ohio Highway Patrol felt nega-

---

[200] Id.

[201] Daniel J. Steinbock, *The Wrong Line Between Freedom and Restraint: The Unreality, Obscurity, and Incivility of the Fourth Amendment Consensual Encounter Doctrine*, 38 San Diego L Rev 507 (2001). The sentiment of one motorist in Lichtenberg's survey is perhaps typical: "I don't think they would have searched the car then and there if I refused to sign the [consent] form, but I didn't know what would have happened beyond that." Lichtenberg, *Voluntary Consent* at 272 (cited in note 157), subject #3614.

[202] Steinbock, 38 San Diego L Rev at 272 (cited in note 201). According to one motorist in Lichtenberg's survey: "Yeah, if I refused, he would get pissed-off and detain me longer." Lichtenberg, *Voluntary Consent* at 269 (cited in note 157), subject #01185.

[203] As is well known to many citizens who live in communities where police presence is pervasive, the consequences of being perceived by police as "uncooperative" are sometimes much more severe than a simple negative affective reaction on the part of the law enforcement officer. See, for example, Tracey Maclin, *Black and Blue Encounters*, 26 Valp U L Rev 243 (1991).

tively affected by the police encounter. Rather than feeling that their response to the police had a "dignity and weight of its own," they instead felt afraid and reported that their respect for the police had diminished.[204]

After the search happened to them, most respondents (60%) reported that they thought about it often—about once a day.[205] When asked about how they felt about the experience, a small proportion of respondents (26%) made positive or neutral comments, such as the following:

> I wish they would do it more.[206]

> I'm just glad I had nothing to hide.[207]

> I guess they were just doing their job.[208]

A large majority (74%), however, had decidedly negative feelings about the experience:

> I don't know if you ever had your house broken into or ripped off . . . [it's] an empty feeling, like you're nothing.[209]

> People probably know me because I own my own business. It was embarrassing. It pissed me off . . . they just treat you like a criminal and you ain't done nothing. . . . I think about it every time I see a cop.[210]

> I feel really violated. I felt like my rights had been infringed upon. I feel really bitter about the whole thing.[211]

> I don't trust [the police] anymore. I've lost all trust in them.[212]

Thus, consent search encounters with police often have a substantial impact on people—they do not forget about the experience

---

[204] For example: "I knew I wouldn't be going to jail for not replying, but I knew I might be detained. . . . There's a foggy area between knowing your rights . . . and something like a policeman disliking the way you answered a question. . . . [I] had to reply to avoid trouble." Lichtenberg, *Voluntary Consent* at 265 (cited in note 157), subject #16633.

[205] Id at 282 n 38.

[206] Id at 283, subject #05168.

[207] Id at 284, subject #13688.

[208] Id at 284, subject #07267.

[209] Id at 285, subject #11091.

[210] Id at 283, subject #14735.

[211] Id at 285, subject #15494.

[212] Id at 288, subject #12731.

quickly, and most people, in this sample at least, had lasting negative attitudes toward the incident (and sometimes toward the police) as a result.[213] Finally, unlike people who are discovered carrying unlawful contraband, innocent citizens who are subjected to coercive consent searches have no practical recourse—it is difficult to prove a constitutional violation even when their privacy interests protected by the Fourth Amendment were violated, and in any event the amount of money damages recovered is likely to be quite small.[214]

B. THE HARM OF THE CONSENT FICTION:
   CONFLICT IN THE LOWER COURTS

That the Court's Fourth Amendment consensual encounter doctrine is founded upon a legal fiction is not a secret. For example, in his widely used treatise, Professor Wayne LaFave begins the first sentence of his discussion on the doctrine by referring to "[t]he so-called consent search."[215] Professor William Stuntz asserts that because "hardly anyone feels free to walk away from a police officer without the officer's permission," the Court's free-to-terminate test is merely the nominal standard for seizure; the

---

[213] The Court in the past has recognized that there is a cost associated with police inspection of the person (pat-downs) or personal effects of citizens. For example, Chief Justice Warren stated in *Terry v Ohio* that when a police officer accosts an individual and restrains his or her freedom to walk away, and conducts a pat-down of that person's body, such a procedure is "a serious intrusion upon the sanctity of the person, which may inflict great indignity and arouse strong resentment, and it is not to be undertaken lightly." *Terry v Ohio*, 392 US 1, 17–18 (1968). And, more recently, the Court acknowledged the intrusiveness of a police officer's tactile examination of a bus passenger's carry-on luggage, and compared this with the intrusiveness of a police officer's physical inspection of a person's clothing described in *Terry*. *Bond v United States*, 529 US 334, 337–38 (2000).

[214] A civil lawsuit alleging violations of the Fourth Amendment may be brought against federal officers, see *Bivens v Six Unknown Named Agents*, 403 US 388 (1971), or under 42 USC § 1983 against state officers. Success rates are low. See Theodore Eisenberg, *Section 1983: Doctrinal Foundations and an Empirical Study*, 67 Cornell L Rev 482, 550–51 (1982). Injuries are often difficult to prove. See Daniel J. Meltzer, *Deterring Constitutional Violations by Law Enforcement Officials: Plaintiffs and Defendants as Private Attorneys General*, 88 Colum L Rev 247, 284 (1988).

[215] Wayne R. LaFave, 4 *Search and Seizure: A Treatise on the Fourth Amendment* § 8.1 596 (West, 3d ed 1996). Other authors have explicitly argued that the Court's doctrine regarding consensual encounters and consent searches is characterized in practice by pervasive lack of consent. See Tracey Maclin, *Justice Thurgood Marshall: Taking the Fourth Amendment Seriously*, 77 Cornell L Rev 723, 792–95 (1992); William R. O'Shields, Note, *The Exodus of Minorities' Fourth Amendment Rights into Oblivion*, 77 Iowa L Rev 1875 (1992).

real standard is whether the level of police coercion is reason-able.[216]

This would account for how the Court persists in reaching con-clusions that fly in the face of scientific findings about the psychol-ogy of compliance and consent and that many ordinary people find implausible. The "real" standard—whether the police conduct was within the bounds of "acceptable" coercion under the circum-stances (no guns drawn, no explicit threats uttered)—functions as the decision rule that permits individual Justices to make an initial private, internal judgment about whether to uphold the admission into evidence of the contraband police discovered. The basis of that judgment is that the police behaved responsibly and did not cross the line that defines acceptable police behavior. The "nomi-nal" standard is then trotted out in the Court's written opinion to justify the police officers' invasion of the citizen's privacy. The reasoning employed to effectuate the nominal standard, by now familiar, goes something like this: The police officer asked permis-sion. The citizen granted it. A reasonable person in the situation would have felt free to not grant permission. Therefore encounter and subsequent search were consensual.

Perhaps the "real" standard can be made workable, as Professor Stuntz suggests.[217] It may be no more vague than the nominal stan-dard, given that both standards must take into account all of the surrounding circumstances that came into play in the particular context. The important point, however, is that in the current state of the law, the Court's stated definitions of seizure and voluntary search are a sham. This is, indeed, a worrisome state of affairs for several reasons.

First, the Court's stated definitions of seizure and voluntary search have already (even prior to the reaffirmation of those defi-nitions under *Drayton*) produced disagreement in the lower courts. Indeed, the most likely reason that the Court granted certiorari in *Drayton* was the lower courts' clashing interpretations of seizure and voluntary search in bus sweep cases after *Bostick*. This is under-standable, given that the courts below in *Bostick* had already applied virtually the same test subsequently articulated by the Court and had concluded that the defendant had been unlawfully seized or

---

[216] Stuntz, 111 Yale L J at 2170 n 102 (cited in note 155).

[217] Id at 2174 n 115.

that the search had been coerced. In *Bostick*, the Court remanded the case back to the Florida courts with instructions that essentially said, "Wrong conclusion. Try again."[218] Shortly after *Bostick* was decided, Professor Wayne LaFave remarked that "*Bostick* lends itself to a rather chilling interpretation: that lower courts are expected not to interfere with bus sweep procedures."[219] Thereafter, the Florida state courts upheld the consent search in every published bus sweep consent search case in the 11 years between *Bostick* and *Drayton*, regardless of the facts, consistently reasoning in each case that the defendant felt free to refuse.[220] The Eleventh Circuit, on the other hand, interpreted *Bostick* more literally and evaluated each bus sweep case before it under the totality of the circumstances. As a result, the post-*Bostick* Eleventh Circuit sometimes found that the seizure was unlawful or that the search was not voluntary.[221] The practical result was that prosecutors in Florida who wanted to be sure that the search in their bus sweep case would be upheld arranged to bring charges in state court rather than in federal court.

This lack of consistency also played itself out in other jurisdictions. Some courts adopted an approach like that of the Eleventh Circuit and ordered suppression of evidence on the grounds that a reasonable passenger in the situation would not have felt free to

---

[218] In *Bostick*, the Court's remand instructions were actually "We remand so that the Florida courts may evaluate the seizure question under the correct legal standard." *Bostick*, 501 US at 437. The "correct" legal standard as articulated by the Court was in reality scarcely different from the standard originally applied by the Florida Supreme Court. As one commentator has remarked, "the Court seems so certain that there was no seizure in the instant case that it virtually reads the question it supposedly remanded right out of the case." Wayne R. LaFave, *Two Hundred Years of Individual Liberties: Essays on the Bill of Rights*, 1991 U Ill L Rev 729, 752 (1991).

[219] Id.

[220] See, for example, *Hemingway v State*, 762 S2d 957 (Fla App 2000); *Ramos v State*, 758 S2d 741 (Fla App 2000); *Mondestin v State*, 760 S2d 1062 (Fla App 2000); *Stubbs v State*, 661 S2d 1268 (Fla App 1995); *State v Hunter*, 596 S2d 158 (Fla App 1992); *State v Kuntzwiler*, 585 S2d 1096 (Fla App 1991).

[221] *United States v Washington*, 151 F3d 1354 (11th Cir 1998); *United States v Guapi*, 144 F3d 1393 (11th Cir 1998). Interestingly, in *Guapi*, the bus driver stated under oath that he thought passengers were not free to leave the bus without being searched. 144 F3d at 1396–97. Courts in most other federal circuits as well as many state courts generally interpreted *Bostick* in such a way that resulted in virtually all bus sweep consent searches being deemed voluntary. See, for example, *United States v Broomfield*, 201 F3d 1270 (10th Cir 2000); *United States v Boone*, 67 F3d 76 (5th Cir 1995); *United States v Garcia*, 103 F3d 121 (4th Cir 1996); *United States v Graham*, 982 F2d 273 (8th Cir 1992); *State v Hernandez*, 64 SW3d 548 (Tex Ct App 2001); *Stevenson v State*, 961 P2d 137 (Nev 1998). But there were some exceptions. See cases cited in notes 222–28.

terminate the encounter in light of the fact that the police did not advise passengers that they could choose not to cooperate.[222] (The Ninth Circuit even suppressed evidence from a consent search in a case where the police did in fact advise passengers of their right not to cooperate but where the majority held that the warning was misleading.[223]) Other courts gave no special weight to the absence of police advice to passengers that they could choose not to cooperate and upheld consent searches under those circumstances.[224] Some courts considering bus passenger cases post-*Bostick* ordered evidence suppressed in cases where the police threatened the use of a drug dog;[225] other courts denied motions to suppress where the police threatened the use of a drug dog.[226] Some courts ordered evidence suppressed when the passenger questioned the officers' authority to search ("Don't you need a warrant?" "Do I have a right to privacy?").[227] Another court upheld a search even where the passenger appeared to hesitate after granting consent.[228]

The Court's response to the disorder in the lower courts was to grant certiorari in *Drayton* and simply repeat the same standard for consensual encounters and voluntary searches already articulated in *Bostick*.[229] *Drayton* did clarify that the absence of police

---

[222] See *People v Bloxson*, 517 NW2d 563 (Mich App 1994); *State v Talbert*, 873 SW2d 321 (Mo App SD 1994); *United States v Lopez*, 1999 WL 494007 (D Or 1999).

[223] *United States v Stephens*, 206 F3d 914 (9th Cir 2000) (holding that the police announcement that passengers were free to leave amounted to a "Hobson's choice" of submitting to a search or missing the bus).

[224] See, for example, *United States v Portillo-Aguirre*, 131 F Supp 2d 874 (WD Tex 2001); *United States v Outlaw*, 134 F Supp 2d 807 (WD Tex 2001); *United States v Gant*, 112 F3d 239 (6th Cir 1997); *United States v Broomfield*, 201 F3d 1270 (10th Cir 2000); *Stubbs v State*, 661 So2d 1268 (Fla App 5th Dist 1995); *State v Hernandez*, 64 SW3d 548 (Tex Ct App 2001); *Hemingway v State*, 762 So2d 957 (Fla App 4th Dist 2000).

[225] *United States v Brumfield*, 910 F Supp 1528 (D Colo 1996); *United States v Barrett*, 976 F Supp 1105 (ND Ohio 1997); *State v Vikesdal*, 688 So2d 685 (La App 2d Cir 1997); *Mitchell v State*, 831 SW2d 829 (Tex Ct App 1992); *United States v Garzon*, 119 F3d 1446 (10th Cir 1997).

[226] *United States v Jones*, 914 F Supp 421 (D Colo 1996); *United States v Bobo*, 2 Fed Appx 401 (6th Cir 2001); *Stevenson v State*, 961 P2d 137 (Nev 1998).

[227] *United States v Randolph*, 789 F Supp 407 (DDC 1992); *Mitchell v State*, 831 SW2d 829 (Tex Ct App 1992).

[228] *Burton v United States*, 657 A2d 741 (DC 1994).

[229] In the bus sweep cases in which the search was found to be invalid, the Eleventh Circuit considered the fact that the police did not advise passengers that they had a right not to cooperate. In reversing the Eleventh Circuit's decision in *Drayton*, the Court admonished the Eleventh Circuit for having adopted a per se rule that invalidated bus sweep searches whenever the police don't advise passengers of their right to refuse. While the

advice to passengers that they need not cooperate was a factor like any other and did not receive any special weight in the totality of the circumstances analysis.[230] But in the end, *Drayton* did little to resolve the lack of consistency in the lower courts. Instead, it essentially affirmed Professor LaFave's "chilling interpretation" of *Bostick:* lower courts are expected to refrain from interfering with bus sweeps. Thus, after *Drayton*, the safest course for lower courts deciding the validity of consent searches in bus sweep cases would be to craft their totality of the circumstances analyses in a way that results in a finding that the search was voluntary and the encounter consensual (regardless of the actual circumstances). But what is a lower court to do when it encounters a bus sweep case involving a new fact (not present in *Drayton*) that suggests that perhaps this particular situation involved coercion, such as a threat to use a drug-sniffing dog? Having adopted a nominal standard for consensual police-citizen encounters and voluntary consent to search that is actually fictitious, the Court has left the lower courts in the unenviable position of deciding cases without the benefit of knowing how to apply the Court's "actual" (though unarticulated) standard. This is a recipe for continued confusion.[231]

Eleventh Circuit does not appear to have explicitly adopted such a bright line rule, it may be the case that in its analysis of the totality of the circumstances, the absence of police warnings effectively tipped the scale in the direction of finding coercion.

[230] *Bostick* had left some ambiguity about this. The majority stated, "Two facts are particularly worth noting. First, the police specifically advised Bostick that he had the right to refuse consent." 401 US at 432. A few lower courts subsequently interpreted *Bostick* to stand for the proposition that because the presence of police warnings is a fact "particularly worth noting," the absence of police warnings weighs especially heavily in the totality of the circumstances analysis. See *United States v Guapi*, 144 F3d 1393, 1395 (11th Cir 1998) ("the absence of such notice is an important factor in this case").

[231] The lower courts' difficulty in applying the current standard for voluntary consent to search is exacerbated by the fact that, because the question of voluntariness is determined on a case-by-case basis, by considering the totality of the circumstances, this encourages the police—who have no concrete guidelines as to which methods are acceptable—to apply as much pressure as is necessary in each case to obtain consent. The lower courts, already faced with the difficult task of assessing all of the circumstances contributing to pressures on the suspect to consent, must factor into their assessment the incentives of the police to minimize the appearance of any pressure at a suppression hearing. For example, at the hearing on the motion to suppress the illegal narcotics found on Drayton's and Brown's person, the arresting officer emphasized repeatedly his own polite manner toward the bus passengers that day. *Drayton*, Respondent's Brief, Joint Appendix at 51, 99, and 101. This incentive structure is similar to that existing under the pre-*Miranda* voluntariness regime, in which case-by-case review left police without adequate guidance and subtle incentives to allow interrogation pressures to spiral out of control. See Stephen J. Schulhofer, *Reconsidering Miranda*, 54 U Chi L Rev 435, 451–52 (1987).

C. THE HARM OF THE CONSENT FICTION: DIMINISHED
   RESPECT FOR THE LAW

The Court's continued articulation of a fictional standard for the definitions of seizure and voluntary consent threatens a different kind of harm as well. As many other scholars have argued, the law works not only because of the sanctions it threatens but also because of the messages it expresses.[232] One possible manifestation of law as an expressive instrument is that when people notice that the legal system regulates behavior in a way that makes sense, they are more likely to comply with the law.[233] Indeed, empirical evidence suggests that citizens who feel that the law is worthy of respect tend to comply more with particular laws.[234] On the other hand, perceived injustices in the legal system have subtle but pervasive influences on people's deference to and respect for the law in their everyday lives.[235] Americans are culturally attentive to law and are concerned when they perceive injustice in the legal system. This attentiveness to legal rules and results is especially likely for the law of consent searches, in part because so many people are personally affected by them (as discussed above), but also because the issue of racial profiling has resulted in a great deal of public attention to consent searches in the popular press.[236] When people perceive the legal system to be unjust, the diminished respect for

---

[232] See Robert Cooter, *Expressive Law and Economics*, 27 J Legal Stud 585 (1998); Dan M. Kahan, *What Do Alternative Sanctions Mean?* 63 U Chi L Rev 591 (1996); Lawrence Lessig, *The Regulation of Social Meaning*, 62 U Chi L Rev 943 (1995); Richard McAdams, *A Focal Point Theory of Expressive Law*, 86 Va L Rev 1649 (2000).

[233] See Paul H. Robinson and John M. Darley, *The Utility of Desert*, 91 Nw U L Rev 453 (1997).

[234] Tom R. Tyler, *Why People Obey the Law* (Yale, 1990).

[235] Janice Nadler, *Flouting the Law: Does Perceived Injustice Provoke General Non-Compliance?* Unpublished manuscript (2002).

[236] See, for example, *Most Recent Traffic Stop Data Show Little Change; Black Drivers Still Stopped at Higher Rate*, Washington Post T03 (June 6, 2002) ("Black and Hispanic drivers are having their vehicles searched at a rate greater than that in which both groups are stopped"); Mike Connell, *Search After Traffic Stop Raises Question of Equal Treatment*, Times Herald (Port Huron, MI) 7B (May 19, 2002) ("once they were pulled over, black males were 70% more likely than white males to be searched without evidence of a crime—so-called consent searches"); *Group to Inform Drivers of Rights in Searches*, New York Times B5 (May 9, 2002) ("consent searches . . . have been the focus of the fight over racial profiling"); John M. Glionna, *Oakland Police: Success Story or Scandal?* Los Angeles Times pt 2, p 1 (Dec 3, 2001) (outlining accusations by the ACLU against the Oakland Police of using racial profiling in consent searches, and noting that the California Highway Patrol had declared a moratorium on consent searches).

the legal system that follows can potentially destabilize the law-abiding behavior of ordinary people. Because people have reasons for obeying the law that are apart from the threat of sanctions, obedience to law is vulnerable to diminished respect produced by perceptions of injustice. According to the Flouting Thesis, when people perceive the law as unjust, they are less likely to comply with legal rules governing everyday behavior.[237]

I have demonstrated the Flouting Thesis empirically in a different context in which I show that the perceived injustice of a particular law can lead to lower levels of expressed willingness to comply with other laws, even those distinct from and unrelated to the source of the perceived injustice.[238] For example, a person who reads a newspaper story about a (perceived) unfair change in the tax code is more likely, on average, to express a future intent to flout other laws, such as parking regulations and copyright restriction, compared to a person who read about a similar but fair law. This research suggests that the fiction that pervades the Court's Fourth Amendment consent search jurisprudence, if known to citizens, can trigger the very kind of lack of moral authority that leads to noncompliance with other unrelated laws. If the *Drayton* Court's conclusion that a reasonable passenger on the bus would feel free to refuse the officers' requests to search and terminate the encounter is perceived by citizens as unjust, this perception can trigger general flouting of the law in everyday life.[239]

It is tempting to dismiss this concern on the grounds that most citizens do not read and are unaware of Supreme Court decisions like *Drayton*, so there is little danger that decisions like *Drayton* or *Bostick* will result in diminished respect for law and increased flouting.[240] While it is undoubtedly true that the vast majority of

---

[237] Nadler, *Flouting the Law* (cited in note 235).

[238] Id. In an experimental demonstration of the Flouting Thesis, some participants were given newspaper stories to read that were about laws widely perceived to be unjust. Others read newspaper stories about perceived just laws. Later, in a seemingly unrelated study, all participants indicated their personal willingness to engage in various examples of unlawful behavior, such as drunk driving, shoplifting, speeding, etc., all unrelated to the laws in the newspaper stories. People who were exposed to unjust laws via newspaper stories were more willing to flout (unrelated) laws in their everyday lives than people exposed to just laws in the newspaper.

[239] These very sentiments were expressed by motorists interviewed in Lichtenberg's survey. See Lichtenberg, *Voluntary Consent* (cited in note 157).

[240] Most citizens undoubtedly did not hear about the *Drayton* opinion, but some did. Shortly after the Court issued its decision in *Drayton*, syndicated columnist James J. Kil-

citizens will never become aware of particular decisions announced by the Court, the effects of those decisions often seep into popular awareness. This is especially true for decisions such as *Drayton* that directly bear on topics that are considered hot-button issues of the moment. With respect to *Drayton*, the associated hot-button issue is racial profiling of citizens by police. For several years prior to *Drayton*, media attention had been focused intensely on the government's use of consent as a justification for searching African-American and Hispanic motorists, who had been stopped by police in disproportionate numbers.[241] For example, the press has reported that blacks and Hispanics are more likely to be targeted for consent searches once they have been stopped.[242] Consent searches of motorists have played such a large role in the racial profiling debate that the most populous state in the nation, California, recently declared a moratorium on consent searches by highway patrol officers.[243] *Drayton* concerned consent searches on buses rather than on highways, but the issue of disproportionate police targeting of members of racial and ethnic minorities for consent searches is raised indirectly by *Drayton* because of the demographic realities of intercity bus travel.[244] Because of this, there is a possibility that *Drayton* will further fan the flames of the racial profiling debate, even if citizens never hear about the case directly.

Once perceptions of injustice in the law take hold, the negative effects of these perceptions can become manifest very broadly. In

---

patrick wrote an editorial published by many local newspapers across the country. In it, he openly mocked the Court's reasoning in *Drayton*. Kilpatrick quoted from a portion of the majority opinion which stated, "'Nothing would suggest to a reasonable person that he or she was barred from leaving the bus or otherwise terminating the encounter,'" to which Kilpatrick retorted, "Ho, ho, ho, and call the Tooth Fairy to the stand!" The *Augusta Chronicle* ran Kilpatrick's column under a headline entitled, *Justice Kennedy Disconnected from Reality* (July 21, 2002), p A04. It is therefore somewhat plausible that such publicity has direct effects on citizens' respect for law, although these direct effects may be small. There are also more widespread, indirect effects, as I argue in the remainder of this section.

[241] See note 236.

[242] See, for example, *Most Recent Traffic Stop Data Show Little Change; Black Drivers Still Stopped at Higher Rate*, Washington Post T03 (June 6, 2002) (cited in note 236); Connell, *Search After Traffic Stop Raises Question of Equal Treatment*, Times Herald (Port Huron, MI) 7B (May 19, 2002) (cited in note 236).

[243] See *Group to Inform Drivers of Rights in Searches*, New York Times B5 (May 9, 2002) (cited in note 236); Glionna, *Oakland Police: Success Story or Scandal?* Los Angeles Times pt 2, p 1 (Dec 3, 2001) (cited in note 236).

[244] Intercity bus passengers are disproportionately poor, nonwhite, and less educated. See O'Shields, 77 Iowa L Rev at 1899 n 211 (cited in note 194).

the study cited earlier,[245] people who read newspaper stories about the unjustness of civil forfeiture and tax laws later expressed a greater willingness to flout laws that were completely unrelated to the newspaper stories that were the source of the perceive injustice. There is reason to think that the Court's consent fiction has already generated perceptions of injustice. After *Bostick* and *Robinette*, the popular press had a difficult time reconciling the Court's standard with common sense justice. One commentator remarked that "by the [C]ourt's weird reasoning, you can 'voluntarily' consent to a search even if you think your cooperation is compulsory."[246] The *Drayton* decision comes at a time of intense public debate about the propriety of consent searches and amidst accusations that the police use consent searches as a tool to target racial and ethnic minorities improperly.[247] Even citizens who never hear directly about the Court's decision in *Drayton* are likely to be exposed in some fashion to this widely publicized debate, to which *Drayton* now has indirectly contributed. To the extent that *Drayton* provides fodder for those who would believe that the law gives free rein to police who target racial and ethnic minorities for consent searches, it also contributes to perceptions among some citizens who are attentive to this debate that the law is unjust. Such perceptions generally can lead to decreased respect for and compliance with the law as a whole.

V. CONCLUSION

It may be the case that, on balance, it is desirable to permit police to board intercity buses and pose questions to passengers and, in some circumstances, conduct searches of baggage and persons, especially with the current need to be vigilant about potential risks of terrorism. In this way, it is understandable that the *Drayton* Court scrupulously avoided announcing rules in drug cases that would restrict the ability of police to investigate terrorism and other serious threats to public security.

On the other hand, in its effort to be sensitive to the order-

---

[245] See Nadler, *Flouting the Law* (cited in note 235).

[246] Stephen Chapman, *"Voluntary" Consent and Other Judicial Fantasies*, Chicago Tribune C23 (Nov 24, 1996).

[247] See note 236.

maintenance needs of the government,[248] the Court has promulgated a standard for determining the bounds of consensual police-citizen encounters and voluntary searches that struggles against a wealth of social science evidence, that subjects many innocent people to suspicionless searches and seizures against their will, and that produces disagreement and confusion in the lower courts. It may be that large-scale, suspicionless searches of passengers on common carriers is a price that we ought to be willing to pay to stem the flow of illegal narcotics transported on intercity buses and trains.[249] If this is the determination that underlies the decision in *Drayton*, then the Court should have explicitly stated it and justified it—rather than relying on the implausible assertion that bus passengers, when they are individually confronted by armed police officers who want to search them, feel free to ignore the police or outright refuse their requests.

---

[248] See David Sklansky, *Traffic Stops, Minority Motorists, and the Future of the Fourth Amendment*, 1997 Supreme Court Review 271; Carol S. Steiker, *Counter-Revolution in Constitutional Criminal Procedure? Two Audiences, Two Answers*, 94 Mich L Rev 2466, 2468 (contending that since the 1960s the Court has become "more accommodating to assertions of the need for public order.").

[249] Of course, it is somewhat self-serving for scholars, policymakers, and judges, many of whom do not travel frequently on intercity buses and trains, to determine that this sacrifice is one worth making when it is others (especially those who are politically vulnerable) who bear the burden of the sacrifice. This kind of self-serving "sacrifice" is reminiscent of an ironic moment in the movie *Shrek*, when Lord Farquaad announces to his constituency, "Some of you may die, but it's a sacrifice I am willing to make."

SUSAN R. KLEIN AND
JORDAN M. STEIKER

THE SEARCH FOR EQUALITY IN
CRIMINAL SENTENCING

For the last two terms, the U.S. Supreme Court has been rocked by the aftershocks of two independent yet equally significant criminal sentencing revolutions. The first, brought on by the Court itself in the 1970s, was the constitutionalization of capital sentencing procedures pursuant to the Eighth Amendment's Cruel and Unusual Punishments Clause. This death-penalty jurisprudence has had the laudable goal of attempting to reduce, if not eliminate, discrimination and disparity in the selection of those defendants to receive the ultimate penalty. Though initiated with cautious optimism, this revolution has been a dismal failure. State schemes have not significantly reduced sentencer discretion at the penalty phase of capital trials, and the results of such schemes have not been demonstrably more consistent than those obtained in the era preceding federal judicial regulation. A concurrent revolution with a similar goal occurred in the non-capital area, though this one was instituted legislatively. Congress passed the Federal Sentencing Act in order to impose rationality and to reduce discrimination and other disparities in criminal sentencing for non-capital cases. Almost half of state legislatures subsequently followed suit. Unlike

Susan R. Klein is the Baker & Botts Professor in Law at the University of Texas at Austin School of Law, and Jordan M. Steiker is the Cooper K. Ragan Regents Professor in Law at the University of Texas at Austin School of Law.

AUTHORS' NOTE: We would like to thank Sara Beale, George Fisher, Danny Richman, and Carol Steiker for their helpful comments, and John Pearson and Donna Strittmatter for their research assistance.

the capital context, however, this revolution has enjoyed considerable success in ensuring similar treatment for similarly situated defendants.

These parallel efforts to enhance equality in capital and non-capital criminal sentencing have not been discussed together in the academic literature. In Section I of this article, we will trace this parallel development in the capital and non-capital arenas, evaluate their success in ensuring equality, and determine whether any lessons can be transferred from one context to the other.

The current approach to non-capital sentencing represents a striking departure from early American history. Although the English practice in colonial times approached sentencing as a largely ministerial task, this approach soon gave way to a system of indeterminate sentencing in which judges, later aided by parole boards, enjoyed essentially unguided discretion in selecting an appropriate sentence within a wide range prescribed by the legislature.

The Federal Sentencing Commission in 1984 replaced the pure judicial-discretion paradigm with an administrative-sentencing system. In this regime, the selection of those facts regarding the offender and her offense that are relevant to setting the punishment, as well as the weight to be given to each fact, are supplied by a statutorily-authorized Sentencing Commission, and the sentencing hearing is conducted without the full panoply of criminal procedural guarantees afforded a criminal defendant at trial. The move from the judicial-discretion model to the administrative model for sentencing has been largely successful in insuring equality of similarly situated, non-capital defendants in a relatively efficient manner. A shift back to pure judicial discretion or to the criminal procedural model, where the jury must find all facts relevant to sentencing, would halt the sentencing reform movement.

A determinate sentencing system employing the administrative model offers two significant advantages over the system it replaced: it enhances the opportunity for equality in non-capital sentencing, and transparency in sentencing decisions. Only through comprehensive guidelines implemented by judges can we promote similar treatment for similarly situated non-capital defendants. Judges, rather than jurors, view a sufficient number of cases to determine which defendants warrant harsher or more lenient sentences, and produce decisions that establish precedent and provide a basis for factual and legal review on appeal. Moreover, without a guidelines system, judges (or juries) are free to implement any particular punishment theory to which they subscribe, or, worse, to indulge in invidious discrimination. A published guidelines system, even one developed by an unelected sentencing commission, is more democratic than discretionary judge or jury sentencing because it publishes in advance all information relevant to sentencing determinations. If the public believes a particular penalty or sentencing factor is inappropriate, it can make revisions through the democratic process in a way not possible when these factors were hidden.

In capital sentencing, states have historically conferred virtually unfettered discretion on juries to choose between life and death. Although the Court first rejected constitutional challenges targeting such unguided discretion, the Court subsequently held that states must offer some structure to capital sentencing if they are to retain the death penalty. Over the past thirty years, states have attempted to rationalize the death penalty decision through detailed sentencing instructions. But the resulting statutes still confer substantial discretion on capital decision makers, and the effort to ensure consistency across cases has been notably less successful than in the non-capital context. In fact, federal constitutional regulation of the death penalty has arguably produced a less desirable capital sentencing regime, because contemporary instructions often obscure the ultimate moral choice capital sentencers must confront.

In Section II.A, we will discuss the most recent threat to the administrative model in the non-capital context: the holding in *Apprendi v New Jersey* that any fact, other than a prior conviction, that increases the prescribed maximum penalty for an offense must be found by a jury beyond a reasonable doubt.[1] The broadest application of this rule would have foreclosed the Federal Sentencing Guidelines and their state guideline counterparts as a matter of practice because it is simply too cumbersome to have juries make all fact-findings necessary to apply the guidelines. Moreover, even if it were feasible to have juries administer guide-

---

[1] 530 US 466 (2000) (Stevens, Scalia, Souter, Thomas, and Ginsburg, JJ, writing for the majority; Thomas and Scalia, separately concurring; and Rehnquist, CJ, O'Connor, Kennedy, and Breyer, JJ, dissenting).

lines, juries could not be relied upon to implement such guidelines in a consistent fashion. The Supreme Court's rejection of this broad *Apprendi* theory last term in *Harris v United States*[2] insures the continued viability of the administrative model in the non-capital context.

In Part II.B, we will discuss the failure of the administrative model in the death penalty context. Meaningful equality across cases cannot be secured through a guideline-like approach to capital sentencing. The success of the guidelines approach in the non-capital area cannot be recreated for capital sentencing for a number of reasons. In non-capital cases the guidelines establish different penalty ranges, whereas in the capital context the choice is binary: death or not death. Moreover, unlike in the non-capital context, it is extraordinarily difficult to quantify factors deemed relevant in a death penalty proceeding, particularly on the mitigating side. Finally, because there is less need in the capital area for judges as sentencers, *Apprendi* is less of a threat to equality values in death penalty law than it was to equality values in non-capital sentencing. Thus, the Court's extension of the *Apprendi* rule, in *Ring v Arizona*,[3] to aggravating circumstances in capital cases will not undermine reform. In addition, there are independent reasons in the capital arena to prefer jury to judge sentencing, such as sustaining the connection between the community and those imposing the death penalty.

We conclude with some final thoughts regarding the tension between equality norms and the commitment to jury sentencing. The Court's decisions in *Apprendi*, *Harris*, and *Ring* reflect an appropriate accommodation of these competing norms. In the non-capital context, *Apprendi* sufficiently protects the role of the jury, while *Harris* justifiably elevates practice over theory to ensure equality. In the death penalty context, equality has been the focal point of contemporary regulation, but, unfortunately, the sentencing phase of capital trials is perhaps the aspect of the capital sentencing system least amenable to systemization through guidelines.

---

[2] 536 US 545 (2002) (Kennedy, O'Connor, Scalia, JJ, Rehnquist, CJ, writing for the plurality; Breyer, J, concurring; and Thomas, Stevens, Souter, and Ginsburg, JJ, dissenting).

[3] 536 US 584 (2002) (Ginsburg, Scalia, Kennedy, Souter, and Thomas, JJ, writing for the majority, with Breyer, J, concurring, O'Connor, J, Rehnquist, CJ, dissenting).

I. Parallel Developments in Sentencing Reform from the 1970s to the Present

A. SUCCESSFUL REFORM IN NON-CAPITAL SENTENCING

The English practice at the time of our nation's founding was determinate sentencing of those convicted of a felony offense; there was one possible sentence for each offense, imposed after a jury verdict based on proof beyond a reasonable doubt of every element constituting that offense.[4] Thus the particular sentence (usually death) followed inexorably from the face of the felony indictment and the jury verdict. It made no difference whether judge or jury pronounced that certain judgment, or whether the offense was created by common law or statute.[5] This system never fully took hold in colonial America. After only a few years, amid the widespread view that whipping and capital punishment had lost their deterrent power, the desire to mitigate "pious perjury," the belief that death was a disproportionate penalty for some crimes, and the new philosophy that solitude and hard labor in a penitentiary would reform the criminal, the trend toward mandatory capital offenses began to reverse.[6] In the late eighteenth century, Massachusetts decreased the number of crimes punishable by death. Within several decades, Massachusetts initiated an experiment looking to newly built penitentiaries for crime control and the reform of offenders, and many states[7] and the federal government soon followed.[8] These new sentencing regimes provided minimum and maximum sentencing ranges and allowed judges, at their dis-

---

[4] *Apprendi*, 530 US at 477; J. Archbold, *Pleading Evidence in Criminal Cases* at 44 (15th ed 1862).

[5] See, e.g., *Apprendi*, 530 US at 477–82.

[6] See generally Morton J. Horwitz, *The Transformation of American Law 1780–1860* (Harvard, 1977); Nancy J. King and Susan R. Klein, *Essential Elements*, 54 Vand L Rev 1457, 1506–07 (2001) (noting that decades later England followed the American trend); Deborah Young, *Fact-Finding at Federal Sentencing: Why the Guidelines Should Meet the Rule*, 79 Cornell L Rev 299 (1994).

[7] See Adam J. Hirsch, *The Rise of the Penitentiary; Prisons and punishment in Early America* at 11–12 (Yale, 1992); David Rothman, *The Discovery of the Asylum: Social Order and Disorder in the New Republic* at 49 (Little Brown, 1990); Kate Stith and A. Jose Cabranes, *Fear of Judging: The Sentencing Guidelines in the Federal Courts* at 16 (Chicago, 1998).

[8] For example, of the 22 crimes enacted by the first Congress in 1790, six were punished by hanging, 13 provided only a maximum sentence, and two set the punishment at four times the value of the property involved. See 1 Stat 112 (1790).

cretion, to set the penalty within the range.[9] By the nineteenth century, most of these discretionary sentences in non-capital cases were imposed by a judge, although several non-federal jurisdictions did practice jury sentencing.[10]

Beginning in the late nineteenth century and ending in about the 1970s, both state and federal judges exercised their discretion pursuant to the rehabilitative or medical approach to sentencing, under the belief that experts in correction would "treat" the criminal.[11] The judge depended upon the parole office to determine when a felon had been sufficiently reformed to warrant release.[12] This highly discretionary, indeterminate sentencing regime was necessary to implement the "prevalent modern philosophy of penology that the punishment should fit the offender and not merely the crime."[13]

The rehabilitative model began to unravel in the 1960s and 1970s. Two concurrent concerns led to its demise and precipitated the sentencing reform movement. First, liberals and conservatives alike increasingly regarded the rehabilitation model as a failure.[14] Three-quarters of a century of data appeared to confirm that parole authorities were unable to identify whether and when any particular offender had been reformed, and studies indicated that the programs offered in penitentiaries were unable to reign in the rampant recidivism rate.[15]

---

[9] Hirsch, *The Rise of the Penitentiary* at 8–14, 57 (cited in note 7); Lawrence M. Friedman, *Crime and Punishment in American History*, 77–82 (Basic Books, 1993).

[10] See Charles O. Betas, *Jury Sentencing*, 2 Natl Parole & Probation Assn J 369 (1956); Note, *The Admissibility of Character Evidence in Determining Sentence*, 9 U Chi L Rev 715 (1942).

[11] See, e.g., George Fisher, *Plea Bargaining's Triumph*, 109 Yale L J 857, 1055 (2000); Alan Dershowitz, *Indeterminate Confinement: Letting the Therapy Fit the Harm*, 123 U Pa L Rev 297 (1974); Comment, *Considerations of Punishment by Juries*, 17 U Chi L Rev 400, 401 n 6 (1949) (explaining that many states limited jury sentencing in non-capital cases during this period because the "disposition of offenders is a problem for specialists in criminology and psychiatry.").

[12] *Mistretta v United States*, 488 US 361 (1989); Sandra Shane-Dubow et al, *Sentencing Reform in the United States: History, Content, and Effect* (Government Printing Office, 1985); Francis A. Allen, *The Decline of the Rehabilitative Ideal* at 3–7 (Yale, 1981).

[13] *Williams v New York*, 337 US 241, 247–48 (1949).

[14] See Jay Miller et al, *Sentencing Reform* at 1–6 (National Center for State Courts, 1981); Allen, *The Decline of the Rehabilitative Ideal* (cited in note 12); Senate Report No 98-225 (1983) (referring to the "outmoded rehabilitation model" for federal criminal sentencing).

[15] See, e.g., Miller et al, *Sentencing Reform* at 6–12 (cited in note 14); Dale G. Parent, *What Did the United States Sentencing Commission Miss?* 101 Yale L J 1773 (1992); Douglas Lipton et al, *The Effectiveness of Correctional Treatment: A Survey of Treatment Evaluation Studies* at 523 (Praeger, 1975); Robert Martinson, *What Works—Questions and Answers About Prison Reform*, Public Interest 22 (Spring 1974).

Second, experience revealed that the broad judicial discretion required by the rehabilitation model resulted in unwarranted disparities in sentencing similarly situated defendants, with such factors as geography,[16] race,[17] gender,[18] socioeconomic status,[19] and judicial philosophy[20] accounting for much of the difference. An enormous and inexplicable disparity was found in pre–Federal Sentencing Guidelines indeterminate sentencing regimes on both the state[21] and federal[22] levels, whether the sentencer was judge or jury,[23] and whether the study was historical[24] or simulated.[25] This

---

[16] Roszel C. Thomsen, *Sentencing in Income Tax Cases*, 26 Fed Probation 10 (1962); Ilene H. Nagel and John L. Hagan, *The Sentencing of White-Collar Criminals in Federal Courts: A Socio-Legal Exploration of Disparity*, 80 Mich L Rev 1427, 1453 (1982). The Eastern District of New York, which employed sentencing councils, nevertheless displayed disparity both within itself and in relation to the rest of the Circuit. Shari Seidman and Hans Zeisel, *Sentencing Councils: A Study of Sentence Disparity and Its Reduction*, 43 U Chi L Rev 109, 145 (1975) (finding 30–40 percent disparity between individual judges, and that sentencing councils were able to reduce roughly 10 percent of this disparity).

[17] See, e.g., Beverly Blair Cook, *Sentencing Behavior of Federal Judges: Draft Cases 1972*, 42 U Cin L Rev 597, 615 (1973); William W. Wilkins, Jr., et al, *The Sentencing Reform of 1984: A Bold Approach to the Unwarranted Sentencing Disparity Problem*, 2 Crim L F 355, 359–62 (1991).

[18] Ilene Nagel, *Structuring Sentencing Discretion: The New Federal Sentencing Guidelines*, 80 J Crim L & Criminol 883, 895–97, and nn 73–84 (1990) (reviewing the empirical studies documenting the sentencing impact of race, gender, and socioeconomic status).

[19] Id.

[20] Paul J. Hofer, Kevin R. Blackwell, and Barry Rubach, *The Effect of the Federal Sentencing Guidelines on Inter-Judge Sentencing Disparity*, 90 J Crim L & Criminol 239, 240 (1999); Kevin Clancy et al, *Sentence Decisionmaking: The Logic of Sentence Decisions and the Extent and Sources of Sentence Disparity*, 72 J Crim L & Criminol 524, 542 (1981) (reporting the results of evaluation by 264 federal judges of sixteen hypothetical cases and finding that only in three cases did a majority of the judges seek the same sentencing goal).

[21] William Austin and Thomas A. Williams III, *A Survey of Judges' Responses to Simulated Legal Cases: Research Note on Sentencing Disparity*, 68 J Crim L & Criminol 306 (1977) (performing analysis similar to that of the Second Circuit study on Virginia state district court judges' hypothetical sentences and finding disparity both in type and magnitude of sentence).

[22] Beverly Blair Cook, *Sentencing Behavior of Federal Judges: Draft Cases—1972*, 42 U Cin L Rev 597 (1973) (examining all 1,852 draft-dodging convictions and finding sentence disparity based on environment, geography, and individual judge).

[23] George William Baab and William Royal Furgeson, Jr., Comment, *Texas Sentencing Practices: A Statistical Study*, 45 Tex L Rev 471 (1966) (performing a regression analysis on 1,720 state felony sentences from twenty-seven different districts and finding evidence of disparity based not only on gender and individual judge but also on whether pretrial release occurred and whether counsel was appointed or retained).

[24] See, e.g., Nagel, 80 J Crim L & Criminol at 895–97 (cited in note 18); Norval Morris, *Towards Principled Sentencing*, 37 Md L Rev 267, 272–74 (1977) (reviewing historical studies and finding that "the data on unjust sentencing disparities have indeed become quite overwhelming").

[25] See Sandor Frankel, *The Sentencing Morass, and a Suggestion for Reform*, 3 Crim L Bull 365 (1967) (recounting an early simulation study carried out at a 1961 workshop of the

welter of empirical data by researchers led to a rallying cry of conservative and liberal judges and policymakers behind Judge Marvin Frankel, the father of the modern sentencing reform movement. Judge Frankel, viewing the status quo as "lawlessness of sentencing," insisted that the unchecked and sweeping powers given to judges in the fashioning of sentences was "terrifying and intolerable for a society that professes devotion to the rule of law."[26]

Out of this perception of the ineffectiveness of rehabilitation programs and the unfairness of sentencing practices, the Federal Sentencing Guidelines[27] and the seventeen state sentencing guidelines regimes[28] were born. Concomitant with the advent of judicial guidelines was the reduction in the number of states permitting juror sentencing, from one-quarter of the states down to five.[29] Jurors sentence offenders with greater disparity than do judges, even judges not utilizing guidelines, "primarily because laypersons bring no experience to the task of sentencing and bear no continued responsibility for it."[30] Just as pre–Federal Sentencing Guide-

---

Sixth, Seventh, and Eighth Circuits, which resulted in widely disparate sentences); Anthony Partridge and William B. Eldridge, *The Second Circuit Sentencing Study: A Report to the Judges of the Second Circuit* (Federal Judicial Center, 1974) (describing study where each judge delivered sentence on approximately twenty real and ten hypothetical presentence reports).

[26] Marvin E. Frankel, *Criminal Sentences: Law Without Order* (Hill & Wang, 1973).

[27] Sentencing Reform Act of 1984, Pub L No 98-473, 98 Stat 1987 (1984). The Act garnered the support of Senators Joseph Biden (D-Delaware), Orrin Hatch (R-Utah), and Strom Thurmond (R-SC). See Stith and Cabranes, *Fear of Judging* at 43–47 (cited in note 7).

[28] See Richard S. Frase, *Is Guided Discretion Sufficient? Overview of State Sentencing Guidelines*, 44 SLU L Rev 425, 446 (2000) (listing the seventeen states currently using guidelines systems and the eight states considering the adoption of such guidelines).

[29] See Note, *Statutory Structures for Sentencing Felons in Prison*, 60 Colum L Rev 1134, 1154, and nn 136–37 (1960) (citing to the jury sentencing statutes in thirteen states); Note, *Jury Sentencing in Non-Capital Cases: An Idea Whose Time Has Come (Again)?* 108 Yale L J 1775 n 65 (1999) (citing to jury sentencing statutes in Arkansas, Kentucky, Missouri, Texas, and Virginia).

[30] Robert A. Weninger, *Jury Sentencing in Non-Capital Cases: A Case Study of El Paso County, Texas*, 45 Wash U J Urban & Contemp L 3, 292 (1994) (regression analysis of random sample of 1,395 felony prosecutions commences between 1974 and 1977, finding greater severity for jury sentencing and greater disparity for almost every offense type); William A. Eckert and Lori E. Exstrand, *The Impact of Sentencing Reform: A Comparison of Judge and Jury Sentencing Systems* (1975) (unpublished manuscript cited in Note, 108 Yale L J (cited in note 29) (comparing sentences before and after Georgia introduced judge sentencing and finding evidence of systematic jury sentencing disparity for aggravated assault offenses); Brent L. Smith and Edward H. Stevens, *Sentence Disparity in the Judge-Jury Sentencing Debate: An Analysis of Robbery Sentences in Six Southern States*, 9 Crim J Rev 1, 4 (1984) (finding the standard deviation in all three jury sentencing states was higher than in the three judge sentencing states).

lines judges were free to impose any sentence for any reason, juries are not compelled to provide reasons for their sentences.

The Federal Sentencing Commission,[31] following marching orders from Congress, crafted the Federal Sentencing Guidelines, which establish a range of determinate sentences for categories of offenses and offenders according to various specified factors. These objective factors concern offense characteristics that make the particular crime more or less serious (such as the use of a firearm, the value of the property involved, and any harm to or provocation from the victim) and offender characteristics that make the particular defendant more or less culpable (such as whether the defendant chose a vulnerable victim, whether he was a leader or follower, whether he accepted responsibility or obstructed justice, and whether he was a career or first-time offender).[32] The Commission compromised between a harm-based, retributive model and a crime-control, deterrence scheme, basing offense levels primarily on an empirical assessment of past sentencing practices.[33] Most states implementing guidelines systems have also incorporated a guidelines manual devised by a sentencing commission.[34]

---

[31] The Commission has seven voting members appointed by the President with the consent of Congress. At least three must be federal judges, and no more than four members can be from the same political party. 28 USC §§ 991–94 and 18 USC § 3553(a)(2). Congress must disapprove of any amendment offered by the Commission or it becomes law, so long as consistent with other Congressional statutes.

[32] Sentencing Reform Act of 1984, 98 Stat 1987 (1984) (cited in note 27). The most recent Guidelines Manual (West, 2002), all 1,626 pages of it, attempts to list every offense and offender characteristic that can play any role in sentencing a defendant. See, e.g., U.S. Sentencing Manual § 2B3.1(b)(2) (use of a weapon during a robbery), § 2B1.1(b) (fraud loss table), § 3A1.1 (hate crime motivation or vulnerable victim), and § 3C1.1 (career offender). Most personal characteristics of the offender unrelated to the offense, such as her age, education and vocational skills, mental and emotional conditions, physical condition (including drug or alcohol dependency or abuse), employment record, community ties, family ties and responsibilities, military service, charitable contributions, and lack of guidance as a youth, are not relevant factors in determining a sentence, and are "discouraged" as a grounds for departure. USSG §§ 5H1.1–5H1.6; 5H1.11–12. Congress has forbidden the Commission from considering the "race, sex, national origin, creed, and socioeconomic status of offenders." 18 USC § 994(d); USSG § 5H1.10.

[33] See, e.g., Stephen Breyer, *The Federal Sentencing Guidelines and the Key Compromises Upon Which They Rest*, 17 Hofstra L Rev 1 (1988); Paul H. Robinson, *Dissent from the United States Sentencing Commission's Proposed Guidelines*, 77 J Crim L & Criminol 1112 (1986).

[34] See, e.g., Richard S. Frase, *Sentencing Guidelines in Minnesota, Other States, and the Federal Courts: A Twenty Year Retrospective*, 12 Fed Sent Rptr 69, 72 (2000); US Dept of Justice, Bureau of Justice Assistance, *National Assessment of Structured Sentencing* 14–17 (1996) (detailing sentencing guideline regimes in the states as of February 1994); Andrew Von Hirsch et al, *The Sentencing Commission and Its Guidelines* at 177–88 (1987) (Appendix, *A Summary of the Minnesota, Washington, and Pennsylvania Guidelines*).

Guidelines transform a judge's job from using her discretion to select a particular sentence from a very broad range to making those factual findings, usually mandated by a commission, that dictate the particular sentence she must impose. In the federal system, these factual findings are made by a judge employing the preponderance-of-evidence standard at an informal sentencing hearing, and the findings establish a defendant's place on a 258-box sentencing grid. The defendant's place along the horizontal axis, which consists of forty-three offense-level categories, is determined by selecting the appropriate offense level from the Sentencing Guidelines Manual. The offense level can then be adjusted upward or downward depending on factual findings of those aggravating and mitigating circumstances listed in the manual, such as whether defendant brandished a weapon or accepted responsibility for the offense. The defendant's place along the vertical axis is determined by the defendant's criminal history. Under this rather mechanical process, the judge's discretion is limited to selecting the sentence within the very narrow range offered by the defendant's place in the grid.[35]

Although everybody loves to hate the Federal Sentencing Guidelines,[36] determinate sentencing guidelines regimes have contributed to two important goals: uniformity and transparency. The Federal Sentencing Guidelines have achieved their highest level of success regarding Congress's stated goal—the reduction of unwar-

---

[35] This discretion is limited to a matter of months of prison time, as within each grid the sentence can vary by only 25 percent. However, in those rare instances where an aggravating or mitigating factor was not taken into account by the sentencing commission or was present to a degree not reflected in the manual, the judge may depart upward or downward, subject to appellate review. See *U.S. Sentencing Guidelines* § 5K2.0 (authorizing departures); U.S. Sentencing Commission, *2000 Sourcebook of Federal Sentencing Statistics* 51, Fig G (noting that, in 2000, 17.9 percent of defendants received downward departures for substantial assistance, 17 percent of defendants received downward departures based upon other grounds, and .7 percent of defendants received upward departures); *Koon v United States*, 518 US 81 (1996) (departures reviewed for abuse of discretion).

[36] See, e.g., Michael Tonry, *Sentencing Matters* (Oxford, 1996); Albert W. Alschuler, *The Failure of Sentencing Guidelines: A Plea for Less Aggregation*, 58 U Chi L Rev 901 (1991); Stephen J. Schulhofer and Ilene H. Nagel, *Plea Negotiations Under the Federal Sentencing Guidelines: Guideline Circumvention and Its Dynamics in the Post-Mistretta Period*, 91 Nw U L Rev; Erik Luna, *Misguided Guidelines: A Critique of Federal Sentencing Policy Analysis No. 458* (Nov 1, 2002); Stith and Cabranes, *Fear of Judging* (cited in note 7); Federal Judicial Center, *The United States Sentencing Guidelines, Result of the Federal Judicial Center's 1996 Survey* (Federal Judicial Center, 1997) (1997 survey concluding that more the two-thirds of federal judges wish to scrap the Guidelines).

ranted disparity in sentencing.[37] Empirical studies indicate that since the Federal Sentencing Guidelines were implemented, differences in sentences are now based primarily on relevant factors such as an offender's criminal history and the particular manner in which the offense was committed, and not unwarranted factors such as the geographic area in which the offense was committed or the sentencing philosophy of the judge.[38] Even those scholars most critical of the Federal Sentencing Guidelines on the grounds of loss of judicial flexibility and prosecutorial evasion admit modest success in reaching the goal of equality.[39] While we could find fewer studies regarding the success of state sentencing guidelines in reducing disparity, what we do know suggests that the experience in the states has been similar.[40]

We are not apologists for the Federal Sentencing Guidelines, nor do we suggest that any present guidelines system is without significant room for improvement. Rather, we claim that an administrative guideline regime enhances the prospects for consistency across cases in the non-capital context, and that much of the

---

[37] See, e.g., U.S. Sentencing Commission, *Sentencing Guidelines and Policy Statements* (1987). The disparity at sentencing must hinge solely on relevant factors such as criminal history and the severity of the offense.

[38] See, e.g., Hofer et al, 90 J Crim L & Criminol at 239, 243 (cited in note 20) (claiming some success for the guidelines at reducing interjudge disparity); James M. Anderson, Jeffrey R. Kling, and Kate Stith, *Measuring Interjudge Sentencing Disparity: Before and After the Federal Sentencing Guidelines*, 42 J L & Econ 271 (1999) ("Our study indicates that the Guidelines [and concomitant statutory minimum sentences] have been successful in reducing interjudge nominal sentencing disparity."); A. Abigail Payne, *Does Inter-Judge Disparity Really Matter? An Analysis of the Effects of Sentencing Reforms in Three Federal District Courts*, 17 Intl Rev L & Econ 337 (1997) (reviewing drug and embezzlement/fraud/theft cases and finding a reduction of disparity for drug cases post-Guidelines and finding more modest success in some district in reducing embezzlement, fraud, theft disparity); U.S. Sentencing Commission, *The Federal Sentencing Guidelines: A Report on the Operation of the Guidelines System and Short-Term Impacts on Disparity in Sentencing, Use of Incarceration, and Prosecution Discretion and Plea Bargaining* (1991) (comparing pre- and post-Guidelines sentences for four major offense types and finding that disparity decreased significantly in all categories).

[39] See, e.g., Joel Waldfogel, *Does Inter-Judge Disparity Justify Empirically Based Sentencing Guidelines*, 18 Intl Rev L & Econ 293 (1998) (arguing that the reduction of interjudge disparity, while statistically significant, does not justify the loss of proportionality in sentencing); Schulhofer and Nagel, 91 Nw U L Rev at 1284, 1286 (cited in note 36) (finding that the Guidelines have reduced disparity in cases going to trial and in 65–80 percent of cases resolved by plea); Alschuler, 58 U Chi L Rev at 901 (cited in note 36) (admitting that the Guidelines impose uniformity in regard to those factors listed, such as harm, but arguing that the Guidelines are faulty because they ignore situational and offender characteristics that reflect culpability and therefore should influence sentences).

[40] State sentencing guidelines in Minnesota have had similar success in limiting disparity. See Hofer et al, 90 J Crim L & Criminol at 262 n 74 (cited in note 20) (collecting studies).

scholarly criticism applies to facets of sentencing that are either
not part of the guidelines regime, or are parts that could be divorced from the guidelines. In other words, the criticism is primarily directed at federal statutes or particular aspects of the Federal
Sentencing Guidelines, rather than at problems inherent in a
guidelines regime.

For example, one serious criticism levied against the Federal
Sentencing Guidelines is that federal prosecutors can circumvent
equality by manipulating offense levels through charge bargaining,
thus giving favorable plea agreements to sympathetic defendants
while preventing judges from doing the same.[41] Although this is a
genuine problem, the perception of unwarranted disparity generated by fact bargaining in negotiating guilty pleas might exceed
the reality.[42] The problem is ameliorated to some extent by the fact
that federal judges are required to sentence defendants for related
uncharged or dismissed conduct so long as that sentence is within
the statutory maximum for the crime to which the defendant pled
guilty,[43] and by the Thornburg memorandum, which prohibits fed-

---

[41] See, e.g., Douglas A. Berman, *Does Fact Bargaining Undermine the Guidelines?* 8 Fed
Sent Rptr 299 (1996); Gerald W. Heaney, *The Reality of Sentencing Guidelines: No End to
Disparity*, 28 Am Crim L Rev 161, 194 (1991) (concluding on the basis of anecdotal evidence
that "the guidelines have the potential to produce a new breed of sentence disparity hidden
from view and controlled primarily by the pressures of the prosecutor's caseload"). But see
Judge William Wilkins, *Response to Judge Heaney*, 28 Am Crim L Rev 795 (1992) (critiquing
Judge Heaney's methodology and finding that prosecutors do not control the Guidelines
process).

[42] See Molly Treadway Johnson and Scott A. Gilbert, *The U.S. Sentencing Guidelines: Results of the Federal Judicial Center's 1996 Survey, Report to the Committee on Criminal Law of
the Judicial Conference of the United States* (Federal Judicial Center, 1997) (reporting that
large majorities of district judges and chief probation officers believe that "plea bargains
are a source of hidden unwarranted disparity in the Guidelines system"). However, in the
only empirical work on disparity in plea situations, Professor Schulhofer and Commissioner
Nagel found that Guideline evasion occurred in only 20–35 percent of guilty plea cases
(see n 36 above). Our intuition matches that of a former U.S. Attorney who served as
chair of the Subcommittee on Sentencing Guidelines of the Attorney General's Advisory
Committee, who wrote that prosecutors follow the Guidelines even in plea negotiations
"in the vast majority of cases," and that evasion will decrease because the principal offenders
were older AUSAs who feel that they know what each case is worth. Joe B. Brown, *The
Sentencing Guidelines Are Reducing Disparity*, 29 Am Crim L Rev 875, 880 (1992).

[43] One of the many Guidelines compromises was between a "real offense" system, where
a defendant is sentenced for whatever she actually did, and a "charge offense" system, where
a defendant is sentenced only for the crime of conviction or plea. See USSG § 1B1.3;
United States v Watts, 519 US 148 (1997) (holding that judge is required to sentence for
related uncharged conduct, even if the defendant was acquitted of that conduct by a jury).
Information regarding related uncharged conduct is found from reviewing the reports of
the federal agents working on the case and a probation department interview with the
defendant. Such conduct is difficult to hide from the judge.

eral prosecutors from accepting pleas except to the most serious readily provable offense.[44] While prosecutors and defense attorneys may attempt to evade a mandated guidelines range for that conduct actually engaged in by misrepresenting the facts of the offense, the case agent and the probation department are not easily fooled. Based upon the Presentence Investigation Report prepared in every criminal case, federal judges should reject any plea agreement that does not reflect the seriousness of the actual offense behavior, or that offers a sentence below the applicable guidelines range, unless other legitimate considerations (e.g., problems of proof) justify the agreement.[45]

Another frequent criticism is that the increased length of sentences under the federal guidelines, coupled with significant reduction in prison time that a defendant receives for "accepting responsibility" (which is accomplished primarily through pleading),[46] gives prosecutors undue leverage to coerce guilty pleas.[47] In fact, much of the ability of prosecutors in the federal system to coerce guilty pleas from favored or disfavored defendants stems from the threat of mandatory minimum sentences[48] and from prosecutors' ability to offer essentially unreviewable downward departures to particular defendants based upon substantial assistance to authorities.[49] This power, confined to the federal system, exists regardless

---

[44] Reprinted in 6 Fed Sent Rptr 347 (1994). This memorandum was moderated by the 1993 Reno Memorandum, reprinted in 6 Fed Sent Rptr 352 (1994). See also USAM 9-27.400 (Sept 1997).

[45] See USSG § 6B1.2 (permitting court to accept plea agreement only if it adequately reflects the seriousness of the actual offense behavior, does not preclude the dismissed conduct from being considered as relevant conduct, or departs from the applicable guidelines range for a justifiable reason); Fed Rules of Crim Proc 11(e)(1)(C) (authorizing judge to reject a binding plea that incorporates a sentencing range contrary to the Guidelines).

[46] See USSG § 3E1.1, offering a two- or three-level decrease in based offense level for accepting responsibility for one's criminal conduct. For a defendant with a base offense level of 30, this can translate into a reduction from 97–121 to 70–87 months of imprisonment.

[47] See, e.g., Stephanos Bibas, *Judicial Fact-Finding and Sentence Enhancements in a World of Guilty Pleas*, 110 Yale L J 1097 (2001); Luna, *Misguided Guidelines* (cited in note 36).

[48] See, e.g., Paul D. Borman, *The Federal Sentencing Guidelines*, 16 Thomas M. Cooley L Rev 4 (1999) (distinguishing the Guidelines from a separate and independent federal sentencing phenomenon—mandatory minimum sentences); U.S. Sentencing Commission, *Special Report to the Congress: Mandatory Minimum Penalties and the Federal Criminal Justice System* at ii–iv (1991) (report from the U.S. Sentencing Commission to Congress criticizing mandatory minimums as producing unwarranted disparities among offenders and transferring power from judges to prosecutors).

[49] See 18 USC § 3553(e); 28 USC § 994(n); and USSG § 5K1.1 (allowing court to depart below guideline range and below statutorily required mandatory minimum sentences upon motion of the government stating that the defendant has provided substantial assistance to

of the implementation of the Guidelines. We are sympathetic to critics of the present Federal Sentencing Guidelines regime bemoaning the decline of jury trials over the last ten years.[50] However, the Guidelines are not the primary culprit here: mandatory minimums and the prosecutorial leverage stemming from reductions for substantial assistance are to blame. These sorts of provisions and the acceptance of responsibility reduction could, and perhaps should, be reassessed.[51] The issue, though, is clearly one of degree. It is neither realistic as a matter of practice nor desirable as a matter of policy to wholly remove incentives for defendants to cooperate and to acknowledge guilt (and waive trial). Rather, Congress should ensure that the incentives strike an appropriate balance without reintroducing unaccountable discretion on the part of prosecutors or placing undue coercive pressure on criminal defendants.

A third common criticism of the Federal Sentencing Guidelines is that they offer insufficient procedural protections at sentencing.[52] The Court has held open the possibility of heightened procedures at sentencing hearings for facts triggering particularly long sentences,[53] a possibility about which we offer no opinion. Yet again, this criticism applies even more appropriately to non-Guidelines discretionary systems, where there is no pretense of factual findings, and no appellate review of sentences.

---

the authorities); *Wade v United States*, 504 US 181 (1992) (holding that court can review prosecutor's refusal to file a substantial-assistance motion only if based upon unconstitutional motive). Nationwide, about 19 percent of federal defendants received such departures in 1998. U.S. Sentencing Commission, *1998 Sourcebook of Federal Sentencing Statistics* (Table 26), United States Sentencing Commission website, <http://www.ussc.gov/ANNRPT/1998/sbtoc98.htm>.

[50] George Fisher, *The Balance of Power to Bargain*, in *Plea Bargaining's Triumph* (Stanford, forthcoming 2003) (suggesting that the Federal Sentencing Guidelines have contributed to the decline in jury trials by reducing the availability of judicial leniency).

[51] See, e.g., Frank O. Bowman, *Departing Is Such Sweet Sorrow: A Year of Judicial Revolt on "Substantial Assistance" Departures Follows a Decade of Prosecutorial Undiscipline*, 29 Stetson L Rev 7 (1999) (noting judicial backlash against use of substantial assistance, and predicting that unless the DOJ exercises greater self-discipline, Congress might repeal the provision); Gary T. Lowenthal, *Mandatory Sentencing Laws: Undermining the Effectiveness of Determinate Sentencing Reform*, 81 Cal L Rev 61 (1993).

[52] See, e.g., Sara Sun Beale, *Procedural Issues Raised by Guideline Sentencing: The Constitutional Significance of Single "Elements of the Offense,"* 35 Wm & Mary L Rev 147 (1993) (advocating clear and convincing evidence standard of proof for certain sentence enhancements, and suggesting that the defendant be afforded an opportunity to confront and cross-examine witnesses).

[53] See *Almendarez-Torres v United States*, 523 US 224, 248 (1998).

The most serious criticism of the Federal Sentencing Guidelines is that they have not succeeded in eliminating racial discrimination.[54] While unwarranted interjudge disparity might have been the most potent source of pre-Guidelines disparity, unwarranted racial disparity is the most pernicious. There are two aspects of this claim; the first has nothing to do with the Guidelines, and the second is severable from the administrative model. The primary cause of higher overall sentences for nonwhites is that certain federal crimes committed disproportionately by African-Americans are punished more severely than crimes committed disproportionately by whites.[55] For example, the sentence disparity caused by the penalty differential between powder and crack cocaine is the choice of Congress, and has nothing to do with the Federal Sentencing Guidelines. The second claim is that the grant of authority to federal prosecutors to request judicial reduction of sentences below guidelines ranges (and even below mandatory minimums) based upon substantial assistance to authorities has resulted in some continued racial discrimination.[56] This problem, again, must be placed at the door of Congress and not the Commission. This authority is statutory, and hence would remain even if the Federal Sentencing Guidelines were repealed.[57] Most state sentencing regimes based upon the administrative model do not grant such power to prosecutors.

In fact, the racial discrimination criticism, along with the equally common charges from scholars that the Federal Sentencing

---

[54] See, e.g., David B. Mustard, *Racial, Ethnic, and Gender Disparities in Sentencing: Evidence from the U.S. Federal Courts*, 44 J L & Econ 285, 311 (2001) (arguing that a large difference in the length of sentence exists on the basis of race, gender, education, income, and citizenship).

[55] Douglas McDonald and Kenneth Carlson have demonstrated that the average-sentence disparity between blacks and whites relies extensively on the 100–1 ratio between crack and powder cocaine. Douglas C. McDonald and Kenneth E. Carlson, Bureau of Justice Statistics, *Sentencing in the Federal Courts: Does Race Matter?* 182 (1993); Heaney, 28 Am Crim L Rev (cited in note 41). The Sentencing Commission's two attempts to change the ratio were both, regrettably, rejected by Congress. See Norm Abrams and Sara Sun Beale, *Federal Criminal Law* 308–10 (West, 3d ed 2000).

[56] See *Substantial Assistance: An Empirical yardstick Gauging Equity in Current Federal Policy and Practice* (1998), U.S. Sentencing Commission website, <http://www.ussc.gov/research.htm> (last visited on January 15, 2003) (report by two Commission staff members finding inequities by judges and prosecutors concerning downward departures for substantial assistance; factors such as gender, race, ethnicity, and citizenship were statistically significant in explaining such departures); Mustard, 44 J L & Econ (cited in note 54).

[57] 18 USC § 3553(e); 28 USC § 994(n).

Guidelines have eliminated all moral judgment from the sentencing process[58] and have offered no coherent philosophy of punishment,[59] are criticisms not of a determinate sentencing regime based upon the administrative model, but rather of policy choices made by legislatures. Moral judgments are still being made, but they are now made by the legislature and are applicable to all potential offenders, rather than being made on an ad hoc basis by judges to apply to individual defendants. That the Federal Sentencing Guidelines system is neither flawlessly coherent nor shares the same normative commitments as its detractors is insufficient reason to dismantle it.

This brings us to the second advantage of a determinate sentencing regime—transparency. While many castigate the Federal Sentencing Guidelines as antidemocratic,[60] we believe just the opposite is true. The Sentencing Commission publishes a manual containing the precise sentence to be imposed for each particular crime committed in a particular manner, listing those factors that are relevant or forbidden in determining that sentence and providing the weight to be given each factor. These guidelines are later ratified or rejected through the political process. Thus, if one believes it is unjust to sentence more harshly for drug offenses than for violent offenses, or that the 100 to 1 ratio of punishment of crack to powder cocaine in the federal system is racially discriminatory, one can invoke the democratic process to change the statutory sentence, and the Guideline change would follow automatically.[61] If one believes, for example, that family circumstances should play a role in sentencing decisions,[62] the present ban against

[58] Stith and Cabranes, *Fear of Judging* (cited in note 7).

[59] See, e.g., Marc Miller, *Purposes at Sentencing*, 66 S Cal L Rev 413 (1992); Paul Robinson, 41 Crim L Rep 3174 (1987) (resigning from Commission in frustration over perceived failure to develop a coherent sentencing rationale).

[60] See, e.g., Luna, *Misguided Guidelines* (cited in note 36).

[61] One could do this by voting for representatives who will change the law, or by persuading the judiciary that the punishment is unconstitutional. See, e.g., David A. Sklansky, *Cocaine, Race, and Equal Protection*, 47 Stan L Rev 1283 (1995) (suggesting that the crack: powder ratio violates the Equal Protection Clause).

[62] Compare Myrna S. Raeder, *Gender and Sentencing: Single Moms, Battered Women, and Other Sex-Based Anomalies in the Gender-Free World of the Federal Sentencing Guidelines*, 20 Pepperdine L Rev 905 (1993) (arguing that, as a normative matter, the Guidelines should take account of whether felons are single parents), with Ilene H. Nagel and Barry Johnson, *The Role of Gender in a Structured Sentencing System: Equal Treatment, Policy Choices, and the Sentencing of Female Offenders Under the United States Sentencing Guidelines*, 85 J Crim L &

its consideration in the federal system[63] is now visible in a written document and open to discourse, rather than hidden in a judge- or jury-imposed sentence without an articulated, reviewable rationale.

B. FAILED REFORM IN CAPITAL SENTENCING

Constitutional regulation of the death penalty is a relatively modern development. Four decades ago federal constitutional rulings placed essentially no restraints on state death penalty practices distinct from those applicable to all state criminal proceedings.[64] A confluence of events in the 1960s brought substantial popular and legal attention to American death penalty practices. The civil rights movement and the dramatic upheaval in constitutional criminal procedure wrought by the Warren Court emboldened opponents of capital punishment to seek reform or abolition of the death penalty through the courts.[65]

Although the assault against the death penalty was multifaceted, an important theme in the popular and legal critique focused on the apparent arbitrariness and inequality of state capital schemes in the United States. The number of persons sentenced to death and executed in the mid- to late 1960s represented a small fraction of persons eligible for the death penalty under state law. Many critics suspected that those selected to die were chosen for arbitrary or even invidious reasons.[66]

The constitutional challenge based on arbitrariness focused on the failure of states to articulate any criteria for determining who should live or die. Virtually all states afforded sentencers absolute discretion in deciding punishment. When the Court first addressed the constitutional attack on "standardless discretion" under the

---

Criminol 181, 207 (1994) (suggesting that the just deserts and crime control principles of the Guidelines outweigh the "exogenous utilitarian concerns" of the impact on children).

[63] See note 32.

[64] See, e.g., Hugo Bedau, *The Courts, the Constitution, and Capital Punishment*, 1968 Utah L Rev 201, 228–29 (stating, as late as 1968, that "not a single death penalty statute, not a single statutorily imposed mode of execution, not a single attempted execution has ever been held by any court to be 'cruel and unusual punishment' under any state or federal constitution").

[65] See Stuart Banner, *The Death Penalty: An American History*, 247–66 (Harvard, 2002); Michael Meltsner, *Cruel and Unusual: The Supreme Court and Capital Punishment* (Random House, 1973).

[66] See Banner, *The Death Penalty* at 243–44 (cited in note 65) (discussing concerns about racially discriminatory aspects of the American death penalty system).

Due Process Clause in *McGautha v California*,[67] it emphatically rejected the claim. Justice Harlan, writing for the Court, famously insisted that the effort "[t]o identify before the fact those characteristics of criminal homicides and their perpetrators which call for the death penalty, and to express these characteristics in language which can fairly be understood and applied by the sentencing authority," were tasks "beyond present human ability."[68]

Surprisingly, just a year later the Court revisited the arbitrariness claim, this time under the Eighth Amendment, in *Furman v Georgia*.[69] Perhaps even more surprisingly, a bare majority concluded that all of the capital statutes before the Court[70] (and, by implication, nearly all of the capital statutes then in force[71]) violated the Eighth Amendment. The five Justices in the majority wrote separate opinions identifying various and, to some extent, conflicting rationales for the Court's judgment. Despite their important differences, the opinions of the Justices in the majority centered on arbitrariness: notwithstanding the broad death-eligibility established in most state schemes, relatively few persons were sentenced to death and fewer still were executed in the decade before *Furman*.[72] The paucity of executions in relation to broad death-eligibility was troubling to several members of the Court because there was no reliable evidence indicating that those executed (or sentenced to death) were in any sense the most deserving of death among the death-eligible.[73] Worse still, some members

---

[67] 402 US 183 (1971).

[68] Id at 204.

[69] 408 US 238 (1972).

[70] Along with *Furman*, the Court reviewed three other cases: *Jackson v Georgia*, *Branch v Texas*, and *Aikens v California*. See 403 US 952 (1971) (granting certiorari).

[71] Of the forty state statutes in effect at the time of *Furman*, all but Rhode Island's suffered from the defect of "standardless" discretion and were thus unenforceable in light of the decision. Rhode Island's mandatory death penalty provisions were later effectively struck down when the Court held that the Eighth Amendment requires "individualized" sentencing in capital cases. See *Woodson v North Carolina*, 428 US 280 (1976) (invalidating nondiscretionary death penalty statute).

[72] See, e.g., *Furman*, 408 US at 291 (Brennan, J, concurring) ("The outstanding characteristic of our present practice of punishing criminals by death is the infrequency with which we resort to it."); id at 309 (Stewart, J, concurring); id at 311 (White, J, concurring).

[73] See, e.g., id at 309 (Stewart, J, concurring) ("These death sentences are cruel and unusual in the same way that being struck by lightning is cruel and unusual."); id at 313 (White, J, concurring) ("the death penalty is exacted with great infrequency even for the

of the Court, particularly Justice Douglas, feared that the few individuals caught in the death penalty web were selected for discriminatory, morally irrelevant reasons, such as race or class.[74]

These shared concerns about the alarming chasm between the death penalty in theory and the death penalty in fact led the Court to condemn the absence of legislative guidance in state schemes. Despite Justice Harlan's eloquent rejection of the petitioner's claim in *McGautha* that the death-penalty decision could be rationalized through detailed sentencing instructions, the *Furman* Court seemed to suggest that just such guidance was necessary to save the death penalty in light of the apparent arbitrary and discriminatory aspects of prevailing death-penalty practices.

The apparent hope of the Court was that legislative guidance would ensure that individual sentencing decisions reflect the values of the larger community, because the states would announce in advance their respective "theories" of when death should be imposed.[75] Such guidance promised to address two distinct problems. First, clear standards would limit the risk that "undeserving" defendants would be sentenced to death because their particular juries concluded, contrary to the values of the community as a whole, that the defendant before them was among the truly worst offenders. Second, clear standards would ensure that all potentially "deserving" defendants would be subject to the same sentencing criteria rather than the ad hoc criteria adopted on a case-by-case basis by juries afforded absolute and unguided discretion. Legislative guidance thus held out the possibility that like cases would be treated alike. Not only would all undeserving defendants escape the death penalty; the hope was that clear legislative direction would ensure as well that all (or most) deserving defendants received it.

States responded to *Furman*'s critique of standardless discretion in two ways. Some states appeared to read *Furman* as requiring the removal of sentencing discretion altogether and accordingly

---

most atrocious crimes and [ ] there is no meaningful basis for distinguishing the few cases in which it is imposed from the many cases in which it is not").

[74] Id at 257 (Douglas, J, concurring) (describing the pre-*Furman* capital statutes as "pregnant with discrimination" in their operation).

[75] Carol S. Steiker and Jordan M. Steiker, *Sober Second Thoughts: Reflections on Two Decades of Constitutional Regulation of Capital Punishment*, 109 Harv L Rev 355, 365 (1995).

enacted mandatory statutes that required the death penalty for certain offenses.[76] Most states, however, revamped their statutes to substantially increase the structure of the sentencing decision while at the same time preserving some sentencer discretion to choose between life and death.[77] In these states, previously broad instructions to jurors to decide punishment in accordance with their "most profound judgment"[78] or their "dictates of conscience"[79] were replaced with formulas involving consideration of "aggravating" and "mitigating" factors or "special issues." These latter statutes have emerged as the sole constitutionally permissible vehicles for deciding punishment in capital cases.[80] Having invalidated the poles of standardless discretion and discretionless standards, the Court has directed most of its regulatory efforts in the death penalty area to fine-tuning the permissible middle ground of "guided discretion."[81]

The effort to secure equality in capital cases through guided-discretion statutes has proven elusive for several reasons.[82] To begin with, states have promiscuously used subjective aggravating factors that significantly undermine the effort to limit or constrain discretion. The Model Penal Code death penalty provision, which received little attention pre-*Furman*, led many states down this path post-*Furman* by including as its last aggravating factor that "[t]he murder was especially heinous, atrocious or cruel, manifesting exceptional depravity."[83] Asking a sentencer to separate "especially" heinous from the "ordinarily" heinous crimes is not a

---

[76] See *Woodson v North Carolina*, 428 US 280 (1976) (invalidating North Carolina's mandatory statute); *Roberts v Louisiana*, 428 US 325 (1976) (invalidating Louisiana's mandatory statute).

[77] See, e.g., *Gregg v Georgia*, 428 US 153 (1976) (reviewing Georgia's post-*Furman* approach); *Proffitt v Florida*, 428 US 242 (1976) (reviewing Florida's post-*Furman* approach).

[78] This was the standard instruction given in Ohio and challenged in *Crampton v Ohio*, the companion case to *McGautha*. See *McGautha*, 402 US at 289 (Brennan, J, dissenting) (quoting *State v Caldwell*, 135 Ohio St 424, 425, 21 NE2d 343, 344 (1939)).

[79] *Baugus v State*, 141 So2d 264, 266 (Fla), cert denied, 371 US 879 (1962).

[80] See Steiker and Steiker, 109 Harv L Rev at 371–403 (cited in note 75).

[81] Id.

[82] Jordan M. Steiker, *The Limits of Legal Language: Decisiomaking in Capital Cases*, 94 Mich L Rev 2590, 2624 (1996) (arguing that the effort to achieve consistency across cases "has proven not merely unachievable but counterproductive").

[83] Model Penal Code § 210.6(3)(h) (1980).

promising means of ensuring consistent outcomes. This aggravating factor operates as a catch-all, allowing the sentencer to find death-eligibility if none of the objective criteria (such as the presence of an accompanying violent felony, or commission of the offense during an escape from custody) is satisfied. Part of the problem, no doubt, is that subjective notions such as "heinousness" and "depravity" capture a genuine, if amorphous, community sentiment about what characterizes the "worst" murders. But the use of such criteria, as well as the Court's willingness to tolerate hopelessly indeterminate factors (such as Idaho's factor, which asks whether "the defendant exhibited utter disregard for human life"[84]), certainly undermines any pretense to equal treatment. Unlike the Federal Sentencing Guidelines, which by and large rely on strictly objective criteria,[85] state death penalty statutes often include factors that invite sentencers to give voice to their impressionistic responses to the offender and offense.[86]

Moreover, many states have adopted numerous aggravating circumstances.[87] Thus, even in state schemes that rely primarily on objective, nonvague aggravating circumstances, such as committing the murder in the course of a felony,[88] or killing a police officer,[89] the factors collectively suffer from the same defect as individual factors that are impermissibly vague. Instead of guiding sentencers toward a particular "theory" of the worst murders, such factors taken together describe the circumstances surrounding most murders. Empirical work reflects this dynamic, as virtually all persons sentenced to death in Georgia before *Furman* would

---

[84] *Arave v Creech*, 507 US 463, 468 (1993) (sustaining limiting construction by Idaho Supreme Court that the defendant displayed the attitude of a "cold-blooded, pitiless slayer").

[85] See note 32 and accompanying text.

[86] See *Walton v Arizona*, 497 US 639, 655 (1990) (upholding use of "especially heinous, cruel or depraved" aggravating factor).

[87] See, e.g., Ariz Rev Stat Ann § 13-703(F)(1989) (listing ten aggravating circumstances); Colo Rev Stat § 16-11-103(5) (Supp 1994) (listing thirteen aggravating circumstances); Fla Stat Ann § 921.141(5) (West Supp 1995) (listing eleven aggravating circumstances); Utah Code Ann § 76-3-202(1) (West Supp 1992) (listing seventeen aggravating circumstances).

[88] See, e.g., NJ Stat Ann § 2C:11-3.c(4)(g) ("[t]he offense was committed while the defendant was engaged in . . . flight after committing or attempting to commit murder, robbery, sexual assault, arson, burglary or kidnapping").

[89] See, e.g., Fla Stat Ann ch 921.141(5)(j) (Harrison Supp 1991); SC Code Ann § 16-3-20(C)(a)(7) (Law Co-op Supp 1991).

have been deemed death-eligible under Georgia's post-*Furman* statute.[90]

In addition, the Supreme Court's recognition of a broad individualization requirement limits the effectiveness of articulating criteria on the aggravating side. When the Court rejected mandatory death penalty schemes in 1976, it suggested that a defendant must be able to offer any evidence regarding his background, character, or circumstances of the offense.[91] This is exactly the opposite of the practice under the Federal Sentencing Guidelines, where most personal characteristics of the defendant are specifically excluded from sentencing consideration.[92] Subsequent decisions expanded this individualization right in the capital context,[93] basically foreclosing any significant state efforts to channel or limit consideration of the factors a defendant might offer in support of a sentence less than death.[94]

The breadth of the individualization requirement is evident in *Skipper v South Carolina*,[95] a revealing case in which the Court held that a state could not prevent a defendant from presenting evidence of his postcrime good behavior in prison.[96] The state had argued that the individualization requirement should be limited to evidence relating to moral blameworthiness—evidence that actually *mitigates* the severity of the crime. The Court, though, defined "mitigating" not as a corollary to blameworthiness, but as any "basis for a sentence less than death." This diluted conception of mitigation explains, for example, the current ubiquitous practice of a defendant's loved ones testifying about the loss his death would bring to family members and friends. There might be good reasons to allow such a practice, but it certainly undermines the pursuit

---

[90] David C. Baldus, George Woodworth, and Charles A. Pulaski, Jr., *Equal Justice and the Death Penalty: A Legal and Empirical Analysis* at 268 n 31 (Northeastern, 1990).

[91] *Woodson v North Carolina*, 428 US 280 (1976).

[92] See note 32.

[93] *Lockett v Ohio*, 438 US 586 (1978); *Eddings v Oklahoma*, 455 US 104 (1982).

[94] See Carol S. Steiker and Jordan M. Steiker, *Let God Sort Them Out? Refining the Individualization Requirement in Capital Sentencing*, 102 Yale L J 835 (1992) (book review).

[95] 476 US 1 (1986).

[96] The result under the Federal Sentencing Guidelines would be just the opposite. See *United States v Harrington*, 947 F2d 956 (DC Cir 1991) (holding that the defendant's successful participation in a drug treatment program during his pretrial release and posttrial incarceration was not an appropriate grounds for a downward sentencing departure).

of equality, as death will often turn on the eloquence (or attractiveness) of those speaking on a defendant's behalf. The enormous breadth of the individualization requirement also contributed to the Court's decision to reverse its ban on the introduction of victim-impact evidence.[97] The Court indicated that states should not be barred from offering a "quick glimpse of the life which a defendant chose to extinguish"[98] if "virtually no limits are placed on the relevant mitigating evidence a capital defendant may introduce concerning his own circumstances."[99]

As a result of the Court's unconstrained individualization requirement, states are essentially forbidden from developing a cabined theory of the death penalty. A state could not, for example, successfully pursue a purely retributivist approach to capital sentencing. If a state were to enumerate aggravating factors solely focused on moral culpability, the individualization requirement would compel the state to afford a vehicle for the sentencer's consideration of future dangerousness and incapacitation should the defendant choose to argue against death based on his projected behavior. In short, the effort to provide sentencers with a focused set of criteria cannot secure meaningful equality if sentencers are in the end told that they can, indeed *must*, consider any evidence a defendant offers for a sentence less than death. Thus, unlike the Federal Sentencing Guidelines, the "guidance" in contemporary death penalty schemes is illusory. The sentencer is guided only to arrive at a point in which anything and everything else must be considered. The individualization requirement operates as a permanent, powerful "downward departure" mechanism that renders the previous guidance a mere prelude to absolute, unreviewable discretion.

Moreover, even if state schemes were able to limit and codify discretion on the "mitigating" side, their ability to secure consistency across cases would be undermined by their failure to provide any guidance as to the relative weight of various aggravating and mitigating factors. The Federal Sentencing Guidelines are significant not only for their enumeration of sentencing factors, but also

---

[97] *Payne v Tennessee*, 501 US 808 (1991) (overruling *Booth v Maryland*, 482 US 496 (1987), and *South Carolina v Gathers*, 490 US 805 (1989)).

[98] *Payne*, 501 US at 822 (internal quotation marks and citations omitted).

[99] Id.

for the assignment of weights to the various aggravating and mitigating considerations.[100] It is not enough to say what factors matter; consistency requires that sentencing considerations play similar roles in similar cases. In the death penalty context, no state has sought to establish a hierarchy of aggravation and mitigation; sentencers must consult their own consciences to assess whether, for example, a defendant's prior conviction for a dangerous felony matters more or less than a defendant's minimal participation in the instant offense.

The refusal of states to assign weights to relevant factors reflects an important, distinctive feature of capital sentencing. In the noncapital context, the sentencer's role is to set a term of years based upon the legislative determination of the severity of the particular crime the defendant committed and the manner in which he committed it. The sentencer judges the defendant's conduct at the relevant time, not his moral worth, his value to the community, or his capacity for redemption. Death penalty decisions, by contrast, necessarily involve a more global assessment of the defendant's moral culpability and worth as a human being. The Court's insistence on individualized sentencing in capital cases, though perhaps expanded beyond its logical reach, is essential to just capital sentencing. If evidence of a defendant's reduced blameworthiness would make his execution excessive in the eyes of the community, a procedure that precluded consideration of such evidence would impermissibly sever the connection between the death penalty and society.

In non-capital sentencing, the federal government and the states justifiably enjoy greater latitude to restrict consideration of mitigating factors and to focus primarily on the criminal conduct. It is appropriate and constitutional, when life is not at stake, to allow for categorical treatment of mitigation doctrines in substantive criminal law. A state can choose, in short, to assign no weight at sentencing to a mitigating factor that fails to meet some significant threshold. A defendant satisfies the requirements for perfect self-defense, insanity, or duress, or is subject to a particular sentence based primarily upon aggravating factors. To require a full assessment of reduced blameworthiness in the non-capital context would entail overwhelming and unacceptable costs. Not only would crim-

---

[100] The "weight" of each factor translates into a specific number of months by which a sentence is either increased or decreased.

inal sentencing become more difficult and time consuming, but sentencers would invariably differ in their assessment of the significance of all potential mitigating facts (except for those few addressed in the guidelines regimes themselves). The elusive quest for "perfect" justice in the individual case would inevitably lead to unwarranted disparities. When the choice, though, is whether a particular defendant should die, it is imperative for the sentencer to affirm that the defendant deserves death.

Moreover, the death penalty context involves an all-or-nothing decision. The effort to systematically assign weights to aggravating and mitigating factors is more acceptable when such assignments operate along a spectrum, because such a process implicitly acknowledges the tentativeness of the weighting process. To assign weights to aggravating and mitigating factors in the death penalty context would communicate a false sense of precision. Indeed, establishing a hierarchy of aggravation and mitigation would distort a system that already tilts unacceptably in the direction of obscuring the moral responsibility of capital sentencers.[101]

In the end, modern death penalty law does little to ensure consistency across cases. At most, states have articulated an unexhaustive list of relevant considerations, leaving sentencers free rein to decide what other facts might be relevant and how they should be weighed. Notwithstanding the absence of meaningful guidance, state death penalty schemes still manage to confuse and obscure the ultimate moral decision sentencers must make. "Guidance" in the post-*Furman* statutes often comes in the form of mind-numbing details about the respective burdens of proof in establishing or disproving the existence of aggravating and mitigating factors.[102]

---

[101] See Steiker, 94 Mich L Rev at 2624 (cited in note 82) ("Instead of clarifying and distilling the relevant issues in capital cases, the jargon and complexity that pervade contemporary punishment-phase instructions obscure the fundamental moral role that capital sentencers should be expected to assume.").

[102] See, e.g., Ala Code § 13A-5-45(g) (1982) ("When the factual existence of an offered mitigating circumstance is in dispute, the defendant shall have the burden of interjecting the issue, but once it is interjected the state shall have the burden of disproving the factual existence of that circumstance by a preponderance of the evidence."); NCPI-Crim § 150.10, at 27 ("The existence of any mitigating circumstance must be established by a preponderance of the evidence, that is, the evidence, taken as a whole, must satisfy you—not beyond a reasonable doubt, but simply satisfy you—that any mitigating circumstance exists. . . . A juror may find that any mitigating circumstance exists by a preponderance of the evidence whether or not that circumstance was found to exist by all the jurors."); 42 Pa Cons Stat Ann § 9711(c)(iii) (requiring proof beyond a reasonable doubt for aggravating circumstances and proof by a preponderance of the evidence for mitigating circumstances).

Such instructions, along with highly technical directions about how to reach the ultimate verdict,[103] are neither easily understood nor particularly helpful in rationalizing the death penalty decision. The complexity of current instructions is likely to steer sentencers away from the core issues they are expected to decide.

Perhaps more importantly, the net effect of casting the death penalty decision in complicated, math-laden vocabulary is to obscure for many jurors the fact that they retain the ultimate moral decision-making power over who lives and dies. Because contemporary statutes invariably fail to instruct jurors in affirmative terms about the scope of their moral authority and obligation, guided discretion can easily (and wrongly) be experienced as no discretion at all. As one commentator has aptly framed the problem, "giv[ing] a 'little' guidance to a death penalty jury" poses the risk that "jurors [will] mistakenly conclud[e] that they are getting a 'lot' of guidance," thus diminishing "their personal moral responsibility for the sentencing decision."[104]

II. THE APPRENDI REVOLUTION AS APPLIED TO CAPITAL AND NON-CAPITAL SENTENCING

A. THE CONSTITUTIONAL THREAT TO THE "ADMINISTRATIVE MODEL" IN NON-CAPITAL SENTENCING

In a series of cases beginning in the 1950s, the Court has rebuffed constitutional challenges that would have slowed legislative

---

[103] See, e.g., Fla Stat Ann ch 921.141(2) (Harrison Supp 1991) ("After hearing all the evidence, the jury shall deliberate and render an advisory sentence to the court, based upon the following matter: (a) Whether sufficient aggravating circumstances exist as enumerated [ ]; Whether sufficient mitigating circumstances exist which outweigh the aggravating circumstances found to exist; and (c) Based on these considerations, whether the defendant should be sentenced to life imprisonment or death."); Tenn Code Ann § 39-13-204 (1991) ("(f) If the jury unanimously determines that no statutory aggravating circumstances have been proven by the state beyond a reasonable doubt, or if the jury unanimously determines that a statutory aggravating circumstance or circumstances have been proven by the state beyond a reasonable doubt but that such circumstance or circumstances have not been proven by the state to outweigh any mitigating circumstances beyond a reasonable doubt, the sentence shall be life imprisonment. . . . (g) If the jury unanimously determines that: (A) At least one statutory aggravating circumstance or several statutory aggravating circumstances have been proven by the state beyond a reasonable doubt; and (B) Such circumstance or circumstances have been proven by the state to outweigh any mitigating circumstances beyond a reasonable doubt; then the sentence shall be death.").

[104] Joseph L. Hoffman, *Where's the Buck? Juror Misperception of Sentencing Responsibility in Death Penalty Cases*, 70 Ind L J 1137, 1159 (1995).

sentencing reform.[105] The most direct threat to utilizing the administrative model to control judicial discretion and promote equality in sentencing came in a 1989 case challenging the constitutionality of the Federal Sentencing Guidelines. Eight members of the Court rejected the following contentions: first, that the delegation of sentencing authority from Congress to the Federal Sentencing Commission violated the constitutional nondelegation doctrine, and, second, that the Sentencing Reform Act of 1984 violated the constitutional principle of separation of powers.[106]

A more recent and credible threat to federal and state guidelines systems was a case from the 1999 Term, *Apprendi v New Jersey*,[107] in which the defendant challenged judicial fact-finding at sentencing on Sixth Amendment and due process grounds. Apprendi plead guilty to a state weapons offense punishable by a maximum of ten years in prison. Pursuant to a state statute permitting enhanced sentencing for "hate-crimes," the New Jersey trial judge, after finding by a preponderance of evidence that Apprendi "acted with a purpose to intimidate an individual . . . because of race," sentenced him to a twelve-year term.[108] In a five-four ruling generating five separate opinions, the majority reversed Apprendi's sentence, declaring that "any fact that increases the penalty for a crime beyond the prescribed statutory maximum [other than the

---

[105] See, e.g., *William v New York*, 337 US 241 (1949) (concluding that due process does not forbid judicial findings of fact at sentencing without extending compulsory process or the right to cross-examine witnesses to the defendant); *Witte v United States*, 515 US 389 (1995) and *United v Watts*, 519 US 148 (1997) (per curiam) (holding that neither the due process standard of proof beyond a reasonable doubt nor the Fifth Amendment's Double Jeopardy Clause apply at sentencing). A few basic protections have been extended to sentencing; however, these do not threaten the guidelines regime. See *Mempa v Rhay*, 389 US 128 (1967) (extending the right to counsel); *Mitchell v United States*, 526 US 314 (1999) (preserving the Self-Incrimination Clause).

[106] *Mistretta v United States*, 488 US 361 (1989). But see 488 US at 413 (Scalia, J, dissenting).

[107] 530 US 466 (2000). The outcome of this case was foreshadowed by *Jones v United States*, 526 US 227 (1999), where the Court held, 5–4, as a matter of statutory construction, that provisions of the federal carjacking statute which established higher penalties for the offense when it resulted in death or serious bodily injury were elements of the offense rather than sentencing factors, and thus must be proven to a jury beyond a reasonable doubt.

[108] *Apprendi*, 530 US at 471 (see text). The state "hate-crime" statute at issue permitted the judge to raise a second-degree felony to a first-degree felony, potentially doubling the length of the sentence. On remand, Judge Rushdon H. Ridgway reduced Apprendi's sentence to seven years because prosecutors "showed by [only] a 'preponderance of the evidence' that Apprendi's act was racially motivated." Brenan Schurr, *Sentence Cut After Court Reverses Hate-Crime Ruling*, Rec N NJ (July 21, 2000), at A06.

fact of a prior conviction] must be submitted to a jury, and proved beyond a reasonable doubt."[109]

The narrowest holding of *Apprendi*, and the one we endorse, applies the Sixth Amendment jury right, the due process right to proof beyond a reasonable doubt, and the Fifth Amendment requirement of a grand jury indictment[110] to only those facts that could increase the otherwise applicable statutory maximum penalty permitted for an offense. Such an interpretation is not a radical transformation of current criminal law practice. A relatively limited number of federal and state statutes permitted judges, rather than juries, to find those facts that could raise the otherwise applicable statutory maximum sentence for an offense.[111] This narrow rule also leaves unaffected affirmative defenses, statutes imposing mandatory minimum penalties, and determinate sentencing guideline schemes where factual findings increase or decrease sentences within a statutorily authorized range. While all of those devices potentially increase a defendant's sentence, they all do so within the prescribed statutory maximum penalty.

However, the four dissenting *Apprendi* Justices, along with two of the five Justices in the majority, contended that *Apprendi*'s rule could not be so limited. Justice Thomas, in a concurring opinion joined by Justice Scalia, suggested that

> if the legislature . . . has provided for setting the punishment of a crime based on some fact . . . that fact is also an element . . . one need only look to the kind, degree, or range of punishment to which the prosecution is by law entitled for a given set of facts. Each fact necessary for that entitlement is an element.[112]

---

[109] *Apprendi*, 530 US at 490. Justice Stevens, writing the opinion for the Court, was joined by Justices Scalia, Souter, and Ginsburg. The majority excepted the pre-*Apprendi* practice of allowing a judicial finding of recidivism, even when such findings increase the otherwise applicable statutory maximum for the offense, by refusing to reverse *Almendarez-Torres v United States*, 523 US 224 (1998) (5–4) (upholding 8 USC § 1326(b)(2), which authorizes the twenty-year term of imprisonment for alien re-entry if the initial deportation was for commission of an aggravated felony, despite an otherwise applicable statutory maximum of two years imprisonment). That decision is unstable, however, because Justice Thomas, who joined the majority opinion in *Almendarez-Torres*, admitted in his *Apprendi* concurrence that he had made a mistake. *Apprendi* at 520 (Thomas, J, concurring).

[110] A unanimous Court held last term that *Apprendi* "facts must also be charged in the indictment." *United States v Cotton*, 535 US 625 (2002).

[111] See King and Klein, 54 Vand L Rev at 1467, 1547–55 (cited in note 6) (Appendices B and C, listing selected federal and state statutes subject to *Apprendi* challenges).

[112] *Apprendi*, 530 US at 501 (2000) (Thomas, J, concurring).

Based upon this reasoning, Justice Thomas openly advocated the reversal of *McMillan v Pennsylvania*,[113] a 1986 split decision allowing a judicial finding of a fact triggering a mandatory minimum sentence within the applicable statutory maximum penalty.[114] The sentencing enhancement in *McMillan* should have been considered an element because

> the prosecution is empowered, by invoking the mandatory minimum, to require the judge to impose a higher punishment than he might wish. The mandatory minimum "entitl[es] the government . . . to more than it would otherwise be entitled (five to ten years, rather than zero to ten. . . .)"[115]

Justice O'Connor, in a dissent joined by Chief Justice Rehnquist, Justice Kennedy, and Justice Breyer, agreed that the holding in *Apprendi* is irreconcilable with *McMillan*, and insisted "it is incumbent upon the Court . . . to admit that it is overruling *McMillan*."[116]

It seems to us that the same broader interpretation of *Apprendi* would undermine *Patterson v New York*,[117] an earlier decision permitting a legislature to transform what was formerly an element of a criminal offense into an affirmative defense, thus relieving the prosecutor of the burden of proving that fact beyond a reasonable doubt. That Patterson may have committed his homicide under the influence of extreme emotional distress, subjecting him to a manslaughter rather than a murder penalty, clearly changed the "range of punishments to which the prosecution is by law entitled."[118] Unless the legislative label of a fact as a mitigator or aggravator controls (and both Justice Stevens in his majority opinion and Justice Thomas in his *Apprendi* concurrence suggested that the

---

[113] 477 US 79 (1986) (5–4) (due process did not forbid the imposition of a five-year mandatory minimum sentence based upon a judicial finding that the defendant visibly possessed a firearm, where the total sentence imposed did not exceed the ten-year statutory maximum penalty for the underlying felony of aggravated assault).

[114] *Apprendi*, 530 US at 518–23 (Thomas, J, concurring).

[115] Id at 522.

[116] Id at 533 (O'Connor, J, dissenting).

[117] 432 US 197 (1977) (5–3) (holding that New York statute permitting affirmative defense of acting under extreme emotional distress to mitigate crime from murder to manslaughter can, consistent with due process, impose the burden of proving that affirmative defense by a preponderance of the evidence on the defendant).

[118] Justice Thomas, while not mentioning *Patterson*, attempted to escape the clear implication of his test on the viability of affirmative defenses by arguing that "a 'crime' includes every fact that is by law a basis for imposing or increasing punishment (in contrast with a fact that mitigates punishment)." *Apprendi*, 530 US at 501.

legislative label of the fact as a sentencing factor or an element cannot control),[119] there is no obvious way to determine whether the defendant's provocation in *Patterson* should be characterized as an aggravator which increased his punishment from manslaughter to murder or a mitigator which decreased his punishment from murder to manslaughter. As Justice O'Connor astutely noted in her *Apprendi* dissent, whether a fact increases or decreases punishment rests "in the eye of the beholder."[120] Thus, this broader interpretation would have transformed dozens of common affirmative defenses and mitigators, such as insanity, self-defense, diminished capacity, ignorance of the law, and intoxication, into elements of a prosecutor's case-in-chief.[121]

Likewise, Justice Thomas does not deny that his broader interpretation of the elements rule in his *Apprendi* concurrence would invalidate the Federal Sentencing Guidelines and similar state schemes. They clearly contain facts provided by the legislature that establish the punishment to be imposed on a defendant, yet these facts are not committed to a jury or subject to the reasonable-doubt standard.[122] In their separate dissents, Justices O'Connor and Breyer both predicted that the broader rule they believed to be mandated by the majority opinion applies not only to schemes like New Jersey's, under which a factual determination exposes a defendant to a sentence beyond the prescribed statutory maximum, but also to all determinate sentencing schemes in which the length of a defendant's sentence within the statutory range turns on specific factual determinations (e.g., the Federal Sentencing Guidelines).[123]

---

[119] Were the legislative label of a fact to control, the Court could police neither the element-sentencing factor nor the criminal-civil divide. See *Seling v Young*, 531 US 250, 261 (2001) (concluding that only the "clearest proof" that an act denominated civil is punitive in purpose or effect can override legislative label to the contrary).

[120] *Apprendi*, 530 US at 542–43 (O'Connor, J, dissenting).

[121] See, e.g., *Leland v Oregon*, 343 US 790 (1952) (holding that it does not violate due process to require a defendant to prove insanity beyond a reasonable doubt); *Martin v Ohio*, 480 US 228 (1987) (5–4) (holding that it does not violate due process to require a defendant to prove self-defense by a preponderance of the evidence); *Montana v Egelhoff*, 518 US 37 (1996) (5–4) (holding that it does not violate due process to eliminate voluntary intoxication as a consideration in determining mens rea).

[122] Justice Thomas suggested that the Guidelines must constitutionally be considered elements of criminal offenses when he opined that they "have the force and effect of laws." *Apprendi*, 530 US at 523 n 11 (Thomas, J, concurring) (citing Justice Scalia's dissent in *Mistretta v United States*, 488 US 361 (1989)).

[123] 530 US at 549 (2002) (O'Connor, J, dissenting) (the majority opinion "will have the effect of invalidating significant sentencing reform accomplished at the federal and state

Not surprisingly, *Apprendi* generated an immediate circuit split on the issue of whether facts triggering mandatory minimum sentences were subject to its element rule.[124] The issue arose most frequently in prosecutions under two federal statutes: the drug trafficking statute, which triggers mandatory minimum and statutory maximum sentences based on drug quantity, and the federal firearms statute, which triggers mandatory minimum sentences based upon such facts as weapon type and use. The Court granted certiorari last term in *Harris v United States* to determine whether a trial judge finding, by a preponderance of the evidence, that a defendant "brandished" his firearm, leading to a seven-year mandatory minimum sentence under 18 USC § 924(c), violated the Sixth and Fourteenth Amendments after *Apprendi*, where the statute prescribed no maximum penalty.[125]

Harris was the Court's second encounter with § 924(c) in the last three years. The 1988 version of the statute provided that:

> whomever, during and in relation to any crime of violence . . . , uses or carries a firearm, shall, in addition to the punishment provided for such crime of violence . . . , be sentenced for five years, and if the firearm is a short-barreled rifle [or a] short-barreled shotgun to imprisonment for ten years, and if the firearm is a machine gun, or a destructive device . . . , to imprisonment for thirty years.[126]

The term prior to *Apprendi*, a unanimous Court in *Castillo v United States* held, as a matter of statutory interpretation, that the type of firearm used is an element of a substantive crime that must be proven beyond a reasonable doubt to a jury, and not a sentencing

---

levels over the past three decades"). Justice Breyer likewise noted: "the Court's rule suggests a principle—jury determination of all sentencing-related facts—that, unless restricted, threatens the workability of every criminal justice system (if applied to judges) or threatens efforts to make those systems more uniform, hence more fair (if applied to commissions)." Id at 565.

[124] See Nancy J. King and Susan R. Klein, *Aprés Apprendi*, Federal Judicial Center website, <http://www.fjc.gov> (May 2002 version) (listing cases) (originally published at 12 Fed Sent Rtpr 331 (2000)).

[125] Every circuit interpreting 18 USC § 924(c) since *Apprendi* has held that the unstated statutory maximum is life imprisonment, and the firearm type and use are mandatory minimum sentences not subject to *Apprendi*. See, e.g., *Harris v United States*, 243 F3d 806 (4th Cir 2001), cert granted 534 US 1064 (2001); *United States v Carlson*, 217 F3d 986 (8th Cir 2000); *United States v Sandoval*, 241 F3d 549 (7th Cir 2001); *United States v Pounds*, 230 F3d 1317 (11th Cir 2000).

[126] 18 USC § 924(c)(1) (West 1988 ed Suppl V).

factor to be assessed by the trial court.[127] Congress amended the statute after Castillo's trial but prior to the Court's decisions in *Castillo* and *Apprendi*. The current version of the statute is similar to the previous version, though subsection numbers are added before each term of years, all mandatory penalties throughout the statute are converted to mandatory minimums, "possession" is added as an *actus reus*, and no maximum term of imprisonment is provided.[128] The legislative history of the 1998 amendment indicates Congress's intent to reverse *United States v Bailey*, a Supreme Court case making it more difficult to prove that a defendant used or carried a firearm[129] and to increase the mandatory penalty, not to shift what were elements of the crime into sentencing factors.[130] Nevertheless, the Court gave short shrift to the statutory argument; it granted certiorari to resolve the constitutional issue.

This was as attractive a case as possible for the defense. The defendant pled guilty to one count of distributing marijuana, and, after a bench trial, he was found guilty of carrying a firearm in relation to his marijuana offense. Harris sold marijuana out of his pawnshop with an unconcealed semiautomatic pistol at his side. The district judge accepted that it was Harris's ordinary practice to wear this gun, and that he unholstered it only at the undercover agent's request. The district judge also noted that the issue of whether the gun was merely carried, triggering a five-year mandatory minimum sentence, or was brandished, triggering a seven-year mandatory minimum sentence, was a "close question."[131] Had the *Apprendi* elements rule applied and the judge been required to use a beyond-a-reasonable-doubt standard, the defendant's sentence may well have been the lower one. In a four-one-four decision, a plurality led by Justice Kennedy, joined by Justices O'Connor, Scalia, and Chief Justice Rehnquist, and concurred in by

---

[127] 530 US 120 (2000) (reversing Branch-Davidian defendant's thirty-year mandatory sentence based on judicial finding that firearm used in relation to a crime of violence was a "machinegun").

[128] 18 USC § 924(c)(1) (West 2002).

[129] 516 US 137 (1995) ("use" of a gun requires active employment).

[130] The legislative history of this statute is discussed thoroughly in *Harris v United States*, Brief for Petitioner 15–17, 2002 WL 113846.

[131] *Harris v United States*, 243 F3d 806 (4th Cir 2001) (affirming district judge's factual finding in favor of the government and imposition of seven-year sentence for gun offense, to run consecutive to six-month sentence for underlying drug offense).

Justice Breyer, held that "whether chosen by the judge or the legislature, the facts guiding judicial discretion below the statutory maximum need not be alleged in the indictment, submitted to the jury, or proved beyond a reasonable doubt."[132] Thus, voting to limit *Apprendi* in *Harris* were the four *Apprendi* dissenters along with Justice Scalia.[133]

After lamenting in their *Apprendi* dissent that the decision could not be cabined in such a way that it would exclude mandatory minimums and the Federal Sentencing Guidelines, four members of the *Harris* plurality found just such a way. Citing seventeenth-century cases and treatises, they noted the dearth of historical evidence showing that facts increasing a defendant's minimum sentence but not affecting the maximum have been treated as elements.[134] While this is no doubt true, it also begs the question. There can be no historical evidence on these types of statutes because they simply did not exist. A reversion to common law practice does not resolve the issue. Moreover, as Justice Thomas noted in his *Harris* dissent, mandatory minimum statutes limit the jury's role in exactly the same fashion as did the increased statutory maximum in *Apprendi*, by imposing mandatory higher penalties based upon facts not even submitted for their consideration—in this case, the penalty of five years to life increased by 40 percent to a penalty of seven years to life.[135] That these mandatory minimum penalties do not alter the statutory maximum sentence is irrelevant; the defendant actually receives the mandatory minimum sentence, never higher or lower.[136] Justice Breyer appeared to agree with Justice Thomas, though he concurred rather than joined Justice Thomas's dissent. "I cannot easily distinguish *Apprendi v New Jersey* from this case in terms of logic. . . . And because I believe that extending *Apprendi* to mandatory minimums would have adverse

---

[132] *Harris v United States*, 122 S Ct 2406, 2418 (2002).

[133] Justice Scalia, for once, had nothing to say, and offered no explanation as to why he switched sides.

[134] *Harris*, 122 S Ct 2406 at 2416.

[135] As Justice Thomas noted in his *Harris* dissent, the logic of the plurality would describe as constitutional a statute where the mandatory minimum without a judicial finding of brandishing is five years but the mandatory minimum with such a finding is life imprisonment. *Harris*, 122 S Ct at 2424 (Thomas, J, dissenting).

[136] Id at 2425 (Thomas, J, dissenting) (citing to the U.S. Sentencing Commission, 2001 datafile, USSCFYO01, Table 1).

practical, as well as legal, consequences I cannot *yet* accept its rule. I therefore join the Court's judgment."[137]

Justice Breyer's reasoning unfortunately makes the *Harris* holding unstable and puts us in the odd position of hoping that he continues to refuse to "buy a ticket to *Apprendi*-land."[138] Justice Breyer's eventual acceptance of *Apprendi*, coupled with his belief that it should logically be extended to mandatory minimums, may lead in a future term to five votes in favor of the broader elements rule.[139]

Divorced from competing concerns about equality, and ignoring all practical considerations regarding the workings of our criminal justice system, the dissenting and concurring Justices in *Apprendi* and *Harris* make a strong case for insisting that the elements rule is applicable to factual findings relevant to sentencing guidelines, mandatory minimum penalties, and affirmative defenses alike.[140] All are facts provided by the legislature which, if found, require that an increased penalty be imposed. However, while perhaps not compelled by strict logic, we believe *Harris* strikes the appropriate compromise between the Sixth Amendment value of a jury trial and important equality concerns.

Had the dissenters in *Harris* prevailed, the cost would be considerable—the experiment with sentencing reform would have come to an ignoble halt, despite some plausible arguments to the contrary. Sentencing guidelines arguably differ from mandatory minimums in two related respects. Whereas sentencing guidelines preserve a court's discretionary authority to deviate from the prescribed range, mandatory minimums retain less flexibility for the sentencer. In addition, the Federal Sentencing Guidelines could be viewed as less binding because, unlike mandatory minimums, they were promulgated by the Sentencing Commission. However, neither of these distinctions persuasively limits the reasoning of

---

[137] Id at 2420–21 (Breyer, J, concurring) (emphasis added).

[138] *Ring v Arizona*, 536 US 584 (2002), 122 S Ct 2428, 2445 (Scalia, J, concurring).

[139] On the other hand, Justice Breyer's strong allegiance to the Federal Sentencing Guidelines, which he helped create, may lead him to our position—compromise over consistency.

[140] See, e.g., Scott Sundby, *The Reasonable Doubt Rule and the Meaning of Innocence*, 40 Hastings L J 457 (1989) (arguing that any fact identified by the legislature as controlling the sentence must be treated as an element); Mark D. Knoll and Richard G. Singer, *Searching for the "Tail of the Dog"; Finding "Elements" in the Wake of McMillan v Pennsylvania*, 22 Seattle U L Rev 1057 (1999); Andrew M. Levine, *The Confounding Boundaries of "Apprendi-land": Statutory Minimums and the Federal Sentencing Guidelines*, 29 Am J Crim L 377 (2002).

Harris. Though the Federal Sentencing Guidelines permit a federal judge to depart upward or downward where a mitigating or aggravating fact exists not adequately considered by the Sentencing Commission, the difference between this discretion and the discretion exercised by federal judges in regard to mandatory minimums is one of degree and not kind. The existence of some infrequently used discretion[141] to lower a determinate sentence under the guidelines is matched by the like authority to lower a mandatory minimum sentence by invoking the safety-valve provision,[142] to decrease any sentence on Eighth Amendment grounds,[143] or to overturn a jury's failure to find an affirmative defense as against the weight of the evidence. Moreover, with both mandatory minimum penalties and guideline ranges, there is no discretion permitted the fact finder in reaching the initial sentence; she is required to hold a hearing and find that the triggering fact either exists or does not. In both cases that fact, once found, mandates a higher sentence.

Second, one could attempt to distinguish the Federal Sentencing Guidelines from mandatory minimums because they were not enacted by Congress as part of the criminal code, but were instead promulgated by an independent commission in the judicial branch. However, this attempt likewise fails, as both involve legislatively ratified factual circumstances, binding on the judge, that expose defendants to additional punishment without a jury finding beyond a reasonable doubt.[144]

Thus, a broad reading of *Apprendi* in *Harris* would have meant the eventual application of the element rule to factors relevant in

---

[141] The vast majority of those convicted of federal offenses do not receive departures, nor is the refusal to depart appealable. See note 35. However, where a judge does depart on an invalid ground, the sentence is reversed unless the error was harmless. *Williams v United States*, 503 US 193 (1992).

[142] As noted by the Department of Justice in oral argument in *Harris*, judges do retain some discretion to depart below statutory minimum sentences, making them, again, indistinguishable from Guidelines departures. Oral argument in *Harris v United States*, Michael R. Druben, Deputy Solicitor General, p 35, lines 3–12, 3/25/02. See 18 USC § 3553(f), USSG § 5C1.2 (the safety-valve provision); 18 USC § 3553(e), USSG § 5K1.1 (departure below mandatory minimum for substantial assistance to prosecutor).

[143] *Harmelin v Michigan*, 501 US 957 (1991) (Eighth Amendment imposes a proportionality limit on criminal sentences).

[144] In fact, both mandatory minimum sentences and the Guidelines play a much more important role in the defendant's sentence than do statutory maximum penalties. A defendant rarely receives the statutory maximum; she receives the Guidelines sentence, unless trumped by a higher mandatory minimum. *Neal v United States*, 516 US 284 (1996) (mandatory minimum sentence for LSD trumps the lower guidelines).

determinate sentencing schemes. This would have foreclosed the employment of the Federal Sentencing Guidelines and their state counterparts for two reasons. First, as a matter of practice, it simply would have been too cumbersome to have juries make all the fact-finding necessary to apply the Guidelines. In a world where we depend upon at least 90 percent of our criminal defendants' pleading guilty,[145] we could not survive a system in which juries have to make all the findings of fact regarding an offender and his offense necessary to apply federal or state sentencing guidelines. If federal and state prosecutors had to include in the indictment and present to the jury every affirmative defense, statutory mitigator, and guideline fact presently determined by a judge at sentencing, trials would lengthen to the point of unmanageability. Justice Breyer effectively makes this point in his *Apprendi* dissent, where he notes that were a jury required to make every one of the twenty or more factual findings that the Federal Sentencing Guidelines presently require the judge to make in every case, trials would become absurdly long and complicated.[146]

This process would be cumbersome not only because twelve people would have to unanimously agree beyond a reasonable doubt on every factor previously ruled upon by the judge at the sentencing hearing, but because each of these new "elements" would be subject to full constitutional criminal procedural guarantees at trial. Unlike sentencing hearings, that are conducted quickly and informally, each fact would now have to be proven using the Federal Rules of Evidence, calling witnesses (rather than relying on the hearsay testimony of the case agent), and providing defendant full opportunities to cross-examine and confront such witnesses. Thus, instead of hours, we can anticipate days or perhaps weeks for each sentencing hearing. Moreover, we would lose the valuable assistance of the probation department, which presently interviews the defendant, case agent, and other pertinent parties and provides a report to the judge suggesting a certain Guidelines sentence. Under the new regime, defendants would have nothing to gain by consenting to the interview.

Of course, some of these time-consuming factual disputes would be resolved by plea, but not many. Certainly in those 6 percent

---

[145] Wayne R. LeFave et al, *Criminal Procedure* § 1.3q at 21 and n 226 (1999).

[146] *Apprendi v New Jersey*, 530 US at 557–58 (Breyer, J, dissenting).

or so of the cases where no plea agreement can be reached and the defendant puts the government to its burden of proof at trial, we would not expect to see any of these additional factual disputes resolved by plea. Thus, each criminal trial we presently conduct would require even greater resources and time. Second, under current practice some portion of the more than 93 percent who do resolve their cases by plea are unable to reach agreement with the government on all issues. In these circumstances, a defendant pleads guilty to a basic criminal offense with a statutory maximum high enough to please the prosecutor and statutory minimum low enough to please the defendant, and both sides agree to resolve the many factual issues that will determine the defendant's actual sentence at the sentencing hearing.[147] There is no reason to believe that any of these issues would become easier to resolve should *Apprendi* apply globally to the Federal Sentencing Guidelines. Thus, those Guideline issues formerly resolved at an informal sentencing hearing would instead be resolved through a jury trial. Third, we would expect to see an increase in the number of unresolved issues with a broad interpretation of *Apprendi*, and therefore fewer guilty pleas. An extension of *Apprendi* to the Federal Sentencing Guidelines would give a new bargaining chip to the defendant (by raising the burden of proof, excluding hearsay evidence, and applying criminal procedural guarantees to what used to be relaxed sentencing procedures) and thus decrease the prosecutor's chance of successfully convincing the defendant to admit to any particular fact.[148]

Perhaps most importantly, a broad application of *Apprendi*'s rule requiring jury findings as to what used to be sentencing factors under the Guidelines would eliminate much of the equality gained through the administrative model. Federal and state judges personally hear hundreds of criminal cases and read hundreds of additional reported decisions of their brethren. This provides a basis for comparison in making the determination as to whether a particular defendant was a ringleader,[149] whether he abused his posi-

---

[147] Nancy J. King and Susan R. Klein, *Acceptance of Responsibility and Conspiracy Sentences in Drug Prosecutions after Apprendi*, 14 Fed Sent Rptr 165 (2002).

[148] See Nancy J. King and Susan R. Klein, *Apprendi and Plea Bargaining*, 54 Stan L Rev 295 (2001).

[149] See U.S. Sentencing Guidelines Manual, § 3B1.1, providing for a three-level increase based on defendant's aggravating role in the offense, and § 3B1.2, providing for a four-level decrease based on defendant's mitigating role in the offense.

tion of trust,[150] whether he used or carried a weapon,[151] whether he foresaw a particular quantity of narcotics,[152] whether his crime was committed with a sexual motivation,[153] or whether a victim was particularly vulnerable.[154]

In addition to having the appropriate data points, these judges will have been exposed to a wide variety of criminal behavior, and thus not be surprised or outraged by the conduct of any particular defendant. On the other hand, most jurors hear one or perhaps two criminal matters in their lifetimes, and thus have no basis for adequately comparing and contrasting the defendant before them with other defendants. Moreover, laypeople are more likely to be distressed and mortified by the types of criminal behavior that they may see, or influenced by whatever particular crime is being decried in the press at that moment. Thus a sentence given to a particular defendant by a judge or a jury, even when both fact finders are using the same sentencing guidelines, is likely to be quite different. Similarly situated defendants in the administrative model will receive similar sentences, while similarly situated defendants in the individual rights model will receive sentences that depend upon which jury they drew and where they drew it. This proposition is well supported by the numerous studies showing wide disparity in jury sentencing cited in Section I of this article.[155] Finally, it would be practically impossible to establish a system for

[150] U.S. Sentencing Guidelines Manual § 3B1.3, permitting a two-level increase for abuse of position of trust or use of special skill.

[151] See, e.g., U.S. Sentencing Guidelines Manual § 2A5.2 (providing for a five-level increase if a firearm was discharged during the crime of interference with a flight crew); § 2A4.1 (providing for a two-level increase if a dangerous weapon was used during a kidnapping); *Bailey v United States*, 516 US 137 (1995); (using a gun requires active employment); *Muscarello v United States*, 524 US 125, 137 (1998) (possessing a firearm in relation to a crime of violence or drug trafficking crime prohibits "prosecution where guns 'played' no part in the crime."); *State v Shoats*, 772 A2d 1 (NJ Sup Ct, App Div 2001) (requiring a defendant to serve 85 percent of his sentence if defendant used a weapon); *People v Rhodes*, 723 NYS2d 2 (App Div 2001).

[152] 12 USC §§ 841 and 846 (triggering enhanced sentences for particular drug quantity); USSG § 1B1.3(a)(1)(B) (providing that a conspirator's sentence be based on the quantity she knew or should have known was involved in the conspiracy).

[153] *Grant v State*, 783 So2d 1120 (Fla Dist Ct App 2001); *State v Grossman*, 622 NW2d 394 (Minn Ct App 2001).

[154] See, e.g., U.S. Sentencing Guidelines Manual § 3A1.1 (providing for two-level increase for a crime committed against vulnerable victim); *State v Gould*, 23 P3d 801 (Kansas 2001) (abuse of child); *People v Chanthaloth*, 743 NE2d 1043 (Ill App Ct 2001) (brutality to elderly and physically handicapped victim).

[155] See notes 23 and 30.

reviewing jury sentences on appeal, as there will be no written opinion and hence no record of how and why the jury reached a particular sentence.

Apprendi was a sound constitutional decision in several respects—as a matter of doctrine, policy, and Fifth and Sixth Amendment jurisprudence. Without a jury finding beyond a reasonable doubt as to every fact considered important enough by the legislature to increase the statutory maximum penalty to be imposed, the jury's role is relegated to that of a "low-level gatekeeper."[156] This is contrary to common law practice, where the jury made every factual finding necessary to impose the particular punishment. Moreover, the elements rule recognized in *Apprendi*, though not strictly compelled as a matter of logic, is not "meaningless and formalistic."[157] Structural democratic restraints prevent legislatures from redrafting criminal statutes to circumvent *Apprendi* by providing very high maximum punishment for all offenses. As one of us has argued elsewhere, while legislatures have responded in the past to cues from the Court on how to circumvent criminal procedural guarantees through changes in substantive criminal law, the response has not been overwhelming.[158] Moreover, the elements rule fosters transparency in punishment theory and decisions. If the legislature attempts to evade *Apprendi*, it must do so in a public proceeding by changing the law. Many citizens will protest draconian sentences for shoplifting, simple assaults, or drug possession. Finally, the Court has suggested that additional constitutional limits might be imposed if legislatures were to attempt such evasions.[159]

The criminal justice system has absorbed the *Apprendi* decision with no significant changes in any of its institutions or assistance from the legislative branch. Justice O'Connor's description of *Apprendi* as "a watershed change in constitutional law"[160] that threatened to "unleash a flood of petitions by convicted defendants seek-

---

[156] *Jones v United States*, 526 US 227, 243–44 (1999); *Apprendi*, 530 US at 479 n 5.

[157] *Apprendi*, 530 US at 541 (O'Connor, J, dissenting).

[158] King and Klein, 54 Vand L Rev at 1490 and Appendix A (cited in note 6). To date, to our knowledge there has yet to be a criminal statute designed to circumvent *Apprendi*.

[159] *Apprendi*, 530 US at 490 n 16. King and Klein, 54 Vand L Rev at 1535–42 (cited in note 6) (suggesting multifactor test to police element-nonelement divide where legislature redrafts criminal statutes to eliminate elements).

[160] *Apprendi*, 530 US at 524 (O'Connor, J, dissenting).

ing to invalidate their sentences in whole or in part"[161] has not been borne out in practice. In actuality, a relatively small number of federal and state statutes are subject to *Apprendi* challenges.[162] For those statutes that are affected, prosecutors have accommodated *Apprendi* by charging those elements in the indictment for submission to the jury. The floodgates of habeas have not opened, as the rule has not been applied retroactively, and those cases on direct review have been largely disposed of using harmless and plain error analysis.[163]

However, should the Court apply the *Apprendi* rule to mandatory minimum statutes and determinate sentencing regimes, the criminal justice system would collapse and Congress and state legislatures would be forced to take action. The most likely result would be a retreat to the nineteenth-century model of sentencing approved by the Court in *Williams v New York*.[164] Legislatures would provide high statutory maximum sentences, to accommodate the worst offenders, as well as a relatively large penalty range, to accommodate the least culpable offenders, but would be unable to provide any guidance to the judge on selecting the appropriate sentence within this range. Perhaps foreseeing this possible reaction, the Supreme Court wisely rejected theoretical seamlessness in favor of protecting sentencing guideline systems and the equality they promote.

B. THE REVOLUTION THAT WASN'T: APPRENDI'S MINIMAL IMPACT
   ON CAPITAL JURISPRUDENCE AND THE SEARCH FOR EQUALITY IN
   CAPITAL CASES

Throughout this country's history, judge sentencing has been the norm in the non-capital context, and jury sentencing has been the norm in capital cases. When the Supreme Court initiated the modern era of judicial regulation of the death penalty in 1972,[165] virtually all death penalty jurisdictions assigned the decision of life

---

[161] Id at 551.

[162] King and Klein, *Aprés Apprendi* (cited in note 124), Appendices A and B.

[163] Id.

[164] 337 US 241 (1949) (holding that due process does not forbid judicial findings of fact at sentencing without extending compulsory process or the right to cross-examine witnesses to the defendant).

[165] *Furman v Georgia*, 408 US 238 (1972).

or death to juries.[166] But the Court's insistence that states limit arbitrariness in capital cases led several jurisdictions to enhance the role of judges in capital sentencing.[167] Several states made judges the sole decision makers at the punishment phase of capital trials,[168] while others adopted hybrid systems in which judges were authorized to override jury recommendations of life or death.[169]

When the Court considered several of the new post-*Furman* statutes in 1976, the Court sustained the three "guided-discretion" statutes it reviewed,[170] including Florida's scheme, which authorizes a judge to override an advisory jury's recommendation. The death-sentenced inmate in *Proffitt v Florida*[171] did not challenge directly the judicial override provision because in his case the advisory jury had recommended death.[172] The Court nonetheless remarked that a judge-sentencing scheme might better ensure equal treatment across cases in capital proceedings.[173]

Eight years later, in *Spaziano v Florida*, the Court confronted the question left open by *Proffitt:* whether the exercise of a judicial override in a case in which a jury has recommended life violates the Constitution.[174] Although Spaziano contended that the Florida procedure violated the Sixth Amendment jury trial right,[175] the focus of his claim (perhaps in light of *Proffitt*) was that the Eighth Amendment requires jury sentencing in capital cases to preserve

---

[166] *Spaziano v Florida*, 468 US 447, 472 (1984) (Stevens, J, concurring in part and dissenting in part).

[167] Stephen Gillers, *Deciding Who Dies*, 129 Pa L Rev 1, 18 (1980) (stating that "each of the eight states currently opting for judge sentencing made that choice after *Furman*" and that "[t]heir adoption of judge sentencing [was] an apparent attempt to meet *Furman*'s unclear commands").

[168] See Ariz Rev Stat Ann § 13-703 (West Supp 2001); Colo Rev Stat § 16-11-103 (2001) (three-judge panel); Idaho Code § 19-2515 (Supp 2001); Mont Code Ann § 46-18-301 (1997); Neb Rev Stat § 29-2520 (1995).

[169] See Ala Code §§ 13A-5-46, 13A-5-47 (1994); Del Code Ann, Tit 11, § 4209 (1995); Fla Stat Ann § 921.141 (West 2001); Ind Code Ann § 35-50-2-9 (Supp 2001).

[170] See *Gregg v Georgia*, 428 US 153 (1976) (reviewing and sustaining Georgia's post-*Furman* "guided discretion" approach); *Jurek v Texas*, 428 US 262 (1976) (same); *Proffitt v Florida*, 428 US 242 (1976) (same). The Court invalidated the schemes of those states that provided for a mandatory death penalty. See *Roberts v Louisiana*, 428 US 325 (1976); *Woodson v North Carolina*, 428 US 280 (1976).

[171] *Proffitt*, 428 US 242 (1976).

[172] Id at 246.

[173] Id at 252 (opinion of Stewart, Powell, and Stevens, JJ).

[174] *Spaziano v Florida*, 468 US 447 (1984).

[175] Id at 458.

a connection between death sentences and community values. The Court, acknowledging the "appeal" of this claim,[176] concluded that the Eighth Amendment does not prohibit states from empowering judges to make the final decision about the appropriateness of the death penalty and to override a contrary recommendation from a jury.[177]

In *Walton v Arizona*,[178] the Court appeared to lay to rest the final challenge to judge sentencing in capital cases. It sustained Arizona's sentencing scheme in which trial judges make all of the findings of fact regarding death-eligibility without the advice or participation of juries. The Court found unpersuasive the effort to distinguish Florida's hybrid scheme, which it had repeatedly endorsed,[179] from Arizona's "pure" judge-sentencing approach.[180] It also found further ammunition against the Sixth Amendment claim in *Cabana v Bullock*,[181] which sustained the ability of appellate courts to make the so-called *Enmund* finding[182] in cases in which a non-triggerperson is sentenced to death.

Apprendi cast doubt on all that the Court had said before about the permissibility of judge sentencing in capital cases. The *Apprendi* majority found no clear contradiction between its previous capital decisions, including *Walton*, and its conclusion that any fact increasing the penalty for a crime beyond the prescribed statutory maximum must be submitted to a jury and proved beyond a reasonable doubt.[183] Indeed, the Court argued rather lamely that aggravating factors do not increase the potential penalty a defendant

---

[176] Id at 461.

[177] Id at 463–65.

[178] 497 US 639 (1990).

[179] In addition to *Spaziano*, the Court had rejected a challenge to Florida's advisory jury scheme in *Hildwin v Florida*, 490 US 638 (1989) (per curiam) (holding that, under *McMillan v Pennsylvania*, 477 US 79 (1986), aggravating factors in Florida's scheme are not elements of the offense but sentencing factors and thus are not subject to the Sixth Amendment jury trial right).

[180] 497 US at 648.

[181] 474 US 376 (1986).

[182] See *Enmund v Florida*, 458 US 782 (1982) (holding that the Eighth Amendment prohibits as disproportionate the application of the death penalty to a defendant who has neither killed, attempted to kill, nor intended to kill). The Court substantially narrowed *Enmund* in *Tison v Arizona*, 481 US 137 (1987), by sustaining the death penalty for persons who do not satisfy the *Enmund* test but who nonetheless are major participants in dangerous felonies and exhibit reckless indifference to human life.

[183] 530 US 466, 496–97 (2000).

faces even though the failure to find at least one aggravating factor renders the defendant ineligible for death.[184] At least five Justices in *Apprendi*, though, expressed substantial doubts about whether *Walton* remained good law. Justice Thomas, concurring, recognized the tension between *Apprendi* and *Walton*, but suggested that the Constitution's separate demands on the death penalty (both in requiring states to narrow the class of the death-eligible and in forbidding mandatory death penalty schemes) might somehow exempt states from the Sixth Amendment requirement in that context.[185] Justice O'Connor, writing for four Justices in dissent, insisted much more persuasively that *Walton* and *Apprendi* could not coexist because, under Arizona's death penalty statute, the finding of an aggravating circumstance clearly " 'exposes the criminal defendant to a penalty *exceeding* the maximum he would receive if punished according to the facts reflected in the jury verdict alone.' "[186] Justice O'Connor rather pointedly observed that "it is inconceivable" that "a State can remove from the jury a factual determination that makes the difference between life and death" and yet "cannot do the same with respect to a factual determination that results in only a 10-year increase in the maximum sentence to which a defendant is exposed."[187]

Given the expression of these doubts in *Apprendi*, the Court's decision in *Ring v Arizona*[188] to plainly overrule *Walton* came as no surprise. The central question here, though, is whether *Ring*'s extension of Sixth Amendment protections to the capital context undermines the Eighth Amendment values, particularly the concern for equality, which the Court has sought to promote in its ongoing regulation of the American death penalty. For a variety of reasons, *Ring* does not pose a significant threat to such goals.

First and foremost, states' efforts to achieve equality through intricate sentencing instructions have been notably unsuccessful. Unlike in the Federal Sentencing Guidelines context, the range of considerations in capital sentencing remains essentially unregu-

---

[184] Id.

[185] Id at 522–23 (Thomas, J, concurring).

[186] Id at 537 (O'Connor, J, dissenting) (quoting majority opinion, id at 483 (emphasis in majority opinion)).

[187] Id.

[188] 536 US 584 (2002).

lated. As argued above, the Court's broad conception of individualization—extending far beyond truly "mitigating" factors (in terms
of reducing moral culpability)—prevents states from developing
any consistent theory of the goal or goals behind their capital statute; a defendant must be free to argue against the death penalty
on the basis of any plausibly relevant consideration, including evidence of familial sympathy, good character traits, and future good
behavior. At the same time, the enumerated criteria in state death
penalty schemes are often amorphous and subjective, with the result that contemporary sentencing schemes afford sentencers substantial discretion.

Given the lack of clear standards in capital sentencing, judicial
involvement in sentencing is unlikely to contribute to equality
across cases. Judges cannot, as in the Federal Sentencing Guidelines context, ensure that criteria are evenly applied when the criteria simply do not exist. Moreover, capital trials remain relatively
rare events, such that individual state judges are unlikely to encounter sufficient numbers of decisions to develop an internal consistency (much less consistency state-wide). As one commentator
observed, even in Florida, one of the most active death penalty
jurisdictions, each of the 300 or so circuit trials is unlikely to be
involved in more than a handful of capital sentencing decisions.[189]

In addition, the transparency and democracy gains from judicially declared findings under the Federal Sentencing Guidelines
are not available in the capital context, because judges are not obligated to explain the steps leading to their decisions to the same
extent as federal judges applying the Guidelines. In the end, state
judges in capital sentencing often retain the same kind of standardless discretion exercised by jurors, and are similarly free to
decide what facts matter to their ultimate decision and the weight
that they should be assigned. Given the lack of criteria for judges
to apply, appellate review of judicial sentencing in capital cases is
necessarily truncated; in the absence of any rulelike limitations on
sentencing discretion, appellate courts are hard-pressed to second-
guess judicial sentences. Moreover, consistency would in any event
require the availability of appellate review for both death sentences
and sentences less than death. But unlike the Federal Sentencing
Guidelines cases, in which prosecutors can appeal unfavorable judi-

---

[189] Gillers, *Deciding Who Dies*, 129 U Pa L Rev at 58–59 (1980).

cial applications, state laws do not permit prosecutors to appeal decisions by trial judges not to impose death.

Lastly, it is important to note that state judges face unusually strong political pressures in capital cases.[190] In most death penalty jurisdictions, state judges must stand for election,[191] and the death penalty remains a significant factor in the election, retention, and promotion of judges.[192] Given such pressures, judicial sentencing appears less an opportunity for careful calibration of evidence than a vehicle for giving voice to real or imagined popular outrage. The experience with jury overrides in Florida and Alabama, in which judges are much more likely to override toward death than life,[193] reflects the unique pressures of capital litigation. Accordingly, judicial involvement in capital sentencing is less central to, and may actually undermine, the pursuit of sentencing equality.

As a practical matter, *Ring*'s significance is limited because the practice of judge sentencing is quite limited. Only five states have committed the ultimate sentencing decision in capital cases entirely to judges, and of those states, only one—Arizona—has a significant death row population.[194] The four others, Colorado, Idaho, Montana, and Nebraska, have a collective death row of about forty[195] (just over 1 percent of the national death row[196]) and have accounted for less than ten executions over the past thirty-five years.[197]

Moreover, it remains unclear whether *Ring* will apply to the four other states, including Florida and Alabama, which operate "hy-

---

[190] Stephen B. Bright and Patrick J. Keenan, *Judges and the Politics of Death: Deciding Between the Bill of Rights and the Next Election in Capital Cases*, 75 BU L Rev 759 (1995).

[191] Id at 776–85.

[192] Id at 784–94.

[193] Id at 793. For further discussion of jury overrides, see Michael L. Radelet, *Rejecting the Jury: The Imposition of the Death Penalty in Florida* 18 UC Davis L Rev 1409 (1985); Mike Mello and Ruthann Robson, *Judge Over Jury: Florida's Practice of Imposing Death Over Life in Capital Cases*, 13 Fla St U L Rev 31 (1985); Katheryn K. Russell, *The Constitutionality of Jury Override in Alabama Death Penalty Cases*, 46 Ala L Rev 5 (1994).

[194] *Death Row U.S.A.* (NAACP Legal Defense and Education Fund, Inc.), Fall 2002, at 23 (listing Arizona's death row population as 125).

[195] Id (listing Colorado's death row population as 5, Idaho's as 22, Montana's as 6, and Nebraska's as 7).

[196] Id at 1 (listing total death row as 3,697).

[197] Id at 6–7 (stating that Colorado and Idaho have each carried out one execution, that Nebraska has carried out three executions, and that Montana has carried out two executions).

brid" systems in which the jury renders an advisory verdict but the judge makes the ultimate sentencing decision. Although Justice Breyer's concurrence argued for a broad right to jury sentencing in capital cases,[198] the Court maintained that Ring's claim was "tightly delineated"[199] and did not require the Court to revisit *Proffitt*'s conclusion that the Sixth Amendment does not require jury sentencing in capital cases.[200] Instead, the Court held only that juries must make the factual findings essential to death-eligibility, leaving open the possibility that judicial overrides remain a permissible means of allocating sentencing responsibility in capital cases.

The practical reach of *Ring* is further limited by federal habeas doctrines that potentially preclude relief even for those defendants for whom death eligibility was established by a judicial finding. The new standard of review under the Anti-Terrorism and Effective Death Penalty Act permits relief only if a state decision "was contrary to, or involved an unreasonable application of, clearly established Federal law, as determined by the Supreme Court of the United States."[201] Given the Court's abrupt departure in *Ring* from its prior endorsements of judicial sentencing in capital cases, it is unlikely that many habeas petitioners will receive the retroactive benefit of the decision (especially given that the Court's judicially crafted, nonretroactivity doctrine independently limits the availability of relief for defendants whose convictions became final prior to an intervening decision).[202]

Ultimately, the Court's extraordinary focus on controlling sentencer discretion at the moment of decision has proven an ineffective means of ensuring equality in our system of capital punishment. Instead of attempting to tame the death penalty determination at the punishment phase of capital trials, the Court would have done better to ensure equality of opportunity throughout the entire conduct of a capital proceeding. Equality, in short, seems an elusive goal when in the end the sentencer must be permitted to consider all facets of the defendant facing the ultimate punishment; but fairness, defined by reasonable access to investiga-

---

[198] 122 S Ct 2446, 2446–48 (2002).

[199] Id at 2437 n 4.

[200] Id.

[201] See § 104, 110 Stat at 1218–19 (codified as 28 USC § 2254(d) (Supp IV 1998)).

[202] *Teague v Lane*, 489 US 288 (1989).

tion, effective trial representation, and adequate postconviction review, is both a desirable and obtainable aspiration in capital proceedings. These sorts of interests, though, have not been required by the Court's death penalty jurisprudence, which has been notoriously noninterventionist in states' systems for assigning and policing counsel in death cases. The Court reviews deferentially the performance of trial counsel[203] and has refused to require (much less review for competency) counsel in state postconviction proceedings.[204]

Along these same lines, the Court's efforts to impose minimal proportionality limitations concerning the availability of the death penalty have been more successful in reducing arbitrariness than its efforts to rewrite punishment-phase sentencing instructions. Given that the Court cannot ensure equal outcomes via the penalty phase, it is sensible to reduce "overinclusion" by eliminating death eligibility for those persons whose crime or characteristics make them unlikely candidates for the ultimate sanction. The Court's few proportionality limitations, such as its decisions precluding the death penalty for persons convicted of rape,[205] for relatively minor participants convicted as accomplices,[206] and for persons with mental retardation,[207] actually contribute substantially to equality, because they prevent persons with relatively low moral culpability from being grouped with, and treated identically to, the most culpable offenders. The Court should continue down this path, and similarly exempt other groups of offenders, such as juveniles, whose personal moral culpability is ordinarily lower than the "worst of the worst" for whom the death penalty, as a matter of practice, appears to be reserved.

III. CONCLUSION

Not since the Warren Court era has the Court embarked on a significant revolution in constitutional criminal procedure.

---

[203] *Strickland v Washington*, 466 US 668 (1984).

[204] *Murray v Giarrantano*, 492 US 1 (1989) (finding no constitutional right to appointed counsel for indigent defendants in state postconviction proceedings).

[205] *Coker v Georgia*, 433 US 584 (1977).

[206] *Enmund v Florida*, 458 US 782 (1982); *Tison v Arizona*, 481 US 137 (1987).

[207] *Atkins v Virginia*, 536 US 304 (2002).

When the Court decided *Apprendi* two terms ago, it had all the earmarks of a watershed decision. The Court had reversed settled case law and called into question the constitutionality of an emerging core practice in the criminal justice system—the use of judges to make critical findings in capital and non-capital sentencing proceedings. At first blush, one might be tempted to regard this past term as a mixed victory for the incipient revolution. In *Harris*, the Court refused to extend *Apprendi*'s elements rule to factual findings triggering mandatory minimum penalties. But in *Ring*, the Court again reversed settled cases by striking down Arizona's "pure" judicial sentencing approach to capital decision making that it had previously—and unequivocally—embraced.

These two decisions, though, are not of equal significance, and together they represent a victory for the status quo. The stakes in *Harris* were extraordinarily high: the Court's willingness to tolerate judicial fact-findings in that context effectively precludes any global Sixth Amendment challenge to federal and state guidelines regimes and thereby curtails *Apprendi*'s revolutionary potential. *Ring*, on the other hand, represents only a modest footnote to contemporary constitutional regulation of the death penalty.

The irony in this revolution that wasn't is the Court's apparent priority. Despite strong logical claims for extending *Apprendi*'s Sixth Amendment requirements to the fact-findings in *Harris*, the Court appeared to appreciate that this decision was tantamount to a referendum on sentencing guidelines and ultimately balked at the notion of casting aside the new guidelines regimes. Such regimes, though, are the product of relatively short-lived, legislatively initiated experiments to eliminate unwarranted disparities in non-capital sentencing. The effort to secure equality in capital sentencing, on the other hand, has been the core concern of the Court's own, also relatively short-lived, Eighth Amendment regulation of the death penalty. And the Court had previously indicated that judge sentencing in capital cases might be an effective means of securing the equality that the Eighth Amendment requires.

Why would the Court preserve the national experiment with guidelines regimes and yet invalidate a state sentencing practice that itself was adopted in response to Court-identified constitutional commands? We believe it is because the Court recognized that the legislative experiment with guideline schemes is already deeply embedded in contemporary practice and holds substantial promise for enhancing equality in non-capital sentencing. At the same time, the use of judges in capital cases never fully took hold despite the obvious flaws of the pre-*Furman* regime and, perhaps more importantly, has never emerged as an obviously preferable or more effective means of achieving the elusive goal of equality in capital cases. Implicit in the Court's decisions is a pragmatic balancing—ubiquitous in contemporary constitutional interpretation—between the Sixth Amendment trial right and competing concerns for efficiency and equality. Given that the scope of the jury sentencing right was not obviously or clearly established by common law practice, the Court in *Harris* reasonably chose to draw a line between findings necessary to increase the maximum punishment for the offense and findings necessary to trigger mandatory minimum punishments. The Court's conclusion in *Ring* to require jury determination of factors necessary for death-eligibility represented a similar sort of prudential balancing. The purported values served by judicial involvement in capital sentencing were simply insufficient to justify overriding the competing claims for the Sixth Amendment jury trial right. Accordingly, the Court followed the logic rather than the letter of *Apprendi* and refused to indulge *Apprendi*'s unpersuasive suggestion that the jury right need not apply to the capital context.

Our endorsement of the Court's decisions in *Ring* and *Harris* is qualified by our significant reservations regarding current capital and non-capital sentencing regimes. Guidelines will not themselves ensure equality in non-capital sentencing. Substantive choices within guidelines regimes must not unfairly reward or disadvantage particular groups or individuals. Now that guidelines regimes that preserve a judicial role in administrative sentencing appear less vulnerable to global constitutional attack, critics of the Federal Sentencing Guidelines should refocus their attention on those features of federal criminal law that contribute to inequality, such as disproportionate punishment for crack cocaine, prosecutorial overuse and abuse of downward departure authority, excessively punitive mandatory minimum penalties, and other provisions that inappropriately coerce defendants to plead guilty. The existence of guidelines regimes does not obviate the need for sound moral judgments, but instead provides a useful vehicle for giving life to such judgments once made.

In the capital context, the extension of *Apprendi* to the sentencing phase should be understood as a confirmation of the truly modest aspirations of current federal judicial regulation of the death penalty. Precisely because the Court has not and cannot tame the death penalty decision through significant guidance, the Court rightly refused to protect an administrative regime of sentencing in the capital context. *Ring*, then, underscores the weakness of the Court's long-standing but flawed focus on achieving equality through the refinement of capital sentencing instructions. The Court should now redirect its regulatory efforts away from the punishment phase of capital trials to those aspects of capital punishment systems that are both in need of and amenable to reform. Ensuring quality representation, meaningful postconviction opportunities, and robust proportionality review are much more promising means of improving our capital system. Fairness, in short, should replace equality as the overriding goal of constitutional regulation of the death penalty.

JOHN F. DUFFY

THE FESTO DECISION AND THE
RETURN OF THE SUPREME COURT TO
THE BAR OF PATENTS

On January 8, 2002, a crowded courtroom in the Supreme Court witnessed a famous legal and political figure rise from his chair to begin arguments on a case about monopolies. The individual was well qualified for the task. He had written one of the most important books on monopolies in the last half-century,[1] taught antitrust law at the Yale Law School, represented the United States as Solicitor General, and served for six years as a judge on one of the most important federal courts in the nation.[2] In many ways, there was nothing unusual about this scene. Since the dawn of the republic, federal policy toward business monopolies has excited passions both inside and outside of courtrooms. In every period of its history, the Supreme Court has been intimately involved in crafting the federal law of monopolies, and the cases at the Court have frequently attracted some of the most preeminent members of the bar. But this case was different. It did not involve antitrust law—the branch of federal monopoly doctrine that the twentieth-century Court had treated "almost on a par in importance with

John F. Duffy is Professor of Law, William & Mary School of Law.

AUTHOR'S NOTE: I thank Rochelle Dreyfuss, Rich Hynes, Doug Lichtman, John McGinnis, Alan Meese, and Anne Sprightley Ryan for their valuable comments on the drafts of this article.

[1] Robert H. Bork, *The Antitrust Paradox: A Policy at War with Itself* (Basic Books, 1978).

[2] *Biographical Directory of the Federal Judiciary 1789–2000* 387 (Bernan, 2001) (entry for Robert Heron Bork).

the major constitutional controversies that come before it."[3] Judge Bork was arguing a patent case.

The sight of such a prominent figure arguing the intricacies of patent law to the Justices would not have been so unusual in the nineteenth century. The Court then had jurisdiction over all patent appeals from the nation's regional trial courts, much like the modern Federal Circuit has today. The Court's jurisdiction was mandatory, and it would regularly hear several patent cases each term. These cases defined the forefront of federal industrial policy and they attracted some of the best legal minds of the day, including Daniel Webster,[4] Justice Benjamin Curtis,[5] and Chief Justice Salmon Chase[6]—all of whom represented private litigants in Supreme Court patent litigation. The practicing patent bar could even claim as its own Abraham Lincoln, who served briefly as counsel in a patent litigation against Cyrus McCormick (the inventor of the mechanical reaper),[7] authored a famous speech on patent policy,[8] and received a patent on a method he invented for lifting river boats over shoals.[9]

The importance of federal patent law during the nineteenth century can be measured not only in terms of the lawyers attracted to the field, but also in the treatment that the subject received at

---

[3] Philip B. Kurland, *The Supreme Court and Patents and Monopolies* ix (Chicago, 1975).

[4] See Andrew J. King, ed, *The Papers of Daniel Webster: Legal Papers, Volume 3, The Federal Practice* 824–90 (Dartmouth, 1989).

[5] A search of the Lexis database shows that in twelve Supreme Court cases Justice Curtis recused himself from sitting on the grounds that he had served as counsel to one of the parties; eight of the twelve were patent cases. See, e.g., *O'Reilly v Morse*, 56 US 62, 62 (1854); *Le Roy v Tatham*, 55 US 156, 156 (1853).

[6] See John Niven, ed, 1 *The Salmon P. Chase Papers, Journals, 1829–1872* 214–15 & n 41 (Kent State, 1993) (noting Chase's representation of Henry O'Reilly in the patent infringement suit brought by Samuel Morse).

[7] See Harry Goldsmith, *Abraham Lincoln, Invention and Patents*, 20 J Patent Off Socy 5, 20–30 (1938). Lincoln was a counsel for the defendants in the case, as was Edwin Stanton, who would later serve as Lincoln's Secretary of War. The plaintiff, McCormick, retained (among others) Reverdy Johnson, the Maryland statesman. See id at 22.

[8] A phrase from Lincoln's speech—"The patent system added the fuel of interest to the fire of genius"—was inscribed over the entrance to the U.S. Patent Office Building in Washington. See id at 5.

[9] See US Pat No 6469 (1849), at 1 (reciting that "I, Abraham Lincoln, of Springfield, in the County of Sangamon, in the State of Illinois, have invented a new and improved manner of combining adjustable buoyant air chambers with a steamboat or other vessel for the purpose of enabling their draught of water to be readily lessened to enable them to pass over bars, or through shallow water") (available at <http://patft.uspto.gov/netahtml/srchnum.htm>).

the Court. Perhaps the most visible indication of the field's significance can be found in *The Telephone Cases*,[10] which sustained the validity of Alexander Graham Bell's telephone patents. There the Supreme Court consolidated five separate pieces of litigation, heard oral argument over the course of twelve days, and filed a report that filled an entire volume of the *U.S. Reports*. The Court's attention to patent law was hardly confined to a single famous case. Early in the century, Justice Story took a special interest in the field. He wrote an influential article on the patent laws[11] and, both at the Court and on circuit, wrote a number of seminal opinions still found in modern case books. And, even when the Court was drowning in appeals toward the end of the century, retiring Justice William Strong supported a congressional proposal that would have limited the Court's mandatory appellate jurisdiction *except* in patent and copyright cases.[12]

But in January of 2002, the heyday of the Supreme Court patent litigation was long gone. In the last decade of the nineteenth century, Congress removed the Court's mandatory appellate jurisdiction in patent cases. While the Court continued to hear several patent cases per term throughout the first half of the twentieth century, it seemed to lose interest in the field at mid-century, and the Court's patent docket precipitously declined. For the next three decades, the Court averaged barely one patent decision per year, or less than one-third its average from the first half of the century. No Justice during that period could claim more than a passing familiarity with the field—a stark contrast to the nineteenth century, which had, in addition to Story, Chase, and Curtis, Justices such as Joseph Bradley, who authored nearly three dozen patent decisions for the Court; Nathan Clifford, who averaged more than one patent opinion for the Court per year during his twenty-three year career; and William Strong, who wrote more

---

[10] 126 US 1 (1888).

[11] See *On the Patent Laws*, set forth as Note II in the appendix to vol 16 of the US Reports, 16 US (3 Wheat) app 13–29 (1818). The Note is attributed to Justice Story in a variety of sources, including a 1904 edition of this volume of the US Reports edited by Frederick Brightly. See Frederick C. Brightly, ed, *Reports of the Cases Argued and Adjudged in the Supreme Court of the United States, February Term 1818* 302 (1904 ed).

[12] William Strong, *The Needs of the Supreme Court*, 132 N Am Rev 437, 446 (1881) (endorsing a bill that would have curbed appeals to the Supreme Court but that would have left a right of Supreme Court review in patent and copyright cases without regard to the sum in controversy).

than a dozen patent opinions for the Court in just ten years and became renown for his expertise in the field.[13] By 1975, Professor Philip Kurland could conclude that "[p]atents do not bulk large in the present business of the Supreme Court," and that the Court had "relegated the resolution of patent controversies to the lower levels of the federal judiciary."[14]

The Court's withdrawal from the field seemed, at first, to become even more complete after the creation in 1982 of a new specialized court of appeals, the Court of Appeals for the Federal Circuit. The Federal Circuit was created in part because of the Supreme Court's then decades-long neglect of the field, and it was designed to become an expert court with the jurisdiction and capability to unify national patent law. The creation of the Federal Circuit seemed to eliminate any need for further Supreme Court supervision. While containing a fair dose of judge-made law, the patent field is ultimately an area of federal statutory law, and in statutory cases the Supreme Court has long seen its primary function as resolving circuit conflicts.[15] With the creation of the Federal Circuit, circuit splits became impossible (or, at best, extremely unlikely), and there consequently seemed to be no pressing need for Supreme Court review. If a patent decision of the Federal Circuit were important enough to correct, Congress could always do so legislatively. Moreover, continuing neglect by the Court might actually be desirable if a generalist court is more likely than a specialized institution to bungle the law in a highly technical field such as patent law. In fact, neglecting the field—or, rather, neglecting the field even more than it already had been—seemed to be the

---

[13] By contrast, the leading author of Supreme Court patent opinions in the second half of the twentieth century was Justice Clark, who wrote five patent opinions for the Court in seventeen years of service. Justices Douglas and Black each wrote twelve patent opinions for the Court in careers spanning more than three decades; however, each wrote only four of his patent opinions during the second half of the twentieth century. No other Justice produced more than three patent opinions for the Court in the second half of the twentieth century.

[14] Kurland, *The Supreme Court and Patents and Monopolies* at xii (cited in note 3).

[15] See US S Ct Rule 10.1 (explicitly recognizing conflicting circuit positions as a grounds for seeking certiorari). Arthur D. Hellman, *The Shrunken Docket of the Rehnquist Court*, 1996 Supreme Court Review 403, 414 (identifying the resolution of circuit conflicts as "[o]ne of the principal functions of the Supreme Court"). See also William H. Rehnquist, *The Changing Role of the Supreme Court*, 14 Fla St U L Rev 1, 12 (1986) (arguing for the creation of a national court of appeals to resolve circuit conflicts and predicting that, if such a court were created, it would have "the all-but-final say in determining . . . what an act of Congress means").

course that the Court was choosing during the first decade of the Federal Circuit's existence, when the Court's already low rate of granting certiorari in patent cases declined even further.[16] As Professor Mark Janis declared, the Supreme Court seemed to have become "well nigh invisible in modern substantive patent law."[17]

The Court's continued retreat from patent law comported with accepted notions about the likely effects that creation of a specialized intermediate appellate court would have. In the debate over the efficacy and desirability of specialized courts, a general assumption has been that the Supreme Court would have little continuing influence over any area subject to the jurisdiction of the specialized court. A specialized court was expected to impede the ability of the Supreme Court to identify the cases worth a grant of certiorari,[18] to preclude "the thinking of generalists [from] contribute[ing] to the field's development,"[19] and, generally, to produce a "seclusiveness" that would "immunize[] [the specialized field] against the refreshment of new ideas, suggestions, adjustments and compromises which constitute the very tissue of any living system of law."[20] Even those who favor specialized patent courts have gen-

---

[16] In that ten-year period, the Court reviewed only three patent decisions of the new court, and one of those cases was decided summarily, without oral argument. The three cases are *Eli Lilly & Co. v Medtronic, Inc.*, 496 US 661 (1990) (interpreting § 271(e) of the Patent Act), *Dennison Mfg. Co. v Panduit Corp.*, 475 US 809 (1986) (per curiam) (summarily vacating and remanding with instructions for the Federal Circuit to reconsider its decision in light of Federal Rule of Civil Procedure 52(a)), and *Christianson v Colt Industries*, 486 US 800 (1988) (applying the "well-pleaded complaint" rule to determine the scope of the Federal Circuit's jurisdiction over cases "arising under" the patent law). Another patent case reviewed by the Court during this period (1982–92) had been decided by a regional circuit prior to the creation of the Federal Circuit. See *General Motors Corp. v Devex Corp.*, 461 US 648 (1983) (holding that prejudgment interest on infringement damages is ordinarily available).

[17] Mark D. Janis, *Patent Law in the Age of the Invisible Supreme Court*, 2001 U Ill L Rev 387, 387.

[18] See Richard L. Revesz, *Specialized Courts and the Administrative Lawmaking System*, 138 U Pa L Rev 1111, 1159 (1990) ("It is extremely difficult for the Supreme Court to identify, from among all the issues decided by a specialized court of exclusive jurisdiction, those that would have generated a conflict if they had been decided instead by the regional courts of appeals, or those in which the process of dialogue would ultimately have produced a uniform contrary decision in the regional courts of appeals."); see also Rochelle Cooper Dreyfuss, *Specialized Adjudication*, 1990 BYU L Rev 377, 380 ("[i]f circuit conflicts fail to develop [because of the specialized court], Supreme Court activity in the specialized field will diminish").

[19] Dreyfuss, 1990 BYU L Rev at 379 (cited in note 18) (recounting this among the "well rehearsed" arguments against specialized courts).

[20] Simon Rifkind, *A Special Court for Patent Litigation? The Danger of a Specialized Judiciary*, 37 ABA J 425, 426 (1951).

erally assumed—to the extent they considered the role of the Supreme Court at all—that the Court's role in the field would remain minimal.[21] There seemed to be a consensus that the creation of a specialized court would insulate patent law from generalist influence and would diminish the power and perhaps the ability of a generalist Supreme Court to continue effective review over the field. This has been a positive point to supporters of specialized courts, who view a generalist influence to be either unnecessary or even detrimental, and a negative to others who bemoan the loss of generalist influence over the path of the law. But it was assumed to be true by all.

This, then, was the context for the case of *Festo Corp. v Shoketsu Kinzoku Kogyo Kabashuki Co.*[22]—a long and seemingly irreversible decline in the Supreme Court's patent jurisprudence punctuated by the creation of the Federal Circuit. Yet that history, and the assumptions it spawned, could be momentarily forgotten as Judge Bork began his argument for the petitioners. By the time of the *Festo* oral argument, the Court that term had already rendered one important decision on the patentability of plants, *J.E.M. Ag Supply v Pioneer Hi-Bred International*,[23] and granted certiorari in another case concerning the scope of the Federal Circuit's exclusive jurisdiction in patent cases, *Holmes Group v Vornado Air Circulation Systems*.[24] Though three patent decisions in a single term may not seem like an extraordinary number, it is equal to the total number of Federal Circuit patent decisions reviewed by the Court in the first ten years of the specialty court's existence—and these recent grants of certiorari came in an era when the Court has reduced its docket by nearly 50% compared to the 1980s.[25]

---

[21] See, e.g., Henry J. Friendly, *Federal Jurisdiction: A General View* 160 n 29 (Columbia, 1973) (supporting the creation of a specialized patent court that is still subject to Supreme Court review but assuming that the Court's certiorari power would not "be exercised any more frequently than it has in the recent past"); Dreyfuss, 1990 BYU L Rev at 435 n 229 (cited in note 18) (finding it "questionable whether the Supreme Court . . . would provide enough of a generalist perspective" to temper the biases of a specialist court). Other discussions have not focused on the relationship between the specialized court and the Supreme Court. See, e.g., Rochelle Cooper Dreyfuss, *The Federal Circuit: A Case Study in Specialized Courts*, 64 NYU L Rev 1 (1989).

[22] 122 S Ct 1831 (2002).

[23] 122 S Ct 593 (2001).

[24] 122 S Ct 1889 (2002); see also 122 S Ct 510 (Nov 8, 2001) (order granting certiorari).

[25] See Hellman, 1996 Supreme Court Review at 403 (cited in note 15).

Moreover, if the number of patent cases reviewed by the Court could be written off as merely a statistical fluctuation, the Court's attitude toward the cases could not be so easily explained. Consider, for example, the posture of *J.E.M. Ag Supply*. In the case below, a unanimous Federal Circuit panel had held that new plants and seeds can be patented under the general Patent Act, even though they can also receive protection under two specialized statutes (the Plant Patent Act and the Plant Varieties Protection Act). The Federal Circuit panel saw the case as a straightforward application of *Diamond v Chakrabarty*,[26] a two-decade-old Supreme Court decision interpreting the general Patent Act to permit the patenting of "'anything under the sun that is made by man,'" including living organisms.[27] The full Federal Circuit rejected a petition for en banc review without dissent.[28] After a petition for certiorari was filed, the Court called for the views of the United States, and that request produced a response which, one would have thought, would foreclose any possibility of certiorari. The Solicitor General endorsed the Federal Circuit's decision as a correct interpretation of *Chakrabarty*, confirmed that the Patent and Trademark Office had held the same position for fifteen years and had been issuing patents based on that position, noted that the decision did not conflict with any other court of appeals decision or any Supreme Court precedent, and concluded that Supreme Court review was "not warranted."[29] Nevertheless, the Court granted certiorari. Although the Court ultimately affirmed the Federal Circuit on a 6–2 vote, the very grant of certiorari shows that the Court is willing to second-guess a patent decision of the Federal Circuit even if the court's decision is unanimous, is in agreement with a long-held legal position of the Executive Branch, and is not in tension with Supreme Court precedents or pre–Federal Circuit appellate precedents.

The Court's attitude was also evident in the interest that the

---

[26] 447 US 303 (1980).

[27] *Pioneer Hi-Bred International, Inc. v J.E.M. Ag Supply Co.*, 200 F3d 1374, 1375 (Fed Cir 2000) (quoting *Chakrabarty*, 447 US at 309 (quoting S Rep No 1979, 82d Cong, 2d Sess 5 (1952) and HR Rep No 1923, 82d Cong, 2d Sess 6 (1952))).

[28] 2000 US App LEXIS 6911 (Mar 13, 2000).

[29] Brief for the United States as Amicus Curiae, *J.E.M. Ag Supply v Pioneer Hi-Bred International*, No 99-1996, 4 (available at <http://www.usdoj.gov/osg/briefs/2000/2pet/6invit/1999-1996.pet.ami.inv.pdf>).

Court took in *Festo*, which involved a seemingly narrow, arcane issue in patent law. A patentee's right to exclude others is normally defined by the literal language of the patent "claims"—a collection of single-sentence statements set forth at the end of the patent document that, by law, must "particularly point[]out and distinctly claim[] the subject matter which the [patentee] regards as his invention."[30] However, a long-established doctrine known as the doctrine of equivalents also protects the patentee a bit beyond the literal language of claim. This doctrine "casts around a claim a penumbra which also must be avoided if there is to be no infringement;"[31] it might accurately be described as the exception to the general rule that a patentee's rights are defined by the literal language of the claim. But the doctrine of equivalents itself has an exception known as prosecution history estoppel, which limits the application of the doctrine of equivalents where the patentees have amended the patent claims during the prosecution of the patent application. *Festo* concerned the precise scope of prosecution history estoppel and could therefore accurately be described as a case about the exception to the exception to the general rule of patent claim interpretation.

While the grant of certiorari on such an issue is itself a significant indication of the Court's renewed interest in patent law, other aspects of the case reveal even more about the Court's attitude. Five years prior to *Festo*, the Court in *Warner-Jenkinson Co. v Hilton Davis Chemical Co.* reversed another Federal Circuit decision on the doctrine of equivalents, but the *Warner-Jenkinson* Court seemed attentive to the Federal Circuit's expertise and authority in the area. The Court there stated that it was leaving further refinements in formulating the test of equivalence to the Federal Circuit's "sound judgment in this area of its special expertise," and that it was also "leav[ing] it to the Federal Circuit how best to implement procedural improvements to promote certainty, consistency, and reviewability to this area of law."[32] That solicitude was absent in *Festo*. Hints of the change could be heard in the oral argument. If the *Warner-Jenkinson* opinion sounded like an invitation for the Federal Circuit to experiment with new refinements

---

[30] 35 USC § 112 ¶ 2.

[31] *Autogiro Co. of America v United States*, 384 F2d 391 (Ct Cl 1967).

[32] *Warner-Jenkinson Co. v Hilton Davis Chemical Co.*, 520 US 17, 40, 39 n 8 (1995).

and improvements to patent doctrine, Chief Justice Rehnquist seemed to have second thoughts about that approach:

> [I]f we're looking for some sort of certainty in the area, to say that the Federal Circuit has now come up with a relatively new doctrine but they're free to change it if it doesn't work is not the most auspicious recommendation for that doctrine.[33]

And the Chief Justice also seemed eager to reassert the Court's authority in the patent field, as he reminded the respondents' counsel that the ruling below was

> simply an interpretation of our cases. Or it should have been at any rate. And I dare say we're in a better position to interpret our cases than the Federal Circuit.[34]

A unanimous opinion by Justice Kennedy made clear that the Chief Justice's comments were not aberrations. Not only did the opinion rebuke the Federal Circuit for "ignor[ing] the guidance" of Supreme Court case law, it also instructed the Federal Circuit on the approach to prosecution history estoppel that "is consistent with our precedents and respectful of the real practice before the PTO [the Patent and Trademark Office]."[35] These statements are really quite extraordinary given that the Supreme Court had issued precisely two precedents on prosecution history estoppel in the sixty years prior to *Festo* and that a specialized patent court might be expected to have a better sense of "the real practice before the PTO" than a generalist court that has heard only one appeal from a PTO patent action in twenty years.

Festo was not the final indication of a changed attitude in patent cases. One week after the decision in *Festo*, the Court held in *Holmes Group* that the Federal Circuit's exclusive jurisdiction over cases "arising under" the patent laws does not extend to cases hav-

---

[33] Transcript of Oral Argument, *Festo Corp. v Shoketsu Kinzoku Kogyo Kabushiki Co.*, No 00-1543, 2002 US Trans Lexis 1, *28 (Jan 8, 2002). The comment came after the respondents' counsel, in trying to defend the result below, pointed to the Federal Circuit's ability to change its "judge-made law" on prosecution history estoppel. Rehnquist thought that "scarcely an encouraging view." Id. The comments are attributed to Chief Justice Rehnquist by contemporaneous news reports. See, e.g., Tony Mauro, *Court May Curb Festo Rule*, Legal Times 6 (Jan 14, 2002).

[34] Transcript of Oral Argument, 2002 US Trans Lexis at *40 (cited in note 33). Again, the question is attributed to Chief Justice Rehnquist by contemporaneous news reports. See, e.g., Mauro, Legal Times 6 (Jan 14, 2002) (cited in note 33).

[35] *Festo*, 122 S Ct at 1841.

ing patent-law counterclaims if the complaint in the case contains no patent-law claim.[36] The decision overturned a twelve-year-old, unanimous, en banc Federal Circuit precedent. The most interesting aspect of the case, however, is the concurrence by Justice Stevens, who acknowledged that the Court's holding represents a "significant" restriction on the Federal Circuit's exclusive patent jurisdiction and that it might reintroduce circuit conflicts into the patent law.[37] Nevertheless, Stevens welcomed the possibility of circuit conflicts because they "may be useful in identifying [patent] questions that merit this Court's attention" and because "occasional decisions by courts with broader jurisdiction will provide an antidote to the risk that the specialized court may develop an institutional bias."[38]

Despite Justice Stevens's implicit suggestion of "institutional bias" in the Federal Circuit, it would be wrong to think that the Supreme Court's recent attention to patent cases was motivated by a hostility toward, or lack of confidence in, the Federal Circuit. During the 2001 Term, the Federal Circuit had one patent decision affirmed and two reversed (technically, vacated); the court has compiled a similar record over the last seven terms (three patent cases affirmed, five reversed or vacated). But those reversal rates are similar to the general reversal rate for federal appellate courts and are significantly lower than the reversal rate for the Ninth Circuit (which maintains a 4–1 ratio between reversals and affirmances).[39] Moreover, of the two issues presented in *Festo* (both of which concerned the scope of prosecution history estoppel), the Court agreed with the Federal Circuit on one and, while the Court did disagree on the other, the opinion contains nothing like the stinging criticism that the Court has deployed in past cases—most famously in *Vermont Yankee Nuclear Power Corp. v Natural Resources Defense Council*[40]—where the

---

[36] *Holmes Group*, 122 S Ct at 1893–94.

[37] Id at 1897 (Stevens concurring in part and concurring in the judgment).

[38] Id at 1898 (Stevens concurring in part and concurring in the judgment).

[39] The figures are derived from the data from the last three Supreme Court terms. See *The Supreme Court, 2001 Term, The Statistics*, 116 Harv L Rev 453, 461 (2002); *The Supreme Court, 2000 Term, The Statistics*, 115 Harv L Rev 539, 547 (2001); *The Supreme Court, 1999 Term, The Statistics*, 114 Harv L Rev 390, 398 (2000).

[40] 435 US 519 (1978). As then-Professor Scalia wrote, the Supreme Court decision in *Vermont Yankee* was so replete with "finger wagging," "pique" and "direct criticisms of the

Court has believed its precedents were being willfully flouted by a court of appeals.

It would be equally wrong to believe that the 2001 Term presages a return by the Supreme Court to the nineteenth century in matters patent. With a docket of less than one hundred cases, the Court is not in a position to hear five or ten patent cases per term as it did more than a century ago—nor should it. When the Court was hearing over a hundred patent appeals per decade, it was not doing so by choice, and only a small percentage of those cases presented questions of lasting moment to the patent system.

But it would not be wrong to believe that the 2001 Term signals a return of the Supreme Court to the field of patent law. The term was, in fact, the continuation of a process that had begun in the mid-1990s, when the Court began exercising its certiorari power more frequently in Federal Circuit patent cases. The tenor of recent patent opinions shows that the Court is becoming increasingly comfortable in reviewing patent decisions and increasingly interested in directing the development of law in the field.[41] This trend does, however, challenge the standard assumption that the Supreme Court would maintain only a minimal presence in a field subject to the jurisdiction of a specialized appellate court.

The Federal Circuit was created in the hope that the court would develop a unified and coherent body of patent precedents and, to a great extent, the court has fulfilled that aspiration.[42] Yet rather than diminishing the Supreme Court's role in the field, the very success of the Federal Circuit in establishing a definite set of patent precedents may both attract and facilitate Supreme Court review of patent cases. Because the Federal Circuit jurisprudence

---

[lower court decision] that are extraordinary in their sharpness" that "[o]ne suspects that the Court felt, as an institution, that its authority had been flouted." Antonin Scalia, *Vermont Yankee: The APA, the D.C. Circuit, and the Supreme Court*, 1978 Supreme Court Review 345, 369–70.

[41] The Court's interest has continued in the 2002 Term; through January of 2003, the Court has invited the Solicitor General to file amicus briefs on three certiorari petitions from Federal Circuit patent cases. See *Monsanto Co. v Bayer CropScience, S.A.*, 123 S Ct 579 (order of Nov 18, 2002); *Dethmers Mfg. Co. v Automatic Equip. Mfg. Co.*, 123 S Ct 579 (order of Nov 18, 2002); *Micrel, Inc. v Linear Tech. Corp.*, 123 S Ct 404 (order of Oct 15, 2002). These account for 20% (3/15) of the cases in which the Court has requested the Solicitor General's views in the 2003 Term.

[42] See Dreyfuss, 64 NYU L Rev at 6–25 (cited in note 21) (analyzing the early performance of the Federal Circuit and concluding that the court had "fulfill[ed] the expectations of [its] founders concerning both the precision and accuracy of patent law").

has generally increased the value of patents, the field has become a more important component of national economic policy,[43] and this importance is surely one explanation for the Court's renewed interest. But the Federal Circuit may also have increased the Supreme Court's ability to control the development of law in the field. As a unified national patent court, the Federal Circuit has eliminated the need for the Supreme Court to expend resources on resolving relatively minor circuit splits and thereby freed the Court to devote attention to issues of moment in the field. More importantly, the expertise of the Federal Circuit judges tends to illuminate the difficult issues of patent law, making the issues more visible, more comprehensible, and easier to review. *Festo* itself provides a good example. The report of the Federal Circuit en banc decision spans eighty-four pages in the *Federal Reporter* and includes six different opinions.[44] It is difficult to imagine a nonspecialized circuit court devoting such effort to a seemingly minor point in patent law. The extended treatment by the Federal Circuit signaled to the Supreme Court the importance of the issue and provided a rich discussion of the competing interests at stake that increased the Justices' ability to comprehend and review the case. The return of the Supreme Court is thus a sign not of the Federal Circuit's failure as a specialized court, but of its great success.

The Federal Circuit's paradoxical ability to facilitate Supreme Court review raises two important questions: whether the Supreme Court can establish a sufficient presence to influence the field, and whether such influence is desirable. These questions are now relevant to every patent case that comes before the Supreme Court because each case serves not only to resolve a particular point of substantive patent law but also to define further what might be termed the "common law" of the relationship between the Supreme Court and the Federal Circuit. The outer bounds of that relationship are established by a single statute, which grants the Court certiorari jurisdiction over all the courts of appeals, includ-

---

[43] Robert P. Merges, *One Hundred Years of Solicitude: Intellectual Property Law, 1900–2000*, 88 Cal L Rev 2187, 2224 (2000) (noting "over time, [the Federal Circuit] has proven to be a more patent-friendly court than its scattered regional predecessors" and that the court has succeeded in its goal of "strengthen[ing] patents").

[44] See *Festo Corp. v Shoketsu Kinzoku Kogyo Kabushiki Co.*, 234 F3d 558, 562–642 (Fed Cir 2000) (en banc).

ing the Federal Circuit.[45] Within that broad boundary, the Supreme Court is free to decide how that jurisdiction should be exercised. For the Court, therefore, matters of substantive patent law have become intimately bound up with the institutional allocation of power. In deciding any particular substantive patent issue, the Court needs to develop a vision of its appropriate role in the patent system.

This interdependence between institutional allocations of power and substantive patent law provides the organizational framework of this article. Section I analyzes the historical record of the Court's exercise of its patent law jurisdiction. This historical background is necessary for explaining the Court's early presence in, later neglect of, and eventual return to the field of patents. The jurisdictional history also provides some insight into the Court's future roles in the area; in particular, it suggests that, even if the Court decides only a modest number of cases, it can maintain sufficient presence to influence the path of patent law. Section II examines the substantive legal issue involved in *Festo* as a case study in the virtues and vices of the Supreme Court's return to the field. This study shows that the Supreme Court's approach to the substantive patent law in *Festo* is largely similar to the approach it has historically taken in the field. Because patent law is a fairly technical system of property rights, the Court has always behaved conservatively in the area, accepted doctrinal changes only incrementally, and looked to specialized actors in the patent system to take the lead in developing the law. The advent of the Federal Circuit requires nothing different, and the *Festo* decision shows the great virtues of maintaining that approach. The final portion of this article examines the possibilities for the future development of the symbiotic relationship between the Court and the Federal Circuit.

I. The Supreme Court at the Bar of Patents

The history of the Supreme Court's patent jurisprudence can be divided into three discrete time periods based on the character of the Court's jurisdiction: (1) prior to 1891, (2) 1891–1982, and (3) after 1982. During the first time period, the Supreme

---

[45] 28 USC § 1254.

Court was, in almost all cases, the only court in the nation with appellate jurisdiction over patent cases. The Court then provided appellate review for all or nearly all litigants, guaranteed the uniformity of national patent law, and exercised leadership in the field. In each of next two time periods, the Court lost one of those three functions. In 1891, the then new regional courts of appeals were given jurisdiction to hear appeals of right by patent litigants. In 1982, the Federal Circuit was charged with unifying national patent law. The Supreme Court has formally remained the court of last resort, but the question has remained whether the Court could continue to lead in the field even though the Court does not have any of the other responsibilities that it had in previous eras. The history is instructive on this question; it suggests that the Supreme Court's former responsibilities in this field have been unnecessary for maintaining the Court's leadership in the area.

A. PRE-1891: THE SUPREME COURT AS THE NATIONAL
   APPELLATE COURT IN PATENT CASES

While a centralized first tier of appellate review is now viewed as the exception in the federal system, it has been the rule in federal patent law more often than not. Prior to 1891, the Supreme Court performed the role now given to the Federal Circuit; it was *the* national appellate court for all patent cases. For all except the very beginning of this period, circuit courts held exclusive original jurisdiction over patent cases,[46] and the Supreme Court provided

---

[46] Under the Patent Act of 1836, the circuit courts held exclusive original jurisdiction over "all actions, suits, controversies, and cases arising under any law of the United States, granting or confirming to inventors the exclusive right to their inventions or discoveries." Act of July 4, 1836, § 17, 5 Stat 117, 124. That allocation of jurisdiction remained in place until the enactment of the Evarts Act in 1891. See, e.g., Revised Statutes § 629 (ninth paragraph) (codifying the circuit courts' jurisdiction over patent and copyright cases). Between 1800 and 1836, circuit courts also maintained exclusive original jurisdiction over patent infringement suits, which then accounted for most patent cases. See Act of April 17, 1800, § 3, 2 Stat 37, 38 (conferring exclusive jurisdiction); Thomas Sergeant, *Practice and Jurisdiction of the Courts of the United States* 120–21 (2d ed 1830) (locating patent infringement jurisdiction in the circuit courts). Between 1793 and 1800, circuit court and district courts exercised concurrent jurisdiction over infringement trials. See Patent Act of 1793, § 5, 1 Stat 318, 322. The Patent Act of 1790 did not specify which court held original jurisdiction in patent infringement cases, but a 1794 statute strongly suggests that cases had been brought in the district courts. See Act of June 7, 1794, 1 Stat 393 (reinstating district court patent cases that had been dismissed "by reason of" the repeal of 1790 Patent Act by the 1793 Patent Act). Between 1793 and 1836, the district courts also possessed a jurisdiction to declare patents invalid through a special statutory proceeding authorized under § 10 of the Patent Act of 1793. See 1 Stat at 323. That jurisdiction was exercised

appellate review of the circuit court decisions.[47] Though the Supreme Court was never as specialized as the Federal Circuit is today (the Court's patent cases were always only a few percent of its total docket), there are still great similarities between then and now. As is the case today, nearly all appellate decisions in the patent field had national effect,[48] and almost all litigants in patent cases had access to the national appellate tribunal. Indeed, Congress allowed one early jurisdictional limit—the $2,000 jurisdictional amount requirement that generally applied to the Court's appellate jurisdiction—to be waived in patent cases precisely so that "the decisions on patents [could be made] uniform, by being finally settled, when doubtful, by one tribunal, such as the Supreme Court."[49] The policy in favor of national uniformity in patent law has, therefore, ancient roots in the country's law.

For a time, this two-tiered judicial structure succeeded. As shown in figure 1,[50] the Supreme Court maintained a manageable

---

infrequently and generated few reported decisions. See, e.g., *Stearns v Barrett*, 22 F Cas 1175 (CCD Mass 1816) (opinion by Justice Story) (hearing an appeal from a district court decision rendered under § 10 of the 1793 Act); *McGaw v Bryan*, 16 F Cas 96 (SDNY 1821) (setting forth a rare report of district court decision in a § 10 case). Indeed, even prior to the 1836 Act's conferral of all patent jurisdiction on circuit courts, the sum total of district court patent jurisdiction was so slight that one district court described patent cases as being "no part of the ordinary or general jurisdiction of the district court." Id at 99.

[47] Appellate review could be obtained under § 22 of the Judiciary Act of 1789, 1 Stat 73, 84, which granted the Supreme Court power to review, by writ of error, cases originally brought in the circuit courts if the amount in controversy exceeded $2,000. As discussed in the text, Congress gradually eliminated the amount in controversy requirement in patent cases.

[48] The only non-national appellate decision in a patent case during this era appears to be *Stearns v Barrett*, 22 F Cas 1175 (CCD Mass 1816), which, as previously noted, involved an appeal from one of the rare district court decisions rendered under § 10 of the 1793 Patent Act.

[49] *Hogg v Emerson*, 47 US 437, 477 (1848) (interpreting § 17 of 1836 Patent Act, 5 Stat 117, 124, which permitted circuit courts to waive the $2,000 jurisdictional amount requirement generally applicable under § 22 of the Judiciary Act of 1789). In 1861, the jurisdictional amount requirement was eliminated altogether in patent cases. See Act of Feb 18, 1861, 12 Stat 130. By contrast, federal admiralty law during the nineteenth century maintained a three-tiered jurisdictional structure, see, e.g., Judiciary Act of 1789, § 21, 1 Stat 73, 83–84; Erastus C. Benedict, *The American Admiralty: Its Jurisdiction and Practice* § 320 at 179 (1850); and the $2,000 jurisdictional amount limitation on the Supreme Court's appellate jurisdiction was raised to $5,000 in 1875 by the Act of Feb 16, 1875, § 3, 18 Stat 315, 316.

[50] The number of Supreme Court patent cases per term was determined first by searching the Westlaw headnote topic category 291, which purports to include all patent cases. This category is slightly overinclusive. About 3.5% of cases (23 of 655) were identified as not patent cases and removed from the set. In determining whether a case should be classified as not a patent case and removed from the initial set, a fairly inclusive standard was used. Thus, for example, *Osborne v Bank of the United States*, 22 US 738 (1824), was the only case removed from the first half century of the Court's decisions (*Osborne* was apparently

S. Ct. Patent Cases: Five Term Running Average

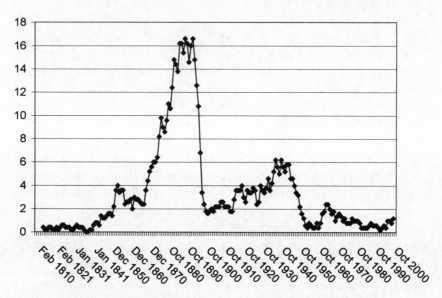

Fig. 1.—Number of Supreme Court patent cases per term averaged over five terms (1810–2000).

patent docket of fewer than four patent cases per term (averaged over five terms) from 1810—the year of the Supreme Court's first patent decision[51]—through the end of the Civil War. Because of

included in the Westlaw category because the court mentioned a principle of patent law in dicta). The first and last fifty years of the set were also examined for underinclusiveness. An independent search discovered no additional patent cases in the 1810–60 period. In the past half century, three cases were added to the count. Two concerned the exclusive patent jurisdiction of the Federal Circuit (*Holmes Group* and *Christianson v Colt Industries*, 486 US 800 (1988)); these were included because, in other time periods, the baseline Westlaw set included cases presenting jurisdictional issues unique to patent law. Also included was one per curiam decision concerning appellate review of patent invalidity rulings (*Dennison Mfg. Co. v Panduit Corp.*, 475 US 809 (1986) (per curiam)). Throughout this article, the number of citations for a case refers to the number of subsequent judicial decisions that cite to the case; the data were drawn from the Lexis/Shepherd's database in late 2002.

[51] The case, *Tyler v Tuel*, 10 US 324 (1810), was quite trivial. The plaintiffs in the case held an unusual "assignment" of patent rights that covered the entire United States, with the exception of four Vermont counties. The issue in case—which arose only because the purported assignment had been poorly drafted—was whether, given the reservation of the four counties, the plaintiffs could be considered the legal assignees of the patent and there- fore entitled to sue for infringement. (Under the statute, assignees but not licensees could bring infringement actions.) In an unsigned, single-sentence opinion, the Court held that the plaintiffs were not assignees and vacated the circuit court's judgment of infringement. In nearly 200 years, fewer than twelve court decisions have cited the case.

the relative youth of the U.S. patent system, the Court decided a relatively high number of significant legal questions. Indeed, this time period contains what is almost certainly the golden age of the Supreme Court's patent jurisprudence—the decade from 1850 to 1859, during which the Court decided at least a half dozen cases articulating fundamental principles of patent law.[52]

This jurisdictional structure did, however, contain an evident flaw: It gave the Supreme Court no control over its patent docket, and the Court could potentially be swamped with trivial appeals. Hints that this possibility might become reality arose even before the Civil War: While a substantial fraction of the Court's patent docket involved significant legal issues, the majority of cases did not, and the fraction of truly significant cases (with significance measured by later court citations) was dropping as time passed.[53]

The real problem began after the end of the war, as the Justices came to be inundated with an enormous flood of mandatory appeals. This problem was, of course, not limited to the Court's patent docket; the Court's appellate docket generally swelled to unmanageable levels.[54] Patent cases were, however, typical of the

---

[52] Important cases decided during this decade include *Gayler v Wilder*, 51 US 477 (1850) (holding that the novelty of inventions is generally to be determined only on the basis of publicly available prior art); *Hotchkiss v Greenwood*, 52 US 248 (1851) (recognizing the doctrine that would eventually be codified as the nonobviousness requirement in 35 USC § 103); *O'Reilly v Morse*, 56 US 62 (1854) (imposing limits on the subject matter that could be claimed in a patent); *Winans v Denmead*, 56 US 330 (1854) (holding that the doctrine of equivalents could be used to expand the rights claimed in the patent); *Brown v Duchesne*, 60 US 183 (1857) (limiting the territorial scope of patent rights); *Kendall v Winsor*, 62 US 322 (1859) (holding that inventors do not necessarily abandon the right to patent even if they delay patenting for long periods). The first four of these cases have each been cited in more than 250 judicial opinions.

[53] The Court decided 69 patent cases during the 1810–65 Terms. Only 19 of those decisions (28%) have been cited in more than 100 court opinions and only 10 (14%) in more than in 150 opinions. By contrast, 35 of those decisions (50%) have been cited in fewer than 50 judicial opinions, and 18 (26%) have been cited in fewer than 25 opinions. The number of significant opinions as a fraction of the total docket also appears to be dropping during this period. While 30% of decisions rendered during the 1810–40 Terms (3 of 10) have been cited in more than 150 judicial opinions, only 12% of decisions rendered during the 1841–65 Terms (7 of 59) have achieved that level of citations.

[54] During the December 1869 Term—less than five years after the end of the war—the Court decided 169 cases, which was more cases than the Court had ever decided during a single term and, in fact, more cases than it had decided during most two-year periods prior to the war. That was just the beginning. Six years later, in the October 1875 Term, the Court decided 200 cases. Over the next 10 years, the Court averaged over 240 decisions per term; one year later, the Court fell just two cases shy of deciding 300 cases in its 1886 Term. The number of cases decided does not give a full picture of situation because, even though the Court was deciding over 200 cases per term, well more than 300 cases were coming to the Court each year. See Strong, 132 N Am Rev at 438 (cited in note 11) (noting

problem. By the early 1870s, the Court was deciding about six patent cases per term, or roughly double its average from the 1850s (which had been the Court's most active decade in patent law prior to the war).[55] By the Court's 1880 Term, the number of patent cases decided had doubled again, and it continued to rise: During its 1880–89 Terms, the Court decided over 150 patent cases—an average of more than fifteen cases per term.[56] In other words, the Court was, on average, hearing more patent cases in one sitting than the modern Court has heard in the two decades since the creation of the Federal Circuit.

Yet the number of truly significant decisions issued by the Court during this period was small compared to the number of mundane cases. Even among the 151 cases decided during the 1880s, it is hard to find more than a dozen decisions that had any lasting moment in the patent system.[57] This is hardly surprising. As the century progressed, the Supreme Court's existing body of patent precedents increased, and fewer fundamental issues had yet to be addressed by the Court. Though the number of patent appeals was swelling, many of the cases could be resolved by fairly straightforward applications of existing precedent. If the Court had control of its docket, such cases would never have come before it.

---

that an average of 390 cases per year were docketed between 1875 and 1880). Since the Court could not keep pace with its docket, it accumulated a backlog of more than a thousand cases by 1880, and parties had to wait several years after docketing their appeals for the Court to hear arguments. Id at 439 (stating that "[c]ases cannot be heard within less than from two and a half to three years after they have been brought into the court").

[55] The average of any five consecutive terms between 1868 and 1875 yields six patent cases per term, plus or minus a fraction of a case. The average through the eight-year period is 6.6 patent cases per term.

[56] As was true for the rest of the Court's docket, patent appeals were being filed faster than the Court could decide them. By the end of the 1880s the Court had a several-years-long backlog of patent appeals. In fact, after the Evarts Act of 1891 eliminated the Court's mandatory appellate jurisdiction in patent cases, the number of patent cases decided by the Court did not drop significantly until four years later because the Court had to clear out the large backlog of cases filed prior to the effective date of the Act. (By law, the new statute eliminating mandatory Supreme Court appellate jurisdiction did not affect any appeal that had been perfected prior to July 1, 1891. See Act of March 3, 1891, 26 Stat 1115, 1116.)

[57] Only 18 cases during this period (about 12%) have been cited more than 150 times in judicial opinions, and this test of significance almost certainly overstates the number of significant opinions. The number of citations needed to qualify as a "significant" opinion should probably be increased for opinions delivered during this era because the amount of patent litigation increased after the Civil War. Since courts tend to cite recently decided opinions more frequently, cases decided during this era tend to have more citations than antebellum cases. If the test of significance is raised to 200 citations, only 11 cases during this period (7%) qualify as significant.

The experience during this period suggests that the Court need not decide a large number of patent cases to have a major effect in the field. One case per term—or perhaps even every other term—may be enough if the case is important enough. Even in its most active decade, the antebellum Court was deciding at most one or two significant patent cases (using court citations as a proxy for significance) every two years.[58] In the postwar era (1866–91), the number of significant opinions was no more than one to 1.5 per term, even though the Court was then deciding an average of about nine patent cases per term.[59] The large bulk of the appeals may have been of consequence to the parties, but they were not greatly important for the functioning of the patent system.

B. 1891–1982: THE FAILURE OF CERTIORARI JURISDICTION
OVER REGIONAL CIRCUITS

By enacting the Evarts Act in 1891, Congress established the now familiar three-tiered federal judicial system and allocated the bulk of mandatory appellate jurisdiction in the system to the newly created regional courts of appeals. Although proposals were made to treat patent cases differently—by, for example, creating a specialized court of patent appeals or by leaving the Supreme Court with mandatory appellate jurisdiction in patent cases—ultimately Congress made patent cases subject to the same three-tiered system that generally applied to other federal cases. The Court thus lost its responsibility for providing patent litigants with appellate review by right and, predictably, its patent docket dropped dramatically.[60] But the Court retained its obligation to ensure the national uniformity of patent law and its power to lead the field.

From the start there were concerns that the Court would not

---

[58] Of 33 patent cases decided in the 1850s terms, only 11 cases (1.1 per term) have been cited in more than 100 judicial opinions, and only five (.5 per term) have been cited in more than 150 opinions.

[59] Of the 341 patent decisions rendered during the 1866–99 Terms, only 61 (18%) have been cited more than 150 times—an average of 1.64 per term. If the threshold of significance is raised to 200 citations, only 42 (12%) opinions qualify—an average of 1.12 per term.

[60] During the first half of the twentieth century, the Court decided about 178 patent cases, an average of 3.5 cases per term. That represents a 75% reduction in the average patent caseload from the 1880s—the last full decade before the Court gained certiorari jurisdiction in the field. The Court was no longer drowning in a flood of patent appeals, but it was still hearing a significant number of patent cases.

be able to maintain uniformity of patent law among the regional appellate courts. Less than a decade after the enactment of the Evarts Act, a committee of the ABA's Section of Patent, Trademark and Copyright Law issued a report that, while affirming "the great utility of [the new courts of appeals] in the general administration of the law," nonetheless concluded "that it is impossible in the nature of things to have under such a system that certainty of uniformity and harmony of administration which is peculiarly necessary to the attainment of justice in dealing with patents and rights under them."[61] That report recommended the creation of a national "Court of Patent Appeals" that would sit in Washington. The report included a mechanism designed to prevent the possibility of overspecialization in the court, which was considered the "the principal objection" to the proposed patent court.[62] The mechanism was not review by the generalist Supreme Court; indeed, the report devoted scant attention to the relationship between the Supreme Court and the proposed patent court.[63] Rather, the report proposed that, with the exception of one permanent chief judge, the specialized court would be staffed by judges from the circuit courts who would be assigned to the court for a period of years by the Chief Justice of the Supreme Court.[64] By relying on judges "trained for their work by experience on the bench in the field of general jurisprudence," the proposal hoped to "give us a court of judges, and not of mere patent lawyers."[65]

By 1920, however, the organized bar retracted its support for a special patent court.[66] The change came partly because the patent bar came to believe that "having the Supreme Court . . . sufficiently in touch with this branch of litigation to understand and appreciate its significance" was an "especially desirable" feature of

---

[61] *Report of Committee of the Section of Patent, Trade-mark and Copyright Law*, 23 ABA Rep 543, 543 (1900).

[62] Id at 548. The objection was considered to be "that a permanent court consisting of judges appointed for life and occupied in the sole work of deciding patent cases would be liable to grow narrow and technical in its views and procedure." Id.

[63] The report stated, without elaboration, that the patent court should be "subject only to that power of review by the Supreme Court which is necessary to keep it, as the Constitution has declared it shall be, the supreme judicial tribunal of the government." Id at 547.

[64] Id.

[65] Id at 548.

[66] See *Report of the Section on Patent, Trade-mark and Copyright Law*, 6 ABA J 505, 507 (1920).

the existing structure,[67] and also partly because, as then-professor Felix Frankfurter and James Landis noted in 1928, "the Supreme Court has shown increasing liberality to review by *certiorari* conflicting patent decisions."[68] The increase in the Supreme Court's patent docket just prior to 1920 can be seen in figure 1. Between 1900 and 1915, the Court was hearing only about two patent cases per term. The rate was double that for most of the next fifteen years and moved higher still in the following two decades.

Nevertheless, although the Court was granting certiorari in a significant number of patent cases during this period, the number of significant opinions remained relatively low. The switch from mandatory to discretionary jurisdiction allowed the Court to double the percentage of significant patent cases on its docket.[69] The experience suggests that the certiorari process by itself is a relatively poor tool for limiting the Court's docket to the significant cases in the field.[70] Certiorari is often exercised to resolve circuit splits,[71] which can arise over the trivial as well as the important. Thus, much of Court's efforts may have harmonized national patent law but not influenced the field in any fundamental way.

The three-tiered system established by the Evarts Act func-

---

[67] *Report of the Committee on Patent, Trade-mark and Copyright Law*, 5 ABA J 440, 445 (1919).

[68] Felix Frankfurter and James M. Landis, *The Business of the Supreme Court* 183 (Macmillan, 1928). See also id at 180–84 (detailing the demise of the patent court proposals). See also 1919 Report, 5 ABA J at 445 (cited in note 67) (noting that the "Court has adopted the practice of issuing writs of *certiorari* where [circuit] conflicts exist" and that "[t]his mitigates the objection to the present system so emphasized in former reports").

[69] During the period from 1900 through 1950, the Court decided 178 patent cases of which 154 were certiorari cases. If the test of significance is citations in at least 150 subsequent judicial opinions, then 40% of the certiorari decisions (61/154) could be viewed as significant. If the test is raised to 200 citations, then the percentage drops to 27% (41/154). Each of these figures is about twice the corresponding figures calculated for the 1866–99 period. Thirty-two cases (21%) were cited 50 or fewer times. Comparing citations of cases from this era to citations of cases in the nineteenth century probably overestimates the significance of the more recent cases. While the more recent cases have been available for citation for less time than older cases (which might decrease somewhat the number of citations of recent cases), the more important effect is likely to be the growth of litigation and reported decisions which, when coupled with the tendency of courts to cite recent decisions, tends to increase the number of citations of recent cases.

[70] This evidence suggests that, contrary to the suggestion of Justice Stevens in his *Holmes Group* concurrence, the circuit conflicts may not "be useful in identifying [patent] questions that merit this Court's attention." 122 S Ct at 1898 (Stevens concurring in part and concurring in the judgment). See also text at notes 36–38.

[71] Though the Court often does not mention its reason for granting certiorari, approximately three dozen (or 23%) of the Court's 154 certiorari decisions during the 1900–50 Terms explicitly mention a circuit split as the reason for granting certiorari.

tioned reasonably well provided that the Court was fairly liberal in granting certiorari to hear patent cases. At mid-century, however, that liberality abruptly ended. In its 1950 Term, the Court decided a single patent case, *Great Atlantic & Pac. Tea Co. v Supermarket Equipment Corp.*[72] During the rest of the 1950s, the Court would decide only four patent cases, thus producing a ninefold reduction in the Court's patent caseload during the 1940s (4.5 cases per term) and a sevenfold reduction from the Court's average in the first half of the twentieth century (3.5 cases per term). In 1960s, the Court's level of interest rebounded very slightly; it averaged just under two patent cases per term, but the average returned to around one case per term in the 1970s. Through the entire period from 1950 through the end of the 1982 Term (the last year in which the Court exercised certiorari over a patent decision of a regional circuit), the Court averaged about one patent case per term (thirty-six cases in thirty-three terms).

The significance of the Court's declining patent docket was magnified by another feature of the docket: The Court was devoting most of its attention not to matters of substantive patent law— that is, the law governing patent validity and the patentee's rights against infringement—but to issues such as venue and procedure,[73] the preemptive effects of the federal patent system on state law,[74] the federal common law of patent licensing (a form of federal preemption of state contract law),[75] and the relationship between the patent and antitrust laws.[76] Out of the thirty-six total patent cases

---

[72] 340 US 147 (1950).

[73] *Brunette Machine Works, Limited v Kockum Industries, Inc.*, 406 US 706 (1972); *Blonder-Tongue Laboratories, Inc. v University of Illinois Foundation*, 402 US 313 (1971); *Schnell v Peter Eckrich & Sons, Inc.*, 365 US 260 (1961); *Fourco Glass Co. v Transmirra Products Corp.*, 353 US 222 (1957); *Sanford v Kepner*, 344 US 13 (1952).

[74] *Kewanee Oil Co. v Bicron Corp.*, 416 US 470 (1974); *Sperry v State of Fla. ex rel. Florida Bar*, 373 US 379 (1963); *Compco Corp. v Day-Brite Lighting, Inc.*, 376 US 234 (1964); *Sears, Roebuck & Co. v Stiffel Co.*, 376 US 225 (1964).

[75] *Aronson v Quick Point Pencil Co.*, 440 US 257 (1979); *Standard Industries, Inc. v Tigrett Industries, Inc.*, 397 US 586 (1970) (affirming lower court judgment by an equally divided Court); *Lear, Inc. v Adkins*, 395 US 653 (1969).

[76] *Dawson Chemical Co. v Rohm and Haas Co.*, 448 US 176 (1980) (antitrust/patent misuse doctrine); *Zenith Radio Corp. v Hazeltine Research, Inc.*, 395 US 100 (1969); *Walker Process Equipment, Inc. v Food Machinery & Chemical Corp.*, 382 US 172 (1965); *Brulotte v Thys Co.*, 379 US 29 (1964) (holding federal patent law preempts state contract law so as to preclude enforcement of a contractual obligation to pay royalties on an invention past the end of the patent term); *United States v Singer Mfg. Co.*, 374 US 174 (1963) (antitrust liability for patent pools); *U.S. Gypsum Co. v National Gypsum Co.*, 352 US 457 (1957) (holding that

decided during the 1950 to 1982 Terms (a thirty-three-year period), nineteen cases fell into one of these peripheral categories.
Substantive patent law was at issue in only seventeen cases—an
average of about one case every two terms.

While the precise reasons for this dramatic drop are not clear,
two contemporaneous events help to explain the Court's retreat
from the field. The first event occurred in 1949, when the Court
by a 6–3 vote invalidated the patent in *Jungersen v Ostby & Barton
Co.* on the grounds that the patentee's improvement (a better
method for casting jewelry) showed no "inventive genius."[77] The
case was merely another in a line of then-recent precedents invalidating patents for want of "genius," but it was significant because
of the concerns voiced in the dissents. Justices Frankfurter and
Justice Burton argued that the case, though having no "serious
consequences for an important industry," nonetheless "raise[d] basic issues regarding the judiciary's role in our existing patent system" because the Court majority was acting "as though [the patent
system] did not exist as it is."[78] In a separate dissent, Justice Jackson
was more blunt. He charged the Court majority with having such
a "strong passion" for striking down patents "that the only patent
that is valid is one which this Court has not been able to get its
hands on."[79] Thus, at least three Justices believed the Court to be
overly hostile to patents and might, therefore, have wanted to keep
the Court from "get[ting] its hands on" more patent cases.

But *Jungersen* is only half of the story. In 1952, Congress enacted a comprehensive revision of the patent laws that, among
other things, overruled the Court's precedents requiring inventive
"genius" as a prerequisite for a valid patent and substituted a statutory test requiring patentable inventions to be not "obvious" mod-
ifications of the prior art.[80] That line of precedents had accounted
for a fifth of the Court's total patent docket in the years preceding
the change,[81] and the new statute was widely viewed as a congres-

patentee could rely on patent infringement and quantum meruit theories to recover damages
against a licensee even though the license had been found unlawful under the antitrust laws).

[77] 335 US 560, 566 (1949).

[78] Id at 568 & 571 (Frankfurter dissenting) (internal quotation omitted).

[79] Id at 572 (Jackson dissenting).

[80] See 35 USC § 103.

[81] In the 1935–49 Terms, the Court decided 15 cases in which the patent was held invalid
for want of invention or inventive genius. Those cases accounted for a full 20% (15 of 74
cases) of the Court's patent docket during the period and for 32% (15/47) if the cases

sional vote of no confidence on a major line of the Court's mid-century patent precedents.[82] The Justices most hostile to patents—Justices Douglas and Black[83]—might have balked at bringing new patent cases to the Court for fear that the new statute might prod moderate members of the Court to take a more favorable view of patents generally. The *Jungersen* dissenters, on the other hand, might equally have feared that the Court's hostility toward patents would not be tempered by the new statute. The risks to each side might explain the dramatic drop in patent cases.

Yet whatever the cause of the drop, the Court would, for the rest of the twentieth century, not hear patent cases with the frequency that it did in the first half of the century. Thus, while the creation of the Federal Circuit would precipitate a decline in Supreme Court patent cases, the reverse is more true: The sharp decline in Supreme Court patent cases at mid-century left circuit patent law largely unsupervised by the Supreme Court. Circuit splits multiplied, and the resulting uncertainty in patent law provided the impetus for the Federal Circuit.[84]

C. POST-1982: THE FEDERAL CIRCUIT AND
THE FACILITATION OF GENERALIST REVIEW

With the creation of the Federal Circuit in 1982, Congress relieved the Court of its responsibility (which it had been neglecting)

---

involving only peripheral patent issues—procedural matters and licensing-antitrust issues—are removed from the count.

[82] According to Giles Rich, one of the drafters of the 1952 Act who would later serve as a judge on the Court of Customs and Patent Appeals and on the Federal Circuit, the Court's decision in *Great Atlantic & Pacific Tea* "clinched the determination to include in the bill what is now 35 U.S.C. 103, in order to get rid of the vague requirement of 'invention.'" Giles S. Rich, *Congressional Intent—Or, Who Wrote the Patent Act of 1952?* in John F. Witherspoon, ed, *Nonobviousness—The Ultimate Condition of Patentability* 1:1, 1:8 (BNA, 1980).

[83] See, e.g., the particularly sharp concurrence by Justice Douglas, joined by Justice Black, in *Great Atlantic & Pacific Tea*, 340 US at 154–58. The concurrence charged the Patent Office with issuing "flimsy and spurious" patents that have to "be brought all the way to this Court to be declared invalid." Id at 158. Justice Black also authored a number of separate opinions that were perceived to be anti-patent and that were joined by Justice Douglas. See, e.g., *Standard Industries, Inc. v Tigrett Industries, Inc.*, 397 US 586, 586 (1970) (Black dissenting); *Aro Mfg. Co. v Convertible Top Replacement Co.*, 377 US 476, 515 (1964) (Black dissenting); *Exhibit Supply Co. v Ace Patents Corp.*, 315 US 126, 137 (1942) (Black dissenting) (arguing that the Court should, sua sponte, invalidate a patent on grounds not argued by any of the parties).

[84] This point was made explicitly in the House Report on the legislation creating the Federal Circuit. See HR Rep No 97-312, 97th Cong, 1st Sess 22 (1981).

of maintaining nationally uniform patent law and returned the jurisdictional structure for patent cases to a system similar to that of the nineteenth century, with a single national appellate court hearing all appeals from the regional trial courts. Initially, the change led to another decline in the Supreme Court's patent docket and, although this drop was not nearly so large (both in numbers and percentages) as the mid-century decline, it seemed at first to signal that the Court would limit itself largely to policing the boundaries and procedures of the patent system while otherwise deferring to the expert judges of the Federal Circuit. In the twelve terms between 1983 and 1994 (inclusive), the Court heard five patent cases, four of which involved issues such as federal preemption of state law, appellate procedure in infringement cases, and the scope of the Federal Circuit's exclusive jurisdiction in patent cases.[85] Even the one case involving a substantive patent issue seemed to be an exception proving the rule: The case, though formally involving the scope of a patentee's rights against infringement, actually turned on the interplay between the Patent Act and the Food, Drug, and Cosmetics Act, a statute outside of the special competence of the Federal Circuit.[86]

At the end of its 1994 Term, the Court seemed destined to maintain a highly marginal role in the patent system. The surprise has been that the Court does not seem to be following that course. In its last seven terms (1995–2001), the Court has decided eight patent cases, or just slightly more than one case per term (see fig. 2). Four of these cases could be explained as being consistent with the Court's pattern of regulating the boundaries of patent law and patent institutions.[87] But the remaining four are harder to

---

[85] See *Cardinal Chemical Co. v Morton Intern., Inc.*, 508 US 83 (1993) (concerning appellate procedure in patent cases); *Bonito Boats, Inc. v Thunder Craft Boats, Inc.*, 489 US 141 (1989) (preemption); *Christianson v Colt Industries Operating Co.*, 486 US 800 (1988) (the scope of the Federal Circuit's exclusive patent jurisdiction); *Dennison Mfg. Co. v Panduit Corp.*, 475 US 809 (1986) (per curiam) (appellate procedure).

[86] See *Eli Lilly and Co. v Medtronic, Inc.*, 496 US 661 (1990). The Court also decided a case concerning the scope of rights under the Plant Varieties Protection Act, 7 USC § 2321 et seq, a patent-like statute administered by the Department of Agriculture that provides exclusive rights over certain types of new plants and seeds. See *Asgrow Seed Co. v Winterboer*, 513 US 179 (1995). This case is not counted as a patent case.

[87] The four concerned the scope of the Federal Circuit's jurisdiction (*Holmes Group*); the States' Eleventh Amendment immunity in patent cases (*Florida Prepaid Postsecondary Education Expense Bd v College Saving Bank*, 527 US 627, 642 (1999)); the application of the Administrative Procedure Act to judicial review of PTO decisions (*Dickinson v Zurko*, 527 US 150 (1999)); and a Seventh Amendment challenge to the Federal Circuit's holding that

S. Ct. Patent Cases: Five Term Running Average
(1950-2001)

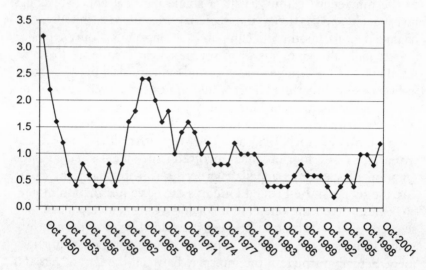

FIG. 2.—Number of Supreme Court patent cases per term averaged over five terms (1950–2001).

explain. *Warner-Jenkinson Co. v Hilton Davis Chemical Co.*,[88] *Pfaff v Wells Electronics, Inc.*,[89] *J.E.M. Ag Supply v Pioneer Hi-Bred International*,[90] and *Festo* all involved nonconstitutional issues falling within the Federal Circuit's patent jurisdiction. In each case, the Supreme Court's grant of certiorari cannot be explained as necessary to maintain the uniform application of federal law or even to resolve a conflict between the Federal Circuit and the legal position of the Executive Branch.[91] Instead, the Court seems to have been motivated by a desire to review the *correctness* of the Federal

---

juries have no role in interpreting patent claims (*Markman v Westview Instruments, Inc.*, 517 US 370 (1996)).

[88] 520 US 17 (1995).

[89] 525 US 55 (1998).

[90] 122 S Ct 593 (2001).

[91] Although the Court in one case stated that it had granted certiorari in part because of the tension between the Federal Circuit decision below and a few pre–Federal Circuit opinions from the regional circuits, see *Pfaff,* 525 US at 60, the Court must have realized that the older circuit decisions posed little risk to the uniform application of patent law that is now dominated by the Federal Circuit's exclusive jurisdiction. Indeed, the Court did not explain its certiorari grant solely in terms of the circuit "split" but also provided, as an additional or alternative reason for granting review, the apparent tension between the Federal Circuit's ruling and the text of the relevant statute. See *id.*

Circuit's patent decision and to assert some degree of supervision over the Federal Circuit—even on statutory issues of patent policy.

This recent experience suggests that the Court will continue to hear patent cases. Perhaps it will average one case per term (roughly the average in the last fifty years), or perhaps half that. If the hopes in creating a court of appeals with nationwide jurisdiction were that such a court would have "the all-but-final say in determining . . . what an act of Congress means"[92] or that the court would be "the probable court of last resort in most of its cases,"[93] those hopes are fulfilled only with emphasis on the exceptions: The Federal Circuit has all *but* the final say and it is the court of last resort in *most*—not all—of its cases.

History suggests that the Court can continue to be important in the field even if it is hearing only five or ten patent cases per decade. Indeed, it could perhaps be as important to the field as it was in the nineteenth century. Influence is driven not so much by the quantity of decisions, but by the quality and authority of those decisions. Even under fairly liberal tests of what constitutes a "significant" patent decision by the Court, the number of such decisions hovered about the level of one per term even during the heyday of the Court's patent docket. Thus, despite the small size of its current patent docket, the Court can continue exercising a leading role in the field if it is able to select the right cases—that is, the important cases—to fill its docket.[94]

It is on this point that a specialized court of appeals with national jurisdiction may actually facilitate the jurisdiction of the generalist Supreme Court by attracting the Court's attention to the important questions in the field. Evidence of this effect can be seen even before the Federal Circuit existed. In the decade before the creation of the Federal Circuit, the Court was already receiving more than half of its patent cases (five of nine) from a specialized

---

[92] Rehnquist, 14 Fla St U L Rev at 12 (cited in note 15).

[93] Howard T. Markey, *The Federal Circuit and Congressional Intent*, 2 Fed Cir Bar J 303, 304 (1992).

[94] It may be true, as Mark Janis writes, that "[n]either the time, temperament, nor resources of the Supreme Court will allow for the implementation of an interventionist approach to patent decision making." Janis, 2001 Ill L Rev at 395 (cited in note 17). But that is true only because Professor Janis defines an "interventionist" approach to mean "exercis[ing] certiorari jurisdiction routinely in patent cases." Id. The Court could, however, be interventionist in the sense of influential even with just a small number of patent cases per term.

tribunal—the Court of Customs and Patent Appeals (CCPA), which then handled appeals from Patent Office actions denying patent applications.[95] If the peripheral patent cases are eliminated, the CCPA's presence in the Court's patent docket is even more dramatic: Only one of the cases taken from a nonspecialized court during this ten-year period involved a core issue of substantive patent law.[96] Thus, in the decade prior to the creation of the Federal Circuit, the Supreme Court was already obtaining nearly all of its substantive patent cases from a specialty court with a national jurisdiction.

At least two effects explain the ability of a specialized court with nationwide jurisdiction to help the Court identify cases meriting review. First, a decision by a national court of appeals such as the CCPA or the Federal Circuit has greater importance than a decision by any one circuit. The decision thus has a stronger claim to review by the Court, and it is also likely to attract a larger number of amicus briefs at the certiorari stage because interested entities— for example, trade associations or firms not party to the particular lawsuit—will have a greater incentive to support a petition for certiorari. Even if the legal analysis in the amicus briefs is not helpful, the sheer number of amicus briefs should give the Court some indication of a case's importance. Thus, for example, the ten amicus briefs filed at the petition stage of the *Festo* litigation (eight briefs supporting certiorari and two opposing) probably gave the Court a reasonable indication of the case's import.[97]

Second, the importance of a case may be signaled by the lower court judges who, because of their expertise, may be better than generalist judges at identifying important issues in the field. Thus, in *Festo*, a set of issues that a generalist might view as minor drew an en banc decision spanning eighty pages in the *Federal Reporter*. If patent appeals were still being heard by regional courts of appeals, it is difficult to imagine any regional circuit de-

---

[95] In the ten terms prior to the creation of the Federal Circuit (1972–81 Terms), the Court decided nine patent cases, five of which came from the Court of Customs and Patent Appeals. See *Diamond v Diehr*, 450 US 175 (1981); *Diamond v Chakrabarty*, 447 US 303 (1980); *Parker v Flook*, 437 US 584 (1978); *Dann v Johnston*, 425 US 219 (1976); *Gottschalk v Benson*, 409 US 63 (1972).

[96] *Sakraida v Ag Pro, Inc.*, 425 US 273 (1976) (holding a patent invalid for obviousness).

[97] Amicus briefs are available at <http://supreme.lp.findlaw.com/supreme_court/docket/2001/january.html>.

voting such a large amount of resources to a patent case.[98] Lengthy opinions like those in *Festo* not only indicate the importance of a case to the Supreme Court; they also thoroughly set forth the various arguments for and against the rule adopted by the lower court. The Supreme Court can be fairly certain that the issue has been thoroughly vetted and is therefore ready for a grant of certiorari.

D. THE POSSIBILITIES FOR THE FUTURE:
   THE INFREQUENT PATENT COURT

The prior discussion suggests that, even if the Court continues to hear fairly small numbers of patent cases, the Court could still play a major role in patent law and policy—indeed, its role could be enhanced by the existence of the Federal Circuit. But this says nothing about whether, or to what extent, the Court should continue to maintain a presence in a field now dominated by an expert lower court.

These questions cannot be answered merely by assuming that one institution is better than the other. Both are staffed by fallible judges; both will reach poor decisions from time to time; there is no a priori reason to believe one institution will necessarily be wiser than the other. But even if we remain agnostic about which court is better in some abstract sense, the institutional differences between the Court and the Federal Circuit do provide some rational basis for deciding the respective roles of the courts.

The most celebrated institutional characteristic of the Federal Circuit is, of course, its specialized jurisdiction in patent cases, and

---

[98] Because a regional court would hear only a fraction of the patent appeals occurring in the nation, it would be less likely to develop an intracircuit split on any particular issue in patent law and therefore less likely to devote full en banc treatment to a patent case. See Fed R App Proc 35 (listing intracircuit conflict as one of two reasons for granting en banc hearing); Tracey E. George, *The Dynamics and Determinants of the Decision to Grant En Banc Review*, 74 Wash L Rev 213, 254–55 (1999) (showing by a statistical analysis that, while most judges will vote for en banc review of an intracircuit conflict, they do not "display the same willingness" to grant en banc rehearing on issues subject to intercircuit conflicts). Furthermore, the generation of multiple, lengthy opinions such as those in the *Festo* en banc is probably more likely when the court's law clerks are motivated to become steeped in the relevant legal issue, and the Federal Circuit tends to attract law clerks with scientific backgrounds who are likely to practice patent law after their clerkships. See Jonathan Ringel, *The Help Desk Clerks Know More Than Law*, Legal Times 71 (Mar 12, 2001) (surveying 36 of 38 Federal Circuit law clerks from one year and finding that 25 clerks possessed degrees in science, math, or engineering; also noting that Federal Circuit law clerks are in high demand by intellectual property firms).

that feature provides the Federal Circuit with an expertise in patent law lacking in the modern Supreme Court. The limits of the Federal Circuit's expertise mark one role for the Supreme Court—policing matters at the boundaries of patent policy and policing the boundaries of the Federal Circuit's jurisdiction. The Court itself seems to recognize this point for, as previously noted, a fairly large fraction of the Court's certiorari grants in Federal Circuit patent cases have concerned the proper relationship between patents and other fields of federal law. The justification for more aggressive Supreme Court supervision need not be that the Federal Circuit's decisions on matters such as administrative or constitutional law are in some way suspect because the Federal Circuit has a specialized jurisdiction in patent law.[99] Rather, the justification is that, in these cases, the Federal Circuit's expertise in patent law does not provide any special reason for resisting certiorari review. The court's decisions are then on an equal footing with decisions of the other circuits, and the Supreme Court should apply its normal policies for certiorari review.

The most important consideration for defining a role for the Supreme Court in patent law is not, however, that the Court exercises jurisdiction generally in a variety of other fields but that it exercises its jurisdiction so infrequently in patent cases. This infrequency can be assumed both because of the reality of the Court's modern docket, which does not leave room for large numbers of cases from any particular area of federal law, and because of the historical record that the Court has not, during any period in which it had control of its docket, been willing to fill more than a small percentage of its docket with patent cases. The infrequency does not mean that the Court is incapable of having an effect on the course of the law, but it does have other implications.

1. *Arbitrating institutional claims to power.* The Court's relative isolation from the day-to-day workings of the patent system may make the Court a particularly good institution for deciding the allocation of decisional power within the patent system. The point

---

[99] See Peter L. Strauss, *One Hundred Fifty Cases per Year: Some Implications of the Supreme Court's Limited Resources for Judicial Review of Agency Action,* 87 Colum L Rev 1093, 1115 (1987) (arguing that specialized institutions such as the Federal Circuit "face handicaps" in "grappling with broad legal issues outside their particular responsibility" because they suffer from "obvious inexperience" with broader questions and because their specialized jurisdiction "can give them a distorted perspective").

here is premised not on the necessary limitations of the Court's docket,[100] but on the desirability of having a more detached institution review Federal Circuit decisions concerning the scope of its own power.

The day-to-day administration of the patent system is lodged primarily with a triad of institutions: the PTO, which is responsible for issuing patents; the district courts, which are responsible for trying infringement actions; and the Federal Circuit, which reviews the work of the other two institutions. Where the Federal Circuit is deciding on the allocation of power among the three institutions, it may suffer from an institutional problem: If the court concludes that a particular power is properly decided by an appellate court, the power redounds to the court itself. In fact, it is hard not to notice that, in cases presenting contested issues concerning the allocation of power in the patent system, the Federal Circuit has consistently pushed decisional power toward itself.[101] Decisions concerning the patent system will, however, have little effect on the Supreme Court's overall power, and that detachment could assist the Court in evaluating the institutions of the patent system and allocating power among them.

2. *Providing stability.* In the early part of the twentieth century, reformers championed specialized institutions—then administra-

---

[100] See, e.g., Samuel Estreicher and John E. Sexton, *A Managerial Theory of the Supreme Court's Responsibilities: An Empirical Study*, 59 NYU L Rev 681 (1984) (arguing that the limitations of the modern Court's docket require the Court's responsibilities to be focused on "manag[ing] a system whose goal is to provide justice").

[101] *Dethmers Mfg. Co. v Automatic Equip. Mfg. Co.*, 272 F3d 1365 (Fed Cir 2001) (refusing to give the PTO deference in its interpretation of its own administrative regulations); *In re Zurko*, 142 F3d 1447 (Fed Cir 1998) (en banc) (holding that PTO patent decisions are subject to a more stringent judicial review standard than the generally applicable standard supplied by the Administrative Procedure Act), revd sub nom, *Dickinson v Zurko*, 527 US 150 (1999); *Cybor Corp. v FAS Techs.*, 138 F3d 1448 (Fed Cir 1998) (en banc) (holding that interpretations of patent claims by district courts are to be reviewed de novo on appeal); *Markman v Westview Instruments, Inc.*, 52 F3d 967 (Fed Cir 1995) (en banc) (holding that juries have no role in interpreting patent claims), affd, 517 US 370 (1996); *Merck & Co. v Kessler*, 80 F3d 1543 (Fed Cir 1996) (holding that the Federal Circuit owes no deference to the PTO's interpretations of the Patent Act). The Federal Circuit's attempt to limit the doctrine of equivalents in *Festo* can also be seen as an example. Patent infringement can be proven either as literal infringement of the patent claims or as infringement under the doctrine of equivalents. The Federal Circuit has held that it determines the scope of claims as a matter of law, while juries decided the scope of equivalents. Limiting the availability of the doctrine of equivalents forces patentees to bring infringement cases under the literal language of the claims rather than under the doctrine of equivalents and thus shifts decisional power in infringement cases toward the Federal Circuit and away from juries.

tive agencies and tribunals—as necessary and desirable because they believed that specialized institutions would be able to adapt law more quickly to the changing needs of modern society.[102] Supervision by a generalized judicial body was anathema to those reformers precisely because it could curb the pace of change. The insight of that era is relevant to the relationship between the Supreme Court and the Federal Circuit, though the point is reversed. A great virtue of infrequent Supreme Court review is its moderating influence on the pace of change.

Patents are alternatively described as a species of property rights or a type of contract between the inventor and the government.[103] Both conceptions of patents suggest the need for stability. As the Court has recognized, "[c]onsiderations in favor of stare decisis are at their acme in cases involving property and contract rights, where reliance interests are involved."[104] In fact, the patent system needs to be reliable and predictable over long periods of time. Patents extend for about two decades under current law. They are intended to allow the investors in intellectual property to recover the investments made many years earlier. Without long-term stability in the patent system, investors could not be certain that they will have a fair opportunity to recover the investments made in creating the intellectual property.

To the extent that it adheres to the normal common-law process of modifying precedents only incrementally,[105] the Supreme Court

---

[102] See, e.g., Harlan F. Stone, *The Common Law in the United States*, 50 Harv L Rev 4 (1936) (theorizing that administrative processes were substituted for common law courts "because the ever expanding activities of government in dealing with the complexities of modern life had made indispensable the adoption of procedures more expeditious and better guided by specialized experience than any which the courts had provided"); id at 18 (observing that administrative bodies having "specialized experience" have set up standards "which the courts could have formulated, if at all, only more tardily and with far greater difficulty"). See also Gerard C. Henderson, *The Federal Trade Commission: A Study in Administrative Law and Procedure* at v (Yale, 1924).

[103] See, e.g., *Florida Prepaid Postsecondary Education Expense Bd. v College Saving Bank*, 527 US 627, 642 (1999) (noting that patents "have long been considered a species of property"); *Bonito Boats, Inc. v Thunder Craft Boats, Inc.*, 489 US 141, 150–51 (1989) (describing the patent as "a carefully crafted bargain" in which the inventor creates and discloses in formation "in return for the exclusive right"); *Markman v Westview Instruments, Inc.*, 52 F3d 967, 984 (Fed Cir 1995), affd, 517 US 370 (1996) (finding "[t]he analogy of a patent to a contract" to be "appropriate").

[104] *Payne v Tennessee*, 501 US 808, 828 (1991).

[105] See *Rogers v Tennessee*, 532 US 451 (2001) (describing "incremental and reasoned development of precedent" as the "foundation of the common law system").

will be able to maintain no more than a glacial pace of change in an area, like patent law, where it decides perhaps only a half dozen cases per century on any particular issue. *Festo* provides a good example. With citations to only eight cases, the Court effectively canvased the universe of its significant precedents on the doctrine of equivalents and prosecution history estoppel from the past 150 years. If the Court's instincts are to change its case law gradually, then an infrequent but steady exercise of its certiorari jurisdiction will likely check any fast shifts that could develop in the case law of a more frequent patent court like the Federal Circuit.

3. *Leading change.* The infrequency of the Court's intervention in any particular issue of patent law makes the Court a poor institution for designing substantive change or for experimenting with possible reforms in the field. In part, this conclusion is simply the converse of the last point: If the Court reviews a particular issue only once every one or two decades, it is more likely to hinder than to help change.

The infrequency of the Court's review also means that the Court will lack expertise of the sort possessed by the Federal Circuit, the PTO, and even certain district courts that routinely adjudicate patent cases. An inexpert institution might fairly be able to evaluate doctrinal experiments in the field, or at least determine whether the doctrinal experiment is such a large departure from existing precedent that it should not be permitted. But developing innovations in the law requires a type of comprehensive knowledge of the field—an appreciation for the interaction between all the various doctrines—that is simply lacking in the Court. Moreover, the Court need not undertake the role of leader. The other institutions in the patent system—particularly the PTO and the Federal Circuit—are better equipped to formulate new doctrine, and their experiments, if unsuccessful, can be more easily abandoned or reversed than can a Supreme Court precedent.

The role adumbrated here for the Court—with a focus on institutional arrangements, a cautious adherence to precedent, and a humble abjuration of any leading role—is in fact the approach that the Court has taken historically in the field. There is no better demonstration of this role than the Court's historical approach in the area of patent law at issue in *Festo*, which concerns the definition of the property rights encompassed within a patent. To that area we now turn.

II. Festo and the Court's Approach to Defining Patent Rights

Festo is a great case to study for many reasons. The prominence of the petitioner's counsel, coupled with the great interest in the case shown by business and the bar (seventeen amicus briefs were filed on the merits), hark back to the era when the Supreme Court frequently entertained important and complex patent appeals. The technicality of the issues in the case demonstrates that the modern Court is unwilling to cede to the Federal Circuit plenary authority over the arcana of patent law. But the most important reason to study *Festo* is that the case is part of a larger history of the Court's attempts to address an extremely difficult legal issue in a specialized area of law. This larger history provides a perfect forum for studying the Court's presence in the field.

A. A TALE OF THE CLAIM AND THE COURT

The ultimate issue in *Festo* is as simple to state as it is hard to resolve: What is the best manner to define property rights in innovations? The difficulty is immediately apparent. Unlike physical property, innovations occupy the realm of the conceptual and, as innovations, they are also new and nonobvious. The task for the law is thus to define accurately rights to incorporeal matters residing on the forefront of human knowledge.[106]

Despite the difficulty of this task, the basic law existing at the time of *Festo* could be defined by three rules: First, patent claims—the formal, single-sentence statements of the invention set forth at end of the patent—provide the primary definition of the patentee's rights against infringement. Second, the doctrine of equivalents is the exception to that rule; it allows patent rights to extend somewhat beyond the literal bounds of the claims. Third, prosecution history estoppel is the exception to the exception; it precludes resort to the doctrine of equivalents where the equivalents measure

---

[106] The problem of fitting language to innovation is not confined to patent law. See Federalist 37 (Madison) in Clinton Rossiter, ed, *The Federalist Papers* 229 (Mentor, 1961) (explaining that drafting a constitution containing "so many important changes and innovations" is difficult because "no language is so copious as to supply words and phrases for every complex idea, or so correct as not to include many equivocally denoting different ideas" and "this unavoidable inaccuracy must be greater or less, according to the complexity and novelty of the objects defined").

of infringement would contradict the patentee's representations and actions during the administrative process of obtaining the patent.

These three rules form the basic framework for *Festo*. The literal language of the patent claims did not cover (or at least were believed not to cover) the accused infringer's products, and so the patentee invoked the doctrine of equivalents. The accused infringer relied on the doctrine of prosecution history estoppel to limit the patentee's rights to the literal terms of the claims. Thus, from the perspective of the patentee in *Festo*, the doctrine of equivalents was a friend—helping to broaden the claims—and the literal language of the claims, an enemy.

Yet less than two centuries ago, in the early nineteenth century, an attorney skilled in patent law would have viewed the posture of *Festo*, to the extent that it would have been comprehensible, as utterly backward. The attorney would have found the concept of prosecution history estoppel unintelligible because there was no prosecution process for obtaining a patent; the Patent Office simply registered and issued patents with no administrative examination to determine their validity. Although the attorney would have understood the concepts of equivalents and claims, he would have viewed equivalents analysis as the primary means of determining infringement and the patent claim as a relatively new legal device designed to help patentees *expand* their rights. The story of how the early nineteenth-century understanding came to be inverted in a modern case such as *Festo* can be told with a surprisingly small number of Supreme Court precedents and, in this tale, we can observe the traditional functioning of the Supreme Court. Rather than leading change in the field, the Court has allowed more specialized institutions—particularly the Patent Office and the patent bar—to develop the law. The Court's role was frequently to provide stability by restraining the pace of change. And where it accepted change, the Court stressed the institutional reasons for reform.

1. *The patent-claiming revolution in the nineteenth century.* Defining the precise scope of property rights is a problem that must be addressed by any patent system, but the early American patent system took an approach that is nearly the complete opposite of the one taken today. In fact, the patent system in the early nineteenth century looked much more like copyright than it does today. Like

copyrights, patents were merely registered; the Patent Office did not attempt to determine the validity of the patent at the time of registration. Patent claims were unknown, and the infringement of a patent was decided by applying a test much like the "substantial similarity" standard still used today to determine infringement of copyrights.[107] The jury would determine infringement by determining whether the defendant's machines (or products or processes) were "substantially, in their principles and mode of operation, like"[108] the invention described in the patent specification (which is the technical description that, by law, must disclose all information to enable the making and using of the invention). This "substantial identity" test was *the* test for infringement and, by the middle of the century, it was equated in name with "the doctrine of mechanical equivalents."[109]

The legal construct now known as the patent claim arose within this legal environment. It arose not from any administrative, judicial, or legislative requirement. Instead, it was an innovation of patent attorneys, and it was formulated to protect and to expand the rights of patentees.

One benefit of early claims is that they could protect an inventor against invalidation of a patent on the ground that the patent did

---

[107] See, e.g., Melville B. Nimmer and David Nimmer, 4 *Nimmer on Copyright* § 13.03[A] at 13–27 (1997) (articulating the modern "substantial similarity" test). Copyright law also requires that the accused infringer have *copied* the copyrighted work; thus, independent creation is a complete defense in copyright law, though not in patent law.

[108] *Odiorne v Winkley*, 18 F Cas 581, 582 (CCD Mass 1814) (Justice Story's instructions to the jury).

[109] Describing the relationship between the substantial identity test and the doctrine of equivalents, the great treatise writer George Curtis (brother of the Supreme Court Justice) wrote:

> It is in relation to this question of substantial identity, that the doctrine of mechanical equivalents becomes practically applicable. This doctrine depends on the truth that the identity of purpose, and not of form or name, is the true criterion in judging of the similarity or dissimilarity of two pieces of mechanism.

George Ticknor Curtis, *A Treatise on the Law of Patents for Useful Inventions in the United States of America* § 310, at 404–05 (1849). Early formulations of the substantial identity test continue to be used in describing the doctrine of equivalents. For example, in 1818 Justice Washington (also on circuit duties) charged a jury "where the machines are substantially the same, and operate in the same manner, to produce the same result, they must be in principle the same." *Gray v James*, 10 F Cas 1015, 1016 (CCD Pa 1817). This charge has frequently been cited as the genesis of a "triple identity" test for determining equivalents. See, e.g., *Hilton Davis Chemical Co. v Warner-Jenkinson Co.*, 62 F3d 1512, 1518 (Fed Cir 1995).

not "distinguish the [invention] from all other things before known."[110] Because the judicial decisions enforcing this statutory requirement denounced "mixing up the new and the old,"[111] some early claims were drafted in the negative, pointing out the portions of the disclosed technology that the patentee thought old and that were thus not claimed as the invention.[112]

Yet claims also delivered another benefit that seems to have been at least as important, and quite possibly more important, in fostering the rise of the claim. From the standpoint of the patentee, judging infringement under an equivalents-type analysis (i.e., the substantial identity test, as it was then known) presented a rather large disadvantage: In determining whether the defendant's machines were "substantially, in their principles and mode of operation, like" the patented invention, the jury had to divine the abstract principles underlying the invention from the drawings and technical description in the patent specification. This inquiry was, as Justice Story recognized in an early circuit case, "often a point of intrinsic difficulty."[113] Or, as Justice Washington put it, "[w]hat constitutes a difference in principle between two machines, is frequently a question of difficulty more especially if the difference in form is considerable, and the machinery complicated."[114] The danger for the patentee was that lay jurors would find no infringement because they would see many superficial differences between the defendant's machine and the description of the patented invention and thus believe the two not substantially identical.

Inventors responded to this problem by developing "claims" in

---

[110] Patent Act of 1793, § 3, 1 Stat 318, 321.

[111] *Evans v Eaton*, 20 US 356, 434 (1822). See also Karl B. Lutz, *Evolution of the Claims of U.S. Patents*, 20 J Patent Off Socy 134, 137–40 (1938) (suggesting that claims arose as a reaction to judicial decisions such as *Evans*); William Redin Woodward, *Definiteness and Particularity in Patent Claims*, 46 Mich L Rev 755, 758–60 (1948) (same). *Evans v Eaton* and the statutory requirement of distinguishing the old from the new should not, however, be viewed as the primary impetus for the development of claims. Claims were beginning to emerge in patent practice at least a decade before *Evans*. Moreover, early claims were often very broad assertions of right, not the narrow claims that might be expected if the patentees' attorneys were merely trying to distinguish the old from the new.

[112] See, e.g., US Pat No 10, col 4, lines 13–15 (stating, in a patent for an improved woodcutting machine, that the "applicant does not claim the invention of a wheel with cutting, or plane irons set therein . . .").

[113] *Odiorne*, 18 F Cas at 582.

[114] *Gray v James*, 10 F Cas 1015, 1016 (CCD Pa 1817).

which they defined their inventions in broad conceptual terms and asserted rights to the invention in those terms.[115] This is why, even before they were required as a matter of law, claims in the modern style first appeared as sweeping assertions of right deployed by aggressive patentees such as Robert Fulton and Samuel Colt.[116] As Justice Story would declare in 1843—seven years after the Patent Act of 1836 required claims as a mandatory part of all patents— claims helped the patentee to "guard[] himself against the suggestion, that his invention consists solely in a particular form . . . and [to] claim the invention to be his, whether the exact form is preserved, or not . . . ."[117] The claim was the friend of the patentee; it helped to expand patent rights.

The Supreme Court's contribution to the patent-claiming revolution was, at first, nothing at all. Only nine Supreme Court patent cases were decided prior to 1836, when statutory law first required patent claims, and none of those cases even hinted that inventors should include in their patent applications anything resembling a patent claim as an aid in defining the patentee's property rights. Thus, even though it held a nationwide mandatory appellate jurisdiction in the field, the Court was in no way responsible for initiating this fundamental shift in the techniques for defining patent rights.

---

[115] Of course, a modern reader might think that, rather than using a formal "claim," inventors could have simply included in their specifications statements like: "The principle of my invention is thus-and-such." In fact, this is precisely what early claims were. The phrase "I claim" was attached to leave no doubt that the inventor was seeking to gain legal rights to the principle of the invention, but otherwise early claims are nothing more than informal attempts to articulate the basic principles that the inventor believed should be the guide to infringement analysis. Formalities grew up only with time.

[116] The origins of the patent claim can be traced back to an 1811 patent to Robert Fulton. See Karl B. Lutz, *Evolution of the Claims of U.S. Patents*, 20 J Patent Off Socy 134, 137 (1938) ("Fulton can perhaps more properly be credited with invention of the 'claim' than of the steamboat"). Fulton's claims to invention were capacious; they included the following bold assertions of right: "I claim as my exclusive right, the use of two wheels, one over each side of the boat to take purchase on the water;" and "[t]his convenience in combining the machinery of Steam boats I claim as my discovery and exclusive right whatever may be the mode by which it is executed." H. W. Dickinson, *Robert Fulton: Engineer and Artist* 313–14 (John Lane, 1913) (reproducing the full specification of Fulton's 1811 patent). Similarly, Colt's basic patent on the revolver included eight broadly drafted claims. See US Pat X9430, at 2–3 (Feb 25, 1836) (available at <http://www.uspto.gov>). Four of the claims were drafted to cover various "principle[s]" employed by the new gun—for example, the "principle of connecting-rod between the hammer and trigger" (claim 4) and the "principle of locking and turning the cylinder" (claim 6). Id.

[117] *Carver v Braintree*, 5 F Cas 235, 238 (CC Mass 1843).

The Court's first significant contributions to the law governing patent claims came in 1854, when the Court decided two major cases on patent claims. Both decisions exercised a moderating influence on the pace of change.

In *O'Reilly v Morse*, the Court invalidated the eighth claim in Samuel Morse's telegraph patent as "too broad, and not warranted by law."[118] In this claim, the last and broadest in Morse's patent, Morse asserted that he was not "limit[ing] [him]self to the specific machinery or parts of machinery described in the foregoing specification" but instead was seeking legal rights to "the essence of [his] invention," which he described as the use of electric current to print signs or letters at a distance.[119] The claim shows the aspiration of early nineteenth-century patentees to extend their rights through progressively more abstract and general claims. But the Justices disappointed those hopes, at least temporarily. For the Court, the patent specification—not the claims—still provided the basic measure of the exclusive rights conferred under the patent: "The specification of this patentee describes his invention or discovery, and the manner and process of constructing and using it; and his patent . . . covers nothing more."[120] And the substantial identity test measured the scope of the patentee's rights: "[A]ny one may lawfully accomplish the same end [as the invention] without infringing the patent, if he uses means *substantially different* from those described."[121]

The other major 1854 case on patent claims was *Winans v Denmead*,[122] which is now cited by the modern Supreme Court as the origin of the doctrine of equivalents.[123] Yet the *Winans* Court was responsible for nothing original; it merely maintained the status quo. In contrast to *Morse*, where the patentee was trying to use the claim form to expand rights, the accused infringers in *Winans* were attempting to use the literal terms of the claim to narrow

---

[118] 56 US 62, 113 (1854).

[119] Id at 112 (quoting US Pat Re 117, at 3 (June 13, 1848)).

[120] Id at 119; see also id ("the patent confers on him the exclusive right to use the means he specifies to produce the result or effect he describes, and nothing more").

[121] Id (emphasis added).

[122] 56 US 330 (1854).

[123] *Festo*, 122 S Ct at 1838; *Graver Tank & Mfg. Co. v Linde Air Products Co.*, 339 US 605, 608 (1950).

the patentee's rights. The claim was directed to a railroad coal car shaped like a "cone"—that is, having a circular cross-section.[124] The defendants' rail car had an octagonal, rather than a circular, cross-section. The Court (in a 5–4 decision by Justice Curtis) held that the patentee was not bound by the restrictive language of the claim and that the defendants' cars infringed because they had been found by the jury "substantially to embody the patentee's mode of operation."[125] This was nothing more nor less than the "substantial identity" test, which was then still the dominant test for infringement.[126]

It was not until twenty-three years after *Winans* that the Court finally declared the "distinct and formal claim [to be] of primary importance, in the effort to ascertain precisely what it is that is patented."[127] But by then, as the Court itself understood, the decision was merely recognizing a reality that had built up below the Court. Explaining its shift from *Winans*, the Court pointed to "[t]he growth of the patent system in the last quarter of a century in this country"—that is, approximately the time since the *Winans* decision—which "has reached a stage in its progress where the variety and magnitude of the interests involved require accuracy, precision, and care in the preparation of all the papers on which the patent is founded."[128] The growth of the patent system not only had led to a more than twenty-fold increase in the yearly output of the Patent Office,[129] but more importantly, had also pro-

---

[124] *Winans*, 56 US at 342 (quoting the patentee's claim). The inventor discovered that the circular cross-section allowed a more even distribution of weight and thus reduced the amount of metal needed to construct the car. See id at 339–40.

[125] Id at 344.

[126] As George Ticknor Curtis (brother of Justice Curtis) stated in his influential 1849 treatise, infringement was understood to be "a copy of the thing *described in the specification* of the patentee, either without variation, or with only such variations as are consistent with its being in substance the same thing." Curtis, *A Treatise on the Law of Patents* § 220 (cited in note 109) (emphasis added). The relative unimportance of claims can be seen in the index of Curtis's treatise, which lists claims only as a subheading of the patent specification and includes no cross-reference to claims under its infringement entries. See id at 581–604. As a later commentator observed, "the courts for a long time did not regard [the claim] as the definitive measure of the scope of the patent" but rather looked to "the whole patent document, including the claims as a guide." Woodward, 46 Mich L Rev at 760 (cited in note 111). The *Winans* decision merely maintained that approach.

[127] *Merrill v Yeomans*, 94 US 568, 570 (1877).

[128] Id at 573.

[129] In 1847, the year in which the *Winans* patent was issued (see US Pat No 5175 (June 26, 1847)), the Patent Office issued about 500 patents, and only about 5,000 patents had been issued since the creation of the examination system in 1836. See <http://www.uspto.

duced "well-settled rules" that left "no excuse for ambiguous language or vague descriptions."[130] Here the Court could not have been referring to its own jurisprudence on patent claiming, which up to this time had been dominated by *Winans* and which did provide, if not an excuse for, at least an accommodation of imprecise patent claims. The "well-settled rules" of patent claiming had instead been constructed by the Patent Office.[131]

In accepting the dominant role of the claim, the Court was careful to consider the effect of claim primacy on the overall legal process of the patent system. For example, one difficulty with aggressively enforcing the limitations of claim language is that unartful drafting could deprive patentees of the fruits of their inventions. But the Court identified a solution to this problem: If the patentee has claimed less than he has a right to, "the law affords him a remedy, by a surrender and reissue."[132] Thus, the strict judicial process was counterbalanced by the administrative reissue

---

gov/web/offices/ac/ido/oeip/taf/issuyear.htm> (listing the issue years of patents). By 1869, the year in which the patent in *Merrill* was issued, and throughout the 1870s, the Patent Office was issuing about 12,000 patents per year. See id.

[130] *Merrill*, 94 US at 573.

[131] The Patent Office began publishing its internal precedents in 1869, and these decisions—which were far more abundant than Supreme Court patent opinions—established and refined the rules of patent claiming. See, e.g., *Ex parte Perrry & Lay*, 1869 Dec Comm'n Pat 3 (allowing redundant claims in a single patent so that "parties [may] put their claims in different forms to prevent misconstructions of them by the public or the courts"); *Ex parte Rubens*, 1869 Dec Comm'n Pat 107, 108 ("strongly condemn[ing]" the practice of using the words "substantially as described" in a patent claim because the phrase has "no fixed legal meaning"); *Ex parte Eagle*, 1870 Dec Comm'n Pat 137 (establishing early rules for "genus" and "species" claims). Indeed, as demonstrated by the following passage from an 1869 decision, the Commissioner of Patents seemed to understand that the Patent Office held chief responsibility for establishing the rules of patent claim drafting practice:

> I know that in [a circuit court decision] Mr. Justice Curtis uses language which seems to imply a different doctrine; but it must be remembered that a claim may be saved by construction, that ought not to have passed the Patent Office in such a form as to make construction necessary to its salvation. The Commissioner ought not to send doubtful claims to the courts. The law makes him the judge in the first instance, and he has no right to turn out his work upon the country botched and blundering, in the hope that some court will patch it up. Many patents never go into the courts, and all patents ought to be so drawn that honest men of ordinary business capacity need not be afraid to deal with them.

Ex parte Thorne, 1869 Dec Comm'n Pat 76, 76–77. Moreover, even before the Supreme Court's decision in *Merrill*, the primacy of claims in defining patent rights was firmly established in the Patent Office's day-to-day decisions, which focused immediately on the claims in determining what rights were being sought by the applicant. See, e.g., id at 76 (following the common administrative form of beginning the analysis with a recitation of the claims); *Ex parte Ackerson*, id at 74 (same); *Ex parte Dean*, id at 77 (same); *Ex parte Webb*, id at 78 (same).

[132] Id at 573.

remedy (a remedy that, as it so happens, was also an innovation of the patent bar and Patent Office[133]). That solution shifts some responsibility from the courts to the Patent Office, which would consider and approve any adjustment to the language of the original claims. But, as the Court noted, that shift was consistent with Congress's decision to impose on the Patent Office the primary "duty of ascertaining the exact invention of the patentee by . . . a laborious examination of previous inventions, and a comparison thereof with that claimed by him."[134] Process considerations, particularly the comparative roles of the Patent Office and the courts, would remain a theme in the Court's jurisprudence on patent claims.

Despite its more rigorous enforcement of the claim limitations, the Court did not wholly abandon the analysis of equivalents. For example, fifteen years after it recognized the primacy of claims, the Court relied on *Winans* to hold that the defendant could be liable for infringement where he had substituted "an old and well known mechanical equivalent . . . to evade the wording of the claims" of the patent.[135] But equivalents analysis had become the exception, not the rule, and it was subservient to claim interpretation.[136] Moreover, process considerations led the Court to create a new limitation on the extent of the patentee's rights, and this further contracted the scope of equivalents. The Court held that, in deciding the scope of patent rights, courts should look to the prosecution history—that is, the record of the Patent Office proceedings by which the inventor obtained the patent—and "strictly construe[], against the inventor, and in favor of the public" any limitations and restrictions introduced by the inventor to overcome rejections imposed by the Patent Office.[137] As applied to the doctrine of equivalents, this practice of restricting the patentee's

---

[133] See *Grant v Raymond*, 31 US 218 (1832) (sustaining the Patent Office's assertion of a power to remedy errors by reissuing a corrected patent even though no statutory provision or judicial decision had previously authorized such a process).

[134] *Keystone Bridge Co. v Phoenix Iron Co.*, 95 US 274, 278 (1877).

[135] *Hoyt v Horne*, 145 US 302, 309 (1892).

[136] *Fay v Cordesman*, 109 US 408, 420 (1883) (holding that every element in a claim "must be regarded as material, leaving open only the question whether an omitted part is supplied by an equivalent device or instrumentality [in the accused product]").

[137] *Sargent v Hall Safe & Lock Co.*, 114 US 63, 86 (1885). See also *Goodyear Dental Vulcanite Co. v Davis*, 102 US 222, 228 (1880) (applying the same doctrine in the context of claims that were narrowed during reissue proceedings).

rights because of the proceedings before the Patent Office would become known as "prosecution history estoppel."

The rise of the claim was not, however, without benefits for inventors. During the 1880s, the Court limited *O'Reilly v Morse* and expanded the ability of patentees to use broadly worded patent claims to extend their rights into the more conceptual realm.[138] Rather than limiting a patentee to "the means he specifies" for accomplishing a particular result (as the *Morse* Court did),[139] the Court in *Tilghman v Proctor* viewed a patent as granting rights on a "conception of the mind" that could be accomplished through "many modes and by the use of many forms of apparatus," all of which need not be disclosed in the patent document.[140]

By 1890, patentees knew that they would usually be bound by the terms of their claims but also that they could reap the benefits of broadly worded claims . . . usually. In *Westinghouse v Boyden Power Brake Co.*,[141] the Court placed one final caveat on the patent-claiming revolution. It held that, just as infringement can be proven even "though the letter of the claims be avoided," "[t]he converse is equally true."[142] This holding would become known as the "reverse doctrine of equivalents," but it was really nothing more than the old "substantial identity" test being applied once again.[143] However, as in the doctrine of equivalents cases, the Court in *Westinghouse* deployed the reverse doctrine as an exception to the now general rule that the claims defined the patentee's rights. Indeed, the primacy of claims is evident from the whole structure of the *Westinghouse* opinion, which extensively analyzed the claims before deciding whether an exception should be made to the normal rule of deciding infringement on the basis of the claims. The case also suggested that the exception would likely remain narrow: the Court found the defendant's product (an improved airbrake for trains) represented a "manifest departure from

---

[138] *Tilghman v Proctor*, 102 US 707, 728–29 (1881). See also *The Telephone Cases*, 126 US 1, 533–35 (1888).

[139] *Morse*, 56 US at 119.

[140] *Tilghman*, 102 US at 728.

[141] 170 US 537 (1898).

[142] Id at 568.

[143] To support its holding, the Court cited *Burr v Duryee*, 68 US 531(1864), a 34-year-old precedent articulating the substantial identity test as it had then existed. See *Westinghouse*, 170 US at 568–69.

the principle of the [plaintiff's] patent";[144] the defendant had actually obtained his own patent on the product accused of infringing;
and four Justices dissented. *Westinghouse* shows the conservatism
of the Court, for even after it had endorsed a switch to measuring
patent rights primarily by the claims, it kept alive the old law for
use in exceptional cases.

At the close of the nineteenth century, the patent-claiming revolution was largely complete, and it had been accomplished with
surprisingly little intervention by the Court. The Court's entire
role—from its temporary resistance to its embrace of the change—
can be recounted with only a few cases. There were, of course,
more cases from that era (particularly from the 1880s) that applied
the relevant doctrines. But the discussions in those cases yield very
little additional insight into the state or development of the law.[145]
Despite the enormous bulk of patent cases decided in the last quarter of the nineteenth century, few cases were anything more than
routine appeals.

2. *Stasis: maintaining equivalents in the age of the claim.* If the
Court's nineteenth-century jurisprudence in this area can be recounted through perhaps a dozen cases, even fewer are needed to
describe the Court's work in the area during the first ninety-five
years of the twentieth century. A summary of the Court's work
during this period is simple: It kept the law from changing much.
In fact, the Court's case law during this period tends to focus
mainly on the application of the law to the facts; the articulation
of the law occurs very briefly, and with a tone of restatement rather
than reform.

A good example of this approach is *Exhibit Supply Co. v Ace Patents Corp.*,[146] which involved a patent on an electric pinball target.
The Court applied the doctrine of prosecution history estoppel to
hold that the defendants could not be held liable under the doctrine of equivalents because the inventor had, during the prosecution, narrowed the claim language so that the claims did not literally cover targets like those manufactured by the defendants.

---

[144] *Westinghouse*, 170 US at 572.

[145] In fact, the Supreme Court opinion in *Festo* cites only two cases decided between 1860 and 1900. See *Festo*, 122 S Ct at 1838–41.

[146] 315 US 126 (1942). The issue involved no circuit split, but the Court was "moved to grant [certiorari] by the nature of the questions presented." Id at 128.

While the discussion of the facts in the case occupies eight pages, the legal discussion is confined to a single paragraph containing nothing more than simple statements of the law with citations of past Supreme Court case law.[147] The Court eschewed any attempt to identify the underlying justifications for the current law or to investigate possible reforms to the existing law.

Similar is *Graver Tank & Manufacturing Co. v Linde Air Products Co.*,[148] which applied the doctrine of equivalents to sustain a finding of infringement on a patent for welding fluxes. As in *Exhibit Supply*, the *Graver Tank* Court provides a legal discussion that seems consciously designed to read like a restatement of existing principles. The restatement effort occupies slightly more space than in *Exhibit Supply*; it covers about three pages. But the discussion in *Graver Tank* did nothing to change the law. At most, the Court slightly modified the justification for the doctrine of equivalents. In the late nineteenth century, the doctrine was justified on the underlying reality that "the substantial equivalent of a thing . . . is the same as the thing itself."[149] *Graver Tank* stresses the limitations of language in capturing the essence of the invention.[150] The subtle shift underscored the increasing dominance of the claim—for it meant that even the justification for the doctrine of equivalents had come to be seen as flowing from the linguistic attributes of the claim.

Graver Tank and, to a less extent, *Exhibit Supply* would both gain a modicum of fame in the later half of the twentieth century, but their prominence was by virtue of default.[151] After 1950, the Court would go nearly a half century without deciding any cases on the doctrine of equivalents or prosecution history estoppel.

3. *The experimental impulse: Warner-Jenkinson.* The Court's return to the law governing patent claims began with the 1996 case *Markman v Westview Instruments, Inc.*,[152] which held that patent litigants have no right under the Seventh Amendment to have ju-

---

[147] See id at 128–36 (facts); id at 136–37 (legal discussion).

[148] 339 US 605 (1950).

[149] *Machine Co. v Murphy*, 97 US 120, 125 (1878).

[150] 339 US at 607 (concluding that the inventor should not be left "at the mercy of verbalism").

[151] For comparison, *Graver Tank* has been cited 1,689 times as of late 2002, and *Exhibit Supply*, 218 times.

[152] 517 US 370 (1996).

ries interpret patent claims, even in cases where there is conflicting expert testimony concerning the meaning of the claims. The Supreme Court's decision had less importance as a matter of theory—claim interpretation had long been considered a matter for courts—and more as a matter of practice: The unanimous Court decision underscored the judicial obligation to resolve claim ambiguities and made lower courts less reluctant to hold elaborate (and frequently dispositive) pretrial hearings devoted to deciding the meaning of claims. *Markman* seemed to have a practical effect at the Court too. The case seemed to whet the Court's appetite for cases on patent claims—or, perhaps more accurately, it gave the Court confidence that it could understand cases about the intricacies of the patent system. After the oral argument in *Markman* and while the case was still pending, the Court granted certiorari in *Warner-Jenkinson Co. v Hilton Davis Chemical Co.*,[153] which presented much more difficult questions concerning the scope of the still vibrant doctrine of equivalents.

Warner-Jenkinson involved a patent on an improved process for filtering out impurities from dyes. The claims defined the steps of the improved process and included limitations concerning the pressures at which the process operated, the size of the membrane pores used in the filters, and so on. Most importantly, the claims specified that the process was to occur "at a pH from approximately 6.0 to 9.0." The defendant's process operated at a pH of approximately 5.0 which, since the pH scale is an inverse logarithmic scale, means that the defendant's process operated at ten times the hydrogen ion concentration. Because the patentee had added the lower pH limit of 6.0 during the prosecution of the patent application, the case presented both the issues of equivalents and of prosecution estoppel.

The Court's decision in *Warner-Jenkinson* highlights the ability of the Federal Circuit to enable more effective exercise of the Supreme Court's jurisdiction in the patent field. Sitting en banc, the Federal Circuit had divided 7–5 and had issued more than sixty pages of opinions in the case.[154] The lengthy opinions not only signaled the importance of the case to the Court but also provided

---

[153] 520 US 17 (1997).

[154] *Hilton Davis Chem. Co. v Warner-Jenkinson Co.*, 62 F3d 1512, 1515–83 (Fed Cir 1995) (en banc).

a menu of alternative positions advanced by judges with expertise and day-to-day responsibility for applying the law in the area. The result is that the case attracted the Court's attention and that the Court was able to examine the issues more thoroughly than it had in at least a century.

The results of the Court's consideration were also predictably conservative and incremental. The Court reaffirmed the continuing vitality of the doctrine of equivalents—an unsurprising holding given the Court's conservative impulses in the field. The Court had long retained equivalents analysis even after it had recognized the primacy of claims; the majority of Federal Circuit judges had voted to retain equivalents in some form; and the United States filed an amicus brief supporting the retention of equivalents analysis.

The Court did add two new components to its law in the field; both contributions continued the historical trend of making equivalents subservient to claim interpretation. First, the Court clarified that equivalents analysis "must be applied to individual elements of the claim, not to the invention as a whole."[155] Thus, the doctrine of equivalents had to follow the structure of claims. This holding was nothing new; it had been the law of the Federal Circuit for a decade.[156] *Warner-Jenkinson* merely entrenched the test in Supreme Court precedent and solidified its authoritative weight.

The Court's second addition to its jurisprudence concerned prosecution history estoppel. A little background is necessary to appreciate this addition. In their initial applications to the Patent Office, inventors typically include relatively broad claims of invention. This approach makes sense from the inventor's perspective because the Patent Office can grant broad rights only if they are sought. Thus, inventors follow an "ask-and-you-shall-receive" approach, filing broad claims and then narrowing them with amendments as the Patent Office rejects the broader assertions of patent rights. The approach, however, carries a certain amount of risk because such narrowing amendments could give rise to estoppel. For example, suppose that an inventor files an initial application claiming all widgets and the Patent Office rejects the claim on the grounds that widgets are already known in the art. The inventor

---

[155] 520 US at 27.

[156] See *Pennwalt Corp. v Durand-Wayland, Inc.*, 833 F2d 931, 935 (Fed Cir 1987) (en banc).

then amends the application to claim only "plastic" widgets, and the Patent Office grants the more narrow claim. That amendment might estop the inventor from arguing in subsequent infringement litigation that a defendant's ceramic or metallic widgets should be viewed as equivalent to the plastic widget claimed in the patent. The theory of estoppel is that, "[b]y the amendment, [the inventor] recognized and emphasized the difference between the two phrases and proclaimed his abandonment of all that is embraced in that difference," and this theory applies without regard to "whether the [patent] examiner was right or wrong in rejecting the [broader] claim as [originally] filed."[157] Thus, even if the Patent Office were wrong in rejecting the broad claim to all widgets, the inventor could still be precluded from relying on equivalents analysis to extend the narrowed claim.

Prior to *Warner-Jenkinson*, the case law required an inquiry into the reasons for the narrowing amendment, with the resulting amount of estoppel adjusted to correspond to "the nature and purpose of an amendment."[158] The case law did not address, however, the question of what to do in cases where the reason for the amendment was unknown (as in *Warner-Jenkinson*). The Court held that the burden was on the patentee to establish the reason for the amendment and, if the patentee could not explain the reason for the amendment, no equivalents analysis would be permitted for the amended portion of the claim. If the patentee did establish a reason, then the court "would decide whether that reason is sufficient to overcome prosecution history estoppel as a bar to application of the doctrine of equivalents to the element added by that amendment."[159] The change at most shifted the burden for establishing the reasons behind claim amendments, and it was less dramatic than the reform urged by the accused infringer, which argued in favor of precluding any equivalents analysis for portions of the claim added during prosecution. Though the change was significant, it was still quite incremental—or at least that is how the Court intended the change.

---

[157] *Exhibit Supply Co.*, 315 US at 136–37.

[158] *Hughes Aircraft Co. v United States*, 717 F2d 1351, 1363 (Fed Cir 1983); see also *Warner-Jenkinson*, 520 US at 30 (rejecting the argument that "the reason for an amendment during patent prosecution is irrelevant to any subsequent estoppel").

[159] 520 US at 31.

Even that incremental change, however, came with a warning. In a concurrence, Justice Ginsburg cautioned that, if the new presumption were applied "woodenly," it could have unsettling retroactive effects because, prior to the Court's announcement of the presumption, patentees would not have had any incentive to memorialize the reasons for their amendments. To show that the Court was "sensitive" to this retroactivity problem, Justice Ginsburg pointed to a footnote in which the Court rejected the broader estoppel rule proposed by the accused infringer because the Court did not want "[t]o change so substantially the rules of the game" in a way that could "subvert the various balances the PTO sought to strike when issuing" existing patents. Justice Ginsburg suggested that, on remand, the Federal Circuit should "bear[] in mind the prior absence of clear rules of the game." The Ginsburg concurrence was joined by Justice Kennedy, the eventual author of the *Festo* opinion, and the concern over disrupting past expectations presaged a major theme in *Festo*.

After it was remanded by the Supreme Court, the *Warner-Jenkinson* litigation settled before any lower court applied the Court's new law of prosecution history estoppel. The Supreme Court's new presumption had, however, plainly increased the importance of estoppel and created many new questions. *Festo* became the litigation where those questions would be addressed.

B. FESTO: THE EXCEPTION THAT ALMOST SWALLOWED THE EXCEPTION

Despite the extensive duration of the *Festo* litigation (which began in 1988),[160] the history leading up to the Supreme Court's decision in the case can be summarized quite succinctly. The Festo Corporation sued the defendants, which were collectively known as the "SMC Corporation," for infringing two of Festo's patents on improved versions of a machine known as a magnetically-coupled, rodless piston assembly. In the district court, Festo conceded (perhaps unwisely) that the literal language of its patent claims did not cover SMC's products, but Festo nevertheless succeeded in establishing infringement under the doctrine of equiva-

---

[160] See Joint Appendix, *Festo Corp. v Shoketsu Kinzoku Kogyo Kabushiki Co.*, No 00-1543, at I-1 (S Ct filed Aug 31, 2001) (docket entries showing filing of complaint).

lents. In 1995, a unanimous panel of the Federal Circuit sustained the district court judgment in Festo's favor and held that prosecution history estoppel did not bar Festo from proving infringement under the doctrine of equivalents.[161] SMC sought certiorari and, after the Supreme Court decided *Warner-Jenkinson* in 1997, it remanded the case back to the Federal Circuit for application of the Court's new law on prosecution history estoppel. It was at this point in the litigation that the *Festo* litigation was chosen by the en banc Federal Circuit to clarify the law of prosecution history estoppel in the wake of *Warner-Jenkinson*.[162] The en banc majority could be fairly described as enthusiastic in applying *Warner-Jenkinson*'s new presumption of estoppel. And, in its enthusiasm, the majority went a bit further too.

Two of the en banc majority's holdings would attract the attention of the Supreme Court. First, the court expansively defined the class of amendments subject to prosecution history estoppel. Estoppel applied not only to amendments made to avoid the prior art, but also to any other "amendment that narrows the scope of a claim for any reason related to the statutory requirements for a patent."[163] Second, the court held that, if an amendment was subject to prosecution history estoppel, then "no range of equivalents [would be] available for the amended claim element."[164] The en banc holdings thus truncated the inquiry that the courts had previously made into the reasons for the amendment. Under the new approach, courts would ask only whether the amendment was made for a "reason related to the statutory requirements for a patent." If so, then equivalents analysis was precluded for the amended portion of the claim.

To see the effect of the en banc decision, consider the perspective of a patentee (like the Festo Corporation) trying to use the doctrine of equivalents for a claim element added by amendment.

---

[161] *Festo Corp. v Shoketsu Kinzoku Kogyo Kabushiki Co.*, 72 F3d 857 (Fed Cir 1995).

[162] Another panel decision rendered after the Supreme Court's remand was vacated by the order granting en banc consideration. That panel decision would have held Festo to be not estopped from asserting an equivalents theory for one of the two patents in the suit and would have remanded the case to the district court for further fact-finding on the reasons for Festo's amendments to the other patent in suit. See *Festo Corp. v Shoketsu Kinzoku Kogyo Kabushiki Co.*, 172 F3d 1361 (Fed Cir 1999).

[163] See *Festo Corp. v Shoketsu Kinzoku Kogyo Kabushiki Co.*, 234 F3d 558, 563 (Fed Cir 2000) (en banc).

[164] Id at 569.

Under *Warner-Jenkinson*, a patentee cannot rely on equivalents analysis for the amended portion of the claims unless the patentee establishes a reason for the amendment. But under the en banc decision, once the patentee establishes a reason for the amendment, then all equivalents would be barred if the reason was related to the statutory requirements for a patent. Since patent claims generally "define[] the scope of a patent grant,"[165] attorneys should never narrow the claims except for reasons related to the statutory requirements for obtaining a patent. Thus, when combined with *Warner-Jenkinson*, the en banc *Festo* decision produced a nice catch-22. Not proving a reason barred equivalents; proving a reason barred equivalents. It was impossible to imagine a realistic scenario where a claim element added by amendment would have been entitled to equivalents.[166] Moreover, since the standard practice of patent attorneys had been first to seek broad patent rights and then to narrow the claims as necessary during the course of prosecution, the effect of the en banc decision would be to eliminate the doctrine of equivalents for many portions of existing patents. Equivalents analysis—the modern exception in the rule that patent rights are defined by the literal language of patent claims— was in danger of being swallowed by the exception to the exception.

The en banc majority did not disguise the effect of its holding; it candidly described its decision as establishing a "complete bar" approach to prosecution history estoppel.[167] The alternative "flex-

---

[165] *Markman*, 517 US at 373 (internal quotations omitted).

[166] The en banc ruling left only one theoretically possible scenario: Equivalents analysis could be used for the amended portion of a claim if the amendment had been made for reasons not related to patentability. However, the possibility of that scenario arising—which was already slight because attorneys generally should not, and generally do not, amend claims except for reasons related to patentability—was made even more remote because the en banc majority held that, to establish the reasons for amendments, a patentee may rely only on evidence found in the publicly available prosecution file. This rather unique evidentiary rule allowed the Federal Circuit to keep control over the new *Warner-Jenkinson* presumption of estoppel, for otherwise the court would have needed to remand *Festo*—and perhaps many other cases litigated prior to *Warner-Jenkinson*—for further factual development in district court. The evidentiary rule also, however, reinforced the practical impossibility of applying equivalents to amended portions of patent claims. If an attorney did not have a reason relating to patentability for narrowing the claims, the narrowing of the claims is almost certainly an error since, by assumption, the broader claim conferring greater rights would have been issued by the PTO. But for the patentee to escape prosecution history estoppel, the fact of the error had to be recognized and memorialized in the publicly available prosecution file.

[167] *Festo*, 234 F3d at 569.

ible" approach to estoppel—which required the courts to inquire into "the nature and purpose of an amendment" and to exclude only those equivalents "that would vitiate limitations expressed before the Patent Office"[168]—had been shown by experience to be "unworkable," and so the court abandoned it.[169] Evidence as to the magnitude of this change could be found within the record of the *Festo* litigation itself (which, like many other patent cases, has extended over a long period of time). During the trial in 1994 (the case began in 1988), SMC's counsel at one point declared "[t]his is not really a prosecution history estoppel case."[170] That statement is ironic given that *Festo* was destined to become the first Supreme Court case on prosecution history estoppel in sixty years, but was also a good barometer of the preexisting law. In 1994, sophisticated legal counsel could fail to see that the entire *Festo* litigation turned on prosecution history estoppel precisely because the doctrine was then a relatively modest exception to the doctrine of equivalents, not the "complete bar" that the Federal Circuit would make it after six more years of litigation.

The biggest surprise in the *Festo* litigation came when the Supreme Court granted certiorari to review the Federal Circuit's en banc decision. In concluding its analysis in *Warner-Jenkinson*, the Court had seemed ready to cede further development of the doctrine of equivalents to the Federal Circuit, for it stated:

> We expect that the Federal Circuit will refine the formulation of the test for equivalence in the orderly course of case-by-case determinations, and we leave such refinement to that court's sound judgment in this area of its special expertise.[171]

This language was not missed by the Federal Circuit. The en banc majority in *Festo* reminded the reader that "Congress specifically

---

[168] *Hughes Aircraft Co. v United States*, 717 F3d 1351, 1363 (Fed Cir 1983) (quoting *Autogiro Co. of America v United States*, 384 F2d 391, 401 (Ct Cl 1967)). See also *Warner-Jenkinson*, 520 US at 30 (rejecting the argument that "the reason for an amendment during patent prosecution is irrelevant to any subsequent estoppel").

[169] *Festo*, 234 F3d at 575.

[170] Joint Appendix, *Festo Corp. v Shoketsu Kinzoku Kogyo Kabushiki Co.*, No 00-1543, at I-141 (S Ct filed Aug 31, 2001) (setting forth portions of the trial transcript); see also *Festo*, 72 F3d at 863 (quoting this statement by counsel). Even during *Festo*'s first appearance at the Federal Circuit in late 1995, the court introduced the estoppel issue as a minor factual dispute that had been raised only to a limited extent at trial. See id at 863–64.

[171] 520 US at 40.

created the Federal Circuit to resolve issues unique to patent law, [citing *Markman*], such as those regarding prosecution history estoppel" and then relied on *Warner-Jenkinson* to declare that "[i]ssues such as the one before us in this case are properly reserved for *this court* to answer with 'its special expertise.'"[172] The court seemed ready, even eager, to assume the power that it thought had been ceded to it. And, in truth, the Federal Circuit had the numbers on its side. At the time of the en banc decision, the Supreme Court had tackled exactly one doctrine of equivalents case (*Warner-Jenkinson*) in the last half century. That case could have easily been viewed as an aberration, for it was granted while the Court had before it an interesting constitutional case on the role of the jury in claim interpretation (*Markman*). Further intrusion by the Court into the Federal Circuit's domain was unexpected.

The Court, of course, did intrude, and it did so in a way that seemed consciously designed to underscore the differences between the Court and the Federal Circuit: The specialized Federal Circuit produced seven opinions spanning eighty pages in the *Federal Reporter*; the opinions were brimming with citations and footnotes and presented a menu of possible approaches to the law in this area—precisely the sort of product to be expected from a more specialized institution at its best. The Court's opinion was simple, unanimous, and only seventeen pages long; it had no footnotes and cited only eleven precedents; and yet it showed a deep appreciation of, and respect for, the broad contours of the historical development of law in this field—precisely the sort of product to be expected from a generalist institution at its best. The Court's opinion seemed to reassert the competence of a generalist institution to contribute to the field.

The first of the two questions on which the Court granted certiorari concerned the class of amendments that could generate estoppel. Festo argued that estoppel should be limited to those amendments that are needed to distinguish prior art. Other amendments, Festo argued, "govern merely the form in which a patent application must be cast."[173] As the Court recognized, Festo's argument on this point was weak. For example, an amend-

---

[172] 234 F3d at 571–72 (quoting *Warner-Jenkinson*, 520 US at 40; emphasis added).

[173] Reply Brief for Petitioner, *Festo Corp. v Shoketsu Kinzoku Kogyo Kabushiki Co.*, No 00-1543, *5 (filed Nov 30, 2001) (available on Lexis at 2000 US Briefs 1543).

ment would not be related to overcoming prior art if it had been made in response to an objection that the applicant had not "enabled"—that is, taught others how to make and use—the full scope of the subject matter claimed. Yet such an amendment could hardly be considered a mere formality since, as the Court had noted in a decision announced just weeks before the *Festo* oral argument, an enabling disclosure is generally considered "the *quid pro quo* of the [patentee's] right to exclude."[174] In rejecting Festo's argument, the Court reiterated this basic point.[175] Furthermore, the Court noted that if Festo was concerned about "truly cosmetic" amendments, then it need not worry because such amendments "would not narrow the patent's scope" and thus not raise any estoppel.[176] Thus, the Court rejected Festo's argument and affirmed the Federal Circuit's broad view that any amendment narrowing the scope of a claim could give rise to estoppel.

The second question presented to the Court was whether the "complete bar" rule was the correct approach to prosecution history estoppel. In its favor, the Federal Circuit's "complete bar" rule would have created fairly clear legal rules concerning the definition of patent rights. For claim elements that had not been added by amendment during patent prosecution, a patentee could rely either on the literal language of the claim or on the doctrine of equivalents in proving infringement. For claim elements that had been added by amendment, the patentee could rely only on the literal claim language because the exception (equivalents analysis) would have been swallowed by its exception (estoppel). The fundamental issue presented to the Supreme Court was whether those legal rules made sense.

In reversing the Federal Circuit, the Court succinctly identified the real difficulty with the Federal Circuit's approach:

> The complete bar . . . approach is inconsistent with the purpose of applying the estoppel in the first place—to hold the in-

---

[174] *J.E.M. Ag Supply, Inc. v Pioneer Hi-Bred Int'l, Inc.*, 122 S Ct 593, 604 (2001). Amendments designed to overcome nonenablement objections can be seen as the mirror image of amendments designed to avoid the prior art: The latter are necessary to avoid claiming material already discovered; the former, to avoid claiming something not yet discovered by anyone (including the applicant).

[175] See *Festo*, 122 S Ct at 1840 (noting that patent rights are given to an inventor "in exchange for" an enabling disclosure).

[176] Id.

ventor to the representations made during the application process and to the inferences that may reasonably be drawn from the amendment. By amending the application, the inventor is deemed to concede that the patent does not extend as far as the original claim. It does not follow, however, that the amended claim becomes so perfect in its description that no one could devise an equivalent. After amendment, as before, language remains an imperfect fit for invention. . . . The amendment does not show that the inventor suddenly had more foresight in the drafting of claims than an inventor whose application was granted without amendments having been submitted. It shows only that he was familiar with the broader text and with the difference between the two. As a result, there is no more reason for holding the patentee to the literal terms of an amended claim than there is for abolishing the doctrine of equivalents altogether and holding every patentee to the literal terms of the patent.[177]

The great strength of this reasoning is its generality. The basis of prosecution history estoppel, the Court recognized, is *estoppel*—which is a general legal concept precluding a party from taking a position that contradicts a previous position. If the patent rule of prosecution history estoppel is to remain comprehensible as an estoppel doctrine, it has to have some connection to the inventor's conduct during prosecution and the inferences that can be fairly drawn from that conduct. And—this is the only observation about patent practice that the Court needed to make—it is not a fair inference from every claim amendment that the applicant has perfected the ability to apply language to invention.

Of course, the Court's reasoning on estoppel is not a complete answer. Even if the Federal Circuit's complete bar rule could not be justified as a true estoppel doctrine, perhaps it might be justified on some other grounds. For example, it might be considered a punitive rule designed to discourage applicants from submitting broad claims in their initial applications to the PTO.[178] But the Court had other reasons for rejecting the complete bar, and it is in these reasons that we can see the characteristics that define the Court as an institution—its conservatism and institutional focus. The Court instructed the Federal Circuit to "be cautious before

---

[177] *Festo*, 122 S Ct at 1840–41.

[178] This justification is asserted in a recent academic article. See R. Polk Wagner, *Reconsidering Estoppel: Patent Administration and the Failure of Festo*, 151 U Penn L Rev 159 (2002).

adopting changes that disrupt the settled expectations of the inventing community," restated its view that "the doctrine of equivalents and the rule of prosecution history estoppel are settled law," and located "responsibility for changing [the equivalents and estoppel rules] with Congress."[179] And the Court also approached the issue with a good sense of the broad sweep of history. The infrequency of the Court's forays in the area helped; in citing a half dozen of its precedents, the Court was able to canvass a century and a half of its law on the doctrine of equivalents and prosecution history estoppel.

The Court's generalist instincts were also evident in its attention to the PTO's role in the patent system. Representing the PTO in *Festo*, the Solicitor General filed an amicus brief warning that the Federal Circuit's complete bar rule would disrupt the prosecution process by "discourag[ing] the give-and-take between the PTO patent examiners and applicants that leads to more refined claims."[180] That warning seemed important to the Court, for it cited, as one reason for overturning the Federal Circuit's rule, the desire to maintain an estoppel rule that is "respectful of the real practice before the PTO."[181]

Ultimately, in crafting a specific test for determining the scope of estoppel, the Court embraced "the approach advocated by the United States," which the Court deemed "sound." The approach imposes the burden on the patentee to show that "the amendment cannot reasonably be viewed as surrendering a particular equivalent."[182] The Court listed three circumstances in which the patent could meet that burden:

> The equivalent may have been unforeseeable at the time of the application; the rationale underlying the amendment may bear no more than a tangential relation to the equivalent in question; or there may be some other reason suggesting that the patentee could not reasonably be expected to have described the insubstantial substitute in question.[183]

---

[179] *Festo*, 122 S Ct at 1841.

[180] Brief for the United States as Amicus Curiae Supporting Vacatur and Remand, *Festo Corp. v Shoketsu Kinzoku Kogyo Kabushiki Co.*, No 00-1543, *21 (filed Aug 31, 2001) (available on Lexis at 2000 US Briefs 1543).

[181] *Festo*, 122 S Ct at 1841.

[182] Id at 1842.

[183] Id.

Two of these three scenarios were cribbed from the Solicitor General's brief.[184] The Court's adoption of the United States's view—which is, of course, the PTO's view—shows that the Court was not taking a leading role in field. Instead, the Court was choosing between the competing positions offered by the two specialized actors in the patent system, the Federal Circuit and the PTO. That approach recognizes the limits of the Court's own institutional competence and provides a model for the Court's intervention in future cases.

C. THE LESSONS FROM FESTO

Festo may seem an unlikely piece of litigation to become a celebrated patent case. The amount of money at stake in the case was not exceptional (the judgment on appeal was for less than $5 million).[185] The case did not involve a famous invention as in *Morse* or *The Telephone Cases*. The legal issue in the case—the proper scope of the exception to the exception to the rule for defining patent rights—seems soporific and utterly trivial compared to such worthy Supreme Court cases as *Diamond v Chakrabarty*, which held that life itself can be patented.[186] But in fact *Festo* was a perfect case for defining the future of patent claiming and, more generally, the future of the Supreme Court at the bar of patents. It was perfect precisely because it was so ordinary.

1. *The devil with the details.* For a generalist Court such as the Supreme Court, one immediate problem presented by patent cases is that they are likely to involve a great amount of technological detail that the Court is ill-suited to evaluate. The difficulty here is compounded by the empirical fact that the vast majority of valuable inventions are not the pioneering new advances that introduce whole new fields of technology, but are rather incremental ad-

---

[184] Brief for the United States as Amicus Curiae at *25–26 (cited in note 180).

[185] See *Festo Corp. v Shoketsu Kinzoku Kabushiki, Ltd.*, Civ Act No 88-1814-PBS (D Mass, Oct 27, 1994), reprinted in Appendix to Petition for Writ of Certiorari, *Festo Corp. v Shoketsu Kinzoku Kogyo Kabushiki Co.*, No 00-1543, *211a (filed Apr 9, 2001) (available on Lexis at 2000 US Briefs 1543) (entering judgment based on a jury verdict for $4,739,183). The actual amount of money at stake was somewhat greater because the jury verdict had calculated damages only through the end of the trial. The trial judge was going to "determine an amount of damages on the same [basis] as awarded by the jury" for later infringements. Id. The defendants were also enjoined from continuing infringement but, by the time the case reached the Court, both patents at issue had already expired.

[186] 447 US 303 (1980).

vances to existing technologies.[187] In other words, most inventions are what might be termed "normal," not "revolutionary," innovations.[188] Thus, not only are the details of patent cases likely to be difficult for generalist judges to understand, but in addition the details are likely to seem so minor as to not be worth the effort to understand. In short, the cases are likely to be technologically complex and boring too.

The two patents at issue in *Festo* followed this pattern. They covered very normal, incremental inventions, and they give a good sense of the problem faced by a generalist Court in adjudicating a patent case. For example, consider the improvements covered by the earlier of the two patents owned by Festo. The general technology of magnetically-coupled, rodless-piston assemblies (a technology predating Festo's patents) consists of three basic parts: (*a*) a hollow hydraulic tube, (*b*) a solid cylindrical piston that slides inside the tube, and (*c*) a donut-shaped "follower" that slides along the outside of the tube. The piston is made to slide back and forth inside the tube by hydraulic pressure (e.g., by pumping fluid into one end of the tube and out of the other end). Both the piston and the follower contain magnets designed to attract each other through the wall of the tube so that the follower will move along the outside of the tube whenever the piston slides along the inside.[189] The earlier of the two Festo patents covered an improved device having three distinct features, including (*a*) a "plurality" of coupling magnets on the piston and follower (rather than just a single magnet on each), (*b*) cushions on each side of the piston to prevent the piston from damage when it reaches the ends of the hydraulic tube, and (*c*) "a pair of resilient sealing rings situated

---

[187] See, e.g., Eric von Hipple, *The Sources of Innovation* 131–207 (Oxford, 1988) (finding that small improvements are often important to progress).

[188] Cf. Thomas S. Kuhn, *The Structure of Scientific Revolutions* 6 (Chicago, 1962) (distinguishing between "normal science," which occupies the time of most scientists, and "scientific revolutions," which occur infrequently and lead to major shifts in the prevailing paradigms of scientific analysis).

[189] This description of the technology is drawn from the Festo Corporation's two patents, US Pat No 3,779,401 (Feb 17, 1972) and US Pat No 4,354,125 (Oct 12, 1982). The advantage of the device is that it allows the hydraulic system to remain completely sealed and yet to move things outside of the hydraulic tube. (For simplicity, certain features and variations of the technology are not mentioned. For example, the tube is described as a hydraulic tube, but the device can also be constructed with a pneumatic tube, with air pressure rather than fluid pressure pushing the piston to and fro. Such variations are irrelevant to the case.)

near opposite axial ends" of the hydraulic piston.[190] This last part—the "pair" of sealing rings—was one portion of the claim language for which Festo tried to invoke the doctrine of equivalents.[191] The device made by the defendant, SMC Corporation, employed a single "two-way" sealing ring (a ring with lips on both sides) located on one side of the piston, and so Festo was trying to rely on the doctrine of equivalents to establish the infringement of the SMC device.

If it seems utterly trivial to distinguish between two *one-way* sealing rings located on *both sides* of the piston versus one *two-way* sealing ring located on *one side* of the piston, it must be remembered that the contribution covered by the patent was also very small. The distinction between the different types of sealing rings is only a small sample of the complexity in the case; for the other patent at issue, Festo invoked the equivalents analysis for two separate portions of the claims, each of which presented similar factual difficulties. Thus, to understand the effect of the various legal doctrines on the subject matter of the case, a court must immerse itself in some rather dense facts. This truth presents a seemingly insurmountable barrier to the Supreme Court's ability to maintain an effective presence in the field, for how can the Supreme Court achieve such a presence if it has neither the time nor inclination to become familiar with the necessary details of a patent case?

The Supreme Court overcame this problem with an elegant solution. It simply asserted that "the precise details of the [invention's] operation are not essential here."[192] Here we see a wise precedent for the Court's involvement in patent cases, and perhaps too in other cases requiring specialized knowledge. The insight is that, while the application of the law to the facts of any particular patent case is difficult, the law being applied need not be. The issue in *Festo* is a good example: The complexities of the case are utterly irrelevant to understanding the legal issue, which is the estoppel effects of actions taken, and representations made, before one particular administrative agency (the Patent Office). The arguments made before the Court—which concerned the unfairness of

---

[190] US Pat No B1 3,779,401, at col 2, lines 2–15 (reissue certificate issued Oct 25, 1988).

[191] The function of the sealing rings is to "form a tight fluid seal" so that the hydraulic fluid does not simply flow around the piston. US Pat No 3,779,401, at col 2, line 13.

[192] *Festo*, 122 S Ct at 1835.

a retroactive decision, the need for stability in property rights, the aspiration for precise definitions of property rights, and the practical limits of language—do not require any particular knowledge of technology. A generalist Court can comprehend these matters; indeed, it may have a broader perspective on them than does a court immersed in the details of a specialized field of law.

2. *The practical ability of the court to contribute to the field.* Overcoming the problem of daunting technological details will, however, mean little if the Court's rulings are not faithfully applied by the lower court with jurisdiction over the specialized field. Moreover, the solution to the detail problem might increase the possibility of noncompliance since, if the Supreme Court is blissfully ignorant of the devil in the details, then a willful lower court could easily disguise noncompliance with the Court's directions. Of course, noncompliance may be hard to hide if one or more of the specialized judges dissent and call attention to the point. But even then the Supreme Court might view the cost of correcting such noncompliance as too high, principally because the Court would then have to examine the details of the case. The result could be that, even with periodic intervention, the Court's effect in the patent field would be negligible. The history of the *Warner-Jenkinson* and *Festo* cases, however, provides some reason to expect that a specialized court will not be recalcitrant, and indeed might welcome the Court's intervention.

On the surface, the history of *Warner-Jenkinson* and *Festo* seems to provide support for a theory advanced by Judge Posner that specialized courts might exhibit dramatic vacillations in jurisprudence.[193] The theory is that experts in a field tend to align themselves with warring factions. A court staffed by experts is then likely to be sharply divided so that a few appointments will tip the balance between one faction and the other. *Warner-Jenkinson* and *Festo* seem to bear out this conjecture. In the first case, a 7–5 majority took an expansive view of the doctrine of equivalents and a narrow view of prosecution history estoppel. Four years later, after four of the judges were replaced with new appointees, the court in *Festo* divided 8–4 in favor of a very expansive view of estoppel, with three of the four new appointees in the majority.

_____

[193] See Richard A. Posner, *The Federal Courts: Challenge and Reform* 251 (Harvard, 1996).

Yet, in reality, the court's switch had nothing to do with the new appointments. Between the Federal Circuit's en banc decisions in *Warner-Jenkinson* and *Festo*, three of the judges who favored a narrow view of equivalents in *Warner-Jenkinson* left the court; they were replaced by precisely three judges who also took a narrow view of equivalents in *Festo*. Only one judge who voted for a broad view of equivalents in *Warner-Jenkinson* had left the court, and he was replaced by a new judge who voted for a broad view of equivalents in *Festo*. Thus, neither side gained or lost from new appointments. The difference was that three judges who favored a broad view of equivalents in *Warner-Jenkinson* switched and voted to limit equivalents (by expanding estoppel) in *Festo*.[194]

The Federal Circuit's change—which was not caused by new appointments—might possibly be explained by the Supreme Court's reversal in *Warner-Jenkinson*. Judges who initially favored a broad application of equivalents might have switched positions in an attempt to carry out the Court's new precedent. Oddly enough, this experience may bear out another of Judge Posner's theories—that judges enjoy (gain utility from) "compl[ying] with certain self-limiting rules that define the 'game' of judging."[195] In short, judges like to play by the rules, and one of the rules of appellate judging is that Supreme Court precedent must be followed. If this is so, a generalist Supreme Court might have more ability to control the jurisprudence of a specialized lower court than has previously been thought, and the problem of recalcitrance may be more imagined than real.[196]

3. *Institutions and (legal) innovations.* Even though one major theme in the Supreme Court's *Festo* opinion is that the patent law needs stability, this theme should not be interpreted as requiring the patent law to remain frozen. Nor should the Court be viewed as admonishing the Federal Circuit against trying to innovate. After all, the Court in *Warner-Jenkinson invited* the Federal Circuit to undertake reforms. The Court's rejection of one possible

---

[194] The three were Chief Judge Mayer, Judge Clevenger, and Judge Schall, who wrote the *Festo* majority.

[195] Richard A. Posner, *What Do Judges and Justices Maximize? (The Same Thing Everybody Else Does)*, 3 S Ct Econ Rev 1, 28 (1993).

[196] Judge Posner, for example, has argued that "decisions by a specialized court resist effective control by a higher generalist court." Posner, *The Federal Courts* at 257 (cited in note 193).

change (the complete bar rule) should not chill the Federal Circuit's future attempts to adopt different reforms, even though some of those reforms might also be reversed by the Supreme Court.

In fact, the development of legal techniques for defining patent rights is already continuing. Even as *Festo* was being decided, a new en banc decision from the Federal Circuit extended an estoppel-like theory to *unamended* claims. The case, *Johnson & Johnston Associates v R.E. Service Co.*, held that a patentee cannot use the doctrine of equivalents to reach equivalents expressly disclosed but not claimed in a patent.[197] In a concurring opinion in that case, Judge Rader suggested a much more ambitious reform—that, in all circumstances, patentees should be precluded from relying on the doctrine of equivalents to "capture subject matter that the patent drafter reasonably could have foreseen during the application process and included in the claims."[198] That proposed rule, like the Court's test in *Festo*, demands only that patent claim drafters perform reasonably, judged at the time of the claim drafting, and retrospective inquiry would permit the change to proceed gradually, following the developing norms of actual patent practice. Unlike the *Festo* rule, Judge Rader's proposal would apply globally, that is, even to unamended claims. That, however, may be a virtue, for the *Festo* Court itself noted that the fact of amendment should not be viewed as signaling a radical shift in the ability of the drafter to capture the invention. Even prior to *Festo*, the judges of the Federal Circuit had already begun an internal debate on the merits of Judge Rader's proposal.

While the Federal Circuit will almost certainly continue generating refinements in patent doctrine, there is, however, another specialized institution that might also usefully contribute to the development of the law in this area: the PTO. In its recent cases, the Supreme Court has dropped broad hints that it would welcome the PTO's assistance in refining the law governing patent claims. In *Warner-Jenkinson*, the Court recognized the agency's "primacy" in ensuring that the claims cover the patent applicant's invention.[199] And the Court rejected the petitioner's suggestion to elimi-

---

[197] 285 F3d 1046 (Fed Cir 2002) (en banc).

[198] Id at 1057 (Rader concurring).

[199] *Warner-Jenkinson*, 520 US at 33.

nate equivalents on all amended claim elements because the Court was "extremely reluctant to upset the basic assumptions of the PTO" or to "subvert the various balances the PTO sought to strike" in processing existing patent applications.[200] Arguing for the petitioner in *Festo*, Judge Bork suggested that, if the law of prosecution history estoppel were to be changed dramatically, then the PTO should undertake the change via an administrative rule-making which, under settled administrative law, would have only prospective effect.[201] That suggestion drew attention from the bench, and it was raised again in Bork's rebuttal.[202] In its final opinion, the Court took an even more pro-PTO position: It adopted wholesale the position that the agency articulated in the amicus brief that it and the Solicitor General filed on behalf of the United States.[203]

The cases strongly suggest that, in controlling the path of the law in this area, the Supreme Court is looking to the PTO for guidance as much as it is looking to the Federal Circuit. Moreover, the PTO has a large wellspring of power in this area precisely because the agency approves the language of patent claims. For example, consider how the agency could have responded if the Supreme Court had left the Federal Circuit's "complete bar" rule intact and the agency thought that rule too harsh. The most obvious response would be for the agency to allow patent applicants to include language expressly claiming "equivalents" whenever they amend their claims.[204] But the agency need not clutter up every claim with repeated invocations of "equivalents." It could just as easily permit the patentee to reference equivalents once in the preamble to the claims. Indeed, some savvy firms are already doing this. Amazon.com was recently issued a patent that contains this preamble to its claims: "It is intended that the scope of the invention be defined by the following claims *and their equivalents*: . . . ."[205]

---

[200] Id at 32 & n 6.

[201] Transcript of Oral Argument, *Festo Corp. v Shoketsu Kinzoku Kogyo Kabushiki Co.*, No 00-1543, 2002 US Trans Lexis 1, *9 (Jan 8, 2002).

[202] Id at *9 & *47.

[203] See text at notes 182–84.

[204] See, e.g., US Pat No 6,418,989 (July 16, 2002) (claiming "support wedges or the equivalent").

[205] US Pat No 6,449,601, col 21, lines 61–62 (Sept 10, 2002) (emphasis added).

Yet the PTO need not even clutter any part of the claims with express mention of equivalents. The agency could just as easily write a rule stating that all claim elements (amended or un-amended) encompass equivalents to the element unless equivalents are expressly *disavowed* in the claim. Of course, the PTO is unlikely to take that position in the wake of *Festo* because the agency en-dorsed precisely the position adopted by the Court. The agency could, however, write a more nuanced rule that provides clearer parameters governing the loss of equivalents through amendment.

Rulemakings of the sort suggested above would, in fact, be broadly consistent with the role that the agency has long filled in this area of patent law. In fact, one historical explanation for the survival of the doctrine of equivalents is that the Patent Office would usu-ally reject claims including the word "equivalents" because the word was unnecessary—all claims would be construed to include equivalents.[206] Rulemakings would also present the Supreme Court with the perspectives of another expert body which, in turn, could help the Court exercise its jurisdiction in this area more effectively.

D. POSTSCRIPT: AND WHAT OF FESTO?

In the years to come, *Festo* will surely be cited as one of the major cases on prosecution history and, more generally, on the law

---

[206] See *Ex parte Haasz*, 1873 Dec Comm'n Pat 170, 171–72 (holding that the phrase "or equivalents" should be "inhibited" in patent claims because no "useless word or phrase ought ever to be allowed in a claim" and "[i]t is well known to those versed in patent law, that equivalents are comprehended in every claim whether specified or not"); see also Wil-liam C. Robinson, *The Law of Patents for Useful Inventions* § 516 at 128–29 (Little, Brown, 1890) (stating that equivocal words are not permitted in patent claims and that "[o]f this character is the word 'equivalent;' for as a true 'equivalent,' in the sense of the Patent Law, is always covered by the Claim"). Prior to the *Haasz* decision, the Patent Office had viewed the phrase "or equivalents" as "unobjectionable" even though it "add[ed] nothing that the applicant not be entitled to without them." *Ex parte Continental Windmill Co.*, 1870 Dec Comm'n Pat 74, 74. The PTO's current Manual of Patent Examination Procedure seems to follow the earlier view; it does not prohibit patent applicants from expressly claiming "equivalents" and indeed recognizes that "broadening modifiers are standard tools in claim drafting in order to avoid reliance on the doctrine of equivalents." Patent & Trademark Office, *Manual of Patent Examination Procedure* § 2173.05(b), at 2100–2196 (8th ed 2001) (available at <http://www.uspto.gov/web/offices/pac/mpep/mpep.htm>). But even in the absence of any express claim to equivalents, examiners are required, in determining patent-ability of the claim, to consider "[a]ll subject matter that is the equivalent of the subject matter as defined in the claim, even though specifically different from the definition in the claim." Id § 904.01(b), at 900–951; see also *Haasz*, at 1873 Dec Comm'n Pat at 171 (noting that the determination of equivalents "constitutes the major part of the duties of the exam-ining corps" and rejecting the argument that "it is for the courts to determine what consti-tute equivalents").

governing the definition of patent rights and on the relationship between the Federal Circuit and the Supreme Court. But to the parties in the case, the Court's decision in *Festo* will be just another step in a very extended course of litigation. As the *Festo* litigation grinds into its fifteenth year, the Federal Circuit has already begun the proceedings required by the Supreme Court's remand. In a September 20, 2002, order, the court required briefing on four questions covering the allocation of decisional power among the jury, the trial court, and the appellate court in applying the Court's new presumption (question 1), the factors relevant to applying the Court's test (question 2), and the application of the test to the case at hand (questions 3 and 4).[207]

The Federal Circuit could answer those questions in a way that, in effect if not in name, restores a complete bar. The court would merely have to hold that the application of the Court's test is a matter of law for the courts and that, in rebutting the presumption, the patentee is limited to the evidence available in the public prosecution record. Those rules would clearly dictate a loss for Festo Corporation. They would also foreclose escape from prosecution history estoppel for the vast majority, indeed perhaps all, of existing patentees, who would not have known to memorialize such evidence in their prosecution files. Such a result would require the creation of an exceptional evidentiary rule for use only in this particular corner of patent law, and it would also be inconsistent with the Supreme Court's emphasis that its test should not be interpreted as "just the complete bar by another name."[208]

There is, however, no particular reason to think that the Federal Circuit will try to undermine the Court's decision in *Festo*. As noted above, the *Warner-Jenkinson* and *Festo* litigations suggest that the Federal Circuit does try to follow the Court's directions faithfully. Three principles are particularly important for guiding the Federal Circuit's decision on remand. First, the allocation of decisional power should be broadly consistent with the law on estoppel issues generally. As the Court's *Festo* decision stresses, one flaw in the Federal Circuit's "complete bar" approach to estoppel was that it had lost all connection to general concepts of estoppel.

---

[207] See *Festo Corp. v Shoketsu Kinzoku Kogyo Kabushiki Co., Ltd.*, 2002 US App LEXIS 19734 (Sept 20, 2002).

[208] *Festo*, 122 S Ct at 1842.

That mistake should not be repeated. In other areas, concepts of equitable estoppel are treated as mixed questions of fact and law. District courts, not juries, find the relevant facts; appellate courts review the facts deferentially and review the application of the legal standard de novo.[209] There is no good reason for deviating from this approach in this area of patent law. Indeed, the general approach to estoppel seems to comport with the Court's opinions both in *Warner-Jenkinson*, which described prosecution history estoppel as a check on the jury's application of equivalents,[210] and in *Festo*, which demands a factual inquiry into expectations of those "skilled in the art."[211]

Second, a key theme in the Court's *Festo* opinion is that changes in the patent doctrine must not "destroy[] the legitimate expectations of inventors in their property."[212] There is a fundamental connection between that theme and the standard ultimately adopted by the Court, which turns on whether "at the time of the amendment one skilled in the art could not reasonably be expected to have drafted a claim that would have literally encompassed the alleged equivalent."[213] A great virtue of this retrospective inquiry is that it allows change to proceed gradually. Expectations reasonable in 1982 (when one of Festo's two patents was issued) or in 1988 (when the other Festo patent was amended during reexamination) might be unreasonable for patents issued after the *Warner-Jenkinson* and *Festo* decisions. The Federal Circuit is familiar with making such retrospective inquiries in other areas of patent law— particularly in applying patent law's nonobviousness doctrine, which requires an invention to have been not obvious to persons skilled in the art *at the time of the invention*. In applying that doctrine, the Federal Circuit has repeatedly warned against the dangers of "hindsight" reasoning: Inventions often appear easy after they have been invented.[214] A similar approach should be followed in applying the estoppel test. After fourteen years of litigation in

---

[209] See, e.g., *Tyler v Union Oil Co.*, 304 F3d 379 (5th Cir 2002); *United States v Walcott*, 972 F2d 323, 325 (11th Cir 1992).

[210] *Warner-Jenkinson*, 520 US at 39 n 8.

[211] *Festo*, 122 S Ct at 1842.

[212] Id at 1841.

[213] Id at 1842.

[214] See, e.g., *In re Dembiczak*, 175 F3d 994 (Fed Cir 1999).

the *Festo* case, the problems with Festo's claim language—and the solutions to those problems—are apparent. But that is irrelevant. The relevant inquiry is not even what was *possible* when Festo wrote its claims, but rather what was *reasonable* to expect of the inventor and the attorney at that time.[215] The challenge for the Federal Circuit and for district courts is to apply that test without imposing unrealistic demands.[216]

Third, at some point the Federal Circuit has to place some premium on stabilizing the law in this area so that a case like *Festo* does not become a technological version of *Jarndyce v Jarndyce*. The parties in *Festo* have endured two trips to the Supreme Court and three full opinions from the Federal Circuit, with a fourth on the way. While further possible reforms are always possible in the law—and the Supreme Court's new test for prosecution history estoppel leaves many ambiguities—such future refinements should probably await another case.

III. The Return of the Court

The return of the Supreme Court to the field of patents has the odd property of seeming at once to be both real and unreal, terrible and propitious. As Judge Bork concluded his argument in the *Festo* case—as the Court finished an hour of debating the finer points of patent law with one of the leading attorneys of our time—the return seemed real. By end of the 2001 Term, however, it seemed an illusion. The Court was busy with its normal complement of constitutional cases, and *Festo* and the other patent cases

---

[215] The Supreme Court's test tends to conflate the roles of inventor and attorney. The test is based on the abilities of "one skilled in the art" in "draft[ing] a claim." *Festo*, 122 S Ct at 1842. But there are two relevant arts at issue here. One is the technological art that is the subject of the patent, which is the province of the inventor; the other is the art of patent claim drafting, which is the province of the attorney. Though the Court's test appears to require an inquiry only into what can be reasonably demanded from the attorneys, that inquiry requires some understanding of the language available in the particular technological art.

[216] The Supreme Court's test requires judgment about the difficulty of drafting good claims. Yet this is a point on which at least some judges of the Federal Circuit seem to have quite different views than the Justices of the Supreme Court. Compare the Court's view—"the nature of language makes it impossible to capture the essence of a thing in a patent application," *Festo*, 122 S Ct at 1837—with that of Judge Lourie, who joined the Federal Circuit's en banc majority and who wrote separately to express his confidence "that competent patent attorneys can readily craft their claims to cover" even complicated subjects. *Festo*, 234 F3d at 597 (Lourie concurring).

decided during the term seemed an insignificant portion of the Court's docket.

Yet, for the patent bar, the return is real. Despite its complexities, patent law can be organized into perhaps eight to ten fundamental issues. In the last decade, the Court has produced important opinions touching on about half of those issues. More importantly, the Court's willingness to review even legally complex patent cases (such as *Warner-Jenkinson* and *Festo*) reminds the actors in the patent system—including the attorneys litigating patent cases, the judges deciding those cases, and the PTO officials administering the system—that Supreme Court review *is* a real possibility, and that possibility affects the strategies that the various actors take in developing the law.

The return of the Court is, however, not necessarily a good thing. If after its long neglect the Court returned with an aggressive agenda of its own making, there would be every cause for alarm. When it has had an agenda, the Court has not been entirely helpful to the field, and those times are not far from current memory: Less than fifty-five years ago, Justice Jackson accused the Court of having a "strong passion" for striking down every patent that the Court could "get its hands on."[217] While a modern Court with an agenda would likely face resistance from the new specialized appellate court, such a power struggle between the Court and the Federal Circuit would be as unseemly as it would be unhelpful.

But the modern Court does not seem to have returned to the field with its own agenda. It is instead relying on the specialized actors themselves to identify the critical points of current doctrine that merit the Court's attention. Divisive en banc opinions from the Federal Circuit are likely to continue to attract certiorari, as are petitions filed on behalf of the PTO. Perhaps also the Court is entertaining claims that the Federal Circuit's current doctrine has strayed beyond the parameters of the Court's patent jurisprudence.

Applying those parameters to govern its grants of certiorari in patent cases, the Court is likely to limit its intervention to a few specific areas. One very good candidate for review is the law governing whether an invention is not "obvious" at the time of inven-

---

[217] Id at 572 (Jackson dissenting).

tion.[218] The centerpiece of the Federal Circuit's case law in this area is the so-called "suggestion test"—an invention will be considered nonobvious (and thus patentable) unless the existing art at the time of the invention contained a "suggestion" to make the invention. This test, which tends to make even seemingly trivial developments patentable, is entirely the Federal Circuit's product. It has no basis in the Supreme Court's case law and may, in fact, be inconsistent with the Court's most recent pronouncement on the subject (though that precedent is now more than a quarter century old).[219] There are also indications that the PTO is not entirely satisfied with this test, and that a conflict may be brewing between the agency and the Federal Circuit.[220] None of this is to say that the Court will necessarily reject the doctrine developed by the Federal Circuit; it is only to suggest the Court is likely to end its long absence from this doctrinal area soon.

Beyond the obviousness doctrine, a few additional issues seem likely to attract the Court's attention in the near future, but the number is not large.[221] The more important point is that, for any particular issue, the Court and the Federal Circuit seem likely to complement each other. For the Court, the Federal Circuit has identified the important issues in the field and provided the Court with a panoply of possible approaches to them. For the Federal Circuit, the Court has provided stability by adding the weight of its authority to doctrines previously announced by the Federal Circuit (as in *Markman, Warner-Jenkinson, J.E.M Ag Supply*, and even, in part, *Festo*) and by checking the Federal Circuit's experimental impulses where its innovations are insufficiently incremental (as in *Festo*). And the Court also serves to reconcile the Federal Circuit's

---

[218] See 35 USC § 103 (requiring an invention to be not "obvious" in order for it to be patentable).

[219] *Sakraida v AG Pro Inc.*, 425 US 273 (1976).

[220] See, e.g., *In re Lee*, 277 F3d 1338 (Fed Cir 2002) (chastising the PTO for "refus[ing] to follow circuit precedent" in a case where the agency had "rejected the need for [finding] any specific hint or suggestion" to support its obviousness determination) (internal quotations omitted).

[221] The standards applied by the Federal Circuit in reviewing district court interpretations of patent claims generated a fairly lengthy set of opinions in a 1998 en banc decision. That issue or a similar issue involving the allocation of power between the Federal Circuit and the district courts may yet attract the Court's review. Also, the PTO has recently published guidelines concerning the requirement that patent applicants identify a utility for their inventions, see *Utility Examination Guidelines*, 66 Fed Reg 1092 (2001), and those guidelines may eventually lead to a conflict between the PTO and the Federal Circuit.

power with the roles of the other institutional actors in the patent system and to provide more historical perspective for the ongoing development of the law.

Because of the existence of the Federal Circuit, patent cases at the Supreme Court now come with a subtext. Each case serves not only to resolve a patent issue but also to define further the roles of the generalist and specialist courts. We can only hope that, as that process continues, each institution will be mindful not only of its strengths, but of its weaknesses too. For the Supreme Court, this means recognizing the limitations of its expertise and refraining from trying to lead the development of the law. The Court should not be embarrassed to do as it did in *Festo*—where it copied the solution proposed by the United States. It should hesitate to do what it did in *Warner-Jenkinson*—where it modified the doctrine of prosecution history estoppel in a way not suggested by the petitioner, the Federal Circuit, or the United States. For the Federal Circuit, the task is not to avoid leading, for it has the expertise to reform and perhaps even to experiment with the law. Despite the ultimate reversal, the Federal Circuit need not be apologetic about what it did in *Festo*. Reform efforts do not always strike the right balance immediately; failed experiments are no cause for alarm. The difficult task for the Federal Circuit comes in implementing the Supreme Court's approach after the Court has reversed a decision. As a specialist court, the Federal Circuit has the practical ability to thwart the Supreme Court. But the combination of a generalist Supreme Court and a specialized appellate court can function—or, at least, can function effectively—only if the generalist court's acceptance of its limited competence is matched by the specialized court's acceptance of its limited authority. In other words, the combination can work if each institution practices the virtue of humility.

DANIEL J. MELTZER

THE SUPREME COURT'S
JUDICIAL PASSIVITY

The Supreme Court's constitutional federalism decisions have not
only drawn enormous attention but have frequently been characterized as a form of judicial activism. Less attention has been paid
to recent Supreme Court decisions on subconstitutional matters,
where, by contrast, the Court exhibits a form of selective judicial
passivity. In the subconstitutional arena, it is striking, on the one
hand, how the Court has sought, across a broad range of subject
matters, to reduce the role of judicial lawmaking and to refuse to
take responsibility for shaping a workable legal system in the everyday disputes that come before the judiciary without great fan-
fare. I will illustrate this claim by focusing initially on four decisions over the past two Terms that are extremely varied in subject
matter, but in all of which the Court sounds the theme that its
power (or, more generally, that of the federal courts) is sharply
limited and that Congress has primary, if not exclusive, responsibility for fleshing out the operation of schemes of federal regulation. Several of these cases might be viewed as quite mundane,
but that feature itself plays into some of the arguments that I will
advance.

Daniel J. Meltzer is Story Professor of Law, Harvard Law School.

AUTHOR'S NOTE: This article is an expanded version of an address that I gave at the
Workshop of the Federal Courts Section of the AALS on May 17, 2002. I am grateful to
Howell Jackson, John Langbein, Judith Resnik, and David Shapiro for comments and helpful discussions, as well as to the participants in the Harvard Law School Summer Workshop
series. David Bitkower, Anna Lumelsky, and Beth Schonmuller provided helpful research
assistance. I am grateful for support from the Harvard Law School's Summer Research
Program.

On the other hand, while the Court frequently articulates the supposed limits of its role quite forcefully, it does not consistently operate within those limits.[1] In an important contemporaneous set of decisions—those involving statutory preemption—the Supreme Court has been willing to recognize in the federal courts a broad lawmaking power, based upon policy judgments about how best to further the purposes of federal enactments. Indeed, the Court exercises that power to preempt quite unself-consciously, as if it is self-evident that federal courts, unaided by textual direction in the statute itself, should make the substantive judgments necessary to ensure that federal statutory schemes are not impeded by state or local measures. Here, the Court takes on exactly the judicial role that the first set of decisions rejects.

Having put forward that contrast, I will offer an explanation of why the two sets of decisions exhibit such disparate approaches. One ingredient of the explanation could be viewed as a rather crude kind of result-orientation: preemption cases tend to enlist the deregulatory sympathies of a majority of the current Justices, and those sympathies may impel them to engage in a form of judicial lawmaking that they purport to disfavor elsewhere. But the preemption decisions also illustrate, in my view, that the approach that the Court articulates in other areas is not a tenable one and

---

[1] Of course, inconsistency is not limited to subconstitutional decision making. The current Supreme Court, for example, favors judicially imposed restrictions on national authority and deference to state and local lawmaking, but those general inclinations are not strongly in evidence, for example, in the majority or concurring opinions in *Bush v Gore*, 531 US 98 (2000).

Recently, Bradley Joondeph argued that *Bush v Gore* is not inconsistent with the Court's federalism cases; he suggests that the Court's federalism revolution has been restricted to cases raising questions of the scope of congressional power, and that when such questions do not exist, the Court often supports national power at the expense of the states—notably in preemption and dormant Commerce Clause decisions. Bradley W. Joondeph, *Bush v. Gore, Federalism, and the Distrust of Politics*, 62 Ohio St L J 1781, 1803 (2001). That description seems largely accurate, but does not explain why the two sets of cases should be treated differently, or, more particularly, why the rhetoric of state autonomy, so prominent when congressional power is in question, counts for so little in other cases that pose a deeper challenge to state regulatory authority. Moreover, *Bush v Gore* rested not on preemption or dormant commerce grounds, but rather on the Fourteenth Amendment, and the claim that the Rehnquist Court has broadly interpreted the Fourteenth Amendment as restricting state action is somewhat overbroad to say the least. By the same token, the suggestion in the Chief Justice's concurring opinion in *Bush v Gore* that the Supreme Court should engage in de novo review of a state court's decision of state law is hardly a routine application of established principles. See generally Richard H. Fallon, Jr., Daniel J. Meltzer, and David L. Shapiro, *Hart & Wechsler's The Federal Courts and the Federal System* 66–72 (Foundation, 2002 Supp).

that sympathetic attention to congressional enactments more generally calls for a less passive attitude toward judicial lawmaking.

I will then try to link these arguments to broader debates about statutory interpretation and democratic processes. The approach of judicial passivity, articulated forcefully though followed only inconsistently, would deprive the polity of an immeasurably important source of lawmaking authority, would impose unrealistic demands on the federal legislative process, and would give rise to needless injustices in routine disputes. The Court appears implicitly to recognize all of this in preemption cases, but that recognition fades as the Court moves its attention to other issues of subconstitutional policy.

Compared to judicial activism, judicial passivity may seem undramatic and unthreatening. Yet I hope to suggest that this is not the case, and that the professions of judicial passivity represent a dramatic departure from an important tradition in the Anglo-American legal system, one in which courts have a distinctive responsibility for promoting legal coherence. In this setting, a hesitancy about discharging traditional and important responsibilities can hamstring the effectiveness of legislation as much as does outright constitutional invalidation. No less than its constitutional activism, the Supreme Court's judicial passivity has rendered it more difficult for Congress to legislate effectively.

I. Judicial Passivity Exemplified

Over a broad set of subject matters, recent decisions repeatedly sound the theme that judicial lawmaking of the kind sought by one of the parties is beyond the power of the federal courts, and that, as a result, if anyone is to create the requested rule of decision or to address the particular legal question, it must be Congress. Virtually no one disputes the proposition that Congress's power is far broader than that of the federal courts, or that, constitutional interpretation aside, such lawmaking as the federal courts do undertake must be consistent with the enactments of Congress. But the cases I wish to discuss reach much further, articulating a constricted view of statutory interpretation and of the scope of judicial power to flesh out federal enactments in service of statutory and constitutional purposes.

I must begin, however, with a caveat: with respect to three of the four cases I will discuss, the evidence of judicial passivity is found in dicta rather than in holdings. But in all three of those cases, the dicta appeared over protests in separate opinions about the unnecessary and gratuitous breadth of the majority's reasoning. These dicta, then, were anything but casual or inadvertent. Rather, for a lower court or a lawyer trying to ascertain the present state of the law and its likely future course, these opinions are important signals that one would be ill-advised to ignore.[2]

A. GREAT-WEST LIFE AND ANNUITY INSURANCE COMPANY
   V KNUDSON

The first of these decisions, *Great-West Life and Annuity Ins. Co. v Knudson*,[3] took an expansive view of the degree of congressional foresight and express statutory specification that can be expected in shaping a complex statutory scheme, and a correspondingly narrow view of judicial authority to fashion substantive rules to implement the scheme's purposes. There, a benefits plan regulated by ERISA paid more than $400,000 for the medical expenses, arising from injuries suffered in a car accident, of the wife of a covered employee. The plan had a standard subrogation provision authorizing it to obtain reimbursement from the beneficiary of any recoveries by the beneficiary from a third party for medical expenses. Thereafter, the husband and wife settled a state court action against the car manufacturer for $650,000. More than half of that amount went to the plaintiffs' attorney, and most of the rest was allocated to a Special Needs Trust for the wife's benefit; only

---

[2] See, for example, *Reich v Continental Casualty Corp.*, 33 F3d 754, 757 (7th Cir 1994). There, Judge Posner ruled that the court of appeals should follow dictum in an earlier Supreme Court decision, stating: "The [Supreme Court's] majority opinion goes out of its way to throw cold water on the idea of an implied liability of nonfiduciaries for knowing participation in fiduciaries' misconduct. The discussion is dictum, but it is considered dictum. If we thought the Court had overlooked some point that might have altered its view, we would be less reluctant to buck the dictum. But it appears not to have. . . . Justice Holmes has been derided for claiming in 'The Path of the Law,' 10 Harv. L. Rev. 457, 461 (1897), that the law is merely a prediction of what the courts will do. The theory has many weaknesses, but also a valid core."

The position on nonfiduciary liability taken in the Reich decision was rejected by a number of other circuits and eventually by the Supreme Court, when it resolved the resulting circuit conflict. See *Harris Trust & Savings Bank v Saloman Smith Barney Inc.*, 530 US 238 (2000). But those developments merely illustrate the problems that considered dicta of this kind can generate.

[3] 122 S Ct 708 (2002).

$14,000 (5 percent of the settlement amount net of attorney's fees) was deemed to be for medical expenses. Thereafter, Great-West Life, an insurer that, under an agreement with the plan, had paid most of the expenses and succeeded to its right to subrogation, brought suit to enforce that right; the action was filed in federal court under § 502(a)(3) of ERISA,[4] which authorizes suit for appropriate *equitable* relief to redress violations of a plan.

By a margin of 5–4, the Supreme Court found that the suit lacked merit. Justice Scalia's opinion relied on what he termed the plain meaning of the word "equitable" as excluding the subrogation claim, which he described as a personal liability for a contractual obligation to pay money. In so holding, the Court strictly applied language in a prior decision[5] that had read § 502(a)(3) as authorizing only such relief as was "typically" available in equity— a limitation not found in the statutory text.[6]

The rub in the case comes from the likelihood that ERISA would preempt any action under state law by Great-West Life to enforce its right to subrogation—whether through a simple action for breach of contract or a prior effort to have intervened in the Knudsons' state court lawsuit against the car manufacturer. ERISA contains a far-reaching preemption clause[7] to which the Supreme Court has given broad effect, and despite some recent decisions suggesting a more moderate view of the scope of state law displaced by ERISA,[8] the preemption issue in *Great-West Life* looks to be a serious one. If efforts to enforce the subrogation agreement under state law would indeed be preempted, then the majority's ruling would leave Great-West Life (and, more generally, employee benefits plans) without effective legal recourse to enforce

---

[4] 29 USC § 1132(a)(3).

[5] *Mertens v Hewitt Associates*, 508 US 248, 256–59 (1993).

[6] See 122 S Ct at 712.

The district court, taking the state court settlement at face value, had suggested that Great-West Life could recover, but only the $14,000 that the settlement designated as for medical expenses. See 2000 WL 145374 (9th Cir 2000) (unpublished disposition). The Supreme Court's decision did not rest on the ground that any recovery beyond the $14,000 was unauthorized by the subrogation agreement, but instead on the broader ground that that agreement could not be enforced in a suit under § 502(a)(3).

[7] See 29 USC § 1144(a) (providing that ERISA "shall supersede any and all State laws insofar as they may now or hereafter relate to any employee benefit plan").

[8] See, for example, *Pegram v Hedrich*, 530 US 211 (2000); *New York State Conference of Blue Cross & Blue Shield Plans v Travelers Ins. Co.*, 514 US 645 (1995).

standard subrogation provisions. Justice Scalia acknowledged but did not resolve the preemption problem;[9] he merely suggested that the Court was powerless to do anything about it.

Some may not be greatly concerned about the inability of a benefits plan to enforce its right to subrogation against a woman left quadriplegic by a serious accident. But as a result of this decision, benefit plans under ERISA may in the future be reluctant to make payments to injured individuals because of the uncertainty that subrogation rights will be enforceable. More broadly, subrogation clauses are standard in the insurance industry and indeed make perfectly good sense; they permit injured parties to obtain the benefits they need but not double recovery, and by thus saving money, enable plans to offer lower premiums or to extend other benefits. It is not merely difficult but impossible to imagine that Congress, in enacting ERISA, meant by indirection to upset the legal landscape by precluding enforcement of standard clauses like the one at issue in the *Great-West Life* decision.

That said, the case was not without its complexities. Justice Scalia's major premise—that unless the word "equitable" in § 502(a)(3) has some limit, the Court would be reading the word out of the statute—had not only been endorsed by prior decisions; in addition, as noted above, the Court had previously ruled that § 502(a)(3) authorized only such relief as was "typically available in equity."[10] But as the dissenters and the Solicitor General observed,[11] it would not have been hard to conclude that preventing unjust enrichment was a remedy typically available in equity—a position, indeed, endorsed by the Restatement of Restitution in 1937.[12] Indeed, *avoiding* that conclusion required considerable effort by the majority to distinguish forms of restitution at law from those at equity, and an insistence that judges today should look to the pre-1938 division of law and equity in shaping remedies for a complex modern regulatory scheme enacted in 1974.[13]

---

[9] 122 S Ct at 718.

[10] Id at 712, quoting *Mertens*, 508 US at 256.

[11] See 122 S Ct at 723–26 (Ginsburg dissenting); Brief for the United States as Amicus Curiae at 14–15.

[12] See Restatement of Restitution § 162, comment a (1937).

[13] The ripple effects of the *Great-West Life* decision for ERISA remain to be seen. They may, however, extend well beyond ERISA, for, according to Justice Scalia, the term "equitable relief" appears in seventy-seven provisions of the U.S. Code. 122 S Ct at 716 n 3.

John Langbein has explained with devastating power the flaws in the Court's approach in this and prior cases.[14] Indeed, despite the Court's protestations that it was merely enforcing congressional will, the prior gloss on the scope of § 502(a)(3) was judge-made. To be sure, one might take the view that the problem was not simply with the Court's brand of textualism, but rather that the Court did a poor job of interpreting the term "equitable." That may be true, but there can be little doubt that a more purposive approach to interpreting the statutory language would have helped to avoid reaching a decision so obviously at war with common sense. And if the *Great-West Life* decision, together with ERISA preemption (a statutory doctrine but one, too, with a judicial gloss), would produce so unfortunate a result as to render subrogation clauses unenforceable, one might have thought that the Justices would have felt a responsibility to make appropriate doctrinal adjustments. New statutes do not reenact all aspects of the preexisting legal landscape, and an important feature of responsible interpretation (one supported by the canons against implied repeals of existing statutes and strict construction of statutes in derogation of the common law) is to promote "the value of minimal disruption of existing arrangements consistent with the language and purpose of [a] new law."[15]

Instead, the Court stuck with its precedents and, in particular, with its constricted view of the term "equitable relief." No appeal was made to the tradition of creativity in the development of equity, nor to the fact that *Great-West Life* presented a situation (unknown to English chancery courts) in which federal preemption of common law remedies could leave the moving party with, to use the classic formulation, no adequate remedy at law.[16] Instead,

---

[14] See John H. Langbein, *What ERISA Means by "Equitable": The Supreme Court's Trail of Error in Russell, Mertens, and Great-West* (forthcoming 2003).

For another critique of *Great-West Life* that links it to other restrictions on the remedial powers of the federal courts, as well as to efforts of the Judicial Conference of the United States to persuade Congress to limit the creation of new federal rights that are enforceable in the federal courts, see Judith Resnik, *Constricting Federal Remedies: The Rehnquist Judiciary, Congress, and Federal Power*, 78 Ind L J (forthcoming 2003).

[15] David L. Shapiro, *Continuity and Change in Statutory Interpretation*, 67 NYU L Rev 921, 937 (1992).

[16] Nor did the Court consider whether, in the face of the advance of more than $400,000 in medical expenses, the allocation to medical expenses of only 5 percent of the $650,000 state court settlement constituted fraud on the insurer. Equity, after all, has always been concerned with avoiding fraud and mistake. See Langbein, *What ERISA Means by*

Justice Scalia insisted that "'vague notions of a statute's "basic purpose" are nonetheless inadequate to overcome the words of its text regarding the *specific* issue under consideration.'"[17] He adduced no evidence from the text (and certainly none from the legislative history), however, that § 502(a)(3) itself specifically addressed the enforceability of subrogation provisions.

Alternatively, if ERISA both preempts state remedies and provides no express federal remedy for the enforcement of subrogation rights, the Court might have recognized an implied federal remedy to enforce those rights, fashioning federal common law in a field that, because of the breadth of federal regulation and federal preemption, has been broadly federalized.[18] While the question of the availability of such an implied remedy was not directly presented in the petition for certiorari,[19] it surely was closely related, perhaps closely enough to bring it within the scope of review.[20] Indeed, Justice Scalia did opine on the availability of such a remedy, quoting prior statements by the Supreme Court that ERISA's "'carefully crafted and detailed enforcement scheme provides "strong evidence that Congress did *not* intend to authorize other remedies that it simply forgot to incorporate expressly."'"[21] But the Court's frequent repetition of that view does not mean that it is true, and even that quotation says only that the evidence is strong, not irrebuttable. It is not only plausible but almost certain that *if* ERISA not only preempts state law remedies but also provides no substitute remedy for enforcement of a subrogation clause, Congress "simply forgot to incorporate expressly" a provi-

---

"Equitable": The Supreme Court's Trail of Error in Russell, Mertens, and Great-West (cited in note 14).

[17] 122 S Ct at 718 (quoting *Mertens*, 508 US 248, 261 (1993)).

[18] Compare *Metropolitan Life Ins. Co. v Taylor*, 481 US 58 (1987) (holding that ERISA is one of only two areas in which, because of the extraordinary preemptive power of a federal statutory regime, a state court action that purports to rest on state law may, under the "complete preemption doctrine," be removed to federal court on the basis that the action is preempted under federal law).

[19] That question was: "Whether federal courts have jurisdiction over actions brought by ERISA plan fiduciaries to enforce recoupment provisions in ERISA plans against plan participants or beneficiaries for medical expenses paid for injuries caused by third-party tortfeasors."

[20] The Petitioner's Brief at 38–39 argued in the alternative for a federal common law remedy.

[21] 122 S Ct at 712, quoting *Mertens*, 508 US at 254 (quoting *Massachusetts Mut. Life Ins. Co. v Russell*, 473 US 134, 146 (1985)).

sion that would avoid rendering subrogation provisions entirely unenforceable. An overly broad conception of congressional omniscience and exclusivity, no matter how forceful the arguments for judicial supplementation, is itself a symptom of the problem that I seek to highlight.

B. NORFOLK SHIPBUILDING AND DRYDOCK V GARRIS

I will discuss my second example, *Norfolk Shipbuilding and Drydock v Garris*,[22] only briefly. In this admiralty case, the Court's opinion for the most part followed a sensible approach to judicial lawmaking—but not without a concluding, admonitory dictum suggesting that the future might be different.

The issue in the case—"whether the negligent breach of a general maritime duty of care is actionable when it causes death, as it is when it causes injury"[23]—fell at the intersection of two well-established rights of action under the federal common law of admiralty. One recognizes liability for *nonfatal injuries* caused by *negligence*. The second recognizes liability for *wrongful death* caused by *unseaworthiness*. But never before had the Court recognized liability for *wrongful death* caused by *negligence*. Addressing that question, Justice Scalia's brief opinion found no basis for distinguishing deaths resulting from negligence from those resulting from unseaworthiness, nor for distinguishing deaths from nonfatal injuries caused by negligence.[24] The common law method was at work.

The Court proceeded to discuss three federal statutes that provide remedies in maritime cases in other circumstances. As to each, the Court rejected the argument that the statutory failure to provide a remedy impliedly precluded the provision of one under judge-made admiralty law. Such a reading, the Court found, was foreclosed by precedent.

However, the opinion ended on a quite different note, stating (over the protest of three concurring Justices) that "[b]ecause of Congress's extensive involvement in legislating causes of action for maritime personal injuries, it will be the better course, in many cases that assert new claims beyond what those statutes have seen

---

[22] 532 US 811 (2001).

[23] Id at 812.

[24] Id at 815.

fit to allow, to leave further development to Congress."[25] Looking
to the future, the Court suggests—as it had ruled in the present
in *Great-West Life*—that further legal development should be left
at the doorstep of Congress.

C. UNITED STATES V OAKLAND CANNABIS BUYERS' COOPERATIVE

That message was repeated in a third decision that, while formally civil, involved enforcement of federal criminal law. In *United
States v Oakland Cannabis Buyers' Cooperative*,[26] the government
sued to enjoin an organization dedicated to dispensing marijuana
for medical purposes, and the organization's director, from violating the federal Controlled Substance Act.[27] That Act is probably
best known for criminalizing violations of its provisions, but it also
authorizes injunctive remedies against violators.[28] The question before the Court was whether a defendant who supplies marijuana
to seriously ill persons for the purpose of alleviating their pain may
assert a medical necessity defense to the Act's prohibition against
manufacturing and distributing marijuana.

The arguments favoring the defense were hardly overwhelming.
First, on the facts the district court found a lack of proof that the
distributees were in danger of serious harm without marijuana.[29]
Second, the necessity defense, because it is meant to address potential statutory applications that a legislature, had it anticipated
them, would not have favored, is typically unavailable in circumstances in which the legislature has manifested a specific intention
to preclude any such defense.[30] And that was likely the case here:
while the Act permits many controlled substances to be prescribed
for medical purposes, it declares that Schedule I substances, of
which marijuana is one, may not be. Thus, it was little surprise
that the Court, without dissent, found that no necessity defense
was applicable on these facts.

But once again the majority opinion, this time authored by Jus-

---

[25] Id at 820, citing *American Dredging Co. v Miller*, 510 US 443, 455 (1994).

[26] 532 US 483 (2001).

[27] 84 Stat 1242, 21 USC § 801 et seq (1988).

[28] 21 USC § 882.

[29] See 532 US at 487.

[30] See, for example, Model Penal Code § 3.02.

tice Thomas, ranged a good deal further. After noting, correctly,[31] that the necessity defense in general is somewhat controversial,[32] he added this rather bold statement: "[U]nder our constitutional system, in which federal crimes are defined by statute rather than by common law, see *United States v Hudson*, 7 Cranch 32, 34 (1812), it is especially so." Thus, "as an initial matter, we note that it is an open question whether courts ever have authority to recognize a necessity defense not provided by statute."[33]

Three concurring Justices objected to the breadth of this language, and, pointing to a relatively recent Supreme Court decision that seemed to acknowledge that a judge-made necessity defense exists in appropriate circumstances,[34] contended that the question treated as open by Justice Thomas had in fact been settled.[35] They might, however, have taken issue with Justice Thomas's "open question" more broadly, by focusing not merely on the necessity

---

[31] See, for example, John T. Parry, *The Virtue of Necessity: Reshaping Culpability and the Rule of Law*, 36 Houston L Rev 397 (1999).

[32] 532 US at 490.

[33] Id.

[34] Id at 500–01, citing *United States v Bailey*, 444 US 394 (1980) (setting forth limitations on a necessity defense when raised by a prisoner who escapes to avoid greater harm threatened if he remained confined).

[35] In an opinion concurring in the judgment, Justice Stevens suggested in addition that the defendants in this case fell outside of any necessity defense as they, unlike seriously ill patients, did not personally face the same choice of evils. 532 US at 500 n 1. One can understand that these defendants, who appeared to be campaigning for broader use of marijuana rather than responding to localized circumstances of an emergency nature, were not the most appealing parties to claim a necessity defense. But *if* seriously ill users indeed were entitled to a defense—a point that Justice Stevens called a "difficult issue" but wished to leave open—it is far from clear that a person who assists an actor in choosing the lesser of two evils is not also entitled to the defense. Of course, a distributor of marijuana does not face the same choice faced by a seriously ill person, but that would be true of any person from whom the ailing individual obtained marijuana. Because there will ordinarily be many potential distributors, it would never be "necessary" that any one distributor choose to supply a particular distributee, since someone else might. But the net result of that approach would be to deny the defense to any distributor, in which case the ailing person might have a right to use the drug but anyone who supplied it would be subject to prosecution. Compare *United States v Haney*, 287 F3d 1266 (10th Cir 2002) (where a prisoner would be entitled to a duress defense to a criminal charge of attempting to escape from prison in order to avoid a threat of harm, a confederate who helped the prisoner attempt to escape but was not personally subject to the threat of harm may also raise the defense of duress); Richard H. Fallon, Jr., Daniel J. Meltzer, and David L. Shapiro, *Hart & Wechsler's The Federal Courts and the Federal System* 190 (Foundation, 4th ed 1996) ("*Hart & Wechsler*") (suggesting, in discussing *Griswold v Connecticut*, 381 US 479 (1965), that where a prohibition on the use of contraceptives by married individuals violated their constitutional rights, a doctor may not be convicted on the theory that, in prescribing contraceptives, he was an accomplice to the crime of illegal use by married persons).

defense but on defenses to federal criminal liability generally. Federal decisions have long recognized common law defenses: the best-known (but not the only) examples are self-defense[36] and the insanity defense[37] (which was a common law rule until Congress in 1984 supplanted the judge-made defense with a statutory version).[38] If a defense based on necessity, rather than, for example, on self-defense, is a bad idea—either in general or in particular circumstances—that raises a question of policy, not of judicial authority. More broadly, just as the interpretation of ERISA should presume the continuity of the prior law of subrogation, the interpretation of the Controlled Substances Act should presume the continuity of the prior law (and prior interpretive approaches) regarding defenses. To suggest otherwise, even in dictum, would be quite revolutionary.[39]

In this respect, the majority was entirely unconvincing when it suggested that *United States v Hudson and Goodwin*, in which the Supreme Court held nearly two centuries ago that the federal courts lack power to establish common law crimes, supported the claim of a lack of power to consider recognition of a necessity defense. Quite apart from political considerations that may have shaped that decision,[40] *Hudson* derived in significant part from a

---

[36] See, for example, *Brown v United States*, 256 US 335 (1921).

[37] See, for example, *Shannon v United States*, 512 US 573 (1994) (Thomas, J) (citing numerous federal decisions recognizing a judge-made insanity defense to federal prosecutions).

[38] See the Insanity Defense Reform Act of 1984, Pub L No 98-473, 98 Stat 2057, codified at 18 USC §§ 17, 4241–47.

For other judge-made defenses, see, for example, Paul Robinson, 1–2 *Criminal Law Defenses* §§ 81 (abandonment of inchoate crimes), 141 (public authority), 177 (duress), 209 (entrapment) (West Group, 1984).

[39] Thus Judge Easterbrook, hardly an apostle of federal common lawmaking or of broad statutory construction, has written (albeit in an opinion in a hypothetical case) that "[a]ll three branches of government historically have been entitled to assess claims of justification—the legislature by specifying the prohibition and allowing exceptions, the executive by declining to prosecute (or by pardon after conviction), and the judiciary by developing defenses." Frank Easterbrook, *The Case of the Speluncean Explorers Revisited*, 112 Harv L Rev 1913, 1913–14 (1999).

[40] According to Stewart Jay, *Origins of Federal Common Law: Part Two*, 133 U Pa L Rev 1231, 1323 (1985), "*Hudson* was decided in a peculiar setting of partisan disturbance, and grew out of a fear that we can scarcely appreciate today—the belief that there was a scheme afoot to install a consolidated national government through incorporation of the British common law." See also Note, *The Sound of Silence: United States v Hudson & Goodwin, the Jeffersonian Ascendancy, and the Abolition of Federal Common Law Crimes*, 101 Yale L J 919 (1992) (arguing that *Hudson* represented a change in practice influenced greatly by the Jeffersonians' political triumph in 1800 and their opposition to the Alien and Sedition laws).

concern about the scope of federal lawmaking powers vis-à-vis the states.[41] Surely the Court was not suggesting that the scope of defenses to federal statutory crimes should be left to *state* law.[42]

The *Oakland Cannabis* decision makes an interesting contrast with a decision handed down the very same day, *Rogers v Tennessee*.[43] There, a *state court*, in the course of upholding a murder conviction for a death that occurred fifteen months after the fatal stabbing, abolished the common law rule that death in a homicide must occur within a year and a day of the criminal act. That change in the law sustained a murder conviction that would otherwise have had to be set aside.

The U.S. Supreme Court affirmed the judgment, rejecting the claim that the state court's retroactive expansion of criminal liability denied due process. The Justices split 5–4, but not along the usual lines, with Justice O'Connor writing the majority opinion and Justices Scalia and Thomas joined in dissent by Justices Stevens and Breyer. The majority did not dispute that a state *legislature's* retroactive abolition of the year-and-a-day rule would violate the Ex Post Facto Clause, but it refused to equate the Ex Post Facto Clause's limits on legislative expansion of crime with the Due Process Clause's limits on judicial expansion of crime. The majority thus rejected, as mere dictum, the suggestion in *Bouie v City of Columbia*[44] that the Due Process Clause provides the same protection against retroactive judicial expansion of criminal liability that the Ex Post Facto Clause provides against retroactive legislative expansion.[45] Instead, Justice O'Connor wrote, "the common law . . . presupposes a measure of evolution that is incompatible with stringent application of ex post facto principles," for such an application would "unduly impair the incremental and reasoned

---

[41] See 11 US at 33 ("The powers of the general Government are made up of concessions from the several states—whatever is not expressly given to the former, the latter expressly reserve."). Accord, John Calvin Jeffries, Jr., *Legality, Vagueness, and the Construction of Penal Statutes*, 71 Va L Rev 189, 192 n 9 (1985).

[42] Moreover, there are distinctive constitutional concerns associated with retroactive judicial *expansion* of criminal liability in the context of a particular prosecution that do not apply to retroactive *contraction* of liability resulting from recognition of a defense. See generally Jeffries, 71 Va L Rev at 190 (cited in note 41).

[43] 532 US 451 (2001).

[44] 378 US 347 (1964).

[45] *Rogers*, 532 US at 460–61.

development of precedent that is the foundation of the common law system."[46]

If the *Oakland Cannabis* case differs from *Rogers v Tennessee* with respect to judicial authority, it must be that *state* courts have more authority to adjust the bounds of state criminal liability than *federal* courts possess with regard to federal criminal liability predicated upon congressional legislation. And this difference in judicial role must be so great, indeed, that the result in *Rogers* is permissible (and formulation of a defense in *Oakland Cannabis* perhaps even unthinkable), despite the fact that the Constitution limits the retroactive expansion of criminal liability (as in *Rogers*) but does not, of course, limit retroactive contraction of liability (as when a new defense to a criminal charge is recognized).

There are, of course, many arguments why state common law courts have broader lawmaking authority than federal courts, but the most persuasive of these sound in federalism rather than in separation of powers.[47] It is difficult indeed to think that the formulation by federal judges of defenses that might narrow the scope of federal statutory liability would constitute an incursion on state authority.

D. CORRECTIONAL SERVICES CORP. V MALESKO

My last example involves the relationship of judge-made law to the federal *Constitution*. In *Correctional Services Corp. v Malesko,*[48] a federal prisoner housed in a halfway house operated by a private contractor alleged that he suffered injuries from the contractor's alleged negligence in refusing to permit the prisoner to use an elevator. The prisoner filed a so-called *Bivens* claim[49]—an implied right of action for damages for violation of his constitutional rights. Here, too, the case was not a strong one in a variety of respects. First, the complaint (alleging only negligence) did not seem to state a meritorious claim under the Cruel and Unusual

---

[46] Id at 461.

[47] See note 159. See generally *Hart & Wechsler* at 756–57 (cited in note 35).

[48] 122 S Ct 515 (2001).

[49] See *Bivens v Six Unknown Named Agents of the Federal Bureau of Narcotics*, 403 US 388 (1971).

Punishment Clause.[50] Second, in *FDIC v Meyer*,[51] the Supreme Court had held, however unpersuasively, that no *Bivens* action lies against a federal agency (as distinguished from a federal officer), even when Congress had waived the agency's sovereign immunity. It would hardly have been a stretch to hold that any *Bivens* action with respect to privately operated correctional facilities extends only to suits against individual employees and not to suits against the organization itself. That, indeed, was the position on which the Solicitor General's Amicus Brief rested.[52]

In his opinion for the Court, Chief Justice Rehnquist, who regularly had voted against recognizing *Bivens* liability,[53] mentioned both of these points[54] but did not stop there, instead offering a dramatic new reading of the *Bivens* cause of action. Most have understood *Bivens* and succeeding decisions as holding that when a federal official violates an individual's constitutional rights, a damages remedy is presumptively available absent some reason to preclude it. (*Bivens* actions are, however, subject to very broad immunities that in the end often defeat recovery.) The Supreme Court itself had disposed of a number of cases acting on this apparent assumption,[55] and Congress appears to have been operating on

---

[50] See, for example, *Hope v Pelzer*, 122 S Ct 2508, 2514 (2002) (reiterating that the question under that Clause is whether officials acted with "deliberate indifference" to an inmate's health or safety).

[51] 510 US 471 (1994).

[52] See Brief for the United States as Amicus Curiae Supporting Petitioner at 11–26.

[53] Thus, he dissented in *Carlson v Green*, 446 US 14 (1980), and *Davis v Passman*, 442 US 228 (1979), and joined the majority in refusing to recognize a *Bivens* right of action in *Schweiker v Chilicky*, 487 US 412 (1988), *Bush v Lucas*, 462 US 367 (1983), *Chappell v Wallace*, 462 US 296 (1983), and *United States v Stanley*, 483 US 669 (1987).

[54] 122 S Ct at 521–23.

[55] See, for example, *Dickerson v United States*, 530 US 428, 442 (2000) (apparently approving a lower court decision upholding the availability of a *Bivens* right of action for a denial of due process in custodial interrogation); *Behrens v Pelletier*, 516 US 299 (1996) (due process claim relating to dismissal from employment); *Cleavinger v Saxner*, 474 US 193 (1985) (alleged violation by prison disciplinary body of rights under the First, Fourth, Fifth, Sixth, and Eighth Amendments); *Harlow v Fitzgerald*, 457 US 800 (1982) (claim of illegal discharge under the First Amendment).

This is not to say that the Supreme Court has invariably recognized a *Bivens* right of action. See note 53. But the decisions refusing to do so have been based on more particular reasons for not implying a damages remedy—for example, comprehensive congressional regulation of the area, or distinctive concerns respecting the military—rather than on challenges to the premise that a *Bivens* remedy is presumptively available when a federal official violates constitutional rights. See generally *Hart & Wechsler* at 870–73 (cited in note 35).

the same understanding.[56] Much as the Constitution evolves by virtue of common law decisions, which then becomes part of the constitutional framework against which future constitutional disputes are resolved,[57] judicial decisions like *Bivens* become part of the subconstitutional framework on which not only later decisions, but also subsequent congressional enactments, are based. Respecting that framework is a counsel of humility, reflecting doubts about the wisdom of rejecting judgments that were carefully arrived at and that have been reaffirmed or at least accepted over a period of years.[58]

But in *Malesko*, the Chief Justice seemed willing to ignore that framework. He suggested that *Bivens* recognized a claim for money damages "in limited circumstances," and added: "in 30 years of

---

[56] A good example is the Federal Employers Liability Reform and Tort Compensation Act of 1988, PL 100-694, which provided, in damage actions against federal employees for common law torts committed within the scope of their employment, both for a broadened immunity and for recharacterizing the action as one against the United States under the Federal Tort Claims Act (FTCA). In general, the 1988 Act made the FTCA the exclusive remedy when plaintiffs seek money damages for tortious conduct of a federal employee acting with the scope of employment, 28 USC § 2679(b)(1), but the exclusivity provision expressly left open the right of plaintiffs to sue federal employees under *Bivens* for constitutional violations, see id § 2679(b)(2)(A). The House Report accompanying that Act explains: "Since the Supreme Court's decision in *Bivens*, supra, the courts have identified this type of tort [a constitutional tort] as a more serious intrusion of the rights of an individual that merits special attention. Consequently, H.R. 4612 would not affect the ability of victims of constitutional torts to seek personal redress from Federal employees who violated their Constitutional rights." HR Rep 100-700, 100th Cong, 2d Sess, 1998 USCCAN 5945, 5950.

Similarly, when in 1974 Congress amendment the FTCA to embrace a broad range of intentional torts committed by law enforcement officials, a committee report accompanying a bill that was later embodied in that amendment described *Bivens* as holding "that the Fourth Amendment and elementary justice require that there by [sic] a right of action against the Federal agents for illegal searches conducted in bad faith or without probable cause." S Rep No 588, 93d Cong, 2d Sess, 1974 USSCAN 2789, 2790. Although the extension was designed "as a counterpart to the *Bivens* case and its progeny, in that it waives the defense of sovereign immunity so as to make the Government independently liable in damages for the same type of conduct that is alleged to have occurred in *Bivens* (and for which that case imposes liability upon the individual Government officials involved)," id at 2791, the FTCA expressly preserved *Bivens* remedies as a supplement to common law tort liability, rather than suggesting (as the Court did in *Malesko*) that the availability of a common law remedy provides a basis for refusing to recognize a *Bivens* remedy.

See also, for example, the Senate Report on the Judicial Immunity Restoration Act, S Rep No 465, 101st Cong, 2d Sess 1990, 1990 WL 201715 at 2 ("In *Bivens*, 403 U.S. 388 (1971), the Supreme Court enunciated the doctrine of 'constitutional tort,' which subjects Federal officials to suits for violation of Federal constitutional rights in a manner equivalent to 42 U.S.C. 1983 actions against State officials.").

[57] See David A. Strauss, *Common Law Constitutional Interpretation*, 63 U Chi L Rev 877 (1996).

[58] Id at 891.

Bivens jurisprudence we have extended its holding only twice, to provide an otherwise non-existent cause of action against individual officers . . . , or to provide a cause of action for a plaintiff who lacked any alternative remedy for harms caused by an individual officer's unconstitutional conduct."[59] In particular, in emphasizing that the plaintiff is not "in search of a remedy as in *Bivens* or *Davis* [*v Passman*[60]]," his opinion gave prominence to a point that had been rejected (or whose rejection had at least been presupposed) in prior cases—that a constitutional tort remedy should be implied only when state remedies are inadequate.[61] The notion that a federal remedy for violation of a federal constitutional right should be withheld when state law supplies a remedy is in tension with both the constitutional understanding set forth nearly a century ago in *Home Telephone & Telegraph Co. v City of Los Angeles,*[62] and with at least four decades of constitutional tort litigation ushered in by the 1961 decision in *Monroe v Pape.*[63] Those decisions recognized that federal constitutional rights (*Home Telephone*) and federal remedies for violation of those rights (*Monroe*) do not depend upon what state law provides. And if *Home Telephone* and *Monroe* established those points with regard to action under color of state law, the *Bivens* decision followed and applied that same under-

---

[59] 122 S Ct at 521.

[60] 442 US 228 (1979).

[61] Id at 523. Indeed, this is clearest in the holding in *Carlson v Green*, 446 US 14 (1980), which upheld a *Bivens* action despite the availability of recovery against the United States under the Federal Tort Claims Act, see note 56.

It is true that, in *Carlson*, the Court suggested four ways in which the *Bivens* remedy might be more effective than the FTCA remedy: (a) an action against the individual wrongdoer is a more effective deterrent than an action against the government; (b) unlike the FTCA, the *Bivens* remedy permits punitive damages; (c) a *Bivens* plaintiff can opt for jury trial, unavailable under the FTCA; and (d) the FTCA applies only to conduct that would be actionable under state law if committed by a private person, whereas uniform federal rules govern the extent of *Bivens* liability. However, the Court failed to mention countervailing advantages of the FTCA remedy: that plaintiffs need not surmount the considerable barrier of qualified immunity, and that the United States is the ultimate deep pocket. Indeed, the Supreme Court has since found remedies to be adequate that have all of the "defects" of the FTCA that *Carlson* noted. See *Bush v Lucas,* 462 US 367 (1983) (upholding as an adequate substitute for a *Bivens* remedy a statutory scheme providing relief only against the government, without punitive damages or jury trial); *Parratt v Taylor,* 451 US 527 (1981) (upholding as an adequate state postdeprivation remedy, which provides all the process that is due, a state tort remedy similar to the FTCA in the respects noted above), overruled in part on other grounds by *Daniels v Williams,* 474 US 327 (1986).

[62] 227 US 278 (1913). But cf *Parratt,* 451 US 527; *Hart & Wechsler* at 1151–52 (cited in note 35).

[63] 365 US 167 (1961).

standing with regard to action under federal law. Equally fundamentally, *Bivens* was one of many landmark decisions recognizing that federal courts have authority to fashion appropriate remedies for violation of federal constitutional rights—a point explained cogently by Justice Harlan in his separate opinion in the *Bivens* case itself.[64] But the Chief Justice's opinion seems to throw back upon Congress primary responsibility for fashioning damages remedies for violations of federal rights.

Indeed, the approach suggested by *Malesko* would have required a very different analysis in the *Bivens* case itself. It is true that the Court's opinion in *Bivens* suggested that the Fourth Amendment often protects interests not protected by state law, and that "[t]he interests protected by state laws regulating trespass and the invasion of privacy, and those protected by the Fourth Amendment's guarantee against unreasonable searches and seizures, may be inconsistent or even hostile."[65] But the Court nowhere inquired whether, on the facts of the case, Webster Bivens could have obtained adequate redress under New York tort law. Given the allegations of flagrant misconduct in the case, it was quite possible, as the Second Circuit had noted in *Bivens*,[66] that the plaintiff could have sued successfully under state law for trespass and false imprisonment.[67] Thus, it is doubtful that the *Bivens* case itself fits the characterization that the *Malesko* opinion gives to the *Bivens* line of cases generally—cases in which the plaintiff "lacked any alternative remedy for harms caused by an individual officer's unconstitutional conduct."[68]

In *Malesko*, a concurrence by Justice Scalia, joined by Justice Thomas, went still further than the majority. Emphasizing (as the Court had mentioned) that *Bivens* was the product of an era in which the implication of remedies for violation of statutory rights was far more prevalent than it is today (when, under the Court's

---

[64] See 403 US at 398–411. See generally *Hart & Wechsler* at 847–77 (cited in note 35).

[65] 403 US at 394; see id at 391–94.

[66] See 409 F2d 718, 725 (2d Cir 1969).

[67] Before the Supreme Court in *Bivens*, the Solicitor General's Brief for the Respondents at 32–38 elaborated the New York State precedents that would support such recovery, as well as recovery for battery and mental distress. The Brief also stated that the United States may be liable, under the Federal Tort Claims Act, for trespasses committed by federal officers.

[68] 122 S Ct at 521.

decisions, implication is virtually never appropriate[69]), Justice Scalia found "even greater reason to abandon" the earlier approach "in the constitutional field, since an 'implication' imagined in the Constitution can presumably not even be repudiated by Congress."[70] (His premise that Congress lacks power to repudiate a *Bivens* action is hardly unassailable.[71]) Thus, he said that he would limit *Bivens, Davis v Passman,*[72] and *Carlson v Green*[73] "to the precise circumstances that they involved."[74]

If the *Bivens* decision once seemed, as a general matter, to extend constitutional tort remedies against federal officials as broadly as 42 USC § 1983 does against state and local officials,[75] and to confirm the authority of federal courts to fashion appropriate remedies for violation of federal constitutional rights, *Malesko* suggests that the future may look different. As support for the Court's decision, the Chief Justice, like Justice Scalia, referred to the Court's retreat, when considering remedies for *statutory* duties, from its earlier willingness to imply private rights of action.[76] That shift in approach did not lead immediately to wholesale repudiation of earlier decisions recognizing implied rights of action under federal statutes; instead, the Court said that those decisions were the product of a different era, in which Congress was legislating against a legal framework of far easier implication of private remedies, and that it was appropriate to take into account the "contemporary legal context" against which a particular statute was passed.[77] But the

---

[69] See, for example, *Alexander v Sandoval,* 532 US 275 (2001). See generally *Hart & Wechsler* at 840–41 (cited in note 35).

[70] 122 S Ct at 524.

[71] See, for example, Henry P. Monaghan, *Foreword: Constitutional Common Law,* 89 Harv L Rev 1 (1975); *Hart & Wechsler* at 876–77 (cited in note 35).

[72] 442 US 228 (1979) (recognizing an implied damages claim for an alleged violation of the Equal Protection Clause in the context of employment on a congressional staff).

[73] 446 US 14 (1980) (recognizing an implied right of action under the Cruel and Unusual Punishment Clause for failure to provide medical attention to a federal inmate).

[74] 122 S Ct at 524.

[75] See, for example, the Senate Report on the Judicial Immunity Restoration Act, S Rep No 465, 101st Cong, 2d Sess 1990, 1990 WL 201715 at 2 ("In *Bivens,* 403 U.S. 388 (1971), the Supreme Court enunciated the doctrine of 'constitutional tort,' which subjects Federal officials to suits for violation of Federal constitutional rights in a manner equivalent to 42 U.S.C. 1983 actions against State officials.").

[76] See id at 519 n 3; id at 523 (Scalia concurring).

[77] See *Merrill Lynch, Pierce, Fenner & Smith, Inc. v Curran,* 456 US 353, 378–79 (1982); *Cannon v University of Chicago,* 441 US 677, 698–99 (1979).

Court's most recent decision in this line, *Alexander v Sandoval*,[78] repudiated the view that earlier enactments should be interpreted under the legal standards in effect when the statute was passed. Thus, while the Court has yet to overturn a prior decision that, in an era of freer implication, had upheld such a remedy under a statutory scheme, *Sandoval* could be viewed as setting the stage for that possibility; and if that development in fact takes place, *Malesko* suggests that remedies for violations of constitutional duties may follow the same path.

II. Preemption and the Judicial Role

The decisions just discussed show that the Supreme Court's declarations about its lack of power to flesh out federal enactments extend over a broad range of subject matters. But as I have noted, such judicial passivity is not found uniformly in the Court's recent subconstitutional decisions. Far and away the most important set of recent decisions looking the other way—decisions in which the Court has been willing to engage in creative lawmaking to supplement positive law—are those involving statutory preemption of state and local law.

A. PREEMPTION JURISPRUDENCE

The Court's recent preemption decisions do not suggest that in formulating the appropriate rule of decision, courts should hew closely to textual directives in congressional statutes. Even such textualists and skeptics about federal common lawmaking as Justices Scalia and Thomas have said that " 'the existence of conflict cognizable under the Supremacy Clause does not depend on express congressional recognition that federal and state law may conflict.' "[79] To be sure, preemption can be based on express language in a statutory preemption clause,[80] but the preemptive effect of federal enactments reaches well beyond such textual directives.

Indeed, even where Congress has enacted an express preemption

---

[78] 532 US 275 (2001).

[79] *Crosby v National Foreign Trade Council*, 530 US 363, 390 (2000) (Scalia concurring in the judgment, joined by Thomas) (quoting id at 388 (majority opinion)).

[80] See, for example, *Lorillard Tobacco Co. v Reilly*, 533 US 525, 541 (2001); *Cipollone v Liggett Group, Inc.*, 505 US 504, 517 (1992).

clause, the Court has occasionally decided cases without relying upon it, resting instead on general preemption principles[81] or at least interpreting the specific language of a particular statute's preemption clause in light of those general principles.[82] In the same vein, when interpreting ERISA's preemption clause, which on its face reaches extraordinarily broadly, Justice Scalia himself has endorsed recent decisions refusing to give literal application to the statutory text. He argued that the statutory language, which calls for preemption of "all State laws insofar as they . . . relate to any employee benefit plan,"[83] "provides an illusory test, unless the Court is willing to decree a degree of pre-emption that no sensible person could have intended—which it is not."[84] In addition, the Court has not consistently taken textual preemption clauses to be exclusive: it has stressed that "at best," its body of preemption decisions "supports an inference that an express pre-emption clause forecloses implied pre-emption; it does not establish a rule."[85] Finally, the Court has affirmed that neither an express preemption provision nor a savings clause "bar[s] the ordinary working of conflict preemption principles."[86]

Thus, a robust set of implied preemption principles operates not only when a statute contains no express preemption clause but, often, even when it does. The principles are familiar ones. The Court recognizes so-called field preemption based on an "implication from the depth and breadth of a congressional scheme that

---

[81] See, for example, *Boggs v Boggs*, 520 US 833, 841 (1997); *Buckman Co. v Plaintiffs' Legal Comm.*, 531 US 341, 348 and n 2 (2001).

[82] See generally Karen A. Jordan, *The Shifting Preemption Paradigm: Conceptual and Interpretive Issues*, 51 Vand L Rev 1149, 1158–65 (1998).

[83] 29 USC § 1144(a).

[84] *California Div. of Labor Standards Enforcement v Dillingham Constr., N.A.*, 519 US 316, 335–36 (1997) (Scalia concurring).

[85] *Freightliner Corp. v Myrick*, 514 US 280, 289 (1995); see *Lorillard Tobacco Co.*, 533 US 525; *Geier v American Honda Motor Co., Inc.*, 529 US 861, 872 (2000). For discussion of the somewhat shifting approach to this question, see, for example, Jordan, 51 Vand L Rev at 1158–65 (cited in note 82).

[86] *Geier*, 529 US at 869; accord, *Buckman Co. v Plaintiffs' Legal Comm.*, 531 US 341, 352 (2001).
The Court's departure from textualism is no less true with respect to saving clauses. For example, when interpreting a statutory clause providing that the federal statute "does not exempt any person from any liability under the common law," the Court has "'decline[d] to give broad effect to saving clauses where doing so would upset the careful regulatory scheme established by federal law.'" See *Geier*, 529 US at 868, 870 (quoting *US v Locke*, 529 US 89, 106 (2000)).

occupies the legislative field" that states lack authority to regulate within that field.[87] More often, the Court recognizes what it calls conflict preemption, which displaces state law that "stands as an obstacle to the accomplishment of the full purposes and objectives of Congress."[88]

It is in the implied preemption cases, particularly the so-called conflict preemption cases, that the Court's approach contrasts most sharply with the judicial passivity exhibited elsewhere.[89] That contrast arises not merely from the fact that the Court's conflict preemption jurisprudence is untethered by statutory text, but also from the range of judicial policymaking that is involved in the application of conflict preemption principles. For state law is preempted not only in the situation in which compliance with both federal and state law is a physical impossibility—as would be true, for example, if state law called for judicial determination of certain contractual claims that, under the Federal Arbitration Act, must be determined by arbitration.[90] Indeed, cases in which it is truly impossible to comply with both state and federal law are exceedingly rare.[91]

Rather, the grist of implied preemption jurisprudence is supplied by cases in which the conflict between federal and state law is less stark and depends upon a judicial evaluation of statutory purpose. Consider, for example, *Geier v American Honda Motor Co.*[92] There, the Court first interpreted federal safety regulations as having the purpose of permitting auto manufacturers to choose among a range of passive restraint devices—airbags, automatic seat belts, or others. The Court then held that those regulations preempted a

---

[87] *Lorillard Tobacco Co.*, 533 US at 541; *Fidelity Federal Sav. & Loan Assn. v De la Cuesta*, 458 US 141, 153 (1982).

[88] *Gade v National Solid Wastes Mgmt. Ass'n*, 505 US 88, 98 (1992); see also, for example, *Lorillard Tobacco Co.*, 533 US at 541; *Geier*, 529 US at 869–74.

The Court has recognized that the categories of preemption that it conventionally recites in its opinions are not conceptually distinct. See *Crosby*, 530 US at 372 n 6 and sources cited.

[89] Caleb Nelson has noted that the distinction between express and implied preemption is elusive, as both forms of preemption are ways of giving meaning to a statute. See Caleb Nelson, *Preemption*, 86 Va L Rev 225, 263 (2000). That is true, of course, but express and implied rules rest on quite different interpretive methodologies, and what is notable is that the Court and particular Justices have endorsed implied preemption principles even though elsewhere they express their aversion to the interpretive methodology that underlies them.

[90] See, for example, *Southland Corp. v Keating*, 465 US 1 (1984).

[91] See, for example, Nelson, 86 Va L Rev at 228 n 15 (cited in note 89).

[92] 529 US 861 (2000).

tort action alleging that the defendant manufacturer had been negligent in failing to install airbags.[93] Plainly, the manufacturer could
have complied with both local negligence law and federal regulations by installing airbags, but in the Court's view, doing so would
have deprived it of the option, authorized by federal law, of relying
on other passive restraint devices. Given the Supreme Court's understanding of the federal regulations, *Geier* was a case of "logical
contradiction": when a federal statute authorizes an actor to do Y,
a state or locality may not prohibit Y (even though the actor could
comply with both regimes by not doing Y).[94]

But implied preemption reaches further still. Even when there
is no logical contradiction between federal and state law, the Court
has not hesitated to find what Caleb Nelson calls "obstacle" preemption. Adjudication of preemption claims resting on this basis
requires consideration of a range of policy-laden judgments that
cannot be accommodated to textual interpretation,[95] for the cases
"assume that Congress . . . would not intend to permit a significant
conflict," even when the text does not so provide.[96] Consider, for
example, *Crosby v National Foreign Trade Council*,[97] in which the
Court found that a federal statute imposing economic sanctions on
the nation of Myanmar (formerly Burma) preempted a somewhat
different set of sanctions imposed by the Commonwealth of Massachusetts. This finding of preemption did not rest on any textual
provision in the federal statute, which lacked any express preemption clause. It was not impossible for businesses to comply with
both the federal and state rules. Nor did the Court interpret the
federal act as authorizing specific conduct that the state prohibited.
Instead the Court found that the Massachusetts law presented an
obstacle to achievement of the purposes underlying the federal
statute, by impairing the President's ability to exercise the discre-

---

[93] The tort law involved in *Geier* was that of the District of Columbia rather than of a
state, but that the Court treated the District as on a par with a state for these purposes.

[94] See Nelson, 86 Va L Rev at 260 (cited in note 89).

Peter Strauss is critical of the *Geier* Court's outcome and of its understanding of federal
law, particularly in light of a savings clause in the federal statute. See Peter Strauss, *Courts
or Tribunals? Federal Courts and the Common Law*, 53 Ala L Rev 891, 917–20 (2002). For
present purposes, what is important is not whether the Court was right but rather the
interpretive approach that it followed.

[95] See Nelson, 86 Va L Rev at 278–87 (cited in note 89).

[96] *Geier*, 529 US at 885.

[97] 530 US 363 (2000).

tion that Congress had given him and thereby reducing the economic and diplomatic leverage that he could bring to bear on Myanmar. In so ruling, the Court stated that "[w]hat is a sufficient obstacle is a matter of judgment, to be informed by examining the federal statute as a whole and identifying its purpose and intended effects. . . ."[98] Whether one views this approach as a broad form of statutory interpretation or a form of federal common lawmaking—the boundary between the two is anything but distinct[99]—it depends on a judicial role entirely different from that underlying the four decisions discussed above.

Another recent preemption decision that exemplifies the same kind of judicial role is *Buckman Co. v Plaintiff's Legal Committee*,[100] a state law fraud action based on the claim that a manufacturer of federally regulated medical devices had defrauded the FDA. The Court ruled that to permit that state law action to proceed would impair the operation of the federal regulatory scheme: it would increase the burdens on applicants beyond those that Congress had contemplated, deter "off-label" use of medical devices that Congress did not wish to deter, and burden the FDA with additional and unwanted information. The Court's conclusion, then, was that state law conflicted not with any textual provision but rather with purposes that the Court ascribed to federal regulation[101]—so much so that the Court decided the case on that basis, without even considering whether the express preemption provision found in the Food and Drug Act applied. Consider how hard that approach is to square with the statement in *Great-West Life* that " 'vague notions of a statute's "basic purpose" are nonetheless inadequate to overcome the words of its text regarding the *specific* issue under consideration.' "[102]

It should be clear that one cannot view preemption decisions merely as straightforward applications of the Supremacy Clause.

---

[98] Id at 373.

[99] See *Hart & Wechsler* at 755–56 (cited in note 35). For a discussion of the close relationship between preemption principles and federal common lawmaking, see Monaghan, 89 Harv L Rev at 12–13 & n 69 (cited in note 71).

[100] 531 US 341 (2001).

[101] The Court also reasoned that policing fraud directed at federal regulatory agencies is an inherently federal matter, so as to make any presumption against preemption inappropriate. Id at 347. But that conclusion, too, is based on a policy-based inference rather than on a textual directive.

[102] See text accompanying note 17.

That Clause provides only that *if* state law conflicts with federal law, federal law prevails; it supplies a rule of priority,[103] but its operation requires prior identification of the rule of federal law with which state law is said to conflict. In implied preemption cases like *Crosby* and *Buckman*, that rule of decision is not found in statutory text, but instead is essentially fashioned by the court as a matter of federal common law.[104]

The Court's willingness to engage in this kind of judicial lawmaking is no minor matter. In the 1999, 2000, and 2001 Terms, the Court decided twelve preemption cases,[105] a significant portion of the Court's docket in nonconstitutional cases. Indeed, it has been suggested that of all the questions concerning gaps in federal regulatory statutes, preemption issues "arise more frequently than any other recurring statutory issue,"[106] as virtually every federal statute preempts some state laws.[107] And while some of the Court's

---

[103] See Nelson, 86 Va L Rev at 252 (cited in note 89); Monaghan, 89 Harv L Rev at 22 n 116 (cited in note 71).

[104] Indeed, many decisions conventionally viewed as implied preemption decisions do not differ in substance from a decision like *Boyle v United Technologies Corp.*, 487 US 500 (1988) (recognizing a federal common law defense to state tort liability for federal military contractors), which is conventionally viewed as a federal common law decision. Both preclude state law from operating in whatever domain preemption, or the federal common law defense, is thought to operate. See Richard H. Fallon, Jr., Daniel J. Meltzer, and David L. Shapiro, *Hart & Wechsler's The Federal Courts and the Federal System* 723–29 (Foundation, 5th ed, 2003); Nelson, 86 Va L Rev at 278–79 (cited in note 89); Viet D. Dinh, *Reassessing the Law of Preemption*, 88 Georgetown L J 2085, 2107–09 (2000).

Jack Goldsmith has suggested that federal common lawmaking is a more significant matter than preemption, for the former "authorizes courts to go beyond mere preemption of state authority and actually 'legislate' the federal rule of decision." Jack Goldsmith, *Statutory Foreign Affairs Preemption*, 2000 Supreme Court Review 175, 204. It may often be true that the range of judicial discretion is relatively narrower in preemption cases, as only two options exist (to preempt or not), whereas in what Goldsmith would call federal common law decisions, there may be more than two options about how to formulate a rule of decision (e.g., about the precise circumstances in which there might be a medical necessity defense, or the scope of a damages remedy for violation of a constitutional duty). That contrast, however, can be overdrawn, for in preemption cases there are often difficult questions about the scope of preemption. In any event, the more fundamental point remains: whatever the bounds of judicial discretion, in both kinds of cases the federal courts are engaged in a kind of policymaking analysis rather than in textual interpretation, and in both cases the judgments they reach may be quite debatable.

[105] See cases cited in notes 108–09. See also *Verizon Maryland Inc. v Pub. Serv. Comm'n of Maryland*, 122 S Ct 1753 (2002) (upholding jurisdiction of federal court to entertain telecommunication carrier's claim that the order of a state utility commission requiring reciprocal compensation for telephone calls to Internet Service Providers violates federal law, without reaching the merits of that claim).

[106] Gregory E. Maggs, *Reducing the Costs of Statutory Ambiguity: Alternative Approaches and the Federal Courts Study Committee*, 29 Harv J Leg 123, 150 (1992).

[107] Id.

recent decisions rested exclusively or primarily on express preemption clauses in federal enactments,[108] at least an equal number involved the application of implied preemption principles.[109]

Especially notable in preemption cases is the departure of the Court—and, notably, of Justices who embrace textualism—from the interpretive approach that they otherwise endorse. If, as Justice Scalia said, the statutory reach of ERISA's preemption clause provides an "illusory test, unless the Court is willing to decree a degree of pre-emption that no sensible person could have intended,"[110] why doesn't his interpretation of the availability of equitable remedies in *Great-West Life* restrict the enforceability of subrogation clauses to an extent that no sensible person could have intended? Or, to make a similar point, if federal courts have power to fashion federal common law rules calling for preemption—whether or not a statute has an express preemption clause—why cannot federal courts seeking to implement a statutory scheme fashion a different kind of federal common law rule—whether it is a federal right of recovery in *Great-West Life* or a defense to a federal criminal prosecution in the *Oakland Cannabis* case?

B. JUDICIAL SELECTIVITY

The implied preemption cases provide an interesting counterpoint to two different trends. The first contrast is between the

[108] See *Lorillard Tobacco Co.*, 533 US 525; *Egelhoff v Egelhoff*, 532 US 141 (2001); *Norfolk Southern Ry. Co. v Shanklin*, 529 US 344 (2000); *Rush Prudential HMO, Inc. v Moran*, 122 S Ct 2151 (2002). See also *Pegram v Herdrich*, 530 US 211, 236–37 (2000) (referring only incidentally to ERISA's preemption clause in holding that mixed eligibility decisions by HMO physicians are not fiduciary decisions under ERISA, and, accordingly, that ERISA does not preempt state law malpractice and fraud claims about such physicians).

[109] See, for example, *Buckman Co. v Plaintiff's Legal Committee*, 531 US 341, 352 (2001); *Crosby*, 530 US 363; *Geier*, 529 US 861; *Locke*, 529 US 89. See also *Raygor v Regents of the University of Minnesota*, 534 US 533 (2002) (interpreting tolling provision of federal supplemental jurisdiction statute as inapplicable to claims against unconsenting states that are dismissed under the Eleventh Amendment, 28 USC 1367, and thus holding that federal law does not preempt application of state statute of limitations); *Circuit City Stores, Inc. v Adams*, 532 US 105 (2001) (interpreting the Federal Arbitration Act as applicable to employment contracts other than for transportation workers, and thus as preempting state law insofar as it calls for judicial determination of state law employment discrimination claim); *City of Columbus v Ours Garage and Wrecker Serv.*, 122 S Ct 2226 (2002) (holding that a savings clause in federal statute that exempts from a statutory preemption clause specified regulations promulgated by a state also exempts such regulations when promulgated by a locality under authority delegated by the state).

[110] *Dillingham Constr., N.A.*, 519 US at 335–36.

approach taken by individual Justices in preemption cases and the approach that the same Justices take to issues of *constitutional* federalism.[111] In its decisions that limit the scope of Congress's legislative power under Article I and under § 5 of the Fourteenth Amendment,[112] elaborate an anticommandeering principle,[113] and recognize a broad constitutional doctrine of state sovereign immunity,[114] the Court's majority seeks to promote and protect state autonomy.[115] A freewheeling preemption jurisprudence, by contrast, limits state autonomy, and, as my colleague Richard Fallon recently noted, of thirty-five preemption cases decided since Justice Thomas joined the Court, nearly two-thirds found state law preempted in whole or in part.[116] The five Justices most protective of state autonomy in constitutional federalism cases are the Justices who most often join opinions finding state laws preempted; of eight non-unanimous preemption decisions in the 1999, 2000, and 2001 Terms, Justice Scalia voted to preempt in all eight, the Chief Justice and Justices O'Connor and Kennedy in seven each, and Justice Thomas in six. By contrast, the four Justices most supportive of national authority in constitutional federalism cases are those who most often vote to uphold state activity that has been challenged as in conflict with national programs; in those same eight

---

[111] This contrast has been much noted. See, for example, Nelson, 86 Va L Rev at 229 (cited in note 89); Richard Fallon, The *"Conservative" Paths of the Rehnquist Court's Federalism Decisions*, 69 U Chi L Rev 429, 432 (2001); Frank B. Cross, *Realism About Federalism*, 74 NYU L Rev 1304, 1310 (1999); Dinh, 88 Georgetown L J at 2087 (cited in note 104); David B. Spence and Paula Murray, *The Law, Economics, and Politics of Federal Preemption Jurisprudence: A Quantitative Analysis*, 87 Cal L Rev 1125, 1128–30 (1999); Calvin Massey, *Federalism and the Rehnquist Court*, 53 Hastings L J 431, 464 (2002).

[112] See, for example, *Board of Trustees of University of Alabama v Garrett*, 531 US 356 (2001); *United States v Morrison*, 529 US 598 (2000); *College Sav. Bank v Florida Prepaid Postsecondary Educ. Expense Bd.*, 527 US 666 (1999); *City of Boerne v Flores*, 521 US 507 (1997); *United States v Lopez*, 514 US 549 (1995).

[113] See, for example, *Printz v United States*, 521 US 898, 935 (1997); *New York v United States*, 505 US 144 (1992).

[114] See, for example, *Alden v Maine*, 527 US 706 (1999); *Seminole Tribe of Florida v Florida*, 517 US 44 (1996); see also *Garrett*, 531 US 356, and *Florida Prepaid*, 527 US 666.

[115] See, for example, Massey, 53 Hastings L J at 464 (cited in note 111); Daniel J. Meltzer, *State Sovereign Immunity: Five Authors in Search of a Theory*, 75 Notre Dame L Rev 1011, 1050–51 (2000); John C. Yoo, *Sounds of Sovereignty: Defining Federalism in the 1990s*, 32 Ind L Rev 27 (1998).

[116] Fallon, 69 U Chi L Rev at 462 (cited in note 111). See also Joondeph, 62 Ohio St L J at 1795 (cited in note 1) (reporting that since Justice Thomas was confirmed, of twenty preemption cases where the lower courts had divided, the Supreme Court found preemption in twelve and partial preemption in two others).

cases, Justices Souter, Ginsburg, and Breyer each voted to preempt only twice and Justice Stevens never voted to preempt.[117]

A second contrast, and the one on which I will focus primarily, lies entirely at the subconstitutional level. That contrast is between the more freewheeling judicial approach in the preemption decisions and the broad declarations of judicial passivity in the four cases that I described at the outset. In all four of those decisions, the Chief Justice and Justices O'Connor, Scalia, Kennedy, and Thomas joined in the Court's declarations of its powerlessness to fashion a rule of decision,[118] although those same Jus-

---

[117] The following table shows the votes of the various Justices in preemption decisions in the 1999, 2000, and 2001 Terms of the Court. The Justices are identified by first and last initial, in order of seniority. "Y" is a vote to preempt, "N" a vote not to preempt.

Name of Decision	WR	JS	SO	AS	AK	DS	CT	RG	SB
City of Columbus v Ours Garage and Wrecker Service, Inc., 122 S Ct 2226 (2002)	N	N	Y	Y	N	N	N	N	N
Rush Prudential HMO, Inc. v Moran, 122 S Ct 2151 (2002)	Y	N	N	Y	Y	N	Y	N	N
Raygor v Regents of Univ. of Minnesota, 534 US 533 (2002)	Y	N	Y	Y	Y	N	Y	Y	N
Lorillard Tobacco Co. v Reilly, 533 US 525 (2001)	Y	N	Y	Y	Y	N	Y	N	N
Egelhoff v Egelhoff, 532 US 141 (2001)	Y	N	Y	Y	Y	Y	Y	Y	N
Circuit City Stores, Inc. v Adams, 532 US 105 (2001)	Y	N	Y	Y	Y	N	Y	N	N
Buckman Co. v Plaintiffs' Legal Committee, 531 US 341 (2001)	Y	Y	Y	Y	Y	Y	Y	Y	Y
Crosby v National Foreign Trade Council, 530 US 363 (2000)	Y	Y	Y	Y	Y	Y	Y	Y	Y
Pegram v Herdrich, 530 US 211 (2000)	N	N	N	N	N	N	N	N	N
Geier v American Honda Motor Co., Inc., 529 US 861 (2002)	Y	N	Y	Y	Y	N	N	N	Y
Norfolk Southern Ry. Co. v Shanklin, 529 US 344 (2000)	Y	N	Y	Y	Y	Y	Y	N	Y
United States v Locke, 529 US 89 (2000)	Y	Y	Y	Y	Y	Y	Y	Y	Y
Total votes for preemption (out of 12 decisions)	10	3	10	11	10	5	9	5	5

---

[118] In only one of them (*Garris*) did any of the four "liberal" Justices (Justice Stevens) join the majority opinion without qualification; otherwise, the four liberals either dissented or concurred in the judgment or in part. (Justice Breyer did not participate in the *Oakland Cannabis* decision.)

tices are the ones who most freely find that a federal statute implicitly preempts federal law. The contrast in rationales is all the more striking because in one important respect—the extent to which they interfere with state autonomy—the preemption decisions might be viewed as occasions for less rather than more free-wheeling judicial intervention. And it would be just as possible in preemption as in other cases for the Justices to adopt a passive approach, saying that it is for Congress to specify whatever preemptive effect it wishes a statute to have.

How can one explain this notable contrast in judicial attitude? Not, I believe, on the basis that the questions at issue in the preemption cases are necessarily more important than those in the cases exhibiting greater passivity. Rather, I want to suggest that preemption analysis appears to engage the sympathies of all of the Justices, but particularly those in the majority. As a result, those Justices seem to appreciate the need for broader judicial lawmaking in preemption cases, to ensure that congressional purposes are not undercut by judicial passivity. However, that need for judicial harmonization is hardly unique to preemption cases; it exists elsewhere, but perhaps it is easier for those Justices to overlook insofar as the congressional purposes that would be served have less appeal.

1. *Result-orientation.* One possible explanation for the difference in approach lies in the fact that a claim of federal preemption ordinarily serves as an actual or potential defense to state law liability. The Court seems more willing, at least in civil cases, to recognize federal common law defenses to potential liability under state law than to recognize affirmative rights of recovery.[119] If one assumes, albeit somewhat crudely, that conservative Justices are more likely to be ideologically predisposed against government regulation, the differing results in preemption cases may not be entirely surprising: preemption, after all, invalidates governmental regulation at the state or local level.[120]

---

[119] See, for example, *Boyle*, 487 US 500 (1988) (recognizing a federal common law defense to state tort liability for federal military contractors).

[120] One might seek to test this kind of crude explanation against the background of related developments in administrative law. For example, Jerry Mashaw has suggested that the *Chevron* doctrine, see *Chevron USA, Inc. v NRDC, Inc.*, 467 US 837, 865–66 (1984), is at odds with the view that plain meaning methodology (particularly with respect to the refusal to recognize implied rights of action) serves to undermine liberal statutes. For *Chevron*, he suggests, "supports the broad policy discretion of the implementors of the positive or wel-

Ruth Colker and Kevin Scott have recently argued that for most of the Justices, the willingness to invalidate state action (whether on the ground of statutory preemption or on constitutional grounds) relates to whether the state action is viewed as "liberal" or "conservative" in orientation, and that conservative ideology may cause Justices who are generally pro-federalist to invalidate state action.[121] They find, in addition, that Chief Justice Rehnquist and Justices Scalia, Kennedy, and Thomas are significantly more likely to vote to invalidate state action on the ground of preemption than on other grounds.[122] Richard Fallon, in an insightful though less quantitative analysis, found that "when federalism and substantive conservatism come into conflict, substantive conservatism frequently dominates."[123]

---

fare state." See Jerry L. Mashaw, *Textualism, Constitutionalism, and the Interpretation of Federal Statutes*, 32 Wm & Mary L Rev 827, 834 (1991). Of course, as Mashaw proceeds to elaborate, matters are more complex than that: one important dimension is the distribution of views among regulators, on the one hand, and lower court judges on the other. The political valence of *Chevron* may look different in an era of conservative regulators and liberal judges (which may have been the situation in 1984) than one featuring liberal regulators and a more conservative judiciary (which may have been the situation ten years later). See id at 834–35.

The Court appears to some to have been narrowing the reach of *Chevron* in recent years, either by overturning agency interpretations of statutes that did not seem clearly to conflict with the statutory text, see, for example, *FDA v Brown & Williamson Tobacco Corp.*, 529 US 120 (2000); *MCI v AT&T*, 512 US 218 (1994), or by holding that *Chevron* deference does not apply to certain kinds of informal agency decisions, see *United States v Mead Corp.*, 533 US 218 (2001). An observer who believes strongly in the explanatory power of result-orientation might explain that development as permitting greater scrutiny, by a judiciary heavily influenced by twelve years of Republican appointments, of liberal regulatory initiatives undertaken during the Clinton administration.

For conflicting views of whether judges on the District of Columbia Circuit use *Chevron* deference selectively to further ideological goals, see Richard L. Revesz, *Environmental Regulation, Ideology, and the D.C. Circuit*, 83 Va L Rev 1717 (1997); Frank B. Cross and Emerson H. Tiller, *Judicial Partisanship and Obedience to Legal Doctrine: Whistleblowing on the Federal Courts of Appeals*, 107 Yale L J 2155, 2168–72 (1998); see also Harry T. Edwards, *Collegiality and Decisionmaking on the D.C. Circuit*, 84 Va L Rev 1335 (1998) (contesting "political" accounts of judging on the D.C. Circuit); Note, *Disagreement in D.C.: The Relationship Between the Supreme Court and the D.C. Circuit and Its Implications for a National Court of Appeals*, 59 NYU L Rev 1048, 1066 n 95 (1984).

[121] Ruth Colker and Kevin M. Scott, *Dissing States? Invalidation of State Action During the Rehnquist Era*, 88 Va L Rev 1301, 1343–45 (2002).

[122] Id at 1342.

[123] See Fallon, 69 U Chi L Rev at 434 (cited in note 111); see also Frank B. Cross and Emerson Tiller, *The Three Faces of Federalism: An Empirical Assessment of Supreme Court Federalism Jurisprudence*, 73 S Cal L Rev 741, 760–62 (2000) (finding that conservative and liberal Justices were more likely to use federalism to support conservative and liberal plaintiffs, respectively, and more likely to use it to defeat liberal and conservative plaintiffs, respectively).

The *Oakland Cannabis* case does not necessarily conflict with that view. Though it was strictly a civil case, the defendants could be viewed as in essentially the same position as criminal defendants, seeking to limit the application of federal drug prohibitions. The defendants were thus advancing a "liberal" position, and one that was rejected by a conservative majority.

To the extent that the Supreme Court's approach to fashioning law varies on the basis of whether, to put it crudely, the rule favors civil plaintiffs or civil defendants, one argument sometimes offered to justify that variation is that upholding a plaintiff's right to sue under federal law carries with it a right to invoke federal court jurisdiction, whereas fashioning a federal defense does not. (The difference results from determining the existence of "arising under" jurisdiction on the basis of a well-pleaded complaint.[124]) The argument continues by asserting that in our system of checks and balances, the federal courts should not determine the extent of their jurisdiction; that decision is for Congress.[125]

The proffered justification falls short, however, descriptively, conceptually, and normatively. Descriptively, it turns out that at the same time that the Court has declared its unwillingness to recognize implied rights of action (typically in actions by one private party against another), it has consistently recognized a particular kind of implied right of action—that asserted by plaintiffs (often businesses) seeking a federal court injunction against officials charged with enforcing state or local laws to which the plaintiff is subject and which the plaintiff alleges to be preempted. Recognition of that implied right of action permits such cases to be brought in federal court under the "arising under" jurisdiction,[126] rather than requiring the regulatee to await state court enforcement and then proffer a federal defense to the enforcement action (a posture that would not be removable under the federal question jurisdiction). Just last Term, in *Verizon Maryland Inc. v Public Service Commission of Maryland*,[127] the Court reiterated that the plain-

---

[124] See *Hart & Wechsler* at 907–13 (cited in note 35).

[125] See, for example, *Cannon v University of Chicago*, 441 US 677, 730–31 (1979) (Powell dissenting); Mashaw, 32 Wm & Mary L Rev at 842–43 (cited in note 120).

[126] The leading precedent, because the most explicit, is *Shaw v Delta Air Lines, Inc.*, 463 US 85 (1983), but it is hardly the first. See, for example, *Ray v Atlantic Richfield Co.*, 435 US 151 (1978); *Hines v Davidowitz*, 312 US 52 (1941).

[127] 122 S Ct 1753, 1758 (2002).

tiff's claim that state regulation "is pre-empted by a federal statute
. . . presents a federal question which the federal courts have jurisdiction under 28 USC § 1331 to resolve."[128] Thus, it is not the
case that the Court has refused to fashion federal common law
rules when doing so provides the basis for the exercise of federal
jurisdiction.[129]

Beyond the descriptive problem lies a conceptual one. "[L]iti-
gants do not come labeled as 'plaintiffs' and 'defendants' as a matter of preexisting Platonic reality," and "[w]hether one is a plaintiff
or a defendant * * * is itself contingent, a product of our remedial
and substantive rules."[130] Thus, a business contending that state
law is preempted may be a defendant (in a state law enforcement
action brought either by an injured party or by the state itself) or
a plaintiff (in a federal action seeking to enjoin enforcement of
state or local regulations). It cannot be that a court may decide a
preemption issue in the first situation but may not decide the identical issue in the second because recognizing a right to injunctive
relief, through which the preemption issue would be decided,
would carry in its wake federal question jurisdiction.

Normatively, it is difficult to defend a pattern of federal common lawmaking on the basis that the Court seeks to avoid expanding federal court jurisdiction. The point is not merely that it
is difficult to justify a substantive tilt in favor of federal common
law defenses and against federal rights of action.[131] For suppose

---

[128] Id at 1758 (quoting *Shaw v Delta Air Lines, Inc.*, 463 US 85, 96 n 14 (1983)). Although
the majority treated the case as one, like *Shaw*, involving a claim that state law was preempted, in fact the claim was (in the words of Justice Souter's concurring opinion) that
"the Maryland Public Service Commission has wrongly decided a question of federal law
under a decisional power conferred by" a federal statute. 122 S Ct at 1763 (Souter concurring).

[129] To be sure, the Supreme Court ruled in 1989 that many if not most suits seeking
injunctions against state regulation alleged to be preempted could be brought under 42
USC § 1983, an express federal right of action. See *Golden State Transit Corp. v City of Los
Angeles*, 493 US 103 (1989). Hence, from today's vantage point, one might claim that it
was Congress, not the courts, that opened the doors of the federal courthouse to claims
of preemption. But long before the *Golden State* decision, the Court had upheld *implied*
rights of action by plaintiffs seeking to enjoin state or local regulation as preempted, and
indeed has continued to recognize this line of authority in upholding jurisdiction. See note
126 and accompanying text. And the *Verizon* decision, though it came thirteen years after
the *Golden State* decision, did not even mention § 1983.

[130] *Hart & Wechsler* at 912 (cited in note 35).

[131] Of course, the potential pattern of federal common law rules is more complicated than
claims and defenses. For example, federal common law might negate a state law defense
to a federal statutory claim, which would both help plaintiffs and not create federal district
court jurisdiction that did not already exist. See, for example, *Dice v Akron, Canton & Youngs-*

that Congress amended the jurisdictional statutes to permit federal defense removal (as many have recommended).[132] It seems doubtful that recognition of federal common law defenses (as in many preemption cases, or, to take a different example, as in *Boyle v United Technologies Corp*.[133]) would become less appropriate because it would now confer federal question jurisdiction on removal. (Nor does it seem that prior rulings would have to be overturned because they now would have jurisdictional consequences.) *Per contra*, if, as was true until 1875,[134] there were no general federal question jurisdiction, it seems doubtful that recognition (presumably by state courts of general jurisdiction) of implied rights of action to enforce federal statutory or constitutional provisions would become more appropriate because suit could not be filed in or removed to federal court.

The deepest concerns about federal common lawmaking, or about a broad judicial role in statutory interpretation, relate not to federal question jurisdiction but rather to the allocation of lawmaking authority and its possible impact on state autonomy. In this respect, the Court's endorsement of preemption decisions, which involve not only judicial policymaking but also the prohibition of state regulatory authority, is particularly striking.[135] One would expect that Justices sympathetic to protecting state sovereignty would be particularly disinclined to engage in purposive, nontextual interpretation of a federal statute[136] where the effect of this form of lawmaking is to displace otherwise valid exercises of state and local regulatory authority. But, as previously noted, the pattern is just the reverse.

---

town R.R. Co., 342 US 359 (1952) (disallowing, as a matter of federal common law, a state law defense—that the plaintiff, in signing a fraudulently obtained release, had relinquished his rights—to a federal claim).

[132] See, for example, American Law Institute, Study of the Division of Jurisdiction Between State and Federal Courts, proposed § 1312, at 187–207 (1968) (proposing that removal be permitted for federal defenses (other than lack of personal jurisdiction or failure to comply with the constitutional or statutory requirements of full faith and credit) that would be "dispositive of the action," id at 197); Donald L. Doernberg, *There's No Reason for It; It's Just Our Policy: Why the Well-Pleaded Complaint Rule Sabotages the Purposes of Federal Question Jurisdiction*, 38 Hastings L J 597 (1987).

[133] 487 US 500 (1988) (recognizing a federal common law defense to state tort liability for federal military contractors).

[134] See *Hart & Wechsler* at 878–80 (cited in note 35).

[135] Compare *Boyle*, 487 US at 517 n 2 (Brennan dissenting).

[136] See, for example, Jordan, 51 Vand L Rev at 1201–28 (cited in note 82).

2. *Preemption and the need for judicial implementation.* The result-oriented explanation clearly has some force, but one should be careful not to overstate its significance. First, four of the twelve recent preemption decisions were unanimous.[137] Second, where the Justices divided, they sometimes did not do so in ways that would be predictable to those using attitudinal models of judicial behavior.[138] Third, despite some cases featuring sharp divisions among the Justices about the preemptive effect of a particular statutory scheme,[139] the opinions did not include broadside denunciations of judicial lawmaking. Indeed, one of the most striking features of the preemption decisions is that all of the Justices appear to accept as common ground a broad judicial role in formulating rules of decision that are not tied to statutory text, as well as the general preemption principles that are to be applied in each case.

Although one cannot be at all certain why that role is accepted as a matter of course in preemption decisions but not elsewhere, I would offer this hypothesis: the Justices, when they recognize the importance of a particular federal objective, are alert to the need to assume a more common-law like role to ensure that the objective is not threatened and to harmonize a complex body of federal and state law. Preemption issues present a particularly strong case for a robust judicial role.[140] The aspiration to have Congress resolve all issues relating to a statutory scheme up front seems particularly misplaced, or at least overly optimistic, in the preemption context. Even a Congress aware that a new enactment may present preemption issues and eager to try to resolve them would find it enormously difficult to specify in advance which of the common law and statutory rules of fifty states (and, in some

---

[137] See *Locke*, 529 US 89; *Buckman Co.*, 531 US 341; *Crosby*, 530 US 363; *Pegram v Herd-rich*, 530 US 211 (2000).

[138] See, for example, *Geier*, 529 US 861 (where Justice Stevens's dissent from the finding of preemption was joined by Justices Souter, Thomas, and Ginsburg); *City of Columbus*, 122 S Ct 2226 (where only Justices O'Connor and Scalia voted to preempt); *Raygor*, 534 US 533 (where Justice Ginsburg joined the "conservatives" in voting to preempt). Accord, Strauss, 53 Ala L Rev at 907 (cited in note 94).

[139] See, for example, *Moran*, 122 S Ct 2151 (5–4).

[140] That fact may also help to explain why proposals in Congress generally to restrict the judicial role in finding federal preemption have not been enacted. See, for example, S 1214, 106th Cong (1999), which would have provided that no statute enacted thereafter should be construed to have any preemptive effect unless (i) the statute expressly states otherwise, or (ii) there is a "direct conflict" between the statute and the preempted measure "so that the two cannot be reconciled or consistently stand together."

cases, of tens of thousands of localities) should be displaced. Such a task would require not merely the identification of all such laws with which a federal statutory scheme may intersect, but also careful thought about the way(s) in which each such state or local law might be applied and the compatibility of such applications with the federal statutory program. If that were not daunting enough, Congress would also have to anticipate the range of laws not yet passed that might in the future come into conflict with a federal statutory scheme.

The difficulties and burdens of such an undertaking would be overwhelming. Congress would have to analyze and pass judgment upon many possible applications of state law that may never materialize in practice. And each potential intersection of state and federal law would have to be examined with something of the careful attention to pertinent facts and argumentation that the adversary process can provide when a preemption question has crystallized in litigation. Congress would then have to develop an adequate verbal formulation that would properly distinguish the applications of state law that should be preempted from those that should not be. It is little wonder that the Court has not thought it realistic to expect Congress to specify the preemptive effect of federal enactments to this degree.

But while not all areas of federal law are equally complex, the difficulties just mentioned in the preemption area are hardly discontinuous with those in other areas. ERISA is a prime example: the issue in *Great-West Life* is only one of many important and unexpected questions that have arisen under that complex scheme. Even necessity defenses like the one at issue in *Oakland Cannabis*, though they arise rather infrequently, can pose difficult issues that are hard to anticipate by statutory formulation.[141] Preemption

---

[141] For example, the Model Penal Code's provision on necessity (section 3.02), resting on starkly consequentialist premises, provides that:

Conduct that the actor believes to be necessary to avoid a harm or evil to himself or to another is justifiable, provided that:
(a) the harm or evil sought to be avoided by such conduct is greater than that sought to be prevented by the law defining the offense charged; and
(b) neither the Code nor other law defining the offense provides exceptions or defenses dealing with the specific situation involved; and
(c) a legislative purpose to exclude the justification claimed does not otherwise plainly appear.

It has never been clear to me why this provision would not by its terms privilege the conduct in a famous example given by Judith Thomson, that of a surgeon who kills an

cases, that is, do not uniquely call for a robust judicial role; they are continuous with the problems that arise in other areas. What is not continuous is the Court's approach to lawmaking across different areas.

III. The Limits of Congressional Capacity

If I am right that the Court's recent decisions reflect an inconsistency about the judicial role in subconstitutional cases, what is the proper approach? My submission is that the burden of fashioning the pertinent rules of decision with regard to the implementation of positive federal law is not sensibly placed on the national legislature alone. Plainly, a complex set of political and institutional arguments bear on this question. My approach will be somewhat suggestive, seeking to meld concrete examples to broader observations without essaying a comprehensive review of the voluminous literature and arguments that bear on this matter.

A. WHY CONGRESS?

The conventional arguments in favor of leaving matters to Congress—arguments for a narrow, textual approach to statutory interpretation and against a generous conception of federal common lawmaking—are straightforward. One set of arguments is political and constitutional: Congress is democratically accountable; its lawmaking processes are expressly recognized in Article I, Section 7; and those processes, structured by the separation of powers and federalism, protect against improvident legal regulation and, more distinctively, against incursions by the national government on the authority of the states. A second set of arguments relates to comparative advantage: Congress has a range of expertise, as well as a capacity to make necessarily arbitrary decisions, that courts lack. Relatedly, particular decisions, if left to courts, may be resolved differently from the way that the legislature would have resolved

---

innocent person in order to harvest his organs, thereby saving the lives of five persons in need of organ transplants and who otherwise would perish. See Judith Jarvis Thomson, *Rights, Restitution, and Risk* 94–116 (Harvard, 1986). But, as Eric Rakowski notes, "nobody, to my knowledge, would condone trading one life for five" in this situation. Eric Rakowski, *Taking and Saving Lives*, 93 Colum L Rev 1063, 1064 (1993).

them had it done so itself.[142] A final set of arguments relates to the smooth operation of the legal system: legislative resolution of questions up front clarifies the law, and spares lawyers, clients, and the legal system the costs of uncertainty (including all of the planning, legal research, and litigation necessary to respond to or to eliminate uncertainty).[143]

Given that the line between statutory interpretation and federal common lawmaking is indistinct,[144] it would make little sense to address only purposive interpretation or federal common lawmaking rather than both. Thus, it is not a surprise, for example, to find Justice Scalia, the avatar of textual interpretation and the author of the *Great-West Life* decision, writing that in the federal courts, "with a qualification so small it does not bear mentioning, there is no such thing as common law."[145] Although Justice Scalia has not been a purist in refusing to formulate federal common law,[146] the general resistance that he has expressed to judge-made rules of decision underlies not only the *Malesko* decision but also the broad and gratuitous dicta in *Oakland Cannabis* and *Norfolk Shipbuilding*.

In many respects, it is hard to disagree with the aspiration to have legislatures resolve matters up front. Who, after all, wishes to embrace incomplete legislation or statutory ambiguity as an objective? And some efforts to increase the scope of advance legislative specification seem entirely salutary. For example, Congress, acting in 1990 in response to a recommendation of the Federal Courts Study Committee,[147] enacted a general four-year statute of limitations for all civil actions "arising under an Act of Congress enacted after the date of the enactment of this section" that do not themselves specify a limitations period for particular rights of action.[148] Congress, unlike the courts, has the capacity to select a

---

[142] See Robert Katzmann, *Courts and Congress* 48–49 (Brookings Institution, 1997).

[143] See Maggs, 29 Harv J Leg at 126–30 (cited in note 106).

[144] See text accompanying note 99.

[145] Antonin Scalia, *A Matter of Interpretation: Federal Courts and the Law* 12 (Princeton, 1997).

[146] See, for example, note 104 (discussing *Boyle v United Technologies Corp.*, 487 US 500 (1988), and text accompanying note 156 (discussing *Semtek International, Inc. v Lockheed Martin Corp.*, 531 US 497 (2001))—both majority opinions authored by Justice Scalia.

[147] See Report of the Federal Courts Study Committee 93–94 (1990).

[148] 28 USC § 1658. Indeed, the Congress might have gone further still. Section 1658 does not address the question of what statute of limitation should govern civil actions

necessarily arbitrary time period. And although a careful analysis of the nature of different causes of action might lead an intelligent lawgiver to prescribe different limitation periods for each, the alternative to congressional selection of a uniform four-year period was, ordinarily, borrowing a state limitations period—a period that did not necessarily serve the needs of a particular statutory scheme better than the four-year default rule.[149] This is an example of a statutory problem that can be addressed at the outset without enormous difficulty.[150]

But even the new statute of limitations provision falls short of being a model of complete congressional specification. For example, the statute does not define when a cause of action accrues or in what circumstances the limitations period is tolled; those issues are left to the courts to resolve. In this respect, it can be seen as consistent with an understanding of the difficulties that inhere in any assumption that it is desirable to structure a legal system on the premise that only Congress is empowered to make the decisions necessary to establish workable schemes of federal regulation. This is not to deny that, constitutional limitations aside, legislative policymaking prevails over judicial policymaking; that is a given.[151]

---

brought under the manifold federal statutes on the books prior to December 1, 1990 (the date on which the general limitations period was enacted) that do not themselves specify any limitations period. Thus, as to those statutes, courts still must wrestle with the question whether to select a limitations period from federal law, see, for example, *Agency Holding Corp. v Malley–Duff & Associates, Inc.*, 483 US 143 (1987), or to borrow (as is the norm) one from state law, see, for example, *Johnson v Railway Express Agency, Inc.*, 421 US 454 (1975). If the latter option is selected, courts must decide *which* state limitations period to select—or, as Judge Posner put it, "which round peg to stuff in a square hole." *Short v Belleville Shoe Mfg. Co.*, 908 F2d 1385, 1393 (7th Cir 1990) (concurring opinion).

It is also uncertain whether § 1658 applies to an amendment to an existing statute that creates a new federal cause of action (or expands an existing one) but contains no specific limitations period. For a recent case outlining three different approaches that the courts of appeals have taken with regard to this question, see *Harris v Allstate Ins. Co.*, 300 F3d 1183 (10th Cir 2002).

The uncertainties that persist make one wonder whether Congress might not have been wiser to provide in § 1658 that the four-year default limitations period would also apply to all causes of action arising after the effective date of the statute—even those as to which settled precedent had established a different limitations period.

[149] See generally *Hart & Wechsler* at 820–26 (cited in note 35).

[150] Another example, frequently given, is the culpability states associated with the elements of various federal criminal offenses. See, for example, Report of the Federal Courts Study Committee 91 (1990); Maggs, 29 Harv J Leg at 144 (cited in note 106).

[151] See, for example, Daniel A. Farber, *Statutory Interpretation and Legislative Supremacy*, 78 Georgetown L J 281, 281 (1989); Peter L. Strauss, *The Common Law and Statutes*, 70 U Colo L Rev 225 (1999); Mashaw, 32 Wm & Mary L Rev at 839 (cited in note 120).

Nor is it to suggest that federal judges can make law whenever Congress could;[152] rather, restraining the reach of federal common lawmaking leaves the primary lawmaking role to Congress, in whose political processes the states have considerable influence.[153] These points have long been acknowledged even by enthusiastic proponents of federal common lawmaking.[154]

But here, as elsewhere, one can have too much of a good thing. Thus, Bradford Clark argues that the Supremacy Clause is limited to the Constitution, laws, and treaties; that laws means only those laws adopted pursuant to Article I, Section 7; and that Article III's definition of arising under jurisdiction is similarly limited. On that view, not only administrative regulations and valid executive orders but also federal common law would neither bind the states under the Supremacy Clause nor provide the basis for district court or Supreme Court jurisdiction.[155] That would be a rather radical proposition. If I understand this line of argument, state courts, for example, would not violate the Supremacy Clause if they denied federal judgments any preclusive effect, for, as the Supreme Court has made clear (in an opinion by Justice Scalia), that preclusive effect is a product of federal common law.[156]

More broadly, the difficulty with any argument that seeks to

---

[152] For such a suggestion, see Louise Weinberg, *Federal Common Law*, 83 Nw U L Rev 805 (1989).

[153] See, for example, Bradford R. Clark, *Separation of Powers as a Safeguard of Federalism*, 79 Tex L Rev 1321, 1342–46 (2001).

Whether the "political safeguards of federalism" are today less robust or different in character than they were in the past, and the extent to which they argue against judicial enforcement of constitutional limitations on national authority, are plainly important but distinct questions. For varying analyses, see, for example, Herbert Wechsler, *The Political Safeguards of Federalism: The Role of the States in the Composition and Selection of the National Government*, 54 Colum L Rev 543 (1954); Jesse H. Choper, *Judicial Review and the National Political Process* (Chicago, 1980); David L. Shapiro, *Federalism: A Dialogue* (Northwestern, 1995); Lynn A. Baker, *Putting the Safeguards Back Into the Political Safeguards of Federalism*, 46 Vill L Rev 951 (2001); Lewis B. Kaden, *Politics, Money, and State Sovereignty: The Judicial Role*, 79 Colum L Rev 847 (1979); Larry D. Kramer, *Understanding Federalism*, 47 Vand L Rev 1485 (1994); Larry D. Kramer, *Putting the Politics Back into the Political Safeguards of Federalism*, 100 Colum L Rev 215 (2000).

[154] Compare, for example, Paul J. Mishkin, *Some Further Last Words on Erie—The Thread*, 87 Harv L Rev 1682 (1974), with Paul J. Mishkin, *The Variousness of "Federal Law": Competence and Discretion in the Choice of National and State Rules for Decision*, 105 U Pa L Rev 797 (1957). More recently, the point has been voiced in a stronger form by commentators who seek to curtail the role of judicial lawmaking. See, for example, Scalia, *A Matter of Interpretation* (cited in note 145); Clark, 79 Tex L Rev (cited in note 153).

[155] See Clark, 79 Tex L Rev at 1336 (cited in note 153).

[156] See *Semtek International, Inc. v Lockheed Martin Corp.*, 531 US 497 (2001).

ground judicial passivity in the elaboration of legislative processes in Article I, Section 7 is that this provision says nothing either about the proper methodology for interpreting statutes passed according to the specified procedures or about the appropriate role of federal common lawmaking.[157] The federal Constitution emerged, after all, from an American political tradition that also recognized bicameralism and (in some state constitutions) an executive veto,[158] but those features did not suggest that American courts were not to play their traditional common law role or that judicial lawmaking is illegitimate because undemocratic.[159] Again, this is not to equate the lawmaking powers of federal courts with those of the state courts;[160] it is merely to suggest that simple appeals to democracy or to the structure set forth in a constitution (federal or state) for the enactment of legislation cannot by itself answer the question of the appropriate judicial role.

---

[157] Accord, Cass R. Sunstein, *Must Formalism Be Defended Empirically*, 66 U Chi L Rev 636, 662–66 (1999); David A. Strauss, *Why Plain Meaning?* 72 Notre Dame L Rev 1565, 1573 (1997).

[158] See generally Gordon S. Wood, *The Creation of the American Republic 1776–1787* at 202–55, 446–53, 552–53 (North Carolina, 1969).

[159] Accord, Strauss, 53 Ala L Rev at 892 (cited in note 94) (asking rhetorically whether the drafters of Article III "imagined something other than a court, as that term would then have been conventionally understood, something different in kind from the black-robed members of state judiciaries?").

Put differently, the case for textual and passive statutory interpretation and against common lawmaking, insofar as that case is based on the fact that legislatures are politically accountable and judges are not, applies not only to federal but also to state judges. Although federal separation of powers notions do not bind the states, see *Crowell v Benson*, 285 US 22, 57 (1932); *Dreyer v Illinois*, 187 US 71, 83–84 (1902), it remains true in broad terms that states share a commitment to conceptions of separation of powers that is very similar to federal conceptions. Even if one views *elected* state judges as just as representative as elected legislators and governors (which seems to me a considerable overstatement), judicial lawmaking in the states does not have to overcome the obstacles to legislation created by bicameralism, the scarcity of legislative time (which in states with part-time legislative sessions is scarce indeed), and the need to secure the Executive's assent or a legislative supermajority. Yet in state legal systems, common lawmaking has been thought to be indispensable rather than in derogation of the constitutional structure of the legislative process. See Larry Kramer, *The Lawmaking Power of the Federal Courts*, 12 Pace L Rev 263, 269–73 (1992).

[160] Among the differences between them are these: (1) some state courts operate under reception statutes that can be viewed as delegations of lawmaking authority (although that understanding of the statutes may be quite anachronistic, see Kramer, *The Lawmaking Power of the Federal Courts* at 280); (2) while states generally follow separation of powers principles similar to those of the federal Constitution, there are differences as well (e.g., Nebraska has a unicameral legislature); and (3) federal common lawmaking, like federal lawmaking generally, takes place against a background of state law, see *Hart & Wechsler* at 521–22 (cited in note 35), whereas sharp limits on state common lawmaking might give rise to a vacuum in lawmaking authority.

The question of the proper interpretation of statutes and the proper role of federal common lawmaking is ultimately a question of political and constitutional theory,[161] but as Cass Sunstein has noted, that normative question cannot be intelligently addressed without considerable attention to matters that are far more empirical and pragmatic.[162] The empirical judgments are, however, difficult to make rigorously, and I am more pessimistic than Sunstein about how far an empirical research agenda could help to resolve these questions.[163] (There is insight as well as overstatement in the quip that there are two kinds of empirical questions: those one can answer and those worth asking.)

In any event, I would like to offer a few observations, which do not purport to be based on systematic and rigorous empirical study (if indeed such study is possible in this context) about whether the attitude of judicial passivity that I have described well serves the polity. That attitude places two kinds of demands upon Congress: initially, to seek to reduce to textual expression all questions that might arise under a statutory scheme, and second, when that has failed, to correct ex post any resulting problems revealed by litigation or otherwise. Imposition of those demands on Congress is undesirable for a number of interrelated reasons.

B. THE LIMITS OF CONGRESSIONAL FORESIGHT

Consider, initially, the question in *Great-West Life*—does ERISA leave a health insurance plan without any federal remedy for breach of a subrogation obligation, even if state remedies may well be preempted? It is farfetched to claim that this result was intended by Congress, or furthers the purposes of Congress when it enacted the remedies it did in ERISA and preempted others; it is equally farfetched to claim that the result is desirable. And at least insofar as one can tell from the briefs, this situation is not one in which Congress seems to have mandated an outcome that, however dysfunctional or peculiar, was the result of interest group politics or voting behavior of the sort that is grist for the mill of

---

[161] Accord, Mashaw, 32 Wm & Mary L Rev at 838–41 (cited in note 120).

[162] Sunstein, 66 U Chi L Rev (cited in note 157).

[163] For discussion of some of the problems, see, for example, William N. Eskridge, Jr., *Norms, Empiricism, and Canons in Statutory Interpretation*, 66 U Chi L Rev 671 (1999).

public choice theory.[164] Rather, it seems most likely that Congress simply failed to realize that a court might take what Congress did in ERISA as rendering standard subrogation obligations unenforceable.

Shortcomings of this nature may be particularly common in the American system of lawmaking, which, as many have noted, lacks the party discipline and executive control of the legislature that characterizes parliamentary systems.[165] The latter are, accordingly, more conducive to the enactment of comprehensive statutes that reflect a coherent, integrated viewpoint and that can be rapidly

---

[164] See generally Daniel A. Farber and Phillip Frickey, *Law and Public Choice: A Critical Introduction* (Chicago, 1991); Symposium, 74 Va L Rev 167–518 (1988).

John Manning has recently stressed that "lines drawn by a clear statutory text may reflect unrecorded compromises among interest groups, the effects of unknowable strategic behavior, or even an implicit legislative decision not to engage in costly bargaining over greater textual precision." John F. Manning, *The Absurdity Doctrine*, 116 Harv L Rev (forthcoming 2003). One might view the legislative history surrounding § 502(a)(3) as consistent with Manning's view, if that view is broadly conceived. According to one close observer of the process, the limitation in § 502(a)(3) was maintained because of concern that the courts, which were then wrestling with the question whether punitive damages were available under the Age Discrimination in Employment Act, would take the authorization of legal relief in § 502(a)(3) of ERISA as a signal that punitive damages should be available under the ADEA. The decision with respect to ERISA, however, was not meant to exclude punitive damages under § 502(a)(3), for there were state cases indicating that courts of equity could award punitive damages. Nor was the decision meant to embrace anything like the limitation later engrafted on § 502(a)(3) as limited to relief "typically available" in equity; rather, it was meant to fudge the issue. See Letter from Michael S. Gordon to John H. Langbein, June 14, 2002 (on file with author).

With respect to Manning's general point, it is always possible that seemingly absurd textual directives are explicable by the kinds of explanations that he posits. There is an empirical question here, perhaps not decisive but important, and yet probably unknowable, and that is how often those explanations, rather than, for example, the conventional concerns about limited legislative resources, limited foresight, and the limits of language, are at work.

Whatever the empirical reality, there is also a legal or constitutional question about the appropriate judicial role. Manning is a sophisticated textualist, who acknowledges that textual meaning depends on context and that context includes social and linguistic conventions. 116 Harv L Rev (forthcoming). The question then remains whether part of the context is an understanding that Congress does not seek absurd results or, more broadly still, that congressional legislation should be interpreted to fit within well-established traditions in the legal framework. Manning endorses some interpretive practices that have that character—for example, the practice of reading culpability requirements or defenses into federal criminal offenses whose text prescribes neither. Id. But the background tradition that Congress did not intend strict liability in criminal offenses, for example, is merely a more specific version of an interpretive approach that ascribes to Congress certain purposes that call for legal rules beyond those plainly specified in text. After all, strict criminal liability is neither unconstitutional nor unheard of, and so Congress might well have sought to impose it. But the presumption remains to the contrary, even when the statute does not specifically prescribe otherwise, for reasons that seem to me generalizable, as I explain in text.

[165] See, for example, Jeremy Waldron, *The Dignity of Legislation* 4 (Cambridge, 1999) (referring to Great Britain).

amended if gaps or problems are revealed. In our system, the Executive Branch, though it helps to shape legislation, does not control its course as do executive ministries in many parliamentary systems.[166] And within the Congress, party cohesion is often absent and agreement between House and Senate must be reached, leading inevitably to compromises and eleventh-hour revisions. Finally, American legislative drafting is less professional and centralized than that in a number of other countries.[167] For all of these reasons, federal legislation is likely to be partial, unintegrated, reactive, and lacking in coherence.[168]

The challenges faced in seeking to construct a comprehensive legislative program—for example, when passing a statute like ERISA that aspires to occupy the field as a complete and coherent unit—arise not simply from our tradition of separation of powers and our legislative and political cultures. Rather, those challenges are heightened by the division of lawmaking authority in a common law system between legislature and courts and in a federal system between the national and state governments. In general, legislation is set against—it presupposes—the existence of the common law, and federal legislation, though perhaps less interstitial today than when Henry Hart and Herbert Wechsler famously so labeled it in 1953,[169] is set against a background of state and local law. Thus, federal legislation builds on, absorbs, or incorporates state common law. Even the federal tax code, as comprehensive a statutory framework as federal law provides, fits this pattern; for example, in specifying certain treatment for married taxpayers, it does not purport to define marriage but leaves that to state law. Federal law does not purport to be a complete corpus juris, like the Napoleonic Code, nor is lawmaking authority located exclusively in a national legislature. Rather, fitting new federal enactments into a complex existing structure of disjointed federal statutes and a plethora of state statutory and common law regimes is an enormous challenge.

---

[166] See Strauss, 70 Colo L Rev at 231 (cited in note 151); Richard A. Posner, *Pragmatic Adjudication*, in Morris Dickstein, ed, *The Revival of Pragmatism* 250 (1998); Sunstein, 66 U Chi L Rev 66 U Chi L Rev at 658–59 (cited in note 157).

[167] See Sunstein, 66 U Chi L Rev at 659 (cited in note 157).

[168] Id at 234–41.

[169] See Henry M. Hart, Jr. and Herbert Wechsler, *The Federal Courts and the Federal System* 435–36 (Foundation, 1953).

That challenge is enhanced when one considers the enormous range of what Americans ask Congress to undertake. Already, as Richard Stewart has noted, "[t]he demands on Congress' agenda far exceed its capacity to make collective decisions."[170] Whether one compares today's Congress to that of 1789 (or indeed, to that of any era in our past), or to the legislature of any other nation in the world, the magnitude of the job of lawmaking imposed on our House and Senate is rivaled by few other legislative institutions. The breadth of those responsibilities, when viewed against the limited time and attention that legislators can devote to any single one of the myriad of bills under consideration, seriously tests any interpretive approach premised on the capacity of Congress to resolve up front all important questions relating to a statutory scheme.[171]

Often, if federal law leaves gaps or uncertainties, they are appropriately filled with state law, relieving Congress of the obligation to re-create in every statute a background set of accepted legal rules.[172] But at least in some of the cases I have discussed, where federal law has gaps or oddities, *state* law does not provide an appropriate default rule. Indeed, in *Great-West Life*, the problem arises precisely because the preemptive effect of ERISA very likely excludes state law from contributing to the solution of legal problems relating to benefits plans. If that is so, it falls either to Congress or the federal courts to ensure that the statute is workable.

Of course, the judicial-legislative relationship is a dynamic one;[173] positive political theory and institutional views of legislation suggest that judicial approaches to lawmaking could have long-term effects on legislative behavior.[174] It is at least possible that the more creative judicial attitude that I advocate may make legislatures less careful at the outset.[175] In this regard, it is some-

---

[170] Richard B. Stewart, *Beyond Delegation Doctrine*, 36 Am U L Rev 323, 331 (1987).

[171] See generally James J. Brudney, *Congressional Commentary on Judicial Interpretations of Statutes: Idle Chatter or Telling Response?* 93 Mich L Rev 1, 20–26 (1994).

[172] See, for example, *Hart & Wechsler* at 521–22 (cited in note 35).

[173] Cass R. Sunstein and Adrian Vermeule, *Interpretation and Institutions*, 101 Mich L Rev (forthcoming 2003).

[174] See generally Jonathan Macey, *Separated Powers and Positive Political Theory: The Tug of War Over Administrative Agencies*, 80 Georgetown L J 671 (1992).

[175] See William N. Eskridge, Jr., Philip P. Frickey, and Elizabeth Garrett, *Cases and Materials on Legislation: Statutes and the Creation of Public Policy* 782–833 (West Group, 3d ed

times asserted that shortfalls in legislative specification reflect
buck-passing by politicians seeking to avoid offending some interest group or another or to evade accountability.[176] No one can
doubt that such behavior occurs, but there are alternative and more
attractive ways of describing the same phenomenon. To begin
with, agreement is generally costlier to reach when one tries to
specify terms more precisely.[177] Moreover, achieving a consensus
that minimizes controversy may be important to advancing a bill
on the legislative calendar.[178] And statutory ambiguity may be necessary in order to obtain agreement within each of the two legislative chambers, and among the House, Senate, and President, in a
political context in which agreement is difficult to obtain.[179] (Even
on the Supreme Court, where agreement among only five individuals suffices, similar behavior is anything but unheard of: as Chief
Justice Rehnquist reports, Chief Justice Hughes "said that he tried
to write his opinions clearly and logically, but if he needed the
fifth vote of a colleague who insisted on putting in a paragraph
that did not 'belong' * * * , in it went, and let the law reviews
figure out what it meant."[180])

Moreover, lack of clarity in legislation—whether through ambiguous language or lack of a provision at all—often reflects something other than a conscious effort by legislators to avoid offending
an interest group or to gloss over potential conflicts with ambiguous language. An absence of textual specification may equally reflect the incapacity of legislators, no matter how willing to try to
resolve statutory uncertainties, to anticipate all of the uncertainties
that will arise, as well as the difficulties of crafting language that,
in the myriad contexts to which it is applied, will avoid ambiguity.[181] Thus, the supposition that a refusal to rely on legislative

---

2001) ("*Cases and Materials on Legislation*"); Adrian Vermeule, *Interpretive Choice*, 75 NYU
L Rev 74, 103 (2000).

[176] See, for example, Strauss, 72 Notre Dame L Rev at 1574–75 (cited in note 157) (describing though not endorsing the argument).

[177] See, for example, Colin S. Diver, *The Optimal Precision of Administrative Rules*, 93 Yale
L J 65, 73 (1983).

[178] See Brudney, 93 Mich L Rev at 23–24 (cited in note 171).

[179] See Posner, *The Revival of Pragmatism* at 250 (cited in note 166).

[180] William H. Rehnquist, *The Supreme Court: How It Was, How It Is* 302 (William Mor-
row, 1987).

[181] See Katzmann, *Courts and Congress* at 61 (cited in note 142); Felix Frankfurter, *Some
Reflections on the Reading of Statutes*, 47 Colum L Rev 527, 528 (1947).

history might induce legislators to increase textual specificity,[182] even if sometimes correct, would address only a small part of the problem of statutory incompleteness. To put the point concretely, the hypothesis that Congress, had it been absolutely certain when enacting ERISA that the courts would follow a passive interpretive approach, would have anticipated the question in *Great-West Life* and enacted a statutory provision resolving it, simply seems implausible.

This is not to say that Congress can never respond to judicial signals: for example, it has done so frequently (although often, in the end, to no avail) when the Supreme Court announced its clear statement rules governing statutes purporting to regulate the states and to abrogate Eleventh Amendment immunity.[183] But while there may be good reason for certain kinds of clear statement rules, the more general proposition that a court should view itself as a kind of disciplinarian, whose role it is to force Congress to act in certain ways, seems to me lacking in force as a normative prescription. (A logical instantiation of this approach, it has always seemed to me, would be for courts, when facing statutory ambiguities, to announce the rule that they think would most seriously obstruct congressional purposes; that, after all, should get their attention![184]) There is, indeed, an irony in an attitude that begins with professions of judicial modesty and legislative supremacy but that evolves into one of a judicial parent disciplining the errant legislative child. As Jonathan Siegel aptly put it, "i[n] the name of preserving legislative power, the textualists actually reduce it, by compelling Congress to meet an impossible standard of drafting perfection before its instructions can be carried out properly."[185]

Although a wide variety of commentators have proposed a wide variety of interpretive approaches designed to induce a correspondingly wide variety of congressional responses, or have more generally assumed that interpretive practices will affect legislative

---

[182] See, for example, Vermeule, 75 NYU L Rev at 103–04 (cited in note 175).

[183] For a list of such statutes, see, for example, Daniel J. Meltzer, *The Seminole Decision and State Sovereign Immunity*, 1996 Supreme Court Review 1, 32 nn 149–50.

[184] Accord, Einer Elhauge, *Preference-Estimating Statutory Default Rules*, 102 Colum L Rev 2027 (2002).

[185] See Jonathan R. Siegel, *What Statutory Drafting Errors Teach Us About Statutory Interpretation*, 69 Geo Wash L Rev 309, 325 (2001).

behavior,[186] they supply little reason to believe that congressional decision making responds to that kind of signal. As Judge Posner remarked some time ago, "There is no evidence that members of Congress, or their assistants who do the actual drafting, know [any supposed code that Congress uses when it writes statutes] or that if they know, they pay attention to it. . . . We should demand evidence that statutory draftsmen follow the code before we erect a method of interpreting statutes on the improbable assumption that they do."[187] Particularly in the absence of such evidence, it seems to me that even if legislatures pass the buck more often than some think they should, in the end the courts must take responsibility for the legal results generated by their decisions.

There is, finally, a conservative argument, in the sense of Burkean conservatism, against judicial passivity, and that is simply that it constitutes a significant departure from historic norms. Congress has not legislated on the assumption that courts would be powerless to flesh out statutory enactments. For example, in defining defenses to federal crimes, our tradition has not been to borrow state law defenses (so that the scope of self-defense or necessity would differ, depending on the state in which a federal prosecution is brought) but rather to have federal uniformity. Thus, in fashioning defenses, the task falls either to Congress or to the federal courts. The point is not that Congress could not fashion criminal law defenses; after all, many state criminal codes do so. But for more than two centuries, Congress has generally left criminal defenses to be fashioned by judges, unless and until displaced by statute.[188] That is the background against which a decision like *Oakland Cannabis* was rendered, and Justices as different as Scalia and Stevens have both stressed the importance of providing Congress with a consistent interpretive approach against which it can legislate.[189] If nothing else, a radical shift in operating as-

---

[186] See, for example, Jonathan R. Macey, *Promoting Public-Regarding Legislation Through Statutory Interpretation: An Interest Group Model*, 86 Colum L Rev 223 (1986); Bernard W. Bell, *R-E-S-P-E-C-T: Respecting Legislative Judgments in Interpretive Theory*, 78 NC L Rev 1253, 1259 (2000); Jane S. Schacter, *Metademocracy: The Changing Structure of Legitimacy in Statutory Interpretation*, 108 Harv L Rev 593, 595 (1995); Cass R. Sunstein, *Interpreting Statutes in the Regulatory State*, 103 Harv L Rev 405, 457–58 (1989).

[187] Richard A. Posner, *Statutory Interpretation—in the Classroom and in the Courtroom*, 50 U Chi L Rev 800, 806 (1983).

[188] See text accompanying notes 34–39.

[189] See, for example, *Finley v United States*, 490 US 545, 556 (1989) (Scalia); *Landsgraf v USI Film Prods.*, 511 US 244, 272–73 (1994) (Stevens).

sumptions like that reflected in the dicta in *Oakland Cannabis* demands considerable justification.[190] And in this respect, although the phrase "judicial passivity" may not sound especially dramatic or radical, in fact it is both.

C. THE LIMITS OF CONGRESSIONAL RESPONSE EX POST

One might seek to defend judicial passivity on a different ground: if the results reached by courts exhibiting that attitude are deemed unsatisfactory, Congress will step in and solve the problem, by overriding the unsatisfactory decision in accordance with the views of democratically elected representatives. And, indeed, one could take that response one step further: it is possible in theory that a Congress confronted with a passive judiciary may be more alert to the importance of monitoring judicial decisions and to remedying the statutory gaps, ambiguities, or difficulties that such decisions are likely to reveal.[191]

But here, too, the hypothesis that a kind of judicial formalism or passivity will produce the posited congressional response is only a hypothesis. Professors Eskridge, Frickey, and Garrett assert that there is no evidence to support it, and they, knowledgeable commentators all, suggest that "the most knowledgeable commentators are skeptical."[192]

Indeed, one might question whether even textualists fully subscribe to the premise. After all, Justice Scalia himself has suggested that when the plain meaning of a statute would lead to an absurd result, rather than following the text and relying on Congress to override the absurd outcome, courts should instead depart from the plain meaning.[193] That position presupposes that within the

---

[190] Compare Strauss, 63 U Chi L Rev at 891–94 (cited in note 57).

[191] See Sunstein and Vermeule, 101 Mich L Rev (cited in note 173).

[192] Eskridge et al, *Cases and Materials on Legislation* at 783 (cited in note 175); see also Vermeule, 75 NYU L Rev at 94–95 (cited in note 175) (discussing the possibility that legislators create text and legislative history primarily for audiences other than judges).

[193] See, for example, *INS v Cardoza-Fonseca*, 480 US 421, 452 (1987) (Scalia concurring in the judgment); *Green v Bock Laundry Machine Co.*, 490 US 504, 527 (1989) (Scalia concurring in the judgment) (when confronted with statutory language that produces an absurd result, it is appropriate "to observe that counsel have not provided, nor have we discovered, a shred of evidence that anyone has ever proposed or assumed such a bizarre disposition"). For criticism of that approach, see generally Manning, 116 Harv L Rev (cited in note 164).

legal system, or particular regulatory regimes, there exist some norms, values, and understandings that provide a basis for concluding that a particular result is indeed absurd.[194] And more broadly, sophisticated commentators sympathetic to textual interpretation note that it need not be acontextual and that language should be construed in light of, *inter alia*, the statute as a whole, other statutes in related areas, administrative interpretations, prior judicial constructions, and background presumptions reflected in various canons of construction or clear statement rules.[195] Once that much is accepted, the question arises whether the context should not be extended, in decisions like *Oakland Cannabis* or *Great-West Life*, to include other aspects of the legal system (for example, long-standing legal doctrines or assignments of institutional responsibility).[196]

Beyond those questions lie two other concerns. The first is that the proposed solution of congressional revision might itself be viewed as unfaithful to the democratic aspirations that are said to support it. For if a judicial decision fails properly to interpret the enactment of one Congress, the uncertain possibility of curative legislation by a second Congress does not necessarily undo any mistake; the second Congress, after all, is composed of different actors and may not reflect the same balance of attitudes or political forces as the first or present the same opportunities for addressing a particular problem given the legislative agenda.[197] As a result, an interpretation that was in some sense wrong or unfaithful to the original legislation may not be susceptible to legislative correc-

---

[194] See Siegel, 69 Geo Wash L Rev at 333 (cited in note 185).

[195] See, for example, Mashaw, 32 Wm & Mary L Rev at 835–36 (cited in note 120); Frederick Schauer, *The Practice and Problems of Plain Meaning: A Response to Aleinikoff and Shaw*, 45 Vand L Rev 715, 739 (1992); Manning, 116 Harv L Rev (cited in note 164).

[196] See, for example, Siegel, 69 Geo Wash L Rev at 324, 335 (cited in note 185); William N. Eskridge, Jr., *Dynamic Statutory Interpretation* 45–47 (Harvard, 1994). See also Shapiro, 67 NYU L Rev at 921 (cited in note 15).

John Manning agrees that the absurdity exception cannot be reconciled with the premises of textualism, but moves in the opposite direction, seeking to require courts to uphold absurd outcomes so long as the statutory text, even after taking appropriate account of context, is clear—subject, however, to the possibility that the absurd outcome is unconstitutional because not rational under the Due Process Clause, or at least that, under the doctrine of constitutional avoidance, the court should interpret the statute as not producing the absurd result so as to avoid raising a constitutional question. See Manning, 116 Harv L Rev (cited in note 164).

[197] Compare William W. Buzbee, *The One-Congress Fiction in Statutory Interpretation*, 149 U Pa L Rev 171 (2000).

tion.[198] That observation does not tell us what a "correct" initial interpretation would be, but it does raise at least one concern about any theory that places great reliance on the prospect of legislative override.

Second, one must recall that the very institutional factors that are said to guard against improvident lawmaking—bicameralism and the need for presidential assent; the ideological diversity of our parties and the lack of strong party control; the power of individual subcommittees and committees to kill legislation and the difficulty of circumventing committee control; and the scarcity of legislative time—also make it difficult to enact remedial amendments. Even where the need for statutory amendments is identified, such amendments, no less than the original legislation itself, must compete to get on the legislative agenda; and any legislative efforts must pass through many veto-gates that threaten to prevent enactment.[199] Put in economic terms, passing legislation is a complex and resource intensive activity; legislative capacity is a scarce commodity; and there is, accordingly, a considerable opportunity cost to any approach that is premised on the need for Congress repeatedly to revisit statutory issues.[200] That is particularly so if, as some political scientists have argued, interest groups are more effective in blocking than in securing the enactment of legislation.[201]

---

[198] See, for example, William N. Eskridge, Jr. and John Ferejohn, *The Article I, Section 7 Game*, 80 Georgetown L J 523 (1992); see also Strauss, 53 Ala L Rev at 538 (cited in note 94).

[199] See, for example, William N. Eskridge, Jr. et al, *Cases and Materials on Legislation* at 5–6, 61–62, 66–68 (cited in note 175); McNollgast, *Legislative Intent: The Use of Positive Political Theory in Statutory Interpretation*, 57 L & Contemp Probs 3, 11 (1994); Kenneth A. Shepsle and Barry R. Weingast, *The Institutional Foundations of Committee Power*, 81 Am Pol Sci Rev 85, 89 (1987).

[200] See generally Brudney, 93 Mich L Rev at 17–26 (cited in note 171); cf. Maggs, 29 Harv J Legis at 129–30 (cited in note 106) (noting the costs to the legislature when its initial draftsmanship is inadequate, thus requiring legislative effort to correct a judicial interpretation that is more likely to have been in error).
I have made a similar observation with regard specifically to federal common lawmaking, noting that "legislative inertia and the political safeguards of federalism are ultimately a double-edged sword. They help explain why the authority to make federal common law is nowhere near so broad as congressional authority to legislate, but also argue that federal common lawmaking may be necessary to fill in the interstices of congressional and constitutional mandates or otherwise to deal with matters of important national concern." Daniel J. Meltzer, *State Court Forfeitures of Federal Rights*, 99 Harv L Rev 1128, 1170 (1986) (footnotes omitted).

[201] See Kay Lehman Schlozman and John T. Tierney, *Organized Interests and American Democracy* 314–15, 395–96, 398 (Harper & Row, 1986).

We have a Congress that has been wrestling with balancing the budget, federal tax policy, fast-track trade negotiation authority for the President, significant amendments to the federal bankruptcy laws, creation of a new Department of Homeland Security, corporate accountability, possible invasion of Iraq, judicial nominations, health care legislation on such topics as prescription drug coverage for seniors and the right to sue HMOs, and many other large and complex questions. In that context, an issue like the enforceability of subrogation clauses in ERISA plans may get lost in the shuffle,[202] or, alternatively, escape correction because of a legislative stalemate today among the interest groups concerned with ERISA. Indeed, consider a far more significant issue—the scope of preemption under ERISA generally. Though the decisions interpreting ERISA's preemption clause are widely viewed as a mess, Congress has not intervened to clean things up, leading one commentator to observe that "it is a great deal more difficult for Congress to correct flawed statutes than it is to enact them in the first place."[203]

And in thinking about the likelihood of legislative attention, it is important to recall that the relevant universe is not merely Su-

---

[202] One study found that of the relatively small number of overrides of Supreme Court decisions, a disproportionate number emerged from Judiciary Committees of the House and Senate. See Michael E. Solimine and James L. Walker, *The Next Word: Congressional Response to Supreme Court Statutory Decisions*, 65 Temp L Rev 425, 449 (1992).

In some respects, the low visibility of an issue may make corrective legislation easier, if some organized constituency seeks legislative revision. For discussions emphasizing the importance of interest group activity in securing legislative overrides, see, for example, Beth Henschen, *Statutory Interpretations of the Supreme Court: Congressional Response*, 11 Am Pol Q 441, 451 (1983); Harry P. Stumpf, *Congressional Response to Supreme Court Rulings: The Interaction of Law and Politics*, 14 J Pub L 377, 391–92 (1965); Solimine and Walker, 65 Temp L Rev at 446–48. At the same time, the low profile of these issues may also make it harder to get them on the legislative agenda at all.

[203] Catherine L. Fisk, *The Last Article About the Language of ERISA Preemption? A Case Study of the Failure of Textualism*, 33 Harv J Leg 35, 99 (1996).

Of course, in theory, legislative drafting could be better and federal legislation more coherent. There are examples at state levels (and in other countries), and suggestions at the federal level, of mechanisms for improving legislation in the first instance and for prompter and more reliable legislative response when problems surface. See, for example, Eskridge et al, *Cases and Materials on Legislation* at 408–09 (cited in note 175); Katzmann, *Courts and Congress* at 67–68 (cited in note 142). It would be foolish to suggest that something in the platonic nature of the American legislative process makes it impossible ever to improve congressional capacity to anticipate, resolve, and respond to problems. At the same time, if the life of the law is not logic but experience, the experience to date creates the most serious doubts that if the Court seeks to leave most every decision relating to a federal program to Congress, its institutional processes are up to the task.

preme Court decisions[204] (much less prominent or controversial Supreme Court decisions[205]) but federal court decisions generally. For the Supreme Court's proclamations on the proper judicial stance shape the behavior of lower federal courts, few of whose decisions will be reviewed by the Supreme Court. And while this proposition deserves more study, there is reason to believe that the likelihood that lower court decisions will regularly be reviewed by, and, when appropriate, revised by Congress is extremely low.[206] Congress lacks the resources consistently to monitor all decisions by other institutions (agencies as well as courts) charged with implementing federal legislation.[207] For example, it is noteworthy that one study found that congressional staff members were unaware of the majority of recent statutory decisions of the D.C. Circuit that the judges thought warranted congressional attention.[208] Other studies have found that, on average, between seven and nine lower federal court decisions were overridden annually.[209] To make sense of those numbers, one would have to know to what they should be compared—the number of statutory interpretations by

---

[204] See, for example, William N. Eskridge, Jr., *Overriding Supreme Court Statutory Interpretation Decisions*, 101 Yale L J 331 (1991); Solimine and Walker, 65 Temp L Rev (cited in note 202).

[205] Thus, for example, Professors Sunstein and Vermeule illustrate their point that interpretive techniques might conceivably affect the likelihood of legislative override by pointing to two well-known examples of textual decision making that was modified by Congress: (1) the amendment of the Delaney Clause of the Food, Drug, and Cosmetic Act, 21 USC § 348(c)(3)(A) (1994), which had been interpreted literally as imposing an absolute ban on carcinogenic substances in processed foods, see the Food Quality Protection Act of 1996, Pub L No 104-170, 110 Stat 1489 (1996), and (2) the amendment of the Endangered Species Act after a literal interpretation had blocked an important dam in order to protect the snail darter, see Pub L No 95-632, 92 Stat 3751, 3752-60 (1978) (creating an administrative procedure for exempting projects from the Act) and Pub L No 96-69, 93 Stat 437, 449 (1979) (legislating an exemption for the dam at issue in the Supreme Court case). See Sunstein and Vermeule, 101 Mich L Rev (cited in note 173).

[206] See, for example, Charles E. Lindblom, *The Policymaking Process* 2–7 (Prentice-Hall, 2d ed 1980) (whether a legislative solution to a problem is enacted depends on confluence of saliency of problem and capacity of groups to formulate a favored solution, mobilize support, and find a receptive political environment).

[207] See, for example, Stewart, 36 Am U L Rev at 330–31 (cited in note 170).

[208] See Katzmann, *Courts and Congress* at 73–76 (cited in note 142).

[209] Stefanie A. Lindquist and David A. Yalof, *Congressional Responses to Federal Circuit Court Decisions*, 85 Judicature 61, 64, 68 (2001) (finding that over a nine-year period, there were 120 provisions in bills reported out of committee that were responses to a federal *court of appeals* decision and that only sixty-five such bills were enacted, or roughly seven annually); Eskridge, 101 Yale L J at 337–38 (cited in note 204) (finding over a twenty-four-year period that 200 *lower federal court* decisions were overridden by statute, an average of roughly nine annually).

the lower courts, or perhaps more precisely, the number that might be viewed as erroneous or somehow ripe for legislative review. Despite the absence of those numbers, the authors of one of those studies seem safe in concluding that "Congress responds to only a minute percentage of cases decided by the courts of appeals, even though the majority of appeals court decisions involve the application of federal statutes."[210]

Finally, even in the rare case in which a congressional response to a problem is forthcoming, judicial passivity creates obvious interim problems. Dismissing these as transition costs is all too easy; an insurer whose subrogation clause is rendered unenforceable, or a criminal defendant denied a legitimate defense because of baseless judicial protestations of powerlessness, would not and should not be satisfied if years later Congress fixes the problem so that others will not be similarly victimized in the future. By the same token, there is a cost to judicial integrity if courts are obligated to render decisions that seem unfair to the litigants and the broader community, and whose unfairness is effectively confirmed by legislative amendment. That cost is hard to quantify, but one should not forget that compliance with law depends to a considerable extent upon perceptions that the legal system is fair,[211] and, hence, an interpretive approach that gives rise to results perceived as unfair, even in the short term, has costs that radiate beyond the dissatisfactions of particular litigants.

IV. THE LIMITS OF ASPIRATIONS FOR LEGISLATIVE
     COMPLETENESS

Thus far, I have been arguing against the wisdom of an approach that lays at Congress's door the responsibility for specifying all aspects of subconstitutional decision making. Whether or not one agrees with that view, one might also believe it preferable

---

[210] Lindquist and Yalof, 85 Judicature at 68 (cited in note 209).

[211] Compare Paul H. Robinson and John M. Darley, *The Utility of Desert*, 91 NW U L Rev 453, 486–87 (1997) (noting, in the context of discussing a criminal code, that social science literature supports the proposition that a code's credibility "depends on it being perceived as a trustworthy guide to assigning liabilities according to the community's perception of which actions are moral, which are immoral," and that "the higher the credibility of the code . . . , the more . . . [people] will be inclined to behave in compliance with the code").

for Congress, when it can, to take political responsibility for resolving matters up front. Indeed, the Federal Courts Study Committee stated that it would be desirable if Congress could somehow
be motivated to use a checklist to ensure that new statutes address
each of a broad range of issues that are often not addressed by a
particular provision.[212] Examples of such issues include the scope
of preemption, the existence of federal and state court jurisdiction,
the nature of any requirement of exhaustion of administrative remedies, the permissible scope for arbitration or other private dispute
settlement mechanisms, severability, the availability of private
rights of action, the scope of remedies, the extent of official immunity, and retroactivity.[213]

I wish, however, to raise at least some questions about that view,
and thus to advance a stronger thesis: not only is it unrealistic to
expect Congress to be able to resolve all issues up front in statutory
text, but there are many instances in which a congressional effort
to do so is likely to be less successful than leaving matters to be
worked out by judicial decision. The aspiration for legislative resolution ignores what Justice Jackson called "the recognized futility
of attempting all-complete statutory codes,"[214] the dynamic quali-
ties of the law, and the limitations of congressional decision making. Often the pertinent legal question "is difficult, if not impossible, to answer in gross. And the courts are functionally better
adapted to engage in the necessary fine tuning than is the legislature."[215] Thus, one should not automatically assume that legislative
decision making as to such matters is superior.

---

[212] Report of the Federal Courts Study Committee 91 (1990). See also Katzmann, *Courts
and Congress* at 65–66 (cited in note 142).

[213] This list is a subset of a fuller list provided in the Report of the Federal Courts Study
Committee 91 (1990). See also Maggs, 29 Harv J Legis at 142–48 (cited in note 106).

[214] *D'Oench, Duhme & Co. v FDIC*, 315 US 447, 469–70 (1942) (Jackson concurring). For
an elaboration of the point, see H. L. A. Hart, *The Concept of Law* 128 (Oxford, 2d ed
1994) ("It is a feature of the human predicament (and so of the legislative one) that we
labour under two connected handicaps whenever we seek to regulate, unambiguously and
in advance, some sphere of conduct by means of general standards to be used without
further official direction on particular occasions. The first handicap is our relative ignorance
of fact: the second is our relative indeterminacy of aim. If the world in which we live were
characterized only by a finite number of features, and these together with all the modes
in which they could combine were known to us, then provision could be made in advance
for every possibility. . . . This would be a world fit for 'mechanical' jurisprudence.").

[215] David L. Shapiro, *Jurisdiction and Discretion*, 60 NYU L Rev 543, 574 (1985). Shapiro's
argument focuses on questions of jurisdiction but has broader applicability.

This is a difficult proposition to establish rigorously, but I will try to offer a set of illustrations that I think are highly suggestive. The first is preemption. As noted above, under both ERISA and other statutes, the courts have refused to take statutory language literally, or to treat textual directives on preemption as being exclusive, when to do so would seem to require counterproductive results. Recall, on the one hand, Justice Scalia's description of the preemption clause in ERISA: it "provides an illusory test, unless the Court is willing to decree a degree of pre-emption that no sensible person could have intended—which it is not."[216] Recall, on the other hand, the willingness of courts to apply implied preemption principles even when a statute contains an express preemption clause.[217] Both of these interpretive approaches illustrate that even Justices who champion textual interpretation and often urge judicial passivity recognize, in practice, the limited capacity of Congress to legislate up front and the superiority of judicial fine-tuning.[218]

In further illustration of the proposition I advance, I wish to consider two other examples of legislative-judicial interplay with regard to statutory schemes in the area of federal jurisdiction: the supplemental jurisdiction statute, and the question of retroactivity of the 1996 amendments to the federal habeas corpus jurisdiction. (Several additional examples are discussed in the margin.[219]) These examples are not chosen at random, to be sure, but they are, I believe, powerful examples because of certain features that they share. First, the issues presented, rather than being complex or novel, were limited and well defined. Second, for the most part the issues in each of these illustrations do not implicate matters of strong social division or rapid economic, technological, or attitudinal change; rather, because they fall within recognized bodies of law that rest on well-established understandings, these issues should be relatively susceptible to crisp and effective congressional specification. Third, the issues were for the most part not ones

---

[216] *California Division of Labor Standards Enforcement v Dillingham Const., N.A., Inc.*, 519 US 316, 335–36 (1997) (Scalia concurring).

[217] See text accompanying notes 79–86.

[218] For a forceful discussion of the superiority of the courts to Congress in delineating the appropriate scope of preemption, see Susan J. Stabile, *Preemption of State Law by Federal Law: A Task for Congress or the Courts?* 40 Vill L Rev 1 (1995).

[219] See notes 229, 254.

about which intense interest group activity made it difficult for Congress to seek a coherent solution.[220] Finally, in at least one of the examples, Congress had expert outside help in drafting.[221] The foregoing conditions make these examples ones in which legislative capacity to get things right at the outset ought to be higher than the norm. But I believe that these illustrations show that even in relatively "easy" contexts, exclusive reliance on legislative specification in textual provisions is not to be preferred to reliance, instead, on a broader judicial role in giving meaning to federal statutes in an effort to create a workable legal regime.

A. SUPPLEMENTAL JURISDICTION AND 28 USC § 1367

My first tale, of pendent party jurisdiction and the supplemental jurisdiction statute, is familiar to all teachers of civil procedure and federal jurisdiction. In *Finley v United States*,[222] a majority of five Justices took a stingy view of judicial authority in fleshing out the meaning of congressional grants of "arising under" jurisdiction.[223] The opinion acknowledged that grants of federal question jurisdiction carry with them implicit authority to exercise pendent jurisdiction over closely related state law claims that a plaintiff asserts against the same defendant(s) who are being sued on the federal claim. But that acknowledgment of accepted doctrine was grudging; the majority viewed it as being in tension with the principle that the federal courts may not transcend the jurisdiction Congress has granted.[224] (Of course, to recognize that principle hardly an-

---

[220] This claim requires some qualification in the case of one of the illustrations, the 1996 amendments to the federal habeas corpus jurisdiction. Those amendments, in the large, were quite controversial and involved considerable lobbying on opposing sides. But the particular issue on which I focus—the retroactive effect of the amendments—does not appear to have been in the vortex of interest group politics. I do not, however, mean to generalize here about retroactivity issues, about which there is sometimes a sharp clash of interests in the legislative process, as was true, for example, with respect to the Civil Rights Act of 1991. See *Landsgraf v USI Film Prods*, 511 US 244, 256–57 (1994).

[221] See the immediate following discussion of the enactment of the supplemental jurisdiction statute, 28 USC § 1367.

[222] 490 US 545 (1989).

[223] Jurisdiction in *Finley* was based not on § 1331, but rather on the specific and exclusive grant of subject matter jurisdiction over actions arising under the Federal Tort Claims Act. See 28 USC § 1346(b). For discussion of the government's position in *Finley*, which was that pendent party jurisdiction was unavailable in the context of that particular jurisdictional grant, see David L. Shapiro, *Supplemental Jurisdiction: A Confession, an Avoidance, and a Proposal*, 74 Ind L J 211 (1998).

[224] 490 US at 547–48, 556.

swers the question of how narrowly or broadly to construe a particular grant of jurisdiction that Congress has made.) Seeking to confine the precedents upholding jurisdiction over pendent claims, Justice Scalia's opinion tried to distinguish them from the situation before the Court in *Finley*, which involved so-called pendent party jurisdiction—supplemental jurisdiction over a state law claim against a party who is *not* a defendant on the federal law claim to which the related state law claim is appended.[225] In so doing, he acknowledged that the Court's decision could be modified by Congress, an observation that some took as an invitation to Congress to enter the fray.

The following year, the Federal Courts Study Committee, in one of its very few recommendations for expanding rather than contracting federal subject matter jurisdiction, urged Congress to override *Finley* and authorize the exercise of supplemental jurisdiction over pendent parties.[226] In turn, Congress, after obtaining the aid of three academic experts in drafting a supplemental jurisdiction provision,[227] enacted the measure now codified as 28 USC § 1367.

Despite that assistance, the new statutory provision presented a number of hard interpretive questions and had quite a few unforeseen consequences. For § 1367, in addition to overruling *Finley*, appeared, in ways that those associated with its drafting apparently did not anticipate or intend, to have narrowed supplemental jurisdiction in some respects, to have broadened it in others, and in the process to have created a fair measure of confusion.[228]

---

[225] Thus, for example, Justice Scalia's broad statements that a grant of jurisdiction "over claims involving particular parties does not itself confer jurisdiction over additional claims by or against different parties," 490 US at 556, ignored then-existing practice in extending supplemental jurisdiction over, for example, third-party claims—claims often in the nature of contribution or indemnity and thus (like pendent party claims) often raising distinct factual issues even when premised on the primary claim.

[226] See Report of the Federal Courts Study Committee 47 (1990).

[227] Thomas D. Rowe, Jr., Stephen B. Burbank, and Thomas M. Mengler, *Congress Accepts Supreme Court's Invitation to Codify Supplemental Jurisdiction*, 74 Judicature 213, 216 (1991).

[228] For some of the leading articles discussing the provision, see Richard Freer, *Compounding Confusion and Hampering Diversity: Life After Finley and the Supplemental Jurisdiction Statute*, 40 Emory L J 445, 474–86 (1991); John B. Oakley, *Recent Statutory Changes in the Law of Federal Jurisdiction and Venue: The Judicial Improvements Acts of 1988 and 1990*, 24 UC Davis L Rev 735 (1991); Thomas Rowe, Stephen Burbank, and Thomas Mengler, *Compounding or Creating Confusion About Supplemental Jurisdiction? A Reply to Professor Freer*, 40 Emory L J 943 (1991) (and subsequent rebuttals and surrebuttals in the same issue); Denis F. McLaughlin, *The Federal Supplemental Jurisdiction Statute—A Constitutional and Statutory*

One might respond that Congress could have done better. But while that is obviously true in theory and may seem particularly so in hindsight, this episode illustrates how unlikely it is that a conception of the judicial role that throws everything into the lap of statutory drafters will work well in practice. Not often does Congress have a relatively narrow issue, like that raised by § 1367, that appears to have been relatively free of partisan or interest group pressures, and also have at its disposal the kind of expert assistance that was available in this case.[229]

Analysis, 24 Ariz St L J 849 (1992); Arthur D. Wolf, *Codification of Supplemental Jurisdiction: Anatomy of a Legislative Proposal,* 14 W New Eng L Rev 1 (1992); Joan Steinman, *Supplemental Jurisdiction in § 1441 Removed Cases: An Unsurveyed Frontier of Congress' Handiwork,* 35 Ariz L Rev 305 (1993). See also Siegel, 69 Geo Wash L Rev at 320–23 (cited in note 185).

[229] Another illustration of the shortcomings of congressional drafting, even when focused on a narrow question and relatively free from interest group politics, involves the amendment of the federal officer removal statute, 28 USC § 1442(a)(1). In *International Primate Protection League v Administrators of Tulane Educational Fund,* 500 US 72 (1991), the Court unanimously ruled that § 1442(a)(1), although it authorized removal of actions against officials of federal agencies, did not authorize removal of actions against federal agencies themselves. The Court relied heavily on § 1442(a)(1)'s wording and its grammar (particularly the absence in one place of a comma). But it proceeded to reject the contention that its interpretation was absurd, asserting that the issue of an agency's immunity was far more straightforward (and thus less hazardous to litigate in a possibly hostile state court) than was the immunity of a federal official.

That explanation was makeweight, for with extremely limited exceptions, the jurisdictional statutes generally express a clear preference for permitting the federal government to seek federal court resolution of all questions of the authority of federal agencies or officials to act, and of all suits in which the United States is a party. Indeed, most waivers of federal sovereign immunity are limited to federal court. See, for example, *Aminoil USA, Inc. v California State Water Resources Control Bd.,* 674 F2d 1227, 1233 (9th Cir 1982). And the Court's decision gave plaintiffs like those in the *Primate Protection* case, who were seeking specific relief (as to which Congress has waived federal sovereign immunity), the option of bringing a state court action either against the agency (which could not be removed) or against its officials (who could and inevitably would remove to federal court). Giving plaintiffs rather than the United States the forum choice in a suit challenging federal official action is unusual to say the least.

Congress evidently shared that view and five years later passed a statute that, both the House and Senate reports indicated, was meant to overrule the *Primate Protection* decision, authorizing removal by agencies of the United States, as well as by the United States itself. See Federal Courts Improvement Act of 1996, Pub L No 104-317, § 206, 110 Stat 3847; S Rep 104-336, 104th Cong, 2d Sess 31 (1996); H Rep 104-798, 104th Cong, 2d Sess 19–20 (1996). However, the draftsmanship of the 1996 Congress, like that of its predecessor in 1948, left something to be desired. The amended provision permits removal by any of the following defendants: "The United States or any agency thereof or any officer (or any person acting under that officer) of the United States or of any agency thereof, sued in an official or individual capacity for any act under color of such office . . . ." Under the interpretive methodology of the *Primate Protection* decision, one would give considerable weight to the presence or absence of commas, and note that the amended section has no comma between "the United States or any agency thereof," on the one hand, and "any officer . . . of the United States or any agency thereof," on the other. Such a comma would have indicated that the succeeding phrase, "sued in an official or individual capacity for any act under color of such office," modifies only "officer of the United States or of any

A more recent development in the saga of supplemental jurisdiction, although it involves action not by Congress or the courts but rather by the American Law Institute (ALI)—a "private legislature"—further illustrates my theme. A number of years after § 1367 was enacted, the ALI commenced a Federal Judicial Code Project, a key element of which is a proposed revision of the supplemental jurisdiction statute.[230] That revision was designed to promote the basic objective that gave rise to the enactment of § 1367—that is, to overrule the *Finley* decision and to confer pendent party jurisdiction—while clearing up the interpretive problems that had arisen under § 1367. The ALI's proposed revision of § 1367 was drafted by an extraordinarily careful and knowledgeable Reporter. Rather than trying to sketch a few basic principles to be implemented by the courts, the Reporter, concerned that the Court's approach in *Finley* required greater textual specification, prepared a detailed statutory provision. Successive drafts were subjected to the ALI's laborious and exhaustive processes: review by an advisory committee of academics, judges, and lawyers, followed by consideration by the ALI's Council and ultimately by its full membership. The proposal was also the subject of considerable academic commentary.[231] Few legislative proposals in Congress receive anything approaching the level of careful drafting, expert attention, and prolonged review characteristic of the ALI's processes.

But after the ALI had approved the proposed revision of § 1367, Professor Hartnett discovered that it did not in fact achieve what

---

agency" rather than "the United States or any agency thereof"; but there being no comma, the amended provision permits the United States or an agency thereof to remove only when it is "sued in an official or individual capacity for any act under color of such office"—perhaps a null set and surely a peculiar category.

I rather think that even those Justices enamored of text and disdainful of legislative history would not have the temerity to say again that the statute does not authorize a federal agency to remove in cases in which the plaintiff does not purport to sue the federal government "in an official or individual capacity for any act under color of such office"—whatever that would mean. Perhaps this is a case where literalism would lead to an "absurd result," which, even the textualists say, licenses them not to be textualists. See text accompanying note 193. But if I am correct in predicting that textualism will not rule this time around, one may fairly wonder whether it had to have ruled in *Primate Protection*. And at a minimum, this episode, too, highlights the shortcomings of congressional drafting and, as a result, the hazards of a judicial approach that places excessive faith in the comprehensive omniscience of legislative drafting.

[230] For the relevant portion of the approved proposal, see ALI Federal Judicial Code Revision Project, Tentative Draft No. 2 (1998).

[231] See, for example, *Symposium: A Reappraisal of the Supplemental-Jurisdiction Statute: Title 28 USC § 1367*, 74 Ind L J 1 (1998).

was intended.[232] The Reporter had stated that the draft provision "preserves the rule of *Owen Equipment & Erection Co. v Kroger*"[233]—a decision that took a narrow view of the reach of supplemental jurisdiction in diversity cases.[234] Whether wisely or not, the ALI Project, from the outset, sought to codify the *Kroger Equipment* holding. But Professor Hartnett demonstrated that, in fact, the provision failed to do so in a certain set of cases—a failure that had escaped the collective attention of all (myself included) who had carefully pored over successive drafts.

There is a lesson in this story. Watching the ALI prepare draft statutes is not like watching the manufacture of sausage; it is rather more like watching an extremely serious and equally slow movie. But even the best informed and most deliberative efforts to address a problem of moderate complexity with a comprehensive statutory solution—efforts in this case that were free from the kind of overt lobbying and interest group influences commonly present in Congress and that have afflicted other ALI activities[235]—came up short. It makes one appreciate all the more the wisdom of Justice Jackson when he spoke of the futility, at least in our legal/political culture, of all-encompassing legislative codes.[236]

The Supreme Court's decision in *Finley* compelled Congress to take action, unless it wished to live with what was widely viewed as a very unfortunate result. But with academics heavily involved, it is unsurprising that Congress (or, later, the ALI) would take seriously Justice Scalia's approach in *Finley* when deciding how to draft a measure overruling it. Absent the judicial self-abnegation that I

---

[232] See Edward A. Hartnett, *Would the Kroger Rule Survive the ALI's Proposed Revision of § 1367*, 51 Duke L J 647 (2001). The article is one part of a four-part colloquy on *Supplemental Jurisdiction, the ALI, and the Rule of the Kroger Case* in that issue of the Duke Law Journal, featuring an exchange between Hartnett and John Oakley, the Reporter for the ALI Project.

[233] 437 US 365 (1978). In *Kroger Equipment*, an Iowa citizen brought a diversity action against a Nebraska citizen, who in turn filed a third-party complaint against an Iowa citizen. The Supreme Court ruled that when the plaintiff subsequently amended her complaint to name the third-party defendant as an additional defendant, there was an absence of complete diversity and that plaintiff's claim against the third-party defendant could not be heard on a theory of ancillary jurisdiction.

[234] John B. Oakley, *Integrating Supplemental Jurisdiction and Diversity Jurisdiction: A Progress Report on the Work of the American Law Institute*, 74 Ind L J 25, 44 (1998).

[235] See, for example, the *Symposium on the American Law Institute: Process, Partisanship, and the Restatements of Law*, 26 Hofstra L Rev 567–834 (1998).

[236] See text accompanying note 214.

am now decrying, Congress could have thrown the problem back to the courts, as my colleague David Shapiro has urged.[237] Congress could have passed a brief, general amendment overturning the result in *Finley* while leaving to the courts the task (in which they had been engaged, in cases like *Kroger Equipment*, prior to the *Finley* decision) of elaborating the standards for supplemental jurisdiction in a fashion that was viewed as consistent with the complete diversity rule, the jurisdictional amount requirement, and other relevant jurisdictional policies.[238]

If Congress could have taken that approach in 1990 after the *Finley* decision, the question arises whether it should have required an act of Congress in 1990 to impel the Supreme Court and the courts generally to take on that kind of role. How much better off we would have been had *Finley* never aspired to place responsibility for fine-tuning the contours of supplemental jurisdiction on the Congress and had Congress not therefore felt obliged to enact a comprehensive codification that proved to be full of pitfalls.

B. RETROACTIVITY OF THE 1996 AMENDMENTS
TO THE HABEAS CORPUS JURISDICTION

My second example, by contrast, is one in which Congress did not try to resolve all the issues up front, and in which the courts proceeded to implement the statute, filling in the gaps as needed. The statute in question is the Anti-Terrorism and Effective Death Penalty Act of 1996[239] (AEDPA), which amended a number of existing provisions in the habeas corpus jurisdiction and supplied a number of new ones as well. Because AEDPA took effect on April 24, 1996, more than six years ago, for the most part questions of the retroactivity of its provisions have receded into the past. But that was not so immediately after the Act's effective date.

The Act expressly addresses retroactivity only with respect to the provisions of its Chapter 154, which is limited to capital cases, and then only when a state has been found to have established a mechanism for the provision of counsel in state postconviction

---

[237] Shapiro, 74 Ind L J at 218 (cited in note 223) (suggesting it would be preferable were Congress to "enact a law establishing the principle of supplemental jurisdiction, and then * * * leave all or most of the details to be worked out by the courts").

[238] See id.

[239] Pub L No 104-132, 110 Stat 1214.

proceedings that meets specified statutory conditions. AEDPA provides that the provisions of Chapter 154 "shall apply to cases pending on or after the date of enactment of this Act."[240]

As matters turned out, this express retroactivity provision had little effect, for it was not until 2001 that a state was found to have satisfied the conditions that bring those provisions into play.[241] But this one effort to prescribe retroactivity in express statutory terms does not inspire confidence. Among the provisions of Chapter 154 is a new statute of limitations of 180 days; prior to the enactment of AEDPA, there was no statute of limitations for any habeas petitioner. Had any state been found on or shortly after the enactment of AEDPA to have satisfied the statutory conditions that make Chapter 154 operative, then a prisoner on death row whose conviction became final 181 days earlier and who had not yet filed a habeas petition would have been time-barred—in circumstances in which one could not have said that he was sleeping on his rights. Indeed, a petition filed prior to April 24, 1996, but more than 180 days after the limitations period began to run, would have been timely when initially filed but would have been rendered untimely after AEDPA took effect, by virtue of the retroactively applicable limitations period.

Had such a situation arisen in practice, perhaps a court would have ignored the retroactivity provision, unwilling to believe that Congress meant to depart from the view that newly enacted "statutes of limitations must allow a reasonable time after they take effect for the commencement of suits upon existing causes of action"[242] or to transform a timely petition into an untimely one. But a review of the committee reports reveals no awareness of any potential problem.

While in practice the express retroactivity provision of Chapter 154 never took effect, a number of other retroactivity issues, in-

---

[240] Section 107(c), 110 Stat 1226.

[241] See *Spears v Stewart*, 267 F3d 1026 (9th Cir 2001), amended and superseded by 283 F3d 992 (9th Cir 2002). Even that conclusion is subject to dispute. The panel in *Spears* carefully analyzed Arizona's system and found that it met the statutory conditions, but also refused to enforce the provisions of Chapter 154 in the case at bar because Arizona had not complied with its own rules requiring timely appointment of postconviction counsel. On rehearing, eleven judges joined in whole or in part in an opinion, dissenting from the denial of rehearing en banc, that characterized the panel's opinion as dictum.

[242] *Block v North Dakota*, 461 US 273, 286 n 23 (1983) (internal quotation marks omitted).

volving the more general statutory amendments found in Chapter 153, which apply to all postconviction habeas petitions, were soon raised. As to these provisions, AEDPA contains no textual provision concerning retroactivity. One issue that initially divided the circuits was whether the core provision of Chapter 153, which limits the scope of federal habeas review of state court determinations,[243] applies to petitions filed prior to the Act's effective date. When the question reached the Supreme Court in *Lindh v Murphy*,[244] it ruled, 5–4, against retroactive application in this situation. The majority relied primarily on the negative implication of the retroactivity provision in Chapter 154, which it read "as indicating implicitly that the amendments to chapter 153 were assumed and meant to apply to the general run of habeas cases only when those cases had been filed after the date of the Act."[245] There was, however, a more than respectable argument, made forcefully in the Chief Justice's dissent,[246] for a contrary conclusion, surely as a matter of policy, and even notwithstanding any possible negative implication of the retroactivity provision in Chapter 154. If nothing more, the decision in *Lindh* shows the potential perils of Congress's addressing an issue like retroactivity in piecemeal fashion.

Of course, Congress could have tried to avoid those perils by addressing the question of retroactivity comprehensively, indicating, for each distinct provision of the Act, just when and in what circumstances it would take effect. But if Congress's efforts with regard to Chapter 154 do not inspire confidence about its capacities, the pattern of decisional law reveals just how nuanced and far-sighted Congress would have had to have been in order to have taken that more comprehensive approach. For the judge-made rules about retroactivity vary quite a bit from provision to provision, depending on the provision's purpose and effect.

For example, AEDPA has a one-year statute of limitations for habeas petitioners generally that runs from the latest of four specified dates. (Unlike the 180-day provision for capital petitioners, that provision does not depend on the state's satisfying any preconditions.) But the courts of appeals ruled that petitioners had,

---

[243] 28 USC § 2254(d).

[244] 521 US 320 (1997).

[245] Id at 327.

[246] See id at 337–45 (Rehnquist dissenting).

in addition, a one-year grace period from the effective date of AEDPA in which to file. Those rulings permitted a petition to be filed until April 24, 1997—even if more than one year had already passed from the specified dates in the statutory provision—in order to avoid any retroactive effect.[247]

Similarly, courts have not mechanically applied AEDPA's tightened limitations on the filing of successive petitions when the prisoner's prior petition was filed before AEDPA took effect. In such cases, some courts have found that application of the tightened limitations was inappropriate and instead applied the pre-AEDPA law;[248] others refuse to apply the tightened limitations if the prisoner can establish reliance on the pre-AEDPA law[249] but do apply them when no detrimental reliance has been shown.[250] At the same time, more than one circuit has ruled that a distinct aspect of the new rules governing successive petitions—requiring that the court of appeals rather than the district court decide whether a successive petition may be filed—should be fully retroactive.[251]

A last question concerns the applicability of a provision in AEDPA that amends the procedure through which a habeas petitioner who loses in the district court may obtain the right to appeal. In *Slack v McDaniel*,[252] the Supreme Court held that this provision does apply to cases pending in the district courts on the effective date of AEDPA so long as appellate proceedings were not initiated until after that effective date.

There are reasons for each of these various holdings, and thus it is not impossible that a far-sighted legislature could have written

---

[247] See, for example, *Nichols v Bowersox*, 172 F3d 1068, 1073 (8th Cir 1999) (en banc); *Wilcox v Florida Dep't of Corrections*, 158 F3d 1209, 1211 (11th Cir 1998).

The Supreme Court's decision in *Lindh* held only that Chapter 153's provisions *do not* apply to petitions filed *before* April 24, 1996. While most courts have ruled that the core provision in Chapter 153—the limitation in § 2254(d) on the scope of federal habeas review—*does apply* to petitions filed *after* that date, the courts have recognized, in Judge Luttig's words, that the *Lindh* decision "left open the possibility . . . that it would not apply the new provisions of chapter 153 even to a post-enactment petition if doing so would result in an impermissible retroactive effect." *Mueller v Angelone*, 181 F3d 557, 568 (4th Cir 1999).

[248] See, for example, In re *Hanserd*, 123 F3d 922, 933 (6th Cir 1997).

[249] See, for example, *Burris v Parke*, 95 F3d 465, 468 (7th Cir 1996) (en banc).

[250] *In re Medina*, 109 F3d 1556, 1563 (11th Cir 1997).

[251] See, for example, *Graham v Johnson*, 168 F3d 762 (5th Cir 1999); *In re Minarik*, 166 F3d 591 (3d Cir 1999).

[252] 529 US 473, 479–82 (2000).

a more detailed set of retroactivity provisions calling for essentially the pattern of results that the courts have given us. If so, much time and energy spent in litigating these questions could have been spared.[253] But what is possible is hardly likely. Moreover, it is important to recall that what may now appear, with hindsight and after careful consideration of concrete cases and adversary argument, to be a clear or sensible or obvious solution to a set of problems may in fact have been far more difficult to anticipate in the abstract. The clumsiness of the retroactivity provision in Chapter 154 hardly leaves one optimistic about Congress's capacity to work out in advance a refined and sensible approach to retroactivity of the various provisions of a statute like AEDPA.

One could multiply the examples of statutes in which textual specification seems to have backfired.[254] The point is not that Con-

---

[253] In addition, such statutory specification would have resolved a question on which the circuits remain divided—whether exemption from the retroactive application of the successive petition provisions requires proof of detrimental reliance.

[254] See, for example, note 229.

Jonathan Siegel, in *What Statutory Drafting Errors Teach Us About Statutory Interpretation*, 69 Geo Wash L Rev at 309 (cited in note 185), discusses another example, from an older enactment, the federal venue statute, 28 USC § 1391, that exhibits many of the same features. See also id at 352–58 (discussing still another example, this one involving 1988 amendments to the diversity jurisdiction statute, 28 USC § 1332, pertaining to aliens).

Still another example reaches back to the 1948 revision of the Anti-Injunction Act, now codified in 28 USC § 2283. In that year, Congress codified a set of exceptions to the general ban on anti-suit injunctions. The Supreme Court has since stressed that the courts are not to add to those exceptions nor to expand them by loose construction. See, for example, *Atlantic Coast Line R.R. Co. v Bhd of Locomotive Eng'rs*, 398 US 281, 286–87 (1970); *Amalgamated Clothing Workers v Richman Bros.*, 348 US 511, 515–16 (1955). In one instance the Court has departed from that approach, recognizing an additional, nonstatutory exception for injunctions sought by the United States—an exception that, in its view, Congress simply failed to anticipate. See *Leiter Minerals, Inc. v United States*, 352 US 220 (1957). But otherwise, the current provision, as the Court has interpreted it, substituted legislative specification for a more flexible system of judge-made law that existed prior to 1948.

There is much, of course, that Congress did not and could not foresee in 1948. A salient example is the phenomenon of class actions unleashed by the 1966 changes to Rule 23 of the Federal Rules of Civil Procedure. Especially pertinent to the problem of anti-suit injunctions are the problems caused by rival class actions in different courts, leading, in the view of some, to both (i) a "reverse auction" that favors defendants and the first set of lawyers to reach a settlement at the expense of class members, and (ii) a "race to the bottom" to find the jurisdiction with the most forgiving standards for certifying classes and/or approving settlements.

The question of the circumstances in which a federal court should be able to enjoin state court actions that threaten to interfere with administration of a pending federal class action is thus an important one. It is also complex, and may depend on such factors as: (i) the kind of federal class action (Rule 23(b)(1), (b)(2), or (b)(3)); (ii) whether the state court action was brought by members of the federal class; and (iii) whether the injunction is sought before certification, after certification but before the time for opting-out in (b)(3) actions, after formulation of a proposed settlement, or after entry of judgment. Congress

gress should always legislate in the most general way so as to leave as much as possible to judicial interpretation; no one would endorse such a position. And, indeed, it is difficult for responsible legislative drafters to determine how far to specify particular matters and how much instead to rely on judicial implementation. But I hope that the argument and examples presented have suggested not merely that calls for Congress to follow statutory checklists are sometimes a bit superficial. These examples also show, more generally, how difficult it is to expect that Congress will, by virtue of detailed textual specification, be able to get things right the first time, or, when initial legislative efforts misfire, to fix things later. There are thus real pitfalls in the assumption that Congress can and should be expected to resolve matters in legislative text without the aid of courts acting as junior partners in shaping a workable legal system.

V. Conclusion

Constitutional activism has been much in the headlines, but I hope I have shown that there is another story line in recent Supreme Court decisions, one of passivity, or, more precisely, of selective passivity, in the realm of subconstitutional decision making. One can offer, as I have, general criticisms of that passive approach as disserving the needs of both Congress and the legal system, and I hope that these criticisms are persuasive in their own terms. But I believe that the critique of judicial passivity gains additional force

---

has not addressed this question, however, and while some lower courts have read the "in aid of jurisdiction" exception to § 2283 as broadly permitting anti-suit injunctions in class actions, see, for example, *Carlough v Amchem Prods., Inc.*, 10 F3d 189, 202 (3d Cir 1993), that conclusion is, to say the least, hardly an obvious one, see Rhonda Wasserman, *Dueling Class Actions*, 80 BU L Rev 461 (2000); Joan Steinman, *Managing Punitive Damages: A Role for Mandatory "Limited Generosity" Classes and Anti-Suit Injunctions?* 36 Wake Forest L Rev 1043, 1091–94 (2001).

In determining whether federal courts may issue anti-suit injunctions, an alternative, and I believe preferable, approach would have been for Congress, in 1948, not to have provided (or for the Court not to have interpreted Congress as having provided) that only Congress may formulate exceptions to the ban. Instead, one could have left intact the pre-1948 tradition in which courts applied the general policy against anti-suit injunctions to particular situations that may call for an exception. Compare David P. Currie, *The Federal Courts and the American Law Institute, Part II*, 36 U Chi L Rev 268, 329 (1969) (proposing a standard under which "The federal courts shall not enjoin pending or threatened proceedings in state courts unless there is no other effective means of avoiding grave and irreparable harm.").

from the very fact that the Justices who endorse such passivity do not in fact exhibit it when facing legal problems that engage their desire to ensure that congressional schemes of regulation are effective. Preemption cases, I have tried to suggest, do appear to engage that desire. While the Justices frequently divide on the merits of particular preemption claims, they all appear to view preemption as important to the workability of federal legal regimes and judicial specification of the scope of preemption as essential to the formulation of a workable doctrine. Implicitly, the Justices reject the proposition that the scope of preemption can be left to Congress to specify in textual directives; indeed, even where Congress has sought to provide such directives, the Court often gives them little weight.[255]

Preemption cases are both consequential and complex, but they are not unique. In many other areas of federal regulation, it is equally implausible to expect that Congress can specify in advance the answer to the complex of questions that over time will arise, and it is equally important for courts to take responsibility for assisting in the creation of a workable legal system. Yet all too often the Supreme Court asserts that it is powerless to take on that role—the very role that it in fact takes on elsewhere. Where such judicial passivity is present, it deprives the polity of an invaluable tool for ensuring the effectiveness of congressional regulation. And the Supreme Court's claim that such passivity is a necessary or proper approach to judicial lawmaking is far less persuasive precisely because the Court's passivity is so selective.

---

[255] Legislatures do, on occasion, enact principles of statutory construction, either in general or in connection with particular measures, and Congress has broad (though not unlimited) power to prescribe such rules. See Nicholas Rosenkranz, *Federal Rules of Statutory Interpretation*, 115 Harv L Rev 2085 (2002). But insofar as the plea in this article may go unheeded by the courts, it seems doubtful to me that Congress can effectively redress the problems that I have addressed by enacting principles of statutory construction calling for a shift in judicial course. Any such congressional effort would be subject to many of the same problems as are efforts to prescribe all of the substantive rules under a substantive regulatory regime. Reducing statutory interpretive practices, which by their nature are complex and contextual, to a statutory code would be extraordinarily difficult. If the *Great-West Life* decision has among its defects an excessive reliance on text, how would one address that problem? By instructing courts to consider the text but not too much? To interpret language in light of context so that the results make sense? Statutory interpretation is an art, and I do not believe that meta-instructions can be shaped with sufficient determinacy that they can effectively order judges who may be otherwise inclined to adopt what Congress might view as a more "correct" approach to decision making.

When compared to judicial activism, judicial passivity may appear to be far less remarkable or important; it surely captures fewer headlines. But in a quite different fashion, judicial passivity poses threats to the effectiveness of congressional legislation every bit as much as does the judicial activism of the Court's constitutional federalism decisions. Genuine deference to and respect for legislative supremacy demands attention to, and retreat from, both approaches.

GEOFFREY R. STONE

THE ORIGINS OF THE
"BAD TENDENCY" TEST:
FREE SPEECH IN WARTIME

It was during and immediately after the First World War that the
Supreme Court first began seriously to consider the meaning of
the First Amendment. The experience of those years has played a
central role ever since in shaping our thinking about the freedom
of speech. In this essay, I consider whether there are new lessons
we can learn from that experience—lessons that may be especially
useful in helping us understand and address the distinctive stresses
of wartime.

We have long recognized that the bad tendency test—the predominant standard in this era for determining whether criticism
of the war was protected by the Constitution—was a misguided
interpretation of the First Amendment.[1] In this article, I show that
the test was also a misguided interpretation of the Espionage Act

Geoffrey R. Stone is the Harry Kalven, Jr. Distinguished Service Professor of Law, The
University of Chicago.

AUTHOR'S NOTE: I would like to thank Shana Wallace, Jake Kreilkamp, Justin Sandberg,
and Elliot Avidan for their invaluable research assistance, my colleagues Albert Alschuler,
Rachel Barkow, Bernard Harcourt, Stephen Schulhofer, and Cass Sunstein for their insightful comments on earlier drafts of this essay, Lynn Chu and Nancy Stone for their
excellent editorial advice, and the Harry Kalven, Jr. Faculty Research Fund of The University of Chicago Law School for financial support.

[1] See, for example, Geoffrey R. Stone, Louis M. Seidman, Cass R. Sunstein, and Mark
V. Tushnet, eds, *Constitutional Law* 1005–44 (Aspen, 4th ed 2002); Frank Strong, *Fifty Years
of "Clear and Present Danger": From Schenck to Brandenburg—and Beyond*, 1969 Supreme
Court Review 41; Bernard Schwartz, *Holmes versus Hand: Clear and Present Danger or Advocacy of Unlawful Action?* 1994 Supreme Court Review 209.

of 1917, a distortion of well-established principles of the criminal law and, ironically, a significantly less speech-protective standard than the test advocated by the Department of Justice.[2] In a sense, this is a case study in how far the courts were prepared to go in order to accommodate the pressures of wartime hysteria.

I. "AN OUTRAGED PEOPLE AND AN AVENGING GOVERNMENT"

When the United States entered World War I in April 1917, there was strong opposition both to the war and the draft. Many citizens believed that our goal was not to "make the world safe for democracy," but to protect the investments of the wealthy. War opponents, including many German-Americans, Irish-Americans, Socialists, Pacifists, and Anarchists, were sharply critical of the Wilson administration.

President Wilson had little patience for such dissent. After the sinking of the *Lusitania*, he warned that disloyalty "must be crushed out" of existence.[3] In calling for the first federal legislation against disloyal expression since the Sedition Act of 1798, he insisted that disloyalty "was not a subject on which there was room for . . . debate," for disloyal individuals "had sacrificed their right to civil liberties."[4] In these and similar pronouncements, Wilson set the tone for what was to follow.

Shortly after the United States entered the war, Congress enacted the Espionage Act of 1917. Although the Act dealt primarily with espionage and sabotage, several provisions had serious consequences for the freedom of speech. Specifically, section 3 of the Act made it a crime for any person willfully to "cause or attempt to cause insubordination, disloyalty, or refusal of duty in the military forces of the United States" or willfully to "obstruct the recruiting or enlistment service of the United States."[5]

---

[2] David M. Rabban and Paul L. Murphy have done splendid work in surveying this terrain, and I draw heavily (and gratefully) on their research. Neither, however, fully considers these facets of the history or reaches the conclusions I set forth in this essay. See Paul L. Murphy, *World War I and the Origin of Civil Liberties in the United States* (Norton, 1979); David M. Rabban, *Free Speech in Its Forgotten Years* (Cambridge, 1997).

[3] Woodrow Wilson's Third Annual Message to Congress, quoted in David M. Kennedy, *Over Here: The First World War and American Society* 24 (Oxford, 1980).

[4] Murphy, *World War I* at 53 (cited in note 2).

[5] Act of June 15, 1917, ch 30, tit I, § 3, 40 Stat 219.

Although the 1917 Act was intended to address very specific concerns relating directly to the operation of the military,[6] aggressive federal prosecutors and compliant federal judges invoked the "bad tendency" test to transform the Act into a full-scale prohibition of seditious utterance. The Wilson administration's stance became evident in November 1917 when Attorney General Charles Gregory, referring to war dissenters, declared: "May God have mercy on them, for they need expect none from an outraged people and an avenging government."[7]

In fact, the federal government worked strenuously to create an "outraged people." Because there had been no direct attack on the United States, and no direct threat to our national security, the Wilson administration found it necessary to generate a sense of urgency and a mood of outrage in order to exhort Americans to enlist, contribute money, and make the many sacrifices war demands.

To this end, President Wilson established the Committee for Public Information (CPI), under the direction of George Creel, whose charge was to promote support for the war. The CPI produced a flood of inflammatory and often misleading pamphlets, news releases, speeches, editorials, and motion pictures, all designed to instill a hatred of all things German.

The CPI actively encouraged patriotic "citizen's groups" to support this effort. These groups not only reported tens of thousands of incidents of suspected "disloyalty" to the Department of Justice, but also engaged with tacit immunity in breaking and entering, bugging offices, tapping telephones, and examining bank accounts and medical records. Vigilantes ransacked the homes of German-Americans and attacked those who questioned the war. In Texas, six farmers were horsewhipped because they declined to contribute to the American Red Cross; in Illinois, an angry mob wrapped an individual suspected of disloyalty in an American flag and then murdered him on a public street.[8]

---

[6] For a review of the legislative history of the Espionage Act, see Geoffrey R. Stone, *Judge Learned Hand and the Espionage Act of 1917: A Mystery Unraveled*, 70 U Chi L Rev 335 (2003).

[7] NY Times 3 (Nov 21, 1917). See Robert Goldstein, *Political Repression in Modern America: From 1870 to the Present* 108 (Schenkman, 1978).

[8] See Meirion Harries and Susie Harries, *The Last Days of Innocence: America at War, 1917–1918* 282–308 (Vintage, 1997); H. C. Peterson and Gilbert C. Fite, *Opponents of War* 18–19 (Wisconsin, 1957); Murphy, *World War I* at 94–95 (cited in note 2); Goldstein,

As John Lord O'Brian, the Head of the War Emergency Division of the Department of Justice, observed shortly after the war ended, "immense pressure" was "brought to bear" in all parts of the country for "wholesale repression and restraint of public opinion."[9] It was, he added, in an "atmosphere" of excessive passion, patriotism, and "clamor" that the laws "affecting 'free speech' received the severest test thus far placed upon them in our history."[10] In this setting, the Department of Justice invoked the Espionage Act of 1917 to prosecute more than 2,000 dissenters during the war for allegedly disloyal, seditious, or incendiary speech.[11]

The story of the Supreme Court in this era is too familiar to require repeating in detail. In a series of decisions in 1919 and 1920—*Schenck, Frohwerk, Debs, Abrams, Schaefer, Pierce,* and *Gilbert*[12]—the Court consistently upheld the convictions of individuals who had agitated against the war and the draft. Although Justices Holmes and Brandeis eventually separated themselves from their brethren and launched a competing tradition within the Court's First Amendment jurisprudence,[13] the Court as a whole evinced no interest in the rights of dissenters. As Harry Kalven observed, these decisions left no doubt of the Court's position: "While the nation is at war serious, abrasive criticism of the war or of conscription is beyond constitutional protection." These decisions, he added, "are dismal evidence of the degree to which the mood of society penetrates judicial chambers." The Court's performance, he concluded, was "simply wretched."[14]

Political Repression at 111 (cited in note 7); Henry Scheiber, *The Wilson Administration and Civil Liberties: 1917–1921* 16–17 (Ithaca, N.Y., 1960).

[9] John Lord O'Brian, *Civil Liberty in War Time*, 62 Rep of the NY Bar Assn 275, 306, 299 (Jan 17, 1919).

[10] Id at 299.

[11] See Murphy, *World War I* at 80 (cited in note 2); Rabban, *Forgotten Years* at 256 (cited in note 2); *Annual Report of the Attorney General of the United States* 47 (1918). More precisely, 2,168 individuals were prosecuted and 1,055 were convicted. See Scheiber, *Wilson Administration* at 46–47 (cited in note 8).

[12] *Schenck v United States*, 249 US 47 (1919); *Frohwerk v United States*, 249 US 204 (1919); *Debs v United States*, 249 US 211 (1919); *Abrams et al v United States*, 250 US 616 (1919); *Schaefer v United States*, 251 US 466 (1919); *Pierce et al v United States*, 252 US 239 (1919); *Gilbert v Minnesota*, 254 US 325 (1920).

[13] See, for example, *Abrams* (Holmes dissenting); *Schaefer* (Brandeis dissenting); *Gilbert* (Brandeis dissenting). See also *Gitlow v New York*, 268 US 652 (1925) (Holmes dissenting); *Whitney v California*, 274 US 357 (1927) (Brandeis dissenting).

[14] Harry Kalven, Jr., *A Worthy Tradition: Freedom of Speech in America* 135–36, 147 (Harper & Row, 1988).

All of this was accomplished by judges who interpreted both the Espionage Act and the First Amendment through the lens of the bad tendency test. The remainder of this essay explores how this came to pass.

II. JUDGES BOURQUIN, AMIDON, AND HAND

The general cast of mind of the legal profession in this era was both politically and jurisprudentially conservative. There was as yet no deeply-rooted commitment to civil liberties within the legal profession, and no well-developed understanding of the freedom of speech. In the absence of any firm judicial precedents protecting this freedom, it was unlikely that many judges would withstand the mounting pressure for suppression.

A few judges, however, did stand fast. Federal District Judge George Bourquin of Montana, for example, presided over the prosecution of Ves Hall, who was alleged to have announced in a series of conversations that "he would flee to avoid going to the war," that "Germany would whip the United States," that "the President was a Wall Street tool," and that "the United States was only fighting for Wall Street millionaires and to protect Morgan's interests in England." Hall was charged with violating section 3 of the Espionage Act.

Judge Bourquin directed a verdict of acquittal, finding that Hall's comments could not be held to violate section 3. Judge Bourquin explained that it is "settled law" that an "attempt" is an effort, "with specific intent to commit specific crimes," which effort fails, but which is nonetheless "of sufficient magnitude and proximity" to its goal that it can fairly be said to have been "reasonably calculated to excite public fear" that the effort might accomplish its goal. Noting that Hall's comments "were made at a Montana village of some sixty people, sixty miles from the railway," and that no soldiers or sailors were "within hundreds of miles," Bourquin concluded that any inference that Hall's remarks had been specifically intended to interfere "with the operations or success of the military," or were reasonably likely to do so, would be "unjustified, absurd and without support in the evidence."

Judge Bourquin observed that the Espionage Act was "not intended to suppress" general "criticism or denunciation, truth or slander, oratory or gossip, argument or loose talk," but only specific "acts that

Congress has denounced as crimes." Congress, he emphasized, "has not denounced as crimes any mere disloyal utterances, nor any slander or libel of the President or any other officers of the United States," unless they meet the requirements of the Act.[15]

Judge Charles Fremont Amidon, a Federal District Judge in North Dakota, also took a strong stance against a broad reading of the Espionage Act. E. H. Schutte, a farmer, was alleged to have stated publicly that "this is a rich man's war and it is all a damn graft and a swindle." Schutte was charged with violating section 3 of the Act. Judge Amidon dismissed the indictment because there was no allegation or evidence that Schutte's comments had been made to an audience containing men who were in the armed forces or eligible for the draft.[16]

In another case, involving John Wichek, a North Dakota banker who had stated that "banks having large holdings of Liberty Bonds are unsafe to keep money in," Judge Amidon instructed the jury that it could not convict unless Wichek had directly affected the attitude of individuals eligible for service in the armed forces.[17] Judge Amidon expressed his general philosophy about these issues in another prosecution, involving an individual who had spoken bitterly in opposition to war profiteering. Amidon observed that "the only way you can produce a change in any political . . . condition is for the people who suffer from that condition to say that the people who are inflicting the sufferings are doing wrong, and speak right out plainly on that subject."[18]

The most important decision in which a Federal District Judge held fast against a broad construction of the Espionage Act was *Masses Publishing Co. v Patten*.[19] *The Masses* was a "revolutionary" journal that regularly featured such authors as Max Eastman, John

---

[15] Judge Bourquin's opinion in *United States v Hall* is reported in 65th Cong, 2d Sess, in Cong Rec S 4559–60 (April 4, 1918). Judge Bourquin also dismissed the charge that Hall had willfully obstructed "the recruiting or enlistment service of the United States" because there was no evidence of actual obstruction and this clause of section 3 did not even cover "attempts to obstruct." Judge Bourquin also observed that to the extent statements like Hall's might cause a breach of the peace that was a matter for state law.

[16] *United States v Schutte*, 252 F 212, 214 (D ND 1918). See Walter Nelles, ed, *Espionage Act Cases* 90–92 (National Civil Liberties Bureau, 1918); Murphy, *World War I* at 208 (cited in note 2).

[17] The jury acquitted. *United States v Wichek*, unreported opinion (D ND 1918), quoted in Murphy, *World War I* at 208 (cited in note 2).

[18] *United States v Brinton*, unreported opinion (D ND 1918), quoted in Murphy, *World War I* at 205–06 (cited in note 2), citing U.S. Department of Justice, *Interpretation of War Statutes*, Bulletin No 132 (1919).

[19] 244 F 535 (S D NY 1917).

Reed, Carl Sandburg, Louis Untermeyer, and Sherwood Anderson. In the summer of 1917, Postmaster General Burleson ordered the exclusion from the mails of the August issue of *The Masses* on the ground that it violated section 3 of the Espionage Act. *The Masses* sought an injunction to forbid the local postmaster from refusing to accept the issue for mailing. The postmaster argued that four cartoons and four items of text violated the Act, thus justifying the order of exclusion.[20]

Judge Learned Hand granted the injunction and prohibited the postmaster from excluding *The Masses* from the mails. Judge Hand began by observing that in times of war it "may be that Congress may forbid the mails to any matter which tends to discourage the successful prosecution of the war."[21] But, he argued, he did not need to resolve the First Amendment issue because, in his judgment, the Act did not reach the material published in *The Masses*.

Hand conceded the postmaster's claim that "to arouse discontent and disaffection among the people with the prosecution of the war and with the draft tends to promote a mutinous and insubordinate temper among the troops."[22] He argued, however, that to read the Act so "broadly would . . . involve necessarily as a consequence the suppression of all hostile criticism, and of all opinion except what encouraged and supported the existing policies."[23]

---

[20] Illustrative of these was a cartoon drawn by Henry J. Glentenkamp entitled "Conscription" and a poem by Josephine Bell entitled "A Tribute." The cartoon depicted a cannon, to the mouth of which is bound the naked figure of a youth, to the wheel that of a woman marked "Democracy," and upon the carriage that of a man marked "Labor." On the ground kneels a draped woman marked "Motherhood" in a posture of grief. An infant lies on the ground beside her. The poem, a "tribute" to Emma Goldman and Alexander Berkman, who were then in jail for opposing the war and the draft, included the following illustrative verse:

> Emma Goldman and Alexander Berkman
> Are in prison tonight,
> But they have made themselves elemental forces,
> Like the water that climbs down the rocks;
> Like the wind in the leaves;
> Like the gentle night that holds us;
> They are working on our destinies;
> They are forging the love of the nations;
>   . . .
> Tonight they lie in prison.

Id at 544.

[21] Id at 538.

[22] Id at 539.

[23] Id.

Hand maintained that such an approach "would contradict the normal assumption of democratic government," and even assuming that Congress would have the power in time of war "to repress such opinion," the exercise of that power "is so contrary to the use and wont of our people that only the clearest expression of such a power justifies the conclusion that it was intended."[24] In these circumstances, Hand concluded that the "language of the statute" does not require such an understanding of its scope.[25]

The challenge for Judge Hand, then, was to articulate the line between lawful and unlawful speech under the Act. Judge Bourquin had focused on the law of attempt to draw this line, arguing that there must be a relatively tight connection between the speech and the feared consequences in order to infer specific intent or find an attempt. Judge Hand took a different approach.

Hand asserted that it "has always" been recognized that one "may not counsel or advise others to violate the law as it stands."[26] Words, he observed, "are not only the keys of persuasion, but the triggers of action, and those which have no purport but to counsel the violation of law cannot by any latitude of interpretation be a part of that public opinion which is the final source of government in a democratic state."[27]

He conceded that speech falling short of express incitement to violate the law can have negative consequences. "Political agitation," he noted, "by the passions it arouses or the convictions it engenders, may . . . stimulate men to the violation of law," and "[d]etestation of existing policies is easily transformed into forcible resistance of the authority which puts them in execution."[28] But,

---

[24] Id at 540.

[25] I had always assumed that Judge Hand's characterization of the legislative history of the Espionage Act was too cavalier and that it was really just a ploy to enable him to cast his opinion in terms of statutory construction rather than constitutional compulsion, and that is certainly the conventional wisdom. See, for example, Rabban, *Forgotten Years* at 265 (cited in note 2) ("[T]he legislative history of the Espionage Act, which Hand never cited in his opinion, demonstrates the congressional intent to punish the very kind of antiwar material that prompted the postmaster to declare *The Masses* 'nonmailable.' "). On examination, however, I have concluded that Judge Hand was right: Congress did not intend the Act to have the severely repressive effect attributed to it by the courts during World War I. For a review of the legislative history and an elaboration of this conclusion, see Stone, *A Mystery Unraveled* (cited in note 6).

[26] *Masses*, 244 F at 540.

[27] Id.

[28] Id.

he reasoned, "to assimilate agitation, legitimate as such, with direct incitement to violent resistance, is to disregard the tolerance of all methods of political agitation which in normal times is a safeguard of free government."[29] This "distinction," he emphasized, "is not a scholastic subterfuge, but a hard-bought acquisition in the fight for freedom."[30]

Judge Hand thus concluded that "[i]f one stops short of urging" others to violate the law, "one should not be held to have attempted to cause its violation."[31] "If that be not the test," he cautioned, "I can see no escape from the conclusion that under this [Act] every political agitation which can be shown to be apt to create a seditious temper is illegal."[32] He declared his confidence that by the language of the Act "Congress had no such revolutionary purpose in view."[33] Applying this approach to the facts of *Masses*, Judge Hand held that neither the cartoons nor the text crossed the line of express advocacy of unlawful conduct.[34]

III. The Triumph of "Bad Tendency"

Few other judges embraced constructions of the Espionage Act similar to those articulated by Judges Bourquin, Amidon, and Hand.[35] Rather, most federal judges had no tolerance for dissenters and no interest in subtle appeals to statutory construction or to the protections of the First Amendment.[36]

The prevailing approach in the lower federal courts is well illustrated by the decision of the United States Court of Appeals in

---

[29] Id.

[30] Id.

[31] Id.

[32] Id.

[33] Id.

[34] Hand's opinion in *Masses* was promptly overruled by the Court of Appeals. *Masses Pub. Co. v Patten*, 246 F 24 (2d Cir 1919). For more on Judge Hand and the *Masses* case, see Gerald Gunther, *Learned Hand: The Man and the Judge* 153–61 (Belknap, 1994); Stone, *A Mystery Unraveled* (cited in note 6).

[35] For other decisions that narrowly construed section 3 of the Espionage Act, see, for example, *Grubl v United States*, 264 F 44 (8th Cir 1920); *Fontana v United States*, 262 F 283 (8th Cir 1919); *Harshfield v United States*, 260 F 659 (8th Cir 1919); *Kammann v United States*, 259 F 192 (7th Cir 1919); *Shilter v United States*, 257 F 724 (9th Cir 1919); *Sandberg v United States*, 257 F 643 (9th Cir 1919).

[36] See Thomas A. Lawrence, *Eclipse of Liberty: Civil Liberties in the United States During the First World War*, 21 Wayne L Rev 33, 70 (1974).

Shaffer v United States.[37] In *Shaffer*, the defendant was charged with possessing and mailing copies of a book, *The Finished Mystery*, in violation of the Espionage Act. The book contained the following passage, which was specified in the indictment:[38]

> If you say it is a war of defense against wanton and intolerable aggression, I must reply that . . . it has yet to be proved that Germany has any intention or desire of attacking us. . . . The war itself is wrong. Its prosecution will be a crime. There is not a question raised, an issue involved, a cause at stake, which is worth the life of one blue-jacket on the sea or one khaki-coat in the trenches.

Shaffer was convicted, and the Court of Appeals affirmed, with the following reasoning:[39]

> It is true that disapproval of war and the advocacy of peace are not crimes under the Espionage Act; but the question here . . . is whether the natural and probable tendency and effect of the words . . . are such as are calculated to produce the result condemned by the statute. . . .
>
> The service may be obstructed by attacking the justice of the cause for which the war is waged, and by undermining the spirit of loyalty which inspires men to enlist or to register for conscription in the service of their country. The greatest inspiration for entering into such service is patriotism, the love of country. To teach that . . . the war against Germany was wrong and its prosecution a crime, is to weaken patriotism and the purpose to enlist or to render military service in the war. . . .
>
> It is argued that the evidence fails to show that [Shaffer] committed the act willfully and intentionally. But . . . he must be presumed to have intended the natural and probable consequences of what he knowingly did.

This approach was embraced by almost every federal court that interpreted the Espionage Act during the course of World War I.[40] Applying this standard, juries almost invariably returned a ver-

---

[37] 255 F 886 (9th Cir 1919).

[38] Id at 887.

[39] Id at 887–89.

[40] See, for example, *Goldstein v United States,* 258 F 908 (9th Cir 1919); *Coldwell v United States,* 256 F 805 (1st Cir 1919); *Kirchner v United States,* 255 F 301 (4th Cir 1918); *Deason v United States,* 254 F 259 (5th Cir 1918); *Doe v United States,* 253 F 903 (8th Cir 1918); *O'Hare v United States,* 253 F 538 (8th Cir 1918); *Masses Publishing Co. v Patten,* 246 F 24 (2d Cir 1917) (reversing Judge Hand's opinion); *United States v Nagler,* 252 F 217 (W D Wis 1918); *United States v Motion Picture Film "The Spirit of '76,"* 252 F 946 (S D Cal 1917). For additional citations, see Rabban, *Forgotten Years* at 256–59 (cited in note 2).

dict of guilty.[41] Rose Pastor Stokes, the editor of the socialist *Jewish Daily News*, was sentenced to ten years in prison for saying "I am *for* the people, while the government is for the profiteers" during an antiwar statement to the Women's Dining Club of Kansas City.[42] D. T. Blodgett was sentenced to twenty years in prison for circulating a leaflet urging voters in Iowa not to reelect a congressman who had voted for conscription and arguing that the draft was unconstitutional.[43] The Reverend Clarence H. Waldron was sentenced to fifteen years in prison for distributing a pamphlet stating that "if Christians [are] forbidden to fight to preserve the Person of their Lord and Master, they may not fight to preserve themselves, or any city they should happen to dwell in."[44] As Paul Murphy observed after reviewing the World War I trials, these judges and juries were clearly "swayed by wartime hysteria."[45]

In 1919, Assistant Attorney General John Lord O'Brian explained that the Espionage Act "was not directed against disloyal utterances." Rather, its "sole aim" was "to protect the process of raising and maintaining our armed forces."[46] In practice, however,

---

[41] See Rabban, *Forgotten Years* at 257 (cited in note 2).

[42] *United States v Stokes* (unreported) (D Mo 1918), rev'd 264 F 18 (8th Cir 1920). See Zechariah Chafee, *Freed Speech* 52–53 (Harvard, 1941); Peterson and Fite, at 185–86 (cited in note 8). See *Mrs. Stokes Denies Assailing Red Cross*, NY Times 13 (May 22, 1918); *Mrs. Stokes Denies Disloyal Intent*, NY Times (May 23, 1918); *Mrs. Rose R. Stokes Convicted of Disloyalty; Illegal to Impair National Morale, Says Judge*, NY Times 1 (May 24, 1918). On March 9, 1920, a federal Court of Appeals overturned Mrs. Stokes's conviction, ruling that that district judge had gone "too far in his charge to the jury" because of his inappropriate "partisan zeal." *Ten-Year Sentence of Mrs. Rose Stokes Overruled by Federal Court in St. Louis*, NY Times 1 (Mar 10, 1920). On November 15, 1921, the government finally dismissed the charges against Stokes. *Mrs. Stokes Freed*, NY Times 5 (Nov 16, 1921).

[43] See Nelles, *Espionage Act Cases* at 48 (cited in note 16).

[44] *United States v Waldron* (unreported) (D Vt 1918). See Chafee, *Free Speech* at 55–56 (cited in note 42). The government was especially aggressive in its prosecution of clergymen who supported peace or conscientious objection. See *Warn Seditious Pastors*, NY Times 16 (March 31, 1918) ("Disloyalty fostered by certain religious sects has been growing in the United States . . . according to Department of Justice officials." The government "regards the preaching of opposition to the aims of this particular war as of seditious nature, and . . . [s]everal German and Austrian preachers and Sunday school teachers have been interned for disloyal utterances, and many others . . . have been warned to desist from criticising the nation's war motives."). Assistant Attorney General John Lord O'Brian declared that "the most dangerous type of propaganda . . . is religious pacifism, i.e., opposition to the war on the ground that it is opposed to the word of God." See Letter from John Lord O'Brian to Rep. Edwin Y. Webb (April 16, 1918), quoted in 65th Cong, 2d Sess, in Cong Rec S 5542 (April 24, 1918).

[45] Murphy, *World War I* at 190 (cited in note 2).

[46] O'Brian, *Civil Liberty* at 299–300 (cited in note 9).

the Act became an efficient tool for the blanket suppression of all "disloyal utterances." Professor Zechariah Chafee concluded that under the "bad tendency" interpretation of the Act, all "genuine discussion among civilians of the justice and wisdom of continuing a war . . . becomes perilous."[47]

IV. THE LAW OF ATTEMPTS: COURTS GONE WRONG?

As already suggested, the Espionage Act was not designed to prohibit "all genuine discussion among civilians of the justice and wisdom" of the draft or the war. Rather, it was enacted to render unlawful *only* those actions that willfully caused or attempted "to cause insubordination, disloyalty, mutiny or refusal of duty in the military or naval forces" or that obstructed "the recruiting or enlistment service of the United States."

The first point worth noting about the prevailing interpretation of section 3 is that it paid little, if any, attention to the specific qualification in the statute that to violate the Espionage Act the speech must have some relation to "the military or naval forces" or "the recruiting or enlistment service of the United States." As Judge Amidon observed in *Schutte* and *Wichek*, to bring an action under the prohibition of the Espionage Act the government had to prove that the speech was likely and intended to affect members of the armed forces or, at least, individuals who were eligible to serve in the armed forces.

Shortly after the war, Assistant Attorney General O'Brian noted that "the evolution" in the interpretation of section 3 in this regard "presents an interesting example of the process of judicial interpretation." "At the outset," he observed, "there was uncertainty as to whether the phrase 'military and naval forces' included only men actually mustered in or whether it included also men within the draft ages." As the war proceeded, however, the federal courts, with "substantial unanimity," moved toward a very "broad view" of this "slenderly worded section" of the Act. As O'Brian concluded, "the standard by which conduct was found to be in violation of the prohibitions of this section was . . . judicial, not legislative in creation."[48]

---

[47] Chafee, *Free Speech* at 52 (cited in note 42).
[48] O'Brian, *Civil Liberty* at 301 (cited in note 9).

Thus, a first objection to the prevailing interpretation of the Espionage Act is that it effectively disregarded an important limitation in the statute. A more faithful interpretation, and one that would have accorded greater protection to the freedom of speech, would have insisted that, in order for speech to fall within the scope of the prohibition, it must be directed primarily and/or specifically at members of the armed forces or those eligible to serve.

But there is a deeper objection. Because there were essentially no instances in which the government could prove that dissident speech had *in fact* caused insubordination, mutiny, refusal of duty, or obstruction of the recruiting or enlistment service, almost every prosecution under the Act had to be framed as an "attempt."[49] This necessarily raises the question, posed by Judge Bourquin, "what constitutes an attempt?"

The law of criminal attempt is one of the most perplexing features of the criminal law.[50] As Judge Bourquin noted in *Hall*, however, it is well settled that to establish an "attempt" the prosecution ordinarily must prove both that the defendant had the specific intent to bring about an unlawful act and that the defendant came sufficiently close to success to warrant governmental intervention. Both elements are essential. Specific intent without proximity does not constitute an attempt, and proximity without specific intent does not constitute an attempt.[51]

---

[49] Indeed, because the provision governing obstruction of the recruiting and enlistment service did not cover attempts, Congress amended the provision in 1918 at the request of the Department of Justice in order to clarify and expand the reach of this prohibition. See O'Brian, *Civil Liberty* at 275 (cited in note 9).

[50] See Joel Prentiss Bishop, 1 *Criminal Law* § 725 (L 5 ed 1872) (the law of attempts is "less understood by the courts" and "more obscure in the text-books" than any other branch of the criminal law). Cf. Glanville Williams, *Textbook on Criminal Law: Involvement in Crime* §§ 1–5 at 368–83 (Stevens & Sons, 1978).

[51] See, for example, *Glover v Commonwealth*, 86 Va 382, 385–86 (1889) (an "attempt in criminal law" requires both the "intent to commit a crime" and "a direct act done towards its commission"); *People v Mills*, 178 NY 274, 284–85 (1904) (an attempt requires both an "intent to commit a crime" and an "overt act . . . such as would naturally effect that result"); *State v Thompson*, 31 Nev 209, 216 (1909) (an attempt requires "intent to commit the crime" and "performance of some act towards its commission"). See also Bishop, 1 *Criminal Law* § 728 at 425 (cited in note 50) ("[a]n attempt is . . . an intent to do a thing, combined with an act which falls short of thing intended"); William L. Clark and William L. Marshall, *A Treatise on the Law of Crimes* § 119 (Callaghan, 2d ed 1912) ("to constitute an indictable attempt to commit a crime, there must be . . . an intent to commit that particular crime" and "an act done in pursuance of such intent, which falls short of the actual commission of the crime"); John Wilder May, *The Law of Crimes* § 183 (Little Brown, 3d ed 1905) ("[i]t is necessary that some act should be done in pursuance of the intent, immediately and directly tending to the commission of the crime").

The element of specific intent is essential because "[o]ne cannot attempt . . . to do an act without the intent to do the act."[52] This seems self-evident, but it is critical. An individual who negligently or even recklessly creates a danger is not guilty of "attempt."[53] Did the defendants convicted under the Espionage Act have the requisite specific intent and, if so, how was this proved? No doubt, some of these defendants specifically intended their speech to cause precisely the harms the Act was designed to prevent (e.g., insubordination, refusal of duty, etc.). But very few of the defendants expressly advocated such conduct, so how did the government prove their intent? In a few instances, the government was able to present letters or other statements of the defendant to demonstrate specific intent to incite unlawful conduct. In the vast majority of cases, however, there simply was no such evidence.[54] To bridge this gap, the government invoked the doctrine of constructive intent.

As illustrated by the opinion in *Shaffer*, courts typically held that the defendant may be "presumed to have intended the natural and probable consequences of what he knowingly did."[55] In theory, this

---

[52] Joseph H. Beale, Jr., *Criminal Attempts*, 16 Harv L Rev 491 (1902). See William M. Blackstone, 4 *Commentaries on the Laws of England* *36 (Cavendish, 2001) (no one can attempt "a crime without an intention to have it done"); Bishop, 1 *Criminal Law* at § 731 at 522 (Little Brown, 9th ed 1923) ("the intent in attempt must be specific").

[53] See, for example, *Simpson v State*, 59 Ala 1 (1877) (recklessness does not establish attempt); *Scott v State*, 49 Ark 156 (1886) (same); *Pruitt v State*, 20 Tex Ct App 129 (1886) (same). But see Oliver Wendell Holmes, *The Common Law* 66–67 (Little Brown, 1881). Holmes argued that "[t]he reason for punishing any act must generally be to prevent some harm which is foreseen as likely to follow that act under the circumstances in which it is done." Thus, "[a]cts should be judged by their tendency under the known circumstances, not by the actual intent which accompanies them," and an act should be "punishable as an attempt, if, supposing it to have produced its natural and probable effect, it would have amounted to a substantive crime." Holmes acknowledged, however, that this was not the law. See Rabban, *Forgotten Years* at 285–98 (cited in note 2); Yosal Rogat, *The Judge as Spectator*, 31 U Chi L Rev 213 (1963). Moreover, his later writing clarified the role of intent in this context. See Oliver Wendell Holmes, *Privilege, Malice, and Intent*, 8 Harv L Rev 1 (1894). For further discussion of Holmes's view, see n 138.

[54] Zechariah Chafee reported: "A lawyer who defended many Espionage Act cases tells me that there was much speculation among his clients as to whether they actually possessed the requisite criminal intent. A few of them admitted to him that they had it," but "most of the defendants had no real intention to cause trouble, and were only engaged in heated altercations or expounding economic doctrines." Chafee, *Free Speech* at 62 (cited in note 42).

[55] See, for example, *Grubl v United States*, 264 F 44 (8th Cir 1920); *Fontana v United States*, 262 F 283 (8th Cir 1919); *Harshfield v United States*, 260 F 659 (8th Cir 1919); *Kammann v United States*, 259 F 192 (7th Cir 1919); *Shilter v United States*, 257 F 724 (9th Cir 1919); *Sandberg v United States*, 257 F 643 (9th Cir 1919).

principle is well known to the law of attempts. If an individual puts poison in the drink of an intended victim, or shoots a handgun directly at an intended victim from a distance of five feet, she can be found to have "attempted" murder, even if the intended victim spilled the drink or the gun misfired, because the defendant can be "presumed to have intended the natural and probable consequences of what she knowingly did." In these circumstances, it is reasonable to presume specific intent, even in the absence of any direct evidence of intent, because the nature of the act is such that it is difficult reasonably to imagine any *other* intent that would explain the act. (Of course, if the defendant does have an alternative explanation, she is free to present evidence to that effect. But in the absence of such evidence, or some other explanatory circumstance, it is quite reasonable to presume a specific intent to murder.)

Now suppose that an individual delivers an impassioned address on a street corner in lower Manhattan in the winter of 1918 in which she proclaims that the draft is unjust because it treats men as chattel, serves only the interests of Wall Street, and is not "worth the life of one blue-jacket on the sea or one khaki-coat in the trenches." Based only on these facts, can one presume with the same degree of confidence as in the prior examples that the defendant had the specific intent to cause insubordination or refusal of duty in the armed forces?

Surely not. In this situation, there are many possible consequences of the speech that the defendant might reasonably have intended. Most obviously, her intent may have been to persuade others to oppose the draft and the war through lawful means. It is impossible to presume beyond a reasonable doubt that this speaker's specific intent was to trigger unlawful conduct. Of course, her specific intent may have been to incite insubordination, but it would hardly be reasonable to *presume* this without substantial additional evidence. What the federal courts did during World War I was to allow juries to infer specific intent from the bare *possibility* that the speaker might have had such an intent. This is not the law of attempt, and it was not the intended meaning of the phrase "attempt" in the Espionage Act.[56]

---

[56] Indeed, the law of attempt may be even more demanding than I have thus far suggested. Many courts have held, for example, that an individual cannot be held guilty of an attempt, regardless of other evidence of specific intent, unless the defendant's act is "of such a nature

The challenge of ascertaining specific intent is especially difficult when a nation is at war. Inquiries into subjective intent are always elusive. There is every danger that a jury, acting in the passion of wartime, will leap to the conclusion that a defendant who has expressed deeply offensive and unpatriotic views must have had a "criminal" disposition. That leap between sharp criticism and criminal intent is all too easy when a juror inherently associates one with the other. Reflecting on the experience during World War I, Zechariah Chafee observed that in time of war neither judges nor juries can reliably "look into the heart of a speaker or writer and tell whether his motives are patriotic or mean."[57]

Judge Amidon also put the point well:[58]

> Only those who have administered the Espionage Act can understand the danger of such legislation. When crimes are defined by such generic terms, . . . the jury becomes the sole judge, whether men shall or shall not be punished. Most of the jurymen have sons in the war. They are all under the power of the passions which war engenders. [During this period, otherwise] sober, intelligent business men . . . looked back into my eyes with the savagery of wild animals, saying by their manner, "Away with this twiddling, let us get at him." Men believed during that period that the only verdict in a war case, which could show loyalty, was a verdict of guilty.

This does not mean that it is impossible to convict a defendant of "attempt" to cause insubordination in the military. But it does

---

that it is itself evidence of the criminal intent with which it is done." John Salmond, *Jurisprudence* § 137 at 404 (Sweet and Maxwell, 7th ed 1924). See, for example, *United States v Cruz-Jiminez*, 977 F2d 95 (3d Cir 1992); *United States v McDowell*, 714 F2d 106 (11th Cir 1983); *United States v Everett*, 700 F2d 900 (3d Cir 1983). See generally Wayne R. LaFave, *Criminal Law* §§ 6.2–6.3 at 548–60 (West, 3d ed 2000). Another, less rigid, approach, exemplified by the Model Penal Code, holds that conduct cannot constitute an attempt "unless it is strongly corroborative of the actor's criminal purpose." See Model Penal Code § 5.01(2). Although this approach offers the prosecution somewhat more flexibility in proving specific intent, it is clearly a standard that could not be met by the Espionage Act prosecutions. See LaFave, *Criminal Law* § 6.2 at 550–52 (cited in note 56). Under this view, an attempt is constituted only if the accused "does an act . . . that can have *no other purpose* than the commission of that specific crime." J. W. Cecil Turner, *Attempts to Commit Crimes*, 5 Cambridge L J 230, 236 (1934) (original text all italicized). Although this standard can readily be satisfied in situations where, for example, the defendant puts poison in the drink or shoots directly at the intended victim, it is far from satisfied in the prosecutions brought under section 3 of the Espionage Act, where the acts of the defendants were almost always much more equivocal.

[57] Chafee, *Free Speech* at ix (cited in note 42).

[58] Quoted in id at 70.

mean that to do so consistent with the traditional criminal law of attempt it is necessary to follow the lead of either Judge Bourquin or Judge Hand. Judge Bourquin dealt with this problem by insisting on a close relation between the expression and the unlawful action. In effect, Judge Bourquin argued that for the government to prove the defendant's specific intent by inference from the "natural consequences" of his speech, it must demonstrate that those consequences were connected to the speech in essentially the same way that intent to murder is connected to the poison in the glass or the firing of the gun.

In his opinion in *Masses*, Judge Hand offered an alternative approach. Judge Hand reasoned that inquiries into specific intent are so elusive, and it is so easy erroneously to infer specific intent in times of national hysteria, that in order to avoid "the suppression of all hostile criticism" the government should be required in all prosecutions for attempt under the Espionage Act to prove that the defendant had expressly advocated unlawful conduct. Judge Hand did not deny that some speakers might in fact have specific intent to trigger unlawful conduct even though they refrained from expressly advocating such conduct, but he concluded that without a test that was objective and difficult to evade, prosecutors, judges, and jurors would leap too quickly to the inference that unlawful intent accompanies disloyal sentiments.[59]

At first blush, Hand's approach might seem extreme. There is, after all, as Judge Hand himself acknowledged, the Marc Antony problem.[60] In fact, however, Hand's approach may be more consonant with the common law than the "bad tendency" approach. As far back as Blackstone, it was recognized that even when a defendant's speech "caused" another to commit a criminal act, the defendant was not guilty of an offense unless he "does yet procure, counsel or command another to commit a crime."[61] Indeed,

---

[59] See Chafee, *Free Speech* at 45 (cited in note 2) (Hand wanted an "objective test" that could be "easily understood by the opponents of the war" so "[t]hey could safely engage in discussion of [the war and] its merits . . . so long as they refrained from urging violation of laws").

[60] Hand noted that a speaker can arouse an audience to violate the law "as well by indirection as expressly," but nonetheless insisted that to violate the Espionage Act the prosecution must prove that the defendant engaged in "direct advocacy of resistance." *Masses*, 244 F at 540–41. See also *United States v Nearing*, 252 F 223, 228 (S D NY 1918), in which Judge Hand observed that "there may be language, as, for instance, Mark Antony's funeral oration, which can in fact counsel violence while it even expressly discountenances it."

[61] Blackstone, 4 *Commentaries* at *37 (cited in note 52).

throughout his discussion of this subject, Blackstone repeatedly uses such words as "commands," "advises," "procures," and "counsels." As Judge Hand observed in another opinion, in cases involving alleged attempts by one person to cause another to commit unlawful acts, "the rule has always been that, to establish criminal responsibility, the words uttered must amount to counsel or advice or command to commit the forbidden acts."[62] That is, they must amount to express advocacy of unlawful conduct.

The second and independent element of the law of attempt is the requirement of proximity between the speech and the unlawful act. Although the federal courts during World War I tended to meld these two elements by presuming specific intent from "bad tendency," they are in fact distinctive elements of the criminal law. Thus, even if there is no question that an individual specifically intends to commit a criminal act, he is not guilty of an "attempt" unless the unlawful act is proximate. This is so because bad intentions are not, in and of themselves, "the concern of the criminal law."[63] A century ago, Professor Joseph Beale observed in his seminal article on the law of attempt that "the sin or wickedness may be as great, . . . but human laws are made, not to punish sin, but to prevent crime and mischief."[64] This was a settled part of the law of attempt at the time of the Espionage Act prosecutions.

Thus, even if a speaker undeniably intends to persuade soldiers to engage in refusal of duty, her speech does not constitute an "attempt" unless there is a sufficient probability that she will succeed. The question of how proximate is sufficiently proximate, and how this proximity should be assessed, has vexed the legal system for centuries.[65] It has been said, for example, that the act "must come dangerously near to success,"[66] that it "must come sufficiently near completion to be of public concern,"[67] that it must

---

[62] *United States v Nearing*, 252 F 223, 227 (S D NY 1918).

[63] Beale, *Criminal Attempts* at 493 (cited in note 52).

[64] Id at 496.

[65] See Joel Prentiss Bishop, 1 *Bishop on Criminal Law* § 669 (T. H. Flood, 8th ed 1892) ("the difficulty is not a small one to lay down rules, readily applied"); LaFave, *Criminal Law* § 6.2 at 544–52 (cited in note 56).

[66] Beale, *Criminal Attempts* at 492 (cited in note 52).

[67] Id at 501.

come "very near to the accomplishment of the act,"[68] and that there must be a "harm which is foreseen as likely to follow."[69] There are no simple or concrete rules in this area of the law. As Justice Holmes remarked when he was still on the Supreme Judicial Court of Massachusetts, "every question of proximity must be determined by its own circumstances, and analogy is too imperfect to give much help."[70]

Nonetheless, under any of the usual formulations of the standard, it is difficult to see how the test could be satisfied in the circumstances of the Espionage Act prosecutions. Indeed, that is part of the reason why the government was never able to present evidence of any *actual* unlawful consequences. Of course, if the test is merely whether the expression *increases* the probability that some soldier might someday be insubordinate, then every criticism of the war or the draft can be transmogrified into an "attempt." By the same ill-reasoning, anyone who criticizes any person could be held to have attempted murder. As Zechariah Chafee noted, "the assassin of President McKinley may have been influenced by the denunciatory cartoons" published in "the Hearst newspapers, but the artist" did not "attempt" to commit the murder.[71]

Another facet of this issue further illustrates the wrong-headedness of the "bad tendency" test as it was applied in the Espionage Act cases. Under the government's theory in these prosecutions, the defendants were "attempting" to obstruct the war effort by generating disaffection in the minds of others who would then themselves commit unlawful acts of insubordination, refusal of duty, etc. Under the common law, however, it was almost unheard of for a court to sustain such a theory of "attempt."

As Professor Beale wrote in 1902, one cannot "attempt" to commit an offense "by the solicitation of another to do an act."[72] Thus,

---

[68] *Commonwealth v Peaslee*, 177 Mass 267, 272, 59 N E 55, 56 (1901).

[69] Holmes, *The Common Law* at 67 (cited in note 53). Most of the modern recodifications state that the defendant's conduct must "constitute a substantial step towards" the unlawful act. LaFave, *Criminal Law* § 6.2 at 545 n 108 (cited in note 56).

[70] *Commonwealth v Kennedy*, 170 Mass 18, 22 48 N E 770, 771 (1897). Justice Holmes also noted in *Kennedy* that because "the aim of the law is not to punish sins, but is to prevent certain external results, the act done must come pretty near to accomplishing that result before the law will notice it." Id at 770.

[71] Chafee, *Free Speech* at 47 (cited in note 42).

[72] Beale, *Criminal Attempts* at 505 (cited in note 52).

a "solicitor to a crime which he does not intend to join in actually committing is . . . not guilty of an attempt."[73] The near universal view is that for an individual who solicits another to commit a crime to be guilty of attempt, the defendant must at the very least have undertaken some additional overt act, such as furnishing the person solicited with the equipment necessary to commit the crime.[74] Given these limitations on the law of attempt, few, if any, of the defendants in the section 3 prosecutions could have been convicted of that offense.[75]

But even if the Espionage Act defendants were not guilty of attempt, were they perhaps guilty of the separate crime of solicitation? At the outset, it is important to note that section 3 expressly prohibits "attempts," not "solicitations." This is not simply a technical distinction, and it is far from evident that it would be appropriate for the federal judiciary to rewrite the statute to convert a prohibition of attempts into a prohibition of solicitations.

More fundamentally, however, the crime of solicitation requires not only that the defendant specifically intend to bring about crim-

---

[73] Id at 505–06. See also Francis Wharton, 1 *A Treatise on Criminal Law* § 179 (Kay & Brother, 9th ed 1885); John W. Curran, *Solicitation a Substantive Crime*, 17 Minn L Rev 499, 501–02 (1933). But see Bishop, *Criminal Law* at § 768(c) at 548 (cited in note 50). For the contemporary view on this question, see LaFave, *Criminal Law* § 6.1 at 534–35 (cited in note 56).

[74] See, for example, *People v Bush*, 4 Hill 133 (NY 1843); *Smith v Commonwealth*, 54 Pa 209, 213 (1867); *McDade v People*, 29 Mich 50 (1874); *Stabler v Commonwealth*, 95 Pa 318 (1880); *State v Harney*, 101 Mo 470 (1890); *State v Bowers*, 35 SC 262, 14 SE 488 (1892); *Ex parte Floyd*, 7 Cal App 588 (1908). For more recent decisions, see, for example, *State v Davis*, 319 Mo 1222, 6 SW2d 609 (1928); *State v Mandel*, 78 Ariz 226, 278 P2d 413 (1954); *Braham v State*, 571 P2d 631 (Alaska 1977); *State v Molasky*, 765 SW2d 597 (1989). See also Wharton, 1 *Criminal Law* at § 179 (cited in note 73) ("the question whether the solicitation is by itself the subject of penal prosecution must be answered in the negative"); Clark and Marshall, *Law of Crimes* at §§ 125, 133 (cited in note 51) ("the better opinion is that solicitation to commit a crime is not an attempt"); T. W. Hughes, *A Treatise on Criminal Law and Procedure* §§ 130, 139 (Bobbs-Merrill, 1st ed 1919) ("the weight of authority . . . sustains the view that solicitation to commit a crime may constitute an independent offense, but not a criminal attempt"); May, *Criminal Law* at § 19 (cited in note 51) ("solicitation to commit a crime is not an attempt"). But see Bishop, 1 *Criminal Law* at § 768(c)(2) at 548 (cited in note 52) ("solicitation can be an indictable attempt . . . without any further . . . overt acts").

[75] Another relevant limitation in the law of attempts is that an effort to commit a crime that is dependent upon the cooperation of another individual who has not yet agreed to act ordinarily will not constitute an attempt. See, for example, *United States v Stephens*, 12 F 52 (D Ore 1882) (defendant's plan to have liquor sent unlawfully into Alaska does not constitute an attempt where no seller has yet agreed to ship the liquor); *People v Murray*, 14 Cal 159 (1859) (defendant's plan to contract an incestuous marriage by marrying his niece does not constitute an attempt where no magistrate has yet agreed to perform the marriage). See Beale, *Criminal Attempts* at 503 (cited in note 52).

inal conduct, but also that the defendant commands, encourages, or requests another person to engage in specific conduct which would constitute a crime.[76] The "essence of the crime of solicitation is 'asking a person to commit a crime.'"[77] Hence, Judge Hand's conclusion in *Masses* that in the absence of express advocacy of criminal conduct, there is no criminal offense of solicitation.[78]

The crucial point here is *not* one about the First Amendment. The point is not that Congress necessarily lacked the constitutional *authority* to declare unlawful all disloyal utterances. It is, rather, that Congress did not *exercise* that authority in 1917 when it prohibited any person to cause or "attempt" to cause insubordination, disloyalty, or refusal of duty in the military or to obstruct the recruitment or enlistment service.[79] If Congress had intended to forbid all disloyal and seditious utterances, it surely knew how to do so.[80] That is not what it did when it enacted the Espionage Act.[81] But, by failing to respect the well-settled boundaries of the

---

[76] See Bishop, *Criminal Law* at § 768(a) at 546 (cited in note 52) (referring to "direct solicitations"); Wharton, *Criminal Law* § 179 (cited in note 73) (using such terms as "counseled," "advised," and "encouraged" to describe the crime of solicitation). See also Model Penal Code § 5.02.

[77] LaFave, *Criminal Law* § 6.1 at 531 (cited in note 56), citing *Gardner v State*, 41 Md App 187, 396 A2d 303 (1979), aff'd 286 Md 520, 408 A2d 1317 (1979). See also Blackstone, *Commentaries* at *36 (cited in note 61); Hale, *Pleas* at 616 (cited in note 61).

[78] Moreover, under the common law, a speaker ordinarily is guilty of solicitation to a crime only if he would have been indictable for the crime itself, had it been committed. See Beale, *Criminal Attempts* at 505 (cited in note 52). See also Chafee, *Free Speech* at 47 (cited in note 42). This would certainly not have been the case in most of the Espionage Act prosecutions.

[79] For a detailed review of Congress's intent in enacting the Espionage Act, see Stone, *A Mystery Unraveled* (cited in note 6).

[80] In 1918, Congress enacted the Sedition Act of 1918, which made it unlawful for any person to utter, print, write, or publish any disloyal, profane, scurrilous, or abusive language intended to cause contempt or scorn for the form of government of the United States, the Constitution, or the flag; or to utter any words supporting the cause of any country at war with the Untied States or opposing the cause of the United States. Act of May 16, 1918, ch 75, § 1, 40 Stat 553.

[81] See Chafee, *Free Speech* at 47–49 (cited in note 42): "[T]he rule has always been that, to establish criminal responsibility, the words uttered must constitute dangerous progress toward the consummation of the independent offense attempted and amount to procurement, counsel, or command to commit the forbidden acts. . . . [T]here is not a word in the 1917 Espionage Act to show that Congress did change the ordinary tests. . . . Every word used, 'cause,' 'attempt,' 'obstruct,' clearly involves proximate causation, a close and direct relation to actual interference with the operations of the army and navy, with enlistment and the draft."

legal concept of "attempt," this is precisely what the federal courts managed to achieve.

The bottom line is this: Congress prohibited any person to "attempt" to cause disruption of the military forces of the United States. But the term "attempt" has never, except in the decisions interpreting the Espionage Act, encompassed actions where the *only* measure of culpability is that the actor could reasonably foresee that his speech might have a "tendency" to increase the likelihood that third parties might commit criminal acts.

V. Why Did the Courts Go Wrong?

Obviously, the tenor of the times created an atmosphere in which it was easy, perhaps inevitable, for courts to go wrong in this direction. But there are other, more subtle, explanations as well.

One such explanation concerns the origins of the "bad tendency" test itself. Blackstone declared that the freedom of speech "consists in laying no previous restraints upon publications, and not in freedom from censure for criminal matter when published."[82] With respect to the latter, Blackstone added that it is legitimate for the state to punish "any dangerous or offensive writings, which, when published, shall . . . be adjudged of a pernicious tendency," in order to preserve the "peace and good order."[83] Because judges and scholars wrestling with the meaning of the freedom of speech in this era focused on whether Blackstone's statement defined the scope of the First Amendment,[84] it was natural for those who accepted this view to assume that speech "of a perni-

---

[82] Blackstone, 4 *Commentaries* at *151 (cited in note 61) (italics omitted).

[83] Id at *152.

[84] Even after the adoption of the First Amendment, Justice Story and other early American commentators accepted the view that liberty of the press was limited to "the right to publish without any previous restraint or license." Joseph Story, *Commentaries on the Constitution of the United States* § 1879 (Brown, Shattuck, 1833); see also James Kent, 2 *Commentaries on American Law* 23 (O. Halsted, 2d ed 1832). Moreover, in its 1907 decision in *Patterson v Colorado*, 205 US 454, 462 (1907), the Court, in an opinion by Justice Holmes, announced that the Constitution prohibited "all such previous restraints upon publications as had been practiced by other governments," but not "the subsequent punishment of such as may be deemed contrary to the public welfare." Thus, it is not surprising that throughout this era commentators focused on the significance of this passage in Blackstone. See Rabban, *Forgotten Years* at 132–37 (cited in note 2). It was not until its decision in *Schenck* that the Court, again in an opinion by Justice Holmes, recognized that "the prohibition of laws abridging the freedom of speech is not confined to previous restraints." 249 US at 51.

cious tendency" may be punished. Hence, the "bad" tendency standard.[85]

But this is all wrong. Whatever else one might think about whether Blackstone's declaration should be understood as defining the scope of the First Amendment, Blackstone in this passage was discussing the freedom of speech, not the law of attempt. The distinction is critical. Blackstone's point was that the liberty of speech does not preclude the government from prohibiting expression that has a "pernicious tendency." Thus, he reasoned, "the liberty of the press, properly understood, is by no means infringed" by laws punishing "blasphemous, immoral, treasonable, schismatical, seditious, or scandalous libels." This was so because such categories of speech have a "pernicious tendency" to undermine "the preservation of the peace and good order."[86]

Following this reasoning, if Congress had expressly prohibited all "disloyal utterances" on the theory that such utterances have a "pernicious tendency" to undermine "the preservation of the peace and good order," and Blackstone's declaration is held to govern the meaning of the First Amendment, then the statutory prohibition would not infringe "the liberty of the press" (assuming, of course, that such utterances do, in fact, have a "pernicious tendency").

But that was not the question posed in the Espionage Act prosecutions. Rather, the question was whether Congress, in enacting the Espionage Act of 1917, had prohibited such utterances.[87] As

---

[85] For a related argument that the bad tendency test derives from Blackstone, see Rabban, *Forgotten Years* at 132–37 (cited in note 2).

[86] Blackstone, 4 *Commentaries* at *151–52 (cited in note 61) (italics omitted).

[87] For example, an individual who purchases an implement that can be used to commit burglary is not, for that reason alone, guilty of *attempt* to commit burglary. Indeed, he would not be guilty of an attempt to commit burglary even if he purchased the implement with the intention of later committing a burglary. This is so because mere "preparation" to commit a crime is not sufficiently proximate to the crime itself to constitute an attempt. On the other hand, the government could make it unlawful for any person to purchase such an implement with the intention of using it in a burglary, or, indeed, to purchase or own such an implement at all. The question, in other words, is not what the government *can* prohibit, but what it *has* prohibited. The same principle governs when the relevant "act" is speech. For example, if X tells Y that Y's wife is having an affair, X is not guilty of attempting to murder Y's wife, even though the disclosure might lead Y to murder his wife. Indeed, even if X discloses this to Y with the intent to cause Y to murder his wife, this would this still would not constitute attempt to murder. On the other hand, the government could (at least under Blackstone's conception of the "liberty of speech") make it unlawful for any person to disclose to one spouse that the other spouse is having an affair, on the theory that such disclosures have a "pernicious tendency" to endanger "the peace and good order."

Judge Hand recognized, the fact (if it is a fact) that Congress could *constitutionally* have prohibited all disloyal utterances does not mean that it *intended* to do so. Rather, in enacting section 3 of the Act, Congress prohibited speech only if it caused or attempted to cause insubordination, refusal of duty, etc. in the armed forces. The passage in Blackstone about "pernicious tendency," which is meant to define the boundaries of the "liberty of speech," does not control the question of statutory construction.

So, what seems to have happened is that judges confused the law of freedom of speech with the law of attempt. They implicitly assumed that if Congress had the constitutional authority to restrict speech having a "pernicious tendency," it necessarily did so. This conflation of Blackstone's definition of the "liberty of the press" with the statutory meaning of "attempt" was analytically disastrous.

Interestingly, Blackstone himself would appear to support Judges Hand and Bourquin on the meaning of "attempt." Anticipating Judge Hand, Blackstone consistently used such phrases as "commands," "advises," "procures," and "counsels" in defining when an individual can be guilty of soliciting a crime. And anticipating Judge Bourqin, Blackstone explained that for an accused to be guilty of murder when he was not physically present at the murder he must have set in motion events "which probably *could not fail* of their mischievous effect." He cites as an example that would satisfy this standard an individual who "incit[es] a madman to commit murder."[88] This is a far cry from the "bad tendency" conception of attempt embraced by the federal courts.

VI. The Astonishing Origins of the "Bad Tendency" Test

It is possible to trace the bad tendency standard as the test of attempts under the Espionage Act directly to the opinion of the Court of Appeals that reversed Judge Hand's decision in *Masses*.[89] This was the first important appellate court interpretation of the Act, and it firmly set the federal courts off in this direction.[90] For this reason, the opinion is worth a close look.

---

[88] Blackstone, 4 *Commentaries* at *35–37 (cited in note 61) (emphasis added).

[89] *Masses Publishing Co. v Patten*, 246 F 24 (2d Cir 1917).

[90] Attorney General Gregory described this opinion as "an early and authoritative ruling by an appellate court to the effect that the criminal intent to obstruct the recruiting service

Judge Rogers began his opinion for the Court of Appeals by invoking the familiar passage from Blackstone on the "liberty of the press." He then distinguished the Espionage Act of 1917 from the Sedition Act of 1798, noting that the former "bears slight resemblance" to the latter. After quoting several impressive statements from Cooley's *Constitutional Limitations*[91] and May's *Constitutional History*[92] about the importance of free speech in a democratic society, Rogers then declared that the purpose of the Espionage Act "was not to repress legitimate criticism of Congress or of the officers of the government, or to prevent any proper discussion looking to the repeal of any legislation."[93]

Judge Rogers then turned to the core question: Had Judge Hand rightly enjoined the Postmaster General from excluding the August 1917 issue of *The Masses* from the mails? Rogers began by

---

or commit other offenses under section 3 may be inferred from the natural and probable effects of the publication and distribution of articles, cartoons, and other published matter." *Annual Report of the Attorney General of the United States* 54 (1918). Zechariah Chafee similarly described the opinion of the Court of Appeals in *Masses* as the decision that established the "doctrine of remote bad tendency in the minds of district judges throughout the country." Chafee, *Free Speech* at 50 (cited in note 42). Because the Court of Appeals decision in *Masses* was the first significant appellate court interpretation of the Espionage Act, it had great influence. As Paul Murphy has observed, after that decision, district court judges could ignore both "the first element of criminal attempt and solicitation—that the effort to commit a crime, though unsuccessful, must approach dangerously near success" and Judge Hand's "test of guilt—that the words must in themselves urge a duty or an interest to resist the law." Murphy, *World War I* at 198 (cited in note 2). After this decision, "[a]ll that had to be shown to sustain conviction was that words uttered or written had a tendency to cause unrest among soldiers or to make recruiting more difficult." Id.

[91] *Masses*, 246 F at 30. "In Cooley's *Constitutional Limitations* that distinguished authority says: 'Repression of full and free discussion is dangerous in any government resting upon the will of the people. The people cannot fail to believe that they are deprived of rights, and will be certain to become discontented, when their discussion of public measures is sought to be circumscribed by the judgment of others upon their temperance or fairness. They must be left at liberty to speak with the freedom which the magnitude of the supposed wrongs appears in their minds to demand; and if they exceed all proper bounds of moderations, the consolations must be, that the evil likely to spring from the violent discussion will probably be less, and its correction by public sentiment more speedy, than if the terrors of the law were brought to bear to prevent the discussion.'" Thomas M. Cooley, *A Treatise on the Constitutional Limitations Which Rest Upon the Legislative Power of the States of the American Union* (Little Brown, 5th ed 1883).

[92] *Masses*, 246 F at 30. "In May's *Constitutional History*, c. 10, it is said that: 'When the press errs, it is by the press itself that is errors are left to be corrected. Repression has ceased to be the policy of rulers, and statesmen have at length fully realized the wise maxim of Lord Bacon, that "the punishment of wits enhances their authority, and a forbidden writing is thought to be a certain spark of truth that flies up in the faces of them that seek to treat it out."'" Thomas E. May, *The Constitutional History of England Since the Accession of George the Third: 1760–1860* (A. C. Armstrong, 3d ed 1886).

[93] *Masses*, 246 F at 31.

rejecting Hand's conclusion that section 3 prohibited speech only if it expressly advocates unlawful conduct: "if the natural and reasonable effect of what is said is to encourage resistance to a law, and the words are used in an endeavor to persuade to resistance, it is immaterial" that the individual did not advise "in direct language against enlistments."[94] In Judge Rogers's view, this was simply "too plain for controversy."[95]

To justify his holding that "it is not necessary that an incitement to crime must be direct," Rogers quoted extensively from Bishop's *Criminal Law*, a leading treatise of the day. On the authority of Bishop, Judge Rogers maintained that "at common law the 'counseling' which constituted an accessory before the fact might be indirect."[96] Finally, turning to the facts at hand, Judge Rogers upheld the Postmaster General's order of exclusion because the Postmaster had reasonably concluded that *The Masses* "contained matter intended willfully to obstruct the recruiting or enlistment service."[97] Judge Rogers added that "the court does not hesitate to say that, considering the natural and reasonable effect of the publication, it was intended willfully to obstruct recruiting."[98]

This was the first federal appellate court decision to interpret the Espionage Act in this manner. As a result of this interpretation, it became possible under the Act to convict dissenters for any utterance that criticized the war, the administration, or the draft. Intention became the central test of guilt, and "this requirement became a mere form, since it could always be inferred from the existence of the indirect injurious effect."[99]

The critical step in Judge Rogers's analysis was his reliance

---

[94] Id at 38.

[95] Id.

[96] Id.

[97] Id at 39.

[98] Id. With respect to the cartoon "Conscription," Judge Rogers reasoned as follows: "[T]his cartoon entitled 'Conscription' . . . seems to us to say: This law murders youth, enslaves labor to its misery, drives womanhood into utter despair and agony, and takes away from democracy its freedom. Its voice is not the voice of patriotism, and its language suggests disloyalty. If counsel wish the court to understand that in his opinion the effect of the cartoon would not be to interfere with enlistment, we are not able to agree with him." *Masses*, 246 F at 36–37.

[99] Murphy, *World War I* at 198 (cited in note 2). See Chafee, *Free Speech* at 50 (cited in note 42).

on Bishop's *Criminal Law*. Here is how Judge Rogers quoted Bishop:[100]

> Every man is responsible criminally for what of wrong flows directly from his corrupt intentions. . . . If he awoke into action an indiscriminate power, he is responsible. If he gave directions vaguely and incautiously, and the person receiving them acted according to what he might have foreseen would be the understanding, he is responsible.

In the light of that passage, it is not surprising that Judge Rogers reached the result he did in *Masses*. But this passage is not in Bishop's discussion of attempt, but in his chapter on "combinations of persons in crime." In this chapter, Bishop addresses the situation "when several persons unite to accomplish a particular object . . . [in] active co-operation."[101] This passage thus relates not to the law of attempt, but to the law of conspiracy. Bishop in this chapter discusses situations in which there is an *agreement* among several individuals to commit a crime *jointly*.

Even more precisely, in this passage Bishop is considering a situation in which, in the context of an agreement to commit a crime jointly, a conspirator mistakenly burns the wrong house. Bishop concludes that, in such circumstances, the conspirator who "commanded" the other "to burn the house of A, and he burn the house of B," is nonetheless "esteemed an accessory to such burning . . . because it was the direct and immediate effect of an act wholly influenced by his command."[102]

---

[100] Bishop, 1 *Criminal Law* at § 641 at 381–82 (cited in note 50). Quoted in *Masses*, 246 F at 38.

[101] Id at § 629.

[102] Id at § 640. Viewed in this light, it may be useful to see the passage in Bishop about co-conspirators from which Judge Rogers quoted only an excerpt: "Every man is responsible criminally for what of wrong flows directly from his corrupt intentions; but no man, intending wrong, is responsible for an independent act of wrong committed by another. If one person sets in motion the physical power of another, the former is liable criminally for its results. If he contemplated the result, he is answerable, though it is produced in a manner he did not contemplate. If he did not contemplate the result in kind, yet if it was the ordinary effect of the cause, he is responsible. If he awoke into action an indiscriminate power, he is responsible. If he gave directions vaguely and incautiously, and the person receiving them acted according to what might be presumed to have been his understanding of them, he is responsible. But, if the wrong done was a fresh and independent wrong springing wholly from the mind of the doer, the other is not criminal therein, merely because, when it was done, he was intending to be a partaker with the doer in a different wrong." Id at § 641.

Astonishingly, it was from Bishop's discussion of a question entirely different from the question presented under the Espionage Act that Judge Rogers derived his conclusion that all that had to be shown to sustain a conviction was that the speech had a tendency to make recruiting more difficult. Whatever else may be said of the dissenters who were prosecuted under section 3 of the Act, they most assuredly were not acting in "combination" with their readers or listeners. Judge Rogers thus drew on a completely inapt analogy and on a completely irrelevant (though accurate) statement of the law of conspiracy.

In another section of his treatise, Bishop addresses the crime of attempt. After noting that "every man is presumed to intend the natural, necessary and even probable consequences of an act which he intentionally performs," Bishop observes that, "in some circumstances, the presumption is conclusive."[103] On this basis, he explains those acts that are "made substantive crimes, not so much on account of their inherent evil, as of their tendency to promote ulterior mischief."[104] For example, libels are unlawful "because they tend to break the peace" and "bawdy-houses" are unlawful "because their tendency is to corrupt the public morals." Bishop explains that with respect to these crimes, "if a man intentionally does the thing" (that is, commit a libel or operate a bawdy-house), "he cannot be heard to say, in his defence, that he did not intend the ulterior mischief." Hence, "these wrongs are substantive crimes, instead of attempts."[105]

Bishop then sharply distinguishes attempts. With respect to attempts, "the jury may take into view the nature of the act, as a matter of evidence, to determine the particular intent with which it was performed."[106] Indeed, " 'they may draw that inference, as they draw all other inferences, from any facts in evidence which, to their minds, fairly proves its existence,' " for " 'intentions can only be proved by acts, as juries cannot look into the breast of the criminal.' "[107] But, Bishop asserts, "they cannot go further" than this, because in the attempt situation the accused "is charged with

---

[103] Bishop, 1 *Criminal Law* at § 734 (cited in note 50).

[104] Id.

[105] Id (italics omitted).

[106] Id.

[107] Id at § 735 n 1, quoting *People v Scott*, 6 Mich 287, 296 (1859).

doing an act deriving its criminal quality . . . from the intent whence it flowed." Thus, "if the prisoner's real intent were not the same which the indictment specifies, he must . . . be acquitted."[108] Moreover, and here is the key, "to draw the intent from the thing, and then increase the thing by adding to it the intent drawn from it, is an absurdity in legal argumentation."[109] Yet this is precisely what Judge Rogers approved in his opinion for the Court of Appeals in *Masses*.[110]

To rebut Judge Hand's argument that express advocacy of unlawful conduct should be required under the Espionage Act, Judge Rogers cited Wharton's *Criminal Law* for the proposition that "at common law 'counseling' which constituted one an accessory before the fact might be indirect."[111] But a fuller reading of Wharton reveals a complete rejection of Judge Rogers's interpretation of the Act:[112]

> "Counseling," to come up to the definition, must be special. Mere general counsel, for instance, that all property should be regarded as held in common, will not constitute the party offering it accessory-before-the fact to a larceny; "free-love" publications will not constitute their authors technical parties to sexual offenses which these publications may have stimulated. Several youthful highway robbers have said that they were led into crime by reading Jack Sheppard; but the author of Jack Sheppard was not an accessory before the fact to the robberies to which he thus added an impulse.

Wharton comments further that "mere words do not constitute an attempt." Indeed, "even when they express illegal purposes," mere words "are often merely speculative, . . . and always belong to a domain which criminal courts cannot invade without peril to individual freedom, and to the just and liberal progress of soci-

---

[108] Id.

[109] Id.

[110] This language from Bishop may go too far. Other authorities of the era suggest that specific intent may be inferred from the circumstances, by analogy to the shooting-a-gun or poisoning-a-drink examples. See Clark and Marshall, *Law of Crimes* at § 121 (cited in note 51) ("the intent need not be proved by positive or direct evidence," but "may be interred . . . from the conduct of the party and the other circumstances"). Hughes, *Criminal Law and Procedure* at § 136 (cited in note 74) ("it is not essential . . . that the specific intent be established by direct evidence," but "it may be inferred from the conduct of the accused and other circumstances"). But no authority suggests that constructive intent, relying on mere bad tendency, is sufficient to satisfy the requirement of specific intent.

[111] Citing Francis Wharton, *Criminal Law* § 266 (Kay & Brother, 11th ed 1912).

[112] Wharton, *Criminal Law* § 265 (cited in note 111).

ety."[113] Perhaps even more to the point, Wharton expressly rejects the proposition that "solicitations to criminality are generally indictable":[114]

> [W]e would be forced to admit, if we hold that solicitations to criminality are generally indictable, that the propagandists . . . of agrarian or communistic theories are liable to criminal prosecutions; and hence the necessary freedom of speech and of the press would be greatly infringed. It would be hard, also, we must agree, if we maintain such general responsibility, to defend, in prosecutions for soliciting crime, the publishers of Byron's *Don Juan*, of Rousseau's *Emile*, or of Goethe's *Elective Affinities*. . . . [T]o make bare solicitations or allurements indictable as *attempts*, not only unduly and perilously extends the scope of penal adjudication, but forces on the courts psychological questions which they are incompetent to decide, and a branch of business which would make them despots of every intellect in the land.

There is no evidence that in enacting the Espionage Act of 1917 Congress intended to change the ordinary meaning of "attempt."[115] The judicial application of the Act in this era clearly reflected "confusion" about the meaning of attempt. Given the uncertain nature of the law of attempt, some degree of uncertainty is not surprising. There was at least some disagreement, for example, whether under the common law solicitation could ever constitute an attempt, whether solicitation required express advocacy of criminal conduct, whether solicitation required an additional overt act, and what degree of proximity was required between the attempt or solicitation and the ultimate criminal act. But however one resolved those questions, one could not wind up with the interpretation of the Espionage Act adopted by the federal courts in this era.

Indeed, the Supreme Court had made all this clear in 1893, a quarter century before the Espionage Act. In *Hicks v United States*,[116] the defendant was charged with encouraging his companion to shoot a third person. The defendant did not expressly incite

---

[113] Id at § 213.

[114] Wharton, *Criminal Law* § 179 (cited in note 73).

[115] See Stone, *Mystery Unraveled* (cited in note 6).

[116] 150 US 442 (1893).

the shooting, and it was unclear from his words whether his specific intent was to encourage the crime. The trial judge instructed the jury that "[i]f the deliberate and intentional use of words has the effect to encourage one man to kill another, he who uttered these words is presumed by law to have intended that effect."[117] The jury returned a verdict of guilty.

The Supreme Court reversed, holding that the jury instruction was "erroneous" because it confounded "the intentional use of the words with the intention as respects the effect to be produced."[118] The Court reasoned that, although the accused "no doubt intended to use the words he did use," he did not necessarily intend his language "to be understood . . . as an encouragement to act."[119] The Court noted that the accused may have spoken "for a different purpose" than encouraging the shooting, even though his words may have "had the actual effect of inciting" the crime.[120] The Court therefore overturned the conviction, holding that the jury should not have been left free to convict "regardless" of the defendant's actual "intention."[121]

What occurred in the federal courts in 1917–1918 was not the consequence of confusion over a technical point of law. It was, rather, the consequence of hysteria. The doctrinal confusion was the effect, not the cause, of the problem.[122]

---

[117] Id at 449.

[118] Id.

[119] Id (italics omitted).

[120] Id.

[121] Id. See also *State v Bosworth*, 170 Ia 329, 345, 152 NW 581, 588 (1915) (citing *Hicks* for the proposition that "the mere use of words, the effect of which is to encourage another to commit a crime, does not make the user thereof an aider and abettor unless he intended them to have that effect").

[122] Throughout this essay I focus on the law of attempt because this was the usual charge in Espionage Act prosecutions. Suppose defendant gives an antiwar speech and several soldiers are prepared to testify for the prosecution that as a result of defendant's speech they decided to desert. Defendant is then prosecuted, not for *attempting* to cause refusal or duty, but for *causing* refusal of duty. In this circumstance, the details of the law of attempt drop away. What, then, must the government prove in order to convict? Under settled law, the government would still have to prove specific intent, but the requirements of express solicitation and proximity might be different. We are cautious about punishing inchoate crimes like attempt and solicitation. But if the defendant actually *causes* criminal conduct, the state interest is more substantial. Thus, in a prosecution under the Espionage Act for actual obstruction of the draft or actual causation of insubordination, the rules governing express solicitation and ex ante proximity might be less stringent than in a prosecution for attempt or solicitation.

VII. The Department of Justice, Bad Tendency, and the Supreme Court

Although several key figures in the Department of Justice in this era were dedicated to civil liberties (at least by the standards of the day),[123] they lost control of the situation. They underestimated the divisions in the nation and the forces the administration had unleashed. Not only was the public swept up in a fierce mood of repression, but prosecutors, judges, members of Congress, and other federal, state, and local officials were swept along with equal ferocity. As Professor Paul Murphy has observed, once "the spirit of intolerance was unleashed . . . containing it was a difficult, if not impossible, task," and "careful distinctions between legitimate and illegitimate behavior, quickly disappeared."[124]

Reflecting on this era shortly after the cessation of hostilities, John Lord O'Brian, the very able and thoughtful Buffalo lawyer who served during the war as Head of the War Emergency Division of the Department of Justice, explained that it had consistently been the view of the Department of Justice that the proper test under section 3 of the Espionage Act was whether, "assuming unlawful intent to be shown, . . . the utterances complained of would have the natural and reasonable effect of producing the result aimed at by the statute." He argued that this was the proper test because "this slenderly worded section was broadly intended by Congress to include every form of activity, by speech or conduct, which was willfully intended by direct or indirect means to obstruct the work of raising and maintaining the national armies."[125]

Is this a sound interpretation of the Espionage Act? Three distinct approaches to the Act emerged in this era. First, as O'Brien argued, the inquiry might focus on the speaker's *intent*. Under this view, criticism of the government is unlawful if the speaker "intended by direct or indirect means" to cause others to violate the law. This approach emphasizes the "badness" of the speaker. In

[123] On several occasions, Attorney General Gregory attempted to limit the excessive zeal of his subordinates and members of the public; Assistant Attorney General John Lord O'Brian was "[p]roperly considered a sensitive civil libertarian in the context" of his times; and even George Creel "spoke out frequently against extralegal actions." Murphy, *World War I* at 16, 88 (cited in note 2).

[124] Id at 72.

[125] O'Brian, *Civil Liberty* at 307–08, 301 (cited in note 9).

the words of Judge Wolverton, in an unpublished opinion that
O'Brian thought stated the argument particularly well:[126]

> A citizen is entitled to fairly criticize men and measures . . .
> and laws and ordinances . . . with a view, by the use of lawful
> means, to improve the public service, or to amend the laws by
> which he is governed or to which he is subjected. But when
> his criticism extends or leads *by willful intent* to the incitement
> of disorder and riot, or to the infraction of the laws of the land
> . . . it overleaps the bounds of all reasonable liberty accorded
> to him by the guarantee of the freedom of speech.

Second, the inquiry might focus on whether the defendant *expressly advocated* unlawful conduct. Under this view, criticism of the
government is unlawful only if the speaker "expressly advocates"
criminal action. This approach distrusts inquiries into intent and
focuses instead on what the speaker actually says. It asserts that
what matters most is not the intent of the speaker, but the *value*
of her speech. If the speaker makes a legitimate contribution to
public debate based on what she actually says, then it should not
matter whether she does so with a "good" or a "bad" intent. In
Judge Hand's view, however, a speaker who expressly advocates
criminal conduct does not make a "valuable" contribution to public debate, and her speech may therefore be punished.[127]

Third, the inquiry might focus on the degree of harm or danger
created by the speech. This is the approach advanced by Judge
Bourquin. Under this view, criticism of the government is protected by the First Amendment unless it creates a substantial danger of causing significant harm. This approach assumes that the
government should not interfere with free expression unless it has
a strong interest in doing so. (This was, of course, the precursor
of the Holmes-Brandeis "clear and present danger" standard.)

---

[126] Id at 308–09 n 15.

[127] As Judge Hand put it in *Masses*, it "has always" been recognized that "one may not
counsel or advise others to violate the law as it stands." Words, he observed, "are not only
the keys of persuasion, but the triggers of action, and those which have no purport but to
counsel the violation of law cannot by any latitude of interpretation be a part of that public
opinion which is the final source of government in a democratic state." 244 F at 540.
Endorsing this position, Chief Justice Rehnquist has argued that "if freedom of speech is
to be meaningful, strong criticism of government policy must be permitted even in wartime," and that "[a]dvocacy which persuades citizens that a law is unjust is not the same
as advocacy that preaches disobedience to it." William H. Rehnquist, *All the Laws But One:
Civil Liberties in Wartime* 178 (Knopf, 1998).

In the abstract, each of these approaches is principled, coherent, and defensible. In theory at least, each could enable the government to restrict especially evil, especially valueless, or especially dangerous expression, without necessarily endangering "that public opinion which is the final source of government in a democratic state." As applied, however, these approaches may produce quite different outcomes. Few, if any, of the Espionage Act defendants could have been convicted under either Judge Bourquin's danger standard or Judge Hand's express advocacy standard; but more than 1,000 individuals were convicted during World War I under the intent standard.

Viewed in this light, there are at least two possible objections to the intent standard: it allows an individual to be punished (1) even though her speech may have contributed positively to public debate and (2) even though it may not have created any significant danger of interfering with the war effort. On the other hand, as Judge Wolverton noted, if we know beyond a reasonable doubt that a speaker specifically intended to induce her readers to violate the law, there must be a lingering unease about allowing her to shield her evil intent behind the cloak of the First Amendment.

In this respect, John Lord O'Brian's statement of what he regarded as the proper test under section 3 is illuminating. In his words, speech is punishable under the Act if, "*assuming unlawful intent to be shown*, . . . the utterances complained of would have the natural and reasonable effect of producing the result aimed at by the statute." Note that in this statement of the test, O'Brian expressly treats "unlawful intent" and "bad tendency" as two distinct elements of the offense. Although this was not the prevailing view in the federal courts, it was the way in which the highest officials of the Department of Justice understood the standard. Indeed, in its briefs for the United States in *Schenck, Frohwerk, Debs,* and *Abrams,* all of which were submitted by O'Brian and Special Assistant Attorney General Alfred Bettman, the Department of Justice consistently defined the standard in this manner.

In these briefs, O'Brian and Bettman emphatically rejected Judge Hand's requirement of express advocacy. In their brief in *Debs,* for example, they stated that Debs "seems to contend that as he did not express [his] unlawful advice in words so direct, plain, and unmistakable as to leave no room whatever for the slightest thought or intellectual process on the part of the jury, no need of any process of inference whatever, the constitutional immunity applies to his speech."[128] They argued that this position would leave the government in the untenable position of being "powerless to punish any incitement to lawlessness, however intentional and however effective, so long as it is concealed in veiled, indirect, or rhetorical language."[129] They rejected this as an implausible construction of the Espionage Act (and of the First Amendment).[130]

On the other hand, O'Brian and Bettman insisted that in order to convict under section 3 the government had to prove *both* that the defendant had a "specific, willful, criminal intent" *and* that he used language having "a natural and reasonably probable tendency to cause the results which have been forbidden by these provisions of the espionage law."[131] In *Schenck*, for example, they argued that the "defendants chose as the recipients of the circulars young men who had been accepted by the draft boards and were simply awaiting the orders to report for duty."[132] This, they reasoned, "is sufficient to support the verdict of the jury that the intent of the defendants was to influence the conduct of persons subject to the draft and to influence that conduct in relation to the draft."[133] Any claim that the defendants "were engaged in a legitimate political agitation for the repeal of the draft law is . . . negatived by this fact that they chose men already drafted and called as the persons to whom to address their arguments."[134] O'Brian and Bettman

---

[128] Brief for the United States in *Debs v United States* 72, in Philip B. Kurland and Gerhard Casper, eds, 19 *Landmark Briefs and Arguments of the Supreme Court of the United States* 688 (Chicago, 1975).

[129] Id.

[130] Id. Bettman and O'Brian carefully distinguished the Sedition Act of 1798 from the Espionage Act of 1917. They argued that whereas the 1798 Act "sought to punish libelous attacks on the Government," the 1917 Act "carefully avoids that pitfall" by restricting only "interference with the process of raising armies." Brief for the United States in *Debs v United States* 83, in Kurland and Casper, 19 *Landmark Briefs* at 677 (cited in note 128). See also Brief for the United States in *Frohwerk v United States* 22–23, in Kurland and Casper, 19 *Landmark Briefs* at 491–92; Brief for the United States in Reply to the Brief of Gilbert Roe in *Debs v United States* 8–9, in Kurland and Casper, 19 *Landmark Briefs* at 763–64.

[131] Brief for the United States in *Debs v United States* at 77, in Kurland and Casper, 19 *Landmark Briefs* at 682 (cited in note 128).

[132] Id.

[133] Id.

[134] Brief for the United States in *Schenck v United States* at 12–13, in Kurland and Casper, 18 *Landmark Briefs* at 1037–38 (cited in note 128). Interestingly, Schenck also argued that this was the appropriate standard. Schenck's brief maintained that "the fair test of protection by the constitutional guarantee of free speech is whether an expression is made with sincere purpose to communicate honest opinion or belief, or whether it masks a primary intent to

never asserted, or even implied, that the requisite intent could simply be inferred from the bad tendency of the leaflets.

Similarly, in *Debs* they expressly endorsed the district judge's instruction to the jury that "disapproval of war is, of course, not a crime, nor is the advocacy of peace a crime under this law, unless the government proves that the defendant had "'the specific, willful, criminal intent'" to bring about a violation of the law, *and* that "'the words have a natural and reasonably probable tendency to cause the results which have been forbidden by these provisions of the Espionage Act.'"[135] In their effort to demonstrate the sufficiency of the evidence on the issue of intent, O'Brian and Bettman pointed expressly to Debs's prior statements and speeches on the theory that such evidence demonstrated his specific intent to encourage draft evasion during his speech in Ohio. They never argued that Debs's intent could or should be inferred from the mere "bad tendency" of the speech itself.

This suggests that at least in its highest reaches, and at least in its arguments before the Supreme Court, the Department of Justice understood the difference between specific intent and bad tendency, and saw them as separate and distinct requirements under the law.[136] This is certainly more in line with the common law doctrine of attempts than the approach that prevailed in the lower federal courts. This also sheds new light on the Supreme Court's opinions in *Schenck*, *Frohwerk*, and *Debs*.[137] Whatever else one

---

incite to forbidden action, or whether it does, in fact, incite to forbidden action." Brief for Charles Schenck in *Schenck v United States* at 14–16, in Kurland and Casper, 18 *Landmark Briefs* at 1002 (cited in note 128). Schenck argued, however, that his circular did not meet this standard because it was intended to persuade readers to sign a petition to repeal the Conscription Act, not to violate the law.

[135] Brief for the United States in *Debs v United States* at 77, in Kurland and Casper, 19 *Landmark Briefs* at 682 (cited in note 128). Moreover, they point repeatedly to jury instructions in other cases in which the judge drew a clear distinction between specific intent and bad tendency.

[136] Because the Justice Department was highly decentralized, O'Brian and Bettman exercised only modest control over the nation's prosecuting attorneys. There was thus great variation from district to district in the standards applied by federal prosecutors. It is therefore quite possible that O'Brian and Bettman held to a position that differed quite significantly from those adopted and employed by their subordinates. See John Lord O'Brian, *New Encroachments on Individual Freedom*, 66 Harv L Rev 1, 12 (1952) ("The United States Attorneys of the various districts exercised a large measure of discretion in instituting prosecutions and, not immune to popular alarm and hysteria, sometimes became overzealous in their activities."); Scheiber, *Wilson Administration* at 43 (cited in note 8).

[137] In *Frohwerk*, the defendants failed to file a bill of exceptions. Thus, as O'Brian and Bettman noted in their brief to the Court, the "overruling of the demurrer to the evidence

might think of those opinions, if they are read in the light of the government's briefs, it would appear that Justice Holmes was not embracing the most extreme version of the bad tendency/constructive intent standard, which essentially equated all criticism of the war with unlawful intent, but was instead following the lead of the Department of Justice and treating proof of specific intent as a distinct evidentiary requirement.[138] A close reading of the opinions bears this out.[139]

But even casting so positive a light on the position of the Department of Justice, several problems remain. First, there is the question whether the standard of "natural and reasonably probable

---

is not reviewable here." Accordingly, it was proper for the Court to assume that the evidence was sufficient to support the verdict. In such circumstances, O'Brian and Bettman argued persuasively that "[t]he question raised under the First Amendment . . . therefore, comes down to this—whether Congress has a constitutional power to provide punishment for deliberate attempts by means of publication of articles in a newspaper to interfere with the raising an army and the faithful military service of those subject thereto." They added that, in their view, "the constitutional guaranty of free press and speech . . . does not include the right to intentionally attempt to induce others to violate law, whether such attempts be couched in direct or indirect language," for "[t]he right of the community to punish intentional incitement to violation of law is . . . well recognized." As in their briefs in *Schenck* and *Debs*, they do not suggest in *Frohwerk* that intent can be inferred from bad tendency. On the other hand, because the evidence is not properly before the Court, they do not discuss the evidence at trial that might otherwise have supported a finding of specific intent. This also explains the very cryptic nature of Justice Holmes' opinion on this question. Brief for the United States in *Frohwerk v United States* at 11, 18–20, in Kurland and Casper, 19 *Landmark Briefs* at 480, 487–89 (cited in note 128).

[138] Indeed, this understanding of the position of the Department of Justice and of the Court's opinions in *Schenck, Frohwerk,* and *Debs* follows neatly from Holmes's analysis twenty-five years earlier. See Oliver Wendell Holmes, *Privilege, Malice, and Intent,* 8 Harv L Rev 1 (1894). In this essay, Holmes recognized that in some circumstances "a man is not liable for a very manifest danger unless he actually intends to do the harm complained of." Id at 2. This is most often so, Holmes explained, when the individual has "a claim of privilege." Id at 9. Because "every one has a right to rely upon his fellow-men acting lawfully," an individual "is not answerable for himself acting upon the assumption that they will do so, however improbable it may be." Id at 10. Thus, Holmes concluded, "when the wrongful act expected is that of a third person," the defendant may be liable for causing the act *only* if he "intended the unlawful act" to occur. Id at 11. Mere anticipation of the unlawful conduct is insufficient. See Sheldon M. Novick, I *The Collected Works of Justice Holmes* 66–69 (Chicago, 1995) (arguing that *Schenck* incorporated the requirement of specific intent Holmes had explained in *Privilege, Malice, and Intent*).

[139] For a different reading of these opinions, see Rabban, *Forgotten Years* at 285–93 (cited in note 2) (concluding that in these opinions Justice Holmes "judged the intent requirement of the Espionage Act by the tendency of words rather than through an effort to uncover the defendants' actual states of mind"). Although I had long shared this view, a careful reading of the briefs for the United States and the jury instructions has persuaded me that these opinions treat proof of intent as a separate and distinct requirement from proof of "bad tendency," although obviously the probability that the speech will cause unlawful conduct is relevant to the question of intent.

tendency" is equivalent to the proximity requirement for attempts under the common law. Recall that the usual common law formulations require that the act "must come dangerously near to success,"[140] "must come sufficiently near completion to be of public concern,"[141] must come "very near to the accomplishment of the act,"[142] and must threaten a "harm which is foreseen as likely to follow."[143] The facts of most, if not all, of the Espionage Act prosecutions do not meet these standards.

Second, this position fails to acknowledge that the general common law approach to punishing speech because it may cause others to commit unlawful acts falls into the realm of solicitation rather than attempt. And as Judge Hand argued, the law ordinarily requires express advocacy of unlawful conduct to make out the crime of solicitation. (This is important not because the common law "trumps" either a legislative judgment or the Constitution, but because it gives meaning to the statutory word "attempt" and informs our understanding of the First Amendment.)

Third, a standard based primarily on intent, however logical or morally satisfying, fails in practice. Indeed, even during the debates in Congress on the Espionage Act, there was substantial concern about the ability of judges and jurors effectively to distinguish "legitimate" from "illegitimate" intent in a wartime atmosphere of fear, suspicion, and excessive "patriotism."[144]

Undoubtedly, some defendants intended to incite unlawful interference with the war effort. But it is extraordinarily difficult to prove a defendant's subjective intent, and it is especially dangerous to undertake this inquiry when jurors, and even some judges, are already inflamed against the defendant because of his "disloyalty." As Professor Chafee observed, it is especially "in times of popular panic and indignation that freedom of speech becomes important as an institution, and it is precisely in those times that the protec-

[140] Beale, *Criminal Attempts* at 492 (cited in note 52).

[141] Id at 501.

[142] *Commonwealth v Peaslee*, 177 Mass 267, 272, 59 NE 55, 56 (1901).

[143] Holmes, *The Common Law* 67 (cited in note 69).

[144] See, for example, Hearings on HR 291 before the House Committee on the Judiciary, 65th Cong, 1st Sess 12–13, 36–43 (April 9 and 12, 1917) (testimony of Emily Balch and Gilbert Roe). See Stone, *A Mystery Unraveled* (cited in note 6).

tion of the jury proves illusory."[145] If nothing else, our experience with the Espionage Act of 1917 proved this.[146]

VIII. Conclusion

In his amicus curiae brief to the Supreme Court in *Debs*, Gilbert Roe of the Free Speech League argued that if, in practical effect, "Section 3 . . . of the Espionage Law prevents general public discussion of the war . . . because a jury is allowed to find that such discussion is with the specific intent prohibited by the Espionage Law, . . . then the constitutional guarantee of free speech and free press is wiped out."[147] In their reply brief, O'Brian and Bettman responded as follows:[148]

> Mr. Roe claims that by reason of the temper of the public during a war, a law directed at obstruction of the prosecution of the war will inevitably be applied so as to suppress all critical discussion of the war, and that the Espionage Act, as applied by courts and juries, has produced that effect. . . . [But if] a trial be free from prejudicial errors and the verdict finds support in the evidence, then the vice, if any, . . . must either be inherent in the policy of the law under which the case was prosecuted, a consideration falling exclusively within the domain of the leg-

---

[145] Chafee, *Free Speech* at 70 (cited in note 42). Chafee added: "It is true that intention is material in other crimes, such as murder; but in dealing with an overt criminal act like killing the intention is evidenced by many other acts, which are a kind of fact with which the jurymen are familiar and capable of dealing. On the other hand, the intention in making utterances is evidenced (1) by inferences drawn from the supposed bad tendency of the words themselves, and (2) by other utterances, which will also be viewed under the . . . test of bad tendency." Id at 67.

[146] In 1923, Justice Brandeis confided to Felix Frankfurter, then a law professor at Harvard, that "I have never been quite happy about my concurrence in [the] *Debs* and *Schenck* cases." Brandeis confessed that "I had not then thought the issues of freedom of speech out—I had thought at the subject, not through it." Brandeis hastily added, in his own defense, "of course you must remember . . . that when Holmes writes, he doesn't give a fellow a chance—he shoots so quickly." Melvin I. Urofsky, *The Brandeis-Frankfurter Conversations*, 1985 Supreme Court Review 299, 323–24. Holmes himself was less than happy with these decisions. Within a year, he admitted that he "greatly regretted his misfortune" in having the "disagreeable task" of writing these opinions. Rabban, *Forgotten Years* at 294 (cited in note 2), quoting letters in the spring of 1919 from Holmes to Harold Laski, Sir Frederick Pollock, and Baroness Moncheur.

[147] Brief of Gilbert E. Roe, as Amicus Curiae in *Debs v United States* at 47–48, in Kurland and Casper, 19 *Landmark Briefs* at 748–49 (cited in note 128) (italics omitted).

[148] Brief for the United States in Reply to Brief of Gilbert E. Roe as Amicus Curiae in *Debs v United States* at 3–4, in Kurland and Casper, 19 *Landmark Briefs* at 758–59 (cited in note 128).

islative branch of the Government, or must be one which the President alone, by act of executive clemency, can correct. Mr. Roe's plea amounts to an appeal to this court to ignore the constitutional limitations of its functions and correct what he conceives to be a mistaken legislative policy or mistaken, though lawful, verdicts.

Interestingly, this response does not rebut Roe's characterization. Rather, it rests upon a very narrow conception of constitutional law. Assuming, as the brief for the United States does, that "Congress has not the power to punish belief or opinion as such," and that "[t]he right to criticize the Government's policies and actions is so essential to democracy, that in any definition of the freedom of speech and press, that right would be acknowledged,"[149] then why is it self-evident that the Act does not violate the First Amendment if its effect *in actual practice* is "to prevent general public discussion of the war"? This is the closest the Department of Justice came in this era to acknowledging a fundamental gap in its understanding of the Act and the First Amendment.[150]

Perhaps the most astute analysis of these issues at the time is the largely overlooked convocation address delivered at Columbia University in 1921 by University of Chicago Law School Dean James Parker Hall.[151] Hall notes that the Espionage Act was "bitterly attacked" as a "departure from one of our greatest political traditions," and that it was "defended in language equally strong."[152] Although the "needs and passions of war time create an atmosphere unfavorable to the discussion of such questions," it should be possible, he says, to do better "[t]wo years after the cessation of armed conflict."[153]

Hall then asserts that "it is nowhere seriously argued by anyone whose opinion is entitled to respect that direct and intentional incitations to crime may not be forbidden by the state." But he then

---

[149] Brief for the United States, in Reply to Brief of Gilbert E. Roe as Amicus Curiae in *Debs v United States* at 2, in Kurland and Casper, 19 *Landmark Briefs* at 757 (cited in note 128).

[150] Edward Corwin reached a conclusion similar to that of O'Brian and Bettman. See Edward S. Corwin, *Freedom of Speech and Press Under the First Amendment: A Resume*, 30 Yale L J 48 (1920).

[151] James Parker Hall, *Free Speech in War Time*, 21 Colum L Rev 526 (1921).

[152] Id at 528.

[153] Id.

observes, as did Judge Hand, that to circumvent such a rule, "shrewder" people, "[i]nstead of urging resistance to the draft," will "argue in passionate and extravagant language how outrageous and . . . tyrannical a draft law is," they will "bitterly and mendaciously attack the motives of their opponents," and they will "picture the undeniable risks of battle . . . in colors as lurid and frightful as imagination can conceive them."[154] These "shrewder" people will "say that they are only arguing to influence public opinion to repeal or amend the draft law, and that, so long as they do not *directly* counsel *resistance* to [the law] as it stands, they are protected in whatever they say as political agitation for its alteration."[155]

"But," Hall recognizes, "what they say . . . *does* induce in some or many persons exactly the same resistance to the draft as if it were more directly urged," and this may often be "exactly what is intended by the utterer." This is a problem because a "genuine believer in constitutional government can hardly afford to take the position that in war time men can lawfully be forbidden to attempt in good faith to secure changes in the laws."[156] To escape this dilemma, the "genuine believer in constitutional government" puts forth an argument that "is theoretically simple and satisfactory: If the utterer in fact *intends* his language to induce evasions of the draft, . . . he shall be liable to punishment; but if in fact he intends only to influence public opinion to bring about a change of law . . . he shall go free."[157]

Hall observes that there "are legal precedents in abundance for such a distinction," both in the criminal and civil law, where "a man is . . . liable for a certain result only if he intends it." On this premise, "our believer in constitutional government" passes the Espionage Act, which forbids "utterances *intended* to produce certain results injurious to the conduct of the war." Hall notes that although this distinction may be theoretically sound, there is a serious question about how "it really work[s] in practice."[158]

Dean Hall next addresses the "problem" of the jury. "[I]f public opinion favors the war," jurors "are almost always impatient of

---

[154] Id.

[155] Id at 531.

[156] Id.

[157] Id at 532 (emphasis added).

[158] Id at 532.

adverse criticism, and almost certain to regard it as inspired by improper motives." In general, "those in opposition will be . . . believed to be disloyal." In such circumstances, the defendant "is all too likely to be condemned chiefly because what he says is disliked, rather than because he actually intends to induce unlawful conduct." Indeed, the "distinction between trying to induce men to *change* a law rather than to *disobey* it does not bite deeply into the minds of a jury who personally think as badly of one effort as of the other."[159]

Hall thus concludes that "once you grant that you can punish a speaker not merely for literally direct incitement, but for language likely to incite and so intended, some cases are sure to . . . be decided erroneously" and this approach will certainly "cut off some useful criticism." Hence, "we have to choose between competing goods and ills." Hall reasons that in "ordinary times the social interest in free discussion so plainly outweighs all possible gains from its suppression that probably only . . . direct incitements . . . may be forbidden." But during "an important war," the "state may lawfully limit the ordinary freedom of speech . . . if this can be thought reasonably necessary for the public welfare," and this is so even if the restriction will of necessity be "susceptible of mistakes and abuse."[160]

Thus, Dean Hall meticulously (albeit implicitly) traces the logical steps in the argument from the bad tendency test, to Judge Hand's opinion in *Masses*, to the arguments of O'Brian and Bettman. In the end, he finds that it all comes down to a "choice" between "a speedier successful ending of the war, or a freer public discussion of it."[161]

Of course, one can disagree with Dean Hall's judgment of which is the more important interest, or even with how he defines the choice. After all, and this is *critical*, "a freer public discussion" may in fact lead to "a speedier successful ending of the war," so the "choice" Hall poses may miss an essential element of the balance. But even if one agrees in the abstract with Dean Hall's assessment, there is an additional question: Does the experience during World

---

[159] Id at 533.

[160] Id at 534–35.

[161] Id.

War I, for which we can now exercise the power of hindsight, bear out his "choice"?

Hall himself addresses this. What of the possibility, he asks, that "our war-time restrictions" of speech "were not really needed, but were the product of an excitement and quasi-panic that deprived men of the power of judging in calmness" what restrictions were needed? He says this question can be answered only by considering "the states of mind" of those who were in the circumstances they confronted.[162] "One who is repelling assault and battery," for example, "is not required at his peril to judge of the proper limits of self-defence with the detachment of a bystander." Rather, in "appraising the correctness of his decision, the court will take into account his naturally excited state of mind," for he "need only decide as well as could fairly be expected . . . under such circumstances of provocation and excitement."[163]

"It is doubtless true," Hall concedes, that "during the late war, men of . . . intelligence and credulity believed there was much greater danger from pro-German and treasonable activities than was in sober truth the case." But, he argues, by analogy to the assault and battery example, if we consider the magnitude of the "emergency," the "temper of the country," the "stress of war," and the "imperfect information available" at the time, it "seems impossible to say" that the government's actions were in their "essential features unreasonable."[164]

Is Dean Hall correct that viewed from within the circumstances of World War I the actions of the government cannot fairly be adjudged "unreasonable"? Even if that is so, is that the right question? Our concern ought not to be whether we would hold Wilson, Gregory, Creel, or O'Brian liable for their conduct, but whether we can learn from our experience and do better the next time. If the government's actions during World War I were "reasonable" in light of the "emergency," the "temper of the country," the "stress of war," and the "imperfect information available," but nonetheless failed to meet our national aspirations, how can we come closer to our aspirations in the future?

---

[162] Id at 535.

[163] Id at 536.

[164] Id.

DENNIS J. HUTCHINSON

"THE ACHILLES HEEL" OF THE CONSTITUTION: JUSTICE JACKSON AND THE JAPANESE EXCLUSION CASES

Robert H. Jackson's dissenting opinion in *Korematsu v United States*[1] has always been a puzzle to both his admirers and his critics. The decision itself upheld the criminal conviction of a Japanese-American citizen for refusing to leave a restricted area on the West Coast during World War II, and it was commonly understood to uphold not only exclusion but also relocation of all Japanese— some 120,000 citizens and noncitizens alike—from the West Coast shortly after Pearl Harbor.[2] Jackson dissented on the ground that a criminal conviction that turned on the race of the defendant violated the Constitution. But unlike his fellow dissenters, Owen J. Roberts and Frank Murphy, Jackson accepted that the military enjoyed the power to arrest and detain even citizens during a wartime emergency, and he refused to hold that the "courts should have attempted to interfere with the Army in carrying out its task."[3]

Dennis J. Hutchinson is William Rainey Harper Professor in the College and Senior Lecturer in Law, the University of Chicago.

AUTHOR'S NOTE: I am grateful to John Q. Barrett, David P. Currie, Jack Goldsmith, Philip Hamburger, Tom Merrill, Richard Posner, David Roe, Cass Sunstein, and William Wiecek for comments on a preliminary draft, and to Lee Saladino for research assistance. The essay is offered for David Wigdor, Assistant Chief of the Manuscript Division of the Library of Congress, who for more than two decades has been colleague, consummate professional, and friend.

[1] 323 US 214, 242 (Jackson, J, dissenting) (1944).

[2] The Court did not reach the issue of the constitutionality of detention. See text at notes 70 ff.

[3] 323 US at 248.

The implication of his position—condemning criminal prosecution but refusing to condemn the underlying military power—was that he would stand idle had the dissenters prevailed and the federal government had then defied the decision. He thus left the impression of someone voting "present" on a monumental aye-nay issue. To Charles Fairman, who saw Jackson's career as a "shining mark"[4] in the Court's history, the equivocal position was simply "wrong."[5] To Eugene V. Rostow, author of a searing and influential critique of the decision, Jackson "wrote a fascinating and fantastic essay in nihilism":[6] "What Justice Jackson is saying seems to be this: Courts should refuse to decide hard cases, for in the hands of foolish judges they make bad law. The ark of the law must be protected against contamination."[7]

The puzzle of Jackson's position in *Korematsu* can be understood as the outgrowth of conflicting impulses, never resolved, that were prompted by two prior cases involving the military, the war power, and the Court: *Ex Parte Quirin*[8] was decided in 1942 and *Hirabayashi v United States*[9] a year later. Indeed, Jackson's opinion in *Korematsu* is in substance simply an updated edition of an opinion that he worked through multiple drafts that were never circulated while *Hirabayashi* was pending. Those earlier, unpublished struggles with the fundamental war powers and the role of the courts show the elements of his thinking much more clearly than the much-criticized *Korematsu* dissent. Jackson often drafted opinions that he later withdrew if the Court changed tack or if he was persuaded that his separate views were a personal indulgence at the expense of institutional clarity or authority. The unpublished drafts, of which more than a dozen survive in archives,[10] seem to

---

[4] Charles Fairman, *Robert H. Jackson: 1892–1954—Associate Justice of the Supreme Court*, 55 Colum L Rev 445 (1955).

[5] Id at 453 n 30.

[6] Eugene V. Rostow, *The Japanese American Cases—A Disaster*, 54 Yale L J 489, 510 (1945) (cited hereafter as Rostow).

[7] Id at 511.

[8] 317 US 1 (1942).

[9] 320 US 81 (1943).

[10] Two have been posthumously published in professional journals: Arthur S. Miller and Jeffrey H. Bowman, *"Slow Dance on the Killing Ground": The Willie Francis Case Revisited*, 32 DePaul L Rev 1 (1983) (see also the same authors, *Death by Installments: The Willie Francis Case* (Greenwood, 1988)); Bernard Schwartz, *Chief Justice Rehnquist, Justice Jackson and the Brown Case*, 1988 Supreme Court Review 245.

be written more to convince the author than his colleagues. Why Jackson declined to publish his views in *Hirabayashi* and why he added more rhetoric than substance to his views in *Korematsu* is a function of the internal dynamics of the Court, of the use to which the decision in *Hirabayashi* was put as soon as it was decided, and of his own genuine anxieties over the real power of courts and law.

Justice Jackson came to the cases with powerful biases. As Solicitor General (1938–40) he had defended the New Deal in the wake of the so-called Constitutional Revolution of 1937,[11] in which the Supreme Court abruptly changed course and reread the Commerce and Due Process Clauses to uphold central features of Franklin D. Roosevelt's "second hundred days"—most notably the Wagner Act[12] and the Social Security Act.[13] Jackson traced the Court's road to Damascus, and celebrated the new learning, in *The Struggle for Judicial Supremacy*, which he completed in 1940.[14] As Attorney General (1940–41) he continued to develop his views of broad legislative and strong executive power, including advice to Roosevelt justifying the provision of naval destroyers to Great Britain in return for military base lease agreements even absent Congressional approval.[15] As war became more imminent, he oversaw implementation of the Alien Registration Act of 1940,[16] which required registration and fingerprinting of all noncitizens, and the Nationality Act of 1940,[17] which regulated issues of citizenship loss and expatriation. He also developed contingency plans for arresting suspected enemy aliens,[18] although he worried that the power could easily be used indiscriminately to "over-intern." Years later, he recalled: "The problem, of course, in the matter was to

---

[11] See, generally, William E. Leuchtenburg, *The Supreme Court Reborn: The Constitutional Revolution in the Age of Roosevelt* (Oxford, 1995).

[12] *NLRB v Jones & Laughlin Steel Corp.*, 301 US 1 (1937).

[13] *Helvering v Davis*, 301 US 610 (1937).

[14] (Knopf, 1941), cited hereafter as Jackson.

[15] William E. Leuchtenburg, *Franklin D. Roosevelt and the New Deal, 1932–1940* 304–06 (Harper & Row, 1963).

[16] 54 Stat 670 (1940). See further note 97 below.

[17] 54 Stat 1137 (1940).

[18] See various memorandums: "Re: Internment of dangerous persons in the event of war," April 1941, Box 90, Robert H. Jackson Papers, Library of Congress, Manuscript Division (cited hereafter as RHJP).

avoid security risks having an opportunity to work harm to our effort if war came. But there was a second purpose that was even as pressing. We wanted to avoid over-internment, the creation of unnecessary situations of internment of persons on whom families or infirm persons were dependent, interference with the labor supply through reckless internment, and the internment of persons solely for careless statements they had made prior to the outbreak of war."[19] Later, when Jackson began preliminary work on his memoirs, he counted among the three most important achievements of his Attorney Generalship "development of the government's legal philosophy concerning" the "war powers of the President."[20]

Robert Jackson was appointed to the Supreme Court in the summer of 1941, Franklin D. Roosevelt's seventh appointee in the four years since the Court's *volte-face* in the spring of 1937. In late July of 1942, the war came to the Court in the form of *Ex Parte Quirin*, in which eight German saboteurs—including two American citizens—sought habeas corpus relief from their trial by a military commission. Jackson's experiences as Attorney General framed his views when the Court nervously asserted jurisdiction over *Quirin*. The Court denied relief on July 31, 1942, by order after a Special Session; all but two of the putative saboteurs were executed after trial by a military commission appointed by the President; and the Court then spent weeks trying to forge an opinion justifying its decision. Jackson circulated memoranda to his colleagues arguing that the Court had no business reviewing the President's order establishing the military commissions: "I think we are exceeding our powers in reviewing the legality of the President's Order and that experience shows the judicial system is ill-adapted to deal with matters in which we must present a united front against a foreign foe."[21] The specter of wholesale habeas corpus proceedings was unacceptable to him: "The fact that the Court comes out right by sustaining the President in this instance does not justify the

---

[19] VI *Reminiscences of Robert H. Jackson* 283, D'Angelo Law Library, University of Chicago (transcript of interviews with Columbia University Oral History Project).

[20] Jackson, *Autobiography* 18, unpublished ms, D'Angelo Law Library, University of Chicago Law School. The other two were "the concept of the German-Soviet war of aggression" and the "right of a neutral to give aid to a victim of aggression, short of war." The fragmentary ms carries a transcription date of "6-8-44."

[21] Memorandum of Mr. Justice Jackson, Oct 23, 1942, at 8, Box 124, RHJP.

entertainment of the prisoners' complaint against his procedure; it only obscures the mischief of which the process in our own hands and in those of nearly one hundred District Courts is capable."[22] His conclusion was cast in rhetorically ominous tones: "I press this view because in the long run it seems to me that we have no more important duty than to keep clear and separate the lines of responsibility and duty of the judicial and of the executive-military arms of government. Merger of the two is the end of liberty as we in this country have known it."[23] Chief Justice Harlan Fiske Stone's eventual opinion for the Court, issued October 29, 1942, did not adopt Jackson's extremely restrictive scope of review, but fudged the matter by finding history on the side of the President and the Commission, and unanimity was achieved.[24] Jackson's thinking about the war power continued to rest on a foundation presuming strong executive power and a correspondingly modest—if any—role for the judiciary. Six months later, the unequivocal position he staked out in *Quirin* would be sharply tested.

I. HIRABAYASHI V UNITED STATES

Less than ninety days after Pearl Harbor, President Roosevelt issued an executive order on February 19, 1942, authorizing the Secretary of War and designated "military commanders" to prescribe "military areas" from which "any or all persons may be excluded," as a precaution against espionage and sabotage.[25] A series of subsequent orders by Lieutenant General J. L. DeWitt, Military Commander of the Western Defense Command, designated "the entire Pacific Coast" (to an average depth of forty

---

[22] Id at 8–9.

[23] Id at 10.

[24] The case has been extensively covered, most recently by G. Edward White, *Felix Frankfurter's "Soliloquy" in Ex Parte Quirin: Nazi Sabotage & Constitutional Conundrums*, 5 Green Bag 2d 423 (2002). The classic treatments are David Danelski, *The Saboteurs' Case*, 1 J S Ct Hist 61 (1996); Michael R. Belknap, *The Supreme Court Goes to War: The Meaning and Implications of the Nazi Saboteur Case*, 89 Milit L Rev 59 (1980). Robert Cushman, *Ex Parte Quirin et al.—The Nazi Saboteur Case*, 28 Cornell L Q 54 (1942), is a thorough contemporary account.

[25] The most sustained account of the program and the litigation it produced is Peter Irons, *Justice at War* (Oxford, 1983; California, 1993) (cited hereafter as Irons). As comprehensive as Irons's account is, it suffers from lacking access to the Jackson Papers, which were not donated to the Library of Congress until 1985.

miles) to be such a restricted military area, and provided for the exclusion from the area and relocation of persons of suspect loy- alty, alien enemies, and all persons—alien and citizen alike—of Japanese ancestry. A War Relocation Authority was established by Executive Order to carry out DeWitt's orders, and on March 21, 1942, Congress provided criminal penalties for violations of the military orders. Shortly thereafter, General DeWitt imposed a cur- few on aliens and all persons of Japanese ancestry (between the hours of 8 P.M. and 6 A.M.) in one of the primary areas. Despite the unvarnished racism of the program, civil liberties organizations kept remarkably quiet during the early months of the operation, perhaps because fears of invasion on the West Coast refused to wane as the first five months of 1942 witnessed one Japanese vic- tory after another over the Allies in the Pacific. Singapore fell Feb- ruary 9, several islands were taken, and Java surrendered March 9. The Japanese forces were expanding their perimeter seemingly at will. The only relief to buffeted Allied morale came April 18, when Tokyo was bombed in a surprise raid by aircraft from the USS *Hornet*, but the victory was psychological and not military. The American home front was thus split between fear and anger over the Japanese juggernaut when the relocation program was imple- mented. Allied victory at Midway Island in early June of 1942 marked a turning point, but tensions, if not security risks, still sim- mered when *Hirabayashi v United States* arrived in early 1943 at the Supreme Court in the form of questions certified by the Court of Appeals for the Ninth Circuit.

Gordon Hirabayashi was a senior in the spring of 1942 at the University of Washington in Seattle, where he had been born to Japanese alien parents. He violated the curfew imposed by General DeWitt on May 9, 1942, and was indicted for that offense as well as for failing to report on May 11 and 12 to a designated area for processing at a "Civil Control Station."[26] (What the indictments omitted, but what everyone knew, is that the station was the first step toward assignment in a detention camp.) Hirabayashi was con- victed on both counts and received concurrent sentences of three months imprisonment on each count. At trial, he contended unsuc- cessfully that the charges against him were unconstitutional on two grounds: that DeWitt's orders were an unconstitutional delegation

---

[26] *United States v Gordon Kitoshi Hirabayashi*, 46 F Supp 657, 658 (WD Wash 1942).

of legislative authority to the executive, and that as a loyal American citizen he could not be penalized for a crime that turned on his ancestry without violating the Due Process Clause of the Fifth Amendment. Francis Biddle, who had succeeded Jackson as Attorney General in 1941, wanted the constitutionality of the program settled quickly by the Supreme Court, before the end of Term, if possible.[27] So the Justice Department persuaded the Ninth Circuit, over a bitter and hasty dissent by Judge William Denman,[28] to certify the constitutional questions to the Supreme Court. The Supreme Court overrode the certification process, however, and directed the entire record be certified "so that the case could be determined as if brought here by appeal."[29] Oral argument was held May 10 and 11, 1943.

On the second day of argument in *Hirabayashi*, the Court also heard argument on a preliminary question in another case testing the constitutionality of the relocation program. Fred Korematsu, another American citizen of Japanese ancestry, had been found guilty of remaining in a military area after having been ordered to leave. He was sentenced to probation for five years, and he appealed. The Ninth Circuit certified to the Supreme Court the question whether Korematsu could appeal his conviction; the circuit court doubted that it had jurisdiction, since it viewed probation as preliminary to final sentencing and thus not a "final and appealable order" under the Judicial Code. The Supreme Court ignored heated pleas by Korematsu's counsel to reach the merits of the constitutionality of the conviction, and answered the certified question with a unanimous and matter-of-fact "yes" in less than five pages on June 1.[30]

The Supreme Court thus knew that the constitutionality of the relocation program would be before it one way or another, sooner or later. The issue was whether it should be reached in *Hirabayashi*. The nettle of the constitutional issue was nicely grasped by Justice Jackson during argument in *Hirabayashi*: "We all agree that the government may not say in peacetime that it is a crime for a de-

---

[27] Irons at 182–83.

[28] Judge Denman's dissent is printed in Brief for Appellant, *Hirabayashi v United States*, No 870 (October Term 1942), A33–48.

[29] 320 US at 85.

[30] *Korematsu v United States*, 319 US 432 (1943).

scendent of an Irishman to do what would not be a crime if committed by a descendent of another national,"[31] he pointedly said to Solicitor General Charles Fahy—a Catholic of Irish descent and a friend of Jackson. "The basis of the discrimination is therefore in the war powers."[32] Fahy replied that "What makes it reasonable now is the war power and the circumstances of war," but he would not "admit" that there was any discrimination involved in the case.[33]

Jackson had been unsympathetic at oral argument to Hirabayashi's claim based on the delegation doctrine, but he was clearly troubled by what he referred to as the "ancestry" point. On the one hand, as his unfiled opinion in *Quirin* amply demonstrated, he would be the last member of the Court to second-guess the President—and, here, the Congress—on the exercise of the war powers during time of war. On the other hand, he feared that judicial deference to the "war powers" would create a precedent that ancestry was a constitutionally legitimate basis of classification by the government in some circumstances. His primary fear was that the emergency that justified the classification would eventually be forgotten, leaving the constitutionality of the classification as the lesson of the cases.

Some time between the conclusion of oral arguments on May 11 and the conference on May 17 when the Court met to discuss and vote on the case, Jackson prepared a 2,300-word draft opinion.[34] The draft does not have the finished appearance of many of his other working drafts, with citations and case analysis; rather, it appears to be more a *cri di coeur*. None of the ambivalence he felt during oral argument had been resolved. The only unequivocal conclusion is the bottom line: "Hence I would reverse these convictions and order these indictments dismissed, leaving the enforcement of these military measures to the military authority."[35] Thus, Jackson appeared to assume that both convictions, for violating the curfew and for refusing to report, would be reached by the Court. If so, he was unwilling to sustain either conviction.

---

[31] Irons at 225.

[32] Id.

[33] Id.

[34] Undated draft, Box 128, RHJP.

[35] Id.

His unwillingness traced a rather contorted path. The opinion began, after stating the facts, with a candid statement of what Jackson saw as the issue: "So the question we face is whether a citizen of the United States may be classified according to ancestry for unequal treatment before the law. In normal times and circumstances, I suppose we would unhesitatingly answer, 'No.' The question is therefore, whether the war power in which these orders are grounded requires or permits a different answer."[36] The next paragraph telegraphed the answer, in a phrase that recurs in his draft opinions in this case but which was not used in a published opinion until six years later in a First Amendment case: "Nothing in the Constitution requires it to be construed as a suicide pact. It recognized the existence of a war power which it does not define or expressly limit."[37] But he then went on to say that "the exercise of the war power, at least within the limits of good faith and decent judgment, is not susceptible to judicial review."[38] Without scrutinizing the basis for the orders in detail, he discussed them sympathetically, wished other means had been available or used, acknowledged the hardships on the evacuees, but pointed out that "the war power in time of stress cannot be halted by considerations of individual hardship or even injustices."[39] He concluded "that these military orders were permissible exercise[s] of the war power and that the courts should neither interfere with their military execution nor attempt to review in individual hearings military steps to prevent or punish infractions thereof."[40]

But that did not end the case for Jackson. "The Army's use of the war power is quite a different matter than making the courts agencies for its execution."[41] He then set up his Solomonic solution to the issue he had created. Realizing that the military may overstep the guidelines of the Constitution in using the war power, he wrote, "But when traveling outside the realms of clear constitutional right, I think it far safer to our ultimate liberties if the

---

[36] Id.

[37] Id. Compare *Terminiello v Chicago*, 337 US 1, 37 (Jackson, J, dissenting) (1949).

[38] Undated draft, Box 128, RHJP.

[39] Id.

[40] Id.

[41] Id.

executive travels alone."[42] The heart of the judicial problem was simple:[43]

> Temporary or local departures from the strict lines of the law are less dangers if there is an agency of government that can aid to restore the balance when the emergency has passed. But if the Judiciary go arm-in-arm with the Executive through constitutional short-cuts, how can the courts ever perform this duty? Judicial commitments become recorded as precedents. The courts cannot be extricated from an unconstitutional course or unconstitutional principles rooted out of its practice merely by an election, as can be done in the case of the President or Congress. There is no room for temporary or local constitutional judgments by the Court and if ever in normal times we are able to hold to the rights of the citizens, we disable ourselves if we become committed and compromised in emergency.

Jackson then condemned the classifications used in the cases in angry terms: "However proper this rough-and-ready sorting out by the military for emergency orders, I think it an utterly inadmissible principle upon which to base criminal law to be applied by the American Courts. It is the principle of the Ghetto, of the Bill of Attainder, of decrees of condemnation of races and confiscation of their goods."[44] He then concluded by washing his hands, at least precedentially, of the matter, with the notion that he would reverse the convictions. "There is more danger that liberties will be devitalized through patriotic straining by the Judiciary to find theories to support orders which necessity appears to dictate than that they will be overthrown through frank but unrationalized overstepping by the Executive power."[45]

---

[42] Id. The sentence echoes one of Jackson's favorite lines from what appears to have been his favorite poet, Rudyard Kipling: "Win by his aid and the aid disown—/He travels the fastest who travels alone!" "The Winners," in *Rudyard Kipling's Verse: Definitive Edition* 530 (Doubleday, Doran, 1940). A framed print of a solitary man, bearing the final line of the poem, was displayed in Jackson's offices throughout his career. Eugene C. Gerhart, *America's Advocate* 48 (Bobbs-Merrill, 1958). See also note 91 below and accompanying text.

[43] Undated draft, Box 128, RHJP.

[44] Jackson's reference to the "ghetto" may have been inspired by news coverage of the uprising of the Warsaw Ghetto, which was crushed by Nazi forces May 16, 1943, and which occurred as he was drafting his opinion.

[45] Undated draft, Box 128, RHJP.

The draft opinion gives the appearance of a judge who wants to have his constitutional cake and eat it (or let the executive eat it), too. But the line Jackson sketched in his draft was one that for him did what was necessary to give the Army and the President the room it needed in dark hours of war without permanently committing the courts to bad constitutional law on the rights of citizens. The Janus-like resolution of the case (which is similar to his eventual position in *Korematsu* on the merits a year later) is less strange than the extraordinary lengths he was willing to go—at least by implication—to keep the precedential record clean. Jackson understood that his position could be trumped by an Executive eager to enforce its edicts simply by declaration of martial law (which had happened in Hawaii almost immediately after Pearl Harbor[46]) and concomitant suspension of habeas corpus. (Jackson, who had studied the issue before the war while he was still Attorney General, assumed that the President could suspend habeas corpus without congressional authorization—a dubious assumption in light of the constitutional text,[47] notwithstanding the outcome of *Ex Parte Merryman* during the Civil War.[48]) That would let the military have its will and let the judiciary, which would be unlikely to disturb suspension of the writ, keep a clean conscience.

It was not necessary for Jackson to live with the desperate implications of his draft dissent, at least immediately. When the Court met in conference on May 17, both Chief Justice Stone and Justice Hugo Black urged that *Hirabayashi* be disposed of on grounds as narrow as possible.[49] Because Hirabayashi had received concurrent sentences for his offenses, the Court elected to decide only the question of the constitutionality of the curfew and leave the more disquieting issues of relocation to another day.[50] An emergency

---

[46] See *Duncan v Kahanomoku*, 327 US 304, 307–08 (1946).

[47] Art I, sec 9, cl 2 prohibits suspension of habeas corpus "unless when cases of rebellion or invasion," a decision implicitly committed to Congress, not the President.

[48] 17 F Cas 144 (CC Md 1861) (Taney, CJ, sitting as Circuit Justice). President Abraham Lincoln refused to comply with Taney's issuance of a writ. Congress eventually ratified Lincoln's suspension of the writ. Act of March 3, 1863. 12 Stat 755. Cf. *Ex Parte Milligan*, 4 Wall 2 (1866).

[49] Irons at 231.

[50] Justice Horace Gray provided the classic statement of the concurrent sentence doctrine: "in any criminal case a general verdict and judgment on an indictment or information containing several counts cannot be reversed on error, if any one of the counts is good

curfew was much less a curtailment of civil liberty than internment, even if both were grounded on racial classifications, and so Jackson switched his tentative vote for reversal to affirmance. Only Justice Frank Murphy appeared to be committed to reversal at the end of the conference.

Although the Court had voted to ameliorate the gravity of the racial discrimination it was countenancing, Jackson continued to prepare an opinion—now a concurrence—to reinforce his anxieties about the precedential force of the decision. In successive drafts of May 21, 29, and June 1, he spelled out in more detail his ambivalence to the Court's proposed resolution of the case, but the theme that he emphasized is highlighted by a passage that appears in each draft and that served as the first sentence of the draft dated May 21: "When this Court judges an incident it makes a precedent, and a precedent may introduce a new principle into the law of the Constitution."[51]

The draft opinion of the Court circulated from the Chief Justice to the other Justices on May 30. Jackson prepared two more editions of his own opinion shortly after that, but there is no evidence that he circulated his work to his colleagues. Once Stone took the narrow way out, there was less reason for Jackson to write separately. Moreover, both Justice Douglas and Justice Murphy were circulating opinions, and there was great pressure from both Stone and Justice Felix Frankfurter for the Court to unite behind one opinion, as it had in *Quirin*. Frankfurter's campaign to get Murphy to suppress his opinion, or at least to change it from a dissent to a mild concurrence, has been frequently detailed.[52] Whatever remaining temptations Jackson may have had to publish his opinion were apparently extinguished by June 8, if an entry in Felix Frankfurter's diary is accurate: ". . . the Chief has had a long talk

---

and warrants the judgment, because, in the absence of anything in the record to show the contrary, the presumption of law is that the court awarded sentence on the good count only." *Claassen v United States*, 142 US 140, 146–47 (1891) (internal citations omitted). The Court had recently reaffirmed use of the concurrent-sentence doctrine in a prosecution under the Espionage Act of 1917, *Gorin v United States*, 312 US 19, 33 (1941).

[51] May 21 Draft Opinion, Box 128, RHJP.

[52] Irons at 243–46. Sidney Fine, *Frank Murphy: The Washington Years* 443 (Michigan, 1984) (cited hereafter as Fine). See also Fine, *Mr. Justice Murphy and the Hirabayashi Case*, 33 Pac Hist Rev 195 (1964).

with Jackson who is very eager to join the Chief's opinion and the Chief is confident he can meet a number of suggestions that Jackson made."[53] We will never know what those suggestions in fact were, but later events suggest that Jackson was willing to swallow Stone's opinion and the result silently on condition that Stone emphasized—as he eventually did three times[54]—that the affirmance of Hirabayashi's conviction went only so far as the curfew order and reached no "orders differing from the curfew order."[55] At the end of the day, *Hirabayashi* was unanimous, although anxious separate concurrences were filed by Douglas,[56] Murphy,[57] and Rutledge.[58]

Jackson's fears, first aired in the spring of 1940 while he was Attorney General, about overinternment of "enemy aliens"[59] had suddenly materialized in nightmarish proportions. His anxieties over pitting the Court against the military—first developed in detail in *Quirin*—still counseled hesitation: if the Court second-guessed the military judgment in question, civilian courts would be faced with countless habeas corpus petitions, which was undesirable, and even worse, the government might refuse to comply with orders requiring release of detainees (which had happened in *Ex Parte Merryman*[60]), and that would defeat the rule of law. Jackson's final draft opinion, which he apparently abandoned after Stone capitulated to his requests at their meeting on June 8, rehearsed and elaborated on the earlier drafts. It began with a vivid metaphor.[61]

---

[53] Joseph Lash, ed, *From the Diaries of Felix Frankfurter* 252 (Norton, 1975) (cited hereafter as Lash). The date in Lash's text, June 6, is a misprint: the first Tuesday in June, 1943, was the June 8.

[54] 320 US at 101, 102, 105.

[55] Id at 105.

[56] Id.

[57] Id at 109.

[58] Id at 114.

[59] See text at notes 18–19 above.

[60] See note 46 above.

[61] The opinion is labeled "Rev of 6-4-43 not used." Box 128, RHJP. Jackson apparently did not send the draft to the Court's in-house printer. The text is a combination of passages cut from an earlier draft and handwritten riders and interlineations. The draft published here represents Jackson's deletions with strike-throughs. Poor condition of the original document precludes photoreproduction.

SUPREME COURT OF THE UNITED STATES

No. 870—October Term, 1942

Gordon Kiyoshi Hirabayashi

vs.

The United States of America

On Certificate from the United States Court of Appeals
for the Ninth Circuit

[   ]

Mr. Justice JACKSON, concurring.

The Court is sustaining a novel exercise of the war power,
which I regard as the Achilles Heel of our constitutional system. The issue here is raised by creation of an offense extraordinary in American law.

Citizens of this country by birth are convicted of a crime,
an indispensable element of which is their ancestry. An act otherwise innocent becomes in them a crime only because their
ancestors were Japanese. The same conduct at the same time
and place would not be criminal if their parents were of any
other national origin—even German or Italian. It is a little
startling that guilt should attach to one because he springs from
ancestors as to whom he had no option, or belongs to a race
from which there is no way to resign. To classify citizens according to their ancestry for frankly unequal standing before
the law is, to say the least, difficult to reconcile with either our
constitutional tradition or even our professions.[1]

This crime is made such by combining penal sanctions prescribed by Congress with prohibitions prescribed by military
order. The only serious constitutional question, as I see it, is
the effect of the discriminatory effect of the order.

---

[1] See Yick wo v. Hopkins, 118 U.S. 536; Buchanan V. Warly [sic], 245 U.S.
60; Terrace v. Thompson, 263 U.S. 197; Yu Cong Eng v. Trinidad, 271 U.S.
500; State v. Darnell, 166 N.C. 300. *Contra:* Carey v. Atlanta, 143 Ga. 192;
Harden v. Atlanta, 147 Ga. 248; Harris v. Louisville, 165 Ky. 559; Hopkins
v. Richond, 117 Va. 692.

The question, therefore, is whether we ~~will~~ should sustain as an exercise of the war power a discrimination we would probably strike down as an exercise of legislative power. ~~The Court's answer is that we will. I do not disagree with the result, but~~ We must also make a choice between two ways of reaching ~~it, and the choice is of some importance.~~ such a result. One is to uphold the order, as the Court does, because ~~that "due process of law" permits~~ such discrimination is constitutional when there is a rational basis for it; the other is to ~~hold that~~ let the order stand because it is beyond our power to review. ~~I am not sure which is the better way, but I am sure that the alternative should be exposed if for no other purpose than to fertilize legal thinking on an important and little explored subject.~~

The Constitution recognizes existence of a war power which it does not define or expressly limit. It is wisely left to unfold as events might call forth. It was left to the vigilance succeeding generations to conform its exercise as much as possible to the spirit of our institutions. ~~It was a power not practical to subdivide or to subject to the usual scheme of checks and balances.~~ Grounded in necessity, the power must be measured chiefly by necessity.

I agree with the implication of the Court's opinion that this war power is not an absolute one wholly removed from our examination. If it were, it would approximate Lenin's definition of a dictatorship, which is only, as he said, "an authority relying directly on force, and not bound by any law."[2] Men in high position have advocated this view of the war power,[3] but such has never been the doctrine of this Court.[4]

~~If we are to judge the war power by legal standards as is~~

---

[2] Lenin, The Proletarian Revolution, p. 18.

[3] Thaddeus Stevens said he "would not stultify" himself by supposing that a certain measure was constitutional, but he voted for it regardless of its constitutionality. Congressional Globe, 37th Cong., 3rd Sess., pp. 50-51. Senator Sumner took much the same view, saying "War cannot be conducted *in vinculis.* In seeking to fasten upon it restraints of the Constitution, you repeat the ancient tyranny which compelled its victims to fight in chains. Glorious as it is that the citizen is surrounded by the safeguards of the Constitution, yet this rule is superseded by war which brings into being other rights which know no master." Congressional Globe, 37th Cong., 2d Sess., p. 2196. See Randall, Constitutional Problems Under Lincoln, pp. 30-31.

[4] Although this Court considered the validity of the war power as exercised in the Civil War, narrowly sustaining in some cases (Prize Cases, 2 Black 635; Miller v. United States, 11 Wallace 268; Stewart v. Kahn, 11 Wallace 493), and condemning it in others (Ex Parte Milligan, 4 Wallace 2; see also Ex Parte Merryman, 17 Fed. Cases 144) it was chiefly concerned with the division of the war power between Congress and the President—not an issue here. This Court also reviewed the constitutionality of acts in connection with the First World War (Selective Draft Cases, 245 U.S. 366; McKinley v. United States, 249 U.S. 397). These cases afford little light on the basic questions here.

assumed in this case, we must stand buy those standards if they hereafter lead to a conclusion against the government. It would in my opinion be the duty of this Court in a proper case, if convinced that an exercise of the war power was out of constitutional bounds, to pronounce the illegitimacy of its orders and absolve loyal citizens from the moral duty and legal obligation of support and obedience. The appearance of now being guided by a rule of law that would be abandoned if it happened to work the other way should be avoided by a court that has regards for the profession's belief in its intellectual integrity. And if we are not prepared to follow this test to such a conclusion, we should renounce review entirely.

But the consequences of a clash between judicial power and the war power, particularly in the midst of a foreign war, would be so grave that as much so far as is consistent with out duty we should minimize occasions upon which it might happen. It is one thing to reserve the power to say that we will not recognize the war power when it is shown to be invoked in clear bad faith, or as a pretext for effecting internal policies, or resort to it upon judgment so wild as to lack all rational foundation; it is another to say that even when properly invoked in dealing with foreign wars we will review specific orders made in its exercise. We may say that we will not approve military invasion of the proper field of civilian government, but it is something else to say that where military authority admittedly has a job to do we will review how it does it. We may even when it is properly in play disapprove use of military power from being used as a cloak to impose cruel or oppressive denial of civil rights on citizens outside the military realm without claiming power to review denials within an area present to proximate to military operations. Which bear an obvious elation to the military problem. I do not think the war power is absolute, to be invoked at will, terminated only at pleasure and meanwhile bound by no law.

Since, however, the situation on the West Coast plainly required intervention of military power to put it in a state of defense and these orders deal with military precautions as to the presence of men of Japanese stock back of our lines of defense against Japanese attack in a war Japan is trying to give the aspect of a race war, I see no reason to go further, unless it be required by the circumstance: This is not a case where we are asked to issue our writ to interfere with the military arm of the government. It is a case where courts are asked to become auxiliary to the military power by using criminal procedure to sanction military orders. It seems to me that this presents our power of review at its maximum—certainly as

~~great as we could exert by an independent attack on military proceedings by habeas corpus. But the Court does not weigh this circumstance as affecting the scope of review.~~

The Court tests the specific order in question against the requirements of the constitutional provision that no person "shall be deprived of life, liberty or property without due process of law." It has been well termed a "clause of convenient vagueness."[5] It is this provision as to the meaning and application of which the Court long has been and is currently divided.[6] If we are to test the validity of war measures by the "due process" concept without some working definition of it, we apply to a war power of indefinite content a maximum of indefinite meaning and come out with a result respectable only as an expression of personal opinion.[7] It is worse than idle to profess that legal standards determine the present result if they are not so settled and firm that we would stand by them should they hereafter lead to a decision against the government.

If we cannot set out ~~there are not~~ fairly definable legal standards to guide us, it would be better in my opinion both for the war and for the law that we refrain altogether from considering the validity of these military orders. To substitute the mere personal opinion of judges for the personal will of the Executive only ~~would~~ substitutes a theorizing absolutism for a practical one.

~~But~~ We are even less able to use legal standards to test these military measures than to test many executive ones that we have always refused to review. Specific orders involved detailed exercise of discretion, and wide indeed must be the discretionary powers of those who wield the war power in the field of actual or prospective hostilities.

If we are realistic in the matter, we will agree that such military decisions as we have here are not susceptible of intelligent judicial review, even if amid the pressures of war they could

[5] See Judge Charles M. Hough, Due Process of Law Today, 32 Harvard Law Review 218.

[6] See Charles Grove Haines, The History of Due Process of Law after the Civil War, 1 Selected Essays on Constitutional Law, 268, and Hough, *supra*, note 5.

[7] There is of course no equal protection clause applicable to the Federal Government. But Chief Justice Taft, referring to the Fifth Amendment, said: "It, of course, tends to secure equality of law in the sense that it makes a required minimum of protection for everyone's right of life, liberty, and property, which the Congress or the legislature may not withhold. Our whole system of law is predicated on the general fundamental principle of equality of application of the law. 'All men are equal before the law;' 'This is a government of laws, and not of men;' 'No man is above the law,'—are all maxims showing the spirit in which legislatures, executives, and courts are expected to make, execute, and apply laws." Truax v. Corrigan, 257 U.S. 312, 332.

have really impartial review. They are peculiarly executive in character, influenced by events and predictions of events in foreign quarters as well as at home. ~~Military decisions~~ They differ, too, from administrative decisions or legislative acts in that their basis often cannot be disclosed to the public without danger of reaching the enemy. Neither can they be secretly communicated to us. Should we act on confidential information, we would lose character as an independent branch of government.

We must also admit that the impact of official action on the individual, which is the usual criterion for judgment in ~~constitutional~~ "due process" cases, can have only limited consideration from the war power. Citizens are necessarily classified without judicial hearings on considerations unrelated to their conduct and subjected to military discipline under which their normal constitutional rights are habitually denied, with none of the safeguards against arbitrary authority which we extend even to the least worthy in civilian life.[8] But if every citizen could claim his peace-time immunities with hostilities going on, the war power would be of little use as a war power. We must not hedge the war power with restrictions which will make the Consitution a suicide pact.

~~Since, however,~~ The situation on the West Coast plainly required intervention of military power to put it in a state of defense. ~~and~~ These orders deal with military precautions as to the presence of men of Japanese stock back of our lines of defense ~~against Japanese attack~~ in a war Japan is trying to give the aspect of a race war. I see no reason to go further, unless it be required by the circumstance: This is not a case where we are asked to issue our writ to interfere with the military arm of the government. It is a case where courts are asked to become auxiliary to the military power by using criminal procedure to sanction military orders. It seems to me that this presents our power of review at its maximum—certainly as great as we could exert by an independent attack on military proceedings by issuing writs of habeas corpus. It can only harass the government with litigation and hoax a people already suffering many injustices to suggest that in another way and on another day we may afford them in individual trials of loyalty issues. If we are ever to review the basis of these orders today is the time to do it where Congress has laid them in the lap of the courts to enforce. It is only this fact, which none of my colleagues think of significance, which makes me doubtful whether I am right in choosing between unhappy alternatives

---

[8] Articles of War, Title 10, U. S. C., c. 36.

the one I consider least evil—to decline to examine the factual basis of these orders. Of course the existence of a war power resting on force, so vagrant, so centralized, so necessarily heedless of the individual is an inherent threat to liberty. Its exercise makes free men uneasy. They feel defenseless against it.

But I would not lead people to rely on this Court for defenses that seem to me wholly delusive. If they ever let the war power fall into irresponsible and unscrupulous hands, the courts wield no power equal to its restraint. So long as And when it is in hands whose good faith we have confidence, there is every urge upon us to we are likely to find adequate any reason which led sustain orders that there is upon the President to make them. An occasion may be imagined when the war power would be so dangerously projected into civilian life that this Court would make a great issue by challenging it. But it is idle to expect that under the pressures of foreign war we will precipitate such an issue over local and temporary orders.

Hence, I question the wisdom as well as the legality of our review by any conventional legal standards of specific military measures in an area of probable operations and dealing with matters obviously related to the prosecution of the war. I am not dreamy enough to imagine that in areas of military operations and in times of anxiety those in charge will or can always observe the limitations that bind civil authority. They may overstep temporarily and locally as a matter of necessity. But if we review and approve, we accept what were otherwise an incident into the body of the law as a principle. To avoid giving the impression that we are hampering the war we adopt constructions which distort the law and compromise our institution, do little to insure civil liberties, and perhaps disable ourselves through bad precedents from helping their restoration when peace comes. I contemplate any construction of the due process clause which will make it approve this order as ultimately a more dangerous thing than the promulgation of the order.

That the war power, has never overwhelmed our constitutional system is not due to the power of this Court, but to the fact that military power during each emergency so far has been in the hands of a Commander in Chief devoted to a political system in which authority is controlled by law, and whose ultimate aim was to preserve free institutions. Each crisis so far has been handled by those in Executive authority trained in the tradition of the law, and their fidelity to the Constitution on the whole does not suffer by comparison with that of the Court. There has been, it is true, temporary excesses of executive power,[9] but they have proved to be incidents in the larger policy of preserving and perpetuating our free institutions. The chief restraint upon those who command the physical forces of the country in the future as in the past must be their ~~political~~ responsibility to the political judgments of their contemporaries and ~~their responsibility~~ to the moral judgments of history. I would leave the political departments of government to face the accountability without embarrassing their lawful acts by litigation or rationalizing their questionable ones by judicial decision.

---

[9] The course pursued by Lincoln in the days following the attack on Fort Sumter has been thus described:

"Borrowing the phraseology of the Militia Act of 1795, he described the secession movement as comprising 'combinations too powerful to be suppressed' by the ordinary processes of the Courts and the powers of the marshals, and from this premise drew the conclusion that he was authorized to summon the total man power of the nation as a species of *posse commitatus* in order to overcome the illegal combinations, and to adopt such other measures as he deemed essential to success. Thus he embodied the militia into a voluntary army, added 23,000 men to the Regular Army and 18,000 to the Navy, pledged the credit of the United States for a quarter of a billion dollars, paid out two millions from unappropriated funds in the Treasury to persons unauthorized to receive it, closed the Post Office to 'treasonable correspondence,' proclaimed a blockade of the Southern ports, suspended the writ of habeas corpus in various places, caused the arrest and military detention of persons 'who were represented to him' as being engaged in or contemplating 'treasonable practices'—and all this either without one whit of statutory authority or with the merest figment thereof." Edward S> Corwin, The President: Office and Power, p. 157.

James Parker Hall has pointed out a reason for Lincoln's discriminatory action too often overlooked, although perhaps it does not amount to a legal defense: "During the Civil war it was deemed politically inexpedient to legislate against disloyal utterances in general. In the earlier stages of the contest Lincoln earnestly sought to hold the border slave states in the Union. He was represented as praying: 'Oh, Lord, we earnestly hope that Thou wilt favor our cause, but we *must* have Kentucky.' Men not irreconcilably of southern sympathies were to be won over, if possible, by the methods of persuasion. Many utterances that in Massachusetts would have been treated as clearly indicative of disloyalty, in Kentucky were the natural expressions of men sorely perplexed and reluctant to make a decision that either way was fraught with such sorrow. Legislation applying to all laike would have been unjust and alienating to the border-state doubters, and would have been widely criticized as an illustration of the despotism so often charged against Lincoln by his opponents. But without the sanction of legislation the federal government arrested by the thousand men whom it knew or suspected to be dangerous or disaffected, and confined them, without charges and without trial, in military prisons as long as it saw fit—and public opinion generally acquiesced in this as a fairly necessary measure of war-time precaution. The number of such executive arrests has been variously estimated at from 20,000 to 38,000. The War Department records, confessedly very incomplete, show over 13,000." James Parker Hall, The University Record, Vol. VII, No. 2, April 1921.

I do not know that the ultimate cause of liberty has suffered, and it may have been saved, by these questionable arrests. I am sure the cause would have suffered if this Court had rationalized them, as Constitutional.

These and many other excesses of the Civil War period are more thoroughly covered by Randall, Constitutional Problems under Lincoln.

Hirabayashi was decided on June 21, 1943. A week earlier—co-incidentally, on Flag Day—the Court invalidated compulsory flag salutes in public schools by an 8–1 vote in *West Virginia State Board of Education v Barnette*,[62] overruling a 1940 decision, *Minersville School District v Gobitis*,[63] that had gone the other way by the same vote. Jackson's opinion for the Court in *Barnette* is one of his most eloquent and memorable, and ironically that may have contributed in some small part to his suppression of the draft in *Hirabayashi*. Jackson's law clerk, John F. Costelloe, pointed out the paradox between the positions developed in *Barnette* and in *Hirabayashi* in a memorandum while both cases were nearing resolution:[64]

> And it looks a little funny to have the First Amendment talk one way to the school board of Indiana when it doesn't expressly apply to the states (or apply at all except by virtue of a good healthy historical error sired by judicial confidence), and talk another way to the President. The Court begins to look like a small boy willing to give the raspberry to his smaller brethren, but very deferential to his larger and tougher ones. And it begins to look funny when one remembers all the Justices but one lined up with *Gobitis*, an opinion handed down when France was falling, but several recanted when the going looked a lot easier.

The memorandum did not challenge Jackson's draft opinion with respect to its posture toward Hirabayashi's case—at least directly—but Jackson may have winced at the comparison. Costelloe, who had been Jackson's first clerk and who stayed on for a second term,[65] closed his memo with a pointed challenge to the basic premise of the *Hirabayashi* draft:[66]

> This Court's protection against catastrophe from the military isn't "wholly delusive." It could be the only body with sufficient prestige to raise the issue. It could perform an important function in marshalling its historical wisdom and giving a moral

---

[62] 319 US 624 (1943).

[63] 310 US 586 (1940).

[64] JFC to RHJ, 6-3-43, Box 128, RHJP.

[65] On Jackson's relationship with Costelloe, see John Q. Barrett, *Robert Jackson on "What the Law's Going to Be"—At Least Until Its "Gelding,"* 6 Green Bag 2d 125 (2003).

[66] JFC to RHJ, cited in note 64. Costelloe also pointed out that Stone's opinion for the Court in *Hirabayashi* belied the famous declaration by Stone that government decisions affecting "discreet and insular minorities" were subject to more searching judicial inquiry than economic regulations. *United States v Carolene Products*, 304 US 144, n 4 at 152–53 (1938).

judgment. No respectable and trusted segment of the press is likely to have sufficient prestige. If Henry Luce and all his pictures and patter had it that the military was in the right, and this Court refused to say it was wrong, the chances are that no stand would ever be made against the military; *sed quare* if the Court came out and said it was wrong. If civil liberties and other constitutional guarantees can get along without the Court in war time they can do the same in peace.

Jackson remained unmoved, but Costelloe had put his finger on a central and unacknowledged problem with Jackson's draft opinion. Jackson, fearing that the Court could not challenge the executive branch during wartime, was gambling that a minor deprivation of civil liberties was the price of preserving the Court's power in peacetime, but the gamble depended on the assumption that when the war ended the proper balance of power between the judiciary and the rest of the government would be restored, almost as if nothing had happened. Costelloe was pointing out that the assumption might be wrong with respect both to the duration of the war and peacetime.

II. Korematsu v United States, Ex Parte Endo

Six months after *Hirabayashi* was issued, on December 2, 1943, the Court of Appeals for the Ninth Circuit decided *Korematsu* on the merits.[67] The lower court's treatment of the case, both procedurally and substantively, was not a model of judicial responsibility. In a two-page opinion, the court, sitting en banc, upheld Korematsu's conviction for refusing to leave the restricted area. The result was not unexpected, to say the least, but the disposition was remarkable in two respects. First, the court heard no oral arguments after the Supreme Court had remanded the case on the issue of appealability; the only oral argument in the case, which only touched the merits lightly, had been in February of 1943. Second, Judge Curtis Dwight Wilbur's opinion for the Court drove a tank through Chief Justice Stone's narrow and limited holding in *Hirabayashi*:[68]

---

[67] *Toyosaburo Korematsu v United States*, 140 F2d 289 (1943).

[68] Id at 289–90. Judge Wilbur, then 76 years old, was an 1888 graduate of the United States Naval Academy and Secretary of the Navy in the Herbert Hoover administration. Hoover appointed him to a new seat on the court in 1929.

> These decisions [*Hirabayashi* and its companion, *Yasui*] involve
> the portions of the proclamations of General DeWitt imposing
> curfew restrictions upon Japanese citizens of the United States
> of Japanese ancestry. The Supreme Court held the curfew re-
> strictions valid. The Supreme Court did not expressly pass
> upon the validity of the evacuation order which is involved in
> the case at bar. However, the Supreme Court held that under
> the Constitution the Government of the United States, in
> prosecuting a war, has power to do all that is necessary to the
> successful prosecution of a war although the exercise of those
> powers temporarily infringe some of the inherent rights and
> liberties of individual citizens which are recognized and guar-
> anteed by the Constitution. We are of the opinion that this
> principle, thus decided, so clearly sustains the validity of the
> proclamation for evacuation, which is here involved, that it is
> not necessary to labor the point.

He added that the questions of discrimination based on race and
"ancestry" "were also considered and decided by the Supreme
Court contrary to the contentions of the appellant" in *Hirabayashi*
and thus required "no further elaboration by this court."[69]

The Supreme Court granted certiorari in *Korematsu* less than
four months later, on March 27, 1944,[70] but oral arguments could
not be scheduled until the beginning of the next Term, a month
before Franklin D. Roosevelt would stand for his fourth term as
President. It has never been clear why the Court voted to grant
Korematsu's petition. The Director of the War Relocation Authority, who was responsible for implementing the exclusion and
detention policies, had been suggesting publicly since March 11,
1943, that the exclusion orders should be rescinded, and the focus
of public debate by the spring of 1944 was how, not if, the program should be scrapped.[71] The prospects for Allied victory in
both the Pacific and in Europe were rising, so there was no pressing need for the Supreme Court to certify the scope of the war
power during earlier, more perilous, circumstances. A simple denial of certiorari would have left the war power intact without, as
Jackson had worried in the *Hirabayashi* deliberations, providing a
precedent from the Supreme Court validating racial discrimination. In fact, Justice Wiley Rutledge's law clerk recommended de-

---

[69] Id at 290.

[70] 321 US 760 (1944).

[71] Irons at 269.

nying Korematsu's petition for certiorari. He pointed out that, strictly speaking, Korematsu's case raised only the question of the constitutionality of the exclusion order, not the question of the constitutionality of the detention camps.[72] Since other cases were pending that raised the question of the constitutionality of detention, the clerk saw little point in granting the petition: "To take the case in order to bless it, when other and more important questions are in the offing, is of questionable statesmanship."[73] There is no evidence available as to why certiorari was granted. The best guess now is that several of the Justices—probably Roberts, Douglas, Murphy, Rutledge, and even Jackson—wished to cabin *Hirabayashi* due to the sweeping construction the Ninth Circuit had placed upon it and in light of the breadth with which the evacuation program had swept since its inception.

The pivotal issue in the case was whether the detention scheme was properly before the Court, or whether the case was technically limited to noncompliance with an exclusion order from the prohibited zone, which was the ground of Korematsu's conviction. The government conceded that he "would have found himself for a period of time, the length of which was then not ascertainable, in a place of detention," but insisted that "this detention, which did not become actual," was not "an issue in the case."[74]

At the Court's conference of October 16, 1944, when *Korematsu* was discussed, the Court split five-to-four to uphold Korematsu's conviction.[75] The dissenters on that day were Roberts, Douglas, Murphy, and Jackson. There was consensus that the decision should be limited to exclusion from the area and should not reach the issue of the constitutionality of detention; that issue was presented by a companion case, *Ex Parte Endo*.[76] There was nonetheless heated debate over the government's power to detain, and some question about the basis used by the government to identify those who would be detained. Jackson said he did not think DeWitt's exclusion order was "something we have got to accept

---

[72] Undated certiorari memorandum, Box 119, Wiley B. Rutledge Papers, Library of Congress Manuscript Division.

[73] Id.

[74] Brief for the United States at 28–29.

[75] Irons at 323.

[76] 323 US 283 (1944).

without any inquiry into reasonableness."[77] (During oral argument, Jackson had pointedly asked one of Korematsu's counsel about "what standard" the Court should use to review General DeWitt's military judgment,[78] and at another point he sharply questioned Solicitor General Fahy over disputed facts in DeWitt's final report on the program.[79]) The Court appears to have been divided as bitterly as the tentative vote indicated. Stone and Black stated that *Hirabayashi* supported affirmance of Korematsu's conviction. Roberts thought *Hirabayashi* did not go that far, and Douglas emphasized "no constitutional authority to arrest without probable cause."[80] Jackson noted only his vote, not his reasons. His notes on Murphy's vote underscore that division in the conference room: "[Murphy] frowned [and recalled that he] dissented and then changed. Thinks wrong in *Hirabayashi*."[81]

Chief Justice Stone assigned the opinion of the Court to Black. The first draft of Black's opinion was circulated November 8 and was, in the apt phrase of Peter Irons's blow-by-blow account of the Court's deliberations in *Korematsu*, "little more than a carbon copy of Stone's opinion in the *Hirabayashi* case."[82] Black had no trouble preventing defections from his majority, although he yielded to several suggestions by Stone and Frankfurter. Douglas drafted a perplexing dissent (which he later withdrew when he switched sides to join Black's opinion),[83] but the real fireworks were ignited by the dissents of Roberts, Murphy, and Jackson. When Murphy received his copy of Jackson's draft dissent November 30, he sent it to his clerk with the inscription: "Read this and perish! The Court has blown up on the Jap case—just as I expected it would."[84]

---

[77] Irons at 322.

[78] Id at 314.

[79] Peter Irons, *Fancy Dancing in the Marble Palace*, 3 Const Comm 35, 49 (1986) (transcript of oral argument for the government in *Korematsu*) (cited hereafter as Irons II).

[80] Conference Notes, Box 128, RHJP. For a synthetic recreation of the conference on *Korematsu* and *Endo* (based on the notes of Justices Douglas, Murphy, and Jackson), see Del Dickson, ed, *The Supreme Court in Conference (1940–1985): The Private Discussions Behind Nearly 300 Supreme Court Decisions* 687–93 (Oxford, 2001).

[81] Conference Notes, Box 128, RHJP.

[82] Irons at 327.

[83] Id at 333–38.

[84] J. Woodford Howard, *Mr. Justice Murphy: A Political Biography* 333 (Princeton, 1968) (cited hereafter as Howard).

Jackson's opinion was written more in anger than in sorrow over the Court's proposed disposition of the case. He rambled for fifteen printed pages, repeating his argument in the suppressed *Hirabayashi* opinion, condemning the Court's ratification of racial classifications in the present case, recalling Lincoln's constitutional excesses during the Civil War, and even pointing out—in a two-page footnote quoting from an amicus curiae brief—the factual defects underlying DeWitt's judgments. He again used his metaphor identifying the war power as the "Achilles Heel" of the Constitution. The opinion was poorly organized and internally contradictory (he said that courts should not review the factual basis of military orders, but he could not resist the long footnote that seemed to do just that), but it was, again as Irons notes, a "slashing attack"[85] on Black's proposed opinion for the majority, and the Court was "thr[own] into turmoil."[86] The attack may have helped to buoy Murphy's inclination to pull out the stops in his own dissent.

Black recirculated his opinion, incorporating the changes suggested by members of his thin but firm majority, on December 8. Jackson recirculated his dissent, which had been in printed form since November 13 (although not circulated until November 30), the same day. This time the draft was cut dramatically to five pages. Gone were the references to Lincoln and the footnote cribbed from the amicus brief. Jackson repeated the nub of his argument from the unpublished *Hirabayashi* opinion: Courts should not review exercises of the war power, but the military should not expect civil courts to enforce orders based on that power. He thus was able to focus his fire on what continued to be his deepest reservations about the Court's behavior in the case. His final opinion, which tracked the December 8 circulation, warrants extended rehearsal:

> Much is said of the danger to liberty from the Army program for deporting and detaining these citizens of Japanese extraction. But a judicial construction of the due process clause that will sustain this order is a far more subtle blow to liberty than the promulgation of the order itself. A military order, however

---

[85] Irons at 332.

[86] Id.

unconstitutional, is not apt to last longer than the military emergency. Even during that period a succeeding commander may revoke it all. But once a judicial opinion rationalizes such an order to show that it conforms to the Constitution, or rather rationalizes the Constitution to show that the Constitution sanctions such an order, the Court for all time has validated the principle of racial discrimination in criminal procedure and of transplanting American citizens. The principle then lies about like a loaded weapon ready for the hand of any authority that can bring forward a plausible claim of an urgent need. Every repetition imbeds that principle more deeply in our law and thinking and expands it to new purposes. All who observe the work of courts are familiar with what Judge Cardozo described as "the tendency of a principle to expand itself to the limit of its logic." A military commander may overstep the bounds of constitutionality, and it is an incident. But if we review and approve, that passing incident becomes the doctrine of the Constitution. There it has a generative power of its own, and all that it creates will be in its own image. Nothing better illustrates this danger than does the Court's opinion in this case.[87]

He then scolded Black's reliance on *Hirabayashi:*

It argues that we are bound to uphold the conviction of Korematsu because we upheld one in Hirabayashi v United States, 320 U.S. 81, when we sustained these orders in so far as they applied a curfew requirement to a citizen of Japanese ancestry. I think we should learn something from that experience.[88]

After pinpointing the three places in Stone's opinion that confined the decision solely to the curfew issue, Jackson underscored the gulf between the two cases:

However, in spite of our limiting words we did validate a discrimination on the basis of ancestry for mild and temporary deprivation of liberty. Now the principle of racial discrimination is pushed from support of mild measures to very harsh ones, and from temporary deprivations to indeterminate ones. And the precedent which it is said requires us to do so is Hirabayashi. The Court is now saying that in Hirabayashi we did decide the very things we there said we were not deciding. Because we said that these citizens could be made to stay in

---

[87] 325 US at 245–46.

[88] Id.

their homes during the hours of dark, it is said we must require
them to leave home entirely; and if that, we are told they may
also be taken into custody for deportation; and if that, it is
argued they may also be held for some undetermined time in
detention camps. How far the principle of this case would be
extended before plausible reasons would play out, I do not
know.[89]

Jackson cannot have derived any pleasure saying to his colleagues,
in effect, "I told you so." More likely, he now regretted even more
keeping his counsel in *Hirabayashi* when all of his instincts and
experience pointed to foreseeable developments that in fact had
materialized.

His anger over the revitalization of *Hirabayashi* in *Korematsu*
spilled over in the companion case to *Korematsu, Ex Parte Endo.*
Endo was an American citizen who was held in a detention camp
but whose loyalty the government did not challenge. She argued
that her detention was unconstitutional, and her lawyers saw her
case as the vehicle for reaching the issue that the Court had been
dodging since *Hirabayashi* and which it had legitimate grounds for
not reaching in *Korematsu:* whether such detention of an admittedly loyal citizen violated the Fifth Amendment's Due Process
Clause, and its arguably implicit equal protection component.[90]
The Court ordered Endo released from custody but again avoided
the constitutional issue. In a unanimous opinion by Justice Douglas, the Court held that the War Relocation Authority had no statutory basis for confining a concededly loyal citizen. Jackson had
no use for the ingenuity—or disingenuity—of the decision. He
prepared a draft concurrence which he never sent to the printer
nor circulated to his colleagues. It read in full:[91]

---

[89] Id at 247.

[90] Chief Justice William Howard Taft suggested that the Due Process Clause of the Fifth
Amendment contemplated a notion of equal protection, *Truax v Corrigan,* 257 US 312,
332 (1921), but the Supreme Court had not yet expressly ruled on the point.

[91] Box 133, RHJP. The final two lines of the draft are quoted from Rudyard Kipling's
poem "The Old Issue," commemorating the outbreak of the Boer War, Oct 9, 1899. *Rudyard Kipling's Verse: Definitive Edition* 294, 295 (Doubleday, Doran, 1940). Jackson eventually
used the couplet as the final lines of his opening address to the International Military Tribunal at Nuremberg, Nov 21, 1945, available on-line at, inter alia, <www.holocaust-
history.org/works/imt/02/htm/t098.htm>. The couplet appears at t155htm. See also
Youngstown Sheet & Tube v Sawyer, 343 US 634, 654 (1952) (Jackson, J, concurring).

Ex Parte Endo

In this case we have a demand that the Court reach out a protecting arm to a citizen in unlawful restraint. If she were in military custody for security reasons, even if I thought them weak ones, I should doubt our right to interfere for reasons I have stated in Korematsu's case. No such question need trouble us. Miss Endo is now in civilian custody.

This decision and that in Korematsu's case are separated by a wide chasm, and the real question in this case seems to have fallen therein. In Korematsu's case the Court carefully stops short of the question whether an American citizen may be detained in camps without conviction of crime. In Endo's case the Court is careful to start beyond it and to hold no more than that such a citizen may not be held after the government confesses it had no security reason for holding her. I should release her whether it had made that confession or no. She is an American citizen, virtually imprisoned, without charge or conviction of crime, and there has been ample time to place and try such a charge.

The difference in grounds is substantial. No one may as matter of right obtain a certification of loyalty. There is no way by which trial techniques can establish what is in a man's heart if the time to act has not yet come and he has kept his mouth shut. Anyone bent on keeping another in custody may say, and quite rightly, that it cannot be known that his prisoner would not commit crime if he were at large. So the grounds taken by the Court is once available to but few and favored ones.

But under our form of government it has never been thought that a citizen must prove or be admitted to be harmless in order to be free. On the contrary, it has been supposed that it must be charged that he has committed or conspired or attempted or threatened to commit some crime before he could be temporarily detained, and the charge must be speedily proved if he is to be held. The absence of such accusation or conviction, I should think, is sufficient to require the release. She is held only on the basis of "protective custody"—a custody that I gather is almost as uncomfortable for the custodian as for their involuntary guests.

It is said, and may well be true, that if the citizen of Japanese ancestry goes out among our people he or she may be the victim of discrimination or even violence. So it is sought to release them only when [they] have assured employment and can prove some "community acceptance" in a place from which they are not excluded by the military. On a voluntary basis this protection would be wholly commendable and as much is due them.

Of course, when a people is exiled from home on the military judgment that they are potential saboteurs, then they are objects of fear and hatred to the inhabitants of regions to which they are strangers. It does not help them any that this Court adds that the undiscriminating holding is found reasonable. Any humane government would offer them shelter from the storm of prejudice so whipped up against them.

But "protective custody" on an involuntary basis has no place in American law. The whole idea that our American citizens' right to be at large may be conditioned or denied by community prejudice or disapproval should be rejected by this Court the first time it is heard within these walls. To fail is to betray

"Ancient rights, unnoticed as the breath we draw,
Leave to live by no man's leave, underneath the law."

When Jackson drafted the opinion for *Endo*, he was beyond mincing words about the niceties of the war power and its relation to the role of the civil courts. *Endo* presented the statutorily unauthorized and constitutionally repugnant specter of an American citizen—loyal "or no"—held without charge: for him, that ended the matter, and the majority walked deftly through the decision when adamance was required. Yet Jackson did not file the *Endo* opinion, and he left no evidence of why he did not. Perhaps there was too much pressure for the Court to speak with one voice after "blowing up" in *Korematsu*, although Roberts and Murphy—the other *Korematsu* dissenters—both filed pointed opinions resting their vote on the Constitution.[92] Or perhaps Jackson did not want to rattle the habeas corpus saber too loudly after implying in *Korematsu* that he would allow the Executive to break it by imposing martial law and suspending the writ. Moreover, his draft seemed to focus on the government's lame rationale, expressed in oral argument,[93] for detaining a loyal citizen—fear of reprisals once the detainees returned to their residences on the West Coast. Taken together, the published dissent in *Korematsu* and the fragmentary draft in *Endo* bespoke a man with a sour taste in his judicial mouth: He had been double-crossed, at least jurisprudentially, in *Korematsu* after keeping his peace in *Hirabayashi*—"led down the garden path,"[94] in the apt phrase of Stone's biographer. Yet he was

---

[92] 323 US at 307 (Murphy, concurring), 308 (Roberts).

[93] Irons II at 58.

[94] A. T. Mason, *Harlan Fiske Stone: Pillar of the Law* 677 (Viking, 1956; Archon, 1968).

willing to live with the implications of his position in *Korematsu*, as he confessed seven years later in a speech: "my view, if followed, would come close to a suspension of the writ of habeas corpus or recognition of a state of martial law at the time and place found proper for military control."[95] Jackson worried about the fragility of habeas corpus both at the time he wrote *Korematsu* as well as later. Frankfurter tried to talk him out of his position before *Korematsu* came down by pointing to the risk Jackson was taking.[96] But to Jackson, the risk was worth taking because the costs of the precedent—as he spelled out in his dissent—were simply too high. The threat to habeas corpus, in hindsight more hypothetical than likely, was the price Jackson was willing to pay to avoid having the larger constitutional principle lying "about like a loaded weapon."[97] Thanks in part to Jackson and the other dissenters, and in part to the quick condemnation that the decision richly earned in the public and professional literature,[98] *Korematsu* became—like the Trotsky of Stalin's revisionists—a nonauthority, and the loaded weapon was neutralized.[99]

Korematsu and *Endo* were handed down on December 19, 1944,

---

[95] Robert H. Jackson, *Wartime Security and Liberty under Law*, 1 Buff L Rev 103, 116 (1951–52).

[96] Frankfurter to Jackson, n.d., Box 128, RHJP.

[97] 323 US at 246 (Jackson, J, dissenting). Jackson's memorable image may have been inspired by a letter he received several months before the war began from Zecahriach Chafee, the Harvard Law School authority on freedom of speech. Referring to the Alien Registration Act of 1940, Chafee wrote: "my general conclusion about Title I of this statute is that it will not do much harm if you yourself keep it as a revolver in your bureau drawer to use whenever burglars are ever in the house." Chafee to Attorney General, April 22, 1941, at 2, Box 118, RHJP. (Title I made it unlawful, inter alia, "to interfere with, impair, or influence the loyalty, morale, or discipline" of military servicemen, to "advise, counsel, urge, or in any manner cause insubordination, mutiny, or refusal to serve," or to teach or urge violent overthrow of the government.) Title I was informally known as the Smith Act, which was the basis of prosecution in *Dennis v United States*, 341 US 494 (1951).

[98] See, e.g., Rostow (cited in note 6); Morton Grodzins, *American Betrayed: Politics and the Japanese Evacuation* (Chicago, 1947); Jacobus Ten Broek, Edward N. Barnhart, and Floyd W. Matson, *Prejudice, War and the Constitution: The Anti-Japanese Movement in California and the Struggle for Japanese Exclusion* (California, 1954, 1977); Roger Daniels, *The Politics of Prejudice* (California, 1964).

[99] The Supreme Court never subsequently cited *Korematsu* with approval of its result, only for Justice Black's caveat "that all legal restrictions which curtail the civil rights of a single racial group are immediately suspect." 323 US at 216. Even when racial quotas were first being defended in *Regents of the University of California v Bakke*, 438 US 265 (1978), and in *Fullilove v Klutznick*, 448 US 448 (1980), on the ground that they served a "compelling state interest," not one defender of the quotas was willing to rely on the decision in *Korematsu* by name.

but the decisions were overshadowed by the announcement the day before by the War Department that General DeWitt's mass exclusion orders of 1942 had been revoked. The timing of the decision is significant and hints at deeper issues involving the Justices and their lack of detachment with respect to the war effort. *Endo* was ready to be issued a month before it was announced,[100] but Chief Justice Stone held up release of the decision at the behest of the government so that it would be preceded by announcement that the relocation program was ending.[101] Douglas complained to Stone about the delay, but to no avail.[102] Stone's cooperation with the government was symptomatic of the Justices' contribution to the cause. Justice Frank Murphy had reenlisted in the summer of 1942 and even appeared at the Court's first meeting on *Quirin* in uniform—prompting his colleagues to urge recusal, which he did.[103] Justice Owen J. Roberts headed the commission investigating Pearl Harbor; Hugo Black spoke at a war rally at the President's request; and several Justices, principally Frankfurter and Douglas, provided advice on war-related issues.[104] As Joel B. Grossman has written, "From President Roosevelt's perspective, enlisting the Justices in the war effort was a shrewd strategy: It drew them personally into the prosecution of the war and gave them a personal stake in insuring its success, while using them to legitimate wartime policies."[105] On a personal level, Black and General DeWitt were long-standing personal friends; Frankfurter was close to the Secretary of War, Henry Stimson (who had appointed him to his first government job), and to John J. McCloy, Assistant Secretary of War, who was a former student, close friend, and War Department official responsible for implementing the relocation program.[106] The net result, in Grossman's words, "is a

---

[100] William O. Douglas to Chief Justice, Nov 28, 1944, quoted in Melvin I. Urofsky, ed, *The Douglas Letters: Selections from the Private Papers of Justice William O. Douglas* 105–06 (Adler & Adler, 1987) (cited hereafter as Urofsky).

[101] Irons at 344–45.

[102] Urofsky at 106.

[103] Howard at 275 (cited in note 84); Fine at 404 (cited in note 52).

[104] See generally Joel B. Grossman, *The Japanese American Cases and the Vagaries of Constitutional Adjudication in Wartime: An Institutional Perspective*, 19 U Hawaii L Rev 649, 672–73 (1997).

[105] Id at 673.

[106] Id at 673 at sources there cited.

Court charged with assessing the means to achieve ends to which all the justices were intensely committed. . . . There is no better example of . . . the frailty of judicial independence, in Supreme Court decision-making."[107] There is little direct evidence of how much Jackson knew about his colleagues' contributions to the war effort, although he was close enough to Frankfurter that he must have known of the intimate relationships with Stimson and McCloy,[108] but the entire picture provides a chilling backdrop to Jackson's statement in his *Hirabayashi* draft: "[Military decisions differ] from administrative decisions or legislative acts in that their basis often cannot be disclosed to the public without danger of reaching the enemy. Neither can they be secretly communicated to us. Should we act on confidential information, we would lose character as an independent branch of government."[109]

Beginning January 2, 1945, Endo and more than 50,000 other Japanese would be released from detention. The government thus had Supreme Court precedent for power it no longer wished to use.[110] As the war continued to wind down, the Supreme Court looked more searchingly at assertions of the war power. In the following Term, after the war had ended, the Court held that the invocation of martial law in Hawaii would not prevent habeas corpus from freeing a civilian held pursuant to military authority for purely civilian offenses.[111] Jackson was away from the Court at the Nuremberg trials and did not participate in the decision.

III. The Lessons of the "War Power"

Justice Jackson's unpublished opinions in *Hirabayashi* and *Endo* are now little more than constitutional curios, although they help to cast light on a Justice who could be substantively elusive, notwithstanding all his style and eloquence. At a minimum, the

---

[107] Id at 673.

[108] Frankfurter's diary for 1943 is dotted with numerous entries recounting conversations with both men over the conduct of the war. See Lash at 141–262, passim (cited in note 53).

[109] See Hirabayashi draft, p 5.

[110] The War Department wished to scrap the relocation program as early as the spring of 1943, but President Roosevelt was not so advised until May of 1944. Irons at 269. See text at note 71.

[111] *Duncan v Kahanomoku* (cited in note 46).

drafts show that Jackson's controversial opinion in *Korematsu*—"a curious kind of judicial schizophrenia"[112] is the kindest of the critical judgments—was fueled by the trampling of the Maginot Line he thought had been fixed by *Hirabayashi*. More than that, the drafts provide fragmentary, internal evidence of Jackson's evolving thought about the role of the Supreme Court, especially when faced with decisions posing momentous consequences to the Constitution and to the Court's capacity to protect its political capital. (Worries over the Court's capacity to make its rulings stick are a recurrent theme in Jackson's jurisprudence, especially in momentous cases. The principal examples are the *Steel Seizure Case* in 1952, in which the Court ruled that the President lacked inherent power to seize the steel mills to protect the war effort during the Korean Conflict,[113] and the school segregation cases in 1954.[114]) He began in *Quirin* with the fixed presumption that the Court has no business reviewing military judgments in time of war, and he never deviated from that position even after the war was over and petitions for habeas corpus began to arrive from enemies held overseas under the authority of military tribunals trying war crimes.[115] But when the military attempted to enlist the judiciary, even with congressional approval, in enforcing its decisions, he began to have doubts, as his unpublished opinion in *Hirabayashi* recorded. The Court's decision in *Hirabayashi* was as far as he was willing to go, and even then he went only under duress. But when grave doubts began to be raised over the basis of General DeWitt's exclusion and detention program, Jackson abandoned ship. The question remains why he did not go all the way and condemn not only the detention and exclusion but also its basis, instead of producing the equivocal testament to judicial infirmity that is one of

---

[112] Irons at 332.

[113] *Youngstown Sheet & Tube v Sawyer*, 343 US at 654 (Jackson, J, concurring) ("I have no illusion that any decision by this Court can keep power in the hands of Congress if it is not wise and timely in meeting its problems.").

[114] *Brown v Board of Education*, 347 US 483 (1954). At one point in the Court's deliberation in *Brown*, Jackson prepared a draft opinion which foresaw litigation over enforcement of the decision invalidating state-imposed racial segregation in public schools extending over "two generations" and eventually resulting in a "failure that will bring the court into contempt and the judicial process into discredit." Schwartz at 259–60 (cited in note 10).

[115] See generally Dennis J. Hutchinson, *Justice Jackson and the Nuremberg Trials*, 1996 J S Ct Hist 105, 113. The culmination of his views is *Johnson v Eisentrager*, 339 US 763 (1950).

his doctrinal legacies in *Korematsu*. The answer lies in history lessons he may have learned too well and in the idiosyncracies of his writing habits.

Jackson conceded after the war that his opinion in *Korematsu*, disclaiming power to review military orders, risked inviting the government to frustrate habeas corpus by simply declaring martial law and suspending the writ.[116] But he was moved by what he viewed to be a graver possibility: that if he, and the Court, found the military order constitutionally invalid, and consequently that "100 district courts" began granting relief to detainees, then the War Relocation Authority might refuse to comply with the courts' orders. For Jackson, that would drive a stake through the heart of the rule of law. He thought the possibility hypothetical, if not likely, but he was not willing to take the risk, either in *Korematsu* or in unforeseen cases in the future. In hindsight, the risk now seems far-fetched, but to Jackson it was real. Two episodes shaped his thinking about the problem. In 1935, while working in the Treasury Department, he had watched closely as a peacetime President had contemplated resisting the Supreme Court if it held against his executive order departing from the gold standard.[117] Roosevelt discussed contingency plans with Jackson "in case the court decision went against the government," and Roosevelt declared—in Jackson's words—that "outright defiance of the Court was possible."[118] Roosevelt even prepared a radio address blasting the Court and refusing to abide by its decision should the justices rule against him.[119] The other episode came in 1937 when Roosevelt tried to "pack" the Court when the tide of anti-administration decisions seemed unabating. Jackson, by then an Assistant Attorney

---

[116] See text at note 95 above.

[117] The *Gold Clause Cases* were *Norman v Baltimore & Ohio Railroad Co.*, 294 US 240 (1935); *Nortz v United States*, 294 US 317 (1935); *Perry v United States*, 294 US 330 (1935).

[118] III *Reminiscences* at 46.

[119] The draft address said in part: "To stand idly by and to permit the decision of the Supreme Court to be carried through to its logical, inescapable conclusion would so imperil the economic and political security of the this nation that the legislative and executive officers of the Government look beyond the narrow letter of contractual obligations, so that they may sustain the substance." Quoted in Arthur M. Schlesinger, Jr., *The Age of Roosevelt: The Politics of Upheaval* 258 (Houghton Mifflin, 1960). See further Marian C. McKenna, *Franklin Roosevelt and the Great Constitutional War: The Court-Packing Crisis of 1937* 48 ff (Fordham, 2002); Leuchtenburg, *The Supreme Court Reborn* at 86–88 (cited in note 11). For a recent illuminating account of the litigation, see Seth P. Waxman, *The Physics of Persuasion: Arguing the New Deal*, 88 Georgetown L J 2399 (2000).

General in the Antitrust Division, was an energetic and powerful proponent of the plan.[120] The cumulative lesson was that a President would not let the Supreme Court frustrate his will if the stakes here high enough during a domestic emergency. A wartime President would have even fewer constitutional scruples, as Lincoln's defiance of Chief Justice Roger B. Taney's habeas corpus order in *Ex Parte Merryman* demonstrated. Jackson was haunted by *Merryman*. The final pages of his book *The Struggle for Judicial Supremacy* provides an evocative account of the case as an illustration of the impotency of the judiciary in the face of a willful President.[121] He rehearsed the episode in a lecture several years after the war.[122]

Yet his published dissent in *Korematsu* makes no reference to the Civil War experience he found so telling. Nor does he attempt to explain on doctrinal grounds why an exercise of what he concedes to be unlimited and almost unreviewable executive judgment cannot constitutionally be facilitated by Congressional authorization, although his law clerk gently urged him to resolve what he saw as the palpable "dilemma" in Jackson's opinion.[123] Jackson, in short, begged one of the central questions raised by his approach to the case. The other was whether Korematsu was unconstitutionally convicted because he was subject to a law that made race an element of the crime, or whether the relocation scheme was unreasonable as well as tainted by the racial classification—as the second paragraph of his opinion seems to imply.[124] Those who admire

---

[120] See generally Stephen R. Alton, *Loyal Lieutenant, Able Advocate: The Role of Robert H. Jackson in Franklin D. Roosevelt's Battle with the Supreme Court*, 5 Wm & M Bill of R L Rev 527 (1997).

[121] Jackson at 324–27. Jackson called Taney's opinion granting habeas corpus and pleading with Lincoln to honor the writ "one of the most admirable and pathetic documents in American judicial annals." Id at 326. The response to Taney's pleas "was drowned out by the measured tread of marching feet. Judicial power was all but extinct." Id. Jackson recounted the incident again in his posthumously published Godkin Lectures at Harvard, *The Supreme Court in the American System of Government* 75–76 (Harvard, 1955).

[122] Jackson, 1 Buff L Rev at 109–11 & n 17 at 110 (cited in note 95 above). See also *Youngstown Sheet & Tube v Sawyer*, 343 US at 637 n 3 (Jackson, J, concurring).

[123] PCN [Phil C. Neal] to Jackson, n.d., Box 132, RHJP.

[124] 323 US at 214. The majority purported to apply "rigid scrutiny" to the racial classification, 323 US at 216, but by relying on *Hirabayashi* to sustain the conviction, the decision in effect rested on a "rational basis" standard of review. "[E]xclusion from a threatened area, no less than curfew," said the majority, "has a definite and close relationship to the prevention of espionage and sabotage." Id at 218. The weight of that conclusion depends, of course, on the evidentiary basis for potential espionage or sabotage, which neither Black

Jackson's dissent slide past these analytical problems and celebrate the eloquent denunciation of criminal guilt based on ancestry or the dark realism of his position on military judgments.[125]

The choice to emphasize, in vivid terms, what Jackson saw as the evil and the risks in the case, at the expense of an orderly mustering of all the difficult issues involved, was a frequent rhetorical choice for the Justice. His case files are sprinkled with notes in his hand identifying images or vivid phrases around which he tended to build opinions in highly controversial cases. The *Japanese Exclusion Cases* offer several examples. *Hirabayashi* begins with an arresting metaphor that is never developed and does not clearly suggest precisely what he sees as the scope of the problem presented by the war power. *Korematsu* relies on a homely if grim analogy suggested to him several years before in private correspondence while he was Attorney General (and perhaps reinforced by his habit of keeping loaded firearms at his own residence).[126] What might be described as an out-take of *Hirabayashi* (the Constitution as a "suicide pact") emerged several years later in a closely divided First Amendment case.[127] *Endo* concludes with a couplet that later becomes the final note in his opening speech at Nuremberg.[128] "Justice Jackson," observed Charles Fairman, "had the knack of reducing his contention to a terse proposition of seemingly inescapable cogency."[129] That somewhat backhanded compliment suggests that Jackson often preferred ringing imagery to close analysis, a natural tendency, perhaps, in a trial lawyer, but a liability for an

---

nor Jackson elected to examine, although Jackson had expressed doubts during oral argument about the government's claims on those points. See text at note 79 above.

[125] On the latter point, see John Harrison, *Review: All the Laws But One Be Close Enough for Government Work*, 2 Green Bag 2d 333, 340 (1999) ("powerful insight"); Louis Michael Seidman, *This Essay Is Brilliant/This Essay Is Stupid: Positive and Negative Self-Reference in Constitutional Practice and Theory*, 46 UCLA L Rev 501, 520 1998) ("subtle and remarkable point").

[126] See note 97 above.

[127] See note 37 above. Jackson was so captivated by his image that he never seems to have considered that the "suicide pact" imagery could be used to limit either *Hirabayashi* or *Korematsu* to the extraordinary dangers to the nation posed by wartime, but that in peacetime the government's need to circumscribe civil liberties was substantially diminished. Modern "balancing test" jurisprudence may provide a model, but Jackson had a blind spot to such a possibility.

[128] See note 91. See also note 42 and accompanying text.

[129] Fairman, *Robert H. Jackson—Associate Justice of the Supreme Court* at 447 (cited in note 4 above).

492 THE SUPREME COURT REVIEW [2002

appellate judge. Or was it, in *Korematsu*? Justice Jackson was not a fool, and his clerk had alerted him to what others would naturally identify as one of the gaping holes in his opinion. Perhaps Jackson elected self-consciously to rest on rhetoric and to accept the inevitable criticism that would surely follow. By simultaneously condemning Korematsu's criminal conviction and warning that the Court could only offer cold comfort in the most extreme situations, Justice Jackson turned another controversial wartime case into an indelible and chilling constitutional history lesson.

There were deeper lessons that Jackson could only hint at even after the war was over. He discovered the range of frailties in both the Constitution and in the Court, although he never confused one with the other. The war power may have been the Achilles Heel of the Constitution, but the Court itself revealed its own vulnerabilities, which Jackson viewed as psychological. He watched Stone and Frankfurter, primarily, and Black to a lesser extent, identify themselves as much with serving the Commander-in-Chief as with honoring their judicial commissions; Douglas was not only a presidential adviser, but an aspiring if closeted candidate for Vice-President if not President, all of which compromised his judicial independence; Murphy literally suited up for battle, but was susceptible to pressure from those more committed to the war effort. The combination produced what Justice Oliver Wendell Holmes, Jr., called a "hydraulic pressure"[130] on the cases that came before the Court during the war, a pressure that defeated judicial detachment and made doctrine hostage to total mobilization in the broadest sense. Jackson was not naive and did not expect the judicial process to be an academic seminar, but he resented the Court being commandeered for the duration. The deepest problem in his view was that capitulation to the war effort, for want of a better term, did not necessarily end with demobilization. He tried discreetly to touch on the combination of problems in 1951 in a lecture, mentioned above, entitled "Wartime Security and Liberty under Law."[131]

---

[130] *Northern Securities v United States*, 195 US 197, 401 (1904) (Holmes, J, dissenting).

[131] 1 Buff L Rev at 112. See also Jackson, *The Supreme Court in the American System of Government* at 75 (cited in note 121): "[T]he removal of the Japanese from the West Coast during the War, which seemed to me plainly unconstitutional as applied to citizens, was rationalized as a service to ultimate liberty."

> Judges [like juries] sometimes give way to passion and partisanship. The judicial process works best in an atmosphere of calmness, patience and deliberation. In times of anxiety, the public demands haste and a show of zeal on the part of the judges, whose real duty is neutrality and detachment.
>
> Wartime psychology plays no favorites among rights but tends to break down any right which obstructs its path. And the fall of one weakens others.

Justice Jackson's worries over the latent potency of the Court's decision in *Korematsu* eventually proved to be misplaced.[132] His anxieties over the capacity of the Court to restrain a determined executive during wartime are explained by his experiences before he assumed the bench. The opinion remains unsatisfying and even ominous. At bottom, his puzzling opinion in *Korematsu* appears to be a bet on the future: that the excesses of the executive branch will be self-curing once the emergency expires, and as long as the judiciary withholds its formal approval of those excesses, the Constitution will remain intact. The fallacy of the position is twofold: some emergencies may not be resolved quickly or clearly, and judicial abstention may popularly and even formally be understood as tacit approval. The risk that Jackson ran was that his position in *Korematsu* could result in diminishing the power of the Court while trying to preserve it.

The *Japanese Exclusion Cases* taught Robert Jackson a number of lessons. He never voted to interfere with military tribunals trying war crimes overseas, a bow perhaps to both the war power and to territorialism.[133] Nonetheless, Jackson drew the line when President Harry Truman tried to leverage his power as Commander-in-Chief over what Jackson called a "de facto"[134] war in Korea into the power to defeat property rights at home. The concurrence in the *Steel Seizure Case* is Jackson's most famous and celebrated opinion. With no Congressional authorization for the seizure of the steel mills, and indeed with implicit refusal by Congress to provide such authorization, Jackson found the president's power "at its lowest ebb,"[135] and powerfully argued that Truman's actions were

---

[132] See note 99 above.

[133] See note 115 and accompanying text.

[134] *Youngstown Sheet & Tube v Sawyer*, 343 US at 643.

[135] Id at 637.

unconstitutional. The opening lines of the opinion resonate against the backdrop of the World War II cases:[136]

> That comprehensive and undefined presidential powers hold both practical advantages and grave dangers for the country will impress anyone who has served as legal adviser to a President in time of transition and public anxiety. While an interval of detached reflection may temper teachings of that experience, they probably are a more realistic influence on my views than the conventional materials of judicial decision which seem unduly to accentuate doctrine and legal fiction. But as we approach the question of presidential power, we half overcome mental hazards by recognizing them. The opinions of judges, no less than executives and publicists, often suffer the infirmity of confusing the issue of a power's validity with the cause it is invoked to promote, of confounding the permanent executive office with its temporary occupant. The tendency is strong to emphasize transient results upon policies . . . and lose sight of enduring consequences upon the balance power structure of our Republic.

Jackson closed his opinion with an abbreviated quotation of the couplet he used at the end of his unfiled opinion in *Endo*,[137] and then declared:[138]

> With all its defects, delays and inconveniences, men have discovered no technique for long preserving free government except that the Executive be under the law, and that the law be made by parliamentary deliberations. Such institutions may be destined to pass away. But it is the duty of the Court to be last, not first, to give them up.

He may have been addressing himself as well as his audience.

---

[136] Id at 634.

[137] Id at 654. See note 91.

[138] 343 US at 655 (footnote and paragraph break omitted).